THE SEVERED HAND AND THE UPRIGHT CORPSE

Society of Biblical Literature

TEXTS AND TRANSLATIONS
GRAECO-ROMAN SERIES

edited by
Ronald F. Hock

Texts and Translations 42
Graeco-Roman 12

*THE SEVERED HAND AND THE
UPRIGHT CORPSE*

The Severed Hand and the Upright Corpse

THE DECLAMATIONS OF MARCUS ANTONIUS POLEMO

by

WILLIAM W. READER

in collaboration with
ANTHONY J. CHVALA-SMITH

Scholars Press
Atlanta, Georgia

The Severed Hand
and
the Upright Corpse

THE DECLAMATIONS OF
MARCUS ANTONIUS POLEMO

by
WILLIAM W. READER

in collaboration with
ANTHONY J. CHVÁLA-SMITH

© 1996
Society of Biblical Literature

Library of Congress Cataloging-in-Publication Data
Reader, William W.
   The severed hand and the upright corpse : the declamations of
Marcus Antonius Polemo / by William W. Reader in collaboration with
Anthony J. Chvála-Smith.
      p.   cm. — (Texts and translations ; 42. Graeco-Roman ; 12)
   Includes text of the declamations in Greek with an English
translation.
   Includes bibliographical references (p.   ) and indexes.
   ISBN 0-7885-0282-4 (alk. paper)
   1. Polemo, Antonius, ca. 88–145. Declamationes. 2. Speeches,
addresses, etc., Greek—Translations into English. 3. Speeches,
addresses, etc., Greek—History and criticism. 4. Oratory, Ancient.
I. Polemo, Antonius, ca. 88–145. Declamationes. English and Greek.
II. Chvála-Smith, Anthony J. III. Title. IV. Series: Texts and translations ;
no. 42. V. Series: Texts and translations. Graeco-Roman religion series ; 12.
PA4390.P2D437   1996
885'.01—dc20   96-22492
                                                         CIP

Printed in the United States of America
on acid-free paper

Dedication
to

Eleanor P. Reader

my mother
who shouldered so much
for the sake of her children.

TABLE OF CONTENTS

Acknowledgements

A book like this does not come into being through the efforts of one person alone. In the course of the research and writing many people contributed directly or indirectly. To all those who provided assistance along the way for this book I would like here to express my appreciation and gratitude.

Anthony Chvala-Smith in particular deserves special recognition. In the midst of my work on this book it became clear that the hitherto 'standard' critical edition published by H. Hinck in 1873 could no longer serve as an adequate text base for a modern translation and commentary. It was then — faced with the originally unplanned and daunting task of having to produce a new critical edition of the Greek text alongside the other work — that I turned to Tony and his Greek skills for help. He graciously allowed himself to be enlisted for this task. For over ten months he tirelessly endured with me first the ordeal of collating the manuscripts and then the work of reconstructing the stemma and critical text. Without his assistance it would not have been possible to carry out this text-critical work. He shares the credit for the critical edition (chapter 3) and all the analytical work on the manuscripts that preceded it (chapter 2). It is due to his keen eye, sound judgment, and good humor that the work was finally completed. I want to express my deep appreciation for his collaborative efforts.

To my colleagues in the Religion Department at Central Michigan University also belongs a word of thanks. The department granted me a sabbatical leave for the academic year 1993/94 so that I could undertake the initial research for this book. This meant that they also had to bear the additional teaching load incurred by my absence. For their collective support and individual encouragement thanks are due to Roger Hatch, Robin Hough, Merlyn Mowrey, Guy Newland, David Smith, and Michael Stemmeler. In particular I want to thank David for suggesting the title of this book and Robin for enriching the commentary with his wide-ranging knowledge of mythology. Further, by making the concurrent teaching job easier through their generous assistance, our able and patient department secretaries, Dolores Lawrence (now retired) and Betty Lewis, also helped facilitate the completion of this volume.

Many others too contributed help along the way. To name them all would not be possible. However, I would like to acknowledge the help provided by Steve Dyson of the Classics Department of the State University of New York at Buffalo. He enabled me, while participating in his 1994 National Endowment for the Humanities Summer Seminar on the History and Legacy of the Western Roman Empire, to integrate my work on Polemo into that seminar. His personal support and his making accessible all the library resources of the Classics Department at Buffalo helped considerably to advance the work on this volume.

For supplying microfilms or photographic replicas of the Polemo manuscripts I would like to thank the directors and staffs of the following libraries and archives:

Biblioteca Ambrosiana, Milan, Italy
Biblioteca Apostolica Vaticana, Vatican City / Rome, Italy
Biblioteca Medicea Laurentiana, Florence, Italy
Biblioteca Nazionale, Naples, Italy
Bibliothèque Nationale de France, Paris, France
Bayerische Staatsbibliothek, Munich, Germany
Österreichische Nationalbibliothek, Vienna, Austria
Medieval Institute, University of Notre Dame, Notre Dame, Indiana
Center for Medieval and Renaissance Studies, St. Louis, Missouri

Finally, I would like to express my appreciation to the editor of this series, Ronald F. Hock, for his patience and encouragement in the extended 'birth pangs' for this book. To all those named and unnamed who helped me bring this work to fruition I want to express my heartfelt gratitude.

x

Abbreviations of Ancient Authors and Works

(Authors' names are written plenum, their works are abbreviated.)

Achilles Tatius	
Aelian	
N. A.	*de Natura Animalium*
V. H.	*Varia Historia*
Aeneas Tacticus	
Aeschines	
Aeschylus	
Ag.	*Agamemnon*
Ch.	*Choephori*
Eum.	*Eumenides*
Pers.	*Persae*
Pr.	*Prometheus Vinctus*
Th.	*Septem contra Thebas*
Ammianus Marcellinus	
Amphilochius	
Ep. Syn.	*Epistola Synodalis*
Anacreontea	
Andocides	
Alc.	*in Alcibiadem*
Myst.	*de Mysteriis*
Anthologia Graecae	
An. Gr.	*Anthologia Graecae*
Anthologia Latinae	
An. Lat.	*Anthologia Latinae*
Antiphon	
Apollodorus	
Appian	
B. C.	*Bella Civile*
Hisp.	*Hispanica*
Mith.	*Mithradatica*
Pun.	*Libyca*
Syr.	*Syriaca*
Apollonius Rhodius	
Archilochus	
Aristides	
Pan. (= 13.)	*Panathenaicus*

Aristophanes
Ach.	*Acharnenses*
Av.	*Aves*
Ec.	*Ecclesiazusae*
Eq.	*Equites*
Lys.	*Lysistrata*
Nu.	*Nubes*
Pax	*Pax*
Pl.	*Plutus*
Ra.	*Ranae*
Th.	*Thesmophoriazusae*
Ves.	*Vespae*

Aristotle
An. Pr.	*Analytica Priora*
Ath. Con.	*Athenian Constitution*
Div. Somn.	*de Divinatione per Somnia*
E. N.	*Ethica Nicomachea*
frag.	*fragmenta*
H. A.	*Historia Animalium*
Pol.	*Politica*
Pr.	*Problemata*
Rh.	*Rhetorica*
Top.	*Topica*

Arnobius
adv. Gent.	*adversus Gentes*

Arrian
An.	*Anabasis*
Epict. Dis.	*Epicteti Dissertationes*

Asclepiodotus

Athanasius
Quest. Al.	*Questiones Aliae*

Athenaeus
Deipn.	*Deipnosophistae*

Aulus Gellius

Bacchylides
Dith.	*Dithyrambi*
Ep.	*Epinicia*

Basilius [Caesariensis]
Asc. Meg.	*Asceticon Magnum*
Ep.	*Epistula*
Reg. Mor.	*Regulae Morales*

Callimachus
Callixinus

Cicero
    ad Brut.   *ad M. Brutum Epistulae*
    Div. Caec.   *Divinatio in Caecilium*
    Fin.   *de Finibus*
    Leg.   *de Legibus*
    Mur.   *Oratio pro L. Murena*
    Pis.   *Oratio in Pisonem*
Claudian
    Cons. Stil.   *de Consultatu Stilichonis*
    Gig.   *Gigantomachia*
Clemens [Alexandrinus]
    Paed.   *Paedagogus*
Const. Ap.   *Constitutiones Apostolorum*
Curtius [= Quintius Curtius Rufus]
Democritus
    frag.   *fragmenta*
Dinarchus
    Dem.   *Demosthenes*
Dio Chrysostomus
Diodorus Siculus
Dionysius Byzantius
    Bosp.   *per Bosporum Navigatio*
Dionysius Halicarnassus
    Ant.   *Antiquates Romanae*
    Rh.   *Ars Rhetorica*
Euripides
    Alc.   *Alcestis*
    Andr.   *Andromache*
    Cyc.   *Cyclops*
    frag.   *fragmenta*
    Hec.   *Hecuba*
    Hel.   *Helena*
    Heracl.   *Heraclidae*
    Hipp.   *Hippolytus*
    Ion   *Ion*
    Iph. A.   *Iphigenia Aulidensis*
    Iph. T.   *Iphigenia Taurica*
    Med.   *Medea*
    Or.   *Orestes*
    Ph.   *Phoenissae*
    Sup.   *Supplices*
Eusebius Caesariensis
    H. E.   *Historia Ecclesiastica*

Eusebius Nicomediensis
    Lib. Poen.   *Libellius Poenitentiae*
Eustathius
    Comm. Il.   *Commentarii ad Homeri Iliadem*
                              et Odysseum

Frontinus
    Strat.   *Strategematica*
Galen
    Ars Med.   *Ars Medica*
    Ther.   *de Theriaca ad Pisonem*
    U.P.   *de Usu Partium*
Gregory Nazianzenus
    Vit.   *de Vita sua*
Heliodorus
    Eth.   *Ethiopica*
Herodas
Herodian
Hesiod
    Op.   *Opera et Dies*
    Sc.   *Scutum Herculis*
    Th.   *Theogonia*
Himerius
    Or.   *Orationes*
Hippocrates
    Aër.   *de Aëre Aquis et Locis*
    Aph.   *Aphorismi*
    Cap. Vul.   *de Capitis Vulneribus*
    Epid.   *Epidemiae*
    Hum.   *de Humoribus*
    Prog.   *Prognostic*
    Sept.   *de Septimanis*
    Virg.   *de Virginum Morbis*
Homer
    Il.   *Iliad*
    Od.   *Odyssey*
Horace
    A. P.   *Ars Poetica*
    Od.   *Odae*
Hymni Homerici
    H. Hom.   *Hymni Homerici*
Isidorus
    Etym.   *Etymologiae*
Isocrates

Joannes Chrysostomus
  Coemet.   *de Coemeterio et Cruce*
  hom. in Phil.   *homilia in Philippienses*
  Matt.   *in Matthaeum*
  Pseud.   *de Pseudoprophetis*
Josephus
  A. J.   *Antiquatates Judaicae*
  Ap.   *contra Apionem*
  B. J.   *Bellum Judaicum*
Julian
  Or.   *Orationes*
Libanius
  Arg. Dem.   *Argumenta Orationum Demosthenicarum*
  Decl.   *Declamationes*
  Or.   *Orationes*
Lucan
  Phar.   *Pharsalia*
Lucian
  Alex.   *Alexander*
  Dem.   *Demonax*
  Dial. Mar.   *Diologi Marini*
  Dial. Meretr.   *Dialogi Meretricii*
  Dial. Mort.   *Dialogi Mortuorum*
  Dial. Deor.   *Dialogi Deorum*
  Fug.   *Fugitivi*
  Herm.   *Hermotimos*
  Im.   *Imagines*
  J. Tr.   *Juppiter Tragoedus*
  Nav.   *Navigium*
  Nigr.   *Nigrinus*
  Par.   *de Parasito*
  Phal.   *Phalaris*
  Pr. Im.   *Pro Imaginibus*
  Rh. Pr.   *Rhetorum Praeceptor*
  Salt.   *Saltatio*
  Smp.   *Symposium*
  Tox.   *Toxaris*
  V. H.   *Verae Historiae*
Lycophron
  Alex.   *Alexandra*
Lycurgus
  Leoc.   *Leocrates*

Lysias
    Epit.   *Epitaphion*
Maximus Tyrius
Menander
    Epit.   *Epitrepontes*
    Georg.   *Georgos*
Methodius [Olympius]
    Sym. et An.   *sermo de Symeone et Anna*
Nepos [Cornelius]
    Milt.   *Miltiades*
Nonnus
    Dion.   *Dionysiaca*
Origen
    Cels.   *contra Celsum*
Ovid
    Met.   *Metamorphosis*
Pappus Alexandrinus
    Syn.   *Synagoge*
Persius
Petronius
    Sat.   *Satyricon*
Phalaris
    Ep.   *Epistolae*
Philo [Judaeus]
    Aet.   *de Aeternitate Mundi*
    Cher.   *de Cherubim*
    Cong.   *de Congressu Eruditionis Gratia*
    Ebr.   *de Ebrietate*
    Her.   *Quis Rerum Divinarum Heres sit.*
    L. A.   *Legum Allegoriarum*
    Mig.   *de Migratione Abrahami*
    Mos.   *de Vita Mosis*
    Op.   *de Opificio Mundi*
    Post.   *de Posteritate Caini*
    Prob.   *Quod Omnis Probus Liber*
    Spec.   *de Specialibus Legibus*
    Som.   *de Somniis*
Philo Mechanicus
Philostratus
    Gym.   *Gymnastica*
    V. A.   *Vita Apollonii*
    V. S.   *Vitae Sophistarum*

Phrynichus
    Ecl.   *Eclogae*
Pindar
    Isth.   *Isthmian Odes*
    Ol.   *Olympian Odes*
    Nem.   *Nemean Odes*
    Pae.   *Paeanes*
    Pyth.   *Pythian Odes*
Plato
    Alc.   *Alcibiades*
    Ap.   *Apologia*
    Char.   *Charmides*
    Comp. Arist. Cat.   *Comparatio: Aristides et Cato*
    Crat.   *Cratylus*
    Dem.   *Demodocus*
    Epin.   *Epinomis*
    Euthd.   *Euthydemus*
    Euthphr.   *Euthyphro*
    Gorg.   *Gorgias*
    La.   *Laches*
    Leg.   *Leges*
    Men.   *Meno*
    Mx.   *Menexenus*
    Phd.   *Phaedo*
    Phdr.   *Phaedrus*
    Phlb.   *Philebus*
    Pol.   *Politicus*
    Prot.   *Protagoras*
    Resp.   *Respublica*
    Smp.   *Symposium*
    Soph.   *Sophist*
    Tht.   *Theaetetus*
    Tim.   *Timaeus*
Pliny
    N. H.   *Natural History*
Plutarch
    Ages.   *Agesilaus*
    Alc.   *Alcibiades*
    Alex.   *Alexander*
    Arist.   *Aritides*
    Art.   *Artaxerxes*
    Brut.   *Brutus*
    Caes.   *Caesar*

Plutarch
  Cam.   *Camillus*
  Cim.   *Cimon*
  Dem.   *Demetrius*
  Dio.   *Dion*
  Fab.   *Fabius Maximus*
  Lyc.   *Lycurgus*
  Mar.   *Marius*
  Marc.   *Marcellus*
  Oth.   *Otho*
  Pel.   *Pelopidas*
  Sert.   *Sertorius*
  Sul.   *Sulla*
  Them.   *Themistocles*
  Thes.   *Theseus*

  Apoph. Lac.   *Apophthegmata Laconica*
  Apoph. Lacaen.   *Apophthegmata Lacaenarum*
  Apoph. Reg.   *Apophthegmata Regum et Imperatorum*
  Conj. Pr.   *Conjugalia Praecepta*
  Cons. Ap.   *Consolatio ad Apollonium*
  Cons. Ux.   *Consolatio ad Uxorem*
  Fort. Rom.   *de Fortuna Romanorum*
  Gar.   *de Garrulitate*
  Glor. Ath.   *de Gloria Atheniensium*
  Herod.   *de Herodoti Malignitate*
  Inv. Laud.   *de Se Ipsum Citra Invidiam Laudando*
  Lib. Ed.   *de Liberis Educandis*
  Mul. Virt.   *Mulierum Virtutes*
  Par. Gr. R.   *Parallela Graeca et Romana*
  Quest. Conv.   *Questionum Convivalium Libri*
Pollux
Polyaenus
Pompeius Trogus
    (Epitome in M. Junianus Justinius)
Procopius Gazaeus
  Is.   *Commentarius seu cantena in Isaiam*
Pseudo-Dionysios Areopagita
  E. H.   *de Ecclesiastica Hierarchia*
Ptolemaeus
  Alm.   *Almagest*
Quintilian
Quintus Smyrnaeus

Sallust
    Cat.   *Catilina*
    Jug.   *Jugurtha*
Seneca
    Contr   *Controversiae*
    Ep.   *Epistulae*
    Suas.   *Suasoriae*
Servius
    Verg.   *in Vergilii Carmina Commentarii*
Simplicius
    in Ph.   *in Aristotelis Physica Commentaria*
Sophocles
    Aj.   *Ajax*
    Ant.   *Antigone*
    El.   *Electra*
    O. C.   *Oedipus Colonnus*
    O. T.   *Oedipus Tyrranus*
    Ph.   *Philoctetes*
Suidas (= Suda Lexicon)
Suetonius
    Caes.   *Julius Caesar*
    Gr.   *de Grammaticis*
    Rh.   *de Rhetoribus*
Synesius
    Ep.   *Epistulae*
Tacitus
    Dial.   *Dialogus de Oratoribus*
Terence
    Ph.   *Phormio*
Theocritus
Theophrastus
    Char.   *Characteres*
    H. P.   *Historia Plantarum*
Tzetzes [Johannes]
    Chil.   *Chiliades*
Valerius Flaccus
Virgil
    Aen.   *Aeneis*
Vita Hadriani
    Vit. Hadr.   *Vita Hadriani*
Vitruvius
Xenarchus
    Pent. frag.   *Pentathlum fragment*

Xenophon
Ag.	*Agesilaus*
An.	*Anabasis*
Cyn.	*Cynegeticus*
Cyr.	*Cyropaedia*
Hel.	*Hellenica*
Mem.	*Memorabilia*
Oec.	*Oeconomicus*
Smp.	*Symposium*

Xenophon Ephesius
Zenobius
Ben.	*de Beneficiis*

Abbreviations of Epigraphical and Papyrological Publications

AM   *Mitteilungen des deutschen archäologischen Instituts,*
Athenische Abteilung, Berlin: Mann.

CIG   *Corpus Inscriptionum Graecarum*, ed. A. Boeckh,
Berlin: Reimer, 1828-1877.

DAA   *Dedications from the Athenian Akropolis*, ed. A. E. Raubitschek,
Cambridge, MA: Archaeological Institute of America, 1949.

IG   *Inscriptiones Graecae*, ed. Academia Litterarum Regia Borussica,
Berlin: de Gruyter / Reimer, 1913ff.

OGI   *Orientis Graeci Inscriptiones Selectae*, ed. W. Dittenberger,
Leipzig: Hirzel, 1903-1905.

P. Oxy.   *Papyri Oxyrhynchus*, ed. B. P. Grenfell and A. S. Hunt,
London: Egypt Exploration Fund / Hart, 1898-1927.

SEG   *Supplementum Epigraphicum Graecum*, ed. J. E. Hundius et al.,
Leiden: Brill, 1923-1988.

SIG   *Sylloge Inscriptionum Graecarum*, ed. W. Dittenberger,
Leipzig: Hirzel, 1915-1924.

Biblical and related literature is cited according to SBL conventions.

Abbreviations of Modern Works

AJA	*American Journal of Archeology* New York: Archeological Institute of America
AJP	*American Journal of Philology* Baltimore: Johns Hopkins University Press
ANRW	*Aufstieg und Niedergang der römischen Welt* Berlin: de Gruyter, 1972ff
BAGD	W. Bauer, W. F. Arndt, F. W. Gingrich, F, W. Danker, *A Greek-English Lexicon of the New Testament and* *Other Early Christian Literature*, 2nd ed. Chicago: University of Chicago Press, 1979
BDR	F. Blass, A. Debrunner, F. Rehkopf, *Grammatik des neutestamentlichen Griechisch*, 14th ed. Göttingen: Vandenhoeck & Ruprecht, 1976
BICS	*Bulletin of the Institute of Classical Studies*, London: University of London
BPhA	*Breslauer Philologische Abhandlungen* Breslau: Koebner
CA	*Classical Antiquity* Berkeley: University of California Press
CJ	*Classical Journal* Gainseville: Classical Association
DNTT	*Dictionary of New Testament Theology*, 4 vols., ed. C. Brown, Grand Rapids: Zondervan, 1975
GG	H. Smyth &. G. M. Messing, *Greek Grammar*, Cambridge: Harvard University Press, 1974
GGR	M. P. Nilsson, *Geschichte der Griechischen Religion*, 2 vols. 3rd ed., München: Beck, 1976

GRBS	*Greek, Roman, and Byzantine Studies* Durham: Duke University Press
Hermes	*Hermes, Zeitschrift für classische Philologie*, Berlin: Weidman / Wiesbaden: Steiner
HSCP	*Harvard Studies in Classical Philology*, Cambridge: Harvard University Press
JÖAI	*Jahreshefte des Österreichischen Archäologischen Instituts* Vienna: Österreichisches Archäologisches Institut
JR	*Journal of Religion* Chicago: University of Chicago Press
KP	*Der kleine Pauly. Lexikon der Antike*, 5 vols. ed. K. Ziegler & W. Sontheimer, Stuttgart: Druckenmüller, 1964-1975
LIMC	*Lexicon Iconographicum Mythologiae Classicae*, ed. H. C. Akermann / J. R. Gisler, Zürich / München: Artemis, 1981ff
LPGL	G. W. H. Lampe, *A Patristic Greek Lexicon*, Oxford: Clarendon, 1978
LSJ	H. G. Liddell, R. Scott, H. S. Jones, *A Greek-English Lexicon*, Oxford: Clarendon, 1968
MM	J. H. Moulton & George Milligan, *The Vocabulary of* *the Greek Testament Illustrated from the Papyri* Grand Rapids: Eerdmans, 1976
MPG	J. P. Migne, *Patrologia Graeca* Paris: Migner, et al., 1857-1866
Mnemosyne	*Mnemosyne*. Bibliotheca Classica Batava Leiden: Brill
NovT	*Novum Testamentum* Leiden: Brill

NZ	*Numismatische Zeitschrift* Wien: Selbstverlag der Österreichischen Numismatischen Gesellschaft
OCD	*Oxford Classical Dictionary*, 2nd ed., ed. N. G. L. Hammond & H. H. Scullard, Oxford: Clarendon, 1978
Ph&Rh	*Philosophy and Rhetoric* University Park: Pennsylvania State University Press
RAC	*Religion in Antike und Christentum*, ed. T. Klauser, Stuttgart: Hierseman, 1950ff
RE	*Realencyclopädie der classischen Altertumswissenschaft*, ed. A. Pauly, G. Wissowa, et al. München / Stuttgart: A. Drückenmüller, 1884ff
RhM	*Rheinisches Museum für Philologie* Frankfurt: Sauerlander
RhSt	*Rhetorische Studien* Paderborn: Schöningh
TWNT	*Theologisches Wörterbuch zum Neuen Testament*, 10 vols. ed. G. Kittel / G. Friedrich, Stuttgart: Kohlhammer, 1933-1973
WS	*Wiener Studien*. Zeitschrift für klassische Philologie und Patristik. Wien: Bohlaus
ZNW	*Zeitschrift für die neutestamentliche Wissenschaft* Berlin: de Gruyter
YCS	*Yale Classical Studies* New Haven: Yale University Press

Other Abbreviations

acc	accusative
act	active
aor	aorist
BCE	Before the Common Era
ca.	circa (= approximately)
CE	Common Era
cf.	confere (= compare, see)
dat	dative
ed.	edition / editor / edited
esp.	especially
et al.	et allii (= and others)
etc.	et cetera (= and the rest, and the like)
fem	feminine
frag.	fragment
fut	future
gen	genitive
ibid.	ibidem (= the same)
impf	imperfect
impv	imperative
ind	indicative
inf	infinitive
loc. cit.	loco citato (= in the place cited)
LXX	Septuagint
masc	masculine
mid	middle
MS / MSS	manuscript / manuscripts
neut	neuter
nom	nominative
NT	New Testament
op. cit.	opere citato (= in the work cited)
opt	optative
p. / pp.	page / pages
part	participle
passim	passim (= spread, scattered throughout)
pass	passive
perf	perfect

pluperf	plusquam perfect
plur	plural
pres	present
sing	singular
subj	subjunctive
suppl.	supplement
sc.	scilicet (contraction of: scire licet = it is evident, namely)
voc	vocative
vs.	versus (= against, in contrast with)

Introduction

For the Roman empire as well as for the Christian church the second century CE brought heady times. Particularly in the old Greek-speaking world of the East there was a notable rejuvenation. Nowhere is this more clearly evident than in the remarkable and wide ranging literature produced by that world. Lamentably, many of those works have long since disappeared in the sands of time. Still, many others have survived, including lesser known pieces some of which we are often not even aware. Rediscovering a neglected work can produce an experience not unlike that which we can have rummaging around in an old junk shop. On occasion and unexpectedly we can come across an unusual piece buried amidst a pile of clutter. But until we pick it up and wipe off the dust we often do not appreciate what we have found. It is the act of cleaning, polishing, and examining that elicts our admiration or brings a handsome reward. This book is about picking up the declamations of Marcus Antonius Polemo, dusting them off, and letting their value re-emerge in the daylight.

Polemo (88–144 CE) was the most famous sophist in Smyrna at the same time Bishop Polycarp headed the church there. In the early centuries of the common era Polemo was admired by Greek rhetoricians and Christian preachers alike as a model of eloquence. Yet despite his reputation in antiquity his work has never before been translated into a modern language or examined thoroughly.

The heart of this book is the Greek text of Polemo's surviving declamations (chapter 3). Everything else is supplementary and intended as an aid to understanding this text. The Greek text presented here constitutes a new

1

and comprehensive critical edition, the first such to be published in well over a century. Accompanying it on facing pages is an English translation, the first ever to appear. The commentary following (chapter 4) deals with the full range of issues: philological and stylistic, historical and mythological, literary and rhetorical. The opening review of Polemo's life and work, and of declamations in general and his in particular (chapter 1), puts our text into its historical and literary context. The discussion of the manuscripts and editions (chapter 2 and the appendices) explains the basis upon which the text rests and the rationale for the form here presented. The indices at the end are designed to facilitate independent study of the Greek text and encourage an examination of its relationship to other works in the Greek tradition.

A thick tome about a minor text requires, one might reasonably object, some justification. In response any number of reasons could be easily cited:

(a) the historical man: In his own day and up through the end of antiquity Polemo was recognized as one of the leading sophists in Asia Minor. He was among the foremost intellectual, social, and political elites of Smyrna and a prominent representative of the revival movement known as the Second Sophistic. Moreover, he was also a personal favorite of emperor Hadrian. In short, he was an imposing figure of the second century. A case for this book could be made on the basis of Polemo's historical personage alone.

(b) the geographical place: Polemo was born in Laodicea but lived and worked his entire life in Smyrna. Yet he also privately visited and in his public capacity delivered addresses in the neighboring cities such as Ephesus, Sardis, and Pergamum. Though he travelled widely, it was primarily the important cities of Asia Minor that shaped him and upon which he in turn left his mark. In the end he returned to his birthplace, Laodicea, to die. In the Roman period Asia Minor was especially important both for the revival of Hellenism and for the development of early Christianity (cf. John of Patmos, Ignatius of Antioch, Polycarp of Smyrna, Papias of Hierapolis, Melito of Sardis, to cite but a few well-known names). This present study could be justified on the grounds that it can add to our understanding of this important region in the eastern Mediterranean.

(c) the cultural milieu: In the era of the Roman Principate there emerged a vibrant renaissance of ancient Greek culture. One emblem of this is what Philostratus termed the "Second Sophistic." The old adage, that the Romans subdued the Greeks militarily, but the Greeks conquered the Romans culturally, is not without foundation. Hellenistic culture in the Roman period was vigorous and in part characterized by the polarity between the Asianists and the Atticists, between the new school and the old school, between the progressives and reactionaries. This tension between modernity and nostalgia produced in the second century CE a remarkable creativity and noteworthy literature in many fields (e.g., the works of Plutarch, Galen, Pausanias, Aristides, Dio Chrysostom, Lucian, Philostratus, Cassius Dio, Appian, Arrian, Chariton, Athenaeus, and Phrynichus). An examination of Polemo will necessarily shed additional light on this extraordinarily literate culture. Such illumination, it can be argued, makes a book on Polemo's work well worth the effort.

(d) the rhetorical genre: Polemo's declamations belong to that type of rhetoric known as epideictic, and to that sub-genre called *controversiae*. An examination of Polemo's declamations can not only shed new light on that genre as a literary phenomenon but also on its *Sitz-im-Leben*, its pedagogical function, and its societal role in general. Given the fact that grammar and rhetoric constituted the core of the educational curriculum in antiquity, it is fair to contend that a study of Polemo's declamations should increase our knowledge not only of epideictic rhetoric specifically but also of higher education in the Greco-Roman world in general.

(e) the surviving work: Though Polemo was a prodigious sophist and prolific rhetorician most of his work has unfortunately been lost. Only one pair of declamations in Greek and a portion of his physiognomica in Arabic translation are extant. Since his work, though considerable, has largely disappeared, the little that has survived takes on much greater significance. By way of comparison, what remains of the *oeuvre* of Polemo's older contemporary, Dio Chrysostom, as well as of that of his younger contemporary, Aelius Aristides, is extensive, so that no single piece of their work is all that important by itself. In the case of Polemo's declamations, however, the limited extent of his surviving legacy is rationale enough for a detailed analysis — rarity is what makes a treasure valuable.

Among those who reflect on the indebtedness of our modern civilization to the Western heritage there are at least four important interest groups who should find here much that will repay study.

(1) Those interested in **Hellenism** during the Roman period, particularly in the cultural renaissance known as the "Second Sophistic," should find Polemo's portrayal of Classical traditions and ideals instructive. His notions of valor, nobility, and freedom, his beliefs about the soul and post-mortem existence, his knowledge of Greek history, customs, and mythology, and his

nostalgia for the 'glory' that was Greece — all this shines through in his declamations.

(2) Those interested in **rhetoric** and the history of its development will find here abundant material to illumine the phenomenon, the process, and the tools of the trade. Invention and arrangement, argument and proofs (*ethos, pathos, logos*), *paradigmata* and *sententiae*, encomium and invective, *synkrisis* and *prosopopoeia*, countless figures and tropes — all this is richly illustrated in Polemo's declamations.

(3) Linguists and students of **Greek philology**, be they specialists (lexicographers, grammarians, translators) or beginners (those struggling just to get through elementary Koine or even just past 'It's Greek to me'), will find that Polemo can serve as an instructive case study in word usage, syntactical construction, conditional sentences, classical idioms, and etymology.

(4) Finally, those interested in **early Christianity** and its relationship to the Hellenized cultural milieu will find in Polemo's declamations a rich resource for illumining the language and thought forms of the early church. It is this in particular which has intrigued the present editors — both by training teachers of the NT. The declamations brush any number of topics of importance for the NT and the early church: gods and heroes, the soul and death, social customs and a shame culture, '*arete*' and 'vicarious sacrifice'. With Polemo on the one side and the NT authors, Apostolic Fathers, Apologetes, and Patristic writers on the other, striking linguistic parallels (lexicographic and syntactic) may be observed — whether or not with semantic differences remains to be studied. For items of particular theological interest let it suffice here to highlight two topics which are worth further investigation.

First is the topic of martyr death: Polemo's portrayal of heroic death was composed during, or certainly close to, the Bar Kochba Revolt, the only military conflict Rome engaged in during Hadrian's reign. This war brought death not only to Jewish soldiers on the battlefield, but also to non-combatants who remained loyal to the God of the Covenant and to his Torah. Legendary, for example, is the martyrdom of Rabbi Akiba who died under severe torture with the Shema on his lips. On the Christian side this same era also brought martyrdom to such prominent church leaders as Ignatius under Trajan and Polycarp under Antoninus. Polemo's presentation of heroic death deserves comparison with Jewish, Christian, and pagan martyrologies. Potential implications of this contemporaneity may be worth exploring. Further, one may ask, what connexion might there be, for example, between Polemo's picture of Callimachus pierced with a myriad arrows and say the 5th century legend of saint Sebastian perforated with the countless arrows of Diocletian's legions? And was it later simply coincidence that a manuscript of Polemo's declamations appeared in Italy and was studiously copied there at the same time that saint Sebastian's 'pin-cushion' iconography emerged as so popular in the Italian renaissance?

Second and far more intriguing is the relationship of Polemo's imagery to the topic of Christ's death. Polemo portrays Callimachus achieving the victory by forcing the Persians to shoot all their arrows at him. They emptied their quivers at his upright corpse and, as it were, ran out of ammunition. He defeated the enemy by 'stripping' them of their arms (cf. σκυλεύω, Polemo, B 51; indeed he collected their arrows as 'spoils' of war (cf. λάφυρα, Polemo, B 51). This picture represents, of course, an ironic reversal because ordinarily in war it is the living who strip the defeated dead. What is fascinating in this connection is the *Christus victor* theology that unfolded among the Fathers of the church in the 3rd and 4th centuries. Among other aspects they argued that in death Christ drew to himself all the darts of the devil; he despoiled (cf. σκυλεύω) Satan and gathered all his weapons as λάφυρα (= booty or plunder) — the same peculiar irony as in Polemo! While one might perhaps argue that the general image of Christ rendering the Enemy impotent is rooted in the NT, the specific imagery and terminology (σκυλεύω and λάφυρα) are certainly not found there. It would be worth exploring whether Polemo's declamations may have in fact been the source of this metaphorical language in the later Fathers and the origin of this key soteriological motif in Patristic Christology.

In any case the text of Polemo's declamations will reward study for anyone interested in the manifold relationships between early Christianity and the classical tradition.

Finally, it should be pointed out that this whole book, especially the commentary and indices, is aimed at both professor *and* student. That is to say, it has in mind not only the seasoned scholar who is well grounded in Greek grammar and literature, but *also* the neophyte still memorizing paradigms and agonizing over syntax and for whom the many names and allusions in the text ring no bells. If the mature scholar should sometimes feel that the commentary is carrying owls to Athens, let it be remembered that beginners may be happy for the elementary analysis of syntax and historical references. In any case I have tried to provide the kind of information that I would like to have had in my own early struggles with Greek.

In closing this introduction I would like to point to and take over a comment that Eduard Norden once made. In the foreword to his monumental

work, *Die antike Kunstprosa,* he apologized for its size which he says had
acquired dimensions he never anticipated but which — he discovered as he
worked — could not be avoided. He remarked that "the fear of [writing] the
μέγα βιβλίον (= big book) was the only disturbing element amidst the joy of
seeking and finding."[1] While not claiming for this volume on Polemo's
declamations any resemblance with Norden's great masterpiece, I do admit in
its preparation to having an experience analogous to his.

---

[1] "Die Furcht vor dem μέγα βιβλίον war bei der Freude des Suchens und Findens das
einzige störende Moment." (cf. E. Norden, *Die antike Kunstprosa,* 5. Aufl., Stuttgart:
Teubner, 1958, Vol. I, p. vii). This comment is, of course, an allusion to that famous
aphorism from Callimachus: μέγα βιβλίον, μέγα κακόν (= a big book [is] a big evil). Cf.
Καλλίμαχος ὁ γραμματικὸς τὸ μὲγα βιβλίον ἴσον ἔλεγεν εἶναι τῷ μεγάλῳ κακῷ
(= Callimachus the grammarian used to say that the big book was equivalent to the big
evil), Athenaeus, epit. in init. lb. III p. 72 A, cf. R. Pfeiffer, *Callimachus,* Vol. I, Oxford:
Clarendon, 1949, p. 353, fragment 465. While originally Callimachus' saying may have
been part of his sharp critique directed against Apollonius of Rhodes for trying to revive
epic poetry in his *Argonautica,* in later time it has come to be applied freely to any thick
book. In Norden's case it is a happy irony that instead of a μέγα κακόν he produced a
magnum opus.

Chapter 1

Polemo and His Declamations

Polemo (ca. 88-144 CE) was the preeminent sophist in Smyrna in the first part of the second century and one of the leading figures in the Greek revival movement known as the Second Sophistic. The primary sources for reconstructing his life and work are sparse,[1] and the important secondary literature is not extensive.[2]

The Life of Polemo

Background and Education

Polemo's full name — Marcus Antonius Polemo[3] — is a reminder that he was a grandson of Polemo II, the last king of the Pontus (38-63 CE), who

---

[1] The main sources are [a] his own surviving writings (declamations and physiognomica), [b] Philostratus (*V.S.*[I.25] 529-544), [c] Suidas (Πολέμων), and [d] a few scattered coins, inscriptions, and literary references.

[2] Cf. H. Jüttner, *De Polemonis rhetoris vita operibus arte, BPhA* 8,1, Breslau: Koebner, 1898 [reprint: Hildesheim: Olms, 1968]; J. Mesk, "Die Beispiele in Polemons Physiognomik," *WS* 50 (1932) 51-67; C. J. Cadoux, *Ancient Smyrna* (Oxford: Blackwell, 1938) 254ff; W. Stegemann, *Antonius Polemon, der Hauptvertreter der zweiten Sophistik* (Stuttgart, 1942); W. Stegemann, "Polemon, 10," *RE* 21 (1952) 1320-1357; R. H. Chowen, "Traveling Companions of Hadrian," *CJ* 50 (1954) 122-124; G. W. Bowersock, *Greek Sophists in the Roman Empire* (Oxford: Clarendon, 1969) passim, esp. pp. 120-123; M. W. Gleason, *Embodying the Rhetoric of Manhood: Self-Presentation in the Second Sophistic*, Berkeley: dissertation, 1990 (Ann Arbor: UMI Dissertation Services, 1995) 56-124 [this study has since been published, see the bibliography].

[3] Attested in inscriptions (CIG II 3148 = IGR 4,1431), coins from Smyrna (R. Münsterberg, "Die Münzen der Sophisten," *NZ* 48 {= Neue Folge 8} [1915] 119-124), and epigrams (*An.Gr.* 11.181); cf. C. P. Jones, "Prosopographical Notes on the Second Sophistic," GRBS 21 (1981) 374-377.

could trace his dynasty back to its establishment by the triumvir Mark Antony (cf. Appian, *B.C.* 5.75 [319]; Cassius Dio, 45.25.4; Strabo 12.568, 578). The progenitor of that Polemo family, Zeno the rhetorician (1st century BCE), hailed from Laodicea on the Lycus River (cf. Strabo 12.578). When under the pressure of imperial Rome the royal family of the Polemos abdicated their kingship, they in part took up residence in their home town of Laodicea. That is where Marcus Antonius Polemo was born, and, since at the time of his birth (ca. 88 CE) Laodicea belonged to Phrygia, he could on occasion later be called "the Phrygian" (ὁ Φρύξ, Philostratus, *V. S.* 539).

Inasmuch as he came from an aristocratic family in Laodicea he will have enjoyed a good primary education which typically included a thorough study of grammar. Already as a young boy he showed promise — people saw in him a certain greatness (τι ἐν αὐτῷ μέγα, Philostratus, *V. S.* 530) — and so he transferred to school in Smyrna to study rhetoric under the most famous sophists of his day. The head of the school then was Scopelianus of Clazomenae (the successor of Niketes of Smyrna), a rhetorician of renown who attracted students to Smyrna from all over the Greek-speaking world. Scopelianus' oratorical skills, whether in court pleas, ambassadorial speeches, or declamations, were universally acknowledged. He excelled at extempore speeches, at veiled allusion and ambiguous language, and he was a master at the more challenging themes, particularly those related to the Medes (Philostratus, *V. S.* 511, 518–519, 521). In Smyrna Polemo also studied for four years under Timocrates of Heraclea, a man who prided himself more as philosopher than sophist. His language was fluent, vigorous, and ready (εὐφόρως, σφοδρῶς, ἑτοίμως) and on this account Polemo, who liked such headlong speech (τὴν τοιάνδε ἐπιφορὰν τοῦ λόγου), prized him as teacher and called him the "father of his own eloquence" (πατέρα ... τῆς ἑαυτοῦ γλώττης). When a quarrel broke out between these two teachers over Scopelianus' use of pitch-plasters and hair-removers — a mark of effeminacy and vanity[4] — Polemo sided with Timocrates (Philostratus, *V. S.* 535–536). A certain irony lies here in the fact that later as practising sophist Polemo himself put great stock in external appearances. Any split, however, between Polemo and Scopelianus cannot have lasted long because in 113 CE Polemo, then only 25 years old, stood in for the aging Scopelianus on a embassy to emperor Trajan (Philostratus, *V. S.* 536).

---

[4] Cf. "Look for orators among the smooth and hairless (*valsis atque expolitis*) of today, men only in their lusts" (Seneca, *Contr.* 1 pr. 10).

In his student days Polemo also went to Bithynia to study under the "Golden Mouth," Dio of Prusa (Philostratus, *V. S.* 539). From these early years probably stem some of the humorous sayings attributed to him. Once, when he saw a gladiator dripping with sweat out of terror because of the upcoming combat he said, "You are in agony as though you were about to declaim" (ἀγωνιᾷς ὡς μελετᾶν μέλλων, Philostratus, *V. S.* 541). Such a sentiment fits better the student novice than the mature sophist who rounded off his periods with a smile to show how effortlessly he could speak (cf. Philostratus, *V. S.* 537). The adult Polemo's extravagance with money was prefigured in his student life. That is evident from the episode with Varus, a wealthy and arrogant student from whom Polemo had once borrowed money. Varus imagined himself eloquent and from those to whom he had loaned money he demanded attendance at his own declamations as part of the interest due. When debters did not attend he threatened them with a summons to recover the debt. Varus' parasites reproached Polemo for avoiding the lectures and urged him to come and give signs of approval. So one evening Polemo showed up, but after listening for a while to the student's disorganized declamation filled with solecisms, barbarisms, and inconsistencies, he jumped up and cried "Varus, bring your summons!" (Οὔαρε, φέρε τοὺς τύπους, Philostratus, *V. S.* 541).

Career in Smyrna

Since Smyrna elected Polemo to replace the honored but aging Scopelianus as the city's official representative to Trajan in 113 CE it must be assumed that he already had established himself there as a recognized rhetorician. This would mean that Polemo had begun his career as independent sophist already in his early twenties. His teaching methods and materials will probably have reflected the influences of his own teachers and the rhetorical traditions they represented. For him, however, Demosthenes served as the real model to be emulated. Polemo himself claimed to have received guidance from Demosthenes in his dreams. Indeed, he set up a bronze statue of Demosthenes in the sanctuary of Asclepius at Pergamum which bore the inscription Δημοσθένη Δημοσθένους Παιανιέα Πολέμων κατὰ ὄναρ (= Polemo [set up this statue of] Demosthenes, son of Demosthenes, of Paeania in accordance with a dream).[5] This commemoration constituted a public claim of privileged access to the undisputed source of rhetorical authority. Philostratus spoke of "the Demosthenic quality of his thought ... as though delivered from the tripod" (τὸ Δημοσθενικόν τῆς γνώμης ... ὥσπερ ἐκ τρίποδος), that is, as if it were a divine oracle (*V. S.* 542).

In general, however, Polemo seems to have valued natural talent and quick-witted repartee more than *mimesis* of the ancients. In this regard a Polemonic anecdote is revealing: Once when the proconsul was subjecting a bandit (λῃστής) to torture on the rack and had declared that he could not think up a punishment (τιμωρία) that would be adequate for his crimes, Polemo, who happened to be present, piped up and said "Order him to learn ancient stuff by heart!" (κέλευσον ... αὐτὸν ἀρχαῖα ἐκμανθάνειν, Philostratus, *V. S.* 541). Although Polemo had himself memorized a great wealth of material (πλεῖστα ἐκμαθών), he nevertheless considered this to be the most wearisome of the educational exercises (ἐπιπονώτατον ἡγεῖτο τῶν ἐν ἀσκήσει τὸ ἐκμανθάνειν, Philostratus, *V. S.* 541).

There is no evidence that Polemo put his students through the preliminary exercises (προγυμνάσματα) typical of the rhetorical training of his day. But he clearly required of them the exercises known as declamations (μελέται). The themes will have been posed in part by the audiences, in part by himself. And he certainly will himself have declaimed so as to provide his students with models for their own efforts. It goes without saying that he collected fees for his teaching (cf. Philostratus, *V. S.* 538). His most famous student was without question Aelius Aristides, but other notables also belonged to the ranks of those who learned from him, e.g., Euodianos of Smyrna, Ptolemaios of Naucratis, Herodes Atticus, and possibly Lucian of Samosata.[6]

Besides being a teacher of rhetoric Polemo was also a successful court lawyer, acting in both criminal and civil suits. Even outside of Smyrna he was a sought-after advocate. For example, a wealthy Lydian hired Polemo to defend him in Sardis, paying an honorarium of two full talents (cf. Philostratus, *V. S.* 524–525). It was probably in this capacity as lawyer that he developed a reputation of being better at attack (ἐπιφορά) than defense (ἀπολογία), a criticism that Philostratus says was unfounded (*V. S.* 542).

---

[5] Cf. Phrynichus, *Ecl.* 395; the statue has not survived, but the dedicatory inscription has (cf. C. Habicht, *Die Inschriften des Asklepieions*, Altertümer von Pergamon 8.3 (Berlin: de Gruyter, 1969) 75 # 33.

[6] Cf. W. Stegemann, "Polemo, 10," *RE* 21 (1952) 1325.

In the second century Smyrna was one of the leading Ionian cities; it vied primarily with Ephesus, "the other luminary of Asia" (*alterum lumen Asiae*, Pliny, *N.H.* 5.120) for preeminence. Other cities too had ambitious pretensions — for example, Pergamon, Laodicea, Sardis, Miletus, Colossae, Tralles — but few could rival Smyrna in architecture, culture, and imperial favor. Rome fostered this competitiveness between cities and the spirit of local 'boosterism' because it served the 'divide-and-rule' strategy of the empire. Throughout his adult life Polemo devoted himself to advancing the interests of Smyrna, his home of choice. His efforts, which did not go unrewarded, were, of course, not all selfless; Smyrna's advance brought advantages for him too.

Polemo played an important political role in Smyrna. He brought about "a harmonious and faction-free government" (ὁμονοοῦσαν καὶ ἀστασίαστον πολιτεύειν) arbitrating long-standing differences between the hill and shore residents. When suits arose between citizens about money, Polemo saw to it that they were settled within the city jurisdiction. (Philostratus, *V. S.* 531–532). This policy of harmony and autonomy was obviously designed to keep the Romans, as much as possible, from intervening in the affairs of Smyrna. Some offenders, however, e.g., adulterers, temple desecraters, or murderers, Polemo was only too happy to see turned over to Roman jurisdiction because they needed, as he said, "a judge with a sword in his hand" (δικαστοῦ ... ξίφος ἔχοντος, Philostratus, *V. S.* 532), a reference of course to the Roman *jus gladii* (cf. Rom 13:4).

Because of his political acumen and services Polemo was appointed to a number of offices in Smyrna. Already during Hadrian's rule (117-138 CE) he held the position of στραγηγὸς ἐπὶ τῶν ὅπλων (= General over the Weapons). Some time after 130/131 CE he was named στρατηγὸς διὰ βίου (= General for Life). Further, he occupied the office of ὁ τοῦ Διονύσου ἱερεύς (= Priest of Dionysus) which gave him the right to ride as captain in the sacred trireme when it was brought to the agora in sacral procession during the winter wine-drinking festival of Anthesteria (Philostratus, *V. S.* 531).[7] Finally, Polemo held the post of ἀγωνοθέτης (= President of the Games) at the Olympic Games held at Smyrna in honor of Hadrian. The date of the establishment of these Asian games is disputed, but it probably falls in the period 123-129 CE.[8] In his

---

[7] This commemoration festival celebrated the seemingly miraculous victory of Dionysus' unarmed devotees against a treacherous Chian invasion (cf. Aristides 17.6).

[8] For the various offices which Polemo held in Smyrna cf. Stegemann, op. cit., 1329–1330; for the date when the Hadrianic Games were established, cf. ibid., 1334. For Polemo as office holder cf. also M. W. Gleason, op. cit., 57–65.

capacity as ἀγωνοθέτης Polemo more than once expelled an actor from the contests. Once at the Smyrnaean Games an actor performing Euripides' *Orestes* pointed to the ground while uttering the words "O Zeus" and then raised his hands toward heaven while saying "and Earth" (*Or.* 1496). At that Polemo, who was presiding at the games (προκαθήμενος τῶν 'Ολυμπίων), expelled him from the contest, saying, "This fellow has committed a solecism with his hand (οὗτος τῇ χειρὶ ἐσολοίκισεν)" (Philostratus, *V. S.* 541–542; cf. 535).

As leading citizen and public figure Polemo took every opportunity to foster the improvement and beautification of Smyrna. He managed to get Hadrian to provide generous financial subsidies to Smyrna which were then used to build a large-scale corn market (τά τε τοῦ σίτου ἐμπόρια), a gymnasium which ranked among the most magnificent in Asia (γυμνάσιον ... μεγαλοπρεπέστατον), and an enormous temple on a promontory visible from the sea (νεὼς τηλεφανὴς ὁ ἐπι τῆς ἄκρας), a χαριστήριος νεώς (= thank-offering temple), dedicated jointly to Zeus and Hadrian (Philostratus, *V. S.* 531).[9] This construction brought with it Smyrna's second νεωκορία (= temple guardianship).[10] This 'temple-wardenship' was a jealously coveted sacral office because it made the 'warden city' the seat of the provincial emperor cult, which in turn meant increased revenues through imperial subsidies and pilgrim-tourist traffic.

Finally, on a number of occasions Polemo acted as official ambassador representing Smyrna to the emperor in legal, fiscal, and political matters. The first of these legateships took place in the reign of Trajan (113 CE). Other embassies followed in the reigns of Hadrian (118, 123/124, 133 CE) and Antoninus Pius (143 CE), and some of these took him to Rome. Already on the first embassy Trajan bestowed on Polemo the right of the *libera legatio*, that is, the privilege of traveling on land and sea with all expenses paid. Not only did he retain that right throughout his career, but later Hadrian extended it to all Polemo's descendants as well (cf. Philostratus, *V. S.*, 532). Polemo made full use of his privilege and was notorious for conducting his journeys with ostentatious splendor and a large entourage (Philostratus, *V. S.* 532). External show was essential for a man so self-important.

---

[9] These buildings are mentioned several times by Aristides as emblems of Smyrna's civic pride (17.11; 18.6; 19.3); cf. C. J. Cadoux, *Ancient Smyrna* (Oxford: Blackwell, 1938) 181, 202.

[10] Smyrna attained the first νεωκορία from Rome in 26 CE with the permission to build a Tiberius temple. A third and final neocorate temple was granted to Smyrna in 214/215 CE under Emperor Caracalla (cf. W. Stegemann, op. cit., 1331).

Relations with Contemporary Sophists

Polemo's fame reached far in sophist circles. Moreover, it was natural that other 'professionals' in the 'guild' would want to meet him personally and form their own judgment about him. Among those sophists who heard and met Polemo and whose opinions of him are preserved, the most famous was probably Herodes Atticus. After having heard Polemo deliver the dedication speech at the Zeus temple in Athens in 131/132 CE, Herodes, on a trip to Asia, sought him out in Smyrna. He attended his lectures for three days. Few details about their personal contact are preserved, though Herodes did in a letter to the Consul Varus record the themes of the declamations that he heard, a description of Polemo's style of delivery, and his own reactions. Herodes reported that he listened to Polemo's first declamation as do impartial judges (ὡς οἱ δικάζοντες), to the second as do those who love to hear more (ὡς οἱ ἐρῶντες), and to the third as those who stand in amazement (ὡς οἱ θαυμάζοντες). As payment for what he had heard (μισθὸν τῆς ἀκροάσεως) Herodes sent him 150,000 drachmae. When Polemo refused the money apparently because he had expected more, Herodes added another 100,000 to make the total a quarter million! Thereupon Polemo accepted it without hesitation (προθύμως) as though he were only receiving his due (ὥσπερ ἀπολαμβάνοντα). Henceforth Herodes always praised Polemo profusely (ἐπαινῶν τὸν Πολέμωνα καὶ ὑπερθαυμάζων). On a later occasion in Athens Herodes declaimed on the theme that after the truce in the Peloponnesian war the Greek victory-trophies should be removed. When complimented on his eloquence, his response was, "Read Polemo's declamation [on the same topic] and you will know a [truly eloquent] man (τὴν Πολέμωνος μελέτην ἀνάγνωτε καὶ εἴσεσθε ἄνδρα)" (Philostratus, *V. S.* 538).

The sophist, Marcus of Byzantium, who always looked unkempt (αὐχμηρῶς), once visited Polemo's school unannounced and took a seat inconspicuously in the audience. When Polemo asked for declamation themes to be proposed, some members of the audience who recognized Marcus turned toward him expecting him to suggest a theme. Noticing that Polemo said, "Why do you look to 'the rustic' (τὸν ἄγροικον)? This fellow will not come up with a theme." At that, Marcus retorted, "I will propose [a topic] and I will [myself] declaim." Thereupon Polemo, recognizing him on his dialect, — and no doubt a bit embarrassed at having dropped the unflattering term 'rustic' —

addressed himself to Marcus in an eloquent, flattering, and extemporaneous speech. When they had both declaimed, each enjoyed the admiration of the other (cf. Philostratus, *V. S.* 529).

The aged Dionysius of Miletus once heard young Polemo argue a court case at Sardis and remarked, "This athlete has strength, but not from the wrestling-school" (ἰσχὺν ... ὁ ἀθλητὴς ἔχει, ἀλλ᾽ οὐκ ἐκ παλαίστρας). Upon overhearing this Polemo went to Dionysius and promised him a declamation. When Dionysius came to listen, Polemo first declaimed magnificently (διαπρεπῶς), then he went up to Dionysius, took the stance of a wrestler against him, and jokingly quoted the old proverb: "They were once, they were strong, the men of Miletus" (ἦσάν ποτ᾽, ἦσαν ἄλκιμοι Μιλήσιοι).[11] Thus he turned the ἀθλητής - παλαίστρα picture against the fading rhetorician — and that with a humor that Dionysius apparently accepted. Dionysius acknowledged that Polemo had many admirers and cited some of their opinions: according to some Polemo has "a mouth with twelve springs" (δωδεκάκρουνον ... τὸ στόμα), according to others "they measure his tongue with cubits, like the risings of the Nile" (πήχεσι διαμετροῦσιν αὐτοῦ τὴν γλῶτταν, ὥσπερ τὰς τοῦ Νείλου ἀναβάσεις) (Philostratus, *V. S.* 525).

Every celebrity with admirers also has detractors, and Polemo was no exception. Well publicized was the notoriously nasty dispute between Polemo and Favorinus of Arles. Favorinus practiced his sophist trade in neighboring Ephesus where the long standing rivalry between the two cities provided fertile soil for the strife that arose between Polemo and Favorinus. Favorinus' fiery lectures made inroads in Polemo's sphere of influence and threatened to diminish his own stature. The vain and offended Polemo responded with ridicule, invective, and personal insults. This quarrel spiraled out of control in mutually abusive speeches and writings. The details of this shabby squabble have been described often enough elsewhere[12] and need not be repeated here. The whole mud-slinging business served as a kind of cheap advertisement which helped both sophists achieve more fame. But the ripple effects reached to the imperial court where high officials sided with the one or the other. In the end Hadrian gave the nod to Polemo and let Favorinus fall in disfavor. The obvious sign of Polemo's 'victory' was his receiving the imperial commission

---

[11] This iambic phrase was a proverb for the degenerate (cf. πάλαι ποτ᾽ ἦσαν ἄλκιμοι Μιλήσιοι, Anacreon, *frag.* 81; Aristophanes, *Pl.* 1003).

[12] See most recently M. W. Gleason, op. cit., passim; cf. also Stegemann, op. cit. 1327-1328.

to deliver the festal oration at the dedication of the temple to Olympian Zeus in Athens when with the support of Hadrian it was finally finished in 131 CE.

Relationships with the Emperors

Polemo was born around 88 CE during the reign of Domitian (81-96). It was just about this time that Domitian enacted a number of onerous policies for which his reign is remembered[13] — policies which also helped rouse conspirators against him. In 96 CE Domitian was assassinated in a palace intrigue and he fell to the *damnatio memoriae* of the Senate. Thus his reign ended while Polemo was only an eight year old boy, and his policies will have had little material effect on the development of the young Polemo. Domitian's rule, especially the 'reign of terror' in the later years, however, did make much more welcome the reigns of the subsequent adoptive and Antonine emperors — the 'good,' 'philhellenic' rulers whose policies Polemo consistently worked to his own advantage.

During the long reign of Trajan (98-117 CE) Rome's fortunes were still on the rise. Trajan was a respected soldier, popular with the army, amenable to the senators, and honored by the people. He was a natural leader who did not abuse his powers. In contrast to Domitian he was not *dominus*, but *princeps*. He was personally modest, led a simple life, and fostered traditional Roman values. He is perhaps most remembered for expanding the empire to its farthest extent. Particularly important was the successful conquest and incorporation of Dacia (= Rumania / Bulgaria) through the Dacian Wars (101 and 105 CE) — the last Roman campaign to swell, not drain the Roman coffers. In the following decade Trajan turned his efforts to the East: Arabia was annexed in 106, Armenia in 114, and Mesopotamia in 115. While these eastern annexations were not immune to revolt as those in Europe appeared to

---

[13] For example, (a) he raised military pay and secured the German frontier between the Rhine and the Danube through concerted campaigns. These expenditures, however, brought increased taxation and a drain on the treasury. (b) To reduce competition with domestic agriculture in Italy, Domitian issued an edict that half the vineyards in the provinces should be cut down (cf. Suetonius, *Dom.* 7), a policy that brought an uproar in Asia. (c) He began refashioning his public image as Roman emperor more toward that of a Hellenistic autocrat, assuming divine honors as *dominus et deus.* Those who opposed the emperor cult with contrary philosophical or religious concepts — as did Stoics and Christians — came into conflict with Domitian. (d) As part of his general persecution of the Stoics (cf. Tacitus, *Agr.* 45; Pliny, *ep.* 3.11.3; 9.1.2-3) Domitian banished the philosophers from Italy (cf. Suetonius, *Dom.* 10.3-4; Cassius Dio 67.13.1-4). Resistance to such policies came from many quarters.

be, Trajan's reign was a period of Roman self-assurance. Hence, for Polemo's Ionian Greeks Roman sovereignty was never in dispute.

Trajan's administration was strict, just, and economically sound, but also humane and progressive. In the appointment of his administrators competence counted for something. Nonetheless, as Pliny's correspondence with Trajan shows, the emperor often personally directed the administration and discouraged local initiative. Polemo unfolded his career in this world of patron-client hierarchies, a world in which Trajan was conscious of his imperial mission to secure *felicitas, securitas, aequitas,* and *justitia.* Despite the nostolgia of Polemo — along with the whole Second Sophistic — for the earlier greatness of Greece, he betrayed no inner conflict between Greek ideals and Roman realities. Polemo, like virtually all Hellenistic Greeks, accepted Roman dominance and did his best to adapt to it and make the most of it. It was Trajan who bestowed on Polemo, probably on the occasion of his first ambassadorship representing Smyrna (113/114), the *libera legatio* by sea and by land (cf. Philostratus, *V. S.* 532). That right Polemo will have accepted gladly and he knew how to make use of it as his many travels show. Little else is reported about Polemo's relation to Trajan, but the patronage policies of Trajan's reign will have suited Polemo well and helped him considerably to advance his career.

During the reign of Hadrian (117-138 CE) Polemo reached the height of his career. The transition from Trajan to Hadrian brought important changes to the empire. Hadrian, recognizing that the empire had outstripped its financial and human resources, abandoned the expansionist policies of Trajan. Instead he pursued a policy of rational consolidation within defensible frontiers. From Hadrian's Wall in Britain, to the *Limes* in Germany, to the transfer of eastern provinces to client kings, Hadrian reorganized the military for a highly disciplined but more stationary defense posture. With the exception of putting down the Bar Kokhba Revolt in Judea (132-135 CE), there was little warfare during Hadrian's reign. Prosperity increased across the empire, particularly on the frontiers.

To implement his consolidation policies Hadrian became a traveling emperor like none before or after him. Between 121 and 132 he spent most of his time away from Rome traveling tirelessly through the provinces to learn first hand their problems and to enact effective policies. Hadrian's first journey in the Greek speaking lands of the Eastern empire took place in 123-126 CE. The first two of these years he spent in Asia, Bithynia, and Pontus, the third year in the homeland of Greece proper.[14] It was during his initial stay in Ephesus that Polemo met Hadrian. He must have made a strong impact on the emperor because, as much as was possible for an emperor who often vacillated toward friends and clients, a kind of friendship developed between them.[15] The *libera legatio* which Trajan had bestowed on Polemo Hadrian now extended to Polemo's descendants (cf. Philostratus, *V. S.* 532). And Hadrian invited the well-travelled Polemo to become his own travelling companion; after all Polemo knew the Greek provinces and their leaders, presented a dignified appearance, had a passion for hunting, and above all could provide sophisticated conversation. The extent of their travels together is a matter of dispute, but their journeys will certainly have covered Asia and Greek territories to the north, possibly even including Thrace.

That Hadrian became Polemo's patron if not friend proved to be of enormous advantage not only to Polemo personally, but also to Smyrna. No doubt at Polemo's urging Hadrian provided (both in 123/124 and again 133/134 CE) lavish subsidies for civic building projects in Smyrna (cf. Philostratus, *V. S.* 531, 533) — monies which hitherto had been designated for Ephesus now found their way to rival Smyrna. Many benefits accrued to Polemo thanks to his personal connection with the emperor, but perhaps none is more telling than the fact that Hadrian selected Polemo to deliver the oration at the dedication of the great temple of Olympian Zeus in Athens, a temple that after centuries of dormancy was finally completed at the behest of Hadrian. The Athenians would have no doubt preferred to have one of their own be speaker, but who could contest it when the emperor declared Polemo to be the poet laureate of Greece? The dedication occurred in 131/132 CE and Philostratus describes the event as follows:

"He fixed his gaze as was his custom, on the thoughts that were already taking their place in his mind, and then flung himself into his speech, and delivered a long and admirable discourse from the base of the temple. As the prooemium of his speech he declared that not without a divine impulse (μὴ ἀθεεὶ τὴν περὶ αὐτοῦ ὁρμὴν) was he inspired to speak on that theme" (*V. S.* 533).

---

[14] Cf. B. W. Henderson, *The Life and Principate of the Emperor Hadrian* (New York: Brentano, 1923) 84-89.

[15] A close relationship with Hadrian will probably not have been easy (cf. *professores omnium artium semper ut doctior risit, contempsit, obtrivit* [= he always laughed at, disdained, and degraded teachers of all sorts because he was more learned], *Vit. Hadr.* 15.10).

Twice Hadrian conducted extended trips to Greece (125/126 and 128). These trips are emblematic of his philhellenism.[16] He had, to be sure, a fondness for things Greek, but his philhellenism was more than just a cultural inclination. For Hadrian the Greek heritage was also a political tool for creating cohesion in a multic-ethnic empire. Hadrian's favors toward Polemo need to be seen also in this light. His patronage was as much a matter of political calculation as it was of personal inclination. To advance Polemo meant thus to strengthen the societal fabric of the eastern empire. And Hadrian was guided by astute *Realpolitik*.

Antoninus Pius, the adoptive son of Hadrian, was the successor of Hadrian and the emperor (138-161 CE) under whom Polemo finished out his career. Polemo was fortunate that this new administration did not put him in disfavor because of an earlier incident. When Antoninus was proconsul of Asia Polemo had treated him in a humiliating and insulting fashion. Once, while Polemo was out of town, Antoninus visited Smyrna and took up lodging in Polemo's house because it was the best in Smyrna and belonged to the most notable citizen. When Polemo returned home from his journey late at night to find his own home occupied by the proconsul, instead of accepting that as flattery he rudely turned Antoninus out of his house and compelled him to find other quarters. The affair was reported to Hadrian but he did not pursue it so as not to reopen the wound. Nevertheless, looking ahead, he prepared the reconciliation between Antoninus and Polemo by recording in his last testament that Polemo advised him upon his death to have the imperial power transfered to Antoninus. This tactic apparently performed its intended function because after Antoninus assumed the purple, Polemo remained in the good graces of the emperor. Indeed Antoninus even jested on occasion about Polemo's *faux pas* in Smyrna. Once when Polemo came to Rome Antoninus embraced him and said, "Give Polemo a lodging and don't let anyone turn him out of it" (cf. Philostratus, *V. S.* 534).

In light of Polemo's brilliant career in Smyrna, his sometimes condescending treatment of other sophists, and his close relationship to the emperors, Philostratus characterized Polemo with the oft quoted words: "Polemo was so arrogant (ὑπέρφρων) that he conversed with cities as though from a superior position (ὡς ... ἀπὸ τοῦ προὔχοντος), with emperors as though not from an inferior position (ὡς ... ἀπὸ τοῦ μὴ ὑφειμένου), and with gods as though an equal (ὡς ... ἀπὸ τοῦ ἴσου)" (Philostratus, *V. S.* 535).

---

[16] Cf. B. H. Henderson, op. cit., 105-121.

Disease and Death

In his later years Polemo suffered from a debilitating rheumatoid arthritus (cf. τὰ ἄρθρα ἐνόσει [= the joints were diseased], Philostratus, *V. S.* 535). The disease gradually progressed so far that he could walk only with difficulty or not at all. He customarily had himself carried to his declamations in a litter (φοράδην) because his joints were already so degenerated (διεφθορότων αὐτῷ ἤδη τῶν ἄρθρων, Philostratus, *V. S.* 537). He seems to have endured his condition with some humor. With a pun he exhorted the physicians who attended to what they must have diagnosed as a "petrifying of his joints" (λιθιώντων αὐτῷ τῶν ἄρθρων) to "dig and cut in the stone-quarries of Polemo" (ὀρύττειν καὶ τέμνειν τὰς Πολέμωνος λιθοτομίας, Philostratus, *V. S.* 543). In accordance with popular religion he sought healing at the Asclepius temple in Pergamon. Routinely such shrines had an 'incubation chamber' where the patients were to sleep and await therapy instructions from the god in their dreams.[17] When Polemo followed this customary 'somniation' process at the Pergamon's healing shrine Asclepius appeared to him and told him to abstain from drinking anything cold (ἀπέχεσθαι ψυχροῦ ποτοῦ). Polemo's sardonic response was: "Good sir, but what if you were treating a cow? (βέλτιστε, εἰ δὲ βοῦν ἐθεράπευες;)" (Philostratus, *V. S.* 535). Possibly in this whole matter he took his cue from Aristophanes' spoof on sacral incubation (cf. *Pl.* 654-747). In any case the episode shows that he tried to maintain his humor despite a condition that was increasingly incapacitating him. That will not have been easy because beside the restriction of movement the condition also brought physical pain. Regarding his health he once wrote to Herodes Atticus: "It is necessary to eat, but I do not have hands; it is necessary to walk, but there are no feet for me; it is necessary to endure pain (δεῖ ἀλγεῖν) and then I have both feet and hands" (Philostratus, *V. S.* 543).

As matters got progressively worse and it became clear to him that hope for healing or remission was illusory, he chose voluntary death over dragged out suffering. At the age of 56 (ca. 144 CE), therefore, he had himself brought to his hometown of Laodicea where he could be buried at the family grave site. His tomb was prepared "near the Syrian gate where his ancestors lay," and then in the presence of family and friends he had himself entombed while he was still alive (ταφῆναι δὲ αὐτὸν ζῶντα ἔτι). From inside the tomb he

---

[17] Pausanias' description of the Asclepeion at Corinth is typical: τοῦ ναοῦ δέ ἐστι πέραν ἔνθα οἱ ἱκέται τοῦ θεοῦ καθεύδουσιν [= over against the temple is the place where the suppliants of the god sleep] (2.27.3).

enjoined those bricking up the entrance: "Make haste, make haste, lest the sun see me reduced to silence! (ἔπειγε, ἔπειγε, μὴ γὰρ ἴδοι με σιωπῶντα ἥλιος)." As the opening was being closed he shouted out his last words to those wailing over him: "Give me a body and I will declaim" (δότε μοι σῶμα καὶ μελετήσομαι) (Philostratus, *V. S.* 543–544). This dictum appears to be an allusion to that widely circulated saying of Archimedes: "Give me a standing-place and I will move the world (δός μοι ποῦ στῶ καὶ κινῶ τὴν γῆν)."[18] His final utterance thus was commensurate with the self-importance that characterized his whole career.

Polemo's Personality and Oratory

Polemo was clearly endowed with impressive intellectual abilities. Along with having a remarkable memory and extensive vocabulary he was also quick-witted and sharp-tongued. His natural talent led him, however, to sidestep the rigor of a disciplined theoretical training and to remain rather superficial, a fact that was partly hidden by his polished language and many *bon mots*. Moreover his inborn abilities made him conceited and arrogant beyond all proportion. His royal ancestry and unusual wealth will, of course, also have contributed to his exaggerated self-assurance and sense of importance. Nevertheless, Polemo's rhetoric and oratorical style were regarded by his own world as exceptional — a model which some might aspire to, which few could actually emulate, but at which all had to marvel.

From Polemo himself no treatise on rhetorical theory or practice exists; he apparently was not one for handbooks. Little direct 'how to' advice for students survives, though Philostratus (*V. S.* 539) does record one interesting piece of guidance attributed to him: "Polemo used to say that the works of

---

[18] The quoted wording is from Pappus of Alexandria, *Syn.* 8.1060.1-4. Other versions were also in currency (cf. πᾷ βῶ καὶ κινῶ τὰν γᾶν [= {If there is} anywhere I can stand and I will move the earth], Simplicius of Athens, *in Ph.* 10.1110.5; πᾷ βῶ, καὶ χαριστίωνι τὰν γᾶν κινήσω πᾶσαν [= {If I have} somewhere to stand I will move the whole earth with my *charistion*], J. Tzetzes, *Chil.* 2.130 [The χαριστίων seems to have been a multiple pulley device for lifting or weighing, cf. *Chil.* 3.61]; Ἀρχιμήδης ... ἔγραψεν ὡς τῇ δοθείσῃ δυνάμει τὸ δοθὲν βάρος κινῆσαι δυνατόν ἐστι, καὶ νεανιευσάμενος ὥς φασι ῥώμῃ τῆς ἀποδείξεως εἶπεν ὡς εἰ γῆν εἶχεν ἑτέραν, ἐκίνησεν ἂν ταύτην μεταβὰς εἰς ἐκείνην [= Archimedes wrote ... that with the given force it is possible to move the given weight, and emboldened, as they say, by the strength of his demonstration, he said that if he had had another world, he would have moved this one by going to that one], Plutarch, *Marc.* 14.7).

prose writers needed to be brought out by armfuls, but the works of poets by wagon-loads (ἔλεγε δὲ ὁ Πολέμων τὰ μὲν τῶν καταλογάδην ὤμοις δεῖν ἐκφέρειν, τὰ δὲ τῶν ποιητῶν ἁμάξαις)."[19] The surviving declamations of Polemo cannot be said to actualize this advice. To be sure, they do build on the Marathon traditions first recorded by Herodotus (prose) and do contain a few mentions of Homer and Aeschylus (poets), but these hardly represent 'armfuls', let alone 'wagon-loads' of either. The dearth of allusions to the ancients, however, may be chalked up largely to the fictional setting of the declamations in 490 BCE. Quotations of or allusions to classical authors later than that year would, of course, constitute anachronisms. Given the early fifth century date of the ostensible speakers (Euphorion and Callimachus' father), it is natural that Polemo referred only to Homer and alluded only to Hesiod. The mention of Aeschylus appears only in connection with his being Euphorion's son and a word-smith. Since there is no literary reference to any work of Aeschylus — though his *Persians* may possibly lie in the background — Polemo avoided an open blunder.

Various listeners' descriptions of Polemo's style of rhetoric and delivery were recorded by Philostratus. Fragments of these may be gathered from his work and assembled into an 'impressionist' collage of Polemo as declaimer and rhetor. The theatrical externals — what Philostratus calls Polemo's σκηνή (*V. S.* 537, 595) — were integral to his delivery style. "He would come forward for the declamations with a face relaxed and confident (παρῄει μὲν ἐς τὰς ἐπιδείξεις διακεχυμένῳ τῷ προσώπῳ καὶ τεθαρρηκότι). ... When the themes had been proposed, he did not gather his thoughts in public but withdrew from the crowd for a brief time (τὰς ὑποθέσεις οὐκ ἐς τὸ κοινὸν ἐπεσκοπεῖτο, ἀλλ᾿ ἐξιὼν τοῦ ὁμίλου βραχὺν καιρόν). His utterance was clear and incisive, and there was a wonderful ringing sound in the tones of his voice (φθέγμα δὲ ἦν αὐτῷ λαμπρὸν καὶ ἐπίτονον καὶ κρότος θαυμάσιος οἷος ἀπεκτύπει τῆς γλώττης). ... He used to rise to such a pitch of excitement that he would jump up from his chair when he came to the most striking conclusions in his argument (ἀναπηδᾶν τοῦ θρόνου περὶ τὰς ἀκμὰς τῶν

---

[19] The distinction between prose and poetry was common, but not necessarily precise (cf. πολλὰ γὰρ καὶ τῶν μετὰ μέτρου ποιημάτων καὶ τῶν καταλογάδην συγγραμμάτων [= many of the poems with meter and of the writings in prose], Isocrates 2.7; ὁ ποιητὴς ἐν τοῖς δίχα μέτρου καὶ καταλογάδην αὐτῷ γεγραμμένοις φησίν [= the poet says in his writings without meter and in prose], Plutarch, *Fort. Rom.* 316d; ἐν μέτρῳ καὶ καταλογάδην ὑμνοῦσιν [= they hymn praises in meter and in prose], Julian, *Or.* 1.3a; τὴν ... ποίησιν, ᾗ ...ὕστερον ἐχρήσατο ἐν τοῖς καταλογάδην ἰάμβοις [= the poetry which he later used in the iambic verses in prose], Athenaeus 10.445b).

ὑποθέσεων, τοσοῦτον αὐτῷ περιεῖναι ὁρμῆς), and whenever he rounded off a period he would utter the final clause with a smile, as though to show clearly that he could deliver it without effort (καὶ ὅτε ἀποτορνεύοι περίοδον, τὸ ἐπὶ πᾶσιν αὐτῆς κῶλον σὺν μειδιάματι φέρειν, ἐνδεικνύμενον πολὺ τὸ ἀλύπως φράζειν). At certain places in the argument he would stamp the ground just like the horse in Homer [Il. 6.507] (κροαίνειν ἐν τοῖς τῶν ὑποθέσεων χωρίοις οὐδὲν μεῖον τοῦ Ὁμηρικοῦ ἵππου)" (V. S. 537). When asked his opinion of Polemo, Herodes Atticus quoted a line from Homer: "The sound of swift-footed horses strikes upon my ears (ὠκυπόδων ἀμφὶ κτύπος οὔατα βάλλει [Il. 10.535], thus indicating how resonant and far-echoing was his eloquence (ἐνδεικνύμενος δὴ τὸ ἐπίκροτον καὶ τὸ ὑψηχὲς τῶν λόγων)" (Philostratus, V. S. 539). Others described "Polemo's style of eloquence [as] passionate, combative, and with an echoing ring, like the trumpet at the Olympic games (= ἡ δὲ ἰδέα τῶν Πολέμωνος λόγων θερμὴ καὶ ἐναγώνιος καὶ τορὸν ἠχοῦσα, ὥσπερ ἡ Ὀλυμπιακὴ σάλπιγξ)" (V. S. 542).

Even apart from the delivery, however, Polemo's composition apparently possessed a certain distinctive eloquence. "It was solemn speech, not tedious, but brilliant and inspired (ἡ σεμνολογία οὐχ ὑπτία, λαμπρὰ δὲ καὶ ἔμπνους)." "His ornate rhetoric and technical skill were equal to the argument (ἤρκεσε τῷ λόγῳ ξὺν περιβολῇ καὶ τέχνῃ)" (V. S. 542). In his declamations "he gave free reins to the argument, and yet the ideas preserve the effect of presenting both sides (ἡνία τε ἐμβέβληται τῷ λόγῳ καὶ τὸ ἐπαμφότερον αἱ διάνοιαι σώζουσιν)" (V. S. 543). It is precisely the both-sidedness (τὸ ἐπαμφότερον) which is essential in that declamation sub-genre known as controversiae, the type to which Polemo's surviving declamations belong. As testimony to the plain persuasiveness of Polemo's words Philostratus reports that even after his death when Polemo's last prepared speech on behalf of Smyrna's temple rights was read aloud before emperor Antoninus he gave his decision in accordance with it (Philostratus, V. S. 540).

The Writings and Speeches of Polemo

Most of what Polemo produced no longer survives. Completely lost is his work called *The Histories* (αἱ ἱστορίαι). Its contents are unknown, but it apparently had some pretensions because Phrynichus says that Polemo employed a grammarian (γραμματικός) to correct (ἐπανορθῶν) this work (cf. *Ecl.* 238). That Phrynichus could criticize specific vocabulary (namely: κεφαλαιωδέστατον) in its prooemium shows that the book was still in circulation late in the second century.

While the Greek text of Polemo's work on *physiognomica* was apparently lost early,[20] the work did manage to survive in Arabic translation as well as in a shortened Latin version (late 4th century) and in a Greek paraphrase from the Jewish physician Adamantios (early 4th century).[21] These versions make clear the pseudo-scientific character of the work and the underlying notion that the external physiognomy reflects the internal character and intentions of a person.[22]

It was not primarily, however, for being a writer that Polemo was remembered, but for being a rhetorician. Yet here too, unfortunately, the great bulk of his work does not survive. This may be due in part to the fact that many of his speeches were delivered impromptu while other speeches, though written, were probably too insipid to save. His public or official speeches comprised a range of genres: there were *court arguments* (λόγοι δικανικοί), *ambassadorial speeches* (λόγοι πρεσβευτικοί), and *occasional talks* (e.g., nuptual addresses, funeral eulogies, and invectives against Favorinus).[23] The high point of Polemo's public speaking was probably his speech in Athens (131/132 CE) at the dedication of the completed Zeus temple (cf. Philostratus, *V. S.* 533), but this speech too has unfortunately not survived.

As sophist and teacher of rhetoric Polemo, of course, engaged his life long in the presentation of declamations (μελέται). These will have served a variety of functions — paradigms for students, public entertainment, and competitive exericises to keep the wits sharpened. From this genre of his

---

[20] The Greek *physiognomica* was still read by Origen who mentioned it (ca. 248/249 CE) alongside comparable works from Zopyrus and Loxus (cf. *Cels.* 1.33).
[21] Cf. R. Förster, *Scriptores Physiognomonici Graeci et Latini* (Leipzig: Teubner, 1893) 2 vols.; J. Mesk, "Die Beispiele in Polemons Physiognomonik," *WS* 50 (1932) 51-67.
[22] Cf. M. W. Gleason, op. cit., 125-175.
[23] Cf. W. Stegemann, op. cit., 1341-1342.

speeches the great mass is also lost though the themes of at least ten of Polemo's declamations are recorded:[24]

(1) A theme from pre-Classical Athens: 'Solon demands that his laws be rescinded after Peisistratus has obtained a bodyguard' [ca. 560 BCE] (ὁ Σόλων ὁ αἰτῶν ἀπαλείφειν τοὺς νόμους λαβόντος τὴν φρουρὰν τοῦ Πεισιστράτου, cf. Philostratus, *V. S.* 542). This was a ἐσχηματισμένη ὑπόθεσις (= subject fashioned with figures of speech) belonging to the so-called *ductus simplex* (= plain discourse).[25]

(2) A theme from the Persian Wars: 'The fathers of Cynegirus and Callimachus dispute over the preeminent honor for their sons at Marathon' [490 BCE]. Of all the declamations reported in connection with Polemo, this is the only one whose text has survived (for the theme cf. especially the prooemium). The text and translation are presented in chapter 3 of the present study. The corresponding pair of speeches belongs to the common subcategory of declamations known as *controversiae*.

(3) A theme from the Peloponnesian War: 'The Athenians should return to their demes after the battle of Aegos Potami' [405 BCE] (τοὺς ᾽Αθηναίους μετὰ Αἰγὸς ποταμοὺς ἐς τοὺς δήμους ἀνεσκεύαζεν, cf. Philostratus, *V. S.* 538). Polemo refuted the opinion that defeated Athens should give up its sea empire and be dismantled, and that the Athenians should be banished and spread out in villages.

(4) A theme from after the Peloponnesian War: 'The Greek victory trophies should be taken down once the Peloponnesian war ended in a truce' [404 BCE] (τὰ τρόπαια κατέλυε τὰ ῾Ελληνικὰ τοῦ Πελοποννησίου πολέμου ἐς διαλλαγὰς ἥκοντος, cf. Philostratus, *V. S.* 538). The argument was that such monuments should be removed after the conclusion of peace; there should not be permanent monuments of Greek victories over other Greeks. This theme appears to have been commonly used in school declamations (cf. Pausanias 9.40.8–9; Philostratus, *V. S.* 539; Apsines 219).

(5) A theme from the career of Socrates: 'Xenophon requests to die at the same time as Socrates' [399 BCE] (ὁ Ξενοφῶν ὁ ἀξιῶν ἀποθνήσκειν ἐπὶ Σωκράτει, cf. Philostratus, *V. S.* 542). The argument appears to have been that life is not worth continuing without the presence of the master philosopher.

(6) A theme from the life of Demosthenes: 'Demosthenes denounces himself after the battle of Chaeronea' [338 BCE] (ὁ μετὰ Χαιρώνειαν προσαγγέλλων ἑαυτόν, cf. Philostratus, *V. S.* 542).

---

[24] Cf. the lists in H. Jüttner, op. cit., 40-41 and W. Stegemann, op. cit., 1342-1342.

[25] Cf. H. Jüttner, op. cit., 43.

(7) A theme from the life of Demosthenes: 'Demosthenes urges the Athenians to flee in their triremes at the approach of Philip' [337 BCE] (ὁ ξυμβουλεύων ἐπὶ τῶν τριήρων φεύγειν ἐπίοντος μὲν Φιλίππου, cf. Philostratus, *V. S.* 543).

(8) A theme from the life of Demosthenes: 'Demosthenes pretends that he ought to be punished with death for the affair of Harpalus' [323 BCE] (ὁ δοκῶν θανάτου ἑαυτῷ τιμᾶσθαι ἐπὶ τοῖς Ἀρπαλείοις, cf. Philostratus, *V. S.* 542/543).

(9) A theme from the life of Demosthenes: 'Demosthenes denies taking the bribe of fifty talents' [323? BCE] (ὁ Δημοσθένης ὁ τὰ πεντήκοντα τάλαντα ἐξομνύμενος, cf. Philostratus, *V. S.* 542).

(10) A theme from everyday life: 'The adulterer uncovered' (ὁ μοιχὸς ὁ ἐκκεκαλυμμένος, cf. Philostratus, *V. S.* 542). This, the only recorded a-historical theme of a Polemonic declamation, appears to be about a case of a father committing adultery with the wife of his son — a topic treated both in comedy and in court.[26]

This range of recorded topics probably constitutes a fair representation of Polemo's repertoire of declamation themes — mostly historical topics from the classical period (from the Persian Wars to Alexander the Great) along with a smattering of other kinds of subjects. These themes certainly correspond to the general archaizing tendencies of the Second Sophistic, a movement characterized by nostogia both for the old, 'pure' Attic dialect and for the classical, 'golden' age of Athens.

---

[26] Cf. W. Stegemann, op. cit., 1343; also 1 Cor 5:1-5 where a son is having an affair with his father's wife.

Declamations: Genre and *Sitz-im-Leben*

Aristotle's landmark treatise on classical rhetoric distinguished three basic types (γένη) of speech: δικανικόν, συμβουλευτικόν, ἐπιδεικτικόν (= forensic, deliberative, demonstrative; cf. *Rh.* 1358a36–1359a36). The literary genre known as "declamation"[27] (Latin: *declamatio* = Greek: μελέτη) which first emerged in the Hellenistic era[28] was regarded as belonging in the third group. Declamation did not have the specific practical purpose of winning a case through legal argumentation (forensic rhetoric) or convincing an assembly through political address (deliberative rhetoric). Its goal was not to persuade the listeners to form a judgment about the past or make a decision about the future. Rather it sought simply to impress the audience and win their applause. Declamation revolved around 'invented' topics and served as *practice* for the speaker (μελέτη = exercise), as *entertainment* for the public, or as *display* of the rhetorician's talents (thus, *epideictic* rhetoric). That is to say, declamation was at home not in the forum (court) or the senate (council) but in the school. And with it the school took on the character of a theater in which the rhetorician was at center-stage — not as a pedantic teacher but as a virtuoso performer. His performances were called declamations.

The decline of the Greek city-state and the Roman republic and the rise instead of the principate profoundly affected oratory and rhetoric in the Mediterranean world. When significant political decisions were no longer arrived at through democratic debate but were made by a single ruler at the

---

[27] For overviews on the phenomenon of declamation cf. C. J. Fordyce, "Declamatio," *OCD*, 316–317; W. Kroll, "Rhetorik," *RE*, Suppl. 7, 1119–1124; W. C. Summers, "Declamations under the Empire," *Proceedings of the Classical Association* 10 (1913) 87–102; W. Hofrichter, *Studien zur Entwicklungsgeschichte der Deklamation von der griechischen Sophistik bis zur römischen Kaiserzeit*, Breslau: dissertation, 1935; S. F. Bonner, *Roman Declamation in the Late Republic and Early Empire* (Berkeley: University of California Press, 1949); D. L. Clark, *Rhetoric in Greco-Roman Education* (New York: Columbia University Press, 1957) 213-261; M. L. Clarke, *Rhetoric at Rome* (London: Cohen & West, 1962) 85–99; H. I. Marrou, *A History of Education in Classical Antiquity* (New York: Sheed and Ward, 1956) 194–205, 284–289; G. A. Kennedy, "The Sophists as Declaimers," *Papers Presented at the 105th Annual Meeting of The American Philological Association* (University Park: American Philological Association, 1974) 19-22; D. A. Russell, *Greek Declamation* (Cambridge: Cambridge University Press, 1983).

[28] Its origin in the Greek world was often dated to the time if not the person of Demetrius of Phaleron [ca. 350-280 BCE] (cf. Quintilian 2.4.41). In the Latin world it was traced to the time of Cicero and Calvus (cf. Seneca, *Contr.* I, pr. 12).

top, deliberative rhetoric lost much of its *raison d'être*. When serious judicial decisions were not reached through local courts with juries of peers, but transferred to imperial officials who came in from the outside, forensic rhetoric was drained of much of its life's blood. With the rise of the empire epideictic rhetoric, however, did not suffer the same negative effects. Education and the school remained important, for they provided a means to increase one's influence or to raise one's station within a society built around class and hierarchy. In a world of patrons and clients the skilled speaker is always at an advantage. Thus epideictic rhetoric and declamation became especially popular in the period of the emperors.

The declamations fell into two basic groups. The main sub-categories were the *suasoriae* and the *controversiae*. The sub-category *suasoria*, as the name indicates, presented a persuasive argument for (*suadere* = προτρέπειν) or a dissuasive argument against (*dissuadere* = ἀποτρέπειν) some undertaking (cf. Quintilian 3.8.6). The sub-category *controversia* usually comprised a pair of antithetical speeches which argued two sides of a case or presented two opposing positions. In *suasoriae* the speaker typically 'advised' famous characters from the past what to do at critical junctures in their careers. In *controversiae* the speaker assumed the role of the litigants or their advocates in an imagined law-suit — arguing first on behalf of the one, then on behalf of the other. Because of their 'advisory' nature the *suasoriae* appeared to resemble deliberative rhetoric and because of their 'adversarial' nature the *controversiae* seemed to be like forensic rhetoric.

The subjects or themes (ὑποθέσεις) of declamations, though largely traditional, were fictitious in the sense that they were 'made up' by the speaker or proposed by his audience. On the one hand there were subjects dealing with mythological or historical situations remembered and recreated in the past, and on the other hand there were subjects treating legal or moral dilemmas postulated in the present. In general, figures from the classical past provided the themes for the *suasoriae*, while tangled legal problems posited in the present provided the themes for the *controversiae*. In the former category situations taken from the poets (Homer, the tragedians), historians (Herodotus, Thucydides, Xenophon) and orators (Demosthenes, Aeschines, Lysias) were favorites. In the latter category themes were often drawn from a traditional repertoire of unreal and improbable situations — tyrant killers and rapists, pirates and hostages, disinherited and adopted sons, violated daughters and wayward virgins, thwarted suicides and failed executions, unpaid ransoms and reclaimed dowries, and other such romance-like subjects. In both types of declamation literary license allowed the distortion of received history or the fabrication of bizarre convoluted situations for the sake of sharpening the issue. In contrast to the Latin rhetoricians the Greek sophists preferred historical themes, particularly topics from the history of Athens in the period from the Persian wars to Alexander the Great.[29]

The 'historical' theme of Polemo's extant declamations is in line with this grand tradition of Greek declamations. The subject is not a contorted legal problem depicted in the present but a dispute — undocumented, to be sure, but not inherently implausible — projected into the classical past. Such retrojection was common practice in the Latin *suasoriae*; while not unknown in the Latin *controversiae*, it was much less frequent (cf. Seneca, *Contr.* 6.5; Suetonius, *Rh.* 25.3). The *controversia* form of Polemo's declamations matches that of other published Greek declamations from the second century (cf. Lucian, *Phal.* 1 and 2; and Aristides, many of whose declamations involve speakers on two or more sides of a case).

The theme for a declamation was often determined on short notice or right on the spot. The teacher could assign it to the student and allow some time for preparation, but often audiences proposed the topic and this, of course, allowed little time for organizing one's thoughts. This procedure sharpened one's skill at speaking extemporaneously but it was no business for the faint hearted. On occasion the teacher would declaim before the students to provide for them a model to emulate. As teachers became more recognized their declamations could be presented not just before their students, but also in front of a larger public. In cases of accomplished performances this practice brought fame, even stardom to the rhetorician. Polemo certainly became a celebrity through his impressive and polished declaiming. This whole development led to the declamation becoming a recognized literary form, and in the second century and thereafter a number of distinguished authors (e.g.,

---

[29] Philostratus and Apsines, our two main primary sources (3rd century) on Greek declamation in the Second Sophistic, make this clear. Of the *circa* 45 declamation subjects reported by Philostratus in his *Lives of the Sophists*, 31 are 'historical' (relating to figures like Solon, Demosthenes, Xerxes, and Darius). Some of the speeches are imagined as taking place in a law court, others in a political assembly. Only four of the 45 are clearly judicial and so comparable to Latin *controversiae*, though a few others may be regarded as in this class. In Apsines' rhetorical handbook ($\tau \acute{\epsilon} \chi \nu \eta$ $\acute{\rho} \eta \tau o \rho \iota \kappa \acute{\eta}$) a similar percentage of historical hypotheses is recorded (cf. G. A. Kennedy, op. cit., 19).

Polemo, Aristides, Lucian, Libanius, Himerius) ended up publishing selected declamations.[30]

The fictitious theme of a declamation was posed right at the beginning, and Polemo's declamations conform to this pattern. The theme could be and often was introduced with the words τίνας ἂν εἴποι λόγους (= what words would [so-and-so] say [when ...] ... ?) or τί ἂν εἴποι (= what would [so-and-so] say [when ...] ...?) (cf. *An. Gr.* 9.449-480). For both *suasoriae* and *controversiae* hundreds of topics are known from the ancient world and scores of representative speeches survive.[31]

Advanced students of rhetoric were expected to master both types of declamation. After beginning with grammar and then working through the *progymnasmata* the curriculum[32] culminated in the practice of declaiming. Of the two types of declamation the *controversia* was viewed as by far the more challenging.[33]

The declamations were criticised harshly from many quarters because of their hackneyed themes, their distortions of history and reality, the remoteness of their subject from real life, and their bombastic style.[34] A more withering

---

[30] In earlier times declamations do not seem to have been written out or published. In the first century, for example, Seneca wrote, "In general there are no extant drafts from the pens of the greatest declaimers, or, what is worse, there are forged ones" (*Fere enim aut nulli commentarii maximorum declamatorum extant aut, quod peius est, falsi*, Seneca, *Contr.* 1 pr. 11).

[31] A catalogue of over 400 mythological-historical topics is assembled in R. Kohl, *De scholasticarum declamationum Romanarum argumentis ex historia petitis* (Rhetorische Studien 4; Paderborn: Schöningh, 1915); cf. M. Schamberger, *De declamationum Romanorum argumentis* (Halle: Wischau & Burckhardt, 1917). A broad survey of typical legal topics is found in Seneca's *Controversiae* and *Suasoriae*; cf. T.S. Simonds, *The Themes treated by the elder Seneca* (Baltimore: dissertation, 1896); W.C. Summers, "Declamations under the Empire," *Proceedings of the Classical Association* 10 (1913) 87-102; G. A. Kennedy, op. cit., 19-23.

[32] Philostratus refers to the curriculum as the δρόμος (= path, cf. οὐκ ἀγύμναστον τοῦ περὶ τοὺς σοφιστὰς δρόμου [= not untrained in the curriculum among the sophists], *V. S.* 587).

[33] Cf. *suasoriae quidem etsi, tamquam plane leviores et minus prudentiae exigentes, pueris delegantur, controversiae robustioribus adsignantur* (= the *suasoriae* are entrusted to [mere] boys, as being obviously of less importance and not making such demands on the judgement, the *controversiae* are assigned to the more mature [students], Tacitus, *Dial.* 35.4).

[34] Cf. Seneca, *Contr.* 7.6.24; 10 pr. 12; Suetonius, *Rh.* 1, 5, 6; Juvenal 7.150-177; Tacitus, *Dial.* 35.4; Petronius, *Sat.* 1-6, 10; Pseudo-Quintilian, *Decl.* 279.13; Dionysius Halicarnassus, *Rh.* 10; Philostratus, *V.S.* 595-596; Lucian, *Rh. Pr.* 10, 17-18. For a summary review of the ancient criticisms of declamations cf. S. F. Bonner, op. cit., 71-83; H. Caplan, "The Decay of Eloquence at Rome in the First Century," *Of Eloquence. Studies in Ancient and Medieval Rhetoric* (Ithaca: Cornell University Press, 1970) 160-195.

critique than that credited to the orator Cassius Severus is hard to find: "Everything is superfluous in a declamation — declamation is itself superfluous" (*In scholastica quid non supervacuum est, cum ipsa supervacua sit*, Seneca, *Contr.* 3 pr. 12). Despite the criticisms, however, the genre once established proved to be long-lived — it endured in school and culture for centuries virtually unchanged.[35] *Suasoriae* were deemed to be a good education for those aspiring to administrative posts and the *controversiae* were regarded as valuable training for students preparing for careers in the legal profession. In the West these declamations were part of the curriculum in rhetoric until the collapse of Rome, in the East they survived well into the Byzantine empire. Thus with his declamations Polemo was neither innovator nor catalyst nor iconoclast. Rather he stood in and continued an established tradition, and his declamations must be measured in terms of that tradition.

Polemo's Theme: The Valor of Cynegirus and Callimachus at Marathon

The Battle of Marathon[36]

The golden age of Greece was ushered in by the Greeks repelling the Persian invaders. The Persians had ascended to world power under Cyrus (550–530 BCE) who systematically defeated and annexed the Median empire, Asia Minor, Mesopotamia and the Iranian plateau. His son Cambyses (530-522 BCE) extended the Persian imperial rule to Egypt. Under the third monarch, Darius (522-486 BCE), Persia's expansion efforts were turned toward Europe — something no Eastern empire had ever done before. But these efforts were

---

[35] That in late antiquity declamations could be cast in poetic form was the exception, not the rule (cf. the *controversia* in 285 hexameters, *An. Lat.* 21).

[36] The principal authority is and remains Herodotus 6.107-117. All other texts are either derivative or supplementary (cf. Nepos, *Milt.* 4-6; Plato, *Leg.* 3 [698d–e]; Aristotles, *Rh.* 3.10 [1411a]; *Ath. Con.* 22.2-3; Demosthenes 19.303; Isocrates 4.86-87; Lysias 2.21-26; Xenophon, *An.* 3.2.12; Plutarch, *Arist.* 5; *Herod.* 26-27 [861e-863b]; *Quest. Conv.* 1.10.3 [628d-e]; *Cam.* 19.3; *Glor. Ath.* 7 [349d-e]; Pausanias 1.32.3-5; 10.20.2; 1.15.3-4; 10.11.5; Pompeius Trogus 2.9.8-20 [epitome in M. Junianus Justinius]; Aelian, *V.H.* 2.25; Suidas, Ἱππιας 1). For a solid assessment of the material cf. W. W. How and J. Wells, *A Commentary on Herodotus*, Appendix XVIII "Marathon" (Oxford: Clarendon, 1912) vol. 2, pp. 353-363. Though older, this careful analysis of the sources and reconstruction of the events at Marathon is still fundamentally sound and extremely useful for understanding the battle. Cf. W. K. Pritchett, *Marathon* (University of California Publications in Classical Archeology 4.2; Berkeley: University of California Press, 1960) 137-190.

unsuccessful. In 513 BCE Darius' army crossed the Bosporus and pressed north along the shore of the Black Sea into the land of the Scythians. Their scorched earth policy forced the Persians to retreat. In 499-494 BCE Darius suppressed a revolt of the Greek cities in Ionia; but when he attempted to advance into Greece in 492 BCE storms off Mt. Athos brought his naval forces to a halt. In 490 BCE a larger and more carefully prepared invasion force made a 'frontal' attack on the Greek heartland itself by sailing straight across the Aegean and disembarking on the shores of Attica. That fateful landing occurred in September of 490 BCE[37] on the eastern side of Attica at the bay of Marathon. The Persian general Datis was guided in this choice of landing spot by the renegade Hippias, the former tyrant of Athens (527-510 BCE).

Topographically the oblong plain of Marathon[38] is about 6 miles long and 1½ - 3 miles wide. Though now partially drained, in classical time it was in spots quite marshy. On the one side the plain is bounded by the sea, on the other by abruptly rising mountains. The Persians anchored their ships near the Kynosoura (= Dog's Tail) promontory, a long narrow natural 'jetty' at the northeastern end of the plain which protrudes a mile into the sea and which provided shelter for the boats during the disembarkation. Thus the Persians formed their beachhead on the northeastern part of the plain. The actual size of their force is uncertain: the early sources provide no numbers and later traditions grossly exaggerated the size (into the hundreds of thousands!). But the Persian forces are reasonably estimated today at twenty to thirty thousand — that is, they will have outnumbered the Greeks by two or three to one.

As soon as the Athenians learned of the Persian landing they sent a runner posthaste to Sparta (ca. 150 miles away to the southwest) to request military assistance and themselves marched out to Marathon (ca. 26 miles northeast of Athens) to meet the enemy. They arrived from the southwest and encamped in the hills at the southwestern end of the plain near the sanctuary of Herakles. There they were joined by an allied contingent of 1000 Plateans. The combined Greek forces then totaled around 10,000+ men. They held a strong defensive position and blocked the mountain road to Athens. The Greek

---

[37] For the date of the landing cf. *Marmor Parium* 48, line 62; Aristotle, *Ath. Con.* 22; Plutarch, *Arist.* 5; *Cam.* 19.

[38] The plain was named after the chief town, Marathon, in the old Attic tetrapolis which controlled the whole plain (cf. Strabo 8.7.1; Plutarch, *Thes.* 14.1). The name Marathon (Μαραθών) itself appears to derive from the fennel (μάραθον, cf. Theophrastus, *H.P.* 1.12.2) which characteristically grows all over the plain (cf. Strabo 3.4.9).

high command was vested in the polemarch, Callimachus, who had a staff of ten generals including Miltiades, the traditional architect of the victory.

The two armies faced each other for a number of days without taking action. The Persians were unwilling to attack the Athenians in their strong position because that tactic could not put to effective use the Persian cavalry and bowmen. For their part the Greeks were not minded to leave their position without the awaited Spartan reinforcements. After this 'waiting game' Datis — apparently believing that he was not going to lure the Greeks onto the plain where they would be exposed to the rapid mobility of his cavalry and the superior 'firepower' of his archers, and probably reckoning that his own position would become weaker should help arrive from the Peloponnesus — put his horses back on the ships so as to move against Athens by sea. Miltiades, seeing the Persians in 'transition' posture, convinced Callimachus and the Greek generals that it would be the opportune time to attack.

Hence, the Greek hoplites extended their line to match that of the Persians. They thinned their center, strengthened their wings, and at dawn advanced in double time surprising the Persians and not allowing their archers to get into effective formation. The Greeks had to yield in the center but their flanks squeezed the Persians in a pincher movement which destroyed the invading army. The whole battle was over in one day. Many escaped to their ships, indeed most of the fleet made a successful get-away, but a great number of surrounded Persian infantry were cut down on land (6400 according to Herodotus 6.117). How large in fact the material defeat was may be debated, but the moral effect of the Greek victory was immeasurable. The Greek hoplites had proven to be more than a match for the best soldiers from the East. The remaining Persian force abandoned any further attack on Athens and sailed back to Asia. The Greek dead numbered relatively few (192 Athenians according to Herodotus 6.117; no figure is given for the dead Plateans). More importantly, the blood of the Greek heroes buried at Marathon — and their burial mound is still visible there[39] — became the seed of classical Greek liberty and the stuff of legend for centuries to come.

---

[39] A generation after Polemo Pausanias visited Marathon and described the mound: "On the plain is the grave of the Athenians, and upon it are *steles* giving the names of those who died according to their tribes; and there is another grave for the Boeotian Plataeans" (Pausanias 1.32.3). This famous mound, a tourist site today known as the *Soros* (σωρός), was first excavated by Greek archeologists in 1890-1891 and has since then been re-examined several times. The findings are summarized in J. G. Frazer, *Pausanias's Description of Greece* (New York: Biblo & Tannen, 1965) vol. 2, pp. 433-434 and N. Δ. Παπαχατζῆς, Παυσανίου Ἑλλάδος Περιήγησις: Ἀττικά (Athens: Ekdotike Athenon, 1974) vol. 1, pp. 422-424 who also includes a color photo of the Soros.

The Heroes Cynegirus and Callimachus in Early Classical Tradition

In the first generation after Marathon (490 BCE) there were still thousands of eye-witnesses in Athens who could recount the events and heroic deeds of the great battle. In the second and third generations, of course, these eye-witnesses gradually died off. Their recollections, however, were in part preserved by two 'record-keepers' — an artist and an historian.

(1) Around 460 BCE the Athenians erected on the north edge of their central agora a long colonnaded portico which became known as the Στοὰ Ποικίλη (= Many-Colored [or Painted] Portico). This name derived from the fact that its back wall was decorated with a series of expansive and renowned murals, one of which portrayed the battle at Marathon. The painting of this scene was attributed to various mid-fifth century artists: Polygnotus of Thasos, Mikon of Athens, or Panaenus, the brother of the Athenian sculptor Phidias (cf. Pliny, *N. H.* 35.57, 59; Plutarch, *Cim.* 4.6; Aelian, *N.A.* 7:38). This Stoa Poikile was the same public hall where Zeno of Citium later (ca. 300 BCE) used to teach and where his successors, the "Stoics" (named after that same portico), continued teaching well into the third century CE. The building together with its famous paintings survived the Herulian sack of Athens (267 CE) and was still intact in the 4th century. Himerius, who studied and taught in Athens in that period explained elements of the painting to visiting Ionians (cf. Himerius, *Or.* 10 [59].2). When Synesios mentions (ca. 400 CE) that a [unnamed] proconsul had the paintings removed, he speaks as if this removal were recent (cf. *Ep.* 54.135). Thus throughout the Classical and Hellenistic periods because of its cultural attractions and its central location the Stoa Poikile drew countless visitors of all sorts — philosophers, sophists, students, shoppers, tourists, and just plain loiterers.[40] In Polemo's own day, therefore, the Marathon picture was still intact and it is fair to assume that he viewed it when he was in Athens — and if on no other occasion he was certainly there to deliver the dedication speech at the Temple of Olympian Zeus in 131 CE (cf. Philostratus, *V. S.* 533).

The painting first of all preserved elements of the living mid-5th century oral tradition about Marathon, but then the picture subsequently became itself

---

[40] Cf. Luke's disparaging remark about those hanging around in the agora (cf. Acts 17:17), "Now all the Athenians and the foreigners residing there customarily find nothing else to do with their time than to talk about or listen to some novelty" (Acts 17:21; cf. Aristophanes, *Eq.* 1257–1263; Demosthenes 4.10; Thucydides 3.38.4).

an impetus for continuing and embellishing that tradition. Both this painting
and the traditions connected with it informed the declamations of Polemo. If
the painting could be examined today it would, no doubt, illumine some of
Polemo's formulations. Unfortunately in the present no substantial remains of
the Stoa Poikile survive or are visible. The whole site has been disturbed on its
south side by the modern rail line to the Piraeus while on the north side it is
covered by shops of modern Athens' Ermou business district. Nonetheless,
though nothing of the Marathon mural is archeologically recoverable, there do
exist a number of descriptions of the painting including some from second
century authors only a few decades removed from Polemo.[41] These texts,
supplemented with an analysis of a few extant reliefs depicting (probably) the
battle of Marathon, do allow a partial reconstruction of basic elements of the
painting's composition. On the basis of this evidence several reconstructions of
the mural have been attempted.[42]

The painting was epic in proportion and elaborate in detail. Despite
divergencies in the various reconstructions there is consensus that Cynegirus,
Callimachus, and Miltiades played especially significant roles in the
composition (cf. Aeschines, 3.186; Nepos, *Milt.* 6.3; Pausanias 1.15.3;
Lucian, *J. Tr.* 32). Other famous figures too, whom Polemo names, appeared
in the painting, for example: Polyzelus, Aeschylus, and Datis. The heroes
(Herakles and Theseus) and gods (Zeus, Hera, Athena, Poseidon, Pan)
mentioned by Polemo (cf. Index 7) were also shown in the picture.

Cynegirus, who attempted to hold back a Persian ship, will have been
depicted either with his hand on the verge of being chopped off or with it
already severed. Because of the Marathon mural the severed hand appears to

---

[41] Cf. Demosthenes 59 [*in Neaeram*].94; Aeschines 3.186; Nepos, *Milt.* 6.3; Pliny, *N. H.* 35.57; Pausanias 1.15.1–3; Aelian, *N.A.* 7.38; Aristides 46.174; Lucian, *Dem.* 53; *J. Tr.* 32; *Dial. Meretr.* 8.2; *Nav.* 13.

[42] Cf. C. Robert, "Die Marathonschlacht in der Poikile," (*Hallisches Winckelmannsprogram* 18), Halle: Niemeyer, 1895, pp. 1–126. The careful study from E. B. Harrison, "The South Frieze of the Nike Temple and the Marathon Painting in the Painted Stoa," *AJA* 76 (1972), 353–378, gives the most comprehensive documentation both from the plastic arts and literary texts — including an examination of Polemo's declamations. For an elaborate graphic reconstruction of the entire Marathon mural see the presentation in N. Δ. Παπαχατζῆς, Παυσανίου Ἑλλάδος Περιήγησις: Ἀττικα (Athens: Ekdotike Athenon, 1974) vol. 1, pp. 250–251.

have become a fixed element in the artistic tradition.[43]

Callimachus appears to have been depicted in the painting wounded with arrows. No extant texts referring to the picture explicitly describe Callimachus this way. But Aristides' allusive description [2nd century CE] of Callimachus with the phrase τις καὶ τελευτήσας εἰστήκει περιτοξευθεὶς ὑπὸ τῶν βαρβάρων (= one even when he was dying remained standing, shot to death with arrows by the barbarians, Aristides 13.88) probably derives from the Marathon painting.[44]

(2) Subsequent to the artistic record, Herodotus produced [ca. 433±2 BCE] the first extant literary account of the battle at Marathon (cf. 6.107-117).[45]

In this entire account Cynegirus is accorded merely one sentence: τοῦτο δὲ Κυνέγειρος ὁ Εὐφορίωνος ἐνθαῦτα ἐπιλαμβανόμενος τῶν ἀφλάστων νεός, τὴν χεῖρα ἀποκοπεὶς πελέκεϊ πίπτει (= Further, Cynegirus, the son of Euphorion, fell there after laying hold of a ship's ornament, getting his hand cut off with an axe, 6.114). Immediately prior to this line is a reference to the deaths of Callimachus, the polemarch, and Stesilaus, son of Thrasylaus, a general. Immediately following comes the note that the fallen also included other Athenians as well — both numerous and famous (πολλοί τε καὶ

---

[43] Cornelius Longinus [1st cent. CE?] seems to have regarded a later painting of Cynegirus with his hands still intact as a departure from the graphic tradition:

Οὔ σε, μάκαρ Κυνέγειρε, τοὶ ὡς Κυνέγειρον ἔγραψε

Φᾶσις, ἐπεὶ βριαραῖς ἄνθετο σὺν παλάμαις·

ἀλλὰ σοφός τις ἔην ὁ ζωγράφος, οὐδέ σε χειρῶν

νόσφισε, τὸν χειρῶν οὕνεκεν ἀθάνατον (*An. Gr.* 16.117)

Blest Cynegirus, Phasis did not paint you as Cynegirus

since he presented you with sturdy hands;

But the painter was a wise one, he did not deprive you

of hands, [you who became] immortal because of [your] hands.

A *chreia* from Lucian [2nd cent. CE] also suggests that it was artistic tradition to depict Cynegirus with his hand severed (cf. πρὸς δὲ τῇ Ποικίλῃ ἀνδριάντα ἰδὼν τὴν χεῖρα ἀποκεκομμένον, ὀψὲ ἔφη Ἀθηναίους εἰκόνι χαλκῇ τετιμηκέναι τὸν Κενεγειρον [= On seeing near the Painted Portico a statue with its hand cut off he remarked that it was pretty late in the day for the Athenians to have honored Cynegirus with a bronze statue], *Dem.* 53).

[44] Aristides' description of the Marathon battle speaks of the marsh (ἕλος) into which the Persians were driven (Aristides 13.88). Since this feature was not mentioned in Herodotus, the primary literary source, but did appear in the Marathon mural (cf. Pausanias 1.15.3), it is reasonable to assume that Aristides' allusion to Callimachus derived from the artistic, not the literary source.

[45] For an analysis of Herodotus' text cf. W. W. How and J. Wells, op. cit., 2.109-114; 353-363.

ὀνομαστοί). This 'bracketing frame' around Cynegirus implies that Herodotus viewed him likewise as a notable figure. His patronymic, "son of Euphorion" (father of Aeschylus), identifies him as a brother of the tragic playwrite Aeschylus (who apparently was also depicted in the Poikile painting, cf. Pausanias 1.21.2).

In Herodotus' narrative much more attention was devoted to Callimachus. Identified by his toponymic, ᾿Αφιδναῖος (= of Aphidnae), Callimachus was polemarch that year in accordance with the lot (6.109). Prior to the battle the ten Greek generals were of evenly divided opinion regarding the best tactic — five were for defense, five for offense. Miltiades, who was of the latter mind, went to Callimachus and persuaded him to deliver the tie-breaking vote in favor of attack (6.110). As polemarch Callimachus received the command of the right flank (6.111).[46] In the battle, then, he was killed after proving himself to be a brave man (διαφθείρεται, ἀνὴρ γενόμενος ἀγαθός, 6.114).

Cynegirus and Callimachus in Later Hellenistic Traditions

Both the mural in the Stoa Poikile, which endured over eight centuries, and the account of Herodotus, who as the *pater historiae* (Cicero, *leg.* 1.1.5) was read by all the ancients, fed the later traditions about Athenian heroism at Marathon. The lore was varied and rich. There thrived legends about such figures as Miltiades,[47] Epizelus (= Polyzelus),[48] Echetlus,[49] Cynegirus,[50] and

---

[46] The right wing was not just a position of honor. Greek hoplites, who held the shield with the left hand and the spear with the right, tended in battle gradually to shift to the right in order to stay close to the protection of the next man's shield. This produced a general tendency in battle for the whole hoplite line to squeeze to the right. A disciplined and determined commander was needed to counteract this tendency.

[47] Cf. Aeschines 3.186; Nepos, *Milt.* 6.3; Pliny, *N.H.* 35.57; Plutarch, *Quest. Conv.* 1.10.3; *Comp. Arist. Cat.* 2.1; *Par. Gr. R.* 1 [305b–c]; Pausanias 1.15.3; Lucian, *J.Tr.* 32; Aristides 46.174; Diogenes Laertius 1.56; Suidas, ῾Ιππίας 2.

[48] Cf. Plutarch, *Glor. Ath.* 347d; *Par. Gr. R.* 1 [305b–c]; Aelian, *N. A.* 7.38; Diogenes Laertius 1.56; Suidas, Πολύζηλος and ῾Ιππίας.

[49] Cf. Pausanias 1.15.3; 1.32.5.

[50] Cf. Pliny, *N.H.* 35.57; Pompeius Trogus, 2.9.14–19 (→ Epitome from M. Junianus Justinius); Plutarch, *Comp. Arist. Cat.* 2.1; Plutarch, *Glor. Ath.* 3d; Plutarch, *Par. Gr. R.* 305b–c; Lucian, *Dem.* 53; *J. Tr.* 32; *Rh. Pr.* 18; *Themistoclis Epistulae* 11; Aelian, *N. A.* 7.38; Diogenes Laertius 1.56; Cornelius Longinus, *An. Gr.* 16.117; Himerius 10 [59].2; 2 [6].20–21; Paulus Silentiarius, *An. Gr.* 16.118; Suidas, Κυναίγειρος.

Callimachus.[51] Pliny (*N.H.* 35.57) and Plutarch (*Par. Gr. R.* 1 [305b-c]) rank these last two with Miltiades as generals — a notion which may represent their interpretation of Herodotus 6.114. Other authors though designate Cynegirus as a simple infantryman (cf. *miles* [= soldier], Pompeius Trogus, 2.9.16 → Epitome from M. Junianus Justinius; ἰδιώτης [= private], Polemo, B 18). In any case Cynegirus and Callimachus, who apparently were positioned near each other in the Poikile painting (cf. Aelian, *N.A.* 7.38), were sometimes mentioned together in one breath as being among the most valorous (cf. Pliny, *N. H.* 35.57; Plutarch, *Comp. Arist. Cat.* 2.1-2; *Glor. Ath.* 3 [347d]; Diogenes Laertius 1.56; Libanius, *Decl.* 11.1.2; 14.1.14; 19.1.13). With so much valor exhibited at Marathon the question seems to have naturally arisen how these heroes should be ranked with respect to their valor.[52] Plutarch accorded to Miltiades the chief honor (τὸ πρωτεῖον) of Marathon while allowing that "the second place honors are contested by [the] Sophaneses, Ameiniases, Callimachuses, and Cynegeiruses" (τῶν δευτερείων ἀμφισβητοῦσι Σωφάναι καὶ 'Αμεινίαι καὶ Καλλίμαχοι καὶ Κυνέγειροι), who displayed the greatest valor in those struggles (cf. *Comp. Arist. Cat.* 2.1-2). Plutarch's plural formulation shows that he thinks of these heroes as paradigms.

What captured the imagination in the case of Cynegirus was the violent chopping off of his hand[s] with an axe. The horror and gore required no extra words, thus the focus appears rather to have been on explaining the circumstance and what brought it about. Pausanias' interpretation of the Poikile painting (cf. 1.15.3) suggests that Cynegirus suffered his horrid fate while chasing and killing Persians who were trying to escape from the battle by scrambling into their waiting ships. Other interpreters, however, explain that Cynegirus lost his hand[s] while attempting to hold back a ship itself as it was putting to sea (Plutarch, *Par. Gr. R.* 1 [305c]; Aristides, 13.88; Himerius, *Or.* 2 [6].20-21; Paulus Silentiarius, *An. Gr.* 16.118). This latter is the dominant view and the notion that Polemo works with. One line of tradition has it that Cynegirus lost one hand (cf. Herodotus 6.114; Plutarch, *Par. Gr. R.* 1 [305b-c]; Lucian, *Dem.* 53; *An. Gr.* 11.335; Himerius, *Or.* 2 [6].20-21)

---

[51] Cf. Pliny 35.57; Plutarch, *Quest. Conv.* 1.10.3; *Comp. Arist. Cat.* 2.1; *Glor. Ath.* 347d; *Par. Gr. R.* 1 [305b-c]; Aristides 13.88 [202-203d]; Aelian *N. A.* 7.38; Diogenes Laertius 1.56; Himerius 10 [59].2; 2 [6].20-21; Suidas, Καλλίμαχος and Ἱππίας 2.

[52] Cf. *In eo proelio tanta virtus singulorum fuit, ut, cuius laus prima esset, difficile iudicium videretur* (= In this combat the valor of individuals was so great, that it seemed hard to decide whose renown should be {ranked} first), Pompeius Trogus 2.9.14 (→ Epitome from M. Junianus Justinius).

while another strand says that he lost both hands (cf. Pompeius Trogus 2.9.18-19 [→ Epitome from M. Junianus Justinius]; Cornelius Longinus, *An. Gr.* 16.117; Himerius, *Or.* 10 [59].2; Paulus Silentiarius, *An. Gr.* 16.118). In Polemo's declamations the loss of both hands is the position taken by Euphorion in the first speech; the loss of only the right hand is the position argued by Callimachus' father in the second speech. A very extreme development of the Cynegirus tradition is that after losing first the right hand and then the left he continued fighting with his teeth like a wild beast.[53] This grotesque picture of Cynegirus trying to hold back a trireme with his mouth is rare and not adopted by either father in Polemo's declamations. Throughout the long tradition the focus remained on the severed hand[s].[54]

Post-classical traditions about Callimachus developed also on the basis of the Poikile painting and the Herodotus text. When Hellenistic traditions gave his rank, Callimachus was identified either as polemarch (πολέμαρχος: Plutarch, *Quest. Conv.* 1.10.3 [628d-e]; Pausanias 1.15.3) or as general (στρατηγός: Plutarch, *Par. Gr. R.* 1 [305b-c]; *dux*: Pliny, *N. H.* 35.57). He was remembered particularly for his display of exceptional valor on the

---

[53] Cf. *tum quoque amputata dextera navem sinistra conprehendit, quam et ipsam cum amisisset, ad postremum morsu navem detinuit. Tantam in eo virtutem fuisse, ut non tot caedibus fatigatus, non duabus manibus amissis victus, truncus ad postremum et velut rabida fera dentibus dimicaverit* (= Then also when the right hand was chopped off he grabbed the ship with his left, and he had lost that too, after that he held the ship with his corpse. {They say} such valor to have been in him that he was not fatigued by so much carnage, {that} he was not defeated by the loss of both hands, {that} even dismembered he fought to the end with his teeth just like a mad beast), Pompeius Trogus, 2.9.18–19 (→ Epitome from M. Junianus Justinius).

[54] A humorous late epigram (*An. Gr.* 11.335) underscores this focal point of attention in the tradition:

᾿Ω τλῆμον Κυνέγειρε, καὶ ἐν ζωοῖς καὶ ἀπελθών,
   ὡς αἰεὶ κόπτῃ ῥήμασι καὶ κοπίσιν.
πρόσθε μὲν ἐν πολέμοισι τεῇ πέσε μαρναμένη χείρ·
   νῦν δέ σ᾿ ὁ γραμματικὸς καὶ ποδὸς ἐστέρισεν.

O wretched Cynegirus, both among the living and when departing,
   how always you are hacked by words and axes.
Formerly your hand fell fighting in war,
   and now the grammarian has deprived you also of a foot.

The correct classical spelling of the name is Κυναίγειρος (with a long second syllable αι). In late Hellenistic Greek the diphthong αι took on a pronunciation like the short vowel ε. In Byzantine Greek the two became homophones and were often confused. The "grammarian" reflects this gradually emerging development and opts for the Κυνέγειρος spelling. This later orthography makes the second syllable, of course, short, and thus deprives the name of a 'metrical foot'.

battlefield (cf. Plutarch, *Comp. Arist. Cat.* 2.1-2; *Glor. Ath.* 3 [347d]; *Quest. Conv.* 1.10.3 [628d-e]). Despite many wounds (cf. Plutarch, *Glor. Ath.* 3 [347d]) he continued fighting, and some traditions have it that when he died he had so many arrows and spears stuck in him that he could not fall over because these missiles held his body upright as though he were still alive (cf. Plutarch, *Par. Gr. R.* 1 [305b-c]; Aristides 13.88; Himerius, *Or.* 10 [59].2; 2 [6].20-21; Suidas, Καλλίμαχος; Ἱππίας 2). It is this 'standing corpse' aspect of the Callimachus tradition that Polemo singles out and develops in his declamations.

The Marathon battle in general and the heroes Cynegirus and Callimachus in particular appear to have been standard topics in the declamation genre (cf. Aristides 13.88; Libanius, *Decl.* 11.1.2; 14.1.14; 19.1.13). Indeed, in his parody on the rhetoricians Lucian has the teacher advise the student above everything else to always mention Marathon and Cynegirus without which, he says, no success can be achieved (cf. ἐπὶ πᾶσι δὲ ὁ Μαραθὼν καὶ ὁ Κυνέγειρος, ὧν οὐκ ἄν τι ἄνευ γένοιτο, *Rh.Pr.* 18). More telling in this regard is Lucian's satire Ζεὺς Τραγῳδός (= Tragic Zeus) which presents the Olympians deliberating about how to react to the public philosophical debate taking place at the Stoa Poikile between Timocles the Stoic and Damis the Epicurean. Timocles argued for the providence, beneficence, and intervention of the gods in human affairs while Damis portrayed the gods as immoral, indifferent, and impotent — in short, he portrayed them as irrelevant or non-existent. When it appeared that Damis' position was going to carry the day Herakles volunteered to shake the Stoa Poikile and destroy the whole building on top of the entire lot of disputers and thus stop the insolence. To this suggestion Zeus responded as follows:

"That was a loutish, horribly Boeotian thing you said, Herakles, to involve so many honest men in the destruction of a single rascal, and the Stoa too, with its Marathon and Miltiades and Cynegirus. If these should collapse how could the rhetoricians go on any longer with their rhetoric? (πῶς ἂν τούτων συνεμπεσόντων οἱ ῥήτορες ἔτι ῥητορεύοιεν;)! They would be robbed of the principal topic for their speeches (τὴν μεγίστην εἰς τοὺς λόγους ὑπόθεσιν ἀφῃρημένοι)" (Lucian, *J. Tr.* 32).

Zeus's words represent, of course, an exaggeration — hyperbole is after all the satirist's tool. But they surely also contain something of the truth because parody is not funny unless it somehow corresponds to reality.

From this survey we can see that the general theme in Polemo's declamations, — the valor of Cynegirus and Callimachus at Marathon — if not hackneyed, was at least a traditional favorite. What becomes interesting then is Polemo's own treatment. Particularly striking is Polemo's bombast with the miraculous: the severed hands go on fighting by themselves and the upright corpse continues the battle long after its death. In itself bombast was not unusual among the sophists, but Polemo may have pressed it to its limits. Further, it appears that of the two heroes, it was Cynegirus who attracted more attention in the popular mind. Hence, Polemo's declamations, which clearly want to make Callimachus the 'winner' in the contest of valor, go counter to the more popular pro-Cynegirus viewpoint.

Polemo's Surviving Declamations

Length

Polemo's pair of declamations is a text of respectable length. It comprises ca. 6040 words. In comparison with NT documents the Polemo text is longer than 2 Corinthians (4448 words) or Hebrews (4942 words) but shorter than Romans (7094 words) or 1 Corinthians (6807 words).[55] In the medieval MSS — all written in minuscule script — the declamations typically cover 11 ± 3 double sided folios.[56] Ancient copies of the declamations, in the early centuries written in majuscules, will no doubt have taken up somewhat more (20%-50%?) space.

In the *controversiae* genre to which Polemo's declamations belong it was often the case that the first speech was delivered on one day and the second, contrary speech presented then on the following day. Inasmuch, however, as Polemo's first speech is much shorter than the second — only a little over half the length of the second — the two will in all likelihood have been presented on the same day. This will have allowed the audience to perceive more clearly the corresponding parallels between the two speeches. The subtle contrasting nuances of the two arguments will also then have emerged much more sharply.

---

[55] Cf. R. Morgenthaler, *Statistik des neutestamentlichen Wortschatzes* (Zürich/Frankfurt: Gotthelf, 1958) 164.

[56] In the MSS Polemo's declamations occupy as few as 10, as many as 58 pages (cf. Table 1 in Chapter 2). If one sets aside the extremes at both ends of the spectrum (low 10, 11, 13; high 40, 43, 58), the bulk of the exemplars cover 16 to 28 pages (= 11 ± 3 folios).

Situation and Theme

The declamations are set in the time period shortly after the battle of Marathon (September 490 BCE). The *terminus a quo* is marked by the fact that the fight is over and the Persians have withdrawn (cf. A 21–22, 28–29, 36, 43–44, 47–48; B 2, 12, 14, 28, 43, 47). Regarding the *terminus ad quem* there is a certain inconsistency. Some comments indicate that the dead have not yet been buried (cf. A 49; B 15, 19, 46, 63) while other remarks suggest they have already been interred (cf. A 3, 12, 49). The fictitious situation is best imagined, therefore, two or three days after the battle.

At issue is the question who should deliver the solemn funeral oration at the state ceremony soon to be held in honor of the dead. The matter hangs on the valor of the fallen. The introduction postulates an Athenian νόμος (= law? custom?) according to which the father of the one who died most bravely should have the honor of giving the eulogy (cf. 0; A 1–4; B 1–2). Such a νόμος has never been historically documented — the situation is fictitious.

The contestants in the imaginary debate are the father of Cynegirus (his name is Euphorion) and the father of Callimachus (his name remains unknown). First the one father and then the other makes the case that his own son fought with the greater valor.

Date of Composition

The year when Polemo first delivered or published these declamations cannot be determined with precision. There is no reference to them in any literature of antiquity. It is reasonable, however, to assume that they will not have stemmed from the period before he had achieved some recognition as a sophist, otherwise they would not likely have been preserved. In other words, they certainly should not be dated before his first official ambassadorship on behalf of Smyrna, when Trajan granted him the *libera legatio* (113/114 CE). In view of their theme, however, it might well make more sense to date them later than this, namely after Polemo had visited Athens and had the opportunity to view the famous mural in the Stoa Poikile which depicted the valor of Cynegirus and Callimachus. Detailed information about his travels is lacking. Certainly the various trips he may have made across the Aegean to Athens are unknown. It is, however, historically established that he did go to Athens in 131/132 CE to deliver the keynote address at the dedication of the great Zeus temple there. To date the declamations between that time and his death (132-

144 CE) would mean they belong to the zenith of his career. While that is a fair assumption, there is admittedly nothing in the declamations that points specifically either to a time in the reign of Hadrian (117-138 CE) or Antoninus (138-144 CE).

Outline

Despite the difference in length of the two speeches their structures are similar. Both exhibit a rhetorically standard four part outline:[57]

Exordium	(προοίμιον = opening)	A 1-4	B 1-4
Narratio	(διήγησις = narrative)	A 5-12	B 5-15
Argumentatio	(ἀποδείξεις = proofs)	A 13-33	B 16-50
Peroratio	(ἐπίλογος = summary)	A 34-49	B 51-65

While the correspondences are striking they are not wooden. Variation in the outlines is achieved by the insertion of differing propositions, excurses, *sententiae*, and supporting details.

The Speech for Cynegirus

In his *prooemium* (A 1-4) Euphorion explains the crux of the debate: to determine which of the fallen heroes was most valorous in combat. To the father of that soldier goes the honor of delivering the state funeral oration. The leading candidates are Cynegirus and Callimachus. Without malice toward Callimachus he asserts that the pre-eminence belongs to his own son Cynegirus.

The *narratio* (A 5-11) contrasts the two contestants. Callimachus was obliged as polemarch to go to war, Cynegirus was a volunteer. Callimachus' fame consists in his passive upright posture brought about by the mass of enemy arrows in him; Cynegirus by contrast actively went on the attack against a ship. As infantryman he fought a naval battle — unprecedented — in which he lost both hands trying to restrain a fleeing ship. Appended to the narrative proper is Euphorion's thesis (A 12) that he deserves therefore to be awarded the funeral oration.

The *argumentatio* (A 13-33) presents the proofs. Callimachus' rank as polemarch is not relevant: the rank was obtained by lot and by chance (A 13-

---

[57] This four part division corresponds to the analysis of H. Jüttner, *De Polemonis Rhetoris, Vita Operibus Arte*, BPhA 8,1 (1898) 55-60. The outline is adopted also by W. Stegemann, "Polemon," *RE* 21.2 (1952) 1344.

14), relatives of the polemarch have no special status (A 15), and Miltiades as general had superior rank (A 16). Valor counts, not rank (A 17). The voluntary zeal of Cynegirus counts more than the obligating duty of Callimachus (A 18-19). Youth sacrifices more life than maturity (A 20). Cynegirus fought longer than Callimachus and was more active (A 22-24). Cynegirus was conscious of his deeds, Callimachus was not (A 25-26). Not Callimachus' volition, but the enemy arrows kept him erect (A 27). Cynegirus was a better model to emulate than Callimachus (A 28-29), he instilled more fear in the enemy (A 30-31), and he mounted more individual fights than Callimachus (A 32-33).

The *peroration* (A 34-49) begins with a series of exclamations (A 34-35) which label Cynegirus' hands the "saviors" of Greece. His struggles rivaled those of legendary heroes and were guided by gods (A 35-36). He was the first to restrain a ship and demand the return of Greek captives (A 37-40). The enemy accomplished nothing against his hands (A 41) and even after his hands were severed they continued fighting (A 42). Their prowess is sung in Persia and Sparta and is the pattern for grappling irons (A 42-44). Cynegirus' hands supported Greece, barbarian arrows Callimachus (A 45-46). The funeral speech belongs to Euphorion, and his son Aeschylus will serve as speech writer (A 47-49).

The Speech for Callimachus

The *exordium* of Callimachus' father (B 1-4) praises Athens' νόμος of honoring the dead with a eulogy (B 1), which he is worthy to deliver because Callimachus' post-mortem continuation of the fight was a marvel (B 2-3). His upright corpse showed more valor than Cynegirus' mutilated body did (B 4).

The *narratio* (B 5-15) recounts the events of the Persian invasion at Marathon. When help from Sparta did not materialize, Miltiades sided with Callimachus about going on the offensive (B 5-6), Callimachus commanded the battle and with resolve withstood Persia's most intense assault (B 7-9) forcing the enemy to expend all their arrows (B 10). Even after he died from countless wounds his corpse remained erect and kept fighting (B 11). An excursus of exclamations lauding the upright corpse (B 12) interrupts the narrative. Exhausted and terrified by Callimachus the enemy fled and thereby gave Cynegirus the opportunity for pursuit (B 13-14). As summation of the narrative Callimachus' father contends that the funeral oration should be accorded to him (B 15).

The proofs offered in the *argumentatio* section (B 16-50) are extensive: Callimachus' pre-eminent position in life is rightfully his also in death (B 16-19). Rank counts, and since Miltiades lays no claim to top honors, Callimachus is next in line (B 20-22). Callimachus was a leader, Cynegirus a follower (B 23). The young Cynegirus acted hot-headedly, the mature Callimachus with deliberation (B 24). Callimachus drove back bold attackers, Cynegirus chased fleeing cowards (B 25-28). Callimachus' courageous deeds enabled Cynegirus' cautious actions (B 29-31). Callimachus showed initiative, Cynegirus only copied him (B 32). Cynegirus acted senselessly (B 33-37) while Callimachus achieved his purpose — stripping Asia of its weapons (B 38-39). Callimachus wanted to block the way to Athens, Cynegirus tried to keep the enemies in the land (B 40). Cynegirus worked at cross-purposes with the heroes and gods (B 41) and his own personal ambition brought harm on the Greeks (B 42). Callimachus was a better model for the Greeks than Cynegirus (B 43). Prizes go to the upright not the prostrate (B 44). Cynegirus' endeavors were ineffectual (B 45). Cynegirus' mutilated body has many analogies among the fallen, but no comparison to Callimachus' upright corpse can be found (B 46-47). The etymology of Callimachus' name portended his pre-eminent valor (B 48), his decision precipitated the battle (B 49), and his fight lasted beyond his death (B 50).

The *peroration* (B 51-65) casts Callimachus in epic proportion. Only a Homer could adequately recount his deeds (B 51). A long series of exclamations punctuates his inimitability (B 52-55). He challenged Asia to single combat (B56-57) but its assault was ineffectual (B 58-59). Datis was exasperated and Darius terrified by him (B 60-61). Gods and heroes were on his side (B62). Cynegirus fell from a single blow, but Callimachus rescued the fatherland (B 63-64). Hence, Callimachus' father should recite the victory hymn while as consolation prize Euphorion may sing a dirge for his son (B 65).

Language and Style

Polemo's language mirrored the cultural standards of his time. To identify these, however, with specificity and precision within a limited space is not easy. In the 19th century a vigorous debate raged about the language of the Greek renaissance which flowered in the 2nd century CE. The debate was framed by the polarities: Asianism versus Atticism. However Asianism was defined by the ancients — whether in terms of Eastern geography, Hellenistic chronology, vulgar or 'modern' style (vocabulary and syntax, sentence structure and rhythm) — it was generally a cipher for *corrupta eloquentia*. It was as reaction to this 'linguistic decline' that Atticism emerged, the movement to revive and replicate the 'pure' Attic tongue of the 'Golden Age' of Greece. In Atticism the literary monuments of the 5th and 4th centuries stood as the models to be imitated. The scholarly debate about Asianism and Atticism[58] which has engaged the leading classicists of the last two centuries[59] is too extensive to be recapitulated here. It is enough here to note that the language in Polemo's declamations, while striving to be classically Attic, lies more between the poles of Asianism and Atticism.[60]

The declamations show a wide-ranging vocabulary, most all of which has classical precedent (cf. Index 8). Virtually every type of classical condition — past, present, and future, real and unreal — appears (cf. Index 2). The whole range of classical prepositions is put to use — all the proper and some of the improper (cf. Index 6). Not surprisingly the dual is absent, but it is striking that the optative and subjunctive moods are so infrequent (cf. Index 1). Polemo

---

[58] The whole discussion was in many ways analogous to the century long debate in modern Greece between the proponents of the vernacular (δημοτική) and the advocates of the traditional literary language (καθαρεύουσα). The modern dispute was finally settled in favor of the δημοτική when Papandreiou's socialist party (ΠΑΣΟΚ) came to power in the 1980's.

[59] Cf. W. Schmid, *Der Atticismus in seinen Hauptvertretern von Dionysius von Halikarnassus bis auf den zweiten Philostratus* (4 vols.; Stuttgart: Kohlhammer, 1887-1897); I. Bruns, *Die attizistische Bestrebungen in der griechischen Literatur* (Kiel: Universitäts Buchhandlung, 1896); L. Rademacher, "Über die Anfänge des Attizismus," *RhM* 54 (1899) 351-374; U. von Wilamowitz-Möllendorff, "Asianismus und Atticismus," *Hermes* 35 (1900) 1-52; W. Michaelis, "Der Atticismus und das Neue Testament," *ZNW* 22 (1923) 91-121; F. H. Sandbach, "Atticism and the Second Sophistic Movement," *Cambridge Ancient History* (Cambridge: University Press, 1936) 11.678-689; M. J. Higgins, "The Renaissance of the First Century and the Origins of Standard Late Greek," *Traditio* 3 (1945) 49-100; G. Anlauf, *Standard Late Greek oder Attizismus? Eine Studie zum Optativsgebrauch im nachklassischen Griechisch* (Köln: dissertation, 1960); A. Dihle, "Analogie und Attizismus," *Hermes* 85 (1957) 170-205; A. Dihle, "Der Beginn des Attizismus," *Antike und Abendland* 23 (1977) 162-177; J. Frösen, *Prolegomena to a Study of the Greek Language in the First Centuries A. D. The Problem of Koiné and Atticism* (Helsinki, 1974); T. Gelzer, "Klassizismus, Attizismus und Asianismus," *Le Classicisme a Rome aux 1ers Siècles Avant et Apres J. C.* (Entretiens sur l'antiquite classique 25; Vandoeuvres-Geneve: Fondation Hardt, 1979) 1-55.

[60] H. Jüttner (op. cit.) subjected Polemo's declamations to a detailed linguistic analysis regarding the vocabulary (pp. 62-64), grammar (pp. 65-68), occurrence of hiatus (pp. 68-75), periodic sentence structure (pp. 75-76), use of figures (pp. 76-88), and rhythm of the clauses (pp. 88-112). From the language in the declamations Jüttner (p. 112) concludes that the ancients were justified in saying that Polemo sought to "atticize" (ἀττικίζειν).

shows a predeliction for compound words and articular infinitives. Though he did employ contraction, crasis, and elision, he did not make any consistent effort to avoid hiatus (the succession of two vowel sounds in adjoining syllables), which "Attic more than any other dialect disliked" (*GG*, 46). In matters of orthography it is hard to demonstrate that Polemo did or did not have Attic preferences in spelling or pronunciation.[61]

As a polished speaker Polemo utilized the entire available spectrum of rhetorical and grammatical figures. Chiasm and pleonasm are among his favorites. Polysyndeton and asyndeton are common too along with parechesis and paronomasia. In addition his repertoire also includes the use of brachylogy, hendiadys, hysteron proteron, litotes, oxymoron, isocolon, synecdoche, prolepsis, metonymy, hyperbaton, and a host of other figures, all of which are treated individually in the commentary.[62]

---

[61] The MSS are often divided and the medieval archetype (π) too seems to have been inconsistent in choosing, for example, between σσ and ττ, ρρ and ρσ, νεώς and ναός, and a single or double augment in compound verbs. Even if a tendency could be established in the medieval archetype (π), the unknowable transcription practices of the copyists in the preceding millenium make it impossible to say anything with certainty about the orthography in the original text (Π).

[62] A systematic analysis of all of Polemo's figures and tropes was originally planned as part of a fifth chapter in this book. Such a study would both contributute to the reconstruction of the patterns of sophistic rhetoric in the Greek renaissance and also help to locate Polemo more precisely within that movement. Nevertheless, that analysis has been foregone because it would make this already overly-thick volume even thicker. Moreover, many readers may share the view expressed by the erudite A.T. Robertson (*A Grammar of the Greek New Testament in the Light of Historical Research*, Nashville: Broadman, 1934, p. 1206): "We need not tarry over antiphrasis, ambiguity, hendiadys, hypokorisma, oxymoron, periphrasis, polyptoton, syllepsis, and the hundred and one distinctions in verbal anatomy. Most of it is the rattle of dry bones and the joy of dissection is gone." Despite that view, however, a comprehensive study of Polemo's similes and metaphors does remain a definite *desideratum* because there is material here with important parallels to Christian imagery both in the NT and the church fathers.

Chapter 2

The Manuscripts and the Editions

The Manuscripts of Polemo's Declamations

Eighteen MSS containing all or part of Polemo's declamations are known to the present editors to exist (cf. Table 1 on the following page).[1] All of these were produced between the 13th and 16th centuries and are currently housed in seven European libraries (in Rome, Florence, Milan, Naples, Paris, Munich, and Vienna). It is these eighteen hand written texts which form the basis for the critical edition presented in this volume. Whether this current edition has overlooked any other extant MSS or whether more MSS will come to light — either by chance or through yet-to-be published catalogs of Eastern European libraries and smaller out-of-the-way archives — remains to be seen.

Quite apart, however, from any other MSS of Polemo that might still be added to the text base, the extant ones are but a fraction of all the Polemo MSS that were ever produced over the twelve or more centuries between the original and the extant exemplars. Post-Gutenberg generations are prone to forget the labor intensive process which was required prior to the printing press for the production and replication of books. Those raised in an era of typewriters and word processors sometimes need to remind themselves of the dedication and diligence of ancient and medieval scribes. The drudgery of their copying endeavors is often reflected in the notes which scribes appended at the finish of their work. Some colophons highlight the physical strain ('Writing

---

[1] A cursory overview list of the Polemo manuscripts listed in printed library inventories is provided by R. Sinkewicz, *Manuscript Listings for the Authors of Classical and Late Antiquity* (Greek Index Project Series 3; Toronto: Pontifical Institute of Mediaeval Studies, 1990) microfiche #004: M 20, N 20, B 21. Hinck's MSS denoted with the sigla G and H are not listed by Sinkewicz.

Table 1: Known Manuscripts of Polemo's Declamations

Siglum	Century	Location	Library	MS Number	Folios	Contents
A	13/14	Florence	Biblioteca Medicea Laurentiana	gr. 56, 1	43r-51v	0/A1-B65
B	13	Florence	Biblioteca Medicea Laurentiana	gr. 87, 14	134r-143v	0/A1-B65
C	15	Florence	Biblioteca Medicea Laurentiana	gr. 59, 37	55r-68r	0/A1-B65
D	15	Florence	Biblioteca Medicea Laurentiana	gr. 70, 28	235r-254v	0/A1-B64
E	14	Rome	Biblioteca Apostolica Vaticana	gr. 96 (103)	11r-18v	0/A1-B65
F	14/15	Rome	Biblioteca Apostolica Vaticana	gr. 1297 (Orsini 9)	408v-413r	0/A1-B65
G	15	Rome	Biblioteca Apostolica Vaticana	gr. 1415	23v-52r	0/A1-B65
H	14/15	Paris	Bibliotheque Nationale	gr. 3017	114r-122r	0/A1-B64
I	15	Paris	Bibliotheque Nationale	Ancien gr. 1733	245r-253v	0/A1-B64
J	13	Rome	Biblioteca Apostolica Vaticana	Palatinate gr. 93	10r	0/A1-13
K	15	Rome	Biblioteca Apostolica Vaticana	gr. 928	196v-202v	0/A1-B65
L	15/16	Rome	Biblioteca Apostolica Vaticana	gr. 1898	220r-223v	A1-49
M	14	Naples	Biblioteca Nazionale	gr. III, E, 16 (338)	43v-48v	0/A1-B64
N	15	Naples	Biblioteca Nazionale	gr. II, E, 21 (156)	1r-22r	0/A1-B65
O	14	Milan	Biblioteca Ambrosiana	gr. D, 42 sup.	90r-101v	0/A1-B64
P	15	Milan	Biblioteca Ambrosiana	gr. I, 49 sup.	99r-110v	0/A1-B64
Q	15	Vienna	Nationalbibliothek	Suppl. gr. 135	1r-9v	0/A1-B65
R	15/16	Munich	Bayerische Staatsbibliothek	gr. 99	187r-197r	0/A1-B65

bows the back, pushes the ribs into the stomach, and produces a general debility of the body'), others reflect the plain tedium ('As travellers rejoice to see their homeland, so also is the end of a book to those who toil [in transcribing]').[2] One codex, which among other things includes Polemo's declamations, contains a colophon evocative of what must have often seemed to scribes to be a Sisyphean task. At the end of a related text, Michael Souliardos (a scribe from Nauplion of Argos) noted punctiliously that he had finished that piece of work "in the year 1488, on the seventh day of the month of October, on Saturday, in the fourth hour, during the night."[3] From this pedantic, elongated date one senses his feeling of achievement and relief, and his desire that the reader appreciate at what personal cost he produced the text. Modern readers of Polemo's declamations, as of any ancient work, ought never forget their indebtedness to countless such long-suffering scribes who did not skimp on the midnight oil. What sustained them was not just their love of books but also their conviction that they were producing something that would outlast them. This sentiment is expressed in the frequently found colophon:

ἡ μὲν χεὶρ ἡ γράψασα σήπεται τάφῳ·

γραφὴ δὲ μένει εἰς χρόνους πληρεστάτους.

(= The hand which wrote [this] is rotting in a grave,

but the writing remains for all times.)[4]

The surviving MSS of Polemo's declamations thus may be said to have bestowed on the scribes who produced them a modicum of longevity beyond their natural years. Since, however, those scribes' names are by and large

---

[2] Cf. B. M. Metzger, *Manuscripts of the Greek Bible. An Introduction to Greek Palaeography* (New York: Oxford University Press, 1981) 20.

[3] This note is found on folio 350r of the composite Milan MS gr. I, 49 sup. in the Biblioteca Ambrosiana. The date, time and authorship note reads: ἐν ἔτει ϛϡϙϛῳ μη(ν)ὸς ὀκτωβρ(ίου) ϛ´ ἡμέρ(ᾳ) σαββ(ά)τ(ῳ) ὥρ(ᾳ) δ῾ νυκτός· ινδ: ϛ´ πὰρ᾽ ἐμοῦ Μιχαὴλ Σουλιάρδου ἐκ Ναύπλου Ἄργους. Cf. A. Martini et D. Bassi, *Catalogus codicum graecorum Bibliothecae Ambrosianae* (Mediolani: Hoepli, 1906) vol. 1, pp. 460–461. This notation is equated with the year 1489 by Martini and Bassi, op. cit., p. 460, but with 1488 by M. Vogel and V. Gardthausen, *Die griechischen Schreiber des Mittelalters und der Renaissance* (Zentralblatt für Bibliothekswesen, Beiheft 33; Leipzig: Harrassowitz, 1909 [reprinted Hildesheim: Georg Olms, 1966], p. 318). Michael Souliardos was a prodigious copyist for over thirty years between 1477 and 1509, working in Crete, Italy, and the Peloponnesus (cf. M. Vogel and V. Gardthausen, op. cit., pp. 318–320).

[4] Well over a hundred examples of this colophon have been tabulated in Greek MSS (cf. B. Metzger, op. cit., p. 20, note 35).

unknown, their handiwork brought immortality not so much to them as to Polemo.

The Sigla Designation of the Manuscripts

Extended discussion about and frequent citation of a dozen and a half different MSS requires some 'shorthand' method of reference. As is standard procedure, therefore, in biblical, classical, and medieval studies, each of the extant MSS has been assigned a siglum consisting of a single capital Latin (English) letter. In the interest of clarity regarding the text critical argumentation and evidence an explanation of the assigned sigla is in order.

If one were to start from scratch to assign sigla to the eighteen known MSS, theoretically a reasonable case could be made for at least three different systems:

(1) After first collating the MSS (temporarily using provisional designators) and establishing their *filiation*, sigla could be assigned to the individual MSS which would reflect the MS dependencies and indicate the stemma relationships.

(2) After first arranging the MSS according to their present *geographical location*, perhaps best from south to north (e.g., Naples, Rome, Florence, Milan, Paris, Vienna, Munich), sigla could be assigned to the individual MSS whose citation would show the regional distribution and breadth of attestation.

(3) After first arranging the MSS *chronologically* (in accordance with paleographic indicators and scribal dates in the codices), sigla could be assigned to the individual MSS which would indicate their relative ages.

Each of these approaches has useful features and each has its own shortcomings. However, in all three cases the biggest drawback is the same: the sigla long since assigned to the nine MSS which formed the basis of Hinck's edition (1873) — for over a century now the standard critical text — would have to be revised. And that unfortunately would lead to unnecessary confusion for those who work with Hinck's edition or who want to compare the present volume with Hinck's work.

Hence, in the present publication the assignment of sigla to the MSS builds on the precedent set by Hinck's edition. The sigla attached by Hinck to the nine MSS which he examined are retained in this present edition (A-I). The nine additional MSS which now join the list of Hinck's witnesses have been assigned the subsequent letters of the alphabet (J-R).

Hinck's procedure seems to have combined aspects of the geographical and chronological principles outlined above in approaches 2 and 3. He grouped his MSS first by location (Florence, Rome, Paris), and then within each local group he appears to have arranged the MSS, more or less, chronologically. Then to each MS in the resulting list he assigned in sequence one of the first nine letters of the alphabet (cf. Table 1).

For the sake of continuity the present edition follows Hinck's lead.[5] The 'new' MSS were also grouped first by location (Rome [placed first because it was already represented in Hinck's list], Naples, Milan, Vienna, Munich), and then each local group arranged chronologically). The resulting list of 'undesignated' MSS received then the next nine letters of the alphabet (J - R). The results appear schematically as follows:

Location	Hinck	Reader / Chvala-Smith
Florence	A B C D	
Rome	E F G	J K L
Paris	H I	
Naples		M N
Milan		O P
Vienna		Q
Munich		R

These eighteen Latin (English) capital letters thus designate the known extant Polemo MSS. The exact equivalencies of these sigla designators are shown in Table 1.

In addition to these upper case Latin letters, lower case Greek letters are employed to designate hypothetical, no longer extant archetype MSS. The Greek designators have as far as possible been deliberately chosen with a view to signaling a dependency relationship:

---

[5] Credit for choosing this approach in the assigning of sigla belongs to A. Chvala-Smith. After weighing the designation options he cogently cited the ecclesiastical principle: τὰ ἀρχαῖα ἔθη κρατείτω (= let the old customs prevail), Council of Nicea, canon 6.

Hypothetical Parent MS		Existing Offspring MSS
α	$\rightarrow$	A O
β	$\rightarrow$	B [ρ]
ε	$\rightarrow$	E J [$\nu\ \eta$]
η	$\rightarrow$	H D
ι	$\rightarrow$	I
μ	$\rightarrow$	M F
ν	$\rightarrow$	N C
ρ	$\rightarrow$	R Q M

No Longer Extant Offspring MSS

γ	$\rightarrow$	$\alpha\ \beta\ \iota$
δ	$\rightarrow$	$\mu\ \varepsilon\ \iota$
π	$\rightarrow$	$\gamma\ \delta$
Π	$\rightarrow \rightarrow \rightarrow$	π

π = 11th century archetype

Π = 2nd century original

When evaluating the presentation of MS relationships and the cited evidence it will be useful to keep in mind the distinction between the upper case Latin letters and the lower case Greek letters.

The Relationships Among the Manuscripts

The following discussion about the relationships and dependencies between the MSS presents the evidence which leads to the reconstruction of the stemma of the MSS as shown in Table 2. As the data is presented the reader is urged to keep consulting this diagram for a schematic portrayal of the relationships.

The eighteen extant MSS utilized in this edition fall into two main families (designated γ and δ) each of which is distinguished by its own set of jointly shared variant readings not found in the other family. Within each major family there are also a number of smaller sub-groups identifiable by their own distinctive patterns of divergent readings. The γ branch contains five MSS: AO BQR, the δ branch twelve MSS: MFGK J EL CN DHP. Under a third category, the 'mixed' type, may also be subsumed three MSS: I, M, and Q/Q² (cf. Appendix 1 [Q R ρ] and Appendix 2). The tell-tale sign or 'give-away' for a group or sub-group is a high incidence of shared variant readings peculiar to that group and not found in any other MSS. (For complete documentation of the following footnote references see the critical apparatus and Appendix 2: γ versus δ.)

The Two Major Families: γ and δ

The most important shared readings in the δ group which distinguish it from the γ group are easily enumerated. Most notable are: 24 omissions,[6] 17 transpositions,[7] 81 substitutions,[8] and 3 additions.[9] The obvious and most cogent explanation for all these shared and uniformly distributed differences between the two families of MSS is that each family derives from its own separate and distinctive archetype (designated here as γ and δ).

---

[6] There are four multiple word omissions (B 13, 19, 31, 63) and twenty single word omissions (A 7, 23, 44, 48; B 1, 17, 20, 22, 27, 29, 30, 31, 32, 37, 39, 43, 45, 47, 63, 64).

[7] Nine transpositions involve changes in the order of three or more words (0; A 3; B 8, 11, 18, 22, 23, 53, 60) and eight simply reverse the order of two words (A 12, 23, 37; B 1, 33, 37, 50, 61).

[8] The substitutions are of various types. Sixteen involve replacements with entirely different words (cf. e.g., μάχεσθαι / δέχεσθαι, A 19; γενναιότερον / κυριώτερον, A 33; πλήρης / τρόπαιον, A 32; παιδεύσεως / κελεύσεως, B 23; also A 27, 45, 49; B 16, 17, 18, 22, 27, 33, 50, 53, 58). There are nine changes of a verb prefix (A 8, 25, 42; B 8, 9, 9, 31, 36, 41), six changes of a verb tense (A 14, 48; B 11, 29, 32, 41), and ca. 55 changes in inflexion: in gender (A 4, 14, 34, 34; B 11, 14, 28, 56), in number (A 33, 44; B 30, 33, 37, 40, 51, 62), in case (A 2, 22, 28, 29, 35, 44; B 1, 5, 5, 10, 16, 19, 28, 28, 39, 47, 48, 48, 50, 54, 56, 56, 62), in person (A 31, 41, 42; B 62), in mood (A 28; B 21, 36, 41, 41, 45).

[9] The preposition ἐν is inserted before the locative Μαραθῶνι (A 1; B 62) and the article ὁ before Κυναίγειρος (A 23).

Table 2: The Stemma of the Manuscripts

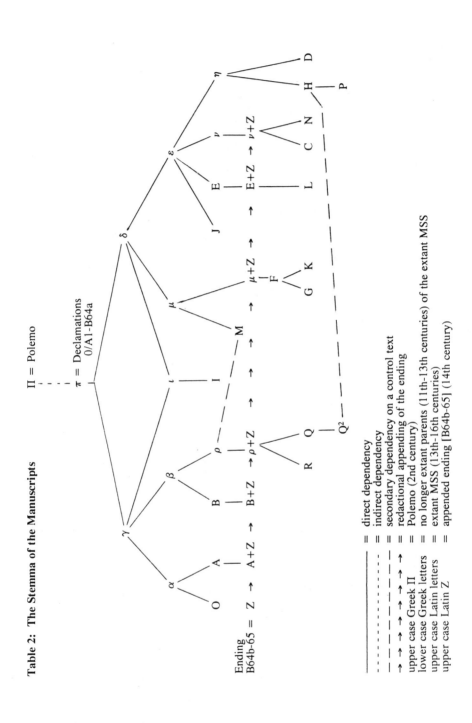

Π = Polemo

π - - - - = Declamations 0/A1-B64a

Ending
B64b-65 = Z

	=	direct dependency
	=	indirect dependency
	=	secondary dependency on a control text
	=	redactional appending of the ending
upper case Greek Π	=	Polemo (2nd century)
lower case Greek letters	=	no longer extant parents (11th–13th centuries) of the extant MSS
upper case Latin letters	=	extant MSS (13th–16th centuries)
upper case Latin Z	=	appended ending [B64b-65] (14th century)

Sub-Groups in the γ Family

A O (→ α)

A and O share about 60 variant readings not found in any other MSS.[10] Since A also has 43 unique variants[11] not found in O, and for its part O has 26 peculiar variants[12] not found in A, neither MS can be explained as having copied from the other. The natural conclusion, therefore, is that A and O are siblings which come from a common parent text (designated here as α).

Q R (→ ρ)

Q and R share nearly 300 variants not occurring in any other MSS. At the same time Q and R each individually exhibit a host of unique variants not found in the other (cf. Appendix 1 [Q R]). Neither, therefore, can have copied from the other. The data is best explained by the presumption that Q and R are siblings having a common parent (designated here as ρ) (cf. Appendix 1 [ρ]). The extremely high number of peculiar variants in ρ means that ρ was an idiosyncratic MS compared with the rest of the MSS. The scribe of ρ was — to put it kindly — much more limited in his abilities than others in the guild.

---

[10] There are six single word omissions (A 11, 19; B 21, 35, 63, 64), five transpositions of word order (A 24, 41; B 27, 55, 60), and seven additions of a single word (A 30; B 21, 29, 29, 37, 51, 56) and most strikingly the addition of the phrase ἀνακάλει νῦν πολλὰ τὸν Κυναίγειρον (B 48). There are some twenty word substitutions (e.g., αὔξεσθαι for ἀξιοῦσθαι, B 19; Μαραθῶνι νίκη ἐδυνάμωσε for Μαραθώνικη δύναμις, B 30; Ἰνταφέρνης for Τισσαφέρνης, B 56; cf. also A 10, 47, 49; B 8, 10, 10, 13, 13, 17, 17, 20, 24, 27, 29, 30, 30, 35, 45, 50, 53). Besides this there are fourteen tense and inflexion changes (A 24, 24, 25, 30, 41; B 22, 36, 38, 41, 62, 62, 63, 63, 63) and fourteen orthographic divergencies (A 20, 20, 40, 41, 46; B 8, 12, 36, 43, 51, 52, 54, 57, 64).

[11] In 29 cases a moveable ν has been added to an end vowel (A 8, 10, 11, 20, 22, 23, 24, 27, 29, 37, 44; B 6, 10, 10, 11, 11, 23, 23, 37, 39, 49, 50, 51, 53, 53, 54, 56, 58, 58). This practice is a clear characteristic of the scribe of A. Most other unique variants are orthographic in nature: six confusion of vowels (A 2, 17, 36, 42; B 17, 19); four wrong accents (B 4, 11, 18, 57); and two omissions of letters (B 5, 12). Not clearly inadvertent are κοινῶν for κοινῷ (A 45) and βεβοασμένον for βεβιασμένον (B 3).

[12] There are six single word omissions (A 6, 32; B 7, 8, 31, 61); one multiple word addition (B 17); four notable substitutions (A 7; B 33, 33, 36); two striking iotacistic variants (οἶσθα for ἦσθα, A 43; λοιπόν for ληπτόν, B 34); three inflexion changes (A 19; B 11, 62); and nine minor orthographic variants (A 5, 38; B 8, 9, 15, 17, 37, 58, 62). Singular is the transposition of the words μεμπτὸς μὲν οὐδεὶς ἦν (B 7).

B ρ [QR] (→ β)

B and QR (→ ρ) share 13 unique readings which do not appear in any other MSS (except occasionally also in the 'mixed' I).[13] The fact that there are hundreds of peculiar readings common to Q and R but not found in B means that Q and R are not dependent on B. For that same reason and because B (13th century) is older than Q and R (15/16th century), B cannot have copied from Q or R. The only convincing explanation is that B and the *Vorlage* of QR (= ρ) are related. That is to say, B and ρ are siblings with a common parent (designated here as β)

Sub-Groups in the δ Family

G K (→ F) / M F (→ μ)

MFGK clearly represent a sub-group of related MSS. There are ca. 160 instances where MFGK share readings together with other δ MSS (cf. critical apparatus), but much more importantly there are 19 instances where MFGK together share readings not found in any other δ MSS.[14] Yet in another 70+ cases M and FKG diverge in their readings.[15] A closer look at the FKG group

---

[13] There are about a dozen substitutions of which some are unusual (Πολύξυλος for Πολύζηλος, A 44; κοπιάσας for πιάσας, B 18; τέχνης for τύχης, B 27). Other substitutions and orthographic variants too involve the change of only one letter or accent (B 3, 8, 10, 18, 26, 29, 44, 50, 54). One lone omission (τόν, 0) completes the composite picture of joint BQR variants.

[14] A number of these involve simply changes of inflexion (gender, B 18; number, A 31, 32, B 51; case, A 8; tense, B 42) or orthographic variants (B 2, 63). Others represent actual word substitutions (συμπλοκήν for ἐμβολήν, B 8; οἰητέον for νοητέον, B 35; συμπερινοστήσεις for περινοστήσεις, B 36; τουτ᾽ εἶδε for τουτὶ δὲ, B 56). Unique transpositions (B 1, 48, 51), omissions (B 27), and additions (B 5, 27, 50, 50) also belong to the common variants peculiar to MFGK.

[15] Ten of these involve omissions in M (0; A 21, 46; B 19, 27, 43, 62) or FKG (0; B 4, 13); two are additions in FKG (A 21; B 38). The great majority are comprised of minor inflexion differences (number, A 11, 33, 35, 59; case, A 33, 37, 37, 49; B 10, 23, 23, 24, 29, 40, 50; mood, A 3; B 22, 62; person, A 31, 47; B 2, 15, 20, 41, 56). But there are also a significant number of different word choices (e.g., μέλη / βέλη, A 42; οἴαν / ἤν, A 45; ῥῖσας / παρακαλέσας, B 18; ἄνθ᾽ / ὠσθ᾽, B 23; ὄψις / σκῆψις, B 33; καλλίστη / ἄριστος, B 50; τελεταῖον / τελευτῶν, B 58; cf. also A 16, 24, 30, 35; B 20, 22, 26, 28, 32, 46, 48, 49, 55, 60). Finally there are some dozen orthographic differences between M and FKG (A 20, 27; B 15, 38, 40, 40, 42, 45, 54, 55, 59).

reveals that there are 23 cases where F and G agree against K,[16] and 42 cases F and K agree against G,[17] but only 10 cases where K and G agree against F, and these few are all trivial, inconsequential differences.[18] All these observations coupled with the palaeographic dating of M (14th century), F (14/15th century), and GK (15th century) lead to two basic conclusions:
(1) G and K are siblings whose parent is F.
(2) F and M are siblings whose parent is no longer extant (here called μ). Finally it needs to be noted that M contains over a dozen and a half readings that are distinctive of the γ family.[19] This means that alongside μ, the main *Vorlage* of M, the scribe of M also used a second *Vorlage* (from the γ family) as a control text. All the evidence points to that text being ρ (the parent text of QR) (see below, The Hybrid Manuscripts [M], and cf. Appendix 1 [Q R ρ]).

J EL CN DHP (→ ε)

The remaining δ MSS not yet discussed, J EL CN DHP, share among themselves over a dozen notably distinctive readings common to this entire group but not occurring in MFKG.[20] These readings common to J EL CN DHP — despite the many differences between the smaller sub-groups — mean that in their lineage they all go back to a common ancestor (designated here as ε). Within this ε branch four separate groups are observable: J EL CN DHP.

---

[16] These are comprised of six substitutions (A 10, 44, 47; B 8, 33, 60), five inflexion changes (B 1, 19, 23, 52, 52), ten orthographic differences (A 23, 28, 30, 42; B 9, 24, 41, 49, 56, 58), one omission (B 25), and one addition (B 1).

[17] These consist of six substitutions (A 5; B 23, 33, 44, 55, 57), five inflexion changes (A 23, 41, 44; B 56, 60), twenty-five orthographic differences (A 7, 9, 14, 14, 25, 25, 30, 40, 46, 49; B 8, 14, 18, 19, 29, 36, 36, 37, 39, 41, 47, 47, 52, 60, 63), four omissions (A 28, 49; B 8, 26), and two additions (A 10, 21).

[18] These divergencies are merely a matter of iotacism (B 1, 5, 32, 38, 47), movable ν (B 37), aspiration (B 36, 44), a dropped letter (A 42), and a vowel confusion (B 20).

[19] Cf. ἐπιτάφιος, 0; ἕδρα, A 23; ἀφῆκε, A 24; οἵαν, A 45; ἐπὶ τὸν αἰγίαλον, B 13; σώματι, B 15; ἐπικαλούμενος, B 22; ἠυθαδιάσατο, B 24; ῥᾳδίως, B 28; μόνον, B 32; ἀγομένων, B 32; τοιαύτην, B 37; τολμή, B 40; ὅς, B 48; τελευταῖον, B 58; ἐστηκότες, B 59; ἁρμόττει, B 62; omission of καί, B 63.

[20] Most of these distinctive readings are striking substitutions: φιλίαις for φιλοτιμίαις (A 3); βέλος for βέλη (A 31); δραμοῦσα for ἐπιδραμοῦσα (A 41); τεθαμμένος for τεθεαμένος (A 44); ὑπό for ὑπέρ (B 3); εἰ περιῆσαν for εἴπερ ἦσαν (B 19); ἐπιμελόμενος for ἐπιμελούμενος (B 22); ἀόριστος for ἄριστος (B 50); ζητούμεναι for ζηλούμεναι (B 56); πρῶτον for πρῶτος (B 56); ἁρμόττον for ἁρμόττοντα / ἁρμόττει (B 62). Two transpositions (δύναμιν ἅπασαν, B 6; παντὶ τολμᾶν, B 27) also are characteristic of this J EL CN DHP group .

J (→ ε) / L (→ E)

J and L pose special cases — both are 'incomplete' MSS. J is less than one full page and contains only O/A 1–13; without any clear reason it simply breaks off in the middle of a sentence. L for its part contains only the first declamation. It was, however, the design of L from the outset — as can be seen from the altered introduction — to contain no more than Euphorion's speech. Because of their truncation, neither J nor L can have served as *Vorlage* for any of the 'complete' MSS in the ε group. This observation is not without significance. The fact that J is the oldest MS in the ε group — palaeographically and codicologically datable to the 13th century (cf. Appendix 1 [J]) — means that the ε archetype must be even older. On the other hand L is the youngest MS in the ε group — to be dated 15th/16th century (cf. Appendix 1 [L]). Its direct *Vorlage* is unlikely to have been, a MS as old as ε.

J has only one peculiar variant reading which specifically narrows its family ties to the ε group — that is the reading φιλίαις instead of φιλοτιμίαις (A 3). Given the brevity of J, however, this is sufficient for family identification. On top of that J has three unique variants unmatched by any other extant MSS.[21] They will thus not have stood in the ε archetype but must be attributed to the scribe of J. These variants, together with the fragmentary nature of the text, set J apart from all other MSS in the ε group as an *unicum*.

L is separated from the CN group by about twenty readings peculiar to that group.[22] L is likewise set off from the DHP group by another dozen readings peculiar to that sub-group.[23] However, L is not set apart from E by any readings unique to E. In fact the one genuinely distinctive reading in E that

---

[21] J alone reads αἱροῦντα instead of ἐροῦντα (A 1) — Byzantine pronunciation of the two was the same. J is also alone in adding μοι after θαυμαστότατοι (A 6) and omitting μάχη before καρτερά (A 10).

[22] In the first declamation the CN group is distinguished by six unique substitutions (βάσεως for βασιλέως, A 9; τἀληθῆ for τἀληθές, A 26; ἀνεδείξατο for ἐπεδείξατο, A 28; πτερομάτων for πνευμάτων, A 35; σῶμα for σέλας, A 36; ἐπιτιμήσεως for ἐπιτιμίας, A 36), three omissions (τὸν τάφον ὃν ἐκόσμησα, A 12; καί, A 22; τὰς ἑαυτοῦ, A 28), one addition (ὁ Κυναιείρου πατήρ, A 49), and a batch of orthographic variants with a difference of one letter (A 10, 16, 23, 27, 31, 35, 41, 41, 43).

[23] In the first declamation the DHP group has three peculiar omissions (καί, A 10; ἐμοὶ δὲ ὀφείλεται τιμῆς παραμυθία, A 13; νῦν πρῶτον ἀνδρὸς μάχην καὶ νεώς, A 36) unmatched in L. Unparalleled in L are also a number of unusual substitutions (Μιλτιάδη for Μιλτιάδην, A 10; ἑαυτῆς for σεαυτοῦ, A 31; ὅλος for ὅλης, A 31; δυνάμεις for δεξιάς, A 31; πρώτως for πρῶτος, A 36; ἀσάλευτα for ἀσάλευτον, A 37; Ἀθηναίους for Ἀθήνας, A 41; πεποίηκας for ἐποίησας, A 44).

sets it apart from the other ε sub-groups is the marginal gloss ἀντίθεσις / λύσις (A 12/13) — and precisely that gloss appears also in L at the same point in the margin. These observations indicate that L is related to E, but not the other sub-groups. It does need to be noted that L diverges from E in at least a dozen small ways.[24] Inasmuch as E (14th century) is a much earlier MS than L (16th century) they are not likely to be siblings. The evidence suggests rather that L is the offspring of E and that the scribe of L was not a careful copyist.

C N (→ ν)

C and N are closely related. There are some 45 peculiar variants shared only by these two MSS.[25] Yet C and N also each have their own unique variants not appearing in the other. The number of these lone variants is far higher in N[26] than in C[27], but in both cases their presence and nature is such as

---

[24] The scribe of L eliminated the introduction explaining the *controversia* because he only intended to copy the first speech. There are also other lesser omissions (A 15, 27, 29). The substitutions are minor (A 3, 4, 8, 11, 19, 27), the spelling variants are of little consequence (A 10, 16, 17, 43), and the transpositions do not change the sense (A 5, 14).

[25] For the twenty common variants in the first declamation see footnote 22. In the second declamation there are another twenty-five variants unique to C and N. These include eleven substitutions (cf. βαλομένοις for βουλομένοις, B 13; σπουδή for σχολή, B 13; βασιλεία for βασιλέως, B 30; βοηθῶν for βοῶν, B 56; also B 1, 1, 2, 29, 36, 56, 59); eight orthographic variants (B 13, 21, 24, 36, 41, 44, 56, 63), two omissions (B 1, 29); three additions (A 49 end; B 23, 24), and a transposition (B 61).

[26] N exhibits three dozen unique variants not shared by C or any other MS. Most important are the dozen unusual substitutions (φανερώτατα for φανερώτερα, A 4; πλῆθος for πλεῖστος, A 8; ἐφ᾽ οἷς for ἐφεῖς, A 16; ἀνέβαλε for ἐνέβαλε, A 20; ἀπέθανε for ἔπαθε, A 23; ἐπέτεινε for ἐπενέτεινε, A 24; μαθεῖν for λαθεῖν, A 30; ἔβλεπε for ἔβλαπτε, B 42; ἀποβάλλων for παραβάλλων, B 44; Φοινικίας for Φοινικίῳ, B 47; ἐπιστώσατο for ἐπιστώσω, B 64). Besides these substitutions there are another 17 orthographic variants due to ioticism (A 12, 12; B 20, 41) or confusion of other homophones (ε/αι, A 40; B 46; ο/ω, B 50) or related sounds (α/η, A 49; α/ε, B 27; υ/ε, B 62; π/τ, A 31; σσ/σ, A 21; ᾽/᾽, A 11, 38), and occasionally a dropped syllable (ἀπώσατο for ἀπεώσατο, B 25; φοράν for φοβεράν, B 31; βιάσθαι for βιάσασθαι, B 33; χαῖρε for ἔχαιρε, B 57). N is also guilty of a few small omissions (τι, A 2; ὦ θεοί, A 41; τό, B 33; πᾶς, B 57). Additions are rare (τέλος at the end of the first declamation and γάρ in B 44).

[27] Instead of ἐπανέτεινε (A 24) C reads ἐπενέτεινε while N has ἐπέτεινε. The phrase πρῶτος καὶ μόνος χειρός (A 32) is transposed in C but not in N. C writes κἂν (A 34) with an unusual iota subscript, κᾂν, a odd orthography not appearing in N. Only C reads πρῶτον in B 19 while N joins all the other MSS with πρῶτος. Likewise C alone has the peculiar iotacistic variant πίστην in B 20, whereas N has the normal πίστιν along with all the other MSS. πρότερον (B 29) is written πρότερων in C, while N has the correct spelling. If N were dependent on C one would expect some of these odd variants to have been replicated in N. That they are not indicates that C was probably not the Vorlage of N.

to preclude that either copied from the other. The evidence thus points to C and N being siblings with a common parent (designated here as *ν*).

D H (→ η) / P (→ H)

The remaining three MSS, namely DHP, are closely related and form their own sub-group. This is clear from the 33 variants that they share among themselves but with no other MSS.[28] Just how the three MSS are related can be seen on the variant patterns they exhibit. In order to keep the discussion within managable limits, variants shared between DHP and other MSS will be ignored here. Only one variant unique to DH against P can be found and it is inconsequential.[29] Similarly there appears only one variant unique to DP against H.[30] However, there are a dozen variants unique to HP against D.[31] Finally each of the three MSS has a 'personality' of its own. D has over a hundred unique variants found in no other MS.[32] This alone shows that D did

---

[28] Most important are the ten omissions peculiar to DHP: three multiple word omissions (ἐμοὶ δὲ ἐφείλεται τιμῆς παραμυθία, A 13; νῦν πρῶτον ἀνδρὸς μάχην καὶ νεώς, A 36; and τὰ δὲ πεφοβημένοι, B 13) and seven single words (καὶ, A 10; κοινοῦ, B 2; ἐκ, B 8; καὶ, B 10; ταῖς, B 19; νηί, B 32; πολλοῖς, B 61). One notable transposition of word order (B 8) is peculiar to DHP. There are seventeen substitutions common to DHP some of which are quite striking (δυνάμεις for δεξιάς, A 31; Ἀθηναίους for Ἀθήνας, A 41; καί τοι for ὅτι, B 6; αὐτὸν for τὸν τάφον, B 15; πολλοί for λοιποί, B 30; τοιοῦτος for τοσοῦτος, B 54; βάλλειν for βασιλεύς , B 56) while others represent simply changes in inflexion (case: A 16; B 25; gender: A 31, 31, 36; number: A 37, 49; B 17, 37; tense: A 44). Finally there is a handful of orthographic variants peculiar to DHP (A 6; B 54, 58, 58, 63).

[29] The unusual aorist παρήγγειλε (B 57) in DH is written in P with a movable *ν*: παρήγγειλεν.

[30] In B 53 D and P read ἀδικασίαν while H has διαδικασίαν with the rest of the MSS.

[31] Notable is a long insertion in the proemium (στιχ οἱ σοι λόγοι κρατοῦσιν ἀπάντων λόγων κἂν Κυναιγείρῳ καὶ Καλλιμάχῳ μάχη ἀντικρατοῦσα ταυτοδυνάμοις λόγοις). Besides this there are a number of striking substitutions (ἀναγκαῖοι against ἀναγκαῖος, 0; συγκινδυνεύσουσιν against συγκινδυνεύουσιν, A 3; ἀφεείς against ἠφίεις, A 31; Ἡρακλέου against Ἡρακλέοις, A 35; μόλις against μόγις, B 15; ὁπλίζομεν against ὠπλίζομεν, B 16; πολέμους against πολέμων, B 26; ἄωρον against ἄφρον, B 35). HP also have omissions (καὶ;, A 19; μέν, B 27) and a transposition (μιᾶς πληγῆς, B 47) not found elsewhere.

[32] Most striking are six multiple word omissions (A 21, 27, 44; B 19, 41, 44) and twenty-two single word omissions (A 4, 21, 32, 38, 41, 45, 45, 45; B 2, 8, 17, 19, 21, 22, 35, 37, 40, 40, 46, 49, 56, 58). Further, there are over thirty unique substitutions (e.g., ποίμνης for πρύμνης, A 11; Ἡρακλέοις for Ἡρακλέους, A 35; κλήματα for βλημάτων, B 10; δι᾽ αὐτοῦ for ὑπὸ τοῦ, B 26; καί for τούς, B 31; cf. also A 5, 24, 26, 28, 30, 30, 35, 40, 44, 44, 46; B 1, 5, 6, 8, 12, 13, 15, 26, 33, 40, 41, 45,46, 50, 53, 53, 60), nine unparalleled additions (A 1, 11, 15, 43; B 25, 39, 41, 52, 59), two transpositions (B 40, 61), and a host of orthographic oddities (A 6, 8, 10, 10, 11, 19, 21, 23, 24, 26, 30, 30, 35, 47; B 1, 1, 3, 6, 8, 12, 17, 19, 27, 36, 44, 44, 45, 47, 53, 54, 56, 56. 56. 59, 60).

not serve as a *Vorlage* for either H or P. Indeed, D is such a wretched MS that no scribe in his right mind would ever have replicated it (cf. Appendix 1 [D]). P for its part has eighteen unique readings unmatched anywhere else.[33] These variants show that P did not serve as *Vorlage* for D or H. It is noteworthy that H has only one unique reading not found in D or P and it is simply an orthographic variant due to a homophone.[34] Taken altogether this constellation of variants points to one conclusion: H and D are siblings with a common parent (designated here as η) and P is the offspring of H.

The Hybrid Manuscripts (I M Q/Q²)

Three of the eighteen MSS are of a 'mixed' type: I, M, and Q/Q² exhibit readings from both the γ and δ families. Behind each of these three MSS, therefore, lies not one *Vorlage* but two. However, in each case the 'mixed' condition came about differently:

I [4th generation] appears to have been copied from a single *Vorlage* (ι) [3rd generation] which itself represented a 'mixed' type (that arose by copying from both γ and δ [2nd generation]).

M [4th generation] copied from two *Vorlagen*, namely μ [3rd generation] and ρ [4th generation].

Q/Q² [5th/6th generation] had yet a different ancestry. Q [5th generation] copied from ρ [4th generation] and then later was corrected by a second scribe who utilized H [5th generation].

This phenomenon of cross-fertilization, therefore, began soon after the medieval archetype π had split into two families and it continued on through to the end of the era of the MSS. Each of the three examples has its own peculiarities.

---

[33] Most important are the omissions, both multiple word (B 50, 50) and single word (A 3; B 50, 52). Of the peculiar substitutions several are striking ($\gamma\nu\acute{\omega}\mu\eta$ for $\dot{\rho}\acute{\omega}\mu\eta$, A 22; $\kappa\alpha\acute{\iota}$ for $\mu\acute{\eta}$, B 17; cf also A 3, 27; B 22, 27). The insertion of $\mu\varepsilon$ after $\pi\alpha\acute{\iota}\varepsilon\tau\varepsilon$ (B 57) is singular. The orthographic variants are due to iotacism (A 3, 23; B 5, 50) or sloppiness (A 9, 26; B 37, 48).

[34] H reads $\pi\rho\acute{\omega}\tau\omega\varsigma$ for $\pi\rho\tilde{\omega}\tau o\varsigma$ (B 48).

I (→ ι → γ/δ)

I has ca. 90 readings found only in the γ family and not in the δ branch;[35] at the same time I has ca. 70 readings attested only in the δ family and not in the γ branch.[36] Thus, numerically speaking, I shows a slight preference for γ over δ. Where γ and δ diverge in word order I follows γ a bit more often than δ.[37] In the case of omissions I is more guided by δ than γ.[38] In the matter, however, of significant substitution variants I clearly preferred γ.[39] From these tendencies, however, it is hard to argue that the primary *Vorlage* was γ and that the secondary *Vorlage* (or control text) was δ. It seems rather that I simply went back and forth eclectically between the two texts. Clear criteria upon which the choices were based are not transparent — it may simply have been a matter of the scribe's subjective *Sprachgefühl*. Indeed, there are instances

---

[35] I sides with γ in the case of forty-six substitutions (A 17, 23, 28, 28, 29, 33, 35, 41, 42, 44, 44, 45, 48; B 1, 5, 9, 9, 10, 13, 14, 16, 17, 19, 22, 23, 27, 28, 28, 31, 33, 33, 36, 39, 40, 41, 45, 48, 49, 50, 50, 50, 54, 56, 56, 58, 62), ten transpositions (0; A 3; B 8, 11, 14, 18, 22, 23, 53, 60), six omissions (A 7, 15; B 9, 22, 27, 31), sixteen orthographic variants (A 1, 25; B 3, 13, 19, 24, 26, 27, 32, 33, 35, 36, 36, 37, 42, 43, 49, 63), and about a dozen hard-to-classify additions/omissions (A 44; B 2, 13, 29, 31, 33, 39, 43, 47, 62, 64).

[36] I sides with δ in the case of thirty-eight substitutions (A 2, 3, 4, 8, 14, 14, 19, 22, 25, 27, 31, 32, 34, 34, 41, 42, 49; B 5, 8, 11, 11, 16, 22, 28, 30, 32, 33, 36, 37, 41, 41, 41, 41, 47, 56, 62, 62, 63), eight transpositions (A 12, 23, 37; B 1, 33, 37, 50, 61), eleven omissions (A 23, 39, 48; B 17, 19, 20, 30, 38, 45, 63, 63), eleven orthographic variants (A 16, 30, 43, 47; B 14, 24, 24, 25, 36, 45), and one uncertain omission/addition (B 29).

[37] I matches the word order of γ in ten cases (0; A 3; B 8, 11, 14, 18, 22, 23, 53, 60) and δ in eight cases (A 12, 23, 37; B 1, 33, 37, 50, 61).

[38] I shows eleven of the omissions in δ (A 23, 39, 48; B 17, 19, 20, 30, 38, 45, 63, 63) and only six of those in γ (A 7, 15; B 9, 22, 27, 31). More importantly though, I replicates three of the four multiple word omissions in δ (τῶν ὀνομάτων, B 19; κυρίους τούς, B 31; ἐκείνου δέ, B 63); only one did I fill in from γ (ἐπὶ τὸν αἰγιαλόν in B 13).

[39] Of the arguably top fifteen most striking word differences I chose γ twelve times (γενναιότερον over κυριώτερον, A 23; βεβηκέναι over συμβεβηκέναιε, A 25; κατέστησεν over παρέστησεν, B 9; ἐστοχάζοντο over κατεστοχάζοντο, B 9; ἐπικαλούμενος over ἐπιμελούμενος, B 22; παιδεύσεως over κελεύσεως, B 23; ἀποβάντες over ἐπιβάντες, B 31; ἀφεψαλωμένης over ἐφεψαλωμένης, δακτύλοις over δακτύλῳ, B 33; σκέψις over σκῆψις, B 33; B 41; Πελοπιδῶν over Πελοπίδαι, B 56; τελευταῖον over τελευτῶν, B 58). In only three of the most notable fifteen cases did I chose δ (δέχεσθαι over μάχεσθαι, A 19; τρόπαιον over πλήρης, A 32; ἐνταῦθα over ἐν ταύτῃ, B 56). In other words when it came to real word choices I preferred γ over δ at a ratio of 4 to 1.

where the scribe could not decide between γ or δ and so instead either simply fudged on the decision[40] or created his own alternate reading.[41]

That I derives from both γ and δ (2nd generation) is clear. What may be debated is whether γ and δ were the parents or the grandparents. In other words, does I belong to the 3rd generation (along with α, β, μ, and ε), or to the 4th generation (itself going back to an already hybrid *Vorlage* [ι] of the 3rd generation which had derived from γ and δ)? Two reasons point more to the latter than the former:

(1) The paleographic dating of I to the 15th century fits the 4th generation better than the 3rd. If I were directly dependent on γ and δ it would not only be the sole example in the collection of a MS with 2nd generation parents but it would also mean that the 2nd generation MSS survived physically much longer than any of the other evidence suggests.

(2) I was the joint work of at least three different scribes (cf. Appendix 1 [I]), yet among the various hands there is no difference in the way γ and δ are utilized. It seems unlikely that such uniformity in the use of two *Vorlagen* could arise from multiple scribes who otherwise exhibit considerable individuality. Much more likely, rather, is that they were all copying from a single, already 'mixed' MS (ι) and thus reflecting its prior merger choices. For these two reasons, therefore, the reconstructed stemma posits a *mixtum compositum* ι in the 3rd generation whose parents were γ and δ (2nd generation): From this 3rd generation hybrid ι was then produced the 4th generation I.

M (→ μ/ρ)

M is a 'mixed type' MS from the 4th generation. Its dominant parent (designated here as μ) was a 3rd generation MS from the δ branch. Its receding parent or control text was ρ, a 4th generation MS from the γ branch. These connections emerge from an analysis of all the M variants. There are some 160 variants which M shares in common with all or most of the other

---

[40] Where γ had read πρῶτον and δ had πρῶτος (B 48), I has πρῶτο with the final letter unclear. Where γ had 'Ερέτρια (with the accent on the antepenult) and δ had 'Ερετρία (with the accent on the penult) (B 54), I has 'Ερετρϊα (with no accent at all but a diaeresis instead).

[41] Where γ probably had read τοι τούτῳ τῷ Καλλιμάχου (or something starting with τοι) and δ had τούτῳ τῷ Καλλιμάχῳ (A 30), I conflated to τούτῳ τῷ Καλλιμάχου (later in the margin a corrector prefixed a τοι to the phrase). Where γ reads πρότερος and δ reads πρῶτος (B 18), I chose neither but wrote πρῷτον.

sub-groups in the δ family (FKG J EL CN DHP);[42] these show clearly that M belongs to the δ branch. More specifically there are about twenty variant readings shared only with the sub-group FKG.[43] Yet there are another dozen readings where M diverges from FKG.[44] All of this means that M and F[KG] have a common archetype (designated here as μ) which belongs to the δ family. M was largely, though not entirely, dependent on that *Vorlage*. Alongside that text M also used another MS, one from the γ branch, which served as a kind of secondary control text and which it occasionally followed instead of its main source. M has 17 readings which are nowhere attested in the δ family, but which do appear in the γ branch. In the variety of attestations for these γ branch readings the only common denominator is QR.[45] Since Q and R (15th/16th century) were produced later than M (14th century), neither can have served as the control text for M. Hence, it must have been their *Vorlage* ρ which M used as its control text. This hypothesis is further undergirded by the very elaborate calligraphy of the initial letters in M, a phenomenon unmatched anywhere except in QR, and hence in all probability also in their *Vorlage* ρ. Finally, this dependency of M upon ρ means that ρ, like its sibling B, was a 13th or early 14th century MS.

Q/Q²

The 'cross-family' influence found in Q/Q² differs from that in I and M in several notable ways. For one thing it is not, in contrast to I and M, an eclectic text drawn partly from the γ branch and partly from the δ branch. Rather Q

---

[42] Cf. the critical apparatus at A 1, 3, 4, 7, 8, 8, 10, 12, 14, 14, 16, 19, 19, 19, 20, 22, 23, 23, 23, 23, 24, 25, 25, 27, 28, 29, 30, 30, 32, 32, 34, 37, 39, 41, 41, 41, 41, 41, 42, 42, 43, 44, 44, 47, 47, 47, 48,; B 1, 2, 3, 5, 8, 9, 9, 11, 11, 11, 12, 13, 13, 14, 17, 17, 18, 18, 19, 19, 20, 20, 22, 22, 22, 22, 23, 23, 23, 24, 25, 25, 27, 27, 27, 28, 28, 29, 29, 29, 31, 31, 31, 32, 32, 32, 33, 33, 33, 35, 35, 37, 37, 38, 38, 38, 39, 39, 39, 42, 43, 43, 45, 47, 47, 47, 48, 54, 54, 55, 56, 56, 59, 61, 62, 62, 62, 63, 64.

[43] Cf. the critical apparatus at A 3, 8, 31, 32; B 1, 5, 8, 18, 19, 27, 27, 35, 36, 42, 48, 51, 51.

[44] Cf. the critical apparatus at A 45; B 13, 26, 29, 40, 41, 46, 48, 50, 50, 56, 59, 63.

[45] Cf. ἐπιτάφιος (M AOR I), 0; ἕδρα (M Q^cmgR^cmg), A 23; ἀφῆκε (M QR), A 24; βαρβάρων (M FKG QR), A 31; οἵαν (M AOBQR I), A 45; ἐπὶ τὸν αἰγιαλόν (M AOBQR I), B 13; σώματι (M QR), B 15; ἐπικαλούμενος (M AOBQR I), B 22; ηὐθαδιάσατο (M AOBQR), B 24; ῥαδίως (M AOBQR I), B 28; μόνον (M QR), B 32; ἀγομένων (M Q I), B 32; τόλμη (M QR N HP), B 40; ὅς (M AOQR I), B 48; τελευταιον (M AOBQR I), B 58; ἑστηκότες (M QR), B 59; ἁρμόττει (M QR), B 62; καί omitted (M QR), B 63.

depended not only primarily, but solely, on a *Vorlage* in the γ branch, a 4th generation MS to which the 43 word ending had been appended; this was the same text from which R also copied, namely ρ + Z. Q qualifies here as a *mixtum compositum* simply because it was later 'overlaid' with ca. 200 corrections deriving from a MS of the δ branch. These corrections, however, were not integrated or blended into the Q text by the original scribe. Rather they were added by a second hand (Q²) in the form of interlinear and marginal glosses (about 100 of each) which appear now alongside the original wording of Q. That is to say, the original readings were not deleted, but left standing together with the readings that were added. It remains unclear whether the second scribe intended for the 'new' readings to fully supplant the original ones, or whether the glosses were simply offered as alternates worthy of equal consideration.

A close analysis of the 'corrections' of Q² leads to H as the *Vorlage* from which these readings were derived. This conclusion is arrived at through a process of elimination. There are about 165 readings in Q² which are shared by all the MSS in the δ branch (MFGK J EL CN HPD).[46] This makes clear that the control text belonged to the δ stem. And this source group can be narrowed: eight corrections in Q² can only have come from the smaller ε subgroup (J EL CN HPD)[47] Further, eight more corrections can only be traced to the yet smaller η sub-group (DHP).[48] From the η sub-group D is eliminated because eight of the corrections in Q² do not correspond to the readings in D.[49] The two remaining MSS (H and P) are close contenders for being the *Vorlage* of Q², but the nod finally goes to H for three reasons: (1) Q had omitted ἐν

---

[46] Cf. A 1, 1, 1, 1, 2, 3, 4, 5, 6, 7, 7, 8, 8, 11, 12, 12, 13, 15, 16, 18, 18, 18, 20, 20, 20, 21, 21, 22, 23, 23, 23, 24, 25, 25, 26, 27, 27, 27, 27, 27, 27, 28, 28, 28, 28, 30, 33, 33, 34, 34, 34, 35, 35, 36, 37, 38, 40, 40, 40, 40, 41, 42, 43, 44, 44, 44, 45; B 1, 2, 3, 3, 4, 5, 5, 5, 5, 6, 6, 6, 7, 8, 9, 9, 10, 11, 11, 11, 11, 11, 12, 12, 12, 13, 14, 14, 16, 17, 17, 17, 19, 21, 23, 23, 23, 23, 23, 24, 24, 24, 25, 26, 26, 26, 27, 27, 28, 31, 31, 32, 32, 33, 33, 33, 34, 34, 37, 39, 39, 39, 41, 41, 41, 43, 44, 45, 47, 48, 49, 50, 50, 50, 51, 52, 53, 53, 54, 55, 56, 56, 56, 56, 58, 59, 62, 62, 62, 62, 62, 63, 63, 63, 63.

[47] Cf. τεθαμμένος (Q² EL CN HPD), A 44; ὑπό (Q² E CN HPD), B 3; πιάσας (Q² E CN HPD), B 18; ἐπιμελόμενος (Q² E CN HPD), B 22; ὡμολόγησε (Q² E CN HP), B 53; ἁρμόττον (Q² E CN HPD), B 62; καὶ τὸν μὲν Ἡρακλέος (Q² E CN HPD), B 64.

[48] Cf. ὅλος (Q² HPD), A 31; δυνάμεις (Q² HPD), A 31; πρώτως (Q² HPD), A 36; Ἀθηναίους (Q² HPD), A 41; πεποίηκας (Q² HPD), A 44; ταύτην (Q² HPD), A 49; τοιοῦτος (Q² HPD), B 54; βάλλειν (Q² HPD), B 56; κατακενοῦντες (Q² HPD), B 57.

[49] Cf. θερμότητα (Q² HP) ↔ θερμοττ´ (D), B 6; μόλις (Q² HP) ↔ μόγις (D), B 15; χορῶν δὲ ᾠδῆς οἱ χοροδιδάσκαλοι (Q² HP) ↔ omitted (D), B 23; ἄωρον (Q² HP) ↔ ἄφρον (D), B 35; ἁμιλλᾶται (Q² HP) ↔ ἁμιλᾶται (D), B 36; νεκρόν (Q² HP) ↔ ὄρθον (D), B 44; δέ (Q² HP) ↔ omitted (D), B 46; ὡμολόγησε (Q² HP) ↔ ὁμολόγηκε (D), B 53.

πολέμῳ in the introduction; Q² supplied it from its *Vorlage*. That reading is found only in H, while P reads ἐν τῷ πολέμῳ. This points to H as parent text. (2) Furthermore, P has several dozen unique readings not found in H and none of which appear in the corrections of Q².[50] It is highly unlikely that Q² would have bypassed all of these readings if P had been its *Vorlage*. (3) Finally, H is a MS of the 5th generation while P, its descendant, is of the 6th generation. As a later correction of Q, a 5th generation MS, Q² is best regarded as belonging to the '6th generation'. From a chronological perspective it seems more likely that a 6th generation scribe would have used a 5th generation MS than its 6th generation offspring. This third argument does not have the weight as the first two, but it does further strengthen the case for H.

The Special Significance of R (→ ρ → β)

Among all the MSS R (if not L) is probably the youngest. Moreover, the deficiencies of R are matched only by those of Q, and exceeded only by the aggregate defects of D. Hence, in comparison with the larger pool of MSS, one would ordinarily attach little value to R. Two considerations, however, compel a much higher estimation of its importance:

(1) Looking to the preceding generation of MSS, R and Q together provide the basis for reconstructing their common parent ρ. That MS, a sibling of B, enables the recovery of β, the common parent of B and ρ. In other words, R makes a significant contribution to reconstructing the stemma of the γ branch of MSS. In addition, the establishment of the existence and wording of ρ also sheds some light on the stemma of the δ branch of MSS. As it turns out, all the γ readings in M (a MS in the δ family) can be satisfactorily explained by assuming that M utilized ρ as a control text alongside its primary *Vorlage* μ.

(2) Looking to the succeeding era of printed editions after the MSS, R also illumines the subsequent developments. The *editio princeps* of Stephanus (1563) which in the main seems to have utilized A, B, and C,[51] frequently

---

[50] Some of the more striking ones are: τοῦτόν (instead of τούτου), A 1; τῷ (instead of τό), A 1; ἱκανός (instead of ἱκανῶς), A 16; τῶν δεινῶν (instead of τῷ δεινῷ), A 22; γνώμῃ (instead of ῥώμῃ), A 22; καλίστων (instead of καλλίστων), A 26; στρατιώτην (instead of στρατιώτῃ), A 27; τόν (instead of τῶν), B 4; καί (instead of μή), B 17; οἴχεται (instead of οἴχηται), B 27; κατέσχε (instead of κατέχει), B 37; βουλωμένῳ (instead of βουλομένῳ), B 48; διέσωσε (instead of διέσεισε), B 54; με (added after παίετε), B 57; παρήγγειλεν (instead of παρήγγελε), B 57.

[51] Cf. Hinck, pp. vi-vii.

made mention of divergent readings in an *"alterum exemplum"* (= another exemplar). His edition also offered in dozens of passages readings not attested in the Florentine MSS. The source of those readings is now clear. In over forty instances those unusual readings are matched only by readings in Q and R.[52] Stephanus's 'other exemplar' appears then to have been one of these two MSS. Fortunately, the data allows us to narrow the field to R. There are seven readings in Stephanus which are not matched by Q but are found in R alone.[53] That Stephanus got these defective readings from the parent ρ (which the otherwise inept Q then would have had to correct) rather than R is more than unlikely. Thus, it was R that served Stephanus as a control text, and since he unfortunately attached more value to R than it deserved and thus included many of its readings in his own printed edition, R continued long after its own time to work its mischief in the early printed editions of Polemo's declamations.

The Ending of the Manuscripts (B 64b-65)

The 43 word ending (from γεννάδα οὕτω to τῶν δικαστῶν) presents a special case in the transmission of the text. Three phenomena in particular need to be registered and accounted for.

(1) Both major text families — γ (AO BQR) and δ (MFKG E CN HPD) — contain MSS *with* the ending (A BQR and FKG E CN) and *without* the ending (O and M DHP). I, which is a 'mixed' product deriving from both families, also does not have the ending. Inasmuch as J (only A1-13) and L (only A1-49) do not contain the second declamation they lie outside consideration.

---

[52] Cf. the following list in which the peculiar readings of QR and Stephanus are cited first followed by the 'mainstream' readings in parentheses: εἶχε τό (εἴχετο) A 9; τοῦτο (ἐστι) A 14; ---- (φημι) A 15; ἦν (--) A 17; ὕστερος (δεύτερος) A 22; ἔδρα (ἔδρασε) A 23; σώματι (σχήματι) A 27; μεμαχημένας (μεμαχημένος) A 28; δὲ ἦ (δέ γε ἦ) A 28; ἀφιείς (ἤφιεις) A 31; ἐπαινεῖ (ἐπαινεῖς) A 33; ἐλευθέρον (ἐλευθέριον) A 36; Καλλίμαχος (πολέμαρχος) A 36; ἀγεννῶν (ἀγεννῆ) A 43; ναύσων [ναύτων] (ναῦς) A 43; μακροτέρου (μακροτέρα) B 12; τηρῆσαν, στῆσαν, ἐάσαν (τηρήσας, στῆσας, εἴασας) B 12; τῶν ἄλλων προτιμωμένῳ (προτιμωμένῳ τῶν ἄλλων) B 19; παραμυθεῖσθαι (παραμυθουμένους/-ης) B 21; ῥύμην (ῥώμην) B 24; ἔσχε (----) B 26; -- (οὐ) B 33; ἐπιφερομένην (ἐπιτιθεμένην) B 34; ὄκνῳ (ὄγκῳ) B 34; ἀπέκοψαν (ἀπέκοψεν) B 39; ὑμῖν (ἡμῖν) B 40; φεύγουσαν (φευγέτω) B 41; τοῦ (---) B 42; ἄπαντες (πάντες) B 43; φοινικῷ (φοινικίῳ) B 47; ἀνάημα (ἄγαλμα) B 52; ὦ (ἦ) B 55; ἀπειλητήρων (ἀπειλητικῶν) B 63; γεννάδαν (γεννάδα) B 64.

[53] Cf. ἐξῆλθε (ἐπεξῆλθε) A 8; τὸ μέτρια (τὰ μέτρια) A 19; ἀφῆκε (ἐφῆκε) A 24; βεβληκέναι (βεβηκέναι) A 25; ἐχομένων (συνεχομένων) A 27. In addition to these five readings there are two more found in both Q and R, but which are 'corrected out' of Q by Q²: τετελεσμένων (τετολμημένων) A 1; ἀκεκαλέσαντο (ἀναμαχέσαντο) B 43.

(2) The relationship between the declamations and the ending is comprised in three different categories:

(a) 14-15th century MSS with the ending *lacking* (O I M DHP).

(b) 13-14th century MSS with the ending *appended* by a second hand (A B E).

(c) 15-16th century MSS with the ending *incorporated* in the first hand (QR FKG CN).

(3) Apart from a few inconsequential variants the text of the ending is *verbatim et literatim* identical in all the MSS which contain it.[54]

Together these observations all point to the same conclusion: The ending is a *latecomer* to the text as transmitted by the extant MSS. Neither γ nor δ, the archetypes behind the two basic familes, contained this ending. This observation is also confirmed by the fact that I, whose *Vorlage* (ι) drew from both γ and δ, does not have it. The appearance of the ending thus *post-dates* the split between these archetypes. In other words, the single parent text behind the division into the two families was also lacking the ending. It was not until the late medieval period that the ending found its way into the MSS. To some Italian MSS it was secondarily appended by a later hand (as in A, B, E — and presumably also in ρ, μ, and ν).[55] A careful comparative analysis of the handwriting in the Florentine MSS A and B shows that in both cases the ending was appended secondarily by the *very same* scribe. This addition will have occurred, of course, after the date of the younger MS and after the two MSS (in separate codices) were being read side by side. That was, at the earliest, in the 14th century. The other 'expanded' 14th century MSS (E, ρ, μ

---

[54] The negligible exceptions to uniformity are the following: (1) The FKG sub-group omits ἐπὶ θαύματι and rearranges the word order of πρῶτον τὸν παῖδα to τὸν παῖδα πρῶτον. (2) The R text, the latest MS, offers a few singular bloopers stemming from the scribe's limited knowledge of Greek: τὴν τὴν ψυχήν (the dittography was deleted but it is unclear by what hand); ἐπὶ ταρίοις (for ἐπιταφίοις); τὴν [instead of τὸν] ἐπινίκιον (a variant stemming from the parent of Q and R); and finally the senseless τῶν τὸν δικαστῶν (for τῶν δικαστῶν). These tiny variants in FKG and R only serve to show that a diversity in readings would naturally have appeared in the endings of many MSS if in fact the ending had been subjected to the same transmission process as the rest of the declamations. As it is, however, the uniformity of the extant endings is evidence that it stems from a single source and that it was not transmitted independently in each MS over a long period of time.

[55] Hinck (p. 38) attributed the ending in F to a second hand but a detailed analysis of the handwriting does not lend credence to this view. The script of the ending shows no appreciable difference over against the rest of the declamations. The paleographical evidence speaks for, not against, the ending coming from the original scribe.

and ν) also had the ending attached to them around the same time.[56] Whether this 'expansion' occurred first in Rome, in Florence, or elsewhere, one cannot say. At any rate, when such 'expanded' MSS were themselves later copied, the ending in the new copies appeared in the first hand, incorporated in the text as is the case in QR ($\rightarrow \rho$), F ($\rightarrow \mu$), KG ($\rightarrow$ F), and CN ($\rightarrow \nu$).

The fact that the wording of the ending is identical in all cases, regardless of the provenance of the MSS, shows that this ending was not subjected to the same individually diversifying transmission process as was the text of the declamations themselves.

For its part the ending appears to have arisen from a single source first introduced into the tradition in the 14th century in central Italy (Florence [AB]; Rome [E]; elsewhere?) where it became established (Florence [C]; Rome [FKG]) and thence found its way to places farther removed (cf. Naples [N], Vienna [Q], Munich [R]).

One may only speculate regarding the origin of this ending. If one entertains the hypothesis that it did derive from an old authentic Polemo MS whose ancestry pre-dated the 'incomplete' or 'defective' archetype (π) behind our extant MSS, one must concede that this hypothetical MS is now lost. Further, this hypothesis would have to grant that only the ending of that hypothetical text form has been preserved, namely by being grafted into the known tradition. Such an hypothesis would thus replace the problem it wanted to solve with another more difficult question: Why was the rest of that hypothetical MS itself not copied and preserved *in extenso*? Was it too worn or too illegible to be servicable? Was it only a fragment which happened to include the ending? No compelling explanation is apparent.

Other than this ending no evidence survives of that putative text because all existing MSS go back to two 'ending-less' *Vorlagen* (γ and δ) which themselves were dependent on the same 'incomplete' parent (π). One may say with certainty that no extant Polemo MS represents a copy of any hypothetical 'third' (i.e., non-γ and non-δ) textual tradition containing the ending.

In view of this, it is more reasonable to assume that the ending is not original or derivative from any ancient textual tradition. More likely it was fabricated by a medieval scholar who, understandably, felt unsatisfied by the abrupt termination of the text at $\tau \grave{o}\nu$ $\mu \grave{\epsilon}\nu$ $\mathrm{^\prime H}\rho\alpha\kappa\lambda\acute{\epsilon}o\varsigma$ (B 64a). To be sure, the

---

[56] Note that M (a 14th century MS without the ending) utilized both μ and ρ *before* they received the ending. On the other hand, F (a 14/15th century MS with the ending) copied from μ *after* the ending was attached to it; both Q and R (15/16th MSS with the ending) copied from ρ *after* the ending had been appended to it.

Table 2: The Stemma of the Manuscripts

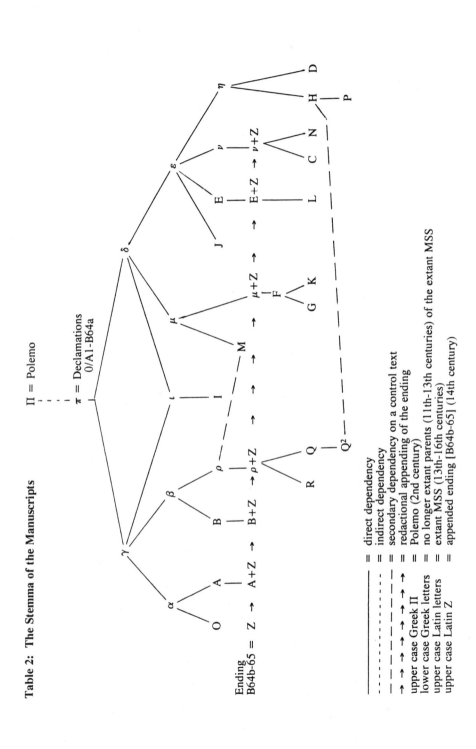

Π = Polemo

π = Declamations 0/A1-B64a

Ending
B64b-65 = Z → A+Z → B+Z → ρ+Z → E+Z → ν+Z
                                    μ+Z

——————————	= direct dependency
‥‥‥‥‥‥‥‥	= indirect dependency
– – – – –	= secondary dependency on a control text
↑ ↑ ↑ ↑ ↑	= redactional appending of the ending
↑ ↑ ↑ ↑ ↑	= Polemo (2nd century)
upper case Greek Π	= no longer extant parents (11th-13th centuries) of the extant MSS
lower case Greek letters	= extant MSS (13th-16th centuries)
upper case Latin letters	= no longer extant parents (11th-13th centuries) of the extant MSS
upper case Latin Z	= appended ending [B64b-65] (14th century)

vocabulary and grammar of the ending may be termed 'Polemonic' in the sense that they are not inconsistent with the rest of the declamations (cf. Appendix 3: The Ending of the MSS). However, a mere 43 words are hardly enough either to verify or falsify authenticity in any methodologically convincing way. In light of the MS evidence, therefore, this present edition regards it as unlikely that the ending goes back to Polemo; it assumes rather that the ending originated in Italy in the 14th century. This hypothesis is, of course, subject to modification should additional evidence (i.e., as yet unpublished papyri or unknown MSS) later come to light. Short of that, however, it is hard to make a compelling argument for the originality and genuineness of the ending.

The Stemma of the Manuscripts and the Reconstruction of the Text

When the observations about the MS branches — two larger families (γ and δ) each consisting of smaller sub-groups — are put together with the evidence for the Ending (B 64a-65 = Z), a composite and coherent picture of the family tree emerges as is shown in Table 2. The reader is urged to study this diagram. It provides — the editors are convinced — a complete and satisfactory explanation for the entire range of variant readings. Moreover it constitutes the basic hypothesis used by the editors for evaluating the variants and reconstructing the medieval archetype (π) from which they all derive.

Six Generations of Polemo Manuscripts

According to the reconstruction of the stemma the eighteen late medieval MSS which provide the basis for this present critical edition constitute the fourth, fifth and sixth generation of MSS all going back to a single medieval progenitor (π). Between that progenitor and the eighteen extant MSS stood another ten intermediate MSS which since have gone lost:

1st generation	(11th century)	π
2nd generation	(11-12th centuries)	γ δ
3rd generation	(12-13th centuries)	α β ι μ ε
4th generation	(13-14th centuries)	A O B ρ I M F J E ν η
Ending appended	(14th century)	A+Z B+Z ρ+Z μ+Z E+Z ν+Z
5th generation	(14-15th centuries)	R Q G K L C N H D
6th generation	(15-16th centuries)	Q^2 P

In the 14th century, in the period of the fourth generation, the hitherto undocumented ending (B64b-65) emerged and was appended to at least six MSS. It appears in a second hand in A, B, and E. It is here assumed that the same 'appending' phenomenon occurred also in ρ, μ, and ν. In the fifth generation four of these 'expanded' MSS were then copied: $\rho+Z$ ($\rightarrow$ Q R), $\mu+Z$ ($\rightarrow$ F), $\nu+Z$ ($\rightarrow$ C N), and probably $E+Z$ ($\rightarrow$ L).[57]

Five MSS derive from other extant MSS: G and K (from F), L (from E), P and Q^2 (from H). Inasmuch as these five do not provide any primary data beyond that of their parent texts (F, E, and H), they are only of secondary value for the recovery of the earlier progenitor π. In rare instances where a reading in F, E, or H is illegible or uncertain the descendent texts may occasionally provide clarification. Other than providing that help, however, they have little independent weight in comparison with the other MSS.

Of the remaining fourteen MSS each is valuable in its own way for recovering the wording of the no longer extant 'parent' and 'grandparent' texts. Agreement in descendant sibling texts reflects the reading in their common parent. Schematically the logic may be presented as follows:

4th generation

$R = Q$ $\rightarrow \rho$
$N = C$ $\rightarrow \nu$
$H = D$ $\rightarrow \eta$

3rd generation

$A = O$ $\rightarrow \alpha$
$B = \rho$ $\rightarrow \beta$
$M = F$ $\rightarrow \mu$
$E = J = \nu = \eta$ $\rightarrow \varepsilon$ (two agreements suffice)

2nd generation

$\alpha = \beta$ $\rightarrow \gamma$
$\mu = \varepsilon$ $\rightarrow \delta$

1st generation

$\gamma = \delta$ $\rightarrow \pi$

---

[57] To be sure, since L did not copy the second declamation, it cannot be demonstrated that L was using the 'expanded' version of E. Nevertheless, the date of L (15/16th century) requires the assumption that its *Vorlage* was the already expanded version of E.

Because ε has more than two direct descendants its wording can almost always be recovered with certainty. The recovery of the other no-longer-extant parent MSS, however, may not always be as simple. Should a pair of siblings agree, the reading of the parent text is, of course, established. When, however, a pair of siblings diverges the recovery process is more complex. Nevertheless, their parent can still often be reconstructed with the help of 'cousins', 'nephews' or other relatives. For example, if A and O diverge, but A has the same reading as B and ρ (i.e. the same reading as 'uncle' β), it may be assumed that A reflects the reading of its parent and the common grandparent γ. In other words, in a family where two pairs of siblings are cousins (e.g., O A and B ρ) agreement among three out of four may be taken as the reading of the common grandparent (in this case, γ). Similarly, in the case of α β and μ ε, when three out of the four agree it may usually be assumed that is the reading of the common grandparent π. Other combinations may be construed by analogy.

In this recovery enterprise one extant MS, namely I, offers special testimony. Its parent (ι) was a *mixtum compositum* which directly utilized both γ and δ as *Vorlagen*. For that reason in certain instances I is a particularly valuable witness and can sometimes provide a 'tie-breaking' vote. Thus, when all the data is taken into account the reconstruction back as far as the second generation (γ and δ) can usually be achieved with confidence in a very high percent of the cases.

In those cases where γ and δ agree, the reading of the single ancestor π may be assumed to have been recovered. In those cases, however, where γ and δ diverge (cf. Appendix 2: γ versus δ) the decision no longer rests simply on an evaluation of the external evidence — the internal evidence must also be considered. At this juncture the text critical judgment of the editors comes into play. Several issues must be pondered.

(1) In the choice between the γ and δ reading the primary question to be answered is: Which of the two readings best explains the rise of the other? The best choice typically lies with the *lectio difficilior* (= the harder reading) — a time-tested principle which is often, though not always, applicable. The more difficult reading is usually to be preferred because when altering a reading scribes tend to make a text smoother, not rougher.

(2) In the choice between γ and δ the old rule of preferring the *lectio brevior* (= the shorter reading) — scribes tend to expand rather than contract a text — is less applicable because in most cases of differing length it is clearly a matter of inadvertent omission rather than scribal insertion.

(3) The question of 'compatibility' may also be considered: Which of the two readings seems to conform better with the vocabulary and style of the rest of the declamations? In other words, the *principle of consistency* may in some instances guide the choice between γ and δ.

(4) When such principles from internal evidence fail to provide clear guidance, then the overall quality of the γ and δ texts may cautiously be taken into consideration. In general and in small ways the δ text is slightly inferior to the γ text. (Appendix 2: γ versus δ, supplies the evidence for the superiority of γ.) Hence, if all other things are equal, the editors are inclined to give the nod to the reading in γ.

While the *verbatim* text of the medieval progenitor (π) may not always be recoverable with absolute assurance, in view of the breadth of the data, the near-certainty of the stemma, and the time-tested text-critical methodology, the text of π can for the most part be reconstructed with a very high degree of probability. That text belonged in all likelihood to the 11th century, it certainly was not any earlier than the 10th century.

Getting back behind that attested medieval text to the second century original (Π) is another matter. Any reconstruction which pretends to bridge the nine century gap has to leave the solid ground of the MSS and resort to conjectures based upon intuition, ingenuity, and subjective judgment. Leaving aside the quest for the original (Π), this edition has set as its goal the reconstruction of the medieval archetype (π). The result rests on the objective evidence cited in the critical apparatus. Reconstruction proposals for the original wording from antiquity (Π) are relegated to a second apparatus of scholarly conjectures (located below the English translation). Some of these are discussed in the commentary.

The Previously Published Editions of Polemo's Declamations

Since the advent of movable type five printed editions of Polemo's declamations have appeared:

Henricus Stephanus,
Polemonis, Himerii et aliorum quorundam declamationes nunc primum editae.
Geneva: H. Fugerus, 1567.

Stephanus Prevosteau,
Πολέμωνος σοφίστου ἐπιτάφιοι λόγοι εἰς Κυναίγειρον καὶ Καλλίμαχον.
Paris: S. Prevosteau, 1586.

Petrus Possinus,
Polemonis Sophistae Orationes quotquot extant, duae.
Toulouse: A. Colerium, 1637.

Joannes Conradus Orellius,
Polemonis Laodicensis Sophistae Laudationes II Funebres.
Leipzig: C. Henricus, 1819.

Hugo Hinck,
Polemonis Declamationes quae exstant duae.
Leipzig: B. G. Teubner, 1873

The *editio princeps* of Stephanus exhibited a text form dependent on the Florentine MSS A, B, and C[58] but also on R (now housed in Munich).[59] The subsequent editions of Prevosteau, Possinus, and Orellius did not undertake independent MS collations or in any way advance matters regarding the establishment of the text. In other words, these editors basically took over, occasionally modifying in small ways, the Stephanus text.

Prevosteau's edition was not available for this study.[60] The fact that the subsequent scholarly literature makes virtually no reference to it suggests that it differed little from what Stephanus had published nineteen years earlier.

Possinus's contributions (in Latin) consisted of a short introduction (nine unnumbered pages), a very brief review of Polemo's life according to

---

[58] Cf. Hinck, op. cit., pp. vi–vii.

[59] For the peculiar and idiosyncratic readings adopted by Stephanus which derive from R cf. above "The Special Significance of R" and Appendix 1 [R].

[60] Like Orellius (p. viii) and Hinck (p. vii) the present editors were not successful in locating a copy of Prevosteau's edition.

Philostratus' *Lives of the Sophists* and the *Suda Lexicon* (five unnumbered pages), a wordy Latin paraphrase (pp. 33–101) appended to the Greek text (pp. 1–31), and some explanatory notes (pp. 102–126). The notes are sometimes useful, particularly in the cross references to classical authors. However, the verbosity of the paraphrase (78 pages of Latin to 31 of Greek) more often than not provides little help in the sticky questions of precise translation.

Orellius was conservative regarding his predecessors, although he did offer occasional emendations and corrections to the Greek text. His work opened with a short preface reviewing the previous editions (pp. iii–xii). Orellius's contributions (in Latin) were threefold: (1) The Latin paraphrase which Possinus had appended to his Greek text was difficult to use because it contained no paragraph numbers to indicate the correspondences in the Greek. Orellius reprinted this Latin paraphrase (a) with corresponding paragraph numbers and (b) placed it on the right hand pages facing the Greek on the left (pp. 2–149). In view of the great disparity in text length (the Latin is 2½ times as long as the Greek) this endeavor to match the two texts unfortunately often diverges by several pages. (2) Orellius supplied at the bottom of every Greek page very useful critical footnotes to the text (also with expansions and corrections, pp. xiii–xvi). Some deal with text reconstruction, many treat grammatical difficulties, and still others cite instructive Classical parallels. His notes uniformly reflect great erudition and acumen. (3) To the text and paraphrase he then appended four related texts: (a) a Greek text (= Diodorus Siculus 8.12.1–16) from Stephanus's edition[61] about two Messenian soldiers excelling in war and afterwards contesting for the pre-eminence in valor (pp. 150–154), (b) the Greek text from Philostratus (*V.S.* 530–544) on the life of Polemo (pp. 156–191), (c) the Greek entry from the *Suda Lexicon* on Polemo (pp. 192–193), and (d) a Latin encyclopedia article on Polemo by J. A. Fabricius (pp. 194–201).

The last edition of Polemo's declamations to appear was that from Hinck in 1873. Based on a broader MS foundation this work placed the declamations on a new footing and represented a significant advance over all previous editions. A concise preface (in Latin, pp. iii–xii) described very briefly the nine exemplars in the MS base, the textual scholarship up to that time, and explained the abbreviation-sigla which appear in the subsequent text. Following the introduction the reconstructed Greek text was printed with —

---

[61] Stephanus did not identify the source of this instructive fragment, but Orellius (p. xv) correctly attributed it to Diodorus Siculus (8.12.1–16), giving credit for identifying the source to Isaac Vossius.

now for the first time — a critical apparatus. This apparatus which gives MS attestation and editorial judgments occupies 20-25% of each page (pp. 3–39). Beyond this no further notes or commentary are provided. Thus, one admirable virtue of the work is its uncluttered brevity. Hinck's text was an important achievement. It constituted the first and only edition with a real critical apparatus, and for over a century now it has served as the standard reference text in the lexica (e.g., LSJ and BAGD) and in scholarly discussions.

Nonetheless, Hinck's edition has notable deficiencies. Apart from the relatively incomplete MS basis of his text for which he cannot be legitimately faulted, Hinck's edition exhibits a number of methodological shortcomings which need to be noted:

(1) Hinck did not (a) collate systematically and in their entirety all nine of his MSS, nor did he (b) note all the variants in the MSS which he did collate, nor did he (c) give the full attestation for the readings that he did cite. In short, his apparatus is woefully incomplete and on occasion inaccurate.

(2) While Hinck did offer some cursory observations about the relationships among the MSS (pp. iv–vii), the question of filiation remained unaddressed. Since he did not carry out a complete collation of the MSS he did not, and could not, systematically analyze the relationships between the MSS. In short, the question of dependencies remained unresolved and no stemma of the MSS was proposed or even attempted.

(3) Consequently and for all practical purposes Hinck — like Stephanus — made the Florentine MSS (ABC) the basis of his reconstruction and he relegated the rest (DEFGHI) to '*et al*' as though they were merely derivative from his prime witnesses. As it turns out, however, none of these other MSS is dependent on his Florentine texts. Furthermore, in many cases Hinck misassessed his MSS. For example, he overvalued A and C while undervaluing F and H. Moreover he neglected E and ignored the important composite character of I. In short, his judgment about the MSS is in need of revision.

(4) Hinck did not recognize or confront the text-critical problem inherent in the ending of the declamations (B 64b-65). The ending is absent in some of his MSS (DHI [now also in OP]); appended by a second hand in others (ABE); and integrated in the first hand in others (CFG [now also in KNQR]). Hinck did not reflect on the MS support for the ending or account for the diverse attestation. In short, he ignored the questions of the origin and authenticity of the conclusion.

(5) Hinck did not provide an explanation of his reconstructive methodology or articulate the criteria whereby the choices between variants

were made. He did not discuss the relative importance attached to external or to internal evidence, nor did he outline the operative principles for evaluating either type of evidence. Consequently, it is often not clear to the text-user why this or that reading has been preferred — the user must retrospectively try to figure out the rationale. In short, Hinck's notes do not guide the reader along the path of the reconstructive logic, and thus his reconstruction of the text is vulnerable to the charge of subjectivity or arbitrariness.

(6) Further, in his introduction Hinck did not make a clear distinction between the earliest recoverable medieval text form and the original Polemo text from the second century. Absent that distinction, the two seem to be equated or confused. Did Hinck mean to reconstruct the oldest medieval form of the text attainable, or did he imagine himself to be recovering the original? One suspects it is the latter. The problem of text changes arising in the intervening thousand years appears to have been by-passed. In short, the specific aim of Hinck's edition remains unclear.

(7) Finally, it is a serious flaw of Hinck's edition that alterations of the wording are all too often undertaken based not on MS evidence but on Hinck's or others' conjectures and the supposed inner logic of the text. Hinck readily took over changes proposed by earlier scholars (Stephanus, Possinus, Orellius, and Jacobs) and himself was especially creative in this regard. Even unanimously attested readings fell prey to Hinck's emendations. In short, in over sixty places Hinck presented a text resting not on MS support but on the conjecture of a *Besserwisser*.[62]

---

[62] These changes are noted in Hinck's apparatus by such words as *scripsi* (26x), *deleui* (13x), *addidi* (2x), *correxi* (3x), *reposui* (1x), *restitui* (1x), *lacunam indicaui* (5x), *conicio* (1x), *deleuerim* (1x), *malim* (3x), *scribendum censeo* (1x), *corruptum ... mutatum puto* (1x) and *fuisse credo* (1x), [= I have written, deleted, added, corrected, rearranged, restored, indicated a lacuna; I conjecture, would have deleted, would prefer, estimate to have been written, surmise as corrupted ... changed, believe to have been]. This practice of liberal alterations is in line with what B. L. Mack and E. N. O'Neil call a "fad of [the] nineteenth century, especially in Germany, whereby ancient texts were frequently re-written to suit modern notions" (cf. "The Chreia Discussion of Hermogenes of Tarsus," *The Chreia in Ancient Rhetoric*, Vol. I. *The Progymnasmata* [ed. R. F. Hock and E. N. O'Neil], Atlanta: Scholars Press, 1986, p. 159). Today, thankfully, such cavalier emendation of ancient texts is out of fashion, but unfortunately bothersome by-products of it still linger on. To cite but two examples: In the text of B 14, instead of the attested πέσῃς or πεσούσης (= you would fall), Hinck printed his own emendation, πεσοίης, noting in his apparatus "scribere ausus sum" (= I am so bold as to write). This wording then, for which there is absolutely no MS evidence, is cited in the LSJ lexicon as attestation for πεσοίης as a classical 2nd singular aorist optative (cf. LSJ, πίπτω)! In A 35 Hinck without any cogent reason emended στολαγωγοῦ to read στολαγοῦ, and this imaginary reading ended up being noted in LS under στολαγωγός!

Nevertheless, despite all these defects Hinck's edition has served as the standard critical text for over a hundred and twenty years now. Today, however, a modern critical edition has become a pressing *desideratum*. A new edition is needed not only because of the noted shortcomings of Hinck's edition, but for other reasons too. The grey age of Hinck's text, which has long been out-of-print, is reason enough to produce a new edition. Furthermore, since Hinck's edition appeared, the number of available Polemo MSS has doubled and the full breadth of this material needs to be exploited. Finally, the burgeoning scholarly interest in the movement of the Second Sophistic, in the history of rhetoric, and in the relationship of early Christianity to the Classical tradition has made a new edition of Polemo's declamations long overdue.

To replace Hinck's text a new critical edition of Polemo's declamations is planned by Teubner Press, to be issued later in this decade.[63] A modern edition embodying the high scholarly standards of the Teubner tradition will certainly be a welcome addition to the repertoire of resources for the study of Greco-Roman antiquity. Lexicographers, classicists, and students of the Second Sophistic, of rhetoric, and of early Christianty will look forward to the appearance of that volume.

The Present Edition

In the meanwhile the new edition presented here intends to meet the need for a modern critical text. It, along with a translation and commentary, is offered in the hope that it will help fill a gap and contribute to our understanding of the Greek renaissance and the thought world of the Hellenized Roman empire. In particular the editors hope that it will shed additional light on the cultural environment of early Christianity in Asia Minor.

This edition makes a conscious effort to avoid the defects of Hinck's edition as outlined above. (1) It offers a comprehensive collation of all the extant MSS and notes all the variants with complete attestation. (2) A detailed stemma of all the MSS is provided, at least in the form of a working hypothesis. (3) Based on a comprehensive analysis of all the data an evaluative

---

[63] According to a letter from Teubner Press (April 5, 1993), work on a new edition of Polemo has been underway for some years. The editorship of this project is in the hands of Hakan Hallberg of Uppsala University's Institute for Classical Languages.

ranking of the MSS is proposed which may lay claim to some objectivity. (4) The text-critical problem connected with the ending (B 64b-65) is faced and a solution is proposed which takes account of the MS evidence. (5) The principles employed in the text reconstruction are spelled out and explained so that the reader may evaluate their cogency. (6) The primary aim of the edition is specific: to recover the earliest attainable medieval form of the text. (7) Apart from a few noted exceptions this edition does not attempt to reconstruct the 'original' text. That project would require additional MS evidence independent from or earlier than the single medieval archetype upon which all the MSS utilized in this edition depend. In those very few instances where the editors have taken the tenuous step of proposing an earlier reading behind the medieval archetype, this is clearly indicated in the text (with square or pointed brackets) and documented in the separate apparatus for conjectures and reconstructions without MS support (printed opposite the Greek text, below the English translation). That is to say, this edition employs conjecture extremely rarely and only as a solution of last resort; reconstructions without MS support are always and necessarily suspect.

Comparison of the Present Edition with Previous Editions

Although five editions of Polemo's Declamations were published prior to this present one, in actuality only two versions of the text have appeared. Stephanus's edition (1567) was, for all practical purposes, reprinted by Possinus (1637) and Orellius (1819).[64] Not until Hinck's edition (1873), based upon independent collations, was there a real departure from the Stephanus text. The current edition (Reader/Chvala-Smith) presents now a third printed version of the text, one which diverges in noticeable ways from Stephanus/Possinus/Orellius on the one hand, and from Hinck on the other. A brief comparison, then, between this new edition and its predecessors is in order.

On the one hand, the wording of this present edition differs from that of Stephanus/Possinus/Orellius in about 210 instances. The large majority (146x = 70%) of these divergencies is due to one single reason: Stephanus's uncritical reliance on R — a late and manifestly inferior MS with hundreds of idiosyncratic variants many of which found their way into his edition. The

---

[64] Since Prevosteau's edition (1586) was not accessible for this current study, its relationship to Stephanus' text cannot be described. It is, however, unlikely that Prevosteau's edition constituted a text independent of Stephanus. Whatever the character of his work, it seems to have made little impact on subsequent scholarship.

deficiencies of R are traceable to two sources: (1) the *Vorlage* of R, namely ρ, was already a seriously flawed MS produced by a scribe with very meager abilities in Greek (cf. Appendix 1 [ρ]). (2) The shortcomings of ρ were then compounded by the ineptitude of the scribe of R, a dutiful but careless copyist also with very limited knowledge of Greek (cf. Appendix 1 [R]).

On the other hand, the wording of this current edition departs also from that of Hinck's edition in about 125 instances. Most of these divergencies from Hinck are attributable to one of two reasons: (1) A full half (64x = 51%) of the cases are due to Hinck's heavy reliance on A — an old and valuable witness but one which had taken over many of the deliberate 'corrections' in its *Vorlage*, namely α (cf. Appendix 1 [A α]). Unfortunately, as a perusal of the critical apparatus makes clear, a host of these scribal 'improvements' have found their way into Hinck's text. (2) Another third (43x = 34%) of this present edition's divergencies from Hinck are due to his frequent and cavalier practice of incorporating conjectural emendations into his text without any MS support.

There is a certain irony in this critique of and departure from Stephanus/Possinus/Orellius and Hinck. A strong influence was exercised on the former by R and on the latter by A. Both of these MSS are members of the family going back to γ (deemed by the present editors to be superior to its sibling δ). Herein lies the irony: the deficiencies of the previous editions derive in large measure from MSS whose ancestry goes back to the better of the two second generation texts (γ and δ).

For all the reasons outlined above this present edition provides a more reliable reconstruction of the oldest recoverable Polemo text than its predecessors.

Versification and Enumeration in Polemo's Declamations

All the medieval MSS of Polemo's declamations clearly indicate, by means of superscriptions, two separate speeches. Beyond that the MSS have no markings for divisions into paragraphs or verses. Greek punctuation marks (, · . ;) are the only signs of divisions. The punctuation, however, varies considerably in the MSS and provides no uniform means of reference.

With the appearance of printed editions of Polemo's declamations a reference system became not only a *desideratum* but also a necessity. Since the publication of the first printed edition of Polemo's declamations by Stephanus in 1567 at least three systems of enumeration have been employed in Polemo's text.

The text in Stephanus's *editio princeps* covered nineteen pages. Initially it was these page numbers which provided scholars a means to refer to specific passages in the declamations. These page numbers from Stephanus are printed at the appropriate points in the inner margins of Hinck's edition of 1873.

Any pericope divisions or paragraph markings which may have been employed in Prevosteau's 1586 edition are beyond the ken of this present volume since no copy of that edition could be located for this study.

Possinus's 1637 edition of the declamations was printed with 33 'paragraph' divisions noted in the outer margins. These numbers continued sequentially through the two speeches together. The logic behind the divisions remains unclear, particularly since paragraph 16 comprises both the last page of the first speech and the initial page of the second speech.

It was Orellius's 1819 edition which introduced the versification currently in use today. The first and shorter declamation he divided into 49 segments, the second and longer one into 65 segments. Orellius's edition printed these numbers in the outer margins alongside the line where the division occurs and then in the text itself clearly separated each verse from the next with an elongated dash. (The printed dash is helpful in the case of B 41 where the number in the margin is mistakenly printed one sentence after the dash.) The impetus for these particular divisions appears to have been the punctuation practice in many of the MSS.

Hinck's 1873 edition took over Orellius's versification. Visually, however, there was a slight modification: while Hinck also printed the verse numbers in the outer margins next to the line with the division, he dropped the dashes in the text with which Orellius had separated the verses — perhaps because there is nothing comparable in the MSS — and simply let the punctuation of the period or question mark suffice to indicate the point of division. In most cases this method works fine, but in several instances, because of the lack of the dashes, Hinck's text contains ambiguities regarding the exact point of division. For example, Hinck inadvertently omitted number 42 in the first declamation and 51 in the second (Orellius too had omitted 51 in his margin). In three passages (B 53, 54, 55) it is on the face of it unclear which punctuation mark on a numbered line represents the verse division; in all three cases it turns out to be the first punctuation mark on the line. In four cases Hinck printed the verse number one line above the actual line with the division (A 43; B 15, 18, 64), and in the case of B 41 Hinck followed the printing error of Orellius's edition by placing the number a full sentence after the (dash) division.

The verse divisions in the present study follow the system initiated by Orellius and continued by Hinck since it is these divisions which modern lexica (LSJ, BAGD) and other reference works utilize when citing Polemo. Only two minor divergencies from the Orellius-Hinck enumeration need be noted:

First, in deference to the syntax the verse division at B 49 in the present edition follows Hinck rather than Orellius; that is, it places the verse division one clause ahead of where Orellius had marked it because this makes much more sense grammatically. Orellius's text had read ὃς πάρεργον τοῖς βαρβάροις ἐγένετο. — ὁ δ' ἐμὸς υἱὸς ... with the dash marking the verse division. However, the preferable reading is ὁ σὸς πάρεργον τοῖς βαρβάροις ἐγένετο, ὁ δὲ ἐμὸς υἱὸς ... In other words, instead of ending one sentence with a relative ὅς clause and beginning another sentence with ὁ δὲ ἐμὸς υἱὸς ... it is better to construe it as a single sentence with the contrast ὁ σὸς ... ὁ δὲ ἐμὸς ..., and not divide it in the middle.

Secondly, for the sake of convenient citation the present edition supplies the number zero (0) to the text of the superscription at the beginning of the book since neither Orellius nor Hinck had attached any number designator to these words.

Finally, the current edition avoids the ambiguities and uncertainties connected with Hinck's edition by printing the verse division numbers right in the text, as is the practice, for example, in many modern English bibles.

Mode of Citation

All modern lexica utilize the Orellius-Hinck versification when referring to Polemo's declamations, but there is no uniformity in the mode of citation. For the sake of brevity this present study utilizes a more concise method than typically appears in the standard lexica. The following comparative examples will suffice to make clear the citation mode used in this present study:

in LSJ:	Polem. Call. 24	Polem. Cyn. 37
in BAGD:	Polemo Decl. 1,24	Polemo Decl. 2,37
in R/C-S:	A 24	B 37

The utilization of the letters A (= the speech of Cynegirus' father) and B (= the speech of Callimachus' father) was prompted by the appearance of these

Greek letters in the superscriptions of Hinck's edition. The use of these letters allows for extreme abbreviation and also sidesteps messy combinations of numbers separated by comma or colon. Given the limited focus of this present work, this mode of citation should not give rise to any ambiguities, uncertainties, or misunderstandings.

The Production of a Critical Greek Text

For those unfamiliar with how a modern edition of an ancient text is prepared a brief explanation may be order. The procedure involves four basic steps. These four phases of work generally follow one another sequentially but they can and often do overlap when the work extends over a longer period of time.

1. The Spade Work — Assembling the Manuscripts

The first step is to identify all the MSS known to contain the text. The minimal data needed comprises codex name, precise folios, and current location. Such information is tracked down in a research library (archive catalogues, monographs, journals, MS listings, and disparate footnotes). Then microfilm or photographic replicas of all the relevant folios must be assembled. This involves letters of inquiry and request, completion of forms, clarifying correspondence, telephone reminders, bank transfers, and other bureaucratic details. Long delays are not uncommon. After the *Papierkrieg* comes the battle with photo-technology. From the obtained films and photographic materials (typically of varying quality and format) readable print copies must be produced. Satisfactory results on the first try may be regarded as good fortune, not as the norm. Despite careful efforts one must reckon with frustrations and failures. Once satisfactory print copies are achieved they must be marked with standard versification — a laborious business. Each MS is then assigned a siglum or abbreviation by which it is identified. This whole process can be time-consuming and marked by bureaucratic glitches, mis-communications, unforeseen expenses, and at times exasperation. Patience and persistence are the requisite virtues.

2. The Grunt Work — Collating the Manuscripts

The next step is to read all the manuscripts, one by one, and line by line — always in comparison with a 'control text'. Every single variant reading needs to be systematically noted — omissions, insertions, substitutions, misspellings, and transpositions. In the case of the present edition of Polemo's declamations this procedure was carried out by the two editors working together. In teamwork — usually in three hour sessions — one would read aloud from a 'control' text, the other would follow in the MS, with the role of 'reader' and 'follower' being reversed every hour. Every divergency was duly noted in accordance with a predetermined system of symbols. Medieval scribal conventions regarding handwriting, shorthand for inflected endings, and abbreviations varied widely. A 'glossary', therefore, of typical script, endings, and idiosyncratic formations had to be gradually assembled for each individual MS. Uncertain readings were settled by joint decision. Such work is sometimes engaging, sometimes *stumpfsinnig*, and always hard on the eyes. Intense bright light and a strong magnifying glass are absolute necessities for this endeavor. This work is by nature slow and laborious. Typically the collation of a single Polemo MS required twelve to fifteen hours with some of the more difficult MSS taking upwards of twenty hours. Tedium and fatigue were fought off with strong tea, regular breaks, and merciless jokes at the expense of the medieval scribes.

3. The Sleuth Work — Determining the Dependencies of the Manuscripts

After the collation of the MSS is completed, the noted divergent readings need to be examined in their entirety. The MSS are then grouped according to patterns of readings. For example, when a number of MSS all exhibit the same omissions, that is ordinarily a sure sign that they are all related. Similarly, when a number of MSS all have the same transposed word order in certain passages that may be taken as a signal that they are connected in some way. Once various groups of MSS have been established, then the task is to determine the nature of the dependencies. Did X copy from Y, or Y from X? Or did both copy from W? Or did all three depend on an earlier, no longer existing archetype? To determine the filiation of the MSS one must pay attention to the paleographic dating, the 'logic' of divergency patterns, and the cumulative weight of scores of probabilities. The solution ultimately depends on a combination of quantitative analysis (statistics) and qualitative analysis (evaluation of peculiar readings). This process of working out the 'family tree' is in some ways akin to solving a jigsaw puzzle. It requires a keen eye, patience, and the ingenuity to test a variety of hypothetical relationships. As far as possible one tries to establish which MSS have 'progenitor' status and which are derivative. Having done that, one is in a position to reconstruct the older archetype(s) from which the existing MSS have come. The goal of this detective work is to construct a diagram which shows the relationships and dependencies of all the MSS. Establishing the stemma, or at least a working hypothesis for the stemma, is a *sine qua non* for evaluating the various divergent readings. For Polemo's declamations the collation data are so extensive and clear that the editors are confident the entire stemma of MSS can be reconstructed with near certainty.

4. The Rescue Work — Recovering the Text of the Progenitor Manuscript

Once the stemma has been posited the work of reconstructing the progenitor or ancestor text can begin. The entire text and all the assembled variants must be worked through word by word. Each variant reading must be evaluated first on the basis of external evidence (= the weight of the MS support) and then on the basis of the internal evidence (= the logic of the variants). The preferred reading is placed in the text, the rest of the variants are noted below in the apparatus. (Ideally the material in the apparatus should be presented in such a way as to allow readers to evaluate the attestation for themselves and come to an independent judgment about it.) The text resulting from this procedure is, of course, an eclectic one. It represents the wording of the hypothetical, no longer extant archetype text from which all the existing MSS derive.

What is presented in the next chapter is such an eclectic text which aims at reconstructing the wording of Polemo's declamations as it appeared in the medieval archetype behind all the extant Polemo MSS. That is, the printed text represents the wording of that lone Byzantine MS which probably came from the Greek speaking world in the East and was brought to Italy in the 11th century.

Chapter 3

The Text and Translation

The Greek Text

The Greek text presented here is that of the medieval (11th century?) progenitor (π) from which all the examined extant MSS derive. The broad stemma and the standard methods of textual criticism allow us to reconstruct with confidence the entire wording of that medieval archetype which no longer exists. No attempt has been made to recover any form of the text earlier than π, let alone get back to the second century original (Π). Without older MS witnesses independent of the π family such a reconstruction is not possible. Absent such evidence all editorial attempts to reconstruct the wording of the original Π are conjectural and methodologically unsound.

The various types of textual changes which can be observed in the six generations (5 centuries) between π and the latest MSS (cf. the critical apparatus) must be presumed to have also occurred to some degree in the nine centuries between the original Π and the medieval descendant π. Hence, one cannot assert that the wording of π presented here matches exactly the form of the original Π. It may well be a close approximation, though how close remains uncertain. The accuracy of the text depends both on the *number* and *quality* of intervening MSS between Π and π. Neither of these factors is knowable. If the known transmission history of six generations over five centuries is retrojected backwards then one can reasonably posit eight or ten intervening generations of MS copies. However, the competence or care of the

87

scribes of those MSS lies beyond our ken. Nonetheless, that π first appeared in medieval Italy suggests that it was brought there from the Byzantine world in the 11th century. This means that in the earlier generations the declamations were copied by Greek speaking scholars, not Latins for whom Greek was a 'learned' or 'foreign' language. That the earlier Eastern copyists did their work in their mother tongue probably means that the text was not subject to as much change as was later the case at the hands of Western scribes.

The English Translation

A translator must take a position in the long-standing debate about whether a translation should be literal or according to sense. Both approaches have their merits and these vary depending on the purpose and audience of the translation. In the case of this work and the series in which it appears, it is presumed that the readers will by and large be academics — classical philologians, NT scholars, historians of the Second Sophistic, and students of rhetoric. With that in mind I have followed the advice of Edgar C. Reinke, my undergraduate professor and advisor in classical languages, who hammered into his students the translation maxim which he received from his doctoral mentor, the great classicist, Paul Shorey: "As literal as possible, as free as necessary." This time-tested principle served throughout as the main guide for the translation presented here.

The Conventions Utilized in the Greek and English Texts

[   ]

Words not represented in the Greek text but which are only implied or which are inserted for the sake of clarity are placed in square brackets [   ]. In the Greek text there are only two such additions (0; B 41), but countless examples in the English. For this practice, however, two exceptions are worth noting:

(1) There are many instances in which the Greek idiom uses the definite article for a person's body parts or actions where English instead ordinarily prefers the possessive adjective. In these cases the Greek has been rendered idiomatically rather than literally, i.e., with the possessive adjective in English rather than the definite article, without noting this by square brackets in the translation. For example: He gave "*his* hands" rather than "*the* hands" (A 28); "*his* soul departed" rather than "*the* soul" (B 47); "he made *his* body to stand" instead of "*the* body" (B 53).

(2) The imperfect of the Greek verb is capable of expressing a variety of meanings (e.g., durative, iterative, inceptive, conative, desiderative, customary action, etc.). When imperfects are rendered with "began to ...," "tried to ...," "wanted to ...," and the like, these words are not usually put in square brackets because these senses are inherent in the verb tense itself and hence are not additions to the text.

{ }

Words in the Greek text which are, despite their presence in the medieval MSS, probably not original but rather secondary interpolations, have been placed within pointed brackets { }. These same pointed brackets are also put around the corresponding phrases in the English translation to indicate the likely secondary nature of the words. There is only a handful of such instances, the most significant of which come at the end (cf. A 16, 40; B 11, 19, 45, 50, 63, 64).

...

Where ellipses have been presumed in the text these are noted with a series of three dots ... The number of dots indicates nothing about the length of the ellipsis. In some cases it could be a single word, in others possibly several lines. There are only nine such instances and these are indicated in both the Greek and English texts respectively (cf. A 2, 39; B 21, 22, 23, 35, 40, 56, 64). In two cases in the English I have ventured to supply what is probably missing, placing it within square brackets (cf. B 22, 56).

Bold Font

In cases where there is uncertainty about the wording in π because the reconstructed readings in the direct offspring (γ and δ) diverge and each is equally plausible, — in such cases the wording preferred by the present editors is printed in bold font to indicate that the choice is debatable. The rival reading may be found in the critical apparatus immediately following the *lemma*. There are 43 such instances in the text, but in most cases the differences between the competing readings are not substantial.

The Greek text and the corresponding English translation are printed on facing pages so that the reader may readily control the accuracy of the translation.

The Critical Apparatus

There are two critical apparatuses. One appears below the Greek text and the other below the English translation; both, however, refer to the Greek text.

The Apparatus Beneath the Greek Text

The apparatus below the Greek text presents a comprehensive tabulation of *all* the variant readings found in the eighteen MSS. Every divergency in the transmitted text down to a single letter is recorded here. Only two qualifications need to be mentioned. First, differences in *accents* are generally ignored. Only in those few cases where the accent is of consequence does the apparatus provide data on divergent MS readings. Such cases are of two types: (a) the distinction between the interrogative τίς and the indefinite τις and (b) the distinction between verb tenses (e.g., present μένω versus future μενῶ). Secondly, differences in *punctuation* are completely ignored. The scribes often set commas indescriminately and no standard rules prevailed in the use of the semicolon, period, and question mark. To record all the punctuation variants would needlessly swell the apparatus to unmanageable proportions without providing any genuinely useful information.

In the critical apparatus the *lemma* (the preferred reading shown in the text) is cited first in **bold print**. The MS attestation for the *lemma* is cited (immediately thereafter) only if this reading has serious rivals. When the attestation is not specifically provided it may be inferred to be all the MSS not named for the variants.

The variant readings (with attestation) are then listed in the order of decreasing likelihood or claim on originality. A single vertical stroke (|) separates the individual variants. A double vertical stroke (‖) marks the end of the variants for a given reading; simultaneously it marks the start of a new *lemma*.

For every variant reading two principles are operative in the ordering of the attestation: (1) *chronology* — earlier MSS are listed before later ones; (2) *quality* — 'superior' MSS are listed before 'inferior' ones. Harmonization of the two principles is not always possible, but within the individual sub-groups the standard order is usually as follows: A O | B Q R | M F [K G] | J E [L] | C N | H [P Q²] D. Among the postulated intermediate archetypes (α [→ AO], β [→ Bρ], ρ [→ QR], ι [→ I], μ [→MF {→KG}], ε [→ JEνη], ν [→ CN], η [→ DH {→PQ²}]) the earlier ones (α β ι μ ε) are weightier than the later ones (ρ ν η). Within these intermediate groups no standard ranking can be established. Each group reading has to be judged on its own merits. Hence, the citation order of the intermediate groups necessarily varies from reading to reading.

When representing attestation in the critical apparatus, groups of three or more MSS are indicated with the Greek letters β, γ, δ, ε, η, μ, and π. These symbols are used only if *all* the descendents in that group share the reading, otherwise the individual MSS are named. Hence, the use, for example, of γ means that the *entire* family of γ MSS (namely, AOBQR) *unanimously* shares the reading. There is an exception to this rule: When a lower case Greek letter is in parentheses or brackets and preceded by an arrow ($\rightarrow$), the Greek letter does *not* refer to a consensus of the descendent MSS, but rather to the archetype MS itself.

The Apparatus Beneath the English Translation

The apparatus below the English translation offers a comprehensive overview of all the conjectures which the editors of printed editions of the declamations have proposed for reconstructing the wording of the original second century Polemo text (II), or at least the wording of an earlier text form behind the medieval archetype (π).

The symbols utilized in the apparatus are listed in the following tables with explanations.

Symbols in the Critical Apparatus beneath the Greek Text.
(This apparatus records all the variants in all 18 examined MSS.)

Symbol		Signification	Explanation
○	=	omission	Word(s) omitted (i.e., not written).
▬	=	deletion	Word(s) deleted (i.e., written, but then excised by erasure, striking through, or marking with dots or other such indicators) and not corrected or replaced.
+	=	addition	Word(s) inserted.
>	=	substitution	Word(s) replaced.
≥	=	correction	Word(s) deleted or crossed out and then either [1] immediately overwritten in place, or [2] corrected immediately following, on the line, or [3] rewritten above, between the lines or [4] corrected in the margin. 1 and 2 ordinarily stem from the first hand; 3 and 4 may derive from the first or a second hand.
╧	=	legitimate orthographic variant	('thumbs up') Same word with legitimate alternate spelling but no difference in meaning. Typical are iotacistic variations ι / ει , Atticistic variations σσ / ττ , variations with or without the movable ν, and elided letters (indicated by an apostrophe).
╤	=	illegitimate orthographic variant	('thumbs down') Same word with inadvertant and unacceptable misspelling arising, for example, from a careless omission, addition, or substitution of letters, or from an otherwise undocumented spelling.

Symbol	Signification	Explanation
ǂ =	ambiguous orthographic variant	Homonym or same word with illegible letters or with an alternate spelling which yields a slight difference in meaning whereby it cannot be determined whether this was deliberate or careless. Typical are variations between a single or double consonant (e.g., λ / λλ, μ / μμ) and variations in the position, form, or existence of an accent. Such tiny differences can, for example, alter the tense of a verb or the meaning of a pronoun (e.g., τίς / τις or μένειν / μενεῖν).
∩ =	transposition	Same words in a different sequence. If the order of two words is reversed, the sign appears alone without further clarification. If the order of three or more words is transposed, then the sign appears with numbers following which indicate the different order.
| =	sub-divider	Separation mark between individual variants all belonging to the same *lemma*.
|| =	divider	Separation mark after the final entry for one *lemma* and before the beginning of the next *lemma*.
. =	unclear letter	A dot below a letter or space indicates that the letter in question is uncertain.
c =	correction	Correction of the original reading whereby it is uncertain whether it stems from the original hand or another hand.
d =	defective	Damage to the MS. For example, a stain, tear, hole, or repair tape means that the text is absent, covered, or otherwise not accessible.

Symbol		Signification	Explanation
i	=	illegible	Script is unreadable. For example the ink is faded, rubbed, or smudged; the letters are too tiny or poorly formed; or the photography is blurry.
u	=	uncertain	Enough text is legible to suggest a reading. The basis, however, is so weak that the editorial judgment could be contested.
mg	=	margin	The reading is located (fully or partially) in the margin.
β	=	BQR	Unanimous consensus of B Q R.
γ	=	AOBQR	Unanimous consensus of A O B Q R.
δ	=	MFKGECNHPD [J] [L]	Unanimous consensus of M F K G [J] E [L] C N H P D. J is to be understood only for 0/A1-13 and L only for 0/A1-49.
ε	=	ECNHPD [J] [L]	Unanimous consensus of [J] E [L] C N H P D. J is to be understood only for 0/A1-13 and L only for 0/A1-49.
η	=	HPD [Q^2]	Unanimous consensus of H P D. Since Q^2 which is dependent on H does not provide a complete witness, it is noted separately.
μ	=	MFKG	Unanimous consensus of M F K G.
π	=	progenitor	The sole medieval (11th century?) progenitor MS from which all 18 extant MSS of the declamations (0/A1-B64a) were derived.

Symbol		Signification	Explanation

Π = Original MS — The original (2nd century) Polemo MS of the declamations from which π ultimately was derived.

Z = Ending — The 43 word ending (B64b-65) which in the 14th century was appended by a second hand to six MSS (namely: A B ρ μ E ν) and which then was subsequently copied in the first hand by seven other MSS (namely: Q R F G K C N).

(→) = archetype — When lower case Greek letters (α, β, γ, δ, ε, η, μ, π, ρ) are preceded by an arrow and noted within paragraph brackets, they do *not* refer to a consensus of the MSS dependent on them, but rather to the archetype MS itself.

Symbols in the Apparatus beneath the English Translation
(This apparatus records all the conjectural reconstructions of the wording
of the 2nd century original text (II) proposed by the previous editors.)

Symbol	Signification	Explanation
h =	Hinck	H. Hinck, *Polemonis Declamationes quae exstant duae,* Leipzig: Teubner, 1873
j =	Jacobs	F. Jacobs, "Adnotationes ad declamationes Polemonis" *Zimmermanns Annals* (1838), pp. 5–11 (cited in Hinck's critical apparatus)
jü =	Jüttner	H. Jüttner, *De Polemonis Rhetoris, Vita Operibus Arte* *BPhA* 8,1; Breslau: Koebner, 1898, pp. 113–116
o =	Orellius	I. C. Orellius, *Polemonis Laodicensis Sophistae* *Laudationes II Funebres in Cynaegirum et* *Callimachum* Leipzig: Teubner, 1819
p =	Possinus	P. Possinus, *Polemonis Sophistae Orationes* Toulouse: Colomerium, 1637
s =	Stephanus	H. Stephanus, *Polemonis, Himerii et aliorum quorunduam* *declamationes, Nunc primum editae* Geneva: Fugerus, 1567
r/cs =	Reader / Chvala-Smith	W. Reader and A. Chvala-Smith, editors of this present edition

The Greek Text

and

The English Translation

0

[Αἱ Μελέται]

Πολέμωνος σοφιστοῦ

εἰς **Καλλίμαχον καὶ Κυναίγειρον**

Νόμου ὄντος 'Αθήνῃσι τοῦ ἄριστα ἀποθανόντος ἐν πολέμῳ τὸν πατέρα
λέγειν τὸν ἐπιτάφιον ὁ Καλλιμάχου καὶ Κυναιγείρου πατὴρ δικάζονται.

---

0 *σοφίστου* Ο FKG ‖ *σοφίστου* + *ἐπιτάφιος* AO QR I MG L ‖
Καλλίμαχον καὶ Κυναίγειρον γ I ∩ 321 δ ‖ **Καλλίμαχον καὶ** Ο L ‖
Κυναίγειρον + ἀπ᾿ τοῦ πατρὸς L | + ἀναγκαίοι πάνυ HP | + ἀναγκαῖος
πάνυ D ‖ *νόμου ὄντος* 'Αθηνῃσι τοῦ ἄριστα ἀποθανόντος ἐν πολέμῳ τὸν πατέρα λέγειν
τὸν ἐπιτάφιον ὁ Καλλιμάχου καὶ Κυναιαγείρου πατὴρ δικάζονται Ο K L ‖ ὄντος +
ἐν I ‖ τοῦ ἄριστα ἀποθανόντος ἐν πολέμῳ τὸν πατέρα ∩ 67123 QR ‖ ἐν + τῷ
P ‖ ἐν πολέμῳ Ο RQ ≥ ἐν πολέμῳ Q² ‖ λέγειν τὸν ἐπιτάφιον ∩ 231 CN ‖
τὸν Ο β I ‖ ἐπιτάφιον Ο J ‖ ὁ > οἱ Q | Ο R ‖ καὶ Κυναιγείρου πατὴρ
∩ 312 I ‖ πατὴρ > πατέρες QR ‖ δικάζονται + στίχ οἱ σοὶ λόγοι κρατοῦσιν
ἀπάντων λόγων κἂν Κυναιγείρῳ καὶ Καλλιμάχῳ μάχῃ, ἀντικρατοῦσα ταυτοδυνάμοις
λόγοις HP ‖

[The Declamations]

0

of Polemo the Sophist
for Callimachus and Cynegirus

Since at Athens [there] is a custom that the father of the one who died most bravely in battle should speak the funeral [oration], the father[s] of Callimachus and Cynegirus plead their cases.

A　　　　　　　ʽΟ Κυναιγείρου πατήρ

1 Ἐπειδὴ τά τε ἄλλα χρὴ καὶ οἰκεῖον εἶναι τοῖς κειμένοις τὸν ἐροῦντα τὸν ἐπ᾽ αὐτοῖς λόγον, φημὶ τούτου μοι προσήκειν μάλιστα, Κυναιγείρου πατὴρ ὢν καὶ τὸ πάντων ἀξιολογώτατον τῶν Μαραθῶνι τετολμημένων ἐκ τῆς ἐμῆς φύσεως τῇ πόλει συμβαλόμενος, ἄνδρα τοῖς βαρβάροις καὶ κατὰ μέρος μεμαχημένον. 2 εἰκὸς μὲν οὖν τι καὶ τὸν Καλλιμάχου ... τῶν ἀρετῇ δευτέρων· ἐγὼ δ᾽ αὐτοῦ τοσοῦτον ἐπειπεῖν τῷ τάφῳ δικαιότερος ὅσῳ τιμῆς ἄξιος πλείονος Καλλιμάχου Κυναίγειρος, στρατιώτης ἀγαθοῦ νεκροῦ, καὶ τὸ σύμπαν ὁπόσῳ τινὶ κρείττων ἀρετὴ σχήματος. 3 ποιοῦμαι δὲ τὴν σπουδὴν οὐ τῶν ἰδίων τοὐμοῦ παιδὸς ἐπαίνων χάριν — ὅστις γὰρ ἂν καὶ λέγῃ τὸν λόγον, τὸν πλεῖστον ἐπὶ Κυναιγείρῳ διαθήσεται — ἀλλὰ τῆς κοινῆς δόξης τῶν ἐπὶ τῷδε τῷ τάφῳ κειμένων οἷς σεμνόν ἐστιν ἂν ὁ Κυναιγείρου πατὴρ εἴπῃ τὸν ἐπ᾽ αὐτοῖς λόγον. ἔσονται γὰρ οὕτως ὁμότιμοι πάντων αἱ χεῖρες τῇ Κυναιγείρου δεξιᾷ· εἰ δὲ μή, ταῖς ἡμετέραις φιλοτιμίαις τὰ τῶν παίδων

A ὁ Κυναιγείρου πατὴρ QR FᵐᵍKGᵐᵍ Eᵐᵍ CN Ο ΑΟ Β Ι Μ J L η ‖ ὁ Ο R ‖ πατὴρ Ο Ν ‖
1 ἐπειδὴ ⧧ πειδὴ (the intended calligraphic ε was not added in the left margin) N ‖ ἐροῦντα > αἱροῦντα J ‖ τούτου > τούτῳ Hᶜ | > τοῦτόν P ‖ μάλιστα + καὶ D ▬ Dᶜ ‖ τὸ > τῷ P ‖ πάντων ⧧ πάντ QR ‖ ἀξιολογώτατον > ἀξιολογούντων R ‖ τῶν + ἐν δ Ι ‖ τετολμημένων > τετελεσμένων RQ ≥ τετολμημένων Q²ᵐᵍ ‖ συμβαλόμενος Β μ EL C η ⧧ συμβαλλόμενος ΑΟ QR I J N ‖ μέρος > μέρη BRQ ≥ μέρος Q² ‖
2 τι Ο Ν ‖ τὸν > τῶν Β | > τιν R ≥ τῶν Rᶜ ‖ Καλλιμάχου γ > Καλλίμαχον δ Ι ‖ ἐπειπεῖν > εἰπεῖν Μ | > ἐπειπῇ R ‖ πλείονος Καλλιμάχου ∩ QR ‖ πλείονος Ο D ‖ Καλλιμάχου + οὐ QR ‖ στρατιώτης > στρατιώτου Μ ≥ στρατιώτης Μᶜ | > στρατιώτ . Q ≥ στρατιώτης Qᶜ ‖ κρείττων > κρεῖττον A ‖
3 δὲ Ο D ‖ τοὐμοῦ > τοῦ ἐμοῦ QR ‖ παιδὸς Ο P ‖ ὅστις + καὶ Q ▬ Qᶜ ‖ λέγῃ ΑΟ Β J E CN | > λέγω Μ ≥ λέγῃ Μᶜ | > λέγοι I FKG HD L QR | > λέγει P ‖ ἐπὶ + τῷ QR ‖ τῷδε τῷ τάφῳ ∩ 231 QR ‖ τάφῳ + ἐπὶ Q ▬ Qᶜ ‖ ἐστιν Ο L ‖ εἴπῃ > εἴποι Μ ‖ οὕτως γ I > . οὕτω δ ‖ ὁμότιμοι πάντων αἱ χεῖρες γ I ∩ 2341 δ ‖ ὁμότιμοι > ὁμοιότιμοι Μ ‖ ἡμετέραις > ὑμετέραις Β | ἡμέραις Q ≥ ἡμετέραις Q² ‖ φιλοτιμίαις ΑΟ Β Ι μ ⧧ φιλοτομίαις QR | > φιλίαις ε ‖ παίδων > παλαιῶν Β ‖

A.   The Father of Cynegirus

1 Since above all else it is necessary for the one who will speak the oration over those who lie dead to be related to them, I assert in this regard that [the oration] should belong above all to me, since I am Cynegirus' father and out of my own physical being I have contributed to the city the most noteworthy of all the deeds of daring at Marathon, a man who fought with one member after the other against the barbarians. *2* It is on the one hand then fair [to say] something also [about] the [fight] of Callimachus ... [though] in terms of valor [he was among] those in second place. But on the other hand I [am] more rightfully suited than he to speak at the grave in the same way that Cynegirus is worthy of more honor than Callimachus, [in the same way that] a soldier [is more worthy] than a brave corpse, and in general [in the same way that] valor is so much more excellent than [outward] appearance. *3* I am zealous not for the sake of the personal praises of my own son — for whoever [delivers] the speech, will devote most of it to Cynegirus — but [for the sake] of the common glory of those lying [dead] at this grave for whom it is an act of respect if the father of Cynegirus delivers the oration over them. For thus the hands of all will be held in equal honor with the right hand of Cynegirus. Otherwise, the [deeds] of the sons are jeopardized along with our

---

Editorial conjectures for reconstructing the wording of the original text (Π) behind the medieval text form (π):

2 τῶν ἀρετῇ δευτέρων with *lacuna* preceeding *r/cs* | with *lacuna* following *h* ‖ στρατιώτης ἀγαθοῦ > στρατιώτης ἀγαθὸς ἀγαθοῦ *o j* | στρατιώτης ἀγαθὸς ἀγαθοὺς *jü* ‖
3 ἐστιν > ἔσται *j* ‖

συγκινδυνεύουσιν. **4** ὁρᾶτε δέ, ὅσῳ δικαιότερος κρατεῖν Κυναίγειρος, ἐπεὶ καὶ κρατῶν ἀπέθανεν. εἰδόσι μὲν οὖν τὰ τοῖς παισὶν ἡμῶν πεπραγμένα τῇ τοῦ παιδὸς θάτερος ἀρετῇ συναγωνίζεται, καὶ λεγόμενα δ' ἔσται τὰ κρείττω φανερώτερα.

5 Καλλίμαχον μὲν ὡς πολέμαρχον ἀνάγκη τῆς ἀρχῆς ἦγεν εἰς Μαραθῶνα καὶ μὴ βουλόμενον ἀμύνασθαι τὴν τῶν βαρβάρων ἀπόβασιν· Κυναίγειρος δὲ ὑπ' ἀρετῆς καὶ τόλμης, ἐθελούσιος, ἐπεὶ καὶ νέος ὢν κομιδῇ, σχεδὸν καὶ πρὸ τῆς ἡλικίας, μετέσχε τῆς ἐξόδου, ἔρωτι δόξης καὶ μεγάλων ἔργων ὀρεγόμενος. **6** ἐν δὲ τῇ μάχῃ πάντες μὲν ἐγένοντο ἄνδρες ἀγαθοὶ καὶ οἱ πεσόντες τῶν στρατιωτῶν καὶ οἱ περιγενόμενοι· θαυμαστότατοι δὲ πάντων ἐφάνησαν οὑμός τε παῖς καὶ ὁ τούτου. **7** ἀλλ' ὁ μὲν τούτου τοῖς βέλεσι τῶν ἐναντίων ἐκθεὶς ἑαυτὸν ὑπ' αὐτῶν τῶν τοξευμάτων τε καὶ βλημάτων περιχυθέντων κατεσχέθη καὶ διὰ τοῦτο ἔμενεν ἐν τῷ τῆς στάσεως σχήματι καὶ ἐδόκει ἑστάναι πεσεῖν μὴ δυνάμενος· καὶ τὸ Καλλιμάχου λαμπρὸν τοῦτό ἐστι μόνον, σχῆμα ζῶντος ἐν νεκρῷ σώματι· **8** ὁ δὲ ἐμὸς Κυναίγειρος ὑπερβὰς τὴν φάλαγγα κᾆτα ἀδεῶς ἐκδραμών, πρὸς αὐτὴν

---

3 συγκινδυνεύουσιν > συγκινδυνεύσουσιν HP ‖
4 κρατεῖν ○ Q ≥ κρατεῖν Q²ᵐᵍ ‖ εἰδόσι ≟ εἰδόσιν QR ‖ ἡμῶν > ἡμῖν QR ‖ πεπραγμένα > πραγματα Q ≥ πεπραγμένα Q² ‖ τῇ ○ D ‖ θάτερος AO B > ἅτερος QR | > θατέρα μ IJECN η | > θατέρου L ‖ κρείττω ≟ κρήττω Q ‖ φανερώτερα > φανερώτατα N ‖
5 μὲν ○ RQ ≥ μὲν Q² ‖ ἀνάγκη τῆς ἀρχῆς ἦγεν ∩ 4123 L ‖ βουλόμενον > ζηλούμενον G ‖ τὴν > τῶν D ‖ ὑπ' ≟ ὑπὸ QR ‖ μεγάλων ≟ μεγάλλων O ‖
6 ἀγαθοὶ > ἀγαθὸν QR ‖ στρατιωτῶν ≟ στρατιοτῶν R ‖ θαυμαστότατοι > θαυμαστότεροι RQ ≥ θαυμαστότατοι Q² | ≟ θαυμαστότοι D | + μοι J ‖ δὲ ○ O ‖ οὑμος AO B ≟ I μ JEL CN R | ≟ οὑμός η Q²? ‖
7 ἐκθεὶς > ἐλθεὶς RQ ≥ ἐκθεὶς Q² ‖ τε γ I ○ δ ‖ περιχυθέντων κατεσχέθη ∩ QR ‖ ἑστάναι ≟ ἐστάναι G ‖ πεσεῖν ≟ πευσεῖν Q ≥ πεσεῖν Q² ‖ τὸ > τὰ R ‖ λαμπρὸν > σεμνὸν MFᵐᵍ ‖ ζῶντος > μόνον O ‖
8 φάλαγγα ≟ φάλαγκα D ‖ κᾆτα AO B ≟ κᾆτ' QR | ○ I μ JECN η | > καὶ L ‖ αὐτὴν > αὐτὸν A ‖

own ambitions for honor. *4* See then how much more suited Cynegirus [is] to hold [the funeral honor], since he died also holding [the enemy ship]. Now then for those who know the deeds done by our sons, the one son competes with the other regarding valor, but when recounted the braver [deeds] will also be more evident.

5 Constraint of office brought Callimachus to Marathon as general-in-chief though without his wishing to ward off the landing of the barbarians. Cynegirus, on the other hand, [motivated] by valor and courage, as a volunteer, when he was also quite young, almost even before adulthood, took part in the expedition, [motivated] by love of glory and yearning for great deeds. *6* In the battle all were brave men, both the soldiers who fell and those who survived. But my own son and the [son] of this [man] appeared most admirable of all. *7* The [son] of this [man], however, after he exposed himself to the enemies' shots was held fast by the very arrows and missiles which were poured over him and because of this he remained in the appearance of the standing posture and seemed to stand since he was not able to fall. And the brilliance of Callimachus is only this, an appearance of being alive in a dead body. *8* My own Cynegirus, on the other hand, after getting past the front line of battle and then running forward fearlessly, made an attack

---

Editorial conjectures for reconstructing the wording of the original text (II) behind the medieval text form (π):

5 τῶν (before βαρβάρων) ○ *o* ‖ ἐπεὶ καὶ > ἐξῄει καίπερ *jü* ‖

ἐπεξῆλθε τὴν ἠόνα ἔνθα δὴ τὸ πλεῖστον ἦν τῆς στρατιᾶς καὶ μαχιμώτατον,

καὶ γυμνὸς σχεδὸν μαχόμενος ἐπέβη τῇ θαλάσσῃ καὶ πρῶτος ἀνθρώπων

ἐναυμάχησεν ἐκ γῆς. 9 πολλὰς μὲν οὖν ἐφόβησε ναῦς, μιᾶς δὲ Φοινίσσης

κατὰ τῆς τρόπιδος χεῖρα μεγάλην ἐπιβαλὼν εἴχετο, μὴ φεύγειν ἐπιτρέπων

τῷ βασιλέως ναυτικῷ. 10 πολὺν μὲν οὖν χρόνον ἡ ναῦς κατείχετο

ἐρηρεισμένη τῇ Κυναιγείρου δεξιᾷ καθάπερ πείσματι· ταύτης δὲ

ἀποκοπείσης τὴν ἑτέραν ἐπέρριψε καὶ καθ᾽ ἕκαστον τῶν Κυναιγείρου μελῶν

ἐγίνετο μάχη καρτερά· κοπείσης δὲ καὶ ταύτης ὁ λοιπὸς Κυναίγειρος

τρόπαιον ἦν. 11 αὐτὸς μὲν οὖν ὡς ὀλίγῃ κατεμέμφετο τῇ φύσει καὶ χεῖρας

ἀπῄτει παρ᾽ αὐτῆς, ἡ δεξιὰ δὲ ἔτι τῆς πρύμνης εἴχετο καὶ φεύγουσιν ἐπὶ

πλεῖστον τοῖς βαρβάροις, καὶ θᾶττον ἀφῆκε τὴν ψυχὴν Κυναίγειρος ἢ τὴν

ναῦν ἡ δεξιά. ἔνθα καὶ θαυμαστὸν ἐγένετο, Κυναίγειρος μὲν ἄνευ χειρῶν

ναυμαχῶν, ἡ χεὶρ δὲ ἄνευ Κυναιγείρου διώκουσα, καὶ νεκρὸς εἰς ἄμφω τὰ

στοιχεῖα πληρώσας ἑαυτοῦ τοῖς μέλεσιν ἔκειτο, γῇ καὶ θαλάσσῃ

μεμερισμένος.

12 ταῦτα ἐμὸν ποιεῖ τὸ νῖκος, διὰ ταῦτα ἐμοὶ τὸν λόγον προσήκειν

---

8 ἐπεξῆλθε O B ≐ ἐπεξῆλθεν A | > ἐξῆλθε QR | > ἐπῆλθε I δ Q² ‖
πλεῖστον > πλεῖον RQ ≥ πλεῖστον Q² | > πλῆθος N ≥ πλεῖστον Nᵐᵍ ‖
μαχιμώτατον > μαχιμώτερον RQ ≥ μαχιμώτατον Q² ‖ τῇ θαλάσσῃ > τῆς
θαλάσσης μ Q ‖ πρῶτος > πρῶτον RQ ≥ πρῶτος Q² ‖
9 ἐφόβησε ≐ ἐφόβησεν G ≥ ἐφόβησε Gᶜ ‖ τρόπιδος ≥ τροπίδος Pᶜ ‖
εἴχετο > εἶχε τὸ QR ‖ βασιλέως > βάσεως CN ‖
10 πολὺν ⇒ πολὺ D ‖ ἐρηρεισμένη BR ⇒ ἐρησμένη Q ≥ ἐρηρεισμένη Qᶜ
| ⇒ ἠρεισμένη I μ J EL CN HP | ⇒ εἰρεισμένη D | > ὡρισμένη AO ‖ τῇ
+ τοῦ QR ‖ πείσματι ⇒ πίσματι R ‖ ἀποκοπείσεις + τὴν δὲ … ταύτης Q ■
Qᶜ ‖ ἐπέρριψε ≐ ἐπέρριψεν A CN | ⇒ ἐπέριψε Q | > ἀπέρριψε K ‖
καθ᾽ ἕκαστον ⇒ καθέκαστον L ‖ τῶν + τοῦ QR ‖ μάχη ○ J ‖ καρτερά >
κρατερά B I ‖ καὶ (before ταύτης) ○ η ‖ Κυναίγειρος + καὶ G ■ Gᶜ ‖
11 ἀπῄτει ⇒ ἀπῄτη D ‖ αὐτῆς + τῆς φύσεως Iᶜ ‖ ἡ + ἡ D ‖ δὲ +
καὶ QR ‖ πρύμνης ⇒ πρύμης RQ ≥ πρύμης Q² | > ποίμνης D ‖ θᾶττον
⇒ τᾶττον QR ‖ ἀφῆκε ≐ ἀφῆκεν A ‖ καὶ (after ἔνθα) ○ AO ‖ ἐγένετο >
ἐγίνετο Q ‖ χειρῶν > χειρὸς L ‖ χεὶρ δὲ ∩ QR ‖ καὶ ○ R ‖ εἰς ⇒ εἴς
I | > εἰς QR N ‖ ἑαυτοῦ τοῖς ∩ QR ‖ θαλάσσῃ > θαλάσσης R ‖
μεμερισμένος > μεμερισμένοι M ‖
12 νῖκος ⧧ νεῖκος N ‖

against the beach itself where the bulk and most warlike [part] of the army was, and fighting almost naked he attacked at the sea and was the first human being to engage in a naval battle from land. *9* Hence, he terrified many ships, and laying a mighty hand against the keel of one Phoenician [ship], he held it fast, not allowing the king's navy to flee. *10* For a long time then the ship was restrained, held fast by the right hand of Cynegirus just as with a ship's line. And when this was cut off he flung his other [hand] upon [it] and against each of Cynegirus' limbs there was occurring an intense battle. And when also this [hand] was cut [off] what remained of Cynegirus was a [victory] monument. *11* He then was blaming nature for being frail and he wanted to demand his hands back from it, but the right hand was still holding on to the stern even while the barbarians were trying to flee as far away as possible, and Cynegirus let go of his soul more quickly than the right hand [let go of] the ship. There also something marvelous occurred: While Cynegirus engaged in a sea battle without hands, the hand without Cynegirus carried on pursuit; and he lay dead, one who with his own limbs served in both elements, having taken part on land and on sea.

12 These things make the victory mine, on account of these things [it is]

Editorial conjectures for reconstructing the wording of the original text (Π) behind the medieval text form (π):

12 ἐμὸν > ἐμοὶ *o* ‖

μᾶλλον δίκαιον· ὑπ᾽ ἐμοῦ γὰρ δεῖ καὶ λέγοντος καλῶς τιμηθῆναι τὸν τάφον

ὃν ἐκόσμησα τῷ πολλῷ μου νεκρῷ. **13** ἀλλ᾽ οὑτοσί φησιν εἶναι πολεμάρχου

πατήρ, ἐμὲ δὲ τῶν ἀκολουθησάντων ἑνός. οὐκοῦν ὁ μὲν ἱκανῶς τετίμηται καὶ

τοὔνομα τῆς ἀρχῆς ἔχει παραμύθιον, ἐμοὶ δὲ ὀφείλεται τιμῆς παραμυθία.

14 ὁ μὲν οὖν πολέμαρχος κλήρῳ καὶ τύχῃ γίνεται· οὔκουν ἀρετῆς οὐδὲ

ἀξιώματός ἐστι τεκμήριον· ἡμεῖς δὲ νῦν ἐξ ἔργων, οὐκ ἐξ ὀνομάτων

φιλοτιμούμεθα ὅτ᾽ οὐδὲν κοινωνεῖ τοῖς δικαίοις τῆς παρούσης ἁμίλλης ἡ τῆς

πολεμαρχίας ἀξίωσις. ἐπολεμάρχησε μὲν οὖν κἂν ἕτερος λαχών, τὰ δὲ

μέγιστα τῶν ἔργων ἀρετὴ καὶ τόλμα φέρει μόνη. **15** δεδήλωται δὲ καὶ τῷ

νόμῳ τὸ μὴ τοῖς τῶν πολεμάρχων οἰκείοις ἀνακεῖσθαι τοὺς ἐπιταφίους· εἰ

γὰρ εἰκὸς ἦν, πάλαι τοῦτο ἂν ἐδέδοκτο· ἐγὼ δὲ καὶ πάντων αἱρετὸν εἶναί

φημι τὸν ἐροῦντα κἂν οὐ πολέμαρχος οὐδὲ πολεμάρχου υἱὸς ᾖ· βελτίων γε

μὴν καὶ δικαιότερος εἰπεῖν χρῆναι λέγειν ὅστις ἀριστέα ἔχει. **16** ταῦτα

διοριζομένῳ Μιλτιάδην ἀμφισβητεῖν ἔδει τοῦ λόγου· καὶ γὰρ στρατηγός

ἐστιν ὃς τοῦ πολεμάρχου καὶ μείζων ἐστί καὶ τὴν μεγίστην ἀρχὴν τοῦ

πολέμου μετακεχειρισμένος {ὁ τοῦ στρατηγοῦ πατὴρ} {ὅπερ ἐστὶν

---

12 μᾶλλον δίκαιον AO B ∩ δ I | > μάλιστα δίκαιον RQ ≥ δίκαιον μᾶλλον Q² ‖ τιμηθῆναι ⸗ τιθηθῆναι RQ ≥ τιμηθῆναι Q² | ⸗ τιμιθῆναι N ‖ τὸν τάφον ὃν ἐκόσμησα Ο CN ‖ marginal gloss next to A12/13: ἀντίθεσις λύσις Fᵐᵍ EᵐᵍLᵐᵍ ‖

13 ἐμὲ > ἐμοὶ R | > ἐμοῦ Q ≥ ἐμὲ Q² ‖ παραμύθιον and the remainder of the text Ο J ‖ ἐμοὶ δὲ ὀφείλεται τιμῆς παραμυθία Ο η ‖ παραμυθία > παραμύθιον EL CN QR ‖

14 καὶ + καὶ R ‖ οὐδὲ ⸗ οὐδ᾽ L ‖ ἐστι > τοῦτο QR ‖ νῦν ἐξ ἔργων οὐκ ἐξ ὀνομάτων ∩ 234561 L ‖ ὅτ᾽ > ὅστ᾽ R | > ᾧστ᾽ Q ‖ τοῖς δικαίοις Ο QR ‖ δικαίοις ≥ δικαίως Iᶜᵐᵍ ‖ ἁμίλλης ⸗ ἀμίλλης G L ‖ τῆς πολεμαρχίας γ > τοῦ πολεμάρχου δ I ‖ ἐπολεμάρχησε γ > ἐπολεμάρχει δ I Q² ‖ οὖν κἂν > οὐκ ἂν B ‖ κἂν ⸗ κἂν G ‖ λαχών ⸗ λαχὸν Q ‖

15 τοῦτο ⸗ τοῦτ. Di | Ο L ‖ τοῦτο ἂν ⸗ τοῦτ᾽ ἂν R | ⸗ τοῦτ᾽ ἀ. ὃν Q ‖ καὶ (before πάντων) Ο Ο ‖ φημι δ Ο γ I | ≥ φημι Q²ᵐᵍ ‖ ὅστις ⸗ ὥστις R ≥ ὅστις Rᶜ | + ἄριστος D (▪? Dᶜ) ‖

16 Μιλτιάδην > Μιλτιάδη η | > Μιλτιάδης Μ ‖ λόγου > λέγειν RQ ≥ λόγου Q²ᵐᵍ ‖ γὰρ Ο Μ ‖ ἐστιν ⸗ ἐστι R | + λέγων Q ▪ Qᶜ ‖ τοῦ (before πολεμαράρχῳ) > καὶ Β ‖ καὶ (after πολεμάρχου) Ο Μ ‖ ἐστί δ I QR ⸗ ἐστιν AO B ‖

more fitting for the [funeral] speech to belong to me; the grave which I adorned with my great dead [son] must be honored by me speaking well. *13* However, this man here says he is the father of a general-in-chief, but that I am [father] of one of those who followed. He, therefore, has been sufficiently honored and the title of the office he has as a comfort, but to me is due a consolation of honor. *14* [One] becomes the general-in-chief then by lot and by chance; [this office] therefore, is proof neither of valor nor reputation. But we now seek after honor based on deeds, not titles, because for those [who are] upright the rank of the general-in-chief's office plays no role in the present dispute about superiority. Indeed another, if he had drawn the lot, would have served as general-in-chief; but valor and daring alone produce the greatest deeds. *15* Further, it has been made clear also by custom that the funeral orations are not to be offered by the relatives of the generals-in-chief; for if this were fair, it would long ago have been decreed. But I maintain that the one who will speak [should] be chosen from among all, even if he is not general-in-chief nor son of a general-in-chief. Whoever has [shown] [the] bravest [deeds] [is] more qualified and more suited to speak, [indeed] to have to do the speaking. *16* It was necessary for Miltiades to wrangle the matter with [the one] determining these things. And in fact it is a general who is even greater than the general-in-chief and has in hand the greatest authority of the war {the father of the general} {which is further removed}. But now having conceded enough to us he himself too has made clear that it is necessary [for

---

Editorial conjectures for reconstructing the wording of the original text (II) behind the medieval text form (π):

12 καλῶς τιμηθῆναι > καλλωπισθῆναι   *j*   ‖
   14 τεκμήριον + ἡ πολεμαρχία   *h*   ‖   ὅτ᾽ > ὥστ᾽   *s* (→ R)   *h*   ‖   δικαίοις > δικασταῖς   *h*   ‖   κἂν > καὶ   *o*   ‖
   15 ἐγὼ > λέγω   *p*   ‖   καὶ (before πάντων) ○   *o*   ‖   φημι ○   *s p o*   ‖   οὐδὲ πολεμάρχου   *jü*   ‖   εἰπεῖν χρῆναι ○   *j h*   ‖   ἀριστέα > ἀριστεῖα   *j*   ‖
   16 μετακεχειρισμένος + οὐ   *j*   ‖   τοῦ στρατηγοῦ ○   *h*   ‖   πατὴρ + αὐτοῦ   *h*   ‖   ὁ τοῦ στρατηγοῦ πατὴρ ○   *jü r/cs*   ‖   ὅπερ ἐστὶν ἀπωτέρω ○   *h r/cs*   ‖

ἀπωτέρω}· νῦν δὲ ἡμῖν ἐφεὶς ἱκανῶς καὶ αὐτὸς δεδήλωκεν ὡς οὐκ ἀπ᾽ ἀρχῆς ἀλλ᾽ ἀπ᾽ ἀρετῆς χρὴ παριέναι ἐπὶ τὸν λόγον. 17 φέρε οὖν ἐπὶ τούτοις κρινώμεθα, ἐπειδὴ καὶ τοὺς ἄλλους πολεμάρχους ὁρᾷς καὶ τοὺς πατέρας αὐτῶν τὴν ἡσυχίαν ἄγοντας.

18 οὐκοῦν τῷ μὲν σῷ παιδὶ καὶ ἀνάγκη τις ἢ ἀρετὴ ἦγεν· ἐξῆρχε γὰρ κἂν τοῖς πρώτοις ἔταττεν αὐτὸν ἡ πολεμαρχία· ὁ δὲ ἐμὸς υἱὸς οὐκ ἀρχὴν αἰδούμενος οὐδὲ ὑπὸ τῆς ἡγεμονίας δυσωπούμενος οὐδὲ ἀκολουθῶν ὀνόματι, αὐτοκράτορι δὲ ἀρετῇ καὶ καθαρᾷ προθυμίᾳ χρώμενος τοιοῦτος ἐφάνη. 19 ἀλλὰ καὶ Καλλίμαχον μὲν νόμος, Κυναίγειρον δὲ τὸ φρόνημα παρέταττε· καὶ τῷ μὲν τὸ χρῶμα οὐδὲ οἷόν τε ἦν λαθεῖν κακῷ γενομένῳ, τῷ δὲ ζῆν ἀφανῶς καὶ τὰ μέτρια μάχεσθαι. 20 Καλλίμαχος μὲν καὶ πρεσβύτερος ὤν, ὥστε καὶ ῥώμην καὶ πεῖραν ἔχων πλείονα, καὶ μέλλων ἐλάττονος ἀμελήσειν βίου πολλὰ μὲν εἶχε τὰ σύμμαχα· θαυμαστὸν δὲ οὐδὲν εἰ κινδυνεύειν ἐτόλμησε· Κυναίγειρος δέ, ἅτε μειράκιον ἐξιών, ἐκ πλείονος μὲν μεγαλοψυχίας τοῦ πλείονος περιεῖδε βίου οὐδὲ τὸ τῆς νεότητος ἄπειρον καὶ

---

16 ἀποτέρω AO B ‖ ἐφεὶς > ἐφ᾽ οἷς FKG N ‖ ἱκανῶς > ἱκανὸς P ‖ οὐκ Ο Q ≥ οὐκ Q²ᵐᵍ ‖ ἀπ᾽ ἀρετῆς ⇌ ἀπαρετῆς L ‖ παριέναι > περιέναι CN ‖
17 τούτοις γ I ≠ τούτ Ε C H (→ ε → δ → π) | > τούτῳ μ N D P | > τούτου L ‖ κρινώμεθα ≠ κρινόμεθα A ‖ πολεμάρχους ⇌ πολειμάρχους Q ≥ πολειμάρχας Q² | ⇌ πολεμάρχας R ≥ πολεμάρχων Rᶜ ‖ τὴν Ο G ‖
18 μὲν Ο RQ ≥ μὲν Q²ᵐᵍ ‖ τις + ἦν QR ‖ ἢ > ἡ M ‖ γὰρ > κἂν Q ≥ γὰρ Qᶜ ‖ κἂν > καὶ N ‖ τοῖς Ο Q ≥ τοῖς Q² ‖ πρώτοις ⇌ πρότοις R ‖ αὐτὸν > ἑαυτὸν M ‖ δὲ > καὶ RQ ≥ δὲ Q²ᵐᵍ ‖
19 καὶ (after ἀλλὰ) Ο HP ‖ μὲν + ὁ B ‖ νόμος ⇌ νόμενος R ‖ παρέταττε ⇌ παρέταττεν A CN | ⇌ παρέταττεν I | ⇌ παρετταταττε D ≥ παρέταττε Dᶜ ‖ τῷ > τὸ QR ‖ τὸ χρῶμα Ο I ‖ οἷον ⇌ οἵαν QR ‖ τε ⇌ τ᾽ QR ‖ ἦν Ο ε ‖ λαθεῖν Ο QR ‖ τῷ > τὸ O ‖ δὲ (after τῷ) + τῷ μ E CN | + τὸ B η L ‖ καὶ (after ἀφανῶς) AO I Ο β δ ‖ τὰ ⇌ τὸ R ‖ καὶ τὰ μέτρια ≠ .. τὰ ...τρια G ‖ μάχεσθαι γ > δέχεσθαι δ I ‖
20 μὲν > δὲ RQ ≥ μὲν Q²ᵐᵍ ‖ ὥστε καὶ Ο Q ≥ ὥστε καὶ Q²ᵐᵍ ‖ ἀμελήσειν ⇌ ἀμελήσεν R ‖ βίου > βίον D ‖ ἐτόλμησε ⇌ ἐτόλμησεν AO | > ἐτόλμα RQ ≥ ἐτόλμησε Q² ‖ δέ Ο D ‖ μὲν Ο RQ ≥ μὲν Q²ᵐᵍ ‖ περιεῖδε ⇌ περιεῖδεν A ‖ βίου > βίον D ‖

the speaker] to come forward for the [funeral] speech not on the basis of office but on the basis of valor. *17* Come then, let us make our choice [based] upon these [criteria], since you see both the other generals-in-chief and their fathers maintaining silence.

18 For your son then [there was] also a certain obligation — or valor led [him]. For he had official authority and the office of general-in-chief stationed him in the front lines. But since my son was not awed by authority nor was he constrained by the leadership role nor was he guided by a title, he appeared as the sort endowed with independent valor and pure eagerness. *19* While law put Callimachus in the battle, highmindedness [put] Cynegirus [there]. And for the one it was not even possible to escape notice if his [skin] color turned bad, while for the other [it was possible] to live unnoticed and to fight in mediocre fashion. *20* Since Callimachus was also older, so that he had both more strength and [more] experience, and since he was likely to be unconcerned about a shorter life [expectancy], he had many things helping him in the fight; it was no wonder if he dared to take risks. Cynegirus, however, inasmuch as he marched forth as a boy, overlooked the longer life [expectancy] because of more bigheartedness, and the inexperience of youth

---

Editorial conjectures for reconstructing the wording of the original text (Π) behind the medieval text form (π):

16 ἀπ᾽ ἀρχῆς / ἀπ᾽ ἀρετῆς > ἐπ᾽ ἀρχῆς / ἐπ᾽ ἀρετῆς *s* ‖

18 τις ἢ > τις ἦν η *s* (→ R) | > τις ἦν καὶ *p* (→ τις ἐπέκειτο μᾶλλον ἢ *p*) | > τις ... (lacuna) ... ἢ *h* ‖ κἂν (= καὶ ἐν) > κἂν (= καὶ ἂν) *s p o* ‖

19 τὸ χρῶμα > διὰ τὸ ἀξίωμα *j* | > τὸ στράτευμα *h?* ‖ ζῆν > ἐξῆν *j h* ‖ ἀφανῶς > ἀσφαλῶς *j* ‖

ἀπόμαχον ἐνέβαλε πολλήν τινα τῇ τούτου τόλμῃ περιουσίαν. **21** ἔτι δέ, Καλλίμαχος ἐν τοῖς πρώτοις ἢ μέσοις τῆς μάχης ἀπέθανεν οὐκ ἀντισχὼν τοῖς πλείοσιν ἔργοις καὶ πόνοις, Κυναίγειρος δὲ μέχρι τῆς τῶν πολεμίων ἤρκεσε φυγῆς, ὥστε ὁ μὲν ἐν μέρει τῆς μάχης ἐξητάσθη μόνον, ὁ δὲ πάντα τὸν πόλεμον διὰ τέλους ἐπολέμησεν. **22** ὁ μὲν ἐν μέσῳ τῷ δεινῷ τὰ πάντα εἱστήκει, καὶ περιὼν ἔτι· Κυναίγειρος δὲ εἰς αὐτὴν τὴν θάλασσαν τὴν Ἀσίαν κατήρραξεν. ἐδεῖτο δὲ ἡ μάχη τῶν διωκόντων, οὐ τῶν ἑστηκότων· τὸ μὲν γὰρ ἀρετῇ καὶ ῥώμῃ καὶ θυμῷ καὶ τόλμῃ καὶ λογισμῷ τὸ διώκειν τοὺς πολεμίους καὶ τρέπεσθαι, ἡ δὲ στάσις πολλάκις ἐκπλήξει μόνῃ καὶ φόβῳ γίνεται. καὶ τοίνυν πρότερον μὲν ἀπέθανε Καλλίμαχος, Κυναίγειρος δὲ δεύτερος· προὐμάχει γὰρ πάντως καὶ τοῦ Καλλιμάχου νεκροῦ. **23** καὶ Καλλίμαχος μὲν ἐξ ὧν ἔπαθε παράσημος ἦν· τὸ γὰρ πλῆθος τῶν ἐπ᾽ αὐτὸν ἐνεχθέντων βελῶν ἀνέστησεν αὐτόν· Κυναίγειρος δὲ ἐξ ὧν ἔδρασε θαυμάζεται, πέμπων τὰς χεῖρας ἐπὶ τοὺς βαρβάρους ὥσπερ ἀποστόλους καὶ τῇ δεξιᾷ πρὸς τὴν

---

20 ἐνέβαλε QR I FKG EL C η | ≠ ἐνέβαλλε B M | > ἀνέβαλε N | > ἀνέλαβε O ≥ ἐνέλαβε Ocmg | > ἀνέλαβεν A ‖ τούτου > τοῦ βίου B ‖
21 δὲ + καὶ FKG ‖ Καλλίμαχος ⚊ Καλίμαχος Q ‖ πρώτοις O D | + ἐν τοῖς πρώτοις G ‖ μέσοις ⚊ μέσσοις N | > μέσα Q ≥ μέσοις Q² ‖ ἀντισχὼν ⚊ ἀντισχὺν RQ ≥ ἀντισχῶν Q² ‖ ἀντισχὼν τοῖς πλείοσιν ἔργοις καὶ πόνοις Κυναίγειρος δὲ μέχρι τῆς τῶν πολεμίων ἤρκεσε φυγῆς, ὥστε ὁ μὲν O M ‖ μέχρι ⚌ μέχρις R ‖ τῆς > τοῖς QR ‖ ἤρκεσε ⚊ ἤρκησε QR | ⚊ ἤρεσε D ‖ τῆς μάχης ⚊ τοῖς μάχοις QR ‖ ἐξητάσθη ⚊ ἐξετάσθη QR ‖ μόνον ὁ δὲ πάντα τὸν πόλεμον διὰ τέλους ἐπολέμησεν O D ‖ ἐπολέμησεν ⚌ ἐπολέμησε P ‖
22 τῷ δεινῷ > τῶν δεινῶν P ‖ τὰ O QR K ‖ πάντα ⚌ πάνθ᾽ HP | > πάντας QR ‖ καὶ (before περιὼν) O CN ‖ περιὼν > περῖὼν M ‖ ἔτι + ἔστη QR ‖ κατήρραξεν ⚌ κατήραξεν μ D ‖ τὸ > τῷ QR ‖ ῥώμῃ > γνώμῃ P ‖ ῥώμῃ καὶ θυμῷ καὶ τόλμῃ ∩ 54321 QR ‖ πολεμίους ⚊ πομι D ≥ πολεμίους Dc ‖ πρότερον O B I μ EL CN D > πρότερος A QR HP ‖ ἀπέθανε ⚌ ἀπέθανεν A QR ‖ δεύτερος > ὕστερος RQ ≥ δεύτερος Q²mg ‖ γὰρ > δὲ M ‖ πάντως > πάντων N ‖
23 καὶ γ O δ I ‖ ἔπαθε ⚌ ἔπαθεν A FG | > ἀπέθανε N ≥ ἔπαθε Nc ‖ παράσημος ⚊ παράσιμος P | ⚊ πέσημος D ‖ τῶν > τὸν D ‖ αὐτὸν > αὐτῶν G | ⚊ αὐτὴ QR ‖ βελῶν > βαλῶν N ‖ ἔδρασε ⚌ ἔδρασεν A | > ἔδρα M | > ἄνδρα RQ ≥ ἔδρα RcmgQcmg ≥ ἔδρασε Q²mg ‖

and ineligibility for military service did not contribute very much advantage in this courage of his. *21* Moreover, Callimachus died at the outset or in the middle of the battle without enduring most of the toils and pains, but Cynegirus held out until the flight of the enemy. Therefore, the one was tested only in part of the fight, whereas the other fought all the battle through to the end. *22* The one had stood completely still in the midst of the danger, even though he was yet alive; Cynegirus, however, dashed Asia shattered into the sea itself. The fight was in need of those who pursued, not those who stood still. Pursuing and routing the enemies comes about through valor and strength and courage and daring and reasoning, but the stationary posture often [comes about] from terror alone and fear. Moreover, Callimachus died first, but Cynegirus second; for he certainly fought out in front of the corpse of Callimachus. *23* And Callimachus was unduly praised because of [the things] which he suffered; for [it was] the mass of arrows which were brought against him [that] caused him to stand erect. Cynegirus, however, is admired because of [the things] which he did, sending his hands against the barbarians just like naval expeditions and contending against the Phoenician oarsmen with his right

---

Editorial conjectures for reconstructing the wording of the original text (II) behind the medieval text form (π):

22 τὰ πάντα > πάντως *s p o* | > ἄπρακτος or ἄπρακτα *j* ‖ ἔτι + ἔστη *s p o* ‖

Φοινίκων εἰρεσίαν ἀμυνόμενος· ὅσῳ δὴ τὸ δρᾶν τοῦ πάσχειν **κυριώτερόν** ἐστι καὶ τοῖς οἰκείοις ὠφελιμώτερον, τοσούτῳ καὶ Καλλιμάχου Κυναίγειρος θαυμασιώτερος καὶ τοσοῦτον αὐτοῦ προτιμότερος. **24** ἡ δὲ ἀγαθὴ προαίρεσις εἰς τὰ καλὰ καὶ ἰδιαιτέρα ἐστι καὶ ἐνδικωτέρα. Κυναίγειρος μὲν αὐτὸς βουλόμενος ἐχρήσατο τῷ περὶ τὰς χεῖρας τολμήματι, Καλλιμάχῳ δὲ ἄκοντι συνέπεσεν ἡ στάσις ἐκ τῆς τῶν βελῶν συμφορᾶς· οὐ γὰρ ἐκ προθυμίας ἑαυτὸν ἐφῆκε καὶ συνεκάλεσε τὰ τραύματα ὥσπερ Κυναίγειρος ἐπανέτεινε τῇ νηὶ τὰς χεῖρας. **25** ἔτι δέ, τοῦ μὲν τὸ θαυμαστὸν ἀναίσθητόν ἐστιν· ἐν γὰρ τῷ μετὰ θάνατον **βεβηκέναι** δόξαν ἡ χάρις οὐκ ἔχει· ἀρετὴ γὰρ οὐκ ἔστιν ἄψυχος· Κυναίγειρος δὲ εἰδὼς καὶ συνιεὶς καὶ δριμείας μὲν ἀλγηδόνας τῆς χειρὸς τεμνομένης ὑπὲρ τοῦ παντὸς στρατοπέδου καρτερῶν, τόλμῃ δὲ τοῦ δεινοῦ τὸ καλὸν πρότερον ποιούμενος ὥστε παρ᾽ ἀμφοτέρων αὐτῷ δικαίως ὀφείλεται θαῦμα μὲν ὧν πέπονθεν, ἔπαινος δὲ ὧν πεποίηκεν. **26** εἰ δὲ δεῖ μηδὲν ὀκνήσαντα τἀληθὲς εἰπεῖν, ἡ μὲν Καλλιμάχου παράδοξος δοκοῦσα στάσις οὐδέν ἐστι· νεκρῷ γὰρ ὅλως τι καὶ πράττειν ἀδύνατον· ἡ

---

23 ἀμυνόμενος ≠ ἀμυνόμενος N | ⲧ ἀκυνόμενος QR ≥ ἀμυνόμενος QᶜRᶜ | ≥ ἀμιλλώμενος FᶜᵐᵍGᶜᵐᵍ | > ἀμιλλῶμενος M ‖ **κυριώτερόν** δ > γενναιότερόν γ I ‖ **τοσούτῳ** > τοσοῦτον RQ ≥ τοσούτῳ Q² ‖ **καὶ** Ο Q ≥ καὶ Q²ᵐᵍ ‖ **Καλλιμάχου** > Καλλιμάχῳ FK ‖ **Κυναίγειρος θαυμασιώτερος** γ ∩ θαυμασιώτερος ὁ Κυναίγειρος δ I ‖ **προτιμότερος** ⲧ προτιμώτερος CN DP ‖
24 δὲ γ I ≟ δ᾽ δ ‖ **προαίρεσις** ⲧ προειραισος Q ≥ προαίρεσις Q² ‖ ἰδιαιτέρα > ἰδιαίτερα Β | > ἰδιώτερον ΑΟ ‖ ⲉ͞ν͞δ͞ι͞κ͞ω͞τ͞έ͞ρ͞α ⲧ εἰδικώτερα Β | > ἐνδικώτερον ΑΟ ‖ **αὐτὸς βουλόμενος** ∩ ΑΟ ‖ **περὶ** > παρὰ I ‖ **προθυμίας** > προμυθίας I ‖ **ἐφῆκε** ≟ ἐφῆκεν Α | > ἐφῆκες D > ἀφῆκε M L RQ ≥ ἐφῆκε Q² ‖ **συνεκάλεσε** ≟ συνεκάλεσεν Α | ≠ συνεκάλεσ ͏ D ≥ συνεκάλεσε Dᶜ ‖ **ἐπανέτεινε** > ἐπενέτεινε C | > ἐπέτεινε M N ‖
25 ἐστιν ≟ ἐστι G R | γὰρ ᐩ φῇ Q | ᐩ φῶ R ‖ **βεβηκέναι** ΑΟ BQ I > συμβεβηκέναι δ Q²ᵐᵍ | > βεβληκέναι R ‖ **συνιεὶς** γ I ≟ ξυνιεὶς δ Q² ‖ **δριμείας** > μυρίας QR ≥ δριμείας Q²ᵐᵍRᶜᵐᵍ ‖ **χειρὸς** > δεξιᾶς RQ ≥ χειρὸς Q²ᵐᵍ ‖ **τεμνομένης** ⲧ τετνομένης K ‖ **τοῦ παντὸς** ∩ QR ‖ **τὸ καλὸν** Ο RQ ≥ τὸ καλὸν Q²ᵐᵍ ‖ **καλὸν** ⲧ καλλὸν DP ‖ **ἔπαινος** > ἔπαινον ΑΟ ‖
26 τἀληθὲς > τἀληθῆ CN ‖ **δοκοῦσα** > δοκοῦντα D ‖ ἐστι ≟ ἐστιν M ‖ **νεκρῷ** > νεκροῦ QR ‖ **πράττειν** ≠ πρά ͏ ειν Ki ‖ **ἀδύνατον** ⲧ ἀδύναται RQ ≥ ἀδύνατον Q² ‖

hand. The degree to which acting is more decisive than being acted upon and more beneficial to the countrymen — to that same degree Cynegirus is more admirable than Callimachus and more to be honored than he. **24** The good course of action for noble [goals] is both more exceptional and more legitimate. Whereas Cynegirus of his own volition employed daring regarding his hands, the standing posture happened to Callimachus without his intent because of the circumstance with the arrows. For [it was] not out of eagerness [that] he threw himself [into the fray] and invited the wounds as Cynegirus [did when he] stretched out his hands against the ship. **25** Besides, the amazing thing of the one is something unperceived [by him]; for [outward] dignity does not have repute when it has occurred after death. For there is no valor without soul. But Cynegirus — since by contrast he knew and was aware of and endured sharp pains when his hand was cut off on behalf of the whole army, and since by virtue of [his] daring he valued what is noble above what is dreadful — [Cynegirus,] therefore, from both sides justly deserves admiration for what he has suffered and praise for what he has done. **26** And if one must speak the truth without holding back anything, the unusual seeming standing posture of Callimachus is nothing because it is impossible for a corpse to do anything at all. But the valor of Cynegirus [was] something most

---

Editorial conjectures for reconstructing the wording of the original text (Π) behind the medieval text form (π):

23 τοσοῦτον > τοσούτῳ *s p o* ‖
26 τι > δὴ *o* ‖

Κυναιγείρου δὲ ἀρετὴ κράτιστον, ζῶντι τετολμημένη. τὸ μὲν Καλλιμάχου

σεμνὸν σχῆμα μόνον ἀργὸν ἦν· τὰ Κυναιγείρου δ' ἔργα θαυμαστὰ μετὰ

καλλίστων σχημάτων. **27** μὴ **παράβαλλε** στρατιώτῃ νεκρὸν μὴ δὲ τῷ

βάλλοντι τὸν πάντα βεβλημένον μὴ δὲ σχῆμα κενὸν ἔργῳ θρασεῖ. ὁ μὲν

Καλλίμαχον ἐπαινῶν ἐπαινεῖ τὰ βέλη τῶν βαρβάρων· ταῦτα γὰρ

ἐμπαγέντα τῇ γῇ καὶ περιπεσόντα τῷ σχήματι καὶ μὴ βουλόμενον ἀνεῖχε καὶ

ὥρθου τὸν νεκρὸν ἐν αὐτῷ τῷ σχήματι τῶν τοξευμάτων δεδεμένον. τί, τῶν

βελῶν ἐν ἀλλήλοις συνεχομένων θαυμαστή γε ἡ στάσις ἐπὶ τοσούτοις

ἐρείσμασι; **28** Κυναίγειρος δὲ ἐπὶ ποίοις σχήμασιν ἢ φίλων ἢ πολεμίων τὰς

χεῖρας ἐπεδίδου τὰς ἑαυτοῦ μεμαχημένος; θαυμαστὸν δέ γε ἢ τίμιον

στρατιώτην Καλλίμαχον λέγεις ὃς τὴν ἀρετὴν νεκρὸς ὢν ἐπεδείξατο; ἡμεῖς

μὲν ἐν γῇ καὶ θαλάττῃ μεμαχήμεθα, ὑμεῖς δὲ ἐν γῇ **μόνῃ**· καὶ ὑμεῖς μὲν

ἀπεμάχεσθε μόνον τοῖς βαρβάροις, ἡμεῖς δὲ φυγεῖν αὐτοὺς ποιοῦντες οὐκ

ἀφιστάμεθα αὐτῶν. **29** εἰ μὲν δὴ Καλλιμάχῳ παραπλήσιοι πάντες

---

26 ζῶντι > ζῶντος EL CN HP | ⥵ ζῶτος D ‖ τὸ > τῷ QR ‖
Καλλιμάχου > Καλλιμάχῳ QR ‖ **σεμνὸν** Ο Q ≥ σεμνὸν Q² ‖ **θαυμαστὰ** +
μὲν QR ‖ καλλίστων ⥵ καλίστων P
27 παράβαλλε β FKG EL ⥵ **παράβαλε** ΑΟ Ι CN η | > παρέβαλλε Μ
‖ **στρατιώτῃ** > στρατιώτην P ‖ **μὴ δὲ τῷ βάλλοντι τὸν πάντα βεβλημένον μὴ δὲ
σχῆμα κενὸν** Ο D ‖ **δὲ** Ο Β ‖ **μὴ δὲ** ⊒ μηδὲ Ι ‖ **κενὸν** > νεκρὸν L HP ‖
βέλη > γένη RQ ≥ βέλη Q²ᵐᵍ ‖ **γὰρ** Ο Q > γὰρ Q²ᵐᵍ ‖ **τῇ γῇ** Ο R ‖
σχήματι > σώματι RQ ≥ σχήματι Q² ‖ **βουλόμενον** ⥵ ζουλούμενον Ι ≥
ζηλούμενον Ιᶜ ‖ **ἀνεῖχε** ⊒ ἀνεῖχεν Α | > ἀνεῖχον QR ‖ **ὥρθου** ⥵ ὄρθου CN
D | > ὥρθουν BQ | ⥵ ὄρθουν R ‖ **νεκρὸν** ⥵ νεκρῶν Q ‖ **αὐτῷ** > τῷ D
≥ αὐτῷ Dᶜ ‖ **τί** ΑΟ QR > ἔτι Β Ι δ | ✛ δὲ RQ ≥ ἔτι Q²ᵐᵍ ‖ **ἐν** (before
ἀλλήλοις) Ο QR L ‖ **ἀλλήλοις** ⥵ ἀλλήλ Q ≥ ἀλλήλοις Q²ᵐᵍ | ⥵
ἀλλήλουν R ‖ **συνεχομένων** > ἐχομένων R ‖ **θαυμαστή γε ἡ στάσις ἐπὶ τοσούτοις
ἐρείσμασι; Κυναίγειρος δὲ ἐπὶ ποίοις σχήμασιν ἢ φίλων ἢ πολεμίων** Ο G ≥ added by
Gᵐᵍ ‖ **τοσούτοις** > τούτοις RQ ≥ τοσούτοις Q²ᵐᵍ
28 Κυναίγειρος > Κυναίγειρον Μ ‖ **ἐπεδίδου** ⥵ ἐπέδου Q ≥ ἐπεδίδου Q²
‖ **τὰς ἑαυτοῦ** Ο CN ‖ **μεμαχημένος** > μεμαχημένας QR ‖ **μεμαχημένος** +
θαυμαστὸν δέ γε ἢ τίμιον L ▬ Lᶜ ‖ **δέ** Ο G ‖ **γε** Ο QR ‖ **στρατιώτην** >
στρατιώτας Q ≥ στρατιώτην Q² ‖ **στρατιώτην** + τὸν G ‖ **λέγεις** γ Ι >
λέγειν δ ‖ **ὃς** > ὡς QR ‖ **ἐπεδείξατο** > ἀνεδείξατο CN ‖ **θαλάττῃ** γ Ι Κ
⊒ θαλάσσῃ MFG ε ‖ **μόνῃ** γ Ι > μόνον δ ‖ **μὲν** Ο QR ‖ **ἀπεμάχεσθε** >
ἀπεμάχεσθαι Ν ≥ ἀπεμάχεσθε Νᶜ ‖ **ἡμεῖς** > ὑμεῖς D ‖
29 Καλλιμάχῳ > Καλλιμάχου QR ‖

excellent [since it was] dared by a living person. The stateliness of Callimachus was merely an inactive appearance; the deeds of Cynegirus, however, [were] admirable with very noble characteristics. **27** Do not keep comparing a corpse with a soldier, nor the one having been struck everywhere with the one striking, nor an empty appearance with a bold deed. The one praising Callimachus praises the arrows of the barbarians; for these [arrows which were] stuck in the ground and surrounding the figure — though without its volition — continued holding up the corpse and keeping [it] erect since it had been bound by the very form of the arrows. Inasmuch as the arrows held together between one another, why [is] the standing position [based] upon such props anything wonderous? **28** But as for Cynegirus, [based] upon what sorts of appearances either of friends or foes was he giving freely his very own hands as he fought? Are you saying that Callimachus [was] an admirable or honorable soldier who exhibited valor when he was dead? We, for our part, have fought on land and on sea, while you [have fought] on land alone. And whereas you only fought off the barbarians, we after making them flee did not let up from them. **29** If all had become like

---

Editorial conjectures for reconstructing the wording of the original text (Π) behind the medieval text form (π):

27 σχήματι + διὰ *j* ‖
28 ἐπεδίδου > ἀπεδίδου *o* ‖ ἢ (after δὲ γε) > καὶ *h* ‖ ἐπεδείξατο + δὲ εἰ *j* ‖

ἐγένοντο, πᾶν ἂν ἡμῶν κατέχωσαν τὸ στρατόπεδον καὶ εἰς Ἀθήνας

ἀναδραμόντες καὶ τὴν ἀκρόπολιν αὐτὴν ἂν εἶχον οἱ βάρβαροι· εἰ δὲ

Κυναίγειρόν τις καὶ ἄλλος ἐμιμήσατο, δίκας ἂν ἔδοσαν ἔτι μείζονας οἱ μετὰ

βασιλέως αὐτοῦ πάντες ἐπὶ τῆς ἠόνος κατακοπέντες καὶ τέλος ἂν **τοὺς**

βαρβάρους ἔσχε χερσαῖα ναυάγια καὶ πάσας ἂν αἰχμαλώτους

ἀναδησάμενοι κεφαλὰς τὰς ναῦς εἴχομεν.   **30** πρὸς δὲ τούτοις, τίνας ἂν

ἐφόβησε πολεμίους ὁ κρυπτόμενος ὑπὸ τῶν πολλῶν βελῶν ἢ τίνας ὤνησε

φίλους;   αὐτῷ γάρ τοι τοῦτο τῷ Καλλιμάχου προβόλῳ καθάπερ τινὶ τῶν

Ἀσσυρίων χωμάτων μέγα φρονοῦντες ἔλεγον·

Οὐ μόνους Ναξίους, οὐ μόνους Ἐρετριεῖς ἀλλὰ καὶ Καλλίμαχον

τοῖς βέλεσιν ἐσαγηνεύσαμεν.

τῶν ἡμετέρων στρατιωτῶν ἕκαστος ὀκνηρότερος ἦν περιπίπτων ἀεὶ φανερῷ

νεκρῷ μὴ βουλομένῳ λαθεῖν ἀλλ᾿ ὥσπερ ἐξεπίτηδες ὑπὸ Μήδων ἐς τὴν

ἡμετέραν ἔκπληξιν ἀνεστηκότι.   **31** σὺ δέ, ὦ τέκνον, ἐθάρσυνας μὲν τοὺς

στρατιώτας τοὺς **σεαυτοῦ** δεικνὺς ὡς Ἀθηναίων ἕκαστος ὅλης νεὼς

βαρβάρου μαχιμώτερος καὶ τὰς χεῖρας οὕτως εὐκόλως ἠφίεις ὡς ἕτεροι

---

29 ἄν Ο L ‖ ἡμῶν > ἡμῖν QR ‖ ἀναδραμόντες > δραμόντες Β ‖
ἄλλος > ἄλλον Β ‖ ἔδοσαν ≐ ἔδωκαν RQ ≥ ἔδωσαν Q² ‖ μείζονας ⚌
μίζονας QR ≥ μείζονας Rᶜ ‖ βασιλέως ⚌ βασίος QR ≥ βασιλείας Rᶜ ‖
τοὺς βαρβάρους δ QR > τοῖς βαρβάροις ΑΟ Β Ι ‖ ἔσχε ≐ ἔσχεν Α ‖
εἴχομεν > ἔχομεν QR ‖
30 πολλῶν Ο QR ‖ αὐτῷ > οὕτω Ι | > αὐτὸ ΑΟ ‖ τοι τοῦτο τῷ
Καλλιμάχου ΑΟ > τούτῳ τῷ Καλλιμάχου Ι ≥ τοι τούτῳ τῷ Καλλιμάχου Ιᶜᵐᵍ |
> τοιούτῳ τῷ Καλλιμάχου Β | > τοι τῷ Καλλιμάχῳ RQ ≥ τοι τούτῳ Καλλιμάχῳ
Q²ᵐᵍ | > τούτῳ τῷ Καλλιμάχῳ δ ‖ καθάπερ ✚ εἰ R | > καθαρεῖ Q ≥
καθάπερ Q² ‖ χωμάτων > χρωμάτων Μ ‖ χωμάτων ✚ καὶ ΑΟ ‖ Ναξίους
> ἀξίους Β ≥ Ναξίους Βᶜ ‖ μόνους > μόνον D ‖ καὶ Ο QR ‖
ἐσαγηνεύσαμεν ⚌ ἐσαγίνευσαμεν D ‖ περιπίπτων ⚌ περίπτων D ‖ φανερῷ >
φανερῶν D ‖ βουλομένῳ ⚌ βουλωμένῳ QR ‖ λαθεῖν > μαθεῖν Ν ≥ λαθεῖν
Νᶜ ‖ ἐξεπίτηδες ✚ ἀλλ᾿ ὥσπερ ἐξεπίτηδες Ο ‖ ἐς Ι MFG E C H ≐ εἰς γ K L
N DP ‖ ἀνεστηκότι > ἐστηκότος Μ ‖
31 ἐθάρσυνας > ἐθράσυνας CN | Ο Ι ‖ μὲν τοὺς ∩ Ι ‖ τοὺς Ο Β
‖ σεαυτοῦ ΑΟ Β FKG L > ἑαυτοῦ Ι Μ E CN QR | > ἑαυτῆς η ‖ ὅλης >
ὅλος ηQ² ‖ βαρβάρου > βαρβάρων μ QR ‖ ἠφίεις > ἀφιεὶς QR HP ‖

Callimachus, the barbarians would have held down our entire army and after racing up to Athens would have taken even the acropolis itself. But if anyone else had imitated Cynegirus, all [the barbarians] along with [the] king himself would have suffered still greater punishments by being cut to pieces on the shore. And finally shipwreck on dry land would have held the barbarians, and by taking the ships in tow we would have taken every person captive. *30* Besides this, what enemies would the one hidden by the many arrows have frightened or what friends would he have benefited? For to the very obstacle of Callimachus — just as to any of the earthen defense embankments of the Assyrians — they, being conceited, would surely say this:

"With our arrows we have swept up in our dragnet

not just Naxians, not just Eretrians, but even Callimachus."

Of our own soldiers each especially timid one would always have been falling in with a conspicuous corpse which did not wish to go unnoticed, but which had been set up purposely, as it were, by the Medes for our own terror. *31* But you, O child, on the one side encouraged your own soldiers by showing that each of the Athenians [was] more warlike than a whole barbarian ship and so you readily were letting loose your hands as others [their] arrows; and on

---

Editorial conjectures for reconstructing the wording of the original text (Π) behind the medieval text form (π):

31 ἠφιεὶς > ἀφιὲν *s o* | > ἀφίησι *p* | > ἀφίει *j* ‖

βέλη, Μήδους δὲ καὶ Πέρσας καὶ Φοίνικας κατέπληττες ἀντιρρόπους δεικνὺς

ταῖς ναυσὶν αὐτῶν τὰς Ἀττικὰς δεξιὰς καὶ δηλῶν ὅτι μόνοις ἀνθρώπων

Ἀθηναίοις χεῖρές εἰσιν ἀθάνατοι. Καλλίμαχον μέν, εἰ μηδὲν ἕτερον,

ἐκάλυψαν οἱ βάρβαροι· σοῦ δὲ φοβοῦνται Φοίνικες τὴν χεῖρα καὶ κειμένην.

32 ὦ Καλλιμάχου πάτερ, ὁ σὸς υἱὸς εἷς ἦν καὶ μίαν ὅλῳ τῷ σώματι μάχην

μεμάχηται· ὁ δὲ ἐμὸς καὶ κατὰ μέρη νενίκηκεν· οὗτος πρῶτος καὶ μόνος

χειρὸς ἀριστείαν ἔδειξεν. ἑνὸς εἶ στρατιώτου πατήρ· ἐγὼ δὲ τὸν πολὺν

Κυναίγειρον ἐκ Μαραθῶνος ἥμισυν ἐδεξάμην· ἑτέρωθι μὲν γὰρ ἡ δεξιά,

ἑτέρωθι δὲ ἡ ἑτέρα χείρ· ὁ δὲ λοιπὸς Κυναίγειρος πλήρης ἦν. **33** ὦ τοῦ

μεγάλου θαύματος. ἐπαινεῖς μὲν σὺ τὸν ἑστῶτα, τὸν ἀκλινῆ, τὸν νεκρόν, τὸν

μηδὲν στήλης διαφέροντα· ἐγὼ δὲ τὸν πεζομάχον, τὸν ναυμάχον, τὸν

πανταχοῦ, τὸν κατὰ **μικρὸν** μέγαν, τὸν ἀντὶ πολλῶν ἕνα.

34 ὦ χεῖρες Μαραθώνιαι, χεῖρες φίλταται κἂν ταῖσδε ταῖς ἐμαῖς χερσὶ

τεθραμμέναι· ὦ σωτῆρες τῆς πάσης Ἑλλάδος· ὦ πρόμαχοι τῶν Ἀθηναίων·

ὦ τῶν στρατιωτῶν ὅλων κρείττονες· ὦ Μαραθῶνος δόξα. **35** ὦ ἡδεῖα δεξιὰ

ἦν ἀνέτειλε τοῖς Ἕλλησιν ἡ γῆ· ὦ δεξιὰ βιαιοτέρα πνευμάτων· σὺ γὰρ

---

31 βέλη > βέλος ε ‖ ἀντιρρόπους ⇌ ἀντιρρότους N ‖ δεξιὰς >
δυνάμεις ηQ² ‖ Ἀθηναίοις ⇌ Ἀθηναίος R ‖
32 ὦ Καλλιμάχου πάτερ ὁ σὸς υἱὸς εἷς ἦν Ο δ I ‖ ἐμὸς + υἱὸς I ‖ μέρη
> μέρος μ ‖ νενίκηκεν ⇌ νενήκηκεν QR ‖ πρῶτος καὶ μόνος χειρὸς ∩ 3214 I
| ∩ 1423 C ≥ 1324 Cᶜ ‖ ἥμισυν > ἥμίσυῃ ταυ Lᶜ ‖ μὲν Ο Ο ‖ δὲ Ο
D ‖ χείρ ὁ > χειρὸς R ‖ πλήρης γ > τρόπαιον δ I ‖ ἦν Ο M ‖
33 ἐπαινεῖς ⇌ ἐπαινῖς E | > ἐπαίνει RQ ≥ ἐπαινεῖς Q² ‖ μὲν > με
G ‖ ἑστῶτα ⇌ ἐτῶλα R ≥ ἑστῶτα R² ‖ στήλης > στήλη M ‖ τὸν
ναυμάχον Ο Q² ≥ τὸν ναυμάχον Q²ᵐᵍ ‖ τὸν πανταχοῦ Ο L ‖ μικρὸν γ I M
> μικρὰ ε FKG ‖ μέγαν > μέσον M ‖
34 Μαραθώνιαι γ > Μαραθώνιοι δ (Mi) I ‖ χεῖρες ≠ χειρ D ≥
χεῖρες Dᶜ ‖ φίλταται > φίλτατοι I ‖ κἂν (= καὶ ἐν) > κἂν (≐ καὶ ἂν)
I G N ‖ ταῖσδε + ταῖσδε Q ▬ Qᶜ ‖ σωτῆρες AO B > σώτειραι δ I QR ‖
τῆς Ο RQ ≥ τῆς Q² ‖ κρείττονες Ο RQ ≥ κρείττονες Q²ᵐᵍ ‖ ὦ Μαραθῶνος
Ο RQ ≥ ὦ Μαραθῶνος Q²ᵐᵍ ‖
35 ἀνέτειλε + κα . G ‖ βιαιοτέρα > βεβαιοτέρα M ‖ πνευμάτων >
πτερομάτων CN ‖ γὰρ Ο B ‖

the other side you were terrifying Medes and Persians and Phoenicians who were trying to compensate, by showing to their ships the right hands of Attica and by making clear that among human beings for Athenians alone hands are undying. Whereas the barbarians, if nothing else, covered Callimachus, the Phoenicians feared your hand even [when it was] lying [severed]. **32** O father of Callimachus, your son was one and he has fought one fight with his whole body; but my [son] has won the victory part by part. He first and alone showed a hand's prowess. You are father of one soldier; but I have received [back] from Marathon half the mighty Cynegirus. For on the one side the right hand and on the other side the other hand [was gone]; but the rest of Cynegirus was intact. **33** — O [hands] of great wonder! — You praise the one who stood, the unbending one, the dead one, the one who differs in no way from a tombstone; but I [praise] the one who fought as soldier, the one who fought as sailor, the one [who fought] everywhere, the one [who became] great little by little, the one [who fought] against many.

34 O Marathonian hands, precious hands and reared by these hands of mine. O saviors of all Greece. O champions of the Athenians. O [hands] stronger than whole soldiers. O glory of Marathon. **35** O sweet right hand which the earth brought forth for the Greeks. O right hand more forceful than winds; for you held fast a ship trying to put to sea. O hand stronger than

---

Editorial conjectures for reconstructing the wording of the original text (Π) behind the medieval text form (π):
31 μὲν (after Καλλίμαχον) > καὶ *s p* ‖
32 γὰρ ○ *o* ‖ πλήρης ἦν $\overset{?}{+}$ τραυμάτων *o* ‖

κατέσχες ναῦν ἀναγομένην· ὦ κρείττων ῥοθίου βαρβαρικοῦ χείρ· σὺ γὰρ ἐρεττομένην ὥρμισας· ὦ στολαγωγοῦ καὶ **μακροτέρας** βελῶν δεξιᾶς δι' ἥν οὐ μάτην ὁ Πὰν ἐξ Ἀρκαδίας ἔδραμεν, οὐκ εἰκῇ Δημήτηρ καὶ Κόρη τῇ μάχῃ παρεγένοντο· ὦ θέαμα τῶν θεῶν ἄξιον. ὦ τρόφιμε τῆς παρούσης Ἀθηνᾶς· ὦ σύντιμε τοῖς Ἡρακλέους ἄθλοις καὶ Θησέως· οἱ μὲν γὰρ ταύρους εἷλκον καὶ λέοντας, σὺ δὲ τὸν τῆς Ἀσίας εἷλκες στόλον. **36** τοῦτο ἦν τὸ δόρυ τῆς Ἀθηνᾶς ἡ Κυναιγείρου δεξιά, τοῦτο δᾷδες τῶν θεῶν χεῖρες ἐλευθέριον σέλας φέρουσαι. νῦν πρῶτον εἶδον ἄνθρωποι ναυμαχίαν ἐν γῇ, νῦν πρῶτον ἀνδρὸς μάχην καὶ νεώς, νῦν πρῶτον ἀντίπρωρον δεξιάν, νῦν ἅμα χεῖρα μὲν ἀφιεμένην, ναῦν δὲ κρατουμένην· οὐ γὰρ ἀπεκόπτετο τοῦ σώματος ἡ χεὶρ ἀλλ' ἀπῳκίζετο. καὶ τῆς πρώτης ἐμνημόνευεν ἐπιτιμίας ὁ πολέμαρχος τῆς ἀλγηδόνος μὴ αἰσθανόμενος. **37** ὦ δεξιὰ ψυχῆς ἰδίας ἀξία, οὕτω τὴν ναῦν ὡς Καλλίμαχος τὰ βέλη κατέσχε τιμωρήσας οἰκείῳ νεκρῷ. ὦ καινὸν ἐπινόημα σώματος. ὦ παῖ, ὦ μέγα θαῦμα, πρῶτος ναῦν ἔδειξας ὑπὸ χειρῶν ὥσπερ ἀγκυρῶν ἀσάλευτον μένουσαν. **38** οἷά σέ φασι βοᾶν, ὦ παῖ, τῆς νεὼς ἐχόμενον·

---

35 **κρείττων** > κρεῖττον I M CN ‖ **ῥοθίου βαρβαρικοῦ χεὶρ** ∩ χεὶρ ῥοθείων βαρβαρικῶν RQ ≥ χεὶρ ῥοθείου βαρβαρικοῦ Q² ‖ **γὰρ** > δὲ QR ‖ **ἐρεττομένην** > ἐρεττομένας QR ‖ **μακροτέρας** γ I M > μακροτέρων ε FKG ‖ **Κόρη** > Κύρη D ‖ **Ἡρακλέους** AO I QR FKG L ≐ Ἡρακλέος B E CN | ⊤ Ἡρακλέου HP | > Ἡρακλέοις D | ≠ Ἡρακλέ Md ‖ **Θησέως** ⊤ Θήσεο. D ≥ Θήσεος Dᶜ ‖ **εἷλκον** > CN ‖
36 **ἦν** + τοῦτο ἦν L ‖ **ἐλευθέριον** > ἐλεύθερον QR ‖ **σέλας** > σῶμα CN ‖ **εἶδον** > εἶδεν RQ ≥ εἶδον Q² ‖ **νῦν πρῶτον ἀνδρὸς μάχην καὶ νεώς** Ο η ‖ **πρῶτον** > πρώτως ηQ² ‖ **ναῦν** > ναῶν A ‖ **ἀπεκόπτετο** > ἀποκέκοπτο QR ‖ **ἀλλ'** ≐ ἀλλὰ Q ‖ **ἐμνημόνευεν** > ἐμνημόνευσεν QR | ⊤ ἐμνημόν I ‖ **ἐπιτιμίας** > ἐπιτιμήσεως CN ‖ **πολέμαρχος** > Καλλίμαχος QR ‖ **ἀλγηδόνος** ⊤ ἀργηδόνος R ≥ ἀλγηδόνος R² ‖
37 **ψυχῆς ἰδίας** γ ∩ δ I ‖ **κατέσχε** ≐ κατέσχεν A | ≠ κατέσχε. G | > κατέσχεσε QR | Di ‖ **οἰκείῳ** > οἰκεῖον FKG Iᵐᵍ | ⊤ εἰκείῳ R ‖ **νεκρῷ** > νεκρὸν FKG ‖ **καινὸν** > κενὸν G ‖ **ἐπινόημα** ≠ ἐπινόη.. G ≥ ἐπινόημα Gᶜ ‖ **σώματος** > σώματι Iᵐᵍ ‖ **ὥσπερ** + ὑπερ ὑπ RQ ■ Qᶜ ‖ **ἀσάλευτον** > ἀσάλευτα η ‖
38 **φασι** ≐ φασὶν ODG ≥ φασὶ G ‖ **βοᾶν** Ο D ‖ **βοᾶν ὦ παῖ** ∩ 231 Ο RQ ≥ 123 Q² ‖

barbarian [oar] thrashing; for you brought to anchorage [a ship] while it was being rowed. O [hand stronger] than a fleet commander and than arrows of a more distant right hand. [O hand] on account of which Pan did not run from Arkadia in vain nor did Demeter and Kore take part in the battle to no avail. O spectacle worthy of the gods. O foster-child of Athena who stands by. O [struggle] co-honored with the struggles of Herakles and of Theseus. For while they were dragging bulls and lions, you were dragging the fleet of Asia. **36** This was the spear of Athena, [namely] the right hand of Cynegirus; this [was] torches of the gods, [namely] hands bearing a freedom flame. Now for the first time people saw a naval battle on land, now for the first time a battle between a man and a ship, now for the first time [they saw] a right hand vying with a prow, now simultaneously [they saw] here a hand being let loose, there a ship being held fast. For the hand was not being cut off from the body, but it was being sent away from home. And his former dignity the general-in-chief was remembering without any sensation of pain. **37** O right hand, worth [as much as] one's own soul; thus he held fast the ship as Callimachus [did] the arrows, avenging a kindred corpse. O fresh purpose of [the] body. O son, O great marvel, [as the] first one you showed a ship remaining motionless [held fast] by hands just as by anchors. **38** What things they say that you shouted, O son, while clinging to the ship!

Editorial conjectures for reconstructing the wording of the original text (Π) behind the medieval text form (π):

35 ὥρμισας > ὥρμησας o ‖ στολαγωγοῦ > στολαγοῦ h ‖
37 κατέσχε > κατέσχες h ‖ τιμωρήσας > τιμωρήσασα h ‖

Νάξον ἀπαιτῶ τὴν ἡρπασμένην,

τὰς ἐν Αἰγαίῳ νήσους ἀπαιτῶ.

ἀπόδοτε καὶ μὴ φεύγετε.

ὦ παῖ μείζω τῆς φύσεως βεβουλημένε· ὦ θρασύτερα ποιήσας τὰ μέλη τοῦ σώματος· ὦ ὁ περινοήσας διὰ τῶν πεδίων καὶ τῶν ὁρῶν ἄγειν ναῦν Ἀθηναίοις αἰχμάλωτον. **39** ὦ δεινῆς μάχης Παναθήναια μεμιμημένης. εἰ τοιαύτας χεῖρας εἴχομεν οἵας σύ, οὐκ ἂν ἐξῆλθον Αἰγαίου, οὐχ ... ὑπεδέξαντο τὰς χεῖρας, ὦ παῖ, τὰς βραδέως πεσούσας, τῇ μὲν οἱ πολῖται, τῇ δὲ οἱ φίλοι Πλαταιεῖς καὶ τὸ λοιπὸν σῶμα πάντες ἐστεφάνωσαν ὥσπερ τρόπαιον. **40** σὺ δέ, ὦ τέκνον, ὡς μηδὲν δεινὸν ὑποστὰς πρὸς τοὺς πολεμίους ἐβόησας·

Τί φεύγετε, ὦ κακοδαίμονες;

στῆτε καὶ τὰς πόλεις ἀπόδοτε ἃς ἐληίσασθε.

αὐτοὶ δὲ ἐκραύγαζον φεύγοντες·

Ὦ τῆς τολμηρίας, ὦ μαινομένης δεξιᾶς, ὦ τοῦ μεγάλου λήμ{μ}ατος·

ἐπιστρέψει τάχα τὴν ναῦν ἡ δεξιὰ πρὸς τὴν ἤπειρον.

41 Δάτιδος δὲ κόπτειν τὴν κεφαλὴν τοῦ τροπαιούχου ἄνωθεν ὁρμήσαντος καὶ

---

38 ἡρπασμένην ⏀ ἡρπασμένην N ‖ βεβουλημένε > βεβουλημένος QR ‖ μέλη > βέλη B ‖ ὁ ○ G ‖ περινοήσας ⏀ περιοήσας Q ≥ περινοήσας Q² ‖

39 μεμιμημένης > μεμιγμένης R | ⏀ μεμιμένης B ≥ μεμιμημένης Bᶜ ‖ εἰ > εἴς QR ‖ εἴχομεν > ἔχομεν R ‖ ὑπεδέξαντο ⏀ ὑπεδέξαν τὸ R ‖ ὑπεδέξαντο + σου γ ‖ τὰς > τῆς R ‖ τῇ (before μὲν) > τὴν QR | > τῷ B ‖ οἱ πολῖται > ἀπολεῖσται R ≥ ἀπολεῖσθαι R² ‖ τῇ (before δὲ) > τὴν QR | > τῷ B ‖ φίλοι ○ HP ‖ πάντες ≠ παντ‥ I ‖
40 ὡς > ὥσπερ D ‖ μηδὲν > μηδεὶς I ‖ ἐβόησας > ἐβόας RQ ≥ ἐβόησας Q² ‖ φεύγετε ≠ φεύγεται Q ≥ φεύγετε Q² | ⏀ ψεύγετε R ‖ ὦ ⏀ ὁ G ‖ ἀπόδοτε ⏀ ἀποδέτε R ‖ ἐληίσασθε > ἐληίσασθαι N ≥ ἐληίσασθε Nᶜ ‖ ἐκραύγαζον > ἔκραζον RQ ≥ ἐκραύγαζον Q²ᵐᵍ ‖ τῆς ○ K ‖ τολμηρίας > τόλμης L ‖ ὦ + τῆς μ ‖ μαινομένης > μαινομένοις Q ‖ λήμματος ≠ λήματος AO D ‖
41 δὲ ○ Du ‖ ὁρμήσαντος ⏀ ὡρμήσαντος CN ‖

"I demand back the captured Naxos,

the islands in the Aegean I demand back.

Return [them] and do not flee."

O son, who wished things greater than nature. O [son] who made the limbs of the body bolder. O [son] who through the plains and the mountains contrived to take captive a ship for the Athenians. *39* O [son?] of the terrible fight having imitated Panathenaic festivals. If we had had such hands as you [had], they would not have gone out of the Aegean, [they would] not .... O son, they would have welcomed your hands which were slow to fall; on the one the citizens [of Athens] [would have bestowed a wreath], on the other the allied Plataeans [would have bestowed a wreath], and all [Greeks] would have crowned the rest of the body with a wreath just like a victory monument. *40* But you, O child, as if submitting to nothing terrible, shouted to the enemy:

"Why are you running, O miserable wretches?

Stay and return the cities which you seized as booty."

And they themselves were shouting as they were fleeing:

"O [you] of insolence, O [you] of crazed right hand,

O [you] of great audacity.

Your right hand is going to turn the ship right around to the land."

41 And when Datis from [the deck] above urged [his men] to cut off the head

---

Editorial conjectures for reconstructing the wording of the original text (Π) behind the medieval text form (π):

38 βεβουλημένε > βεβουλευμένε *s p o* ‖ ὦ ὁ περινοήσας > ὡσπερεὶ νοήσας *s p o* ‖

39 οὐχ with lacuna following *h r/cs* ‖

40 δεινὸν O *s p o* ‖ λήμματος > λήματος *h r/cs* ‖ ἐπιστρέψει > ἐπιστρέφει *o* ‖

ὑπὸ δέους ἀπράκτου μείναντος ἐγείρεται πᾶς ἀνὴρ πρὸς τὴν χεῖρα καὶ μυρία

καμὼν καὶ μηδὲν ἰσχύσας ἐβόησεν ἕκαστος·

   Ἐφ' οἵας ἡμᾶς ἠγάγετε, ὦ θεοί, δεξιάς;

   τί μέλλετε ἄνδρες χαλκόθυμοι;

   ἢ θᾶττόν τις ἡμῶν ἀποτεμνέτω τὴν χεῖρα καὶ ἡμᾶς λυσάτω

   ἢ ἤδη ναῦς διὰ θαλάττης ἐπιδραμοῦσα

   καὶ ἱππικαὶ φάλαγγες διὰ γῆς

   αἰχμαλώτους ἡμᾶς εἰς Ἀθήνας κομιοῦσι.

42 τὰ μὲν οὖν ἄλλα βέλη ταύτης οὐχ ἥπτετο, πελέκει δὲ μεγάλῳ τις αὐτὴν

ὥσπερ δρῦν ἢ πεύκην ἔκοπτεν. ὁ δὲ ταύτης οὐδὲν ἐφρόντισεν ἀφαιρουμένης

ὥσπερ ἀλλοτρίαν χεῖρα διδοὺς περὶ ἣν ὅλον τὸ στρατόπεδον τὸ μὲν ἔπιπτεν

ἐν μέρει, τὸ δὲ ἐμάχετο, καὶ τὰ τραύματα τοῖς στοιχείοις διένειμεν. **43**

ἄξιός γε ἦσθα, ὦ Κυναίγειρε, τῆς Βριάρεω πολυχειρίας ἵνα πᾶσάν μοι τὴν

Ἀσίαν ἐκράτησας· καὶ νῦν πρὸς τοσοῦτον μέρος ἀντήρκεσας ὅσον Νάξον

ἔφερεν, ὅσον Ἐρέτριαν· οἳ ἀπήγαγον βασιλεῖ φήμην οὐκ ἀγεννῆ λέγοντες·

---

41 ἀπράκτου > ἄπρακτον G ‖ **πρὸς τὴν χεῖρα** ○ RQ ≥ πρὸς τὴν χεῖρα
Q²ᵐᵍ ‖ ἐβόησεν γ I > ἐβόησαν δ ‖ **ἕκαστος** ⹂ ἕκαστος R ‖ ἐφ' > .εφ' Q
≥ ὑφ' Qᶜ ≥ ἐφ' Qᶜ ‖ **ἠγάγετε ὦ θεοί** ∩ 231 ΑΟ ‖ ἠγάγετε > ἀγάγετε I
‖ **ὦ θεοί** ○ Ν ‖ **μέλλετε** ⧧ μελετε CN D ‖ **χαλκόθυμοι** ⹂ χαλκεόθυμοι ΑΟ
‖ **ἡμῶν** A BR I FKG L D > ὑμῶν O Q M E CN HP ‖ **ἀποτεμνέτω** ΑΟ QR ⹂
ἀποτεμέτω δ I B ‖ **λυσάτω** ⹂ λυσάστω RQ ≥ λυσάτω Q² ‖ **θαλάττης** γ I ⹂
θαλάσσης δ ‖ **ἐπιδραμοῦσα** β I μ > ἐπιδραμοῦσαι ΑΟ | > δραμοῦσα ε ‖
Ἀθήνας > Ἀθηναίους ηQ² ‖
42 βέλη > μέλη M CN ‖ **ἥπτετο** δ > ἥπτοντο γ I ‖ **ἔκοπτεν** γ >
ἐξέκοπτεν δ I ‖ **ἀφαιρουμένης** ⹂ ἀφαρουμένης F | ⹂ ἀφαιραμένης R | >
ἀφαιρουμένος M ‖ **περὶ ἣν** > περιὴν FG | > περιην K ‖ **ἣν** ○ Ν ‖ **ὅλον**
○ R ‖ **ἐν μέρει** > ἐκ μέρους D ‖ **τὸ δὲ** Ο β I ⹂ τὸ δ' MG N DP | ⹂ τό δ'
FK EL C H | > τῷ δὲ A ‖ **τραύματα** > πράγματα R ≥ τραύματα R² ‖
στοιχείοις ⹂ χείοις Q ≥ στοιχείοις Q² ‖ **διένειμεν** ⹂ διένειμε M ‖
43 ἦσθα ⧧ οἶσθα Ο ‖ **καὶ** ✛ καὶ D ‖ **τοσοῦτον** > τοσοῦτο CN ‖
ἀντήρκεσας > ἐκαρτέρησας HP ‖ **ὅσον** ⧧ ὅ .. Q ≥ ὅσον Qᶜ ‖ **Ἐρέτριαν** γ L
⹂ Ἐρετρίαν I μ E CN HP | Di ‖ **ἀπήγαγον** ⹂ ἀπήγατον R ‖ **ἀγεννῆ** >
ἀγεννῶν RQ ≥ ἀγεννῆ Q²ᵐᵍ ‖

of the 'trophy-winner' and when he remained ineffectual because of fright, every man rouse[d] himself against the hand; both laboring strenuously and availing nothing each one shouted:

"Against what sort of right hands, O gods, did you lead us?

What do you intend, O brazen-hearted men?

Either quickly let one of us cut off the hand and release us,

or forthwith a ship attacking by sea

and cavalry troops by land

will carry us off as captives to Athens."

42 The other arrows then were not affecting this [hand], but someone with a large axe cut it off just as [one would] an oak or a pine. But he took no thought of this [hand] as it was being taken from him as though he were giving someone else's hand for the sake of which the whole army, in part falling and [in part] fighting, was dealing out the wounds amidst the elements. **43** You were deserving, O Cynegirus, of Briareus' multitude of hands in order that you [might have] held fast for me all Asia. And now you held out against such a great contingent as carried off Naxos, as [carried off] Eretria. They brought back to [the] king a not ignoble report saying:

Editorial conjectures for reconstructing the wording of the original text (Π) behind the medieval text form (π):

43 γε > τε *s p o* ‖

Βασιλεῦ, ἐπ᾽ ἄνδρας ἐπλεύσαμεν ἀδαμαντίνους

οἷς κοπτομένων τῶν χειρῶν οὐ μέλει,

ἐπὶ δεξιὰς ὅλαις ναυσὶ παρισουμένας·

καὶ νῦν μόλις ἀνήχθημεν ἐκ Κυναιγείρου.

44 ὦ παῖ, τὰς μὲν σὰς χεῖρας ᾄδουσι Πλαταιεῖς, τὰς δὲ σὰς ἀριστείας

Λακεδαιμόνιοι πυνθάνονται.   ταύτῃ καὶ Πολύζηλος ἠκολούθησε μὴ

τεθεαμένος.   προκατέλαβες Ἀθηναίοις, ὦ παῖ, καὶ τὴν θάλασσαν ἡμῖν

οἰκείαν ἐποίησας·   συνέθου τῷ στοιχείῳ φιλίαν ὑπὲρ τῆς πατρίδος·   ἔδωκας

ὑπὲρ ἡμῶν τῇ θαλάσσῃ τὴν δεξιάν. μιμήσονται χρόνῳ ναυμαχοῦντες τὰ σὰ

σχήματα καὶ γενήσονται ἐκ σιδήρου χεῖρες ἐπὶ ναῦς ἐπιβολάς, ὦ παῖ, τῆς

σῆς μάχης εἰκόνας ἔχουσαι.   **45** καὶ πολλὰ λέγειν ἔχων τῆς σῆς ἀρετῆς

ἐγκώμια, τὰ κάλλιστα κοινῷ νόμῳ φυλάττω.   ἔχεις τοιοῦτόν τινα λόγον

μεγαληγορῆσαι, ὦ Καλλιμάχου πάτερ;   ποίαν τοιαύτην στάσιν οἵαν ἔστησαν

αἱ Κυναιγείρου χεῖρες ἤδη πίπτουσαν τὴν Ἑλλάδα;   τοῦ μὲν γὰρ σοῦ νεκροῦ

βέλη βάρβαρα, τῆς δὲ πάσης Ἑλλάδος αἱ χεῖρες ἡμῶν τὰ σώματα.   **46**

ἄπελθε, παραχώρησον·   ἐρῶ τι καὶ περὶ τοῦ σοῦ παιδός.   καλὸν ἐρῶ λόγον,

ὅτι τοιούτου στρατιώτου Κυναιγείρου πολέμαρχος ἦν.   σὺ δ᾽ ἐπιταφίῳ μὴ δ᾽

43 βασιλεῦ > βασιλεῦς R ‖ ἐπ᾽ > εἰς QR ‖ κοπτομένων ⸗ κοπτώμενων L ‖ μέλει ⸗ μέλλει R ‖
44 χεῖρας Ο RQ ≥ χεῖρας Q²ᵐᵍ ‖ πυνθάνονται ⸗ πυνθάνοντες Q ≥ πυνθάνονται Q² ‖ ταύτῃ FKG ε ≠ ταυτ· Μ | > ταύταις ΑΟ Β Ι | > ταύτας QR | Πολύζηλος ≠ Πολ ΄ζηλος Κ | ⸗ Πολύξυλος β ‖ ἠκολούθησε ≐ ἠκολούθησεν Α Ι | > ἠκολούθησαν QR ‖ μὴ Ο δ | τεθεαμένος ≠ τεθεαμέν ος Α | > τεθαμμένος ε Q² | > τεθραμμένος Κ ‖ Ἀθηναίοις ΑΟ Β Ι > Ἀθηναίους δ QR ‖ ἐποίησας > πεποίηκας ηQ² φιλίαν > φιλίας D ‖ ἡμῶν τῇ > ἡμῖ γῇ RQ ≥ ἡμῶν τῇ Q²ᵐᵍ ‖ θαλάσσῃ ≐ θαλάττῃ L ‖ χρόνῳ > χρόνων D ‖ σα Ο Κ ‖ γενήσονται ἢ γεννήσονται QR ‖ χεῖρες ⸗ ρες D ‖ ἐπὶ ναῦς Ο D ‖ ναῦς > ναυσῶν QR ‖
45 ἔχων ⸗ ἔχον R ‖ κοινῷ > κοινῶν Α D ‖ φυλάττω Ο D ‖ τινα > μοι R | > μένοι Q ≥ τινὰ Q²ᵐᵍ ‖ στάσιν > συστάσιν Β ‖ οἵαν γ Ι Μ > ἦν FKG ε ‖ αἱ Ο D ‖ πίπτουσαν ⸗ σίπτουσαν R ‖ Ἑλλάδος Ο D ‖
46 ἐρῶ λόγον ∩ QR ‖ τοιούτου > τοιοῦτοι D ≥ τοι τοῦτου Dᶜ ‖ Κυναιγείρου > Κυναίγειρος FKG | Ο Μ ‖ μὴ δ᾽ ⸗ μήδ᾽ Ι | ≐ μὴ δὲ ΑΟ | > μὴ QR L ‖

"King, we sailed against men hard as adamant,

to whom it does not matter when their hands are being cut off;

[we sailed] against right hands which were a match for whole ships.

And we just barely put to sea out [of the clutches] of Cynegirus."

44 O son, Plataeans sing of your hands and Lacedaemonians hear tell of your acts of prowess. Even Polyzelos followed this [prowess] though not having beheld [it]. You seized the sea in advance for the Athenians, O son, and you made [it] domestic [domain] for us. You arranged a friendship [pact] with the element on behalf of the fatherland. You gave your right hand to the sea on our behalf. In time naval fighters will imitate your gestures and hands will be produced from iron for assaults [against] ships, O son, [grappling irons] having resemblances to your fight. **45** And while I have many encomiums to say about your valor, by common custom I am noting the best ones. Do you have any such word to boast, O father of Callimachus? What such stance [do you have to boast about] like the sort which the hands of Cynegirus made Greece to stand when it was already falling? The solid substances of your corpse [are] barbarian arrows, while [the solid substances] of all Greece [are] our hands. **46** Go away, step aside. I will say something also concerning your son. I will say a good word because he was general-in-chief of such a soldier as Cynegirus. But don't you start working on the funeral speech

---

Editorial conjectures for reconstructing the wording of the original text (Π) behind the medieval text form (π):

44 χεῖρες > χειρῶν *jü* ‖ ἐπὶ ναῦς ἐπιβολὰς > ἐπὶ ναυτῶν ἐπιβολὰς or ἐπὶ νεῶν ἐπιβολὰς *s p o* | > ἐπὶ ναῶν ἐμβολὰς or ἐπὶ ναῦς καὶ ἐμβολὰς *j* | > καὶ ἐπὶ ναῦς ἐπιβολαὶ or καὶ ἐπὶ ναῦς ἐμβολαὶ *h jü* ‖

45 τὰ σώματα > στερεώματα *j* | > τὰ στερεώματα *h* ‖

ἐπιχείρει πατὴρ ὢν νεκροῦ μὴ δὲ ταφῆναι θέλοντος. **47** ἤδη πάλαι παρελήλυθεν ὁ καιρὸς τῶν ἡμετέρων ἐπιταφίων· πάλαι καὶ πάλαι τέθαπται Καλλίμαχος ὑπὸ τῶν βελῶν. εἰμὶ δέ, ὦ ἄνδρες δικασταί, πρὸς τὸν λόγον ἐπιτηδειότερος τὸν ἐπὶ τῷ **σήματι**· καὶ γὰρ αὐτοῦ πατήρ εἰμι καὶ τῶν μεγάλων ὀνομαστότατος· ἔχω δὲ καὶ γλῶτταν οἵαν ἐκεῖνος δεξιάν. **48** ἐάσατέ με τραγῳδῆσαι τραγῳδίαν ἐπιτάφιον καὶ χορὸν παραγαγεῖν ἐπινίκιον· μὴ φθονήσητε δράματι Μαραθωνίῳ. **49** ἀλλ᾿, ὦ Αἰσχύλε παῖ, τὸν λόγον μοι σὺ ποίησον καὶ συγκόσμησον τὰς Μαραθῶνος μάχας τῷ πατρί. μή με ἀτιμάσητε· χεῖρας ὑμῖν ὁμοίας προτείνω ταῖς ὑπὲρ ὑμῶν κειμέναις. ἔχομαι τοῦ λόγου, λαμβάνομαι τοῦ τάφου. οὐκ ἀφίσταμαι τὸ πολυάνδριον διεξιών, πατὴρ ὢν Κυναιγείρου. ἐπιτίθημι τὰς χεῖρας τῷ σώματι· καὶ ταύτας ὁ θέλων ἀποκοψάτω.

---

46 μὴ δὲ ≐ μηδὲ G ‖
47 πάλαι (after ἤδη) Ο N ‖ **παρελήλυθεν** ⇌ παρελλήλυθεν D ‖ **ἡμετέρων** AO B I M E CN D > ὑμετέρων QR FKG L HP ‖ **πάλαι καὶ πάλαι** all the way to the end of A49: in miniature script from a second hand L ‖ **καὶ** (after πάλαι) > γὰρ AO ‖ **δὲ** (after εἰμὶ) Ο I ‖ **τὸν** (after ἐπιτηδειότερος) A QR L η > τῶν Ο B I μ E CN ‖ **σήματι** QR I FG EL CN > σώματι AO B MK η ‖ **ὀνομαστότατος** ⇌ ὀνομαστότιτος R ≥ ὀνομαστότητος R^c | ⇌ ὀνομαστότατ ̣νε Q ‖ **ἔχω** > ἔχον R ‖ **γλῶτταν** AO B ≐ γλῶσσαν QR I δ ‖
48 με γ Ο δ (Di) I ‖ **τραγῳδῆσαι** AO μ > τραγῳδεῖν β I EL CN HP(Di) ‖ **παραγαγεῖν** AO QR I > παράγειν B μ E(Lu) CN HPQ²(Di) ‖ **Μαραθωνίῳ** ⇌ Μαραθωνιᾳ R ‖
49 Αἰσχύλε > Αἰσύλου FKG ‖ **σὺ** Ο N ‖ **συγκόσμησον** γ > συγκόμισον I FKG ε | > συγκόμι M ‖ **Μαραθῶνος** ≠ Μαραθων.. D ‖ **με** ≐ μ᾿ G | > τε AO ‖ **ἀτιμάσητε** > ἀτιμάσατε N ≥ ἀτιμάσητε N^cmg ‖ **ὑμῶν** > ἡμῶν I M N ‖ **τοῦ** Ο G ‖ **διεξιών** > λαβών G ≥ διεξιών G^cmg ‖ **ταύτας** > ταῦτα QR | > ταύτην ηQ² ‖ **ἀποκοψάτω** + τέλος N^mg | + ὁ Κυναιγείρου πατὴρ CN ‖

because you are father of a corpse wishing not to be buried. *47* The time for [y]our funeral speeches has already long since passed. Long, long ago Callimachus has been buried by the arrows. I am, however, O gentlemen jurors, more suited for the speech at the grave mound. For I am both his father and of the important [persons I am the] most notable [one]. And I have also a tongue as able as [the] right hand he [had]. *48* Allow me to recite the tragic funeral ode and to lead the victory dance. Do not begrudge [me this] at the Marathonian celebration. *49* But, O son Aeschylus, *you* make the speech for me and [*you*] confer honor on the fights at Marathon for the father. Don't you [jurors] dishonor me. I stretch out [my] hands to you like the ones lying [severed] on your behalf. I lay claim to the speech, I take hold of the grave. I am not withdrawing from the mass grave [and] going out, since I am father of Cynegirus. I am putting my hands on the body — let the one who wishes cut these off too.

Editorial conjectures for reconstructing the wording of the original text (Π) behind the medieval text form (π):

47 πάλαι καὶ πάλαι > πάλαι γὰρ καὶ πάλαι *s p o* | πάλαι πάλαι *j* | πάλαι γὰρ πάλαι *h* ‖

49 σώματι > σήματι *s p o h* ‖

Β

εἰς τὸ ἐναντίον

ὁ Καλλιμάχου πατήρ

1 Τὸν μὲν τῆς πόλεως ἐπαινῶ νόμον κοσμοῦντα τὸν τῶν ἀγαθῶν ἀνδρῶν τάφον καὶ λόγῳ. ἔργων γὰρ εὖ πραχθέντων λόγοι ῥηθέντες καλῶς εἰσι τιμή· ἐμοὶ δὲ αὐτῷ μὲν **προσφόρως** τοῦ παιδὸς ἀρετὴ μακροτέρα τῆς ψυχῆς γενομένη, διὰ δὲ τὴν αὐτοῦ Καλλιμάχου προτίμησιν, εἰ ταῖς τῶν πατέρων τιμαῖς ἡ τῶν παίδων ἀνδραγαθία κρίνεται, δείξω τὸν λόγον. **2** Καλλιμάχου γὰρ πατὴρ ὢν παντὸς ἄλλου πρέπω μᾶλλον ἐπὶ τοῦ κοινοῦ βήματος ἑστάναι. ζῶν μὲν οὖν Καλλίμαχος ἡγεμὼν ζῶντος Κυναιγείρου πολέμαρχος ἦν· εἰ δὲ **καὶ** τεθνεὼς ἡττηθήσεται, καὶ τὴν ἀρχὴν καὶ τὴν ἀρετὴν ὑβριεῖται, τὴν μὲν αἰτίαν τῆς πάσης ὑμῖν νίκης γενομένην, τὴν δὲ τὸ μέγιστον παρασχοῦσαν τῶν ἐν Μαραθῶνι θαυμάτων ἄνδρα καὶ χωρὶς ψυχῆς μεμαχημένον καὶ νεκρὸν θανάτου κρείττονα. **3** πεσεῖν μὲν οὖν αὐτὸν καὶ κοινωνῆσαι τοῦ τάφου μόγις ἔπεισα· οὐ γὰρ ἤθελεν ἀπελθεῖν τῆς στάσεως οὐδὲ ὑποπεσεῖν ταῖς ἑτέρων φιλοτιμίαις, οὐκ ἀξιῶν τὸν ὑπὲρ τῆς Ἀσίας ὅλης

Β εἰς τὸ ἐναντίον = ἰς τὸ ἐναντίον F | > ἐκ τοῦ ἐναντίου CN | Ο Mu ‖ ὁ Ο FG R ‖ ὁ Καλλιμάχου πατήρ Ο Mu | + Πολεμῶνος Κ ‖
1 τὸν = ὸν (the intended calligraphic τ was not added in the left margin) F N ‖ ἐπαινῶ > ἐπαινῶν D ‖ τὸν = τὸ D ‖ λόγῳ > λόγων Κ | λόγον QR ‖ ἔργων = ἔργω D ‖ ῥηθέντες καλῶς γ ∩ δ Ι ‖ εἰσι τιμή Ο Q ≥ εἰσι τιμή Q²ᵐᵍ ‖ ἐμοὶ δὲ αὐτῷ μὲν Ο R ≥ ἐμοὶ δὲ αὐτῷ μὲν R²ᵐᵍ ‖ μὲν προσφόρως ∩ πρόσφορος μὲν μ ‖ προσφόρως γ Ι > πρόσφορος δ | + ἡ QR ‖ τοῦ = ποῦ D ‖ τὴν > τοῦ CN ‖ τῶν Ο CN ‖ παίδων ≐ παίδ᾽ R ‖
2 κοινοῦ Ο η ‖ ἑστάναι + τ . G ‖ ἡγεμὼν = γεμῶν QR ‖ καὶ (before τεθνεὼς) γ Ι Ο δ ‖ τεθνεὼς = ταθνεὼς R ‖ ἡττηθήσεται = ἡττηθῆσθαι Q ≥ ἡττηθήσεται Q² ‖ ὑβριεῖται > ὑβριεῖτε μ ‖ ὑμῖν > ἡμῖν M CN D Q | > ἡμῶν R ‖ γενομένην > γεγενημένα QR ‖ ψυχῆς Ο D ‖
3 κοινωνῆσαι > κοινωνεῖν RQ ≥ κοινωνῆσαι Q²ᵐᵍ ‖ μόγις > μόλις β ≥ μόγις Q² ‖ οὐ > οὐδὲ QR ‖ ἤθελεν = ἤθηεν R ‖ οὐδὲ γ Ι ≐ οὐδ᾽ δ ‖ ἑτέρων = ἑ.ταίρων D ‖ φιλοτιμίαις > φιλοτιμίας R ‖ ὑπὲρ > ὑπὸ ε Q²ᵐᵍ ‖

B.

In Opposition
The Father of Callimachus

1 I applaud the custom of the city which adorns the grave of the brave men also with a speech. For after deeds are well done, words spoken eloquently are an honor. Inasmuch as, on account of his prominence, the valor of my son Callimachus lasted longer than his soul, — if the manly bravery of the sons is [to be] decided by the honors [accorded to] the fathers — I will show [that] the speech [should] fittingly [belong] to me. *2* For since I am father of Callimachus I am more suited than everyone else to stand on the public podium. While alive then Callimachus [as] leader was general-in-chief of Cynegirus while he was alive. But if now that he has died he will be [regarded as] inferior, he will be treated outrageously with respect to both his office and his valor. [This valor] was on the one hand the reason for our entire victory, and on the other hand [it] furnished the greatest of the wonders at Marathon, [namely,] a man who fought even without a soul and a corpse stronger than death. *3* I, therefore, barely persuaded him to fall and to have a share in the grave. For he was not willing to leave the standing position nor to succumb to the ambitions of others, because he did not deem the one [ruling] over all Asia worthy of having forced [him] to admit that he had died.

Editorial conjectures for reconstructing the wording of the original text (Π) behind the medieval text form (π):

1 δείξω τὸν λόγον > δέξομαι τὸν λόγον or δείξω τὸν λόγον ἐμοὶ προσήκειν *o* | λήξομαι *jü* ‖

2 Κυναιγείρου πολέμαρχος ἦν > Κυναιγείρου ἦν, πολέμαρχος ὤν *j* | or πολέμαρχος Ο *j h* ‖ καὶ (before τεθνεὼς) > δὴ *j* | Ο *h* ‖

3 καὶ (before κοινωνῆσαι) > οὐ *s* | > ὡς *p* ‖

ὅτι τέθνηκεν ὁμολογῆσαι βεβιασμένον. **4** ἀγαθὸς μὲν οὖν ἦν ὁ Κυναίγειρος καὶ παῖς πατρὸς ἀγαθοῦ, οὐ μὴν ἀγαθῶν κρείττων· ἥττηται δὲ Καλλιμάχου τοσοῦτον ὅσον οἱ κείμενοι τῶν ἑστηκότων καὶ θάρσους ἀγαθοῦ νεκρὸς οὐχ ὁλόκληρος.

5 ὥσπερ δὲ ἅπαν τυγχάνει, καὶ τοῦτο ἐξετάσατε. ἀπέβαινε μὲν εἰς Μαραθῶνα ὁ Δαρείου στόλος μετὰ τὰς **ἐξ Αἰγαίου** τῶν νήσων ἁρπαγάς, τῇ δὲ Ἀττικῇ βοηθεῖν ἔδει τὴν **Λακεδαιμονίων** εἰρωνείαν μὴ περιμένοντας — ὀξὺς γὰρ ὁ κίνδυνος ἦν — καὶ τῷ στρατηγῷ Μιλτιάδῃ τὴν ταχίστην ἐδόκει τρέχειν. **6** ἐνταῦθα ἦγε τὴν δύναμιν ἅπασαν ὁ ἐμὸς υἱός, πολέμαρχος ὢν καὶ κατὰ τὸν νόμον καὶ σπουδὴν ἰδίαν ὅτι θερμοτάτην ἔχων ἔργα μεγάλα καὶ θαυμαστὰ ἐν τῇ μάχῃ παρασχέσθαι· **7** Κυναίγειρος δὲ εἷς τις ὢν τῶν πολλῶν ἠπείγετο. συμμίξαντες δὲ τοῖς βαρβάροις μεμπτὸς μὲν οὐδεὶς ἦν, ἐν δὲ τοῖς ἔργοις Καλλίμαχος ἔδειξεν αὐτοῖς ὅτι πολέμαρχος ἦν. **8** παρακελευσάμενος γὰρ αὐτῷ τὸ σῶμα καὶ τὴν ψυχὴν ὑπὲρ τῆς κοινῆς ἐλευθερίας ἀναλῶσθαι καὶ πρὸς πᾶσαν τὴν δύναμιν βασιλέως ἀντιτάξας

---

3 τέθνηκεν + ὑπ D ▬ Dᶜ ‖ βεβιασμένον > βεβοασμένον A | + marginal gloss: πρὸς τὸν βεβιασμένον + circa 33 illegible letters Iᵐᵍ ‖
4 ἦν Ο FKG QR ‖ ἀγαθῶν > ἀγαθὸν R ‖ κρείττων ⇌ κρεῖττων A ‖ τῶν > τὸν P ‖ νεκρὸς > νεκροῦ RQ ≥ νεκροῦ Q² ‖
5 τοῦτο + νῦν μ ‖ ἐξετάσατε ⇌ ἐξετάσατεν B ‖ ἀπέβαινε > ἐπέβαινε E CN HP | > ἐπέβενε D ‖ τὰς > τὸ R ‖ ἐξ Αἰγαίου γ I > ἐν Αἰγαίῳ δ ‖ ἐξ Αἰγαίου τῶν νήσων ∩ τῶν ἐν Αἰγαίῳ νήσων Μ ‖ ἁρπαγάς > ἁρπάσας RQ ≥ ἁρπαγὰς Q² ‖ τῇ Ἀττικῇ > τῷ Ἀττικῷ B ‖ βοηθεῖν ⇌ θεῖν Q ≥ βοηθεῖν Q²ᵐᵍ ‖ Λακεδαιμονίων γ > λακεδαιμονίαν δ I ‖ εἰρωνείαν ≟ εἰρωνίαν P | Ο I R ‖ περιμένοντας ⇌ περιμένοιας A | > παραμένοντας R | > παρερϊαμένοντας Q ⇌ περιμένοντας Q² ‖ Μιλτιάδῃ ⇌ Μιλτιάδϊ F ‖ τρέχειν > τρέχων B ‖
6 ἦγε ≟ ἦγεν A ‖ δύναμιν ἅπασαν ∩ ε ‖ ἅπασαν ⇌ ἅπασαν Q ‖ ὅτι > καὶ τοι ηQ² ‖ θερμοτάτην γ > θερμότατα I E CN | > θερμόττ D | > θερμοττος Μ ‖ μάχῃ > πόλει RQ ≥ μάχῃ Q²ᵐᵍ ‖ παρασχέσθαι > παρέχεσθαι I ‖ παρασκεύασθαι RQ ≥ παρασχέσθαι Q² ‖
7 μεμπτὸς ⇌ μενητὸς QR ≥ μεμπτὸς Rᶜ | ⇌ μεπτὸς Κ ‖ μὲν Ο Ο ‖ μεμπτὸς μὲν οὐδεὶς ἦν ∩ 341 Ο ‖ ἐν δὲ τοῖς ἔργοις Καλλίμαχος ἔδειξεν αὐτοῖς ὅτι πολέμαρχος ἦν Ο I ‖ αὐτοῖς > αὐτὴν B | Ο RQ ≥ αὐτοῖς Q²ᵐᵍ ‖
8 αὐτῷ > αὐτῷ Ο FK D ‖ ἐλευθερίας > σωτηρίας G ‖ ἀναλῶσθαι I E CN ≟ ἀνηλῶσθαι β μ η | > ἀναλῶσαι ΑΟ ‖ βασιλέως > βασιλέα I ‖

4 Brave indeed was Cynegirus and son of a brave father, [but] certainly no more so than [other] brave [men]. Yet he was inferior to Callimachus to the same degree that those lying [dead] [are inferior] to those having stood and that a corpse without all its parts [is inferior] to courage of a brave man.

5 But just as happens [with] everything [else], examine also this: On the one side, Darius' expedition was disembarking at Marathon after the seizure of the Aegean islands; on the other side, it was necessary to rescue Attica without waiting out the dissembling of the Lacedaemonians — for the danger was acute. Even to the general, Miltiades, it seemed [best] to move very quickly. *6* My own son led the entire force thither, both because he was general-in-chief in accordance with the law and because he had a personal zeal that was burning to produce great and wondrous deeds in the battle. *7* And Cynegirus, since he was one among the many, was being urged forward. And while no one was blameworthy when they clashed with the barbarians, by his deeds Callimachus showed them that he was general-in-chief. *8* For after exhorting himself to expend body and soul on behalf of the common freedom and after ranging himself against the entire force of [the] king as though being

---

Editorial conjectures for reconstructing the wording of the original text (Π) behind the medieval text form (π):

4 θάρσους > ἀνδρὸς *o* ‖
8 αὐτῷ > αὐτῷ *s p o h r/cs* ‖

αὐτὸν ὡς ἂν ἀξιόμαχος ὤν, ἑκὼν πρὸς τὸν Δαρείου στόλον ἔστη τὴν Ἀσίαν **προκαλούμενος** καὶ πᾶσαν ἐκ τῶν νεῶν ἐκχεομένην αὐτὸς ἐδέχετο ῥώμῃ ἀνθρώπων κρείττονι καὶ τόλμῃ παραλόγῳ καὶ παντὶ θυμῷ, καὶ πᾶσι συνεπλάκη κατ' αὐτὸ τὸ τοῦ πολέμου στόμα καὶ κατὰ τὴν ἀκμαιοτάτην τῶν βαρβάρων ἐμβολὴν, καὶ πᾶσιν ἐξήρκεσεν οὔτε τὴν ὄψιν ἐκπλαγεὶς ὑπὸ τοῦ τῆς βοῆς συμμιγοῦς πλήθους οὔτε τὴν βαρβαρικὴν ἰταμότητα κατ' οὐδὲν ἀξιώσας εἶναι φοβερὰν ἀρετῇ. **9** πολὺν δὲ τῶν πολεμίων ἐργασάμενος φόνον καὶ φόβον εἰς τουτὶ αὐτοὺς ὀργῆς τε ἅμα καὶ ἀνάγκης **κατέστησεν** ὥστε τἄλλα πάντα καταλιπόντες τὰ τῆς μάχης χωρία Καλλιμάχῳ πάντες ἐπεχέοντο καὶ Καλλιμάχου πάντες ἐστοχάζοντο καὶ τοῦτο ἦν σπούδασμα ἅπασι τὸ Καλλίμαχον βαλεῖν· τούτου γὰρ παρόντος ἐν τούτῳ εἶναι τὰς Ἀθήνας ἔφασκον. **10** ἔνθα πολλὰ μὲν βελῶν καὶ κοντῶν καὶ ξιφῶν καὶ παντοδαπῶν βλημάτων ὑπεδέξατο, πάσας δὲ αὐτῶν ὑπέμεινε τὰς προσβολὰς ὥσπερ ἐξ ἀδάμαντος ὢν πύργος ἢ τεῖχος ἄρρηκτον ἢ ἀντίτυπος πέτρα ἢ θεὸς ἀνθρώποις μαχόμενος, ἕως πάντα ἀνήλωσε τὰ τῆς Ἀσίας βέλη καὶ καμεῖν ἐποίησε τὴν πολλὴν δύναμιν τοῦ βασιλέως. **11** πολὺν μὲν

---

8 αὐτὸν AO QR I E N DP ≠ αὐτὸν B μ Eᶜ C H ‖ ἂν ○ B ‖ ἀξιόμαχος ⟂ ἀξιώμαχος D ‖ ἔστη + ὖσα̣. E ‖ **προκαλούμενος** δ I > προσκαλούμενος γ ‖ ἐκ ○ η ‖ ἐκ τῶν νεῶν ἐκχεομένην γ I ∩ 4123 μ E CN │ ∩ 423 η ‖ αὐτὸς > αὐτὸ BuQR ‖ ῥώμῃ > τόλμῃ RQ ≥ ῥώμῃ Q²ᵐᵍ │ + φυλλέ H²ᵐᵍ (gloss in lower margin near ῥώμῃ) ‖ καὶ > δὲ R ‖ πᾶσι > πᾶς Ο │ > πᾶσα D ‖ κατ' ≟ κατὰ AO G ‖ αὐτὸ ○ Ο │ τὸ ○ D ‖ ἀκμαιοτάτην ⟂ ἀκμαιότητα E CN ‖ ἐμβολὴν > συμπλοκὴν μ ≥ ἐμβολὴν FᵐᵍGᵐᵍ ‖ ἐκπλαγεὶς ○ G ‖ ἰταμότητα ⟂ ἰταμμότητα QR ‖ ἀρετῇ > ἀρετὴν QR ‖
9 τε δ Q² ○ γ I ‖ ἅμα ⟂ ἄμα Q ‖ κατέστησεν γ I > παρέστησεν δ ‖ τἄλλα > ἄλλα R ‖ μάχης ⟂ μάχες Ο ‖ Καλλιμάχῳ > Καλλιμάχου QR ‖ ἐπεχέοντο καὶ Καλλιμάχου πάντες ○ Q ≥ ἐπεχέοντο καὶ Καλλιμάχου πάντες Q²ᵐᵍ ‖ ἐστοχάζοντο γ I > κατεστοχάζοντο δ ‖ βαλεῖν ≠ βαλλεῖν K D ‖ τούτῳ > τούτοις M ‖ εἶναι τὰς Ἀθήνας ἔφασκον ∩ 4231 QR ‖
10 κοντῶν > ἀκόντων AO ‖ καὶ (after ξιφῶν) ○ η │ + κοντῶν G ▄ Gᶜ ‖ παντοδαπῶν ⟂ πανταδαπῶν QR ‖ βλημάτων γ I M > βλήματα FKG E CN HP │ > κλήματα D ‖ ὑπεδέξατο ⟂ ὑπεδέξα QR ‖ ὑπέμεινε ≟ ὑπέμεινεν A │ ⟂ ὑπεμεινει QR ‖ προσβολὰς > προβολὰς G ‖ ἄρρηκτον ⟂ ἄρηκτον I ‖ ἕως > καὶ ὡς QR ‖ ἀνήλωσε > ἀναλώσαι AO ‖ καμεῖν ⟂ μεῖν Q ≥ καμεῖν Q² ‖ ἐποίησε ≟ ἐποίησεν A ‖

a match for the battle, he willingly stood against the army of Darius and challenged Asia. And as it all streamed forth from the ships he by himself awaited its attack with a superhuman bodily strength and with an incalculable boldness and with all his heart. And he was entangled in close combat with all [the enemies] over against the very jaws of the war and over against the fiercest attack of the barbarians, and he was a match for all. Neither in view of the sight was he panicked by the din of the clamorous shouting, nor did he in any way deem the barbaric insolence to be fearful — [and all this enabled] by [his] valor. *9* And since he was causing much slaughter of the enemy and [much] fear he brought them to this, [namely] that out of anger and at the same time out of necessity they all left all the other sites of fighting and began to stream to Callimachus; and they were all aiming at Callimachus and for everyone this was the endeavor, [namely,] to hit Callimachus. For as long as he was there helping they were saying that Athens was in him. *10* There he submitted himself to many arrows and javelins and swords and all sorts of shots, and he endured all their attacks like a tower [made] out of adamant or an unbreachable wall or a rigid rock or a god fighting against men, until he consumed all the arrows of Asia and made the mighty force of the king to be exhausted. *11* For a long time his soul, striving against nature, held out in

---

Editorial conjectures for reconstructing the wording of the original text (II) behind the medieval text form (π):

8 αὐτὸν > αὐτὸν *s p o h r/cs* ‖ ὑπὸ τοῦ τῆς βοῆς συμμιγοῦς πλήθους οὔτε > ὑπὸ τοῦ πλήθους, οὔτε τὴν ἀκοὴν ὑπὸ τοῦ τῆς βοῆς συμμιγοῦς *j* │ > ὑπὸ τῆς βοῆς συμμιγοῦς τοῦ πλήθους οὔτε *h* ‖

οὖν χρόνον ἐν τῷ σώματι διεκαρτέρησεν ἡ ψυχὴ ἐρίζουσα πρὸς τὴν φύσιν καὶ

εἰς τὴν ἀδύνατον ἀνθρώποις ἀθανασίαν ἐβιάζετο· ἐπεὶ δὲ ἄνθρωπος

Καλλίμαχος ἦν καὶ θνητὸς ἦν καὶ τοῦ σώματος ἀπελθεῖν ἠναγκάζετο τῷ

πλήθει τῶν τραυμάτων, ἀπέθανε μέν, οὐκ ἔπεσε δέ, ἀλλ᾽ ἐξιοῦσα ἡ ψυχὴ

βεβαίως τῷ σώματι μένειν καὶ καρτερεῖν ἐνετείλατο καὶ μάχεσθαι τὴν

δυνατὴν τοῖς ἀψύχοις μάχην. τὸ δὲ ἐπείσθη καὶ βεβαίως ἔμενεν ὥσπερ

ἐρριζωμένον καὶ διὰ τοῦ πολέμου τοιοῦτο{ν} οἷον αὐτὸ ἐξιοῦσα ἔστησεν ἡ

ψυχὴ καὶ πολὺν χρόνον τοὺς βαρβάρους ἐξηπάτησεν· οὐδεὶς γὰρ ᾤετο

τεθνάναι τὸν ἑστηκότα.

12 ὦ Καλλιμάχου καὶ φοβεροῦ νεκροῦ· ὦ στρατιώτου τῆς εἱμαρμένης

πολυχρονιωτέρου· ὦ μακροτέρα τῆς ψυχῆς, ὦ πιστοτέρα τοῦ πνεύματος

ἀρετή· ὦ σῶμα πολλῶν ψυχῶν ἰσόρροπον· ὦ φρόνημα ὀρθόν· ὦ σῶμα

ἔμψυχον· ὦ σῶμα νικηφόρον ὅπλοις καὶ βέλεσι κεκοσμημένον· ὦ πρῶτον

Μαραθῶνος τρόπαιον. ὦ τηρήσας ὀρθὴν τὴν ἐλευθερίαν Ἀθηναίοις, ὦ

στήσας ἐν **αὐτῷ** τὴν Ἑλλάδα, οὐκ εἴασας τὰς Ἀθήνας πεσεῖν.

---

11 χρόνον > χρόνως QR ‖ ἐν τῷ σώματι διεκαρτέρησεν ἡ ψυχὴ γ I ∩ 564123 δ Q² ‖ ἐρίζουσα ⇌ ἐρόζουσα Q ≥ ἐρίζουσα Qᶜ ‖ ἀδύνατον ⇌ ἀδύναται RQ ≥ ἀδύνατον Q² ‖ ἦν ◯ QR ‖ θνητὸς ἦν καὶ ◯ D ≥ θνητὸς ἦν καὶ Dᶜᵐᵍ ‖ τῷ (after ἠναγκάζετο) ◯ RQ ≥ τῷ Q² ‖ ἀπέθανε ≟ ἀπέθανεν A ‖ ἔπεσε ≟ ἔπεσεν A ‖ μένειν > μένει R ‖ ἐπείσθη ⇌ ἐπέσθη RQ ≥ ἐπείσθη Q² ‖ ἔμενεν δ I > ἔμεινεν γ ‖ ἐρριζωμένον ⇌ ἐρριζώμενον A P ≥ ἐρριζωμένον Pᶜ │ ⇌ ἐριζωμένον QR ‖ τοιοῦτον δ I QR > τοιοῦτο AO B ‖ αὐτὸ > αὐτὴ QR ‖ καὶ πολὺν χρόνον τοὺς βαρβάρους ἐξηπάτησεν· οὐδεὶς γὰρ ᾤετο τεθνάναι τὸν ἑστηκότα. ὦ Καλλιμάχου ◯ Q ≥ added by Q²ᵐᵍ ‖
12 ὦ ⇌ ὢ (10 times in B12) B ‖ Καλλιμάχου > Καλλιμάχε O ‖ καὶ φοβεροῦ ∩ RQ ≥ φοβεροῦ καὶ Q² ‖ εἱμαρμένης ⇌ εἱμαρμένης ‖ πολυχρονιωτέρου ⇌ πολο G ≥ πολυχρονιωτέρου Gᶜ ‖ μακροτέρα > μακροτέρου RQ ≥ μακροτέρα Q² ‖ πιστοτέρα > πιστοτέρου RQ ≥ πιστοτέρα Q² ‖ πολλῶν ψυχῶν ∩ μ ‖ ἰσόρροπον ⇌ ἰσώρροπον QR ‖ νικηφόρον ⇌ νηκηφόρον Q │ ⇌ νηκηφίρον R ‖ ὅπλοις ≟ πλοις E ≥ ὅπλοις Eᶜ ‖ πρῶτον > πρῶτος D ‖ Μαραθῶνος ⇌ Μαραθῶ D ‖ τηρήσας > τηρῆσαν QR ‖ ὦ (after Ἀθηναίοις) γ > ὅς δ I ‖ στήσας > στῆσαν RQ ≥ στῆσας Q²ᵐᵍ ‖ αὐτῷ ≟ αὐτῷ AO B I (→ γ) │ ≟ ἑαυτῷ δ QR (→ δ) The pronoun readings in both γ and δ go back to αὐτῷ in π ‖ εἴασας > ἐᾶσαν RQ ≥ εἴασας Q²ᵐᵍ ‖

the body and he tried to force his way into the immortality impossible for humans. But since Callimachus was human he was also mortal, and he was compelled by the multitude of the wounds to depart the body. He died but did not fall; rather, as the soul was leaving it enjoined the body to remain steadfast and to persist and to keep on fighting the fight [as far as] possible for those without a soul. It obeyed and remained steadfast as though rooted even throughout the battle to such an extent that, although the soul had left, it made it [the body] stand and for a long time this completely deceived the barbarians. For no one thought that the one who stood had died.

12 O [valor] of Callimachus and [his] fear-inspiring corpse. O [valor] of a soldier more long-lived than [Fate] allotted. O [valor] longer-lasting than the soul. O valor more trusty than [life's] breath. O body equally matched with many souls. O upright resolve. O animated body. O victory-bringing body adorned with weapons and arrows. O first [victory] trophy of Marathon. O [you who] kept freedom safe for Athenians, O [you who] by yourself made Greece to stand, you did not allow Athens to fall.

Editorial conjectures for reconstructing the wording of the original text (Π) behind the medieval text form (π):
11 καὶ (after ἐρριζωμένον) ○ *h* ‖ τοιοῦτον (→ δ → π) > τοιοῦτο *h r/cs* ‖
12 καὶ φοβεροῦ ∩ *s h* ‖ σῶμα (before νικηφόρον) > σῆμα *h* ‖

13 ἐπειδὴ δὲ οἱ βάρβαροι τὰ μὲν πεπονηκότες, τὰ δ᾽ ἀφωπλισμένοι, τὰ δὲ πεφοβημένοι, τραπέντες ἔφυγον εἰς τὰς ναῦς καὶ τὴν θάλασσαν περιέβλεπον ἄβατον αὐτοῖς Καλλιμάχου τὴν γῆν πεποιηκότος, πολλὴ μὲν ἦν τοῖς βουλομένοις σχολή, εἷς δὲ τῶν ἀκολουθησάντων ἐπὶ τὸν αἰγιαλὸν ἐγένετο Κυναίγειρος καί τινος ἁπτόμενος ἀκροστολίου τὴν χεῖρα ἀπεκόπη ῥᾳδίως ὥσπερ παιδίον καὶ περὶ μὲν τὴν πρύμναν ἔπεσεν ἡ χείρ, περὶ δὲ τὴν χεῖρα αὐτός· ἐμήνυσε δὲ τὸ τῆς χειρὸς τραῦμα ψυχῆς καὶ σώματος τὴν ἀσθένειαν. **14** σὺ δέ, ὦ τέκνον, εἱστήκεις ἔτι καὶ Δάτιδος ἀποπλέοντος ὥσπερ καὶ ταῦτα ἀνδρείως ἐπιτηρῶν, τῶν βαρβάρων τὴν φυγὴν καὶ καθαρὸν γενέσθαι τὸν Μαραθῶνα τῶν πολεμίων, ὡς ἂν ἐπὶ μηδενὸς μάρτυρος ἀλλοτρίου πέσῃς.

15 ταῦτά με ἐπὶ τὸν τάφον ἀναβιβάζει, ταῦτά μοι τὸν ἐπιτάφιον λόγον παραδίδωσιν· ἐμόν ἐστι τοῦ τάφου τὸ κεφάλαιον. τὸν μὲν δὴ μόγις ἐκίνησα καὶ κεῖσθαι σὺν τοῖς στρατιώταις παρεκάλεσα· ὁ δὲ εἰσέρχεται μὲν εἰς τὸν τάφον, ἄξιος δὲ ὑμῖν καὶ ταύτης τῆς τιμῆς τὸν πατέρα τὸν ἐκείνου

---

13 ἐπειδὴ δὲ Ο β Ι > ἐπεὶ δὲ Α ≥ ἐπειδ᾽ δὲ Αᶜ | > ἐπείδ᾽ μ Ε HD | > ἐπεὶ δ᾽ CN P ‖ τὰ μὲν Ο Β ‖ πεπονηκότες > πεποιηκότες RQ ≥ πεπονηκότες ‖ δ᾽ ⇌ δὲ QR ‖ τὰ δὲ πεφοβημένοι Ο η ‖ τὰ δὲ πεφοβημένοι, τραπέντες ἔφυγον εἰς τὰς ναῦς καὶ τὴν θάλασσαν περιέβλεπον ἄβατον αὐτοις Ο Ι ‖ περιέβλεπον > περὶ ἔπ D ≥ περΐἔβλεπον Dᶜ ‖ τὴν Ο Ι ‖ γῆν + ταῦτα Ι ‖ πεποιηκότος > πεπονηκότες D ‖ ἦν > οὖν QR | > ἡ δὲ Μ | Ο Β ‖ βουλομένοις > βαλομένοις CN ‖ σχολή > σπουδὴ CN ‖ ἐπὶ τὸν αἰγιαλὸν γ Ι Μ Ο FKG ε ‖ ἀκροστολίου γ Ι ⇌ ἀκροστόλου μ CN HP Eu Di ‖ περὶ > παρὰ ΑΟ ‖ ἔπεσεν > ἀνέπεσεν Ι ‖ περὶ > παρὰ ΑΟ ‖ αὐτὸς > αὐτοῖς RQ ≥ αὐτὸς Q²ᵐᵍ ‖ δὲ Ο QR ‖
14 εἱστήκεις ⇌ ἑστήκεις G ‖ ὥσπερ καὶ > περὶ RQ ≥ ὥσπερ καὶ Q²ᵐᵍ ‖ ταῦτα γ Ι > ταύτην FKG Ε ηQ² | > ταύτῃ CN | Md ‖ ἐπιτηρῶν τῶν βαρβάρων γ Ι Μ ∩ 231 FKG ε ‖ καθαρὸν > καθαρὰν QR ‖ τὸν > τὴν RQu ‖ ἐπὶ > ὑπὸ QR ‖ πέσῃς δ Ι ⇌ πεσούσης γ ‖
15 ταῦτά με ΑΟ MFK P ⇌ ταῦτα με β Ι Ε CN HD G ‖ ταῦτά μοι ΑΟ Β μ ⇌ ταῦτα μοι QR Ι ε ‖ παραδίδωσι FKG P ‖ ἐστι ⇌ ἐστιν Ο P | τὸν > τὸ D ‖ μόγις > μόλις HPQ² ‖ κεῖσθαι σὺν τοῖς στρατιώταις ∩ 2341 QR ‖ τοῖς > ταῖς D ‖ τὸν τάφον > αὐτὸν η ‖ δὲ (after ἄξιος) + καὶ D ‖ ὑμῖν > ἡμῖν Μ ‖ τῆς Ο QR ‖

13 Then the barbarians — in some cases worn out, in other cases disarmed, and in other cases terrified — turned and fled to the ships; and they were looking to the sea [for rescue] because Callimachus had made the land impassable for them. On the one hand, for those wishing [to pursue] there was plenty of opportunity, on the other hand one of those following to the beach was Cynegirus and when he grabbed hold of some ornament [of a ship] he got his hand cut off easily — just like a little child! The hand fell by the stern, and he himself [fell] by the hand. And the wound of his hand revealed the weakness of [his] soul and body. *14* But you, O child, had still stood, even though Datis was sailing away, courageously supervising as it were also these things, [namely,] the flight of the barbarians and Marathon being purged of the enemies, as if you would not fall in the presence of any foreign witness.

15 These things legitimate my going up on to the grave, these things bestow on me the funeral oration. The chief part of the funeral ceremony is mine. Him then I barely moved and exhorted to lie [dead] with the soldiers, yet he enters into the grave. But at your hands he is worthy even of this honor, [namely] that his own father be chosen to speak over the common

---

Editorial conjectures for reconstructing the wording of the original text (Π) behind the medieval text form (π):

    13 βουλομένοις ... + διώκειν *p j r/cs* ‖ or βουλομένοις > φοβουμένοις *j* | > ἡγουμένοις *h* ‖
    14 πέσῃς > πέσειας *o* | > πεσοίης *h* ‖
    15 ταῦτά με / ταῦτά μοι > ταῦτ᾽ ἐμὲ / ταῦτ᾽ ἐμοὶ *h* ‖

προκριθέντα λέγειν ἐπὶ τῷ κοινῷ σήματι. **16** καὶ γὰρ δίκαιον οὗ ζῶντος ἦν ἡ

κατὰ τὸν πόλεμον ἡγεμονία, τούτου καὶ τεθνεῶτος εἶναι τὰς πρώτας τιμὰς

ἐπὶ τῷ τάφῳ. ἡμεῖς ἤγομεν, ἡμεῖς ἐροῦμεν· ἡμεῖς ὡπλίζομεν, ἡμεῖς

ἐπαινεσόμεθα· παρ᾿ ἡμῶν ἦν τὰ συνθήματα, παρ᾿ ἡμῶν ἔστω καὶ τὰ

ἐγκώμια. **17** μὴ λυπήσητε Καλλίμαχον συνιέντα μὴ **δὲ** καθέλητε τὸν

ἀνεστηκότα μὴ δὲ ἀποχειροτονήσητε τὸν πολέμαρχον τὸν νενικηκότα μὴ δὲ

ἀτιμότερος ἑνὸς καὶ δευτέρου τῶν νενικηκότων παρ᾿ **ὑμῖν** ὀφθῇ. οὐ γὰρ ἐν

τοῖς ὀνόμασι καὶ τοῖς σχήμασι καὶ τῇ στολῇ ἀγγέλλεσθαι χρὴ μόνον τὴν

πολεμαρχίαν ἀλλὰ καὶ ταῖς τῶν ἔργων τιμαῖς ἀξιοῦσθαι τὰς ἀρχάς. **18**

οὕτως οὖν σκοπεῖτε. εἰ τῆς μάχης οἱ παῖδες ἡμῶν περιγενόμενοι τῆς

παρούσης ἠμφισβήτουν τάξεως, τίς **πρότερος** ἂν διεκρίθη; ὁ ἰδιώτης ἢ ὁ

πολέμαρχος; τίς ἐπῄνεσε τοὺς πεσόντας; οὐχ ὁ πιάσας; οὐχ ὁ τάξας; οὐχ

ὁ τοιούτους παρασχών; ἐμοὶ μὲν δοκεῖ. ὑμεῖς δέ, τί; ἆρα οὐκ ἄν, εἰ καὶ

μόνον **ἴσην τὴν ἀρετὴν** ὁ πολέμαρχος τῷ ἰδιώτῃ παράσχῃ, τὸ πλέον ἂν τῆς

---

15 **προκριθέντα λέγειν** ∩ QR ‖ **τῷ κοινῷ σήματι** > τοῦ κοινοῦ σήματος η ‖
σήματι > σώματι M QR ‖
16 **ἡ** Ο M ‖ **τὸν** Ο O QR ‖ **τῷ τάφῳ** γ > τὸν τάφον δ I ‖ **ἐροῦμεν**
δ Q²ᵐᵍ > εὕρομεν γ I ‖ **ὡπλίζομεν** ≠ ὁπλίζομεν HP ‖
17 **λυπήσητε** > λυπήσῃ R ‖ **Καλλίμαχον** Ο D ‖ **συνιέντα** ≠ συνιθέντα
Q ≥ συνιέντα Qᶜ ‖ **δὲ** (before καθέλητε) γ Ο δ I ‖ **καθέλητε** ≠ καθέληται O
≥ καθέλητε Oᶜ ‖ **μὴ** (after ἀνεστηκότα) > καὶ P ‖ **δὲ** (before ἀποχειροτονήσητε)
≐ δ᾿ G ‖ **ἀποχειροτονήσητε** ≥ additional τε written above the -τε ending QR ‖
≥ ἀποχειροτανήσητε Aᶜ ‖ > ἀτιμότερος N ≥ ἀποχειροτονήσητε Nᶜ ‖
ἀποχειροτονήσητε τὸν πολέμαρχον τὸν νενικηκότα μὴ δὲ Ο I ‖ **νενικηκότα** ≠
ἐνικηκότα D ‖ ≠ ἐνικότα RQ ≥ ἐνικηκότα Q² ‖ **δὲ** (before ἀτιμότερος) ≐ δ᾿
QR ‖ **τῶν** ≠ τῶ B ≥ τῶν Bᶜ ‖ **ὑμῖν** AO B I > ἡμῖν δ ‖ > ὑμῶν RQ ≥
ὑμῖν Q² ‖ **ὀφθῇ** > ὀφθείη B ‖ **τοῖς σχήμασι καὶ** Ο Q ≥ τοῖς σχήμασι καὶ Q²ᵐᵍ
‖ **σχήμασι** + καὶ τοῖς ὀνόμασι O ‖ **τῇ στολῇ** > ταῖς στολαῖς η ‖
ἀγγέλλεσθαι I μ E CN H QR ≠ ἀγγέλεσθαι B P ‖ > ἀγάλλεσθαι AO D ‖
ἀξιοῦσθαι > αὔξεσθαι AO ‖
18 **οὕτως** > οὔτι I ‖ **ἡμῶν** > ὑμῶν QR B ≥ ἡμῶν Bᶜ ‖ **περιγενόμενοι**
> παραγενόμενοι ε ‖ **τάξεως** ≠ τάξεος G ‖ ≠ τόξεως M ‖ **πρότερος** AO
B (→ γ?) > πρῶτος δ QR ‖ > πρῶτον I ‖ **ὁ** (before πολέμαρχος) Ο G ‖
πιάσας AO ε Q²ᵐᵍ > κοπιάσας β I ‖ > ῥίσας M ‖ > παρακαλέσας FKG
‖ **ἆρα** ≠ ἄρα A I G ‖ **μόνον** > μόνην μ ‖ **ἴσην τὴν ἀρετὴν** γ I ∩ 231 δ
‖ **παράσχῃ** > παράσχοι RQu ‖ > παράσει D ≥ παράσχῃ Dᶜ ‖ **πλέον** ≐
πλεῖον QR ‖ **τῆς** Ο BR ‖

grave. *16* For [it is] right that the leadership for the war was his while he was living and that the first honors at the funeral be his now that he has died. We were leading; we will speak. We were equipping for war; we will give the laudatio. From us were the signals for battle; let also the eulogies be from us. *17* Do not grieve Callimachus [who is] cognizant, do not pull down the one who stood erect, do not vote against the general-in-chief who won the victory, and let him not be viewed by you as less honorable than one even second [best] of the victors. For the office of general-in-chief ought to be made known not only by the titles and the appearances and the uniform, but the authorities [ought] to be esteemed also by the honors [accorded to] the[ir] deeds. *18* Therefore, look at [it] this way: If our sons had survived the battle and had disputed about the ranking today, who would have been distinguished first? The private or the general-in-chief? Who would have praised the fallen? [Would it] not [be] the one who pressed [them] hard [in training]? [Would it] not [be] the one who marshaled [them]? [Would it] not [be] the one who produced such [soldiers]? It seems [so] to me. And you, what [do you think]? Would you not, even if the general-in-chief exhibited merely the same valor as the private, [would you not] give most of the honor to the high command? By

---

Editorial conjectures for reconstructing the wording of the original text (II) behind the medieval text form (π):

18 πιάσας > ὁπλίσας *h* ‖

τιμῆς τῇ ἡγεμονίᾳ δῶτε; νὴ Δία. **19** οὐκοῦν ἤν, εἴπερ ἦσαν ἀμφότεροι,

προτίμησιν ἔσχε Καλλίμαχος, ταύτην καὶ τεθνεὼς δίκαιος φέρεσθαι· ἐκ γὰρ

ὧν ἦν κρείττων Κυναιγείρου περιὼν περιόντος, ταῦτα καὶ νῦν ἔχει καὶ τὸ

προκεκρίσθαι δοκεῖν δι' ἐμοῦ τοῦ πατρὸς αὐτῷ προτιμωμένου τῶν ἄλλων

πατέρων ὑπάρξει. εἰ δὲ οὐδὲ τὰ τοιαῦτα ἔσται παρὰ τῷ πολέμῳ τεθνηκότι,

ποίων τεύξεται; προεδρία τίς ἔσται αὐτῷ ἐπομένῳ; προετάττετο τῶν

ὀνομάτων τῶν ἐν ταῖς στήλαις γραφομένων πρῶτος {διότι πρεσβύτερος

τούτων ἦν} ἀπὸ τῆς οἰκείας αὐτοῦ γενέσεως, καὶ διὰ τοῦτο δεῖ τὸν ἐπὶ τοῖς

θαπτομένοις λόγον εἰωθότα ἡμῶν ἀκούειν λεγόντων. **20** ὑμεῖς τοιγαροῦν

τὸν στρατηγὸν Μιλτιάδην ἐτιμήσατε θείῳ στεφάνῳ. δικαίως οὖν καὶ τῷ

στρατηγῷ τιμή τις ἐδόθη καὶ τῷ πολεμάρχῳ δὲ γενέσθω γέρας. ὅταν γὰρ ὁ

πατὴρ αὐτοῦ λέγων τὸν λόγον ἀναβιβάσῃ Καλλίμαχον, τότε φωνὴν αὐτῷ

δότε ἐπὶ **τοῦτο** πρὸς πίστιν σωτηρίας μόνον ἐν τῷ σχήματι. **21** εἰ μὲν γὰρ

Μιλτιάδης ὁ στρατηγὸς ἠμφισβήτει τοῦ λόγου, παρεχώρησα ὡς ἀρχῇ

μείζονι· καὶ γὰρ τὸ τὸν ἀποιχόμενον ἄρχοντα ἔλαττον ἢ πρότερον γέρας

---

18 τιμῆς Ο Β ‖ τῇ ἡγεμονίᾳ Α Ι δ > τῆς ἡγεμονίας Ο Β | > τῷ
ἡγεμόνι QR ‖
19 ἤν > ἂν Ο ‖ εἴπερ ἦσαν γ Ι μ > εἰ περιῆσαν ε ‖ δίκαιος >
δικαιότερος D ‖ **Κυναιγείρου** > Κυναίγειρος Μ ≥ Κυναιγείρου Μᶜ | Ο D ‖
αὐτῷ γ Ι > αὐτοῦ δ ‖ **προτιμωμένου** ⇌ προτιμουμένου Ν ≥ προτιμωμένου Νᶜ
| > πρωτιμωμένῳ QR ‖ **προτιμωμένου τῶν ἄλλων** ∩ 231 QR ‖ **πατέρων** Ο
Μ ‖ **ὑπάρξει** > ὑπάρξειν Κ ‖ **δὲ** γ Ι ≑ δ' δ ‖ **παρὰ τῷ πολέμῳ τεθνηκότι
ποίων τεύξεται προεδρία τίς ἔσται** Ο D ‖ **τεθνηκότι** > τεθνηκότος RQ ≥
τεθνηκότι Q² ‖ **προεδρία** ≑ προεδρεία Α ‖ **τίς** Α ΒR Ι ΜFΚ Ε HP > τὶς Q G
CNu | > τῖς Ο ‖ **τῶν ὀνομάτων** γ Ο δ Ι ‖ **ταῖς** Ο η ‖ **πρῶτος** ⇌ πρῶτο
C ≥ πρῶτον Cᶜ ‖ **καὶ** Ο Β ‖ **δεῖ** + τὸ δεῖ Q ▬ Qᶜ ‖ **ἐπὶ** > ἐπιτάφιον Ν
‖ **τοῖς θαπτομένοις λόγον** ∩ 312 Ν ‖ **εἰωθότα** ⇌ εἰωθῶτα D ‖
20 ὑμεῖς > ἡμεῖς Μ ‖ **τὸν** (after τοιγαροῦν) Ο Μ ‖ **Μιλτιάδην** ⇌
Μιτιάδην C ≥ Μιλτιάδην Cᶜ ‖ **δὲ** γ Ο δ Ι ‖ **ἀναβιβάσῃ** > ἀναβιβάσει Ν
| ⇌ ἀναβηβάσῃ D ‖ **φωνὴν** > φωνικὴν R | > φῶσιν Μ ‖ **αὐτῷ** > αὐτὸν
Μ ‖ **τοῦτο** ΑΟ Ι ΜF > τούτῳ β ΚG ε ‖ **πίστιν** ⇌ πίστην C ‖ **μόνον** >
μόνῳ QR ‖
21 ἠμφισβήτει ⇌ ἠμφισβήτη CN ‖ **γὰρ** (after μείζονι· καὶ) Ο ΑΟ ‖ **τὸ**
(after γὰρ) Ο D ‖ **τὸ τὸν** > τοῦτον ΑΟ | > τὸ σὸν QR ‖ **ἄρχοντα** + καὶ
ΑΟ ‖

Zeus, [of course you would]! *19* Therefore, that preeminence which, if both were [alive], Callimachus would have had, even though he has died [should be] his by right. Accordingly then he, if he had survived, would be superior to Cynegirus if he had survived. These things are [so] even now, and the appearance of having been chosen will accrue to him through me the father if I am chosen before the other fathers. And if not even these sorts of things will be [the case] with the one who has died in war, what [other] sorts of things will he meet with? Will there be any front seat privilege for him when he has escorts? He used to be placed first when the names were written on the *steles* {because he was older than them} by reason of his family origin. And on account of this it is necessary to hear us speaking the customary word over those being buried. *20* You accordingly honored the general, Miltiades, with a sacred wreath. Rightly in fact some honor was given even to the general; let there be then also for the general-in-chief a recognition. For when his father, in giving the speech, elevates Callimachus, then give him a voice for this [namely] regarding assurance of preservation only in the appearance. *21* For if in fact Miltiades, the general, had laid claim to the speech I would have yielded as to greater authority. For [that] the departed commander [should] have less recognition than formerly ... it is fair [that] what is lacking of

---

Editorial conjectures for reconstructing the wording of the original text (II) behind the medieval text form (π):

19 δι᾽ ἐμοῦ τοῦ πατρὸς αὐτῷ προτιμωμένου τῶν αλλῶν πατέρων ὑπάρξει   >
ὑπάρξει αὐτῷ δι᾽ ἐμοῦ πατρὸς (αὐτοῦ) τῶν ἄλλων πατέρων προτιμωμένου   ο   ‖   ἔσται
παρὰ τῷ πολέμῳ   >   ἔσται τῷ πολεμάρχῳ   ο | παρέσται τῷ πολεμάρχῳ   h |
ἔσται παρὰ τῷ ἐν πολέμῳ   jü   ‖   τίς   >   τις   h   r/cs   ‖   διότι πρεσβύτερος τούτων ἦν
Ο   h   r/cs   ‖

20 στεφάνῳ. δικαίως οὖν καὶ   >   στεφάνῳ· δικαίως· εἰ οὖν   p   j   ‖   δὲ (after
πολεμάρχῳ)   >   δὴ   j   ‖   δότε ἐπὶ τοῦτο   >   δώσετε λείπουσαν   p   j | δότε ἐπὶ ...
(lacuna) ... τοῦτο   [→ δότε επι{φεροντες λεῖπον} τοῦτο]   h   ‖

21 τὸ τὸν ἀποιχόμενον ἄρχοντα ἔλαττον ἢ πρότερον γέρας σχεῖν εἰκός   >   τοῦτον
ἀποιχόμενον ἄρχοντα οὐκ ἔδει ἔλαττον ἢ πρῶτον γέρας σχεῖν, εἰκὸς γαρ   ο | τοι τὸν
ἀποιχόμενον [ἀπερχόμενον   h]   ἀκοῦντα ἔλαττον ἢ πρότερον γέρας σχεῖν, εἰκός   j   ‖
τοι τὸν ἀποιχόμενον ἄρχοντα ἔλαττον ἢ πρότερον γέρας σχεῖν οὐ συγχωρεῖν εἰκός   jü   ‖

σχεῖν ... εἰκός ἐστι τὸ τῆς μοίρας ἐνδεὲς τῷ πλείονι τῆς τιμῆς

παραμυθουμένης· τούτου δὲ τῆς πείρας ταύτης ἀφεστηκότος τίς

Καλλιμάχου πρότερός ἐστιν; 22 Εὐφορίων, μὴ λύε τάξιν Μαραθωνίαν· μὴ

δ᾽ ... εἰς τὸ πρόσθεν τῷ πολεμάρχῳ δίδωσι **τὸν λόγον ὁ νόμος** τῆς δημοσίας

ταφῆς. καὶ γὰρ εἰ περιὼν **τύχοι**, οὗτός ἐστιν ὁ τὴν πρόθεσιν αὐτῶν

ποιούμενος καὶ καλῶν ἐπὶ τὸν λόγον καὶ παντὸς ἐπιμελούμενος τοῦ τάφου.

23 ἐκ μὲν δὴ τῆς διὰ τῶν ἔργων ... πολλοῦ δεῖ Κυναιγείρῳ πρὸς

Καλλίμαχον εἶναι **παραβολήν**· ὁ μὲν γὰρ ἅπαντας εἰς Μαραθῶνα ἦγε

συνθήματι, ὁ δὲ ἐδέχετο· ὁ μὲν ἐκέλευεν, ὁ δὲ ἐπείθετο· ὧν δ᾽ οἱ πειθόμενοι

καὶ κελευόμενοι ποιοῦσιν, αἴτιοι τούτων οἱ πείσαντες καὶ κελεύσαντές εἰσιν

ὥσπερ μαθητῶν μὲν παιδεύσεως οἱ διδάσκαλοι, χορῶν δὲ ᾠδῆς οἱ

χοροδιδάσκαλοι, ναυτῶν δὲ εὐπλοίας οἱ κυβερνῆται στρατιωτῶν ἀρετῆς οἱ

πολέμαρχοι και στρατηγοί, ὥσθ᾽ ὧν Κυναίγειρος ἐτόλμησε, καὶ τούτων

Καλλίμαχος διδάσκαλος. ἐβόα γὰρ ἐγκελευόμενος·

Μὴ φείδεσθε μήτε χειρῶν μήτε ὀφθαλμῶν μήτε ὅλων σωμάτων.

ὧν δὲ Καλλίμαχος ἐλαμπρύνετο, τούτων οὐδὲν οὔτε εἰς Κυναίγειρον οὔτε εἰς

ἄλλον ἔστι ποιήσασθαι τὴν ἀναφορὰν ἀλλὰ μόνον αὐτὸν τὸν πεποιηκότα.

---

21 παραμυθουμένης > παραμυθουμένους AO | > παραμυθεῖσθαι RQ ≥ παραμυθουμένης Q²ᵐᵍ ‖
22 μὴ δ᾽ ± μηδ᾽ Q ‖ τῷ > τοῦ AO ‖ **δίδωσι** γ I ± δίδωσιν δ ‖ **τὸν λόγον ὁ νόμος** γ I ∩ 3412 δ ‖ **ταφῆς** Ο D ‖ **τύχοι** AO B FKG > τύχῃ I M E CN HP QR | ≠ τύχ ̤ D ‖ **τὸν** > τῶν P ≥ τὸν Pᶜ ‖ **ἐπιμελούμενος** FKG ± ἐπιμελόμενος ε Q² | > ἐπικαλούμενος γ I M ‖ τοῦ γ I Ο δ ‖
23 Κυναιγείρῳ > Κυναίγειρος M ‖ **παραβολήν** FKG ε > παραβολῆς γ I | > παραβολῇ M ‖ ὁ μὲν γὰρ > ...μ ̤ Pi ‖ ἦγε ± ἦγεν A ‖ ἐδέχετο + καὶ QR ‖ **ἐκέλευεν** ± ἐκέλευε D ‖ δ᾽ οἱ > δὴ G ‖ αἴτιοι > αἴτιον B ‖ τούτων > τούτους RQ ≥ τούτων Q² ‖ **τούτων οἱ** ∩ QR ‖ μαθητῶν > μαθητοῦ M ‖ **παιδεύσεως** γ I > κελεύσεως δ Q²ᵐᵍ ‖ χορῶν δὲ ᾠδῆς οἱ χοροδιδάσκαλοι Ο D RQ ≥ χορῶν δὲ ᾠδῆς οἱ χοροδιδάσκαλοι Q²ᵐᵍ ‖ στρατιωτῶν + δὲ δ I Q² ‖ ὥσθ᾽ ± ὥστ᾽ G | > ἀνθ᾽ M ‖ ὧν (after ὥσθ᾽) + ὁ E CN ‖ ἐτόλμησε ± ἐτόλμησεν A ‖ φείδεσθε > φείδεσθαι CN D MGF ≥ φείδεσθε Fᶜ ‖ μήτε χειρῶν μήτε ὀφθαλμῶν AO B I ∩ 3412 δ QR ‖ ἔστι Ο M ‖ τὸν Ο R ‖

[life's] portion [is made up for] by the plus of consoling honor. But now that he has refrained from this undertaking, who is ahead of Callimachus? **22** Euphorion, don't keep on annulling the Marathonian ranking. And don't [keep on annulling the ranking] at the forefront — the custom of the public burial gives the speech to the general-in-chief. For even if he should happen to survive, he is the one who takes care of the laying-out of the [corpses] and invites to the speech and takes charge of the entire funeral.

23 Certainly from the [vantage point] through the deeds ... there has to be a comparison of much with Cynegirus vis-à-vis Callimachus. The one was leading everyone to Marathon with a slogan for battle, the other was heeding; the one was commanding, the other was obeying. [The] reasons why the [ones] who obey and are commanded do things, are those [leaders] who persuade and command — just as the teachers [are the reasons] for education of students, and the choir-teachers [are the reasons] for singing of choirs, and the helmsmen [are the reasons] for good sailing of seamen, [thus] the generals-in-chief and generals [are the reasons] for valor of soldiers. Therefore, Callimachus [was] teacher also of those things which Cynegirus dared [to do]. For he was shouting and urging on,

"Don't spare hands or eyes or whole bodies!"

And for those things by which Callimachus was distinguishing himself the credit is in no way to be given to Cynegirus or to another but alone [to] him

---

Editorial conjectures for reconstructing the wording of the original text (Π) behind the medieval text form (π):

21 σχεῖν followed by lacuna [+ οἰκτείρειν ?] *h* ‖ **Καλλιμάχου** + πατρὸς *j* ‖

22 μὴ δ' followed by lacuna [+ λύε τὴν τάξιν ?] *r/cs* ‖ μὴ δ' εἰς τὸ **πρόσθεν** τῷ πολεμάρχῳ > μηδενὶ πρόσθεν τοῦ πολεμάρχου *s* ‖ αὐτῶν ○ *h* ‖

23 ἔργων followed by lacuna [+ κρίσεως ?] *h* [+ ὄψεως ?] *r/cs* ‖ στρατιωτῶν ἀρετῆς οἱ πολέμαρχοι καὶ στρατηγοί ○ *h* ‖ οὐδὲν > οὐδενὸς *s* | ○ *h* ‖

24 καὶ Κυναίγειρος μὲν νεώτερος ὢν ταῦτα ἠυθαδιάσατο, Καλλίμαχος δὲ

πρεσβύτερος, ὥσθ᾽ ὁ μὲν ἡλικίας θερμότητι τολμηρός, ὁ δὲ ἀνὴρ ἀγαθὸς ὢν

ἀρετῆς ἐβεβαίου κρίσιν καὶ τὴν τοῦ σώματος ῥώμην ἐλάττων καθ᾽ ἡλικίαν

ὑπάρχων ἐκ μόνης ἀρετῆς ὑπερέβαλε. **25** Καλλίμαχος μὲν οὖν ἐν τῇ τῶν

δεινῶν ἀκμῇ τοῖς βαρβάροις παρετάξατο καὶ θαλάττης ἐπιχωριαζούσης

δίκην ἐκ τῆς Ἤλιδος εἰς τὴν Ἀττικὴν τὴν Ἀσίαν ῥέουσαν ἀπεώσατο, ἐν ᾧ

πᾶς ὁ κίνδυνος καὶ τῆς ἀρετῆς ὁ καιρὸς ἦν· **26** Κυναίγειρος δὲ φευγόντων

ἤδη πεφοβημένων, ὑπὸ τοῦ Καλλιμάχου τετραμμένων, δεδιωγμένων, εἰς τὴν

θάλατταν συνεληλαμένων, ἐν ταῖς ναυσὶν ὄντων, λυόντων τὰ ἀπόγεια μιᾶς

νεὼς πρύμνης. ἔστι δὲ τὸ μὲν ἄκρας εὐτυχίας καὶ περιττῆς τινος ἀρετῆς

τῶν κρατίστων πολέμων αὐτοὺς ὑφίστασθαι, τὸ δὲ παντὸς ἤδη καὶ τοῦ

τυχόντος διώκειν τὸν φεύγοντα καὶ τοῖς τετραμμένοις ἐπεμβαίνειν. **27**

οὕτω γὰρ δὴ καὶ γυναῖκες ἀνδράσιν ἐπιτίθενται καὶ κύνες κατὰ λεόντων

θρασύνονται. ὅταν γὰρ τὸ τῶν πολεμίων φοβερὸν οἴχηται, τότε παντὶ

τολμᾶν πρόχειρον καὶ τὸ φρόνημα τῶν ἑλόντων γίνεται οὐκ ἐξ οἰκείας

---

24 ὢν > ὧν R ‖ ἠυθαδιάσατο ΑΟ Bᶜ Μ P ≐ ἠυθαδειάσατο Ι FG E CN H
| ≐ ἠυθαδει.σατο D | ⇌ ἠνθαδιάσατο R | ⇌ ἠυθαυδειάσατο Κ | ⇌
ἠυθαδιάσατο B ≥ ἠυθαδιάσατο Bᶜ ‖ **θερμότητι** > θερμότατος Μ | ≥
θερμότατος Q² ▬ Q²ᶜ ‖ δὲ (before ἀνήρ) γ Ι ≐ δ᾽ δ ‖ **ἀρετῆς** (after ὢν) >
ἀρετὴ CN | ╋ δ᾽ C | ╋ δ Ν ‖ **ἐβεβαίου** > βεβαίου ΑΟ | ╋ τὴν CN
‖ **τὴν** Ο RQ ≥ τὴν Q² ‖ **ῥώμην** ⇌ ῥύμην RQ ≥ ῥώμην Qᶜ ‖ **ἐλάττων** >
οὐκ ἀλάττων RQ ≥ ἐλάττων Q²ᵐᵍ ‖ **ὑπερέβαλε** δ Ι ≠ ὑπερέβαλλε γ ‖
25 **παρατάξατο** γ Ι > ἀντετάξατο δ Q² ‖ **θαλάττης** γ ≐ θαλάσσης δ Ι
‖ **ἀπεώσατο** ⇌ ἀπώσατο Ν ‖ ὁ (after πᾶς) Ο Ι ‖ **ὁ καιρὸς** Ο Κ ‖
26 **ὑπὸ τοῦ** > δῒ αὐτοῦ D ‖ **τετραμμένων** ⇌ τετράμμων G | >
τετραυματισμένων Ι ‖ **δεδιωγμένων** Ο Q ≥ δεδιωγμένων Q²ᵐᵍ ‖ **τὴν** Ο G ≥
τὴν Gᶜᵐᵍ ‖ **θάλατταν** β Ι ≐ θάλασσαν ΑΟ δ ‖ **ἀπόγεια** > ὑπόγεια Κ RQ ≥
ἀπόγεια Q²ᵐᵍ | > ἅπαντα Μ ‖ **νεὼς** ╋ ἔσχε QR ‖ **πρύμνης** > πρύμναν
QR ‖ **ἔστι** > ἔτι QR ‖ **δὲ** > μὲν P ≥ δὲ Pᶜ ‖ **πολέμων** > πολέμους ΗΡ
| > πολεμίων FKG ‖ **ὑφίστασθαι** > ὑφίσταται D ‖ **τὸν** Ο QR ‖ **φεύγοντα**
> φύγοντα Ι | > φεύγοντας QR ‖ **τοῖς** Ο G QR ‖ **τετραμμένοις**
> τετραμμένης Q ≥ τετραμμένοις Q² ‖
27 **δὴ** Ο μ ‖ **κατὰ** ⇌ κα Q ≥ κατὰ Q² ‖ **λεόντων** > ἐχόντων R ≥
λεόντων R² ‖ **οἴχηται** > οἴχεται P ‖ **παντὶ τολμᾶν** ∩ ε ‖ **φρόνημα** >
φρόντισμα Μ ‖

who has acted. *24* Further, since Cynegirus was younger, he did these things rashly, but Callimachus [was] older, so that the one [was] reckless by reason of [the] hot-headedness of youth, but the other, being a brave man, was securing a decision [on the basis] of valor; and although being weaker in bodily strength in accordance with [his] age he prevailed because of valor alone. *25* Callimachus then in the peak of the terrors positioned himself against the barbarians and he drove back Asia as it was streaming into Attica like [the] advancing sea of Elis, in which [situation] every danger was also an opportunity for valor. *26* After they were already fleeing — they had [already] been frightened, routed by Callimachus, pursued, and driven into the sea; they were [already] in the ships loosening the mooring cables — [it was *after* that when] Cynegirus [grabbed hold] of one ship's stern. It is one thing because of utter success and extraordinary valor to withstand those of the fiercest battles; it is [quite] another thing for every chance person to pursue someone [who is] already fleeing and to take advantage of those who have [already] been routed. *27* Thus, indeed, even women set upon men, and dogs are overly bold against lions. For whenever the dread of the enemy is gone, then for everyone [it is] easy to be daring and the high spirit of the [ones] winning arises not out of innate valor but [is] provided by the cowardice

---

Editorial conjectures for reconstructing the wording of the original text (Π) behind the medieval text form (π):

25 ἐκ τῆς Ἤλιδος > ἐκ τῆς Μιλήτου *o* | > ἐκ σύγκλυδος *j* | > σὺν ἤλιδι → συνήλυδα *h* | > ἐκ τῆς ἠόνος Ἤλιδος *jü* ‖

26 νεὼς + ἔσχετο *h r/cs* ‖ αὐτοὺς > ἀθλοὺς *h* ‖

ἀρετῆς ἀλλ᾽ ἐκ τῆς τοῦ πολεμίου κακότητος πεπορισμένον· ἀρετῆς δὲ ἀγὼν

ἐν ἀντιπάλῳ μὲν τῆς δυνάμεως, ἀσταθμήτῳ δὲ τῷ τῆς τύχης κρίνεται. ἃ μὲν

οὖν Καλλίμαχος ἠρίστευσεν ἐν τῷ χαλεπῷ τοῦ δρᾶν καὶ φοβερῷ τοῦ παθεῖν

ἐγένετο, ἃ δὲ ἠθέλησε Κυναίγειρος ἐξουσία μὲν τοῦ ποιεῖν ἦν, ἄδεια δὲ τοῦ

μὴ παθεῖν ἤδη τῶν πολεμίων τὸ χεῖρον ὡμολογηκότων καὶ τὴν ἀναγκαίαν

σωτηρίαν ποριζομένων φυγῇ.   28 ὅλως δὲ τὰ μὲν Κυναιγείρου Καλλίμαχος

παρεσκεύασεν· ἐκ γὰρ τῆς Καλλιμάχου μάχης **πρότερον** γενομένης

καταπλαγέντες οἱ βάρβαροι τὰ νῶτα δείξαντες παρεῖχον τοῖς αὖθις

ἐπιφερομένοις ῥᾳδίαν τὴν δίωξιν· τὰ δὲ Κυναιγείρου δεύτερα καὶ τελευταῖα

πεπραγμένα τῶν Καλλιμάχου λαμπρῶν ἀριστείαν αἰτεῖ.   29 ὥστε καὶ τὸν

τούτου λόγον τῷ θατέρῳ παρασχεῖν. δυνάμεώς ἐστιν ἔργον, οὐκ ἐπιδείξεως·

κράτιστον δὲ ἔργον τῆς τοιαύτης αἰτίας τὸ πρεσβύτατον δύναμις ἐστιν·

ἔργων γὰρ μὴ πρότερον **γενομένων** οὐκ ἂν εἴη ἐπίδειξις. ἀρχὴ δ᾽ οὐκ

ἄκαιρός τις ταῦτα καὶ τῶν ἐπ᾽ αὐτοῖς εὖ τεχνηθέντων αἰτία ὥσπερ τὰ

θεμέλια τῶν οἰκοδομημάτων καὶ τῶν νεῶν αἱ τρόπεις καὶ πάντα ὅσα πρῶτα

---

27 ἀλλ᾽ γ I ≐ ἀλλὰ δ ‖ ἐκ γ I ○ δ ‖ πολεμίου γ I > πολέμου δ ‖ κακότητος ≐ κακόττ I D ‖ ἐν (after ἀγὼν) ○ M ‖ μὲν ○ HP ‖ + τῷ μ ‖ ἀσταθμήτῳ > ἀσταθμήτου QR ‖ ⊤ ἐσταθμήτῳ N ‖ τῷ (after ἀσταθμήτῳ δὲ) > τὸ QR ‖ τύχης ΑΟ δ > τέχνης β I ‖ φοβερῷ ⊤ βοβερῷ Q ‖ μὲν τοῦ ∩ ΑΟ ‖ ἄδεια ⊤ ἀδεία QR | > ἀδεεῖ ΑΟ ‖ δὲ (after ἄδεια) ○ QR ‖ πολεμίων ≠ πολεμίω I ‖ χεῖρον > πρόχειρον M ‖ ὡμολογηκότων ⊤ ὁμολογηκότων D | > διωμολογηκότων QR ‖ καὶ τὴν ἀναγκαίαν σωτηρίαν ποριζομένων φυγῇ ○ I ‖ ποριζομένων ⊤ πορμένων Q ≥ ποριζομένων Q² ‖
28 μὲν Κυναιγείρου ∩ QR ‖ Καλλίμαχος > Καλλίμαχον Β ‖ παρεσκεύασεν > παρεσκεύασθαι QR ‖ πρότερον δ > προτέρας γ I ‖ νῶτα ⊤ νῶνωτα Q ≥ νῶτα Qᶜ ‖ ῥᾳδίαν FKG ε Q² > ῥᾳδίως γ I M ‖ Κυναιγείρου γ > Κυναιγείρῳ δ I ‖
29 τῳ γ I ○ δ ‖ θατέρῳ > θάτερον M ‖ παρασχεῖν > παρασχὼν ΑΟ ‖ δὲ γ I G ≐ δ᾽ MFK ε ‖ αἰτίας ○ Β ‖ πρεσβύτατον > πρεσβύτερον M ‖ δύναμις ⊤ δύμις RQ ≥ δύναμις Q² ‖ γὰρ ○ QR ‖ πρότερον > προτέρων Β | ≠ πρότερων C ‖ γενομένων ΑΟ δ > γινωμένων β I ‖ οὐκ (before ἄκαιρος) + ἂν G ‖ τις + ἦν ΑΟ ‖ ἐπ᾽ > μετ᾽ Β ‖ αὐτοῖς > αὐτῆς QR ‖ εὖ ○ CN | + τε ΑΟ | + γε Β ‖ αἰτία > αἰτίαν QR ‖ νεῶν ≐ νηῶν R ‖ τρόπεις ⊤ τρόπις Β I | > τρόπαι M | + ἔχει I ∎ Iᶜ ‖ πρῶτα > πρῶτον CN | ○ Q ≥ πρῶτα Q²ᵐᵍ ‖

of the enemy. A contest of valor is decided on the one hand by a struggle of might, on the other hand by the uncertainty of chance. What Callimachus bravely excelled at occurred in the hardship of action and the horror of suffering; by contrast what Cynegirus wanted was license to act but with exemption from suffering since the enemies who had already conceded the[ir] inferiority were also providing the necessary security by [their] flight. **28** In short, then, Callimachus prepared things for Cynegirus. Because of Callimachus' fight which took place first, the barbarians, panic-stricken [and] showing their backs, were making the pursuit easy for those attacking afterward. The [deeds] of Cynegirus done subsequently and at the end presuppose [the] prowess of Callimachus' brilliant [actions]. **29** Consequently the repute of this one (= Callimachus) produced [the repute] for the other (= Cynegirus). It is a deed of power, not of showing off. [The] best deed from such a cause is the oldest: might. For if deeds should not first take place, there would be no showing off. These things [were] a not inopportune beginning and cause for the [things] well executed [which were based] upon them, just as the foundations of buildings and the keels of ships and all things

---

Editorial conjectures for reconstructing the wording of the original text (II) behind the medieval text form (π):

29 τὸν τούτου > τοῦτο τὸν h ‖ θατέρῳ > θατέρου jü ‖ τὸ (before πρεσβύτατον) > καὶ o ‖ δύναμις ○ h ‖

καὶ τὴν ἀρχὴν ἰσχυρὰν ἔχει. **30** ὅπερ δὲ ἡ Μαραθωνικὴ δύναμις πρὸς τὰς αὖθις γενησομένας ἁπάσας κατὰ τῶν βαρβάρων, τοῦτο καὶ Κυναιγείρῳ τὰ Καλλιμάχου τολμήματα· διὰ γὰρ τοῦτον ἀνέπνευσαν οἱ λοιποὶ καὶ φεύγοντας ἰδόντες τοὺς βαρβάρους ἐθάρρησαν· πρὸς γὰρ τοῦτον ὁρῶν τις κᾶν ποδῶν καὶ χειρῶν ἤμελει τὸν ὅλου καὶ παντὸς ὑπεριδόντα τοῦ σώματος.

31 ἔτι δὲ Κυναίγειρος μὲν ἐκ γῆς πρὸς ναῦν ἐμάχετο, ἐκ τοῦ βεβαίου καὶ πολλοῦ πρὸς τὸν ἐν τῷ σφαλερῷ καὶ στενῷ, Καλλίμαχος δὲ πρὸς ἰσοστασίους αὐτῷ τοὺς βαρβάρους, ἤδη καὶ γῆς κυρίους, τοὺς ἀποβάντας ἐκ τῶν νεῶν καὶ τὸν Αἰγαῖον δεδουλωμένους καὶ τὴν κατάπληξιν φοβερὰν ἐπιφέροντας ἐκ τῆς τῶν συνειλημμένων Ἑλλήνων ἁρπαγῆς· **32** καὶ Κυναίγειρος μὲν ἴσως καὶ ζήλῳ τῷ πρὸς Καλλίμαχον καὶ φιλοτιμίᾳ, Καλλίμαχος δὲ οὐχ ὑπ' ἄλλου παρωξυμμένος οὐδὲ πρὸς ἕτερον φιλοτιμούμενος ἀλλ' αὐθαιρέτῳ σπουδῇ. καὶ Καλλίμαχος μὲν ἀρετῆς παράδειγμα, Κυναίγειρος δὲ Καλλιμάχου μίμημα, ὁ μὲν τὴν χεῖρα μόνην, ὁ δὲ ὅλα τὰ μέρη τοῦ σώματος· πᾶσι γὰρ μεμάχηται καὶ τοῦ πολέμου πάντα

---

30 **Μαραθωνικὴ δύναμις** > Μαραθῶνι νίκη ἐδυνάμωσε AO ‖ **τὰς** > τὰ R ‖ **τοῦτο** > τούτῳ D ‖ **καὶ** (after τοῦτο) AO QR ◯ B I δ ‖ **Κυναιγείρῳ** > Κυναιγείρου QR ‖ **ἀνέπνευσαν** ⫤ ἀνέπευσαν RQ ≥ ἀνέπνευσαν Q² ‖ **λοιποὶ** > πολλοὶ η ‖ **ὁρῶν τις** MG C P ≖ ὁρῶν τὶς I N H ‖ ✢ ὁρῶν τίς B FK E D ‖ > ὁρῶντες AO QR ‖ **κᾶν** > καὶ QR ‖ **ποδῶν καὶ χειρῶν** ⋂ 321 QR ‖ **ὅλου** > ὅλον QR ‖ **ὑπεριδόντα** > ἠμελήκότα QR ‖
31 **ἐκ γῆς** ◯ G ≥ ἐκ γῆς Gᶜᵐᵍ ‖ **ναῦν** ⫤ ναῦ RQ ≥ ναῦν Q²ᵐᵍ ‖ **τὸν** (after πρὸς) ◯ R ‖ **τῷ** γ I ◯ δ ‖ **στενῷ** ⫤ στεαρ B ≥ στενῷ Bᶜ ‖ **πρὸς** (before ἰσοστασίους) ✛ τοὺς D ‖ **ἰσοστασίους** ⫤ ἰσοσταδίους B ≥ ἰσοστασίους Bᶜ ‖ ⫤ στασίους D ≥ ἰσοστασίους Dᶜ ‖ **τοὺς** (before βαρβάρους) ◯ K ‖ > καὶ D ‖ **ἤδη** ⫤ ἤδε RQ ≥ ἤδη Qᶜ ‖ **κυρίους, τοὺς** γ I ◯ δ ‖ **ἀποβάντας** γ I > ἐπιβάντες δ ‖ **φοβερὰν** ⫤ φορὰν N ‖ ◯ O ‖ **ἁρπαγῆς** > ἁρπαγῶν E ‖
32 **πρὸς** (before Καλλίμαχον) ✛ τὸν QR ‖ **φιλοτιμίᾳ** > φιλοτιμήματι QR ‖ **δὲ** (after Καλλίμαχος) γ I ≐ δ' δ (Di) ‖ **οὐχ ὑπ'** ✢ οὐχὶ π' F ‖ οὐχ ἀπ' R ‖ **παρωξυμμένος** AO B > παροξυνόμενος δ (Di) I Q ‖ παραξυνόμενος R ‖ ✛ ˆ A ‖ **ἕτερον** ⫤ ἔτερον Q ‖ **μόνην** > μόνον QR M ‖ **πᾶσι** ◯ I ‖ **γὰρ** γ ◯ δ I ‖ **μεμάχηται** > μεμάχητο RQ ≥ μεμάχηται Q² ‖

which [come] first also have a beginning [which is] strong.   *30* And what the Marathonian might [meant] for all the [fights?] which would subsequently occur against the barbarians, the bold deeds of Callimachus [meant] this also for Cynegirus. For on account of him the rest caught their breath again and when they saw the barbarians fleeing they took courage.   For whenever anyone looked at him [who was] disregarding his whole and entire body, [that person] did not trouble himself at all about [his own] feet and hands.   *31* Moreover, Cynegirus was trying to fight from land against a ship, from the safe and open [spot] against the [enemy] in the perilous and confined [space]. Callimachus, however, [was fighting] against the barbarians [who were] on an equal footing with him and already masters of the land, who had disembarked from the ships and who had enslaved the Aegean, and who were bringing fearful terror by the[ir] plunder of the captured Greeks.   *32* And whereas Cynegirus probably [was spurred on] both by jealousy toward Callimachus and by ambition, Callimachus [was] not spurred on by another nor desirous to emulate someone else but [was spurred on] by independent zeal. Callimachus, on the one hand, [was] a model of valor, Cynegirus, on the other hand, [was] an imitation of Callimachus. The one [gave] only his hand, the other [gave] all the parts of his body. For he fought with all [his body parts] and all [were]

Editorial conjectures for reconstructing the wording of the original text (Π) behind the medieval text form (π):
30 Μαραθωνικὴ $+$ νίκη   *o*   ‖
31 τὸν (after πρὸς) $>$ τὴν   *h*   ‖

μείζονα. καὶ ὁ μὲν μιᾷ τῶν ἀναγομένων ἐπεχείρησε νηί, ὁ δὲ πρὸς πάνθ᾽

ὁμοῦ τὰ βασιλέως ἔθνη παρετάξατο. **33** ὁ μὲν ἀνόητον ὅλως τὴν ἐπιβολὴν

ἐποιήσατο· ἡ γὰρ ἐλπὶς αὐτῷ τῆς τόλμης ἀδύνατος ἦν. πῶς γὰρ χειρὶ νῆα

ἐλάβετο; τίς δὲ ἂν ἐγένετο τοσοῦτος τῇ δεξιᾷ ὥστε, εἰ μὲν ἠγνόησε

κατασχεῖν οὐ δυνησόμενος, ἀλλὰ προσεδόκησε βιάσασθαι τριήρη δακτύλοις;

ἠλίθιον τὸ τόλμημα. εἰ δ᾽ εἶδεν ὡς τὸ τῆς πείρας ἀδύνατον, ἀλλ᾽ ὡς ἐν τοῖς

ἀμηχάνοις τόλμα κρατεῖ, ἀλαζὼν ἡ προσποίησις ἦν. καὶ οὐκ ἀσφαλὴς οὐδὲ

ἀναγκαία ἡ ἐπίδειξις τοῦ ἀπόρου σχήματος καὶ ματαία ἡ σκέψις διότι οὔτε

ἀλαζὼν οὔτε ἀνόητος ἡ ἀρετή, οἷοι δὲ καὶ τυφλοὶ πόνοι πάντες οἱ περὶ τὰς

ἀδυνάτους ἐπιθυμίας. **34** χρὴ δὲ ὁρᾶν οὐδὲν πρότερον οὐδὲ τέχνην ἔργοις

ἐπιτιθεμένην οὔτε ἀρετὴν λόγοις ἀπειργομένην ὡς τέλος τῆς ἐπιχειρήσεως

εἰ δύνατον ἔτι καὶ ληπτὸν τῇ φύσει καὶ δυναμένῳ καὶ πειρωμένῳ ἀνδρί. ἡ δὲ

ναῦς ὅλη, μεστὴ πληρώματος καὶ τοσαύτης εἰρεσίας συγκεκροτημένης, πῶς

ἦν ἐπιλήψιμος, πῶς ἀγώγιμος τοσούτῳ ὄγκῳ τῆς ἐλπίδος καὶ τῇ προσβολῇ

---

32 καὶ (after μείζονα) Ο QR ‖ ἀναγομένων > ἀγομένων Ι Μ Q ≥
ἀναγομένων Q² ‖ ἐπεχείρησε > ἐπεχείρει QR | > ἐπικεχείρηκε Η | >
ἐπικεχείρηκεν Ρ ‖ νηί Ο η ‖ βασιλέως > βασίλεια Ε CN | > βασιλεῖα Ι
‖ παρετάξατο ⹃ παρετάξετο QR ‖
33 ἀνόητον ⹃ ἀνίητον R ‖ ἐπιβολὴν > ἐπιβουλὴν Ο Κ ‖ αὐτῷ > αὐτοῦ
QR ‖ νῆα ≙ ναῦν Μ ‖ ἐλάβετο > ἐβάλετο G ‖ δὲ γ Ι ≙ δ᾽ δ ‖ δὲ ἂν
> γὰρ QR ‖ ἠγνόησε ⹃ ἠγνώ. σε D ‖ οὐ Ο QR ‖ προσεδόκησε ≙
προσεδόκησεν Α ‖ βιάσασθαι ⹃ βιάσαθαι Ν | Ο ΗΡ ‖ δακτύλοις γ Ι >
δακτύλῳ δ Q² ‖ τὸ (before τόλμημα) Ο Ν ‖ εἶδεν > οἶδεν QR ‖ ἀλλ᾽ ὡς δ
Ι QR > ἄλλως ΑΟ Β ‖ τοῖς > τῆς R ‖ τόλμα > τόλμημα QR ‖
προσποίησις > ποίησις RQ ≥ προσποίησις Q²ᵐᵍ ‖ οὐδὲ ≙ οὐδ᾽ G ‖ ἐπίδειξις
> ἀπόδειξις Ο γ Ι Ε > σκέψις FKG Εᶜ CN η | > ὄψις Μ ‖ ἡ
(before ἀρετή) Ο ΑΟ Β ‖ δὲ (after οἷοι) > δὴ D ‖ πόνοι πάντες γ ∩ δ Ι ‖
περὶ > ἐπὶ RQ ≥ περὶ Q²ᵐᵍ ‖
34 οὐδὲ > οὔτε FKG ‖ ἐπιτιθεμένην ⹃ ἐπιτιθεμένην Ρ | >
ἐπιφερομένην QR ‖ οὔτε ΑΟ ΜΚG ≙ οὔτ᾽ BQ Ι F ε | ≙ οὔτ R ‖
ἀπειργομένην ⹃ ἐπειργομένην QR ‖ ἐπιχειρήσεως ⹃ ἐπίχειρα QR ‖ δύνατον
⹂ δύνατην R ≥ δύνατον Rᶜ ‖ ἔτι > ἐστι R ‖ ληπτὸν > λοιπὸν Ο | >
λεπτῇ QR ‖ πειρωμένῳ ⹃ πειρομένῳ QR ‖ μεστὴ + τοῦ FKG ‖
πληρώματος ⹃ πληρόματος R | ⹂ πληρόματος Q ‖ ὄγκῳ ⹃ ὄκνῳ RQ ≥
ὄγκῳ Q²ᵐᵍ ‖ προσβολῇ > προβολῇ Q ≥ προσβολῇ Q² ‖

more than enough for the fight. The one attacked a single ship of those putting to sea, the other stationed himself against all the hordes of the king together. *33* The one made a completely senseless assault, because hope [for success] of the boldness was impossible for him. For how was he to seize a ship with [one] hand? Who would have become so great with the right hand then, if he had been ignorant about not being able to hold a trireme back, but had expected to overpower [it] with fingers? The recklessness [was] foolish. If, on the other side, he did see thus the impossiblity of the attempt — yet somehow amidst the impossibilities recklessness gets the upper hand — the pretension was bravado. The showing-off of the impracticable gesture [was] neither safe nor necessary, and the thought [was] futile because valor [is] neither swaggering nor senseless. What blind sufferings all those involving impossible desires! *34* It is necessary to regard nothing [which comes] first — not skill applied in deeds nor valor prevented by deliberations — as outcome of the attempt, if [it is] still possible and apprehendible for nature and for a man who is able and tries {??}. The whole ship filled with its crew and so many well-trained oarsmen — how [would it] have been liable to seizure, how [would it have been] vulnerable to capture by such a swelling of hope and

---

Editorial conjectures for reconstructing the wording of the original text (Π) behind the medieval text form (π):

33 κρατεῖ > κυρεῖ *h* ‖ οἷοι δὲ καὶ > ἄνοιοι δὲ καὶ *o* | > οἷοι δὴ οἱ *j* | > οἷοι δὴ καὶ *h* ‖

34 οὐδὲ - οὔτε > οὔτε - οὐδὲ *h* ‖ ἀπειργομένην > ἀπειργασμένην *h* ‖ συγκεκροτημένης > συγκεκροτημένη *o* ‖ πῶς ἦν ἐπιλήψιμος; ○ *o* ‖

τοῦ τολμήματος; **35** *ἢ … μὴ τήν … τινὸς μανικοῦ σχήματος τὸ ἄπειρον τῆς ἐπιθυμίας καὶ τὸ μάταιον τῆς προσβολῆς ἄφρον καὶ ἀπέραντον ἢ ἀνδρὸς οὐ βουλομένου ναῦν λαβεῖν ἀλλ' ἀπολῦσαι. οὔκουν ἀρετὴν ἔτι τὴν ἀνόητον τόλμαν νοητέον ἀλλὰ μανίαν τὴν ἄχρηστον αὐθάδειαν.* **36** *εἴποι δὲ ἄν τις εὖ φρονῶν αὐτῷ·*

Τί *ταῦτα μωραίνεις,* Κυναίγειρε,
τί δ' ἐπιχειρεῖς ναῦν κατέχειν ἀνθρωπίνῃ δεξιᾷ;
τὸ τόλμημά σου φύσιν οὐκ ἔχει.
τίς τοῦτο Γλαῦκος *πόντιος, τίς* Τρίτων *ἐποίησε;*
μόνον δύναται μειράκιον ναῦν ἐπαγαγεῖν
ἢ Ποσειδῶνος *δεξιὰ ἀνέμοις ἁμιλλᾶσθαι;*
περινοστήσεις τοσούτῳ πληρώματι;
συναπάξει σε ἡ ναῦς πλέουσα,
λήσεις πρύμνης ἐξηρτημένος,
αἰχμάλωτος ἀκροστολίου γενόμενος.

37 *γεγόνασιν ἐπὶ ναυσὶ μάχαι καὶ πολλαί· τοιαύτην* Ὅμηρος *διηγήσατο·*

---

35 **ἢ** ○ AO ‖ ***μὴ τήν*** > *τολμητὴν* B ‖ ***τὸ ἄπειρον τῆς ἐπιθυμίας*** ∩ 3412 QR ‖ ***ἄπειρον*** > *ἄπορον* AO ‖ ***ἄφρον*** > *ἄωρον* HPQ^{2mg} ‖ ***ἀπέραντον*** ╤ *ἀπέαντον* F | > *ἀπείραντον* D ‖ **ἢ** (before *ἀνδρος*) > *ἦν* M ‖ ***οὐ*** ○ D ‖ ***βουλομένου*** ╤ *βολομένου* C ‖ ***ἀπολῦσαι*** *μ* E *η* ╤ *ἀπολύσαι* AO BR I CN | ╪ *ἀπολλύσαι* Q ‖ ***ἔτι*** > *ἔστι* QR ‖ ***νοητέον*** > *οἰητέον* *μ* ‖
36 ***δὲ*** (after *εἴποι*) *γ* I ╧ *δ'* *δ* ‖ ***μωραίνεις*** + *ὦ* QR ‖ ***δ'*** AO QR I G ╧ *δὲ* B MFK *ε* ‖ ***κατέχειν*** > *κατασχεῖν* AO ‖ **Γλαῦκος** > Γλαύκων QR ‖ ***πόντιος*** ╤ *πόντινος* Q ≥ *πόντιος* Q^{c} ‖ ***ἐποίησε*** ╧ *ἐποίησεν* QR ‖ ***μειράκιον*** ╤ *μειράκιο* D | ╤ *μειράκι* NC ≥ *μειράκιον* C^{c} ‖ ***ἐπαγαγεῖν*** A B (→ *γ*) > *ἀπαγαγεῖν* *δ* I | > *ἐπαναγαγεῖν* O | > *ἀγαγεῖν* QR ‖ **ἢ** > *ἡ* FKG ‖ ***δεξιὰ*** > *δεξιᾷ* O CN D ≥ *δεξιὰ* D^{c} | > *δεξιὰν* QR ‖ ***ἁμιλλᾶσθαι*** QR I ╤ *ἀμιλλᾶσθαι* AO | > *ἁμιλλᾶται* B MF E HPQ^{2} | > *ἀμιλλᾶται* KG | > *ἀμιλᾶται* CN D ‖ ***περινοστήσεις*** > *περινοστήσας* B | > *συμπεριναστήσεις* *μ* ‖ ***πρύμνης*** > *πρύμναν* M ‖ ***ἐξηρτημένος*** > *ἐξηρτημένης* D ≥ *ἐξηρτημένος* D^{c} ‖ ***ἀκροστολίου*** *γ* ╤ *ἀκροστόλου* I FKG E CN HP | ╪ *ἀκρόστολ* D | ╤ *ἀκροστήλ* M ‖
37 ***γεγόνασιν*** ╧ *γεγόνασι* F ‖ ***μάχαι καὶ πολλαί*** ∩ 231 QR ‖ ***τοιαύτην*** AO QR > *τοιαύτας* B I *δ* Q^{2} | + *καὶ* AO ‖

by the attack of recklessness? **35** Either ... not the ... of some crazed show, the ignorance of the desire and the futility of the attack, senseless and unaccomplishable, or of a man not wishing to capture a ship but to set [it] loose. At any rate, one must not still think of the senseless daring [as] valor, but of the useless willfulness [as] madness. **36** But someone well-minded toward him might say:

"Why are you doing these crazy things, Cynegirus,

and why are you trying to restrain a ship with a human right hand?

Your reckless act is contrary to nature.

What Glaucus of the sea, what Triton [ever] did this?

Can a boy alone draw in a ship

or a right hand vie with Poseidon's winds?

Will you circumvent so great a crew?

The ship will take you away with it when it sails,

you will be unnoticed hanging on the stern,

having become a prisoner of a [ship's] ornament."

37 There have occurred against ships fights, and many [too]. Homer

---

Editorial conjectures for reconstructing the wording of the original text (II) behind the medieval text form (π):

35 ἢ μὴ τήν τινος μανικοῦ σχήματος τὸ ἄπειρον τῆς ἐπιθυμίας καὶ τὸ μάταιον τῆς προσβολῆς ἄφρον > ἢ ὁρμὴ ἦν τινος μανικοῦ λήματος τὸ τῆς ἐπιθυμίας ἄπορον καὶ [τῆς πείρας] τὸ μάταιον καὶ τῆς προσβολῆς ἄφρον j | > ἢ μὴν τινος μανικοῦ τοῦ σχήματος τὸ ἄπορον καὶ τῆς ἐπιθυμίας τὸ μάταιον καὶ τῆς προσβολῆς τὸ ἄφρον h | > ἢ μὴν ἦν τινος etc. jü ‖ ἀπολῦσαι > ἀπολέσθαι j ‖
36 Ποσειδῶνος > παιδὸς j | O h ‖ περινοστήσεις > πάρισος τίς εἰς h
‖

οὐδέ γε εἷλκε τίς ἐκείνας, ἀλλὰ πῦρ **ἐνέβαλλε**, δᾷδας ἐκόμιζεν. αὕτη μόνη κατέχει ναῦν ἡ λαβή. ὁ δὲ σός, ὦ Εὐφορίων, υἱὸς μειράκιον τολμηρὸν ἦν καὶ τοῦ μὲν σώματος κατεφρόνει, μάχεσθαι δὲ εὐβούλως οὐκ ἠπίστατο, οἵαν ἀπώλεσεν εἰκῇ δεξιάν. **38** διὰ ταῦτα Καλλίμαχος μὲν ἁπάντων ἐτύγχανεν ὧν ἠθέλησε, πολλοὺς δὲ ἀφώπλισε, πάντας δὲ ἐφόβησεν, ἐφύλαξε δὲ τὴν στάσιν καὶ τεθνεώς· ὁ δὲ σὸς υἱὸς ὧδε τὴν ἐπίνοιαν ἐκαρπώσατο. **39** καὶ Καλλίμαχον μὲν οὐδεὶς ἀπέκτεινεν, ἀλλὰ κοινὸν ἔργον τῆς Ἀσίας ἐγένετο· πάντα μὲν δόρατα ἐπὶ τοῦτον ἦλθε ψαῦσαι καὶ Καλλιμάχου φιλοτιμούμενα, πάντα δὲ ἀκόντια, πᾶσαι δὲ ἐκενώθησαν φαρέτραι βελῶν, ἅπαντα δὲ τοξεύματα περὶ τοῦτον ἔστη μαρτυρούμενα τὴν κοινωνίαν καὶ πάντα ἀμφισβητοῦντα περὶ τοῦ νεκροῦ· Κυναιγείρου δὲ τὴν χεῖρα ταύτην ἀπέκοψεν ὥσπερ ξύλον. **40** Καλλιμάχου μὲν οὖν ἡ τόλμα καὶ μάχη τοῦτο ἐβούλετο, νικῆσαι τὸν βασιλέως στρατὸν καὶ τὴν Ἀττικὴν αὐτοῖς ἄβατον εἶναι· Κυναίγειρος δὲ φεύγοντας ἡμῖν τοὺς βαρβάρους ἀναιρεῖ καὶ κατεῖχεν ἐν τῇ

---

37 γε Ο D | > χεροῖν QR ‖ **εἷλκε** ⪮ εἷλκεν Α ‖ τίς > τις Ο Q ‖ **ἐνέβαλλε** β MFK Eᶜ CN ⪮ ἐνέβαλε ΑΟ I G Ε η ‖ **ἐκόμιζεν** ⪮ ἐκόμιζε FKG H ‖ κατέχει > κατέσχε P ‖ **ναῦν** > ναῦς η ‖ ὦ Ο B ‖ **μειράκιον τολμηρὸν** γ ∩ δ I ‖ δὲ (after μάχεσθαι) γ I ⪮ δ' δ ‖ **εὐβούλως** ⪯ ἐβούλως D ‖ ἠπίστατο ⪮ ἠπίστετο R ‖ οἵαν ⪮ οἱ αν P ‖
38 ἀπάντων γ Ο δ I ‖ **ἐτύγχανεν** ⪮ ἐτύγχανε FKG | > ἔτυχεν ΑΟ | ‍+ μὲν FKG ‖ ἠθέλησε ⪮ ἠθέλησεν Μ ‖ δὲ (after πολλοὺς) ⪯ δ' G | Ο QR ‖ **πάντες δὲ ἐφόβησεν** Ο R ≥ πάντες δὲ ἐφόβησεν R² ‖ δὲ (before σὸς) Ο B ‖ ὧδε ⪮ ᾧδε F | ⪮ ὧδε Μ Ε ‖ **ἐκαρπώσατο** ⪮ ἐκαρπόσατο R ‖
39 ἦλθε ⪮ ἦλθεν Α ‖ **καὶ** (after ψαῦσαι) Ο δ ‖ **ἀκόντια** ⪮ ἀκόντινα RQ ≥ ἀκόντια Q² | ‍+ καὶ QR ‖ δὲ (before ἐκενώθησαν) ΑΟ B I G ⪯ δ' MFK ε | Ο QR ‖ **ἐκενώθησαν** ⪮ κενώθησαν G ‖ **κοινωνίαν** ‍+ τε Μ ‖ **Κυναιγείρου** γ I > Κυναίγειρος δ (Di) Q² ‖ δὲ (after Κυναιγείρου) ‍+ τις I ‖ χεῖρα ‍+ περὶ τοῦ νεκροῦ Κυναιγείρου δὲ τὴν χεῖρα Du ‖ **ἀπέκοψεν** > ἀπέκοψαν RQ ≥ ἀπέκοψεν Q² ‖
40 Καλλιμάχου > Καλλίμαχον P ‖ οὖν Ο QR ‖ τόλμα ΑΟ B I FKG E C ⪯ τόλμη QR Μ Ν η ‖ **τόλμα καὶ μάχη** ∩ 321 D ‖ τοῦτο > τοῦτον QR ‖ δὲ (after Κυναίγειρος) Ο D | ‍+ καὶ ΑΟ ‖ ἡμῖν > ὑμῖν QR ‖ ἀναιρεῖ ⪮ ἀναριρεῖ Q ≥ ἀναιρεῖ Qᶜ | > ἀνείργε B ‖

recounted such [a fight]. But [it was] not [that] someone was trying to pull those [ships], rather he was trying to set fire [to them], he was bringing in torches. This alone [is] the grip [which] restrains a ship. Your son, however, O Euphorion, was a reckless boy and he thought lightly of his body, yet he did not understand how to fight prudently. What a pointless waste of his right hand! **38** Therefore, Callimachus was achieving everything that he wished: he stripped many of their weapons, he put fear in all, and he kept the standing position even after he had died. Thus your son got his idea as fruit [of Callimachus' labors]. **39** Further, no one [singly] killed Callimachus, but a joint effort of Asia did [it]. All the spears came at him, endeavoring to reach precisely Callimachus, all the javelins too, and all quivers were emptied of arrows, and all [the] missiles around him stood testifying to the communal [effort] and all laying claim to the corpse. But this hand of Cynegirus [somebody] chopped off just like a piece of wood. **40** On the one side, Callimachus' courage and fight had this intent, [namely,] to defeat the king's army and [to make] Attica to be impassable for them. On the other side, Cynegirus both want[ed] to snatch up the barbarians for us while they were

---

Editorial conjectures for reconstructing the wording of the original text (II) behind the medieval text form (π):

39 οὐδεὶς > οὐχ εἷς *o h* ‖ ψαῦσαι καὶ ∩ *h* ‖
40 ἀναιρεῖ > ἀνείργει *j* | > ανεῖργε *h* ‖

χώρᾳ τοὺς πολεμίους καὶ μάχης ἔπραττεν ἀρχὰς δευτέρας. τί ποτε ἂν

ἐποίησεν ἄλλο βασιλεὺς παρών; τοῖς φεύγουσιν ἀνεβόα καὶ τὰς Φοινίσσας

ναῦς ἐκράτει ....

41 Ἄφες ἄφες, Κυναίγειρε, μὴ λαμβάνου.

μένουσιν ἂν λαμβάνῃς,

πάλιν εὑρ[ήσ]ουσιν ἄλλας ἀποβάσεις.

μὴ κράτει ναῦν ὑπὸ Πανὸς δεδιωγμένην

μηδ᾽ ἔχου τριήρους σὺ παρ᾽ Ἀθηνᾶς ἀφεψαλωμένης.

ἀφίησιν αὐτὴν ἡ Δημήτηρ καὶ Κόρη· φευγέτω.

πάρεστι Θησεύς, πάρεστιν Ἡρακλῆς·

ἀλλ᾽ οὐ κατέχουσι τὴν ναῦν ὅτι μὴ συμφέρει.

ἔχω καὶ πνεύματα συγγενῆ μᾶλλον σοῦ κατασχεῖν δυνάμενα·

ἀλλὰ τὰ μὲν ἐκπέμπει τὸν πόλεμον ἐκ τῆς Ἀττικῆς

διὰ τὴν εὔνοιαν τὴν πρὸς ἡμᾶς,

σὺ δέ, ὦ Κυναίγειρε, ναύσταθμον Μηδικὸν τὸν Μαραθῶνα ποιεῖς.

---

40 χώρᾳ > μ ... D ‖ τοὺς ⟓ κοὺς Q ≥ τοὺς Qᶜ ‖ καὶ (before μάχης) ┼ τῆς I ‖ ἀρχὰς γ I > ἀρχὴν FKG ε | > ἀρχῆς Μ ‖ ποτε ⸗ ποτ᾽ G ‖ ἂν (after ποτε) > ἀλλ Ο ≥ ἂν Οᶜ ‖ ἐποίησεν ⸗ ἐποίησε QR ‖ ἐποίησεν ἄλλο ∩ QR ‖ βασιλεὺς ⟓ βασιλ᾽ QR ‖ φεύγουσιν ⟓ φεύγου ... Α ‖ ἀνεβόα > ἂν ἐβόα FKG | ναῦς Ο D ‖
41 ἄφες (after ἄφες) Ο Q > ἄφες Q² ‖ μένουσιν ⸗ μένουσι QR ‖ λαμβάνῃς ΑΟ ΒR > λαμβάνεις Q | > λάβῃς FKG ε > λάβοις I Μ ‖ εὑρ[ήσ]ουσιν > εὕρουσιν Ο Β | > εὕρουσιν Α | > εὕρωσιν QR I FKG ε | > εὕρω Μ ‖ ἄλλας > ἑτέρας QR ‖ Πανὸς > παντὸς R ‖ δεδιωγμένην > δεδιωγμένης Ρ ≥ δεδιωγμένῃ Ρᶜ ‖ μηδ᾽ ἔχου ⸗ μὴ δ᾽ ἔχου QR CN | > μὴ δέχου Μ ‖ παρ᾽ > ὑπ᾽ RQ ≥ παρ᾽ Q² ‖ ἀφεψαλωμένης ΑΟ Β ⟓ ἀφεψαλομένης I | > ἐφεψαλωμένης QR δ ‖ ἡ Δημήτηρ > ἤδη μήτηρ QR ‖ φευγέτω > φεύγουσαν QR ‖ Θησεύς ⟓ Θησσεύς Κ | ⟓ Θυσεὺς CN ‖ Ἡρακλῆς ⟓ Ἡρακλεῖς Ν ≥ Ἡρακλῆς Νᶜ ‖ κατέχουσι ⸗ κατέχουσιν D ‖ τὴν (before ναῦν) ⟓ τῇ Q | > τῆ R ‖ μὴ (before συμφέρει) Ο R ‖ μᾶλλον σοῦ ∩ QR ‖ πόλεμον > πόταμον R ≥ πόλεμον Rᶜ ‖ Ἀττικῆς ┼ ἀλλὰ D ‖ δὲ ⸗ δ᾽ G ‖ ναύσταθμον Μηδικὸν τὸν Μαραθῶνα ποιεῖς ὦ Κυναίγειρε Ο D ‖ Μηδικὸν > Μηδικὴν RQ ≥ Μηδικὸν Q² ‖

attempting to escape, and he was trying to hold back the enemies in the land, and he was starting to bring about [the] beginnings of a second battle. What ever else would [the] king have done, if he had stayed? To those fleeing he would have shouted out and he would have commanded the Phoenician ships

....

41 "Let go, let go, Cynegirus, don't keep holding on!

They [are going to] remain, if you keep holding on;

they will find other landing places again.

Don't keep holding fast a ship driven away by Pan

and don't you keep clinging to a trireme unburnt{?} by Athena.

Demeter and Kore are setting it loose; let it escape.

Theseus is standing by, Herakles is standing by.

But they are not going to hold back the ship

unless it be of some advantage.

I have also kindred winds more able than you to hold [it] back.

However, whereas they are casting the war out of Attica

on account of the[ir] good will toward us,

you, O Cynegirus, are making Marathon a Median harbor.

Editorial conjectures for reconstructing the wording of the original text (II) behind the medieval text form (π):

40 ἀνεβόα > ἂν ἐβόα (→ FKG) *j h* ‖ ἐκράτει followed by lacuna *o j h r/cs* | + τί δ' ἂν εἶπε καὶ ἡ πατρίς; *o* ‖

41 μένουσιν > μενοῦσιν *s p o h r/cs* ‖ εὑρ[ήσ]ουσιν *h r/cs* ‖ μηδ' (before ἔχου) ○ *s p o* ‖ τριήρους > τριήρης *o* ‖ ἀφεψαλωμένης > ἀφεψάλου ἀφιεμένης *o* | > οὐ φεψαλωμένης *j* | > ἀπεψαλμένης *h* ‖ ἔχω καὶ > ἔχει ἡ γῆ *j* ‖

ὦ Κυναίγειρε, τὴν ναυμαχίαν νικήσει βασιλεύς·

τῆς μάχης μόνῳ Κυναιγείρῳ εἴσεται χάριν.

ἄπορον ποιῶν αὐτοῦ τὴν φυγὴν ἀναγκαίαν αὐτῷ τὴν νίκην εἰργάζετο. **42** ἀλλὰ γὰρ οὐ μετὰ τῆς χειρὸς ὡς διανοίας ἡμᾶς ἔβλαπτε — τἀληθῆ γὰρ εἰρήσεται — ἀλλὰ ἄλλως ἐμαίνετο καὶ τὸν Καλλιμάχου νεκρὸν ὁρῶν εὐδοκιμοῦντα ἐπεθύμει μετὰ ἄλλου σχήματος ἀπολέσαι τὴν ἀλαζόνα δεξιὰν ὅπως ἄν ἓν γένηται τῶν Μαραθωνίων διηγημάτων· ἡμεῖς δὲ οὔθ' ἑκόντες οὔτε ἄκοντες οὐδὲν ἐβλάπτομεν. **43** εἰ μὲν δὴ πάντες ὅμοιοι Καλλιμάχῳ κατ' ἐκείνην ἐγένοντο τὴν ἡμέραν, οὐδεὶς ἂν ἐλείφθη τῶν βαρβάρων καὶ πάσας τὰς ναῦς ἂν αὐτῶν κενὰς εἴλομεν· εἰ δέ γε εἶδον εἰς τὰς Κυναιγείρου λαβάς, ἄκοντες ἂν πάντες οἱ βάρβαροι τὴν ἧτταν ἀνεμαχέσαντο. Κυναίγειρος μὲν οὖν οὔτε θάρρος φίλοις οὔτε δέος τοῖς πολεμίοις ἐγένετο, ὃς δράσας οὐδὲν ἀλλ' ἀποτμηθεὶς τὴν χεῖρα ἔπεσεν εὐθὺς ὥσπερ ἑτέραν οὐκ ἔχων ἀλλ' ἐν τῇ δεξιᾷ τῆς ψυχῆς αὐτῷ κειμένης· τὸν δ' ἐμὸν παῖδα οἱ φίλοι μὲν ὁρῶντες ἐν τῇ τάξει μένοντα πάντες ἡδοῦντο, τρέσαντες δὲ ὑπεχώρουν οἱ βάρβαροι. καὶ τὸ σύμπαν, ὁ μὲν ἔπεσεν, ὁ δὲ οὔ.

---

41 ὦ **Κυναίγειρε** (after ποιεῖς) Ο FKG ‖ **νικήσει** γ Μ > νικήσας FKG ε Iu ‖ **βασιλεύς** ≠ βασιλ` QR | > βασιλείαν D ‖ **τῆς μάχης** > τὴν μάχην ΑΟ ‖ **μόνῳ** > μόνον R ‖ **εἴσεται** ≠ εἴσηται Ε ‖ **ποιῶν αὐτοῦ** ∩ Β ‖ **αὐτοῦ** > αὐτῷ RQ ≥ αὐτοῦ Q² ‖ **εἰργάζετο** > εἰργάσατο QR ‖
42 **ἀλλὰ** ≐ ἀλλ' QR ‖ **γὰρ** (after ἀλλὰ) Ο QR ‖ **τῆς** QR I ‖ **ὡς** Ο QR ‖ **διανοίας** > δι' ἀνοίας B FG | > ἀδιανοίας QR ‖ **ἔβλαπτε** ≐ ἔβλαπτεν G | > ἔβλεπε Ν D ‖ **ἀλλὰ** + καὶ QR ‖ **Καλλιμάχου** ε Καλλίμαχον D ‖ **ἐπεθύμει** > ἐπεθύμησε μ ‖ **μετὰ** (before ἄλλου) + τοῦ QR ‖ **ἀλαζόνα** ⚬ ἀλαζώνα D ‖ **ἓν** Ο QR ‖ **τῶν** Ο Iu ‖ **Μαραθωνίων** ⚬ Μαραθώνων RQ ≥ Μαραθωνίων Q² ‖ **οὔτε** γ I ≐ οὔτ' δ ‖
43 **εἰ** > οἱ QR ‖ **ὅμοιοι** > ὅμοια QR ‖ **Καλλιμάχῳ** > Καλλιμάχου QR ‖ **ἂν** (after ναῦς) γ I Ο δ (Du) ‖ **πάντες** > ἀπάντες QR ‖ **ἧτταν** ⚬ ἧτταν Ρ ‖ **ἀνεμαχέσαντο** > ἀνεκαλέσαντο RQ ≥ ἀνεμαχέσαντο Q²ᵐᵍ ‖ **δέος** + δέος Qu ‖ **ἀλλ'** ≐ ἀλλὰ ΑΟ Mu ‖ **ψυχῆς** > ἐμψυχῆς Q ≥ ψυχῆς Qᶜ ‖ **αὐτῷ** Ο QR ‖ **δ'** ≐ δὲ R ‖ **τῇ** (before τάξει) Ο QR D ‖ **δὲ** (after τρέσαντες) Ο Μ ‖ **δὲ** (before οὐ) γ I ≐ δ' δ ‖

O Cynegirus, the king will win the sea-fight;

    he will acknowledge thanks to Cynegirus alone

        for [the outcome of] the battle."

By blocking his escape he was making victory necessary for him. **42** But really not [so much] with his hand as with [his] intention was he harming us — for the truth will be told — yet without reason he was driven mad and when he saw the corpse of Callimachus being held in high esteem he began desiring by means of a different appearance to lose his pretentious right hand in order that he might become one of the Marathonian tales. We, however, were not causing harm in any way — neither intentionally nor unintentionally. **43** If indeed, on the one hand, all had become like Callimachus on that day, no one of the barbarians would have been left [alive] and we would have captured all of their ships empty. If, on the other hand, they had looked at the grips of Cynegirus, involuntarily all the barbarians would have fought back again [from] the defeat. Cynegirus, therefore, became neither a source of courage for friends nor a source of fear for the enemies. He, doing nothing but getting his hand cut off, fell immediately as though he did not have another [one], but [rather as though] his soul were lying [prone] in the right hand. When the friends, however, saw my son remaining in the battle stance, they all stood in awe, but the barbarians began running away like cowards. In summary: the one fell, the other [did] not. **44** If we assume

---

Editorial conjectures for reconstructing the wording of the original text (ΙΙ) behind the medieval text form (π):

41 ὦ (after ποιεῖς) > εἰ *j* ‖ εἰργάζετο > εἰργάζου *h* ‖

42 μετὰ τῆς χειρὸς Ο *h* ‖ ὡς + μετὰ *h* ‖ εὐδοκιμοῦντα > εὐδοκιμήσαντα *o* ‖ γένηται > γένητο *o* ‖

43 ἄκοντες ἂν πάντες > ἄπαντες, ἄκοντες ἂν *j* ‖

44 ἀθλητὰς δὲ εἶναι τοὺς στρατιώτας ὑπολαβόντες πότερον στεφανώσομεν, τὸν ὀρθὸν ἢ τὸν κείμενον, τὸν ἑστηκότα ἢ τὸν ἐρριμμένον; οὐ παύσῃ παραβάλλων ἀνδρὶ χεῖρα καὶ τραῦμα ἐν μυρίοις καὶ τὸν λειποτακτήσαντα τῷ μακροβίῳ νεκρῷ καὶ τὸν ἠκρωτηριασμένον τῷ μέχρι νῦν ὁλοκλήρῳ; ὁ μὲν ἀφῆκε τὴν ναῦν, ὁ δὲ ἐκράτει τῆς ἀσπίδος. **45** λέγε νῦν καὶ τραγῴδει πολλάκις· καὶ γὰρ Αἰσχύλου πατὴρ εἶ καὶ τὴν χεῖρα ὄρος ἐποίεις.

Ἐκ γῆς ἐναυμάχει{ς}·

Δάτις δὲ ἐκ θαλάττης ἐπεζομάχει.

Κατέσχε τὴν ναῦν·

καλωδίου τὸ ἔργον· ἄγκυρα τοῦτο κρεῖττον ποιεῖ. ὁ μὲν ἐλάβετο, ὁ δ᾽ ἀπέκοψε.

Κατέσχε τοὺς πλέοντας·

οἱ δὲ καὶ ὅμως ἐξέπλευσαν. **46** ἄνδρες Ἀθηναῖοι, περιελθόντες τὸ στρατόπεδον τοὺς μὲν εὑρήσετε χειρῶν ἄνευ, τοὺς δὲ ποδῶν, ἑτέρων μὲν οὕς, ἑτέρων δὲ κεφαλὰς ἀποτετμημένας τῶν ἄλλων σωμάτων· πολλοὺς ὁμοίους

44 ἀθλητὰς > ἀθλήτερον QR ‖ δὲ (after ἀθλητὰς) β I ≐ δ᾽ AO δ ‖ ὑπολαβόντες ⇌ ὑπολαμβόντες RQ ≥ ὑπολαβόντες Qᶜ ‖ στεφανώσομεν > στεφανώσωμεν P ≥ στεφανώσομεν Pᶜ ‖ ὀρθὸν > νεκρὸν HPQ²ᵐᵍ ‖ ἢ τὸν κειμένον ○ D ‖ ἑστηκότα ⇌ ἑστηκότα KG ‖ ἐρριμμένον ⇌ ἐρριμένον CN D Q ≥ ἐρριμμένον Qᶜ ‖ παύσῃ + γὰρ N ‖ παραβάλλων ≠ παραβάλων D ι > ἀποβάλλων N ‖ ἐν > ἑνὸς RQ ≥ ἐν Q²ᵐᵍ ‖ μακροβίῳ ⇌ μακρωβίῳ R ‖ καὶ (after νεκρῷ) > δὲ G ‖ ἠκρωτηριασμένον ⇌ ἠκροτηριασμένον D ‖ ἐκράτει + καὶ K ‖ ἀσπίδος > ἀσπίδα FK ≥ ἀσπίδος FᶜKᶜ ι > τρόπιδος I ‖
45 λέγε > λέγει R ‖ τραγῴδει γ I > τραγῳδίαν δ (Md) Q² ‖ εἶ γ ○ δ I ‖ ὄρος > ὄρος AO Eu ‖ ἐποίεις > ἐποίοις QR ι > ἐποίει I ‖ ἐναυμάχεις > ἐναυμάχει I ‖ δὲ (after Δάτις) QR I FK (Md) ε ≐ δ᾽ AO B G ‖ θαλάττης AO QR M η ≐ θαλάσσης B I FKG E CN ‖ κατέσχε ≐ κατέσχεν D ‖ καλωδίου ⇌ καλοδίου R ‖ ὁ δ᾽ > ὅδε D ‖ ἀπέκοψε ≐ ἀπέκοψεν P ‖ οἱ > οὐ R ‖
46 Ἀθηναῖοι ≠ Ἀθην⁻ K ‖ στρατόπεδον > στρατόπαιδον P ‖ εὑρήσετε > εὑρήσεται QR ‖ χειρῶν ἄνευ, τοὺς δὲ ποδῶν ∩ ποδῶν ἄνευ, τοὺς δὲ χειρῶν Q ι πεδω τἄνευ, τοὺς δὲ χειρῶν R ‖ μὲν (after ἑτέρων) > δὲ M ‖ οὕς > οὖσαν R ‖ δὲ (after ἑτέρων) ○ D ‖ ἀποτετμημένας ⇌ ἀποτεμημένας QR ι > ἀπὸ τμημένας D ‖ πολλοὺς + δὲ B ‖ ὁμοίους > ὁμοίως B ‖

that the soldiers are prize-fighters, which of the two will we reward with a crown — the one erect or the one outstretched, the one standing or the one prostrate? Will you not stop comparing a hand with a man, and one wound with myriads, and the one deserting his post with the long-lived corpse, and the one mutilated with the one intact right up till now. The one let loose the ship, the other kept holding fast the shield. **45** Go on boasting then and keep on exaggerating repeatedly! For you are father also of Aeschylus and you were making the hand [into] a mountain:

"From land [he was] fighting a naval battle."

But Datis was fighting a land battle from sea.

"He restrained the ship."

The work of a small rope; an anchor does this better. The one grabbed on, the other lopped off.

"He restrained those trying to sail."

But nevertheless they also sailed away.

46 Men of Athens, if you go around the camp, you will find some [corpses] without hands and others [without] feet; from the other bodies [you will find] in some [cases] an ear, in other [cases] heads cut off. You will see

---

Editorial conjectures for reconstructing the wording of the original text (II) behind the medieval text form (π):

45 ἐναύμαχεις > ἐναυμάχει (→ I)   *h   r/cs*   ‖   δ' (before ἀπέκοψε) > δὲ   *s   p
o*   ‖

ὄψεσθε Κυναιγείρῳ νεκρούς, Καλλιμάχῳ δὲ οὐδένα. τίς γὰρ σοὶ ἰσοστάσιος

νεκρός; τίς γὰρ πιστὸς οὕτω στρατιώτης εἰς μάχην; **47** νῦν σε μᾶλλον, ὦ

Καλλίμαχε τέκνον, ἐθαύμασα Κυναιγείρου πεσόντος ὑπὸ πληγῆς μιᾶς, ὦ

πολλὰ τοιαῦτα λαβὼν τραύματα καὶ μὴ κεκινημένε. οὐδεὶς σὲ Περσῶν

διελὼν ἄπεισιν ὡς τῶν λοιπῶν ἀνθρώπων τὰ σώματα οὐκ ἀκινάκῃ Μηδικῷ, οὐ

κοπίδι Περσικῇ, οὐκ αἰχμῇ Βαβυλωνίᾳ, οὐ πελέκει Φοινικίῳ. ὦ μόνε τῶν

ἀποθανόντων οὐ πεσὼν καὶ μόνε μὴ ζηλούμενε ἔστης μαρτυρούμενος τὴν

νίκην τῷ σχήματι καὶ τῆς ψυχῆς ἀπελθούσης ὅμοιος ἦσθα τῷ μαχομένῳ. **48**

ὦ τοῦ μεγάλου θαύματος· νῦν πρῶτον ἀθάνατος ὤφθη νεκρός. ὦ παῖ,

μάντευμα ἄρα σου τοῦ κάλλους καὶ τῆς μάχης καὶ τοὔνομα ἦν, ᾧ καὶ τὸ

συμβὰν ἄδηλον εἶναι ὄνομα τῷ ἐρευνᾶν βουλομένῳ. **49** ὁ σὸς πάρεργον

τοῖς βαρβάροις ἐγένετο, ὁ δὲ ἐμὸς υἱὸς δι᾽ ἀρετῆς περιουσίαν καὶ τῆς μάχης

ὅλης ἐκράτησε καὶ τῆς νῦν τελουμένης τιμῆς γέγονεν αἴτιος. τῶν γὰρ

ἄλλων πολεμάρχων δειλίαν ἐντιθεμένων τῷ πλήθει ἡ τούτου ψῆφος

προσγενομένη τὴν ὅλην συμβολὴν ἐποίησε καὶ ὅπως δεῖ ἀπομάχεσθαι καὶ

---

46 ὄψεσθε ╪ ὄψεσθαι Q D N ≥ ὄψεσθε N | ⊤ ἔψασθαι R ‖ **Κυναιγείρῳ** ⊤ Κυναιγείρων R ‖ **σοὶ** > σος R ‖ **γὰρ** (before πιστὸς) > δὲ QR ‖
47 πληγῆς μιᾶς ∩ HP ‖ **ὦ** (before πολλὰ) ╪ ˙ G ‖ **πολλὰ τοιαῦτα** ∩ QR ‖ **κεκινημένε** AO BR > κεκινημένος δ I Q ‖ **ἀκινάκῃ** ⊤ ἀκινάκι Q | ⊤ ἀκινὰ R | ⊤ ἀνάκη D ‖ **Μηδικῷ** ⊤ Μηδιῷ FK ‖ **Βαβυλωνίᾳ** ⊤ Βαβυλῶνα R | ⊤ Βαλωνίᾳ D ‖ **πελέκει** ⊤ πελέκϊ FK ‖ **Φοινικίῳ** AO B I KG E C ⊥ Φοινικείῳ MF | > Φοινικῷ QR η | > Φοινικίας N ‖ **οὐ** (before πεσὼν) > μὴ QR ‖ **μὴ** (before ζηλούμενε) AO QR I ○ δ B Q² ‖ **ἔστης** > ἔστη QR ‖ **μαρτυρούμενος** ⊤ μαρτηρούμενος QR ‖ **ἀπελθούσης** + ; η I ‖ **ὅμοιος** ⊤ οἴμοιᾳ QR ‖ **ἦσθα** ⊤ ἦσθαι R ‖
48 μεγάλου ╪ μεγά F ‖ **πρῶτον** AO B E > πρῶτος QR MFK CN DP | ╪ πρῶτο˙ I G ‖ > πρώτως H ‖ **ἄρα** + καὶ D ‖ **σου** AO μ ○ β I ε ‖ **σου τοῦ** AŌ ∩ μ ‖ **καὶ** (after μάχης) QR ‖ **τοὔνομα** ⊥ τὸ ὄνομα QR | > τοῦ νόμου I ‖ **ἦν** + ἀνακάλει νῦν πολλὰ τὸν Κυναίγειρον AO ‖ **ᾧ** γ I M > ὡς FKG ε Q²ᵐᵍ ‖ **βουλομένῳ** ⊤ βουλωμένῳ P ‖
49 ὁ σὸς FKG ε > ὃς AO I QR M ‖ **δὲ** (before ἐμὸς) AO B I K ⊥ δ᾽ MFG ε QR ‖ **δι᾽** ○ QR ‖ **ἀρετῆς** + καὶ ‖ **περιουσίαν** > περιουσία˙ QR ‖ **δειλίαν** ○ D ‖ **ἐντιθεμένων** ⊤ ἐντεθειμένων Q ≥ ἐντιθεμένων Q² | > τιθεμένων B ‖ **προσγενομένη** > προσγινομένη O QR ‖ **ἐποίησε** ⊥ ἐποίησεν A M ‖

many corpses similar to Cynegirus, but no one [similar] to Callimachus. For what corpse [is] equivalent with you? For what soldier [was] so faithful in battle?   *47*   Now, O Callimachus, child, I marveled more at you than at Cynegirus who fell from one blow, O [you who] received so many wounds and have not been moved.   No one of [the] Persians returns to cut you apart as [they do] the bodies of the rest of men — not with a Median sword, not with a Persian cleaver, not with a Babylonian spear, not with a Phoenician axe.   O only one of the dying who did not fall and only one who was not emulated, you stood attesting the victory by your appearance and although your soul had departed you were similar to the one [still] fighting.   *48*   O [fighter] of great wonder!   Now for the first time a corpse appears undying.   O son, even your name (i.e., Καλλίμαχος) then was a prophecy of your nobility (κάλλος) and [your] fight (μάχη), though for the one wishing to inquire after a[nother?] name the result [may seem] to be unclear.   *49*   Your [son] was an incidental bother for the barbarians, but my son because of a superiority of valor both controlled the whole battle and has become [the] reason for the honor now being performed.   For when the other generals-in-chief were being instilled with timidity by the multitude [of the enemy], his vote when added to the whole tally determined that it was necessary to fight it out and he made the

---

Editorial conjectures for reconstructing the wording of the original text (Π) behind the medieval text form (π):

46 σοί ○ *s p o* ‖
47 ζηλούμενε > ζῆν ἀπιστούμενε *h* ‖
48 σου τοῦ ○ *s p* ‖ ἄδηλον ○ *p* ‖ ἄδηλον εἶναι ὄνομα ∩ 321 *h* ‖
ὄνομα + φανεῖται *j* ‖

τολμᾶν ἐκύρωσεν ὥστε παντὸς ἂν καὶ μόνος καὶ μάλιστα τοῦ κατορθώματος

αἴτιος νομίζοιτο.   **50** καὶ τοῦτο μὲν αὐτῷ πρὸς πάντας ἐστί, πρὸς δὲ τὸν

Κυναίγειρον καὶ μάλιστα.   τῷ ἑνὶ γὰρ τούτῳ σε καὶ ἀνανταγωνίστῳ

νικήσομεν ἐρωτήματι.

Κυναίγειρος θαυμαστὸς καὶ τολμηρὸς ἦν ἀνήρ·

οὐ μέχρι τοῦ βίου; οὐ μέχρι τῆς ψυχῆς; ἀλλ᾿ ὡμολόγησε θάνατον καὶ τῷ

κοινῷ τῆς φύσεως ἡττήθη νόμῳ.   Καλλιμάχου δὲ ἡ ἀρετὴ **ἀόριστός** ἐστι καὶ

φύσεως περιττοτέρα μόνη καὶ τὴν ψυχὴν ὑπερβαίνει.   ἀγαθοὺς μὲν

στρατιώτας πολλοὺς εὕροις {Μακεδόνας}, Καλλίμαχον δὲ μόνον ἀνείκαστον

τὸν ἐν τῷ βίῳ μόνον μεμαχημένον, τόν μὴ δὲ ἐν θανάτῳ καμόντα ἀλλὰ καὶ

μετὰ τὸν βίον ἄνδρα ἀγαθὸν γενόμενον καὶ τοὺς κοινοὺς τῆς φύσεως καὶ

ἀρετῆς παρελθόντα ὅρους.

51 ὦ καλλίμαχε καὶ καλλίνικε, ἄτρωτε καὶ πολύτρωτε, πῶς σε ἄν τις

ἐπαινέσειε κατὰ τὴν ἀξίαν; οὐ γὰρ Αἰσχύλου καὶ τοιούτων ποιητῶν καὶ

---

49 τολμᾶν > τὸν ναῦν QR ‖ ἐκύρωσεν ≐ ἐκύρωσε Ο QR ‖ παντὸς > πάντως G ‖ νομίζοιτο > νομίζοντο QR ‖
50 αὐτῷ > αὐτὸ Μ ‖ πρὸς πάντας ἐστί Ο RQ ≥ πρὸς πάντας ἐστί Q²ᵐᵍ ‖ ἐστί ≐ ἐστίν Α Μ | Di ‖ γὰρ Ο R ‖ ἀνανταγωνίστῳ > ἀνταγωνίστῳ Μ ‖ νικήσομεν ≑ νικήσομένων QR ‖ καὶ τολμηρὸς ἦν ἀνήρ ∩ 3412 Ι ‖ ὡμολόγησε ≐ ὡμολόγησεν Α | ≑ ὁμολόγησε Ν | > ὡμολόγει RQ ≥ ὡμολόγησε Q² ‖ τῷ κοινῷ ≥ τοῦ κοινοῦ Fᶜ ‖ ἡττήθη νόμῳ. Καλλιμάχου δὲ ἡ ἀρετὴ **ἄριστός** ἐστι καὶ φύσεως Ο Ρ ‖ νόμῳ ≥ νόμου Fᶜ ‖ Καλλιμάχου > Καλλίμαχον Μ ‖ ἀόριστός ε (→ δ → π) > ἄριστός γ Ι FK | > ἄριστόν G | > καλλίστη Μ ‖ φύσεως (before περιττοτέρα) δ ΑΟ > φύσει β Ι ‖ μὲν (after ἀγαθους) ✝ γὰρ QR ‖ πολλοὺς > πολλὰς R ‖ εὕροις > εὕρηις Ρ ≥ εὕροις Ρᶜ | > εὕρης Β | > εὑρήσης QR ‖ μόνον ἀνείκαστον τὸν ἐν τῷ βίῳ μόνον μεμαχημένον, τὸν Ο Ρ ‖ ἀνείκαστον ≑ ἀείκαστον R ‖ τὸν (after ἀνείκαστον) > τῶν QR Ι D | ✝ μὲν μ CᶜΝ ‖ μόνον (after βίῳ) > μόνων QR ‖ μεμαχημένον > μεμαχημένων QR ‖ μὴ δὲ ΑΟ Β > μηδὲν QR | ∩ δὲ μὴ Ι Ε ΟΝ HD | ∩✝ δὲ μὴ δὲ MF | ∩✝ δὲ μηδὲ Κ | ∩✝ δὲ μήδ᾿ G | > Ο μὴ Ρ ‖ ἐν Ο QR ‖ καὶ μετὰ Ο Q ≥ καὶ μετὰ Q²ᵐᵍ ‖ ἀγαθὸν > ἀγαθεῖν D ‖ γενόμενον ≑ γενώμενον QR ‖ ἀρετῆς ≑ γἀρετῆς Q ≥ ἀρετῆς Q² ‖ παρελθόντα > προελθόντα ΑΟ ‖
51 ὦ (before καλλίμαχε) ✝ καὶ ΑΟ ‖ καλλίμαχε > Καλλίμαχος R ‖ ἐπαινέσειε ≐ ἐπαινέσειεν Α D ‖ ἐπαινέσειε κατὰ τὴν ἀξίαν ∩ 2341 μ ‖ καὶ (before τοιούτων) ✝ τῶν QR ‖ τοιούτων ποιητῶν καὶ ῥητόρων γ Ι > τοιούτου ποιητοῦ καὶ ῥήτορος δ ‖

decision to risk [the fight] with the result that he would be acknowledged [as] solely and most of all responsible for the entire success. *50* And this is [the case] for him with reference to all [the soldiers] but it is is especially [so] with reference to Cynegirus. For in this single and irrefutable question we will prevail over you.

"Cynegirus was an admirable and daring man."
[Was]n't [this the case only] so long as his life [lasted]? [Was]n't [this the case only] so long as his soul [lasted]? Yet he acquiesced to death and was overcome by the common law of nature. The valor of Callimachus, however, is without limits and by itself [is] greater than nature and [it] surpasses his soul. You would find many brave soldiers {Macedonians}, but [you would find] incomparable only Callimachus who in life fought alone and who in death did not tire but who even after [surrendering his] life became a brave man transcending the common limits both of nature and of valor.

51 O noble fighter and noble victor, unwounded and multi-wounded, how would someone praise you as befits your worth? For [you are] worthy not of an Aeschylus and of such poets and orators, but of an epic-tragedy of a

---

Editorial conjectures for reconstructing the wording of the original text (II) behind the medieval text form (π):

50 εὕροις > εὑρήσεις *s p o* ‖ **Μακεδόνας** ○ *j h r/cs* ‖ **μόνον** (before ἀνείκαστον) ○ *s p o* ‖ ἀνείκαστον + ἀνίκητον *s* | + καὶ *j* ‖ γενόμενον ○ *s p o* ‖

ῥητόρων ἄξιος ἀλλά τινος Ὁμήρου τραγῳδίας ἢ τραγικῆς φωνῆς. ὦ κοινὲ

τῆς Ἀσίας σκοπέ· ὦ σκυλεύσας τῷ θανάτῳ τὴν στρατιὰν βασιλέως καὶ

πλεῖστα λάφυρα τῶν βαρβάρων τὰ βέλη κατασχών· ὦ σεμνὸν ἀνάθημα

πολέμου· **52** ὦ καλὸν Ἄρεος ἄγαλμα· ὦ πολέμαρχε πολεμάρχου θεοῦ

δεινὸν εἴδωλον τῆς Ἀσίας τὰ τοξεύματα περιβεβλημένον· ὦ μόνος ἐνδὺς

τὴν τοῦ πολέμου στολήν· ὦ σχῆμα ἐλευθέριον, ὦ σχῆμα Μαραθώνιον· ὦ μὴ

κλίνας τὴν Ἑλλάδα· ὦ τῆς φύσεως περισσότερε· ὦ δύο μεγάλας μάχας

Δαρείῳ καὶ θανάτῳ μεμαχημένε· ὦ κοινὸν καὶ ζώντων καὶ νεκρῶν

κατόρθωμα· ὦ μὴ μετὰ ζώντων τὴν ἀρετὴν ἀφείς· **53** ὦ φρόνημα πλέον τοῦ

βίου· ὦ νεκρὲ ζώντων μαχιμώτερε. εἶχεν ἄρα ψυχὴν ἀριστὴν νεκρὸς καὶ

δευτέραν καὶ μεγίστην διὰ τῆς ἰδίας δυνάμεως πολεμοῦσαν καὶ

ἀγωνιζομένην. ὦ πρῶτος ἡμῖν δείξας ἀνθρώπων νεκροῦ μάχην· ὦ θανάτῳ

τοὺς πρὸς βίον τρέχοντας ἕλκων ἐπὶ διαδικασίαν. τὰ μὲν γὰρ ἄλλα πάντα

ἔπραξεν ὁ Καλλίμαχος, τῷ πολέμῳ δὲ θνήσκων ὡς στρατιώτης πατρίδος

ὑπερμαχῶν ἀθάνατον τὸ σῶμα μετὰ τοῦ σχήματος ἔστησεν· ἔμεινε γὰρ ὡς

ὡμολόγησε τῇ ψυχῇ. **54** ὦ μεγάλη στάσις· ὦ τῇ γῇ σύμψυχε· ὦ ῥίζας ἐξ

---

51 ἄξιος > ἄξιοι RQ ≥ ἄξιος Q² ‖ **τραγῳδιας** ⧺ τραγῳδί F | > τραγῳδίᾳ K | > τραγικοῦ G ≥ τραγῳδίας Gᶜ ‖ ὦ (before σκυλεύσας) > ὁ Q ≥ ὦ Qᶜ ‖ **τῶν βαρβάρων** > τῷ βαρβάρῳ μ ‖ **ἀνάθημα** ⧺ ἀνάθεμα ΑΟ ‖
52 καλὸν ⥊ καλλὸν Q ‖ **Ἄρεος** ≐ Ἄρεως ΑΟ Iᶜ P ‖ **ἄγαλμα** > ἀνάθημα RQ ≥ ἄγαλμα Q²ᵐᵍ ‖ **δεινὸν** Ο P ‖ **Ἀσιας** > ἀξίας B ‖ **μόνος** > μόνον K ‖ **ἐνδὺς** ⥊ εἰδὺς R ‖ **ἐλευθέριον** > ἐλευθερίου B ‖ **περισσότερε** ≐ περιττότερε G | ⥊ περισότερες QR ‖ **δύο** + καὶ D ‖ **ζώντων** (after κοινὸν καὶ) ⥊ ζόντων QR ‖ **νεκρῶν** > νεκρὸν QR ‖
53 νεκρὲ + τῶν QR ‖ **ζώντων** (after νεκρὲ) ⥊ ζώντῳ D ‖ ζώντων **μαχιμώτερε** ∩ I ‖ **μαχιμώτερε** ⥊ μαχιμότερε QR ‖ **ἄρα** + καὶ QR ‖ **ἀριστὴν** > ἀρετὴν ΑΟ | + καὶ QR ‖ **καὶ** (after νεκρὸς) Ο Q ≥ καὶ Q² ‖ ἰδίας > οἰκείας QR ‖ **ἡμῖν δείξας ἀνθρώπων** γ I ∩ 321 δ ‖ **ἐπὶ** Ο H ≥ ἐπὶ Hᶜ ‖ **διαδικασίαν** ⥊ ἀδικασίαν DP | ⥊ διαδικαστ̣ Μ ‖ **Καλλίμαχος** > Πολύμαχος QR ‖ **ὡς** (before στρατιώτης) > ὁ D ‖ **στρατιώτης** ⧺ στρατιώτ F ‖ **πατρίδος** Ο RQ ≥ πατρίδος Q²ᵐᵍ ‖ **τὸ σῶμα μετὰ** > τῷ σώματι D ‖ σῶμα > σ̣μτι I ≥ σῶμα Iᶜ ‖ **ἔμεινε** ≐ ἔμεινεν Α ‖ **ὡμολόγησε** ≐ ὡμολόγησεν Α | > ὡμολόγει RQ ≥ ὡμολόγησε Q² | > ὁμολόγηκε D | > ὡμολόγητο μ ‖ **τῇ** Ο R ≥ τῇ R² ‖ **ψυχῇ** + ὦ μεγάλη ψύχη I ▬ Iᶜ ‖
54 ῥίζας ⥊ ῥίζα η ‖

Homer or of an epic-tragic voice. O common target of Asia! O [you] who in
death stripped the king's army of its arms and who possessed most of the
barbarians' arrows as spoils [of war]! O revered votive offering of war!   *52*
O noble image of Ares!   O general-in-chief, wondrous likeness of [the]
general-in-chief god, enclosed all around with the missiles of Asia! O only
one putting on the garment of war!   O figure of freedom, O figure of
Marathon! O [one] not making Greece lie down! O [one] more extraordinary
than nature. O [one] having fought two great battles — with Darius and with
death! O success shared by both [the] living and [the] dead! O [one] not
leaving valor with the living!   *53* O highmindedness greater than life. O
corpse more warlike than [the] living. As corpse, namely, he had a most
noble soul, both a second and very great one, making war and fighting through
its own power. O first [one] of humans who showed us a corpse's fight! O
[one who] in death dragged to trial those running for [dear] life! For while
Callimachus achieved all the other things, when he died in battle as a soldier
fighting for the fatherland he made his body to stand with the appearance [of
being] undying. For he stood fast since he agreed with his soul.   *54* O
magnificent stance! O [man] of one mind with the land! O [planted man who]

Editorial conjectures for reconstructing the wording of the original text (Π) behind the
medieval text form (π):
51 τραγῳδίας O   jü ‖ ἢ τραγικῆς φωνῆς O   h ‖
52 ζώντων (after μετὰ) > ζωῆς   h ‖
53 δὲ (after πολέμῳ) > καὶ o ‖

ἀρετῆς βαλλόμενος· ὦ φυτὸν Μαραθώνιον. ὦ δήμων βεβαιότερε καὶ νήσων

λαμπρότερε· τοῖς βαρβάροις Ἐρέτρια μὲν ἡρπασμένη πλεῖ καὶ Νάξος

αὔτανδρος ἐν ταῖς ναυσὶν ἐτέθη, Καλλίμαχος δὲ ἀκίνητός ἐστι, τῶν ὁρῶν

στασιμώτερος καὶ τῶν σκοπέλων βεβαιότερος. καὶ γῆ μὲν ἐσείσθη πολλάκις

καὶ νήσους ὅλας εἶδον ἄνθρωποι φερομένας, τὸν δὲ ἕνα νεκρὸν ὁ τοσοῦτος οὐ

διέσεισε πόλεμος.   **55** ὦ τεῖχος Ἀττικῆς ἀρετῆς· ὦ μέγιστον τῶν

Μαραθωνίων θαυμάτων καὶ θειότατον· ὦ τῶν ἐκεῖ φασμάτων ἐξαίρετον.

ἔστη νεκρὸς εὐσχήμων ἐν τῇ πρώτῃ στάσει, νεκρὸς τὸν θάνατον

ἀπιστούμενος, αἰσχυνόμενος πεσεῖν, καὶ γέγονεν ἔμψυχος καὶ τεθνεὼς ὤν. ὦ

βλέπων ἢ μιμούμενος τῆς ψυχῆς τὴν ὁδόν.   **56** ἐγὼ καὶ τὴν ψυχὴν ἐκ τ'

ἀφανοῦς οἶμαι τότε συμμάχεσθαι καὶ παροῦσαν ἐγγυᾶσθαι ἀνέχειν τὸ σῶμα.

ὦ μεγάλῳ φάσματι κεκοσμημένε. τουτὶ δὲ Πολύζηλος, ἐκεῖνο τὸ θαῦμα

Καλλίμαχος ἦν. ἦν μὲν γὰρ καὶ ζῶν ἔτι δεινὸς πολεμίοις καὶ ἀκόρεστος

μάχης ἕστηκε βοῶν·

Ὦ Δαρείου δοῦλοι βάρβαροι,

---

54 βαλλόμενος AO B I > βαλλόμενε δ | > λαμβόμενος QR ≥
λαμπόμενε Q² | ≥ λαμπόμενος R² ‖ **Μαραθώνιον** ⇌ Μαθώνιον QR ≥
Μαραθώνιον Q²R² ‖ **δήμων** > δόμων B ‖ **δήμων βεβαιότερε καὶ νήσων** ∩ 4231
QR ‖ **Ἐρέτρια** β ✦ Ἐρετρία δ Q² | ⇌ Ἐρετρῖα I | ⇌ Ἐνέτρεια AO ‖
Ἐρέτρια μὲν ∩ QR Iᶜ ‖ **ἡρπασμένη** > ἡρπαγμένη FKG | ✦ ἡρπαγμένη E ‖
Νάξος O Q ≥ Νάξος Q²ᵐᵍ ‖ **αὔτανδρος** ⇌ ἄντανδρος R ‖ **ὁρῶν** ✦ ὁρῶν P
‖ **σκοπέλων** ⇌ σκόπλων D | ⇌ ἀκοπέλων R ‖ **γῆ** > μὴ QR ‖ **νήσους** >
νήσεις QR ‖ **δὲ** (before ἕνα) ⇴ δ' G ‖ **νεκρὸν** ⇌ κρὸν D ‖ **ὁ** (after νεκρὸν) O
QR ‖ **τοσοῦτος** > τοσοῦτον QR | > τοιοῦτος ηQ² ‖ **διέσεισε** ⇴ διέσεισεν A
| > διέσωσε P ‖
55 Ἀττικῆς ἀρετῆς ∩ AO ‖ **θειότατον** > θειότερον RQ ≥ θειότατον Q²
‖ **φασμάτων** > θαυμάτων G ‖ **εὐσχήμων** ⇌ εὐσχήμω R ≥ εὐσχήμων Rᶜ ‖
εὐσχήμων ἐν τῇ πρώτῃ στάσει O D ‖ **στάσει** + καὶ R | + νε Q ≥ καὶ Qᶜ
‖ **θάνατον** > ἀθάνατον M ‖ **καὶ** (after ἔμψυχος) O FKG ‖ **ἢ** > ὦ QR ‖
56 τ' ἀφανοῦς ⇌ ταφανοῦς R ‖ **τότε** O RQ ≥ τότε Q² ‖ **ἐγγυᾶσθαι** +
καὶ παροῦσαν Q ▪ Qᶜ ‖ **τουτὶ δὲ** > τουτ' εἶδε μ ‖ **ἦν** (after ἦν) O Q ≥ ἦν
Q²ᵐᵍ ‖ **γὰρ** O QR ‖ **δεινὸς** + τοῖς AO ‖ **ἕστηκε** ⇌ ἑστήκεν A ‖ **βοῶν** >
βοηθῶν CN ‖ **Δαρείου** ⇌ Δρείου RQ ≥ Δαρείου Q² ‖

put down for himself roots by means of valor! O plant of Marathon! O [planted man] more steadfast than lands and more magnificent than islands! Eretria, seized by the barbarians, sets sail, and Naxos, men and all, was placed in the ships, yet Callimachus is immovable, more stationary than the mountains and more steadfast than the peaks. Earth was shaken many times and people saw whole islands carried away, yet such a [great] war did not shake the one corpse. **55** O Attica's wall of valor! O greatest of the Marathonian marvels and most divine! O [portent] par excellence of the portents there! [The] elegant corpse stood in the foremost position, a corpse belying death, being ashamed to fall; and it became instilled with a soul even though it had died. O [corpse] seeing or imitating the way of the soul! **56** I think that even from the unseen [nether world] his soul then continued to fight alongside and that standing by it pledged itself to hold up the body. O [corpse] honored with a great portent. And this very [portent] Polyzelus [saw] — that marvel was Callimachus. For even while still living he was fearsome to enemies, and insatiate in battle he stood shouting:

"O barbarian slaves of Darius,

Editorial conjectures for reconstructing the wording of the original text (Π) behind the medieval text form (π):
55 ἤ (after βλέπων) > καὶ h ‖
56 τουτὶ δὲ > τουτ᾽ εἶδε (→ μ) h r/cs ‖

οὐ Σκύθαι ταῦτα οὐδὲ ποταμὸς

οὐδὲ πλάνης ὅμιλος οὐδὲ ἄμαξαι ζηλούμεναι

ἀλλ᾿ Ἀττική καὶ ... Πελοπιδῶν·

ἐν ταύτῃ ἕστηκα καὶ περιμένω τίς πρῶτος ἀπόλλυται.

καὶ πολλὰ βαλλόμενος καὶ τοξευόμενος

ὥς τισιν ἄνθεσι στεφανούμενος λέγω·

βάλλετε καὶ μὴ φείδεσθε.

τί δ᾿ οὐ βάλλετε;

ἐγὼ δέομαι βελῶν,

ἐπεὶ χωρεῖ τὸ σῶμα τόπον ὑγιῆ ἔχον.

τί τοὺς ἀθλίους Ναξίους,

τί τοὺς ταλαιπώρους Ἐρετριεῖς {ἐμοὶ} περίστητε;

ἐμοὶ τὸ τοῦ πολέμου δίκτυον περιτείνατε.

τίς Δᾶτις, τίς **Τισσαφέρνης**;

ἰδού, ὦ πάντες, ἐγὼ ἕτοιμος.

θυέτω μέ τις, εἰ δύναται·

βασιλεὺς σαγηνευσάτω, εἰ ἔξεστιν.

---

56 Σκύθαι ⧧ Σκύσθαι R | ⧧ κύσθαι Q ≥ Σκύσθαι Qᶜ ‖ **οὐδὲ** (after ταῦτα) ⧧ οὔ δὲ H | > οὐ FKG ‖ **ποταμὸς** > ποταμοὶ M ‖ **ἄμαξαι** ⧧ ἄμαξ QR ‖ **ζηλούμεναι** > ζητούμεναι ε ‖ **Πελοπιδῶν** γ I > Πελοπίδαι δ Q² ‖ **ἐν ταύτῃ** γ > ἐνταῦθα δ I ‖ **πρῶτος** > πρῶτον ε ‖ **ἀπόλλυται** ⧧ ἀπόλυται A QR D ‖ **βαλλόμενος** ⧧ βαλόμενος D ‖ **ἄνθεσι** ⧧ ἄνθεσιν D ‖ **φείδεσθε** ⧧ φείδεσθαι D ‖ δ᾿ (before οὐ) ⧧ δὲ QR ‖ **οὐ** ○ QR ‖ **ἐπεὶ χωρεῖ** > ἐπιχωρεῖ M ‖ **ὑγιῆ** B μ E CN HP ⧧ ὑγιᾶ D | > ὑγιὲς AO QR I ‖ **ἔχον** > ἔχων MG ≥ ἔχον Gᶜ ‖ **Ναξίους** ○ R ‖ **ἐμοὶ** (before περίστητε) > ἐμὲ B ‖ **τὸ** (after ἐμοὶ) ○ D ‖ **δίκτυον** ⧧ δίκτιον R ‖ **περιτείνατε** > παρατείνατε I | > παρατείναται RQ ≥ περιτείναται Q² ‖ **Δᾶτις** + ọ I ‖ **Τισσαφέρνης** I E CN ⧧ Τισαφέρνης B μ HP Di | ⧧ σαφέρης QR | > Ἰνταφέρνης AO ‖ **δύναται** > δυνατὸν QR ‖ **βασιλεὺς** AO B I MK E ⧧ βασιλ᾿ QR G | ⧧ βασιλ᾿ F | > βασιλεῖ CN | > βάλλειν ηQ²ᵐᵍ | (βασιλ᾿ ρ → β → γ → π; μ → δ → π; ν → ε → δ → π) ‖ **σαγηνευσάτω** > σαγηνεύσατε M | ⧧ σηγηνευσάτῳ R ‖

Scythians [did] not [achieve] these things, neither [did] river

   nor nomadic horde nor envied wagons,

      but Attica and [allied Plateia?] of Pelopidae.

In this [Attica] I stand and I wait for who is going to perish first.

   And though [I am] being hit and struck with many arrows

      as though being wreathed with some flowers, I say:

Keep on shooting and don't hold back.

   Why don't you keep on shooting?

I need arrows,

   since my body makes room [for them] [still] having a healthy spot.

Why did you surround the unfortunate Naxians,

   why the pitiful Eretrians {instead of me?}?

      Stretch out the net of the war around *me*.

What Datis, what Tissaphernes [will try]?

   Behold, O all [of you], I [am] ready.

Let someone slay me, if he is able.

   Let [the] king sweep [me] up in the dragnet, if it is in his power."

Editorial conjectures for reconstructing the wording of the original text (Π) behind the medieval text form (π):

56 καὶ (before μὴ φείδεσθε) ○ *s p o* ‖ οὐδὲ (before ποταμὸς) + Ἴστρος *h* (→ *p* Latin "Ister") ‖ καὶ Πελοπιδῶν > καὶ Πέλοπος χθῶν *p* | > ἡ Πελοπιδῶν *j* | ○ *h* ‖ βελῶν + ἔτι *j* ‖ ἐπεὶ χωρεῖ τὸ σῶμα τόπον > βελῶν ἔτι χωρεῖ τὸ σῶμα *j* ‖ ἐμοὶ περίστητε; ἐμοὶ ∩ 213 *h* ‖ Τισσαφέρνης > Ἀρταφέρνης *o h* ‖

57 ἐπεὶ δὲ πᾶς ἀνὴρ ὅλα τὰ βέλη ἐπ᾽ αὐτῷ ἔπηξεν, ἔχαιρε λέγων πρὸς

ἑαυτόν·

Τὴν Ἀσίαν ἀπεδύσαμεν·

καὶ τοῖς συστρατιώταις παρήγγελλε·

Παίετε κατακεντοῦντες αὐτοὺς καὶ μὴ φείδεσθε·

οὐκέτι γὰρ ἔχουσι βέλη.

γυμνοὺς ὑμῖν αὐτοὺς ἐποίησα.

58 οἱ δὲ βάρβαροι πάντες ἐπειρῶντο μὲν καὶ πᾶς ἔβαλλε, κινῆσαι δὲ οὐδεὶς

ἠδύνατο οὐδὲ καθελεῖν τὸν ἄνδρα πεπηγότα οἱ τὰ μεγάλα καθελόντες ποτὲ

χώματα, οἱ βιασάμενοι τὸν Βόσπορον ἄγαν ὄντα ῥοώδη καὶ Σκυθικὴν

θάλασσαν· ἀλλὰ πᾶς μὲν ἔβαλλε καὶ πᾶς ἐφονεύετο καὶ τῷ Καλλιμάχῳ

προσέπιπτεν ὃς καθάπερ προνενευκότι λίθῳ πρὸς θάλασσαν ἐρείσας ἑαυτοῦ

τὸ σῶμα **τελευταῖον** τοιοῦτον εἶπε τὸν λόγον πρὸς ἑαυτόν·

Στῆθι, Καλλίμαχε, ἀκίνητος.

59 οἱ δὲ ὥσπερ τείχει **προσβαλόντες** καρτερῷ πλέον οὐδὲν ἔδρων·

ἐκρύπτετο γὰρ ὑπὸ τῆς τῶν βελῶν περιβολῆς. ἔνθα δὴ πολλοὶ μὲν

---

57 πᾶς Ο Ν ‖ αὐτῷ > αὐτὸν QR ‖ ἔχαιρε > χαῖρε Ν ‖ ἑαυτὸν > αὐτοὺς QR ‖ **ἀπεδύσαμεν** > ἀπεδυσάμην Κ | > ἀποδάσατε RQ ≥ ἀπεδήσαμεν Q² ‖ **συστρατιώταις** ΑΟ Ι ε > στρατιώταις β μ ‖ **παρήγγελλε** Β μ Ε ≟ παρήγγειλεν ΑΟ | ≠ παρήγγελε QR I CN | > παρήγγειλε HD | > παρήγγειλεν Ρ ‖ **παίετε** + με Ρ | **κατακεντοῦντες** > κατακενοῦντες Β ηQ² | > κατακενούντοις QR | > κατακεντᾶτε Μ ‖ **φείδεσθε** > φείδεσθαι Ν ‖ **οὐκέτι** ≟ οὐκ ἔτι Α | > οὐκ ἔστι QR ‖ ὑμῖν > ἡμῖν QR G ‖
58 **οἱ** (before δὲ βάρβαροι) > ἡ R ‖ **ἐπείρωντο μὲν** ∩≟ μὲν ἐπείροντο R | ∩ Q ≥ ἐπείρωντο μὲν Q² ‖ **πᾶς** > πάντες RQ ≥ πᾶς Q²ᵐᵍ ‖ **ἔβαλλε** (after πᾶς) ≟ ἔβαλλεν Α | > ἔβησαν RQ ≥ ἔβαλλε Q²ᵐᵍ ‖ **ἠδύνατο** ≟ ἐδύνατο η ‖ τὸν (before Βόσπορον) Ο D ‖ **ἔβαλλε** (after μὲν) ≟ ἔβαλλεν Κ | ≠ ἔβαλε η ‖ **ἐφονεύετο** ≥ ἐφονεύσατο Μᶜ ‖ **προσέπιπτεν** ≟ προσέπιπτε Ο | ≟ προσέπιπεν R ‖ **πρὸς θάλασσαν** ≟ προθάλασσαν QR ‖ **ἑαυτοῦ τὸ** ∩ QR ‖ **τελευταῖον** γ I Mu > τελευτῶν FKG ε ‖ **εἶπε** ≟ εἶπεν Α ‖ τὸν (before λόγον) Ο Β ‖
59 **στῆθι** ≟ τῆθι R ‖ **Καλλίμαχε** ≟ Καλλίμα D ‖ **προσβαλόντες** β μ Ε ≟ προσβαλλόντες ΑΟ I η | > προβαλόντες CN ‖ **περιβολῆς** > περιδρομῆς Β ≥ περιβολῆς Βᶜ | > παραδρομῆς RQ ≥ περιβολῆς Q²ᵐᵍ ‖ **δὴ** + μὲν D ‖

57 Since every man drove all his arrows into him, he was glad, saying to himself:

"We have stripped Asia [of its weapons]."

And to his fellow soldiers he was giving orders:

"Smite [them], cutting them down, and don't spare [them],

for they no longer have arrows.

I stripped them bare for you."

58 But the barbarians were all trying — and everyone was shooting — yet no one was able to move nor to destroy the man who had become fixed - they [who] once destroyed the great earthworks, they [who] used too much force on the Bosporos despite its being a strong current and a Scythian sea. But everyone was shooting and everyone was being slain and was falling before Callimachus who — just like a rock jutting into the sea — having propped up his own body said to himself some such final word [as this]:

"Stand firm, Callimachus, immovable!"

59 But they, as if attacking a mighty wall, were accomplishing nothing at all. For he was cloaked by the enclosure of the arrows. There indeed many [who

---

Editorial conjectures for reconstructing the wording of the original text (Π) behind the medieval text form (π):

58 ὃς **καθάπερ προνενευκότι λίθῳ πρὸς θάλασσαν** > ὃς καθάπερ προνενευκότα λίθον πρὸς θάλασσαν or ὃς ἐοικὼς προνενευκότι λίθῳ πρὸς θάλασσαν *o* | > ὃς καθάπερ προνενευκὼς τις λίθος πρὸς θάλασσαν *j* | > καθάπερ προνενευκότι λίθῳ θάλασσα ὃς *h* ‖

κάμνοντες ὑπὸ τῶν Καλλιμάχου βλημάτων ἀπώλοντο καὶ πολλοὶ παρ᾿ αὐτὸν

ἔπιπτον ἑστηκότα·   **60**   Δᾶτις δὲ ὁρῶν ὠργίζετο τῷ νεκρῷ καὶ τοῖς

βαρβάροις ἐνεκελεύετο·

Οὐ κλινεῖτε,

οὐκ ἀναιρήσετε τὸν φιλόνεικον νεκρόν;

ἄνθρωπε δαιμόνιε, μετὰ τοσούτων αἰσχύνῃ πεσεῖν;

ἔτι μένεις; ἔτι μάχῃ;

πόσας ἔτι ψυχὰς ἔχεις;

οἴμοι **νικᾷ νεκρὸς ἡμᾶς Ἀθηναῖος.**

ἄνδρες, μηκέτι βάλλετε·

ἀποθνήσκοντες Ἀθηναῖοι γίνονται μαχιμώτεροι.

ὦ δέσποτα Δαρεῖε, τίς σε ἐξηπάτησεν;

ἐπ᾿ ἀθανάτους ἀνθρώπους ἡμᾶς ἔπεμψας πεσεῖν οὐκ εἰδότας.

αἱ δοκούμεναι Πέρσαις καὶ Μήδοις

καὶ Μάγοις τέχναι ἀπρακτοῦσιν·

Ἀθηναίων γὰρ οἱ νεκροὶ μάχονται παρ᾿ αὐτοῖς

καὶ δεξιὰ νεκροῦ πολεμοῦσα μέρος τῆς μάχης ἐγένετο.

61 βασιλεὺς δὲ ἰδὼν αὐτὸν ὀρθὸν ὅπλοις πολλοῖς περιβεβλημένον ἐβόα·

---

59 κάμνοντες > καμόντες M ‖ ὑπὸ (after κάμνοντες) ⚏ ὑπὼν Q ≥ ὑπὸ Qᶜ ‖ ἀπώλοντο ≠ ἀπώλλοντο B | ⚏ ἀπόλοντο RQ ≥ ἀπώλοντο Q² ‖ ἑστηκότα > ἑστηκότες QRM ‖ **60** κλινεῖτε > κινεῖτε B | > αϊνεῖτε Q ≥ κλϊνεῖτε Qᶜ ‖ ἀναιρήσετε ⚏ ἀναιρήσειτε D | > ἀναιρήσεσθε G ‖ **νεκρόν** Ο N ‖ **μένεις** > μὲν εἰς R ‖ **πόσας** > πρὸς N ‖ νικᾷ ⚏ νικᾶν RQ ≥ νικᾷ Q² | > νικᾶς I ‖ νικᾷ **νεκρὸς ἡμᾶς Ἀθηναῖος** γ I ∩ 2341 δ Q² ‖ **Ἀθηναῖος** > ἄνδρες M ‖ ἀποθνήσκοντες > ἀποθνήσκοντι R ‖ γίνονται μαχιμώτεροι ∩ QR ‖ **μαχιμώτεροι** > μαχιμώτερος Q ≥ μαχιμώτεροι Qᶜ ‖ σε ⚏ σ᾿ G ‖ ἐξηπάτησεν > ἐξηπάτηκεν D ‖ ἀνθρώπους ἡμᾶς ∩ AO ‖ εἰδότας > εἰδότι D ‖ **Πέρσαις καὶ Μήδοις** ∩ 321 QR ‖ **Μάγοις** > πάγοις B ≥ Μάγοις Bᶜ ‖ ἀπρακτοῦσιν ⚏ ἀπρακτοῦσι F ‖ καὶ (before δεξιὰ) > οὐ K ‖ **61** δὲ > καὶ R ‖ αὐτὸν ὀρθὸν γ η ∩ I μ E CN ‖ ὅπλοις πολλοῖς περιβεβλημένον ∩ > ὅπλων πολλῶν περιβεβλημένων QR ‖ πολλοῖς Ο η ‖ ἐβόα Ο Ο ‖

were] toiling perished from the wounds [inflicted] by Callimachus and many were falling near him [while he remained] standing. *60* When Datis saw [this] he began to get angry at the corpse and he was enjoining the barbarians:

"Will you not tip [it] over,

will you not carry away the contentious corpse?

Heaven-sent man, amidst so many are you ashamed to fall?

Are you still standing fast? Are you still fighting?

How many souls do you still have?

Woe is me, a dead Athenian is defeating us.

Men, don't shoot any more;

when they die, Athenians become more warlike.

O master Darius, who deluded you?

You sent us men against immortals who do not know [how] to fall.

The skills esteemed among Persians and Medes

and Magians avail nothing.

For the corpses of Athenians fight alongside them,

even a corpse's warring right hand took part in the battle."

61 And when [the] king saw him erect, enclosed by many weapons, he began shouting:

Φεύγωμεν, πλέωμεν·

ἤδη γὰρ ἤγειραν Ἀθηναῖοι τρόπαιον.

τοιαῦτα, τέκνον, παρέσχες τοῖς βαρβάροις δόγματα. **62** ὦ σεμνὸν πολέμου

τέρας· ὦ τῶν συμμάχων θεῶν ἄξιον θέαμα. σὺ μὲν ὦ Πὰν ἐβοήθησας, σὺ δὲ

Ἥρα συνεκρότησας καὶ **Παλλὰς** ὑπερήσπισας ὡπλισμένη. περὶ σὲ μὲν ἔστη

Ἡρακλῆς, ἔστη δὲ Θησεὺς **σεμνυνόμενος·** σὲ δὲ χρὴ καὶ προτιμᾶσθαι τῶν

Μαραθῶνι κειμένων καὶ τὸν πατέρα τὸν σὸν ἐπὶ σοί τε καὶ τοῖς σοῖς

στρατιώταις ἀγορεύειν λόγον ἁρμόττει. **63** τοίνυν, Εὐφορίων, ἀπελθὼν τὸν

σεαυτοῦ νεκρόν, τὸν χαμαί, τὸν ἐν ὄχλῳ **νεκρῶν** καὶ πεπατημένον, θάπτε καὶ

θάπτε τὴν χεῖρα ἣν {τῷ πελέκει τις ἀπέκοψε τὴν Κυναιγείρου δεξιάν} ὅπλῳ

γυναικῶν τις ἔτεμεν {οὐκ αὐτοῦ μὲν ὑπάρχουσαν, ἐκείνου δέ}. ἀκροστόλιον

γὰρ οὖσαν τῆς νεὼς ἀπέκοψεν αὐτὴν καὶ τῶν ἀπειλητικῶν λήρων ἐπέσχε τὴν

61 φεύγωμεν ✝ φεύγομεν A | ⚊ ψεύγωμεν R ‖ ἤγειραν Ἀθηναῖοι
τρόπαιον ∩ 231 D ‖ **τρόπαιον** ⚌ τροπαῖον B ‖ **παρέσχες** > παρέσχε QR ‖
παρέσχες τοῖς βαρβάροις ∩ 231 CN ‖ δόγματα ✝ ...ματα Ou ‖
62 **τέρας** > τέρας QR ‖ **σὺ** (after θέαμα) > σοι AO ‖ ὦ (before Πὰν) >
ὁ AO ‖ **ἐβοήθησας** > ἐβοήθησεν AO | > ἐβόησας RQ ≥ ἐβοήθησας Q² ‖
σὺ (after ἐβοήθησας) > σοι AO ‖ **Ἥρα** ⚊ πέρα RQ ≥ Ἥρα Q²ᵐᵍ ‖
συνεκρότησας > συνεκρότησε O | > συνεκρότησεν A ‖ **Παλλὰς** B (emended
from Πολλὰς in β) ⚊ Πολλὰς AO (→ α → γ → π) QR (→ ρ → β → γ → π) | >
πολλῶν δ I ‖ **ὑπερήσπισας** δ I Q² > ὑπερήσπισεν AO QR | > ὑπερήσβισεν B
‖ **περὶ** > παρὰ B ‖ **ἔστη** (before Ἡρακλῆς) > ἔστιν I ‖ ἔστη (after
Ἡρακλῆς) > ἔστι QR I ‖ **σεμνυνόμενος** μ E C HPQ²(Di) ⚊ σεμνενόμενος N |
⚊ σεμνόμενος QR | > σεμνυνόμενοι AO B I ‖ **καὶ** (after χρὴ) ○ M ‖ τῶν +
ἐν δ Q²ᵐᵍ ‖ **κειμένων** ⚊ κειμένῳ D ‖ **σὸν** > ὼν A | ῶν O | + σὸν N
‖ **ἁρμόττει** γ I Mu > ἁρμόττον E CN HPQ²(Du) | > ἁρμόττοντα FKG ‖
63 **τοίνυν** + ὦ QR ‖ **τὸν** (after ἀπελθὼν) > ταῖς QR ‖ **σεαυτοῦ** ⚊ σεαυτ
K | > ἑαυτοῦ QR ‖ **νεκρῶν** AO (→ α → γ → π) > νεκρὸν B | ○ QR I δ ‖
καὶ (before πεπατημένον) ○ M RQ ≥ καὶ Q² ‖ **θάπτε** (after πεπατημένον) ○ AO
M ‖ **ἀπέκοψε** ⚌ ἀπέκοψεν P ‖ **ἔτεμεν** + ἔτεμεν Q ▬ Qᶜ ‖ **ὑπάρχουσαν** ⚊
ὑπάρουσαν RQ ≥ ὑπάρχουσαν Q² ‖ **ἐκείνου δέ** γ ○ δ I ‖ **ἀκροστόλιον** γ (Qu)
I Q² ✝ ἀκροστόλ E CN (→ ε → δ ?) | ⚊ ἀκρόστολον μ | ⚊ ἀκροστόλου η ‖
γὰρ (after ἀκροστόλιον) γ > δὲ δ I Aᶜᵐᵍ Q² ‖ **καὶ** (after αὐτὴν) ▬ Q² + καὶ
Q²ᵐᵍ ‖ **τῶν ἀπειλητικῶν λήρων ἐπέσχε τὴν** γλῶσσαν ὡς οὖσαν τῶν ἄλλων μερῶν
ἀκρατεστέραν. αἱ μὲν γὰρ ἄλλαι δεξιαὶ ○ Q | + τῶν ἀπειλητηρῶν λήρων ἐπέσχε
τὴν γλῶσσαν ὡς οὖσαν τῶν ἄλλων μερῶν ἀκρατεστέραν. αἱ μὲν γὰρ ἄλλαι δεξιαὶ Qᶜᵐᵍ
‖ **ἀπειλητικῶν** ⚊ ἀπειλητήρων RQᶜ ≥ ἀπειλητικῶν Q² ‖ **ἐπέσχε** ⚌ ἐπέσχεν
A ‖

"Let us flee, let us sail.

For [the] Athenians [have] already erected a victory monument."

Such opinions, child, did you foster in the barbarians. *62* O august marvel of war! O sight worthy of the allied gods! You, O Pan, assisted, and you, Hera applauded, and you, armed Pallas, shielded [Callimachus]. On the one hand Herakles stood by for you, on the other hand Theseus stood by, revered. It is requisite for you to be honored above those lying [prone] at Marathon and it is fitting for your father to deliver [the] speech both for you and for your soldiers. *63* Therefore, Euphorion, go off and bury your own corpse, the one on the ground, the one in the mass of corpses and trampled underfoot, bury too the hand which someone hacked off with a women's weapon {[the hand] belonging not to the latter, but to him} {someone cut off the right hand of Cynegirus with an axe}. For [someone] cut it off since it was [on the] ornament of the ship, and he kept the tongue [of Cynegirus] from [making]

Editorial conjectures for reconstructing the wording of the original text (Π) behind the medieval text form (π):

62 σοῖς στρατιώταις > συστρατιώταις *s* (cf. B 57)

63 ὄχλῳ νεκρῶν + κείμενον *h* ‖ καὶ πεπατημένον > καὶ πεπατημένων *o* | > καταπεπατημένον *j* ‖ τῷ πελέκει τις ἀπέκοψε τὴν Κυναιγείρου δεξιάν Ο *h* r/cs ‖ γυναικῶν > γυναικείῳ *j* ‖

γλῶσσαν ὡς οὖσαν τῶν ἄλλων μερῶν ἀκρατεστέραν. {αἱ μὲν γὰρ ἄλλαι

δεξιαὶ τῶν στρατιωτῶν πρὸ τῶν ἱερῶν θυρῶν ἔμειναν ὑπὸ σπάρτων ἐχόμεναι

ἐν τῷ τῆς λαβῆς σχήματι·} ἡ δὲ τῆς πρύμνης ἀπεκρούσθη μήτε **ξύλου**

κατασχοῦσα Σιδονίων. **64** σὺ δέ, ὦ τέκνον, καὶ τὴν παλαιὰν δόξαν τοῦ σοῦ

πρώτου γένους ἐπιστώσω· αὐτόχθονες μέν ἐσμεν ὡς ἀληθῶς {τρεῖς παῖδες

παλαιοί}, οὕτως ἀνέσχε Καλλίμαχον ἡ μήτηρ καὶ τὸν μὲν Ἡρακλέος,

---

63 γλῶσσαν ⸗ γλῶσαν CN | ⸗ γλῶτταν B I M ‖ ὡς > ὦρ᾽ R ‖
μερῶν > μελῶν OA ≥ μεστῶν Aᶜ ‖ **ἔμειναν** > ἔμεινεν QR ‖ **πρύμνης** ⸗
πρύμνας FKG ‖ **ξύλου** AO ≠ ξύλ FK (→ μ → δ → π) D (→ η → ε → δ → π) | >
ξύλον QR | > ξύλα B I E CN HPQ² | > ξύλων MG ‖ **κατασχοῦσα** + τῶν
B ‖ **Σιδονίων** B I δ (Md) Q²ᵐᵍ ⸗ δονίων QR | > Σιδονίου OA ≥ Σιδονάον Aᶜ
‖

64 παλαιὰν > πάλαι N ‖ **πρώτου** γ > πρῶτος I | ○ δ ‖ **ἐπιστώσω**
≠ ἐπι.σω F | > ἐπιστώσατο N ‖ **μέν** ○ AO ‖ **ἐσμεν** A ≥ ἔσμεν Aᶜᵐᵍ
‖ **καὶ τὸν μὲν Ἡρακλέος** ○ FKG (Mdu) RQ ≥ καὶ τὸν μὲν Ἡρακλέος Q²ᵐᵍ ‖
Ἡρακλέος ⸗ Ἡρακλέους OA ≥ Ἡρακλέως A² | Ἡρακλε.ς I ‖

empty threats on the ground that it is more intemperate than the other [body] parts. {For the other right hands of the soldiers remained before the sacred doors being held by ropes in the form of the grip.} But the [hand of Cynegirus] was knocked off from the stern without gaining possession of Sidonian wood. **64** But you, O child, confirmed the old expectation from your first time of life. We are native to the land in the true sense, {three aged sons}, thus the mother held up Callimachus and the ... of Herakles ...,

---

Editorial conjectures for reconstructing the wording of the original text (II) behind the medieval text form (π):

63 αἱ μὲν γὰρ ἄλλαι δεξιαὶ τῶν στρατιωτῶν πρὸ τῶν ἱερῶν θυρῶν ἔμειναν ὑπὸ σπάρτων ἐχόμεναι ἐν τῷ τῆς λαβῆς σχήματι· ○   j? r/cs ‖ ἄλλαι δεξιαὶ τῶν στρατιωτῶν > πάλαι δεξιαὶ τῶν στασιωτῶν j ‖ μήτε > μηδὲ j h ‖

64 αὐτόχθονες μὲν ἐσμεν ὡς ἀληθῶς ○   r/cs? ‖ τρεῖς παῖδες παλαιοί ○   h   r/cs ‖

The Ending

γεννάδαν οὕτω λαμπρὸν καὶ τόσον ὑπὲρ τῆς πατρίδος σπουδαῖον ὡς ὑπὲρ

αὐτῆς προέσθαι οἱ ἐπὶ θαύματι τὴν ψυχήν.   **65** ἐμὸν τοιγαροῦν, ὦ Εὐφορίων,

εἴη τὸ τοῖς ἐπιταφίοις πρῶτον τὸν παῖδα κοσμεῖν καὶ τὸν ἐπινίκιον τραγῳδεῖν.

σὺ δὲ τὸν σὸν μεθύστερον θρήνει συγχωρούντων τῶν δικαστῶν.

The Ending (= Z):

○ (absent from the MS)
    O   (→ α)
    I   (→ ι)
    M   (→ μ and → ρ   [before Z was appended to μ and ρ])
    HD (→ η)
    P   (→ H)

+ (in a second hand in the MS)
    A (→ α) + Z
    B (→ β) + Z
    ρ (→ β) + Z   [by the time it was copied by Q and R]
    μ (→ δ) + Z   [by the time it was copied by F]
    E (→ ε) + Z
    ν (→ ε) + Z   [by the time it was copied by C and N]

+ (in the first hand of the MS)
    QR (→ ρ + Z)
    F   (→ μ + Z)
    KG (→ F)
    CN (→ ν + Z)

While J and L do not contain the ending, they do not come into consideration here because in them the entire second declamation is also absent.

    64 γεννάδαν QR FKG > γεννάδα A B E CN ‖ ἐπὶ θαύματι ○ FKG ‖ τὴν + τὴν R ▬ Rᶜ ‖
    65 Εὐφορίων ⤳ Ἐφορίων F ‖ ἐπιταφίοις ⤳ ἐπὶ ταρίοις R ‖ πρῶτον τὸν παῖδα ∩ 231 FKG ‖ τὸν (before ἐπινίκιον) > τὴν G RQ ≥ τὸν Qᶜ ‖ τῶν + τὸν R ‖ δικαστῶν + τέλος A B G ∣ + τέλος περὶ Καλλιμάχου R ∣ + τέλο. περὶ Καλλιμάχου Q ∣ + ὁ τοῦ Καλλιμάχου πατήρ C ∣ + ὁ Καλλιμάχου πατήρ N ‖

The Ending

[the] noble one so radiant and so significant for the fatherland that on its behalf he gave up his soul for a marvel.   *65*   Accordingly, O Euphorion, may the first thing at the funeral ceremonies be to honor *my* son and solemnly to recite the victory hymn.   And you sing the dirge for your [son] afterward if the judges assent.

Editorial conjectures for reconstructing the wording of the original text (II) behind the medieval text form (π):
    64 γεννάδαν > γέννημα *h* ‖ οἱ > δὴ *j* | > τοι *h* ‖

Chapter 4

Notes and Commentary on the Introduction (0)

0

Taking their cue from the addition of ἐπιτάφιος after σοφίστου in some MSS (AO QR I MG L) the early editions of the Greek text (Stephanus, Possinus, Orellius) began the superscription with ἐπιτάφιοι λόγοι (= Funeral Orations). The superscription in Hinck's edition presumes an ellipsis: the nominative title before the genitive of authorship (Πολέμωνος σοφιστοῦ) is not expressed. The adjective ἐπιτάφιος (ἐπί + τάφος = *over a tomb*), with λόγος expressed or implied, had by the 4th century BCE become the standard technical term for the *funeral oration* (cf. Plato, *Mx.* 236b; Demosthenes 20.141; Aristotle, *Rh.* 365a31). This traditional title is most certainly not part of the original text, but appears to have originated with the scribe of γ. In actuality these two speeches are not funeral orations spoken to the civic minded at a state ceremony or to mourners at the graveside; rather they are arguments presented to Athenian jurymen (δικασταί, A 47; B 65) explaining why each respective speaker should be the one granted the right to deliver the funeral oration over those fallen at Marathon. Moreover, they do not exhibit the traditional elements or the usual threefold structure of the classical funeral orations, namely: praise, lament, and consolation (cf. Kennedy, *The Art of Persuasion in Greece*, Princeton: Princeton University Press, 1963, pp. 154-166). Praise, of course, does appear, but the other elements are absent. Hence, rather than ἐπιτάφιοι λόγοι or the corresponding Latin *laudationes funebres* already Possinus (pp. 101–102) proposed the Latin legal technical term *divinationes*. However, in jurisprudence *divinatio* (= examination) denoted a proceeding to determine which of several accusers presenting themselves for a case was the most suitable to conduct the accusation in the actual trial (cf. Cicero, *Div. Caec.*; Quintilian 3.10.3; 7.4.33; Suetonius, *Caes.* 55). That situation does not really correspond to the one posed by Polemo, and Possinus's proposal never succeeded in displacing ἐπιτάφιοι λόγοι. Admittedly, much in each speech might also find its way into the eulogy when later delivered. It is worth noting that the traditional Latin title, *declamationes*, describes a different and wider genre. In Polemo's day the term *declamatio* served as the Latin counterpart for the Greek μελέτη (= theme, lecture, exercise, declamation). Herodes Atticus advised listeners who once praised his declamation on war-trophies that if they wanted to know what real eloquence was they should read Polemo's μελέτη (Philostratus, *V. S.* 539). Presumably he was referring to Polemo's no longer extant declamation on τρόπαια, which had argued that there should not be permanent monuments of Greek victories over Greeks (Philostratus, *V. S.* 539). Today, inasmuch as no other μελέται from Polemo are extant beside the so-called ἐπιτάφιοι λόγοι, it is preferable — because no confusion will arise — to use the broader, more accurate Latin 'genre' designation than the narrower, less accurate Greek 'theme' designation as title. Therefore, the English translation opts for this Latin title [in square brackets] as though the Greek text, albeit without MS support, had read the corresponding term μελέτη or μελέται.

In the one-sentence introduction the opening term, νόμος, can denote both the concepts of unwritten *custom* (*mos*) and of written *law* (*lex*). In Polemo it is often difficult to decide which is meant. He can use the term sometimes in the one sense, sometimes in the other (custom: A 15, 45; law: A 19; B 6, 22; "the common law of nature" in B 50 is a case by itself). Here in the introduction — and in the quasi-parallel B 1 — the term seems to encompass both meanings.

Several well-known texts provide the background for the situation referred to in Polemo's introduction. One *locus classicus* is Thucydides' account of the circumstance and content of Pericles' famous funeral oration in the first year of the Peloponnesian war (Thucydides 2.34.1–2.47.1). Thucydides describes in careful detail the public funeral rites conducted by the state for those who had fallen. He explains that the Athenians, in carrying out the ceremony, were following ancestral custom (τῷ πατρίῳ νόμῳ χρώμενοι 2.34.1). As conclusion of the elaborate three day rite after the bones were finally interred, Thucydides says, "a man chosen by the state, who in [public] opinion both seems to be not unintelligent and [who] is pre-eminent in reputation, speaks over them the appropriate praise" (ἀνὴρ ἠρημένος ὑπὸ τῆς πόλεως ὃς ἂν γνώμῃ τε δοκῇ μὴ ἀξύνετος εἶναι καὶ ἀξιώσει προήκῃ, λέγει ἐπ᾽ αὐτοῖς ἔπαινον τὸν πρέποντα, Thucydides 2.34.6). According to Thucydides Pericles began his oration by saying, "Most of those who have spoken here in the past have praised the one who added this oration to the custom on the grounds that it is honorable to speak it over those being buried from the wars" (2.35.1). Both in this comment, which explains the oration as a deliberate addition to the traditional funeral ceremony, and in the earlier one which calls the ceremony a "practice inherited from the fathers" (πάτριος νόμος 2.34.1) the primary meaning of νόμος appears to be *custom*. If, however, "the one who added this oration to the custom" (τὸν προσθέντα τῷ νόμῳ τὸν λόγον τόνδε) could be identified as a law-giver (Solon? Cimon?), then the sense of νόμος might perhaps be shifted toward *law*.

Embedded in Plato's *Menexenus* was a funeral oration well-known to the Greeks; in fact, Cicero says that the speech was so popular that it was read out loud annually at the Athenian commemoration of the war dead (*Or.* 151). Many themes in the *Menexenus* reappear in Polemo; this suggests that Polemo knew the text well. The occasion for this dialogue is that following deliberation "the Council was going to select someone who would speak over the dead" (ἡ βουλὴ μέλλει αἱρεῖσθαι ὅστις ἐρεῖ ἐπὶ τοῖς ἀποθανοῦσι) at the public funeral rites (Plato, *Mx.* 1.234b). Such eulogies are to be delivered "by wise men who do not praise at random, but in speeches prepared long beforehand" (ὑπ᾽ ἀνδρῶν σοφῶν τε καὶ οὐκ εἰκῇ ἐπαινούντων, ἀλλὰ ἐκ πολλοῦ χρόνου λόγους παρεσκευασμένων, *Mx.* 2.234c).

The model speech which Socrates then recites concludes with the remark that the public lamentations were completed κατὰ τὸν νόμον (*Mx.* 21.249c). Here it is not clear if the oration itself is included as part of these mourning rites, and it may be debated whether νόμος here means custom or law.

A third, less-known, post-classical passage from Diodorus Siculus (8.12.1–16) is also particularly illuminating for Polemo's declamations. Diodorus describes a 'trial' contemporary with that in Polemo's text to determine which of two war heroes exhibited the most valor in battle. To be sure, there are differences between Diodorus and Polemo. Diodorus depicts a dispute set in Messenia, not Athens. Moreover it is not fathers of the fallen, but heroes themselves who plead their cases. Nonetheless, the issue is the same: recognition for the most exceptional military valor. And the post-battle 'trial' is held κατὰ τὸν νόμον (Diodorus Siculus 8.12.5). Because of the instructive formal and material parallels with Polemo and because it is less accessible than Plato or Thucydides, the entire Diodorus passage is presented in Appendix 4.

E. P. Parks (*The Roman Rhetorical Schools as Preparation for the Courts under the Early Empire*, Baltimore: Johns Hopkins University Press, 1945, esp. pp. 67–85) and S. F. Bonner (*Roman Declamation in the Late Republic and Early Empire*, Berkeley: University of California Press, 1949, esp. pp. 84-132) have argued convincingly that the Latin rhetorical genre of the *controversiae* or *suasoriae*, to which Polemo's declamations are akin, had in school the function of preparing the student for the conditions in the Roman courts, and they demonstrated that to this end the Latin pro- and contra- school declamations often dealt with specific laws (whether real or fictitious). If a comparable *Sitz-im-Leben* be supposed for rhetorical training in the Greek speaking part of the empire — something that has to be demonstrated — then one might be inclined to give the nod to *law* as the specific sense of νόμος in Polemo's opening line. It is a close call; the translation opts for *mos* over *lex* because that is easier to defend in the absence of clearer evidence.

Whether by law or by custom, there is reliable historical evidence that the Athenian council did formally choose the speaker for the state sponsored funeral ceremonies honoring the war dead. What Polemo appears to have fabricated are the criteria for selection of that speaker. Whereas the primary texts mention as pre-requisites the intelligence, reputation, and eloquence of the candidate, Polemo makes the choice dependent on two different issues which are otherwise historically unattested: (1) which fallen soldier exhibited most clearly pre-eminent valor?   (2) who has parentage (πατήρ) or kinship (οἰκεῖος A 1) vis-à-vis that soldier? The latter is uncontested; it is the former which the two declamations attempt to demonstrate.

In Plato's *Menexenus* the setting is that the Athenian Council was in the process of selecting the speaker of the funeral address at the public ceremony in 386 BCE for the war dead. After due deliberation they reduced the list of candidates to two, Archinus and Dion, then postponed their final decision till the following day (Plato, *Mx.* 234a–b). In his declamations Polemo simulates an analogous situation. Following the battle at Marathon in 490 BCE the Athenian assembly, presumably after careful consideration of candidates, also came up with a short list of two. Before a final decision is reached these two are given an opportunity to make their cases.

In contrast to Plato's *Menexenus* the potential speakers in Polemo are not identified by their own names, but by the names of their sons. While Greek tradition remembered that Callimachus was from the Attic tribe of Aiantis and the township of Aphdna (ca. 10 miles northwest of Marathon) (Plutarch,

Quest. Conv. 628d–e), the name of his father is nowhere attested; hence, it never appears in Polemo. More was known about the family of Cynegirus, information no doubt in part preserved due to the fame of Cynegirus' older brother, the playwright Aeschylus. Their father was Euphorion of Eleusis, an aristocratic landowner of a Eupatrid family (cf. *Marmor Parium*; Chamaeleon, περὶ Αἰσχύλου 39-42; Suidas, Εὐφοριον). The father's name, Euphorion, appears in Polemo (B 22, 37, 63, 65) as does also that of his other son, Aeschylus (A 49; B 45, 51). The name of Euphorion's third son (cf. B 64 — Euphorion? Ameinias?) is never mentioned in Polemo because it was irrelevant to the argument.

The neuter plural accusative ἄριστα is adverbial. This superlative has the same sense which its positive (ἀγαθός) always has in Polemo when used with persons: *brave* (A 2, 2, 6; B 1 4, 4, 4, 24, 50). The introductory superlative formulation of the theme, "dying most bravely," is never thereafter repeated in the text, although etymologically related terms do occur: ἀριστέα (A 15), ἀριστεία (A 32, 44; B 28), ἀρειστεύω (B 27). Instead, in the text itself the theme is expressed repeatedly (35x) with the term ἀρετή. This shift in terminology suggests that the introduction in its present form may have been formulated subsequent to the delivery, when the declamations were later published.

Ἀθήνῃσι is a locative adverb; the ending -σι (like -θι and -ι) denotes the place *where*, *at*, or *in* (*GG*, 342, 1535).

The names of Callimachus and Cynegirus are mentioned in the reverse of the order in which their fathers speak (γ preserves this order; δ adjusts it to the actual order of the speakers). This is the first example of one of Polemo's favorite rhetorical devices, namely *chiasmus*, and it is a hint at the countless figures and tropes to come.

Notes and Commentary on the First Speech (A)

(The Speaker is Euphorion, the Father of Cynegirus)

A.
1

The phrase τὰ ἄλλα joined together with τὲ ... καὶ has the sense of *especially, above all else* (LSJ, ἄλλος II.6; ἄλλως I.3; τε II.1; *GG*, 2980).

The genitive τούτου is difficult. One scribe (Hᶜ) smoothed it to τούτῳ (dative of respect?), another (P) to accusative τοῦτον (i.e., λόγον). The translation takes τούτου to be a loose genitive of connection (= περὶ τούτου, *GG*, 1380-1381; cf. τοῦ λόγου, A 16). The genitive, however, may indeed be a corruption out of an original τοῦτον (ν and υ can on occasion be confused).

Strikingly, Euphorion claims to have contributed from his own 'physique' (φύσις = personal constitution [cf. A 11], not nature in general [cf. A 38; B 11, 34, 36, 50, 50, 50, 52]) the most notable daring *deed* (cf. neuter τὸ ... ἀξιολογώτατον) at Marathon. The epexegetical apposition is more natural, namely, a uniquely fighting *man* (cf. masculine ἄνδρα ... μεμαχημένον).

The phrase κατὰ μέρος μεμαχημένον is unusual and its precise meaning elusive. In the few other instances where Polemo uses κατά with the accusative in the distributive (κατὰ μέρη νενίκηκεν, A 32; τὸν κατὰ μικρόν μέγαν, A 33) it is also hard to determine the exact meaning. The key lies no doubt in the subsequent description of Cynegirus' attempt to restrain the ship: first he grabbed the ship with his right hand, and when that was cut off he tried with his left hand until that too was chopped off (A 10). Those MSS which read μέρη instead of μέρος (BQR [→ β]) represent an assimilation to A 32; μέρος is the *lectio difficilior*. Orellius (pp. 7-8) distinguished the meaning of

191

the plural (= *membratim* = limb by limb) from the singular (= *vel unico corporis membro* = even with a single member of the body). Despite that, he argues, it makes little difference which reading one choses because the sense remains the same: to fight against the enemy *pedententim singulis partibus corporis vel membris* (= by degrees with individual parts or members of the body). Thus Orellius opts for a plural sense as did Stephanus (cf. κατὰ μέρη) and Possinus (cf. p. 34 *trunca ipsa discaptaque membra* [= maimed and mangled members]).

2

The sentence is mutilated. The variants, erasures, and overwriting in the MSS reflect the scribes' struggles to improve the text. εἰκός (= [it is] fair) needs an epexegetical infinitive (e.g., εἰπεῖν [= to say]) and after τι καὶ the sense requires something like [περὶ] τὸν Καλλιμάχου [ἀγῶνα / πόλεμον] (= concerning the struggle of Callimachus). This the translation supplies.

The conclusion of the sentence introduces the central topic at issue: ἀρετή, a term which occurs 35 times in the work (cf. Index 8). Nowhere does Polemo, in contrast say to Plato in the *Meno*, posit or explore definitions of the broad concept ἀρετή. He simply uses the term in a narrow sense to refer to military distinction, merit, or virtue. For Polemo it primarily has the sense of courage, bravery, heroism, and valor in war. While not co-terminous, Polemo's use overlaps in part with the Greek notion of ἀνδρεία (= manliness), a term which he never uses (cf. B 14 which describes Callimachus as acting ἀνδρείως [= courageously]). Essential aspects of the concept emerge not through definition, but through paired synonyms and the narration of the memorable deeds of the two soldiers.

For the construction ἐγὼ ... ἐπειπεῖν ... δικαιότερος cf. the classical δίκαιος εἰμί + infinitive (LSJ, δίκαιος C). The αὐτοῦ is a genitive of comparison with δικαιότερος; the reference is to the father of Callimachus. The neuter correlatives τοσοῦτον ... ὅσῳ indicate a comparison of quantity or degree whereby the ὅσῳ in the comparative clause has the sense of *to the same degree as* the quality mentioned in the principle clause (*GG*, 2468-2473).

The summation (τὸ σύμπαν) of the dispute to follow is the distinction between authentic valor (ἀρετή) and mere appearance (σχῆμα) (cf. οὐ σχήμασι ... ἀλλὰ ἀληθείᾳ τιμῶντας ἀρετήν [= honoring ἀρετή not in appearances, but in truth], Plato, *Epin.* 989c). At issue is substance, not appearance, *Sein, nicht Schein*. The declamations will recall this distinction many times simply by uttering the term σχῆμα (A 7, 7, 26, 26, 28; B 17, 20, 42, 47, 53).

3

Polemo's Atticizing Greek frequently employs crasis (τοὐμοῦ = τοῦ ἐμοῦ) to avoid hiatus (*GG*, 46, 62-69).

Improper prepositions, though common in Attic Greek, seldom appear in Polemo (cf. Index 6). Here χάριν (= for the sake of) is one of the rare occurrences and, as is typical, it is in post-positive position (i.e., after τῶν ... ἐπαινῶν). It needs to be supplied also with the genitive τῆς κοινῆς δόξης.

The evidence for the subjunctive λέγῃ is balanced by that for the optative λέγοι (hence the bold print). The γ and δ families attest both: α (→ A O) and ε (→ J E ν [C N]) had the subjunctive, in β and μ the attestation is divided. The readings of γ and δ, therefore, cannot be established. The MSS themselves show that the change could go in either direction: The optative in I (→ ι) suggests that at least one of its *Vorlagen* (γ or δ) had λέγοι, and yet both γ and δ were in some instances copied as λέγῃ. Conversely, λέγῃ in a *Vorlage* could also appear as λέγοι in a copy (cf. E → L and ε   η → HD). The confusion was, of course, facilitated by iotacism: in Byzantine Greek the endings -ῃ and -οι were pronounced alike. Based on the external evidence alone, therefore, the choice for the reading in the medieval π comes down to a coin toss. From the internal evidence, however, the criterion of style points toward λέγῃ in the original Π since Polemo as a rule used standard and not mixed conditions (cf. Index 2).

Among Hellenistic rhetoricians διατίθημι in the middle voice was the technical term for *delivering* or *reciting* a speech (cf. Polybius 3.108.2; Diodorus Siculus 12.17.5 Dionysius Halicarnassus 11.7; 3.17; Philostratus, *V. S.* 540).

The neuter noun to be supplied with τὰ τῶν παίδων is ἔργα (= deeds) or πεπραγμένα (= things done) as in the following sentence.

4

Polemo plays subtly with the verb κρατέω. Strictly speaking both the infinitive κρατεῖν and the participle κρατῶν are used absolutely, that is without objects. By rights then they should be translated absolutely, e.g., "prevail", the sense being: Cynegirus is suited to prevail [i.e., in the question before the Athenian jury] because he died prevailing [i.e., over the Phoenician ship]. However, inasmuch as he did not in fact gain possession of the ship, the translation opts for a more literal rendering and supplies objects: Cynegirus should *hold* [the honor] since he *held* [the ship].

With the participle εἰδόσι Orellius (p. 10) would supply ὑμῖν: *coram vobis non ignorantibus* (= before you who are not unknowing). However, a less specific reading makes just as good sense: "For [any/those] who know ..."

The form θάτερος is crasis for τὸ ἕτερος, a gender mismatch which though grammatically impossible (neuter - masculine) is documented in the early Hellenistic period (LSJ, ἕτερος). Literally the clause says: " ... the other [one of the two sons] contends along with the valor of the [= my] son ..." This is awkward; the sense is clearly that given in the translation.

The irregular comparative κρείττω is an Attic contraction of κρείττονα (cf. the uncontracted form in B 2): the 'movable' ν drops out and the vowels *o* and α contract in accordance with the rule of progressive assimilation where the *o* dominates and lengthens (*GG*, 134. 51.a, 59). In Polemo there is only one other instance of this Attic contraction (μείζω instead of μείζονα in A 38).

5

The technical term πολέμαρχος (= war-leader, commander-in-chief) which appears here for the first time is mentioned as though needing no explanation (likewise with all subsequent occurrences: A 13, 14, 15, 15, 15, 16, 17, 36, 46; B 2, 6, 7, 17, 18, 18, 20, 22, 23, 49, 52, 52). To assume an understanding of the title is, of course, appropriate for the imagined audience (Athenians in 490 BCE). However, for Polemo and his Ionian listeners six centuries later the parameters of the polemarch's office may not at all have been clear. In early monarchies the polemarch was an adjutant to the king. With the emergence of democracies the polemarch acted as a kind of *primus inter pares* within the staff of generals. Note that in B 49 the στρατηγοί are called πολέμαρχοι. It is to capture this sense that the translation renders πολέμαρχος with *general-in-chief*. In Athenian history, however, the battle of Marathon was the last time that a polemarch acted as military chief of staff. After that the στρατηγοί (= generals) assumed this role and the only 'military' task the polemarch had was overseeing the state ceremonies for the war dead (Aristotle, *Ath. Con.* 58.1; cf. A 15, 16; B 22). His activity was shifted to protecting the resident aliens, the metics with near citizen status, and the representatives of foreign states (Aristotle, *Ath. Con.* 58.2; cf. H. Schaefer, "Polemarchoi," *RE* Suppl. 8 [1956] 1097–1134). Polemo's statements in the declamations thus blur the pre- and post-Marathon distinctions.

Callimachus' actions out of obligation (ἀνάγκη) of office are inferior to those of Cynegirus who acted of his own free will (ἐθελούσιος). The same argument is later repeated (A 18).

Although a number of arguments made about Cynegirus — both *for* (A 5, 18, 20) and *against* (B 13, 24, 37) — are predicated on his youth, his exact age is never mentioned. However, at least five expressions in the text fix his age within a narrow span. He is circumscribed by:

(1) νέος κομιδῇ = *quite young* (A 5; cf. νεώτερος [= younger], B 24). While in Athens νέος could on occasion describe a man up to the age of thirty (cf. Xenophon, *Mem.* 1.2.35), normally it denoted a minor (cf. Thucydides 1.107.2) and was often used in connection with παῖς or κοῦρος (LSJ, νέος). Here certainly the qualifier κομιδῇ disallows an adult.

(2) νεότης = *youth* which is characterized by *inexperience* (ἄπειρον, A 20).

(3) μειράκιον (diminutive of μεῖραξ) = *boy, lad.* This term, used by both speakers (A 20; B 36, 37), can designate a παιδίον = *child* (Plato, *Tht.* 168d-e) or a νεανίας = *youth* (Aristophanes, *Pl.* 1038, 1096), that is, a boy of school age (Aristophanes, *Nu.* 990, 1000; Arrian, *Epict. Dis.* 3.9.8). It designates the stage of life between παῖς (Plato, *Ap.* 18c; *Char.* 154b; *Leg.* 658d) and ἀνήρ (Plato, *Tht.* 173b; *Gorg.* 485a-d). The word denotes one who is ἀγένειος (= not yet showing a beard, Aristophanes, *Eq.* 1373, 1375), that is, a boy in the suitable age for a paederastic relationship (Plato, *Prot.* 315d-e). To be sure, some authors mention μειράκια as old as twenty (Hippocrates, *Epid.* 3.2.8.2; 4.1.15.1; Plutarch, *Brut.* 27.3) but in general the word is used for those somewhat younger.

(4) σχεδὸν καὶ πρὸ τῆς ἡλικίας = *almost even before* [*coming*] *of age* (A 5). The term ἡλικία (cf. ἧλιξ [= of the same age]) is clearly used in the legal sense of maturity, just as ἐνῆλιξ means *in the prime of manhood* or *of age* and ἀφῆλιξ means *not yet of age* in the sight of the law (cf. Phrynichus, *Ecl.* 64; LSJ, sub verba). That is, ἡλικία refers to the age of eligibility or obligation for military service (cf. Thucydides 8.75.3; Demosthenes 4.7; 21.95; Lysias 2.50). The word here is virtually equivalent to the Athenian technical term ἐφηβεία (cf. ἥβη [= youthful prime]), the period of initial military training and service which in classical Athens was set for the age group nineteen and twenty years old (cf. Aristotle, *Ath. Con.* 42; O. W. Reinmuth, "Ephebia", *KP*, 2.287-291). A male reaching the age of eighteen was an ἔφηβος (Aristotle, *Ath. Con.* 42; Pollux 8.105), the point of transition from adolescence to adulthood.

(5) ἀπόμαχος = [*freed*] *from fighting* (A 20). This is a term applied to those unsuitable or ineligible for service by reason of disability or age (cf. Xenophon, *An.* 3.4.32; Arrian, *An.* 5.8.3; 5.27.5).

Taking all these terms into account it must be concluded that Polemo imagined Cynegirus to be a teenager, no more than 17 or 18 years old at the very most. This view does not square well with other known accounts of the battle. The primary report (Herodotus 6.114) mentions in one breath the deaths of Callimachus, the general-in-chief (πολέμαρχος), Stesilaus son of Thrasylaus, a general (στρατηγός), and Cynegirus, son of Euphorion — all standout names among the famous (ὀνομαστοί) Athenians who fell that day. The obvious sense of Herodotus' comment is that Cynegirus was an important figure in Athenian society already *before* the battle. Further, Plutarch goes so far as to say that Cynegirus had been appointed as one of the generals (στρατηγοί) at Marathon (*Par. Gr. R.* 305b–c; cf. *dux*, Pliny, *N. H.* 35.57). Polemo was either unaware of such traditions about Cynegirus' high status or he disregarded them because they did not serve his rhetorical purposes.

There may also be other reasons to suspect that Polemo has 'adjusted' the age and rank of Cynegirus for his own purposes. Given an estimated citizen population in Attica of 140,000 and an available military force exceeding the 9000+ troops they put in the field (cf. R. P. Duncan-Jones, "Population", *OCD*, p. 862; Plutarch, *Par. Gr. R.* 1), it is unlikely that the Athenians sent minors to Marathon. Moreover, Cynegirus' older brother Aeschylus was known to have been born in 525/524 BCE (cf. E. Vogt, "Aischylos", *KP*, 1.192); he was, therefore, 35 years old when he fought at Marathon. Polemo's portrayal would put an age difference between the two brother soldiers of 18 or more years. That seems unlikely in a Greek hoplite corps.

To conclude the point about Cynegirus' age: Polemo's portrayal can serve as an instructive example of his creation of 'historical fiction' or his employment of 'rhetorical license'.

The term ἔξοδος (= going/marching out) has here the specific technical sense of *military expedition* (LSJ, ἔξοδος, I.2).

The synonymous parallelism

ἔρωτι δόξης καὶ

μεγάλων ἔργων ὀρεγόμενος

(= [motivated] by a love of glory and

for great deeds yearning)

is typical of Polemo's love of chiasm and pleonastic expression.

6

The phrase ἐγένοντο ἄνδρες ἀγαθοί (= became brave men) already used by Herodotus to describe the heroic fighters at Marathon (Herodotus 6.114, 117). Indeed, this was his standard expression for those who proved valiant in battle (cf. Herodotus 1.95, 169; 5.2, 109; 7.53; 9.71.75). Like Herodotus (6.114) Polemo applies the phrase also specifically to Callimachus (B 50). When Polemo goes on to describe both Cynegirus and Callimachus as θαυμαστός (= admirable, A 28; B 50), and likewise their deeds (A 11, 25, 26; B 6; cf. A 20, 27), he stands in the tradition of Herodotus who in the prologue to his history stated he intended to record for posterity the θαυμαστὰ ἔργα (= marvelous deeds) of both Greeks and Persians.

οὑμός is crasis for ὁ ἐμός (= the son *of mine, my own* son).

When Euphorion calls Callimachus' father "this man" (τούτου, A 6, 7), or later "this man here" (οὑτοσί, A 13), he is following the common rhetorical practice of referring to an opponent simply with the disparaging demonstrative pronoun (cf. W. W. Goodwin and C. B. Gulick, *Greek Grammar*, Boston: Gunn, 1930, § 1005; for the contemptuous use of οὗτος cf. also BAGD, οὗτος 1.a.α; A. T. Robertson, *A Grammar of the Greek New Testament*, Nashville: Broadman, 1934, p. 697).

7

The circumstance of Callimachus being pierced by so many arrows and spears that these held up his corpse erect is introduced here by Polemo through the mouth of Euphorion who repeatedly returns to this striking image only to deprecate Callimachus' reputation (A 22, 23, 24, 25, 26, 27, 29, 30, 31, 37, 45, 47). Subsequently, by contrast, the father of Callimachus will repeatedly exploit the image in order rather to enhance Callimachus' fame (B 8, 9, 10, 11, 12, 14, 17, 30, 32, 38, 39, 42, 43, 44, 47, 48, 51, 53, 54, 55, 56, 57, 58, 59, 60, 61). This *modus moriendi* for Callimachus is not documented in the classical period. The legend appears to have emerged in the Roman era. It is articulated most succinctly in Plutarch's description of the battle at Marathon (cf. Καλλίμαχος δὲ πολλοῖς περιπεπαρμένος δόρασι καὶ νεκρὸς ἐστάθη [= Callimachus, pierced with many spears, stood upright, although dead], *Par. Gr. R.* 1). This portrait may possibly have arisen out of a simile or hyperbole the sort of which is often found in tales of war. Not uncommon were Roman exaggerations about battlefields so thick with dead that the corpses themselves held each other erect by the sheer press of bodies (cf. *conpressum turba stetit omne cadaver* [= pressed together by the mass {of bodies} every corpse stood upright], Lucan, *Phar.* 1.787; *ita conferti, ut caesorum cadavera multitudine fulta, reperire ruendi spatium nusquam possent, ... miles ... in stipitis modum undique coartatus haereret* [= so crowded together that the corpses of the slain supported by the multitude could nowhere find room to fall, ... {one mutilated} soldier ... pressed from all sides was held erect like a tree stump],

Ammianus Marcellinus 18.8.12). Euphorion dismisses the portrayal of Callimachus' death as mere σχῆμα (= appearance).

8

The term φάλαγξ (singular) does not have here the military organizational sense of *hoplite* or *cavalry corps* (as e.g. the plural in A 41) or Macedonian *phalanx* which it came to have in late classical and Hellenistic times; rather it simply means *line of battle* as in archaic Greek (cf. Homer, *Il.* 6.6; Xenophon, *Cyr.* 1.6.43).

κᾆτα is crasis for καὶ εἶτα (and then).

The assumption here that the Persian commander kept an elite division (μαχιμώτατον [= most warlike]) in reserve back on the shore is unattested, but not implausible. While Herodotus said nothing about the Persian arrangements behind the line at Marathon he did describe how Mardonius, the Persian commander-in-chief at the later battle of Plateia (479 BCE), surrounded himself with a thousand picked men (ἀρίστους ... λογάδας, Herodotus 9.63). However, the assertion that at Marathon the bulk (πλεῖστον) of the Persian force remained on the beach is far less likely. This is an exaggeration calculated to enhance the daring of Cynegirus.

That Cynegirus was nearly naked (γυμνός) does not mean he was devoid of clothing, but without armor (cf. Ἀχιλλεὺς γυμνόν, ἄτερ κόρυθός τε καὶ ἀσπίδος, οὐδ᾽ ἔχεν ἔγχος [= Achilles naked, without helm and shield, nor had he spear]; κτενέει δέ με γυμνὸν ... ἐπεί κ᾽ ἀπο τεύχεα δύω [= kill me naked ... when I have taken off {my} armor], Homer, *Il.* 21.49–50; 22.124–125). In military vocabulary exposed parts of the body not covered by armor are called τὰ γυμνά (Thucydides 3.23; Xenophon, *Hel.* 4.4.12).

The assertion that Cynegirus was the first person to fight a sea battle from land (πρῶτος ἀνθρώπων ἐναυμάχησεν ἐκ γῆς) is introduced here by Euphorion; hereafter he often repeats and expands this point as a weighty element in his argument (cf. πρῶτον ... ναυμαχίαν ἐν γῇ, A 36; and A 11, 28, 33, 35-38, 44). In his rebuttal Callimachus' father takes up the argument and neutralizes it (ἐκ γῆς ἐναυμάχει· Δᾶτις δ᾽ ἐκ θαλάττης ἐπεζομάχει [= he fought a sea battle from land — then Datis fought a foot battle from sea], B 45, cf. B 31). This theme needs to be seen in light of the rhetorical tradition about Xerxes bridging the Hellespont and cutting a canal through the Athos peninsula (cf. Herodotus 7.22-24, 36-37, 55; Aescyhlus, *Pers.* 74-750). His legendary 'marching over the sea and sailing through the land' had become stock items in rhetoric (cf. Isocrates, *Pan.* 89; Lysias, *Epit.* 29; Cicero, *Fin.* 2.34.112; Dio Chrysostom 3.31). Indeed, this paradox had become so hackneyed among

orators that Lucian lampooned it (*Rh. Pr.* 18). Since the Marathonian setting of
Polemo's declamations predated Xerxes, Polemo was kept from directly citing
this cliché. Nevertheless, he could not resist the paradoxical notion of fighting
a sea battle from land. The language Polemo used for this (ἐναυμάχησεν ἐκ
γῆς, A 8; ναυμαχίαν ἐν γῇ, A 36) is reminiscent of Thucydides' description
of the famous battle at Pylos (425 BCE.) where the Spartans were said
virtually to have waged a sea-fight from land (ἐκ γῆς ἐναυμάχουν, Thucydides
4.14.3). This motif found its way into sophists' speeches (cf. ναυμαχία ἀπὸ
γῆς, Aristides, *Pan.* 229) and is applied here by Polemo to Cynegirus as the
inaugurator.

9

That Cynegirus terrified "many ships" and restrained the "king's navy" is
another example of a long series of overstatements to which both speakers are
prone. Hyperbole in Polemo is unabashed.

Polemo identifies the national origin of the ship which Cynegirus attacked
as Phoenician (A 9, 23, cf. A 31; B 40; also Sidonian B 63). Herodotus'
primary account of the battle at Marathon nowhere mentioned Phoenicians,
although he did indicate that in the Persian military build-up the Phoenicians
contributed the major contingent in the fleet (Herodotus 6.6, 14, 25, 28, 33,
34, 41, et al.).

The title of βασιλεύς (= king) without the article is characteristic of
Polemo (A 9, 29, 43, 43; B 8, 32, 40, 40, 41, 51, 56, 61). Ever since
Herodotus this anarthrous expression had become the common designation of
the Persian monarch (cf. Herodotus 3.88, 96, 101; 4.43.87 [altogether 250x]).
Generally it is hard to replicate the anarthrous usage in English without
sounding stilted; hence, the translation always inserts the article in square
brackets before the noun "king". In Polemo's declamations the reference is
uniformly to Darius I, the Achaemenid king of Persia, 521–486 BCE (cf. B 5,
8, 52, 56, 60).

10

The verb κατέχω is used regularly by both speakers to describe
Cynegirus' act of restraining the ship (A 10, 35, 37; B 33, 36, 37, 40, 41, 41,
45, 63). Their differing assessments of the act, however, are expressed in the
verb tenses and qualifiers. Here the passive imperfect (κατείχετο) is qualified
by an accusative of the extent of time (πολὺν χρόνον) as if the duration of
Cynegirus' struggle — its ineffectiveness is, of course, not admitted — had
somehow changed the course of the battle. Later Euphorion uses aorists

(κατέσχες, A 35, 37), as though Cynegirus had actually succeeded in his undertaking. In the refutation the restraining is downgraded to failure and folly through conative imperfects, modal verbs, and other qualifiers (cf. B 33, 36, 37, 40, 41, 41, 45, 63).

The portrayal of the ship having been stayed (ἐρηρεισμένη [√ ἐρείδω = fix firmly]) by the hand of Cyneigirus is made graphic with a simile: "just like with a rope." Polemo likes the adverb καθάπερ ([→ καθ᾽ ἅ περ] = like as if, according as) for introducing comparisons (cf. A 30; B 58). Commonly a πεῖσμα (= boat-rope) is the cable by which a ship is made fast to the land (cf. Homer, *Od.* 10.96; 13.77; Longus 1.28.3; 2.13.1; Appian, *B. C.* 1.7.62).

Whereas Euphorion repeatedly claims that Cynegirus had not only his right hand chopped off, but his left one (τὴν ἐτέραν [= the other one]) too (A 1, 10, 11, 23, 24, 28, 31, 32, 34, 36, 37, 39, 44, 45, 49), Callimachus' father only allows that the right hand was severed (B 13, 32, 33, 36, 37, 39, 43, 44, 45, 47, 63). The mutilated trunk of Cynegirus, with his hands or arms missing, is called a *trophy* or monument of victory. The τρόπαιον (√ τρέπω = turn) was a memorial monument, often set up on a battlefield after the enemy's defeat at the point where the battle *turned* (cf. etymological explanation in Isidorus, *Etym.* 18.2.3; Servius, *Verg.* 10.775.790; Eustathius, *Comm. Il.* 10.465). It could be made of wood (Diodorus Siculus 13.24.5), bronze (Plutarch, *Alc.* 29; Pausanias 5.27.11) or stone (Pausanias 1.33.2; Strabo 4.1.11 [185]). Such monuments were not just emblems of civic or national pride. They had religious significance. They served as sites of sacrifice to the dead or to the gods (cf. IG, II[2], 1006.71; 1008.17; 1028.27), and some had inscriptional dedications to the gods of war (Vitruvius 2.8.15).

11

Polemo's construction ὡς ὀλίγῃ κατεμέμφετο τῇ φύσει is common: καταμέμφομαι (= accuse, blame, find fault with) + dative object of reproach (τῇ φύσει [= his? nature]) + ὡς (= on the ground of, because of, for). With this verb ὡς often expresses the reason for the fault-finding (cf. Plato, *Men.* 71b; Polybius 3.103.3; 5.107.6; Josephus, *B. J.* 5.325; *A. J.* 4.109; Appian, *B. C.* 5.19.9). Here the adjective ὀλίγη has the sense of *weak, feeble* (cf. ἀθυμοτέρη καὶ ὀλιγωτέρη φύσις [= a more fainthearted and weaker nature], Hippocrates, *Virg.* 1; also Homer, *Il.* 16.825). Parallels to Polemo's expression are not hard to find (cf. ἰδίῃ κατεμέμφετο χειρί ὡς ἀπὸ κρητῆρος μηδὲν ἀφυσσαμένη [= he was blaming his own hand for not ladling anything out of the crater], *An. Gr.* 11.57; καταμεμφόμενοι τὴν αὐτῶν φύσιν ... ἢ ἀσθένειαν [= blaming their own nature ... or weakness], Dio Chrysostom 12.11).

Possinus (p. 38) rendered the unusual dative participial construction φεύγουσιν ἐπὶ πλεῖστον τοῖς βαρβάροις as an ablative absolute (*fugientibus enixe barbaris* [= with the barbarians strenuously fleeing]) — the standard Latin counterpart to the genitive absolute in Greek. However, it is probably best construed under the rubric of what Smyth calls a "dative of the participle expressing time," of which he says: "In expressions of time a participle is often used with the dative of the person interested in the action of the subject, and especially to express the time that has passed *since* an action has occurred" (*GG*, 1498).

The prepositional phrase ἐπὶ πλεῖστον is an idiom (= over the greatest distance, as far as possible; LSJ, ἐπί C.I.2.c; πλεῖστος IV.3).

The neuter accusative θᾶττον (comparison of ταχύς) is adverbial: *more quickly*. The statement that Cynegirus relinquished his soul more quickly than his hand let go the ship means that his severed hands continued fighting after his own death. This notion of his continuing post-mortem effectiveness remains undeveloped in the first speech (cf. A 23, 36, 37, 40, 43), but in the second speech a similar claim about Callimachus' corpse going on with the fight after he had died becomes one of the central recurring arguments (cf. B 2, 3, 11, 12, 14, 38, 39,42, 44-48, 50-60).

From the parallel ἄμφω τὰ στοιχεῖα πληρώσας / γῇ καὶ θαλάσσῃ μεμερισμένος (= served in both elements / taken part in land and sea) it is clear that the term στοιχεῖα denotes the *physical elements*: earth and water; that is nothing out of the ordinary. What is lexicographically unusual is that it also at the same time comes close to connoting *branches of the military*: army and navy (cf. ἐν ἀμφοτέροις γὰρ τοῖς στοιχείοις ὁ πόλεμος ἀκμάζει ... εἴτε τῆς πεζῆς ... στρατηγεῖν εἴτε τῆς ναυτικῆς δυνάμεως [= In both elements the war is at its height ... to be general either of the infantry or of the naval force], Chariton, 7.5.7).

12

The twofold ταῦτα (= these things) includes all the arguments made in A 1-11. From them Euphorion deduces a double obligation: (1) the Athenians are obliged to award him the speech; (2) he then is obliged to speak eloquently.

In the phrase τὸν τάφον ... ἐκόσμησα τῷ πολλῷ μοῦ νεκρῷ (= I adorned the grave with my great corpse) the dative of instrument (τῷ ... νεκρῷ) is unusual. Ordinarily a grave is decked *with flowers, wreaths, trophies, or tears*.

13

The deictic suffix -ι added to the demonstrative pronoun (οὑτοσί) has a belittling ring to it: "this fellow here", "this here man" (cf. τούτου, A 6, 7).

From the undisputed distinction in rank between Callimachus and Cynegirus — leader and follower — the two fathers draw opposite conclusions: (a) Callimachus' father: by virtue of Callimachus' title of polemarch his father ought to be awarded the funeral speech; and contrariwise (b) Cynegirus' father: by virtue of that title Callimachus' father has consolation enough; therefore, Euphorion now deserves some compensating recognition.

14

Polemo's assertion that the polemarch at Marathon had been selected by lot was taken over from Herodotus (6.109): ὁ τῷ κυάμῳ λαχὼν Ἀθηναίων πολεμαρχέειν (= the one of the Athenians chosen by the lot to be polemarch). With this claim Polemo unwittingly makes himself guilty of the same anachronism as Herodotus. In point of fact from the time of the 6th century tyranny the archons had been elected from among the aristocrats. The practice of selecting them by lot was not (re-)introduced in Athens until the archonship of Telesinus, i.e., in 487 BCE (Aristotle, *Ath. Con.* 22).

The term τύχη is used in a mundane sense (as also in B 27 where it is parallel with δύναμις). When Polemo mentions gods he usually mentions them in pairs or in groups (cf. A 35–36; B 36, 41, 62); the exceptions are unambiguous (Briareus A 43; Zeus B 18; Ares B 52). There is no need here to capitalize the word as Τύχη as though the goddess Fortuna were being cited. The phrase κλήρῳ καὶ τύχῃ (= by lot and by chance) is a simple *hendiadys*: the two terms together express the same thing.

Aristotle had distinguished τεκμήριον (= *demonstrative* proof) from the fallible σημεῖον (= indication) and εἰκός (= probability) (*An. Pr.* 70b2; *Rh.* 1357b4; 1402b19. In Polemo, however, the term has more the sense of '*argumentative* proof' as distinguished from direct evidence (cf. Plato, *Tht.* 158b-c; parallel with μαρτύριον, Aeschylus, *Eum.* 485).

The contrast here between ἔργα (= deeds) and ὀνόματα (= titles) is paralleled afterward in the opposition between ἔργα and σχῆμα (= appearance) (A 26, 27) or between ἔργον and ἐπίδειξις (= showing off) (B 29). In the current dispute (ἅμιλλη) what matters is inner substance, not outward appearance. Social or military status is irrelevant.

The somewhat clumsy substantized adjective τοῖς δικαίοις (= for the upright) has invited various attempts at 'improvement'. One scribe (I^cmg) altered it to the adverb δικαίως [κοινωνεῖ] (= it *rightly* plays no role); other copyists (QR [→ ρ]) dropped it altogether. Stephanus and Possinus too thought the words suspect and proposed excision. Hinck emended the reading to τοῖς δικασταῖς (= for the judges). Orellius (p. 18) probably offers the best approach: *justus = juste judicaturos* (for the just = for those judging rightly). In other words, the principle of 'class-blindness' is operative *for those* [of the jury] *with integrity*.

The dismissal of Callimachus' rank as a result of chance is framed in the form of a contrary-to-fact condition. This is the first of many unreal conditions which constitute an essential part of Polemo's argumentative repertoire (cf. A 15, 29, 39; B 18, 19, 21, 33, 40, 43; see Index 2). Euphorion's argument against the relevancy of the lot is not as biting as one attributed to Socrates, who is reputed to have said that choosing public officials by lot made as little sense as selecting athletes or ship captains by lot instead of on the basis of competence (cf. Xenophon, *Mem.* 1.2.9; 3.9–10; Aristotle, *Rh.* 1393b4).

Aristotle had classified the adage (γνώμη) as a type of argumentational proof (*Rh.* 1393a25; 1394a-1395b; 1418a17), and it was characteristic of sophistic rhetoricians to punctuate important points by quoting axiomatic sayings (γνῶμαι = *sententiae*). The statement here that "valor and daring alone produce the greatest deeds" looks like such a maxim. The double subject, ἀρετὴ καὶ τόλμα, has a singular verb because the two concepts are thought of as one. Grammatically the adjective μόνη (= alone) belongs to ἀρετή with which it agrees in gender, but according to its sense it modifies both nouns. It stands last in the sentence for rhetorical emphasis.

15

Here νόμος seems to have more the sense of custom than of law (cf. above notes to 0). In post-Marathonian Athens the polemarch was responsible for arranging the funeral honors for the war-dead (cf. Aristotle, *Ath. Con.* 58); presumably this included the funeral oration (cf. B 22). The point that this responsibility applied to the polemarch, but not to his relatives, is an *argumentum e silentio* — Polemo knows of no ancient decree (cf. πάλαι ... ἂν ἐδέδοκτο) declaring the kin eligible to deliver the speech if the polemarch were dead.

κἂν is crasis for καὶ ἄν (= even if).

Euphorion, who himself was an aristocrat (cf. above notes, 0), is here made to voice a democratic sentiment. Historically that is unlikely, but it serves Polemo's argument. Eligibility for the speakership should depend not on status or family connections, but on bravery. ἀριστέα is an anomalous form.

The paroxytonal accent militates against a derivation from the adjective ἄριστος (= finest), the accusative case ending contravenes a derivation from the feminine noun ἀριστεία (= excellence, prowess). Most likely it is a neuter plural derivation from the adjective ἀριστεῖος, α, ον (= belonging to the bravest). Indeed, Jacobs (cf. Hinck, p. 7) posited here the reading ἀριστεῖα (= [the] bravest [deeds]).

16

Subject and predicate of the sentence are clear: Μιλτιάδην ἀμφισβητεῖν ἔδει (= it was necessary for Miltiades to wrangle); beyond that the remaining syntax is less lucid. The phrase τοῦ λόγου is probably a genitive of connection with a verb of saying; i.e., it has the sense of περὶ τοῦ λόγου = to dispute *about the matter* (*GG*, 1380; LSJ, ἀμφισβητέω I.b.3; cf. τούτου, A 1). However, it must be conceded that λόγος in this sense of *matter* or *subject* (LSJ, λόγος, VIII) is without parallel in Polemo for whom it otherwise consistently means *oration* (A 1, 3, 4, 12, 16, 47, 49, 49; B 1, 1, 1, 15, 19, 20, 21, 22, 62) or *word* (A 45, 46; B 34, 58). Problematic is the opening phrase ταῦτα διοριζομένῳ. In his Latin paraphrase (*nunc qui eos sibi fines circumscripserit* = since he had set these goals for himself) Possinus (p. 40) seems to interpret as if he had read an accusative participle, ταῦτα διοριζόμενον, taking the verb as a reflexive middle with Miltiades as subject. In a different interpretation Orellius (p. 21) retained the dative διοριζομένῳ but supplied τῷ νόμῳ as subject (cf. A 15), and explained: *usu et consuetudine, significatione activa*. That is, he apparently takes the verb as a middle functioning like a deponent with active sense, and he takes the dative participle like an ablative absolute (= with usage and custom [determining these things]). In contrast, the English translation offered here attempts to make sense out of the text without adding or changing any words. Like Orellius it takes the participle διοριζομένῳ as a middle with active sense, but it understands the dative as object of ἀμφισβητέω, referring to the *person with whom* the disputing occurs (LSJ, ἀμφισβητέω I.2); that is, the translation takes the subject of the participle to be *Callimachus* who had the *determining* word.

Herodotus (6.109–110) says that prior to the battle the ten leading Greek generals (στρατηγοί) were equally divided about whether to fight or not. The swing vote fell to the polemarch Callimachus; after listening to Miltiades' arguments he submitted the tie-breaking or 'determining' vote. Following Herodotus, Euphorion gives the credit for joining the battle to Miltiades, not to Callimachus.

The assertion that in military matters the στρατηγός is superior to the πολέμαρχος corresponds to the post-Marathonian constitutional reforms, but not to the situation in 490 BCE when the polemarch still served as commander-in-chief (cf. above, notes, 0, 14, 15).

The rest of the sentence, ὁ τοῦ στρατηγοῦ πατὴρ ὅπερ ἐστὶν ἀπωτέρω (= the father of the general, which is more distant), appears to be a corruption. Jacobs tried to make sense out of these words by connecting them to the previous clause (καὶ τὴν μεγίστην αρχὴν τοῦ πολέμου μετακεχειρισμένος) and inserting an οὐ before ὁ πατήρ (= the father of the general does *not* have the greatest war authority). In opposition to such an understanding the English translation takes that previous clause as an epexegetical parallel to μείζων. Hinck viewed τοῦ στρατηγοῦ as an explanatory gloss which, when added, displaced the pronoun αὐτοῦ; he, therefore, bracketed the former and restored the latter. The logic behind this is, however, opaque — at issue here is not the father of the στρατηγός, but of the πολέμαρχος. In any interpretation the neuter singular antecedant of ὅπερ remains obscure. The abstruse phrases ὁ τοῦ στρατηγοῦ and ὅπερ ἐστὶν ἀπωτέρω are perhaps best explained as two muddled scribal glosses which in early medieval time were jotted in the margin and then interpolated by later copyists into the text itself. This interpretation is indicated by the double set of brackets { } { } in the text and translation which suggest that the corruption possibly arose in stages.

The verb παριέναι (√ παρ-εῖμι) — only here in Polemo — has the technical sense of *come forward to speak* (cf. Plato, *Alc.* 1.106c; Demosthenes 18.170; 1.8; Aeschines 3.71, 159).

17

The attestation for the variants τούτοις (γ), τούτῳ (μ N D P), τούτ' (E C H), and τούτου (L) indicates that the progenitor text (π) had a truncated form (τούτ) in which the short-hand mark for the inflected ending was either omitted or ambiguous. Subsequent copyists replicated that form or interpreted it as best they could. The dative ending is certainly preferable to a genitive but whether it was intended as singular or plural is anyone's guess. In any case, the phrase ἐπὶ τούτῳ/τούτοις expresses the condition[s] *upon* which a thing is done (LSJ, ἐπί III.3).

Subjunctives are rare in Polemo (only 17x) and of these only three are hortatory: κρινώμεθα here and φεύγωμεν, πλέωμεν, B 61 (= *let us* choose, flee, sail).

Here (as in B 49) the plural πολέμαρχοι (= generals-in-chief) is synonymous with στρατηγοί (= generals).

The composite construction of ἡσυχία + the verb ἄγω (= keep silence) was common in classical Greek (LSJ, ἡσυχία 4.a), but tended to be replaced by simple verbs in later time (e.g., ἡσυχάζω, σιωπάω). Polemo's expression may be a conscious Atticism.

18

The phrase ἀνάγκη τις ἢ ἀρετὴ ἦγεν is rough and previous editions tried smoothing it in several ways. After τις Stephanus (cf. R) added ἦν (= there was). Instead of ἢ Orellius (p. xiii) wanted to read ἦν καὶ between τις and ἢ (= there was a certain compulsion and valor led [him]). Hinck posited a lacuna. Despite the grammatical difficulty, the meaning seems clear. In theory Callimachus could have been motivated either by the duty of office or by valor; Euphorion asserts the former (resuming the argument in A 5) and leaves the audience to doubt the latter.

Without object the verb ἐξῆρχε appears to mean hold office, be commander (LSJ, ἐξάρχω).

κἀν is crasis for καὶ ἐν. The phrase ἐν τοῖς πρώτοις + τάττω is a standard military expression for posting someone in the foremost position, (cf. ἔστη ... ἐν τῇ πρώτῃ στάσει [= he stood ... in the foremost position], B 55; τῆς πρώτης τεταγμένος μάχεσθαι τοῖς πολεμίοις [= posted in the front rank to fight the enemies], Lysias 16.15; cf. Isocrates 12.180; Chariton 6.9.2).

The threefold parallel, ἀρχὴν αἰδούμενος / ὑπὸ τῆς ἡγεμονίας δυσωπούμενος / ἀκολουθῶν ὀνόματι (= in awe of authority / constrained by the commandership / following a title) is pure but skillful pleonasm. There is enough variety in the cases of the nouns (accusative / genitive / dative) as well as the voices of the verbs (middle / passive / active) so as not to be a flat redundancy.

The parallel of double datives (αὐτοκράτορι ἀρετῇ / καθαρᾷ προθυμίᾳ) makes προθυμία (= zeal, willingness) a constituent element of superior ἀρετή (cf. A 24).

19

Context and argument give νόμος here the sense of law. φρόνημα admits a range of meanings, but here it obviously has the sense of high spirit, courageous resolve in war (cf. Herodotus 8.144; 9.7; Thucydides 2.43.6). Thus, whereas an external νόμος assigned the battle station (παρέταττεν) to Callimachus, an internal φρόνημα did it for Cynegirus. This distinction between extrinxic and intrinsic motivation corresponds to the earlier contrast between ἀνάγκη and ἀρετή (A 5, 18).

The construction is awkward: τῷ μὲν (dative of respect / [dis]advantage?) τὸ χρῶμα (accusative of respect) ... κακῷ γενομένῳ (circumstancial participle with conditional sense) = [literally:] for the one with respect to the color ... if he becomes bad. Possinus (p. 42) took χρῶμα in the sense of skin (cf. LSJ, χρῶμα I) but rendered it not with *cuticula* (= skin) but *pellicula* (= hide) in a *pars pro toto* sense. That is, he paraphrased it in what Orellius (p. 26) calls a *contemptum dictum pro toto corpore* (= a contemptuous saying for the whole body): *si pelliculae timuisset suae* (= if he feared for his hide) — cf. the English idiom "to save his skin". This interpretation is ingenious but unnecessary. Here χρῶμα simply means *skin color, complexion* as it often does in Greek (LSJ, χρῶμα II). Hippocrates regarded a change in skin color (χρῶμα) as a reliable diagnostic indicator (*Aph.* 4.40; 7.61; *Prog.* 2). His medical phrase χρώματα κακοήθη (= wretched skin colors, *Hum.* 8) comes close to Polemo's τὸ χρῶμα κακῷ γενομένῳ. Therefore, the sense of Polemo is this: "For the one [= Callimachus] it was not possible to escape being noticed even if his complexion was only slightly altered because he felt ill-disposed." A loss of color was traditionally taken as a sign of fear or horror (cf. τοῦ μὲν γάρ τε κακοῦ τρέπεται χρῶς, ... τοῦ δ᾽ ἀγαθοῦ οὔτ᾽ ἂρ τρέπεται χρῶς οὔτε τε λίην ταρβεῖ [= for the color of a coward changes, ... but the color of the brave man does not change, nor does he fear much], Homer, *Il.* 279, 284-285; cf. also 17.733; *Od.* 21.412-413; ὠχρήσαντα χρόα [= paling skin color {from fear}], *Od.* 11.529; cf. Aristophanes, *Lys.* 127; Euripides, *Alc.* 174). The point of this graphic image is that because of his high rank no matter what Callimachus might have done, he would have been in the limelight. On the other hand, because of his low station Cynegirus would easily have escaped attention if he had not distinguished himself in battle.

The οἷόν τε ἦν (= it was possible) of the μέν clause needs to supplied also with the infinitives of the δέ clause: [οἷον τε ἦν] ζῆν ἀφανῶς καὶ τὰ μέτρια μάχεσθαι (= [it was possible] to live inconspicuously and to fight modestly) — note the chiastic parallelism. Alongside this reading of γ, there is an alternate reading in δ which may have as much claim to originality: ζῆν ἀφανῶς τὰ μέτρια δέχεσθαι (= [it was possible] to conduct himself inconspicuously [so as] to expect [only] mediocre [assaults]). In the present edition the nod has gone to γ which in general is a more reliable witness to π, the common *Vorlage* of both γ and δ.

20

Callimachus is "older" (πρεσβύτερος, as in B 24 where it is further said that Cynegirus is "younger"). These are not *relative* [older/younger *than*] but *absolute* comparatives [= *very* old/young]. Just as νεώτερος (= younger, B 24) means the same as νέος κομιδῆ (= quite young, A 5), so also "older" has the sense of "quite old", someone of the older generation. No ancient record of Callimachus' birth year has been preserved. Nonetheless, the statement that he was selected as polemarch by lot (A 14) implies that his age is not entirely indeterminate. From the time of Draco's legislation (620 BCE) the minimum age for Athenian office-holders was thirty (Aristotle, *Ath. Con.* 4.3). Further, names of candidates to be selected by lot for the office of ἄρχων (which included the polemarch) were submitted by each Athenian deme — ten from each deme in the time of Solon's reforms (ca. 575 BCE), fifty from each deme in the time of Telesinus' reforms (487 BCE) (Aristotle, *Ath. Con.* 8.1; 22.5). It may be reasonably assumed that for such a high office the deme would only submit names of mature men who had proven themselves. Hence, Polemo surely presumes Callimachus to be at least in middle age. That stands in contrast to Cynegirus who is thought of as a teenager (cf. notes on A 5). This age difference provides Euphorion two arguments for and against each man; the arguments are cited in chiastic order. Callimachus, being older, was (a) physically stronger and more experienced — his feat, therefore, is not so impressive; and (b) he had fewer years life expectancy left — his death, therefore, was not such a big sacrifice. On the other hand, Cynegirus, being younger, (b) could still look forward to many years of life — his death, therefore, meant a greater sacrifice; and (a) his lack of experience and training meant he did not have that 'plus' (περιουσία) which Callimachus enjoyed — Cynegirus' courage, therefore, is all the more impressive. The argument that the older man has little to risk later appeared also on the lips of Polemo's famous student Herodes Atticus: When he once unguardedly let loose a torrent of invectives at Emperor Marcus Aurelius and was warned that he was risking his life he responded, γέρων ὀλίγα φοβεῖται (= an old man fears few things, Philostratus, *V.S.* 561).

The term μεγαλοψυχία (= greatness of soul) was listed by Aristotle as one of the essential component elements of ἀρετή, *Rh.* 1366b5). It stands in stark contrast to μικροψυχία (*E.N.* 4.3.1–38 [1124b]). A man with this quality is ἄριστός and ἀγαθός (= noble and good, 4.3.14–15). A "great-souled man (μεγαλόψυχος) ... braves great danger, and when at risk, [is] not sparing of his life, since [he holds that] it is not worth staying alive by every means" (μεγαλοκίνδυνος δέ, καὶ ὅταν κινδυνεύῃ, ἀφειδὴς τοῦ βίου ὡς οὐκ ἄξιον ὂν πάντως ζῆν, 4.3.23).

In legal parlance ἀπόμαχον (= [exempted] from fighting) is a technical term designating someone *ineligible* or *unfit for military service* by reason of age or disability (Xenophon, *An.* 3.4.32; Arrian, *An.* 5.8.3; 5.27.5; 6.6.5). Legally Cynegirus was underage for combat (cf. τῆς νεότητος = of youth).

21

The phrase ἐν τοῖς πρώτοις ἢ μέσοις (= in the early or middle [stages]) has temporal meaning (contrast spatial sense in A 18). For the assertion that Callimachus died early, Cynegirus late in the battle no evidence is adduced. This was not a point in contention; both speakers hold this view (cf. A 22; B 11, 13-14, 25-30). No ancient accounts of the battle mention the times of death of the two soldiers. Hence, Polemo's view seems to be based upon a syllogistic deduction such as the following:

Major premise: Callimachus was killed by Persians in the *attack* mode (B 9), Cynegirus by them in the *retreat* mode (B 13-14, 26-28, 30).

Minor premise: the Persian assault came at the beginning of the battle when they still had expectations of winning (B 9, 25), their retreat came at the end when their hopes had been dashed (B 13, 26–28).

Conclusion: Callimachus must have died before Cynegirus.

22

The neuter plural accusative τὰ πάντα is adverbial, the equivalent of πάντως (= entirely, wholly, LSJ, πᾶς, D.II.4).

The phrase εἰς αὐτὴν τὴν θάλασσαν τὴν Ἀσίαν κατήραξεν (= he dashed Asia into the sea itself) is rhetorical bombast (cf. κατήραξε δ' εἰς τὴν θάλατταν ἅπαντας [= he dashed them all into the sea], Demosthenes 23.165). The expression καταράσσω εἰς (= dash down, break into pieces) is often used to describe the destruction of a broken and routed army (cf. Herodotus 9.69; Thucydides 7.6; Dionysius of Halicarnasus, *Ant.* 9.58; Arrian, *An.* 5.17.2).

This is the first occurrence of the continent name *Asia* for the Persian invaders, a metonymy which Polemo uses consistently (cf. A 35, 43; B 8, 10, 25, 39, 51, 52, 57; cf. B 3). It has here, as elsewhere, a hyperbolic ring.

In the battle Callimachus stood in one place. On that 'fact' both speakers agree (A 7, 22, 24, 26, 27, 33, 45; B 11, 14, 17, 38, 43, 44, 53, 54, 55, 58, 60, 61,); the difference lies in the *interpretation* each speaker attaches to it — the one negative, the other positive.

In the sentence τὸ μὲν ... τὸ διώκειν (=the [act of] pursuing) the first τό is anticipatory, the second τό resumptive. The reasons for pursuit are given with instrumental datives. The polysyndeton following ἀρετῇ lists four synonyms or component elements of valor: strength, courage, daring, and reasoning. By the end of the speech each of these aspects will be illustrated in Euphorion's argument.

Since the focus is on Cynegirus, a mere two reasons suffice to explain the στάσις (immobile posture) of Callimachus: ἔκπληξις (= terror) and φόβος (= fear) — the former a specific, intense concept (cf. A 30; B 8), the latter a broader, more general one (cf. A 9, 30, 31; B 9, 13, 26, 38).

23

The repeated phrase ἐξ ὧν is a contraction of ἐκ τούτων ἅ (= because of the things which) — the relative pronoun ἅ is attracted into the case of its antecedent, and the antecedent drops out.

The heart of the argument lies in the twice mentioned contrast between the two verbs: ἔπαθε / ἔδρασε and δρᾶν / πάσχειν. The first pair are finite aorist forms which describe the particular case: Callimachus received an action, Cynegirus performed an action. The second pair (in chiastically reversed order) are articular present infinitives which describe the general thesis: the active doing of an action is more decisive (κυριώτερον) and more beneficial (ὠφελιμώτερον) than the passive suffering from an action.

Attestation for the variants κυριώτερον (= more decisive) and γενναιότερον (= more noble) is evenly balanced (δ versus γ) making the choice uncertain (hence the bold print in the text). All previous editions preferred γενναιότερον; yet it seemed to the present editors that κυριώτερον is in better keeping with the point of the distinction between action and passivity.

The sense of the predicative adjective παράσημος (παρὰ + σῆμα = beside the mark) is *falsely distinguished* (cf. παράσημον αἴνῳ [= falsely noted with praise], Aeschylus, *Ag.* 780; Plutarch criticizes parents who carelessly entrust their children to educators who are παράσημοι [= undeservedly recommended], *Lib. Ed.* 4c).

The simile of Cynegirus "sending his [severed] hands against the barbarians *just like naval expeditions* (ὥσπερ ἀποστόλους)" is striking. In classical times the compound ἀπόστολος was a strengthened form of the simplex στόλος (= fleet); in governmental language it became a technical term denoting the dispatch of a *naval expedition*, usually in the context of war (cf. Lysias 19.21; Demosthenes 18.80, 107). Euphorion's use of the plural ἀποστόλους presses the hyperbole to the limit: *each* hand is like a fleet sent to battle the enemy.

The singular εἰρεσίαν (= rowing, oar) has collective sense: *rowers, oarsmen* (LSJ, εἰρεσία II).

24

The term προαίρεσις (πρό + αἵρεσις [√ αἱρέομαι] = *choosing* one thing *before* another), typically a moral or political concept (LSJ, προαίρεσις), is applied here to a preferred military course of action designed to achieve τὰ καλά (= things noble). Cynegirus' active undertaking is more distinctive (ἰδιαιτέρα) and more legitimate (ἐνδικωτέρα) than the passivity of Callimachus.

With grammatical variation the μὲν - δὲ contrast presents a sharp antithesis: αὐτὸς βουλόμενος ἐχρήσατο (= he, himself willing [it], used) — ἄκοντι συνέπεσεν (= to him, not by [his] design, [it] happened). Worth comparing is the medical distinction between a wound inflicted by someone ἐπίτηδες, βουλόμενος (= deliberately, willfully) and an injury that is sustained ἀέκων (= unintentionally) (Hippocrates, *Cap. Vul.* 11).

The additional term συμφορά (= circumstance, chance occurrence; mishap, misfortune) only serves to underscore the happenstance character of the event.

The προθυμία (= eagerness) which characterized Cynegirus (A 18) was absent from Callimachus.

25

The series of contrasts between standing and pursuing (A 22), passivity and action (A 23), intentional and unintentional (A 24), is advanced one more step here with the distinction between ἀναίσθητον (= unperceived) and εἰδώς / συνιείς (= knowing / understanding). The assertion that Callimachus felt no pain applies, of course, not to the initial arrow wounds, but to the multitude of arrows that struck him after he was dead and that ended up supporting his corpse.

The two gnomic remarks about dignity (χάρις) and valor (ἀρετή), which look like parallels, are similar but not identical. Similar in meaning are μετὰ θάνατον (= after death) and ἄψυχος (= lifeless, soul-less). A Hellenistic epitaph calls gravestones στῆλαι ἀψύχων (= monuments of the departed) (cf. W. Peek, *Griechische Grabgedichte*, Berlin: Akademie-Verlag, 1960, # 381.2 [p. 216]). χάρις and ἀρετή are different in content. The former, like σχῆμα, refers to outward appearance (LSJ, χάρις I, archaic objective sense), the latter to inner substance.

Two admirable qualities of Cynegirus are singled out: (1) he was *conscious* of bitter pain and (2) he gave *priority* to what was honorable (τὸ καλόν) instead of to what was fearful (τὸ δεινόν). The statement that Cynegirus' pain and loss of hands was *on behalf of* (ὑπέρ) the whole army appears almost incidental here. Later, the vicarious aspect of both men's 'sacrifice' re-emerges through the same preposition (cf. A 44, 49; B 8, 64). However, this theme is never really developed or exploited in the declamations.

The expression παρ᾽ ἀμφοτέρων (= from both sides) could refer to either (a) Greeks and Persians or (b) supporters of Cynegirus and supporters of Callimachus. Orellius (p. 34) argues for the former. In view of the fact, however, that the only other occurrence of ἀμφότεροι in the text (A 25) refers to Cynegirus and Callimachus, and that the supposed listeners are the Athenian jurymen, the latter interpretation (b) seems more likely.

26

The expression εἰ δεῖ τὰληθὲς εἰπεῖν (= if the truth must be told) is a rhetorical platitude. Countless examples occur in authors of the Second Sophistic (cf. εἰ δεῖ/χρὴ τὰληθὲς/τὰληθῆ εἰπεῖν/λέγειν, Aristides 27.354; 29.373; 46.170; 46.202; 46.262; 53.28; Lucian, *Alex.* 17.1; *Pr. Im.* 12.8; *Dial. Deor.* 21.2; *Dial. Meretr.* 12.2). The expanded phrase μηδὲν ὀκνήσαντα τὰληθὲς εἰπεῖν (= to speak the truth withholding nothing) is also a standard rhetorical flourish (cf. εἰ γέ με δεῖ μηδὲν ὀκνήσαντα εἰπεῖν τὰληθές [= if it is necessary for me to speak the truth witholding nothing], Lucian, *Herm.* 8.13; σαφῶς εἴπατε μηδὲν ὀκνήσαντες [= speak clearly withholding nothing], Libanius, *Decl.* 4.2.13; cf. Dio Chrysostom 77/78.45).

The paronomasia in παρά**δοξ**ος **δοκο**ῦσα (= contrary to expectation [but] apparent) gets lost in the English — unless one could accept a clumsy transliteration: the para**dox**ical **doc**etic stance.

The predicative position of κράτιστον (superlative of ἀγαθός) allows for the change from the expected feminine (cf. ἀρετή) to the neuter gender. This 'neuterizing' has the effect of 'thing-ifying' the valor, almost as if it were an object in and of itself apart from Cynegirus.

The next μέν - δέ contrast plays with two opposing words in a way that is virtually impossible to capture in English. Callimachus' stateliness (τὸ σέμνον) was a (singular) ἀργόν (→ ἀ-εργόν) σχῆμα; Cynegirus' (plural) ἐργά were with noble σχήματα (plural). Callimachus' august stance was an *appearance without deed*; Cynegirus' *deeds* had very noble *appearances* (i.e., *characteristics*).

Without an article the superlative καλλίστων (√ καλός) is an *absolute* superlative: *very* noble (*GG*, 1085).

27

The present (παράβαλλε) and aorist (παράβαλε) imperatives have equal support in the MSS (β and μ had the present, α and ε had the aorist — hence bold print in the text). The difference is subtle. Whereas the aorist (punctiliar) points to a the simple act of comparing, the present (progressive) presumes a series of comparisons — like those appearing afterward in the second speech — as though Callimachus' father had already been making known his arguments informally prior to the official public debate.

Three comparisons (dative [Cynegirus] - accusative [Callimachus]) are rejected in a varied tricolon:

(1) noun / noun (στρατιώτη / νεκρόν [= soldier / corpse])

(2) active participle / passive participle (τῷ βάλλοντι / τὸν βεβλημένον [= the one striking / the one having been struck])

(3) noun adjective / noun adjective (σχῆμα κενόν / ἔργῳ θρασεῖ [= empty appearance / bold deed]).

The third item reverses the case order and resumes the σχῆμα - ἔργον contrast of the previous sentence. Euphorion would say in English: 'There is no comparison between the two!'

Credit for the stance of Callimachus (which is but a σχῆμα!) goes to the intertwined form (σχῆμα) of the Persian arrows. The play on the varied meanings of σχῆμα (appearance - configuration) evades translation. The enemy arrows served as supports (ἐρείσματα) artificially propping up the corpse — like stays which keep a boat on shore upright (cf. Theocritus 21.12).

The formulations in A 27 are artful and more cogent than the arguments hitherto.

28

Euphorion rejects any connection between Cynegirus' actions and "appearances" (σχήματα) which is for him, despite A 26, a negative concept.

The prefix ἐπί in the compound verb ἐπεδίδου could have *directive* sense: he gave *up* his hands *to*; he handed them *over to* [the enemy]. However, more likely it has *intensive* force: he gave *generously*, he surrendered *freely* his hands. This fits well with the picture of Cynegirus' actions as noble (LSJ, ἐπιδίδωμι 3).

With the main verb in the imperfect (ἐπεδίδου) the force of the circumstantial participle μεμαχημένος in the perfect tense is hard to pin down (cf. *GG*, 2069). *Temporal* is grammatically possible: he gave his hands *after having fought*, but this does not appear consonant with the repeated argument that his severed hands continued the fight (A 11, 23, 36, 40). It seems better, therefore, to construe the participle as one of *manner* or *attendant circumstance*. The tense may then be a perfect of *dated past action* or a perfect which suggests the *abiding effects* of his fight (*GG*, 1949, 1946; cf. A 1, 32; B 2, 32, 50, 52).

In the sentence θαυμαστὸν ... Καλλίμαχον λέγεις the infinitive εἶναι is understood (= you say Callimachus [to be] admirable). This standard construction of indirect discourse (verb of saying/thinking + accusative + infinitive) appears also with φημί (A 1, 13, 15, 38), φάσκω (B 9), and οἴομαι (B 11, 56).

The circumstantial participial phrase νεκρὸς ὢν is ambiguous. Is it *temporal* (= when, after he was dead)? *concessive* (= although, even though he was dead)? *attendant circumstance* or *manner* (= and being dead too)? or even *causal* (= since, because he was dead)?   For each of these understandings a certain plausibility might be argued.

The double plurals ἡμεῖς (= we) and ὑμεῖς (= you) are explained by Orellius (p. 36) as a mode of speech used by the legal advocate: "My son, whom I represent in court, so that we say: *my* or rather *our* party ..." If that is the case, why is it so rare in these speeches? It is probably more an expression of family solidarity — biological and personal identity of fathers and sons to such an extent that the fathers were present in the battle in the persons of their sons (cf. A 1). The same tack of corporate participation is also taken by the father of Callimachus (B 16). Similar is the notion of generational identity and corporate personality as found in the Bible (cf. Deut 26:5-9; Exod 20:5-6; Jer 31:29; Ezek 18:2)

The plural formulations restate two arguments for the superiority of Cynegirus: (1) Cynegirus fought so to speak in both army and navy, Callimachus only in the army (cf. A 8, 11, 33, 36; B 45). (2) Callimachus only fought defensively, Cynegirus was agressive to the end.

29

In this passage the words παραπλήσιος (= similar) and μιμέομαι (= imitate) sound the *imitation* theme which the second declamation will take up and counter with alternate terminology (cf. μίμημα [= copy], ὅμοιος [= like], B 32, 43).

In the first contrary-to-fact condition the general subject *all* (πάντες) of the protasis is concretized in the apodosis: *our entire army* (πᾶν ἡμῶν τὸ στρατόπεδον). In the second contrary-to-fact condition the general subject *all* (πάντες) of the apodosis is obviously the βάρβαροι mentioned in the previous and following clauses.

The formulation δίκας (or δίκην) + δίδωμι is standard classical idiom for *suffer punishment, pay the penalty* (LSJ, δίκη IV.3). The dangling accusative τέλος has adverbial sense: *in the end, at last, finally* (LSJ, τέλος II.2.a).

The last clause in A 29 admits several interpretations. An infelicitous string of feminine plural accusatives (πάσας, αἰχμαλώτους, κεφαλάς, τὰς ναῦς) makes it difficult to determine which words belong together and to distinguish the exact objects of the two verbs (ἀναδησάμενοι, εἴχομεν). The noun κεφαλάς is capable of at least two meanings: (a) extremities [of ships] (= sterns or prows) and (b) heads [of people] (= persons) (cf. LSJ, κεφαλή I.2 and II.c/e). The ambiguities may be reduced, but not eliminated, when one notes that a middle participle of ἀναδέω (= fastening by a rope to oneself) often stands with an imperfect active indicative to describe towing a ship: e.g., τὴν [ναῦν] ... ἀναδησάμενοι ἀπῆγον (= taking in tow the [ship] they brought it away, Xenophon, *Hel.* 1.6.21; cf. Thucydides 2.90.6; 4.14.1; Polybius 3.96.3). The English translation offered here links πάσας, αἰχμαλώτους, and κεφαλάς [= people]. However, equally legitimate might be a connection between πάσας, αἰχμαλώτους, and τὰς ναῦς, understood together as object of εἴχομεν; and κεφαλάς [= prows/sterns] as object of ἀναδησάμενοι (= by tying up [the] sterns we would have taken all the ships captive). Such a rendering of the contrary-to-fact apodosis would have in mind Herodotus' assertion that the Greeks captured only seven Persian vessels (Herodotus 6.115).

30

πρός + dative expresses addition so that the phrase πρὸς τούτοις became a common classical idiom: *in addition to these things, besides this* (LSJ, πρός B.III) which continued into the Hellenistic period (BAGD, πρός II.2).

ὤνησε φίλους (= he helped friends): Typically verbs of helping have dative objects, but as early as Homer ὀνίνημι could stand with the accusative (*Il.* 5.205; 7.172; cf. Herodotus 7.141; Euripides, *Hipp.* 314). The construction provides a clean balance with ἐφόβησε πολεμίους (= he frightened enemies).

The answer to the rhetorical question "What enemies ..., what friends ...?" is so obvious — "None!" — that it need not be stated. The graphic portrayal of the imagined Persian reaction to Callimachus' encircled 'pin-cushion' corpse serves as a kind of embellishment to that unstated but understood answer.

The tangle of divergent readings in the MSS goes back to two slight variants in the second generation:

αὐτῷ γὰρ τοι τοῦτο τῷ Καλλιμάχου προβόλῳ   (→ γ)
αὐτῷ γὰρ   τούτῳ τῷ Καλλιμάχῳ προβόλῳ   (→ δ)

The preferable reading is that of γ (generally a better witness) which shows cogent parallels in the comparison.

datives: αὐτῷ ... τῷ ... προβόλῳ / τινι [προβόλῳ understood]
genitives: Καλλιμάχου / τῶν Ἀσσυρίων χωμάτων
accusatives: τοῦτο / [τοῦτο understood]

The basic sentence structure is thus simple: τοῦτο ... [ἂν] ἔλεγον (= this ... they would say) whereby the quote which follows articulates the content of the τοῦτο.

A πρόβολος is literally something that projects (√ προβάλλω = throw before) and hence impedes or hinders (cf. πρόβολον ἐμποδῶν [= barrier before the feet] Plutarch, *Gar.* 510a; cf. Arrian, *An.* 2.21.7; Plutarch, *Caes.* 22). Hence, it could serve as a military description for a defensive fort (φρούριον, Xenophon, *Cyr.* 5.3.11 and 23). Already in classical time it was used metaphorically for persons who stood in the way (cf. Demosthenes 8.61) or acted as protectors (cf. Aristophanes, *Nu.* 1161). Thus there is clear precedent for the use of the term here both as a metaphor for Callimachus and as a comparison with the Assyrian [= Babylonian] defense walls (χώματα) which the Persians had to breach in order to defeat the Mesopotamian empire. In military language the term χῶμα ordinarily denoted an earthen mound thrown up against a city wall or fortification in order to take it (cf. Herodotus 1.162, 168; Thucydides 2.75.1; Josephus, *B. J.* 7 § 304, 306, 313; Appian, *Mith.* 5.30). Polemo's use of χῶμα thus departs from common parlance in that it does not refer to an assault instrument, but to a *defense embankment* (as also in B 58).

The expression μέγα φρονοῦντες (= thinking [overly] big things) is a common idiom for *being presumptuous* (e.g., Thucydides 6.16.4; Xenophon, *Hel.* 5.4.45; 7.1.27; Aristophanes, *Ach.* 988). This remark about Persian arrogance picks up on the recurring theme in Herodotus that the defeat of the Persians was due to their own hybris and the ensuing jealousy of the gods (cf. στρατὸς πολλὸς ὑπὸ ὀλίγου διαφθείρεται ... οὐ γὰρ ἐᾷ **φρονέειν μέγα** ὁ θεὸς ἄλλον ἢ ἑωυτῶν [= A numerous army is destroyed by a small {one} ... for the god does not permit anyone other than himself *to do* {overly} *big thinking*], Herodotus 7.10).

The comparison here of the thicket of arrows to the mesh of a net is an allusion to the Persian practice on captured islands of forming an extended line of soldiers with linked hands who then walked over the entire face of an island to sweep up the population for deportation or enslavement. Herodotus, who first described this procedure, termed it with the verb σαγηνεύω (= catch in a drag-net), a denominative from σαγήνη (= seine net, drag-net) (Herodotus 6.31; 3.149; cf. Strabo 10.1.10; Diogenes Laertius 3.33). As late as the 3rd century CE the capture (ἅλωσις) of the Eretrians was still described like that of fish (ἰχθύων): they were said "to have been netted in and all captured" (σαγηνευθῆναι ... καὶ ἁλῶναι πάντας, Philostratus, *V. A.* 1.23).

In the long series of past contrary-to-fact conditions (A 29–30) the final apodosis omits the particle ἄν (*GG*, 1767) which has to be supplied with the periphrasitic imperfect ἦν περιπίπτων, a rare construction for Polemo. While classical Greek did provide a few precedents for εἶναι with the present participle (*GG*, 1857, 1961), this construction first came into its own in the Koine (cf. G. Björk, ᾊΗν διδάσκων, *Die periphrastischen Konstructionen im Griechischen*, [Skrifter utgivna av Kgl. Humanistiska Vetenskapssamfundet i Uppsala, 32, 2], Uppsala: Almqvist & Wiksell, 1940) — it is uncharacteristic of Atticizing Greek. The point of the argument is that the effects of the upright corpse were more in the interest of the Persians than the Greeks.

31

Given the scene described, the adjective ἀντιρρόπους (= compensating for) is virtually the equivalent of the present participle ἀντιρρέποντας (√ ἀντιρρέπω) with conative sense: *trying to counterpoise*.

Of course Cynegirus showed only one right hand, his own — the plural τὰς ᾽Αττικὰς δεξιάς is *synecdoche*: the whole is used for the part. His hand is an example *par excellence* of what Attic hands are like.

The genitive ἀνθρώπων is probably partitive (= Of [all] men for Athenians alone hands are undying) but it could possibly be construed as possessive with χεῖρες (= For Athenians alone hands of [mortal] men are undying).

If in their abortive invasion the barbarians accomplished nothing else, they did succeed in *smothering* (ἐκάλυψαν) Callimachus *with arrows*. In classical verse the verb καλύπτω (= cover) was often used to describe *burying the dead* (absolutely, Aeschylus, *Th.* 1046; with dative of instrument, e.g., χθονί [= with soil], γῇ [= with earth], χέρσῳ [= with dry dirt], τάφῳ

[= with a grave], Pindar, *Nem.* 8.38; Aeschylus, *Pr.* 582; Sophocles, *Ant.* 28; Euripides, *Ph.* 1633; *Hel.* 1066). Polemo's verb choice here is surely deliberate.

The Phoenicians were only one element in the invading force of the 'barbarians,' but inasmuch as they constituted the major contingent in the Perisan fleet they are fittingly singled out as frightened.

32

The first argument is strained. The logic appears to be that Cynegirus' 'plural' (κατὰ μέρη [= part by part]) is greater than Callimachus' 'singular' (εἷς / μίαν μάχην [= one / one fight]). This resumes a point made in the opening sentence (cf. κατὰ μέρη νενίκηκεν with κατὰ μέρος μεμαχημένον, A 1).

The second argument about the ἀριστεία (= prowess) of Cynegirus' hand is less abstruse. In the rebuttal speech the first argument will be countered with the comment that Callimachus used *all* his body parts while Cynegirus gave *only* his hand (B 32) and the second countered by the reference to the ἀριστεία of Callimachus' brilliant actions (B 28).

The third argument is an expansion of the first: not just *one* hand but *both* were amputated (so also A 10). This is an embellishment of the tradition which originally spoke only of one hand (Herodotus 6.114). The loss of both hands emerged in later tradition (cf. Pompeius Trogus 2.9.18–19; *An. Gr.* 16.117, 118).

The reading πλήρης (= intact [→ γ → π]) is to be preferred over τρόπαιον (= trophy [→ δ]) which is surely an assimilation to the parallels where Euphorion says that Cynegirus' truncated rest (λοιπός) was a war monument (A 10, 39). Here he says it was πλήρης (= complete). Orellius (p. 44) suspected that after πλήρης ἦν (= it was full) there had originally stood the word τραυμάτων but that it has dropped out (= and the rest of Cynegirus was full *of wounds*). However, there is no MS support for this and nowhere else do the declamations make reference to wounds of Cynegirus beyond the loss of his hands. It is best, therefore, to accept the πλήρης and take it in the sense of *intact* (cf. Ovid's comment that in the stalemate battle between Achilles and Cygnus the latter remained unscathed: *sine vulnere corpus sincerumque fuit* [= {his} body was without wounds and uninjured], *Met.* 12.99). For πλήρης in this sense of *complete, whole, with nothing* [else] *missing*, cf. LSJ, πλήρης III.3 and 4; BAGD, πλήρης 2.

33

The vocative noun that should follow the exclamatory particle ὦ is omitted as is frequently the case in Polemo (cf. Index 3). The ellipsis is probably best filled in from the resumptive ὦ in the next sentence: χεῖρες (= hands). Assuming that to be the case, the verse division (# 33) would have been more appropriately placed after this sentence, not before it, because the exclamation serves better as a culminating laudatio for the previous points than as an introduction to the following imperative directed at Callimachus' father.

The *immobility* of Callimachus is denigrated in a hard-hitting asyndeton series (cf. fourfold τόν) which culminates in the comparison of him with a στήλη, a term which designates a variety of upright stone blocks, particularly monuments with inscriptions. Here the context clearly points to a grave marker (cf. LSJ, στήλη II.1).

This is followed by a 'one-up-manship' asyndetic series (cf. fivefold τόν) which praises the *action* of Cynegirus. The staccato summation focuses on three of the arguments that have been made. He fought: (a) both on land and sea (cf. A 8, 11, 23), (b) member by member (cf. A 1, 10, 32), (c) 'single-handedly' against many (cf. A 9).

The substantized adjectives πεζομάχος (= foot-fighter) and ναυμάχος (= ship-fighter) are commonly paired in Greek to indicate the full breadth of military activity (cf. Plutarch, *Alex.* 38.2).

34

The exclamatory ὦ of the earlier sentence (A 33) is now resumed in a crescendo of emotional outbursts (ὦ over 20 times in A 34-39; cf. Index 3). If Euphorion — played by Polemo — had begun his speech sitting, he would certainly be standing by now for this monody. According to his student Herodes Atticus it was Polemo's practice "to jump up from his chair at the peak of the arguments" (ἀναπηδᾶν τοῦ θρόνου περὶ τὰς ἀκμὰς τῶν ὑποθέσεων, Philostratus, *V. S.* 539).

κἂν is crasis for καὶ ἐν. Through his comment about rearing Cynegirus with his own hands Euphorion claims a portion of his son's heroism for himself.

The masculine σωτῆρες (→ γ) derives from π, the feminine σώτειραι (→ δ) is surely a secondary assimilation to the gender of χεῖρες. The term σωτήρ (= savior) was typically an epithet for gods and rulers, but it could be applied also to any humans who provided deliverance or help in some way (cf. W. Foerster, σωτήρ, *TWNT*, 7.1004–1012). Herodotus argued that because they took the lead in the war against Persia the Athenians were the "saviors of

Greece" (σωτῆρες τῆς Ἑλλάδος, Herodotus 7.139). What is unusual and striking in Polemo is the application of this term not to a person or persons, but to a part of a person, to *hands* — as if these were personified. It was extremely rare to speak of an impersonal "savior" (Foerster, op. cit. p. 1005) though there are sparse examples (e.g., a river, Herodotus 8.138; a house or land, Euripides, *Med.* 360).

The substantized adjective πρόμαχος literally means *one who fights out in front*. Epitaphs chiseled on the grave-stones of fallen soldiers commonly employed this descriptor in the memorial tribute to their heroism in battle (cf. W. Peek, *Griechische Grabgedichte*, Berlin: Akademie Verlag, 1960, numbers 36 [p. 62], 46 [p. 64], 125 [p. 92], 130 [p. 96], 169 [p. 118], 206 [p. 136], 457 [p. 268]). This term belonged to the stock presentation of the heroic death — pride in which helped provide consolation to the survivors (cf. R. Lattimore, *Themes in Greek and Latin Epitaphs* [Illinois Studies in Language and Literature 28,1-2], Urbana: University of Illinois Press, 1962, pp. 237–240).

35

Cynegirus' hand is called *sweet* (ἡδεῖα) because the tale about it is *sweet* to the ear or *pleasant* to contemplate (cf. LSJ, ἡδύς I).

The idea that the earth brought forth the hand for Greece expresses the bond between soil and people (cf. *Blut und Boden*), a sense that is particularly strong in communities with an agricultural base. It stands close to the Herodotean notion that in the Persian wars the elements sided with the Greeks.

To say the hand is "stronger than winds" (βιαιότερα πνευμάτων) implies that Cynegirus was holding back a ship with unfurled sails. This image is not entirely consistent with the following statement that the ship was putting to sea (ἀναγομένην) by being rowed (ἐρεττομένην) — but then in a gush of emotion what does consistency matter? Sails are never mentioned and this detail about the wind is nowhere else developed in Euphorion's speech. Nevertheless, in his refutation Callimachus' father pooh-poohs this picture in a biting rhetorical question: "Can a hand vie with Poseidon's winds?" (B 36).

The present stem participle ἀναγωμένον has conative force; it stands for a relative clause with a conative imperfect: ἣ ἀνήγετο (= which was trying to put to sea, cf. *GG*, 1895).

The substantized adjective ῥόθιον (= rushing, roaring, dashing) refers to the turbulence of the oars splashing in the water (cf. ῥοθίοις πλάταις [= with splashing oars], Euripides, *Iph. T.* 1130; ἐρετμοῖς ... γλαυκὴν ἅλα ῥοθίοισι λευκαίνοντες [= making white the blue-green brine with thundrous rowing],

Euripides, *Cyc.* 17); πάντες δὲ μετὰ σπουδῆς ἐλαύνοντες τὸ ῥόθιον ἐφιλοτιμοῦντο πρὸς ἀλλήλους [= rowing with zeal they all competed with each other for the dashing {of the oars}], Diodorus Siculus 13.99; cf. also Euripides, *Iph. T.* 408).

Again, in the rush of exclamations the vocative required with ὦ ... στολαγωγοῦ is omitted. It is to be supplied in harmony with the two previous examples (δεξιὰ βιαιοτέρα / κρείττων ... χείρ) which also stand with genitives of comparison: "O [hand stronger] than a fleet commander!" Hinck's emendation of στολαγωγοῦ (= fleet commander) into an undocumented στολαγοῦ is completely unwarranted.

The "arrows of a more distant right hand" (μακροτέρας βελῶν δεξιᾶς) is a reference to the Persian archer corps. These famed bowmen were depicted in imperial palace reliefs at Persepolis and Susa and duly noted by Herodotus as a formidable element of the Persian military (cf. Herodotus 7.61, 64–67, 77, 92, 158; Heliodorus, *Eth.* 9.14). Their fire-power was immortalized in a legendary *chreia* attributed to Dieneces: When this Spartan was told that the Median archers could unleash enough arrows to block out the sunlight, he responded that it would be pleasant then to fight in the shade (Herodotus 7.226).

The prepositional phrase δι' ἥν (= on account of which [hand]) introduces the parallel relative clauses:

οὐ μάτην ὁ Πὰν ἐξ Ἀρκαδίας ἔδραμεν

οὐκ εἰκῇ Δημήτηρ καὶ Κόρη τῇ μάχῃ παρεγένοντο

Pan did not run from Arcadia in vain

Demeter and Kore did not participate in the battle without purpose.

These clauses bring the gods into the discussion for the first time (cf. Index 7) and make the unheard of assertion that these deities hastened to and participated in the battle *for the sake of Cynegirus' hand!*

Other than the mention of his Arcadian provenance Pan is introduced devoid of all his traditional attributes (e.g., theriomorphic, amorous, pipe-playing, lazy, etc.). The sophist of the Greek renaissance did not readily welcome such 'primitive' aspects in the concept of the divine. But Pan had become embedded in the Marathon traditions and he was not to be left out. Herodotus reported that prior to the battle, when Phidippides made the run to Sparta to request military assistance (which did not materialize) he was met on the way by the god Pan who avowed that he would help the Athenians. Following their victory at Marathon the Athenians, therefore, founded a temple to Pan beneath the acropolis (Herodotus 6.105; Lucian, *Dial. Deor.* [2 Pan and Hermes] 271–272). Polemo's statement that Pan *ran* (ἔδραμεν) from

Arcadia suggests that he retraced Phidippides' route posthaste to provide the help that the Spartans would withhold (Herodotus 6.106).

The assertion that Demeter and her daughter took part at Marathon does not have similar support in legend as does Pan. There is no obvious reason why they should be paired here with Pan as helpers. Neither the Earth-mother goddess of agriculture and fertility nor her daughter, a part-time resident of the netherworld, had a reputation of military intervention. The non-martial character of all the surviving Demeter iconography is indicative (cf. L Beschi, "Demeter," *LIMC* IV.1.844–892; IV.2.563–599). That the ancient cult of these goddesses had strong support — as did Pan — in Arcadia (cf. *GGR*, 1.477–481) or that the Eleusynian mystery cult, in which these two played a central role, was seated in Attica (cf. *GGR*, 1.469–477) does not seem to offer an adequate explanation for their presence here. It may be that dropping the names of a few Olympian gods had simply become part of the standard trappings in a sophist's declamation, so that a deeper connection need not be sought. Nonetheless, it is worth noting that the presence at Marathon of Kore (the unwilling consort of Hades and as such *winter*-time resident of the underworld) is consonant with the tradition that the battle occurred in the late *summer* month of Carneius [= September], 490 BCE, i.e., in the season when she would have been above ground (cf. note at B 5).

A θέαμα (√ θέαομαι = view, gaze at, behold [usually with a sense of wonder]) is frequently a *sight* which gives pleasure (cf. LSJ, θέαμα). Even the gods marvel to behold Cynegirus.

With the vocative τρόφιμε Euphorion addresses his [dead] son as though he were present and listening. Here the substantized adjective τρόφιμος (√ τρέφω [= rear, nourish, foster]) has passive sense: *ward, nursling*. The term could be used of a foundling that had been raised or of an 'adopted' child (cf. LSJ, τρόφιμος III). For example, Ion, son of Apollo and eponymous ancestor of the Ionians, is called the τρόφιμος of his human foster-father Xuthus (Euripides, *Ion* 684). By contrast, in Polemo's declamation it is a human child which is 'fostered' by a goddess (Athena). Indeed, by the time of Polemo Τρόφιμος appears in inscriptions and papyri as a proper name (cf. MM and BAGD, sub Τρόφιμος) — quite possibly as a truncated form with the theophoric element missing.

Of all the gods here named, Athena most suits the scene. Since archaic times she was viewed as "dread rouser of battle-strife, unwearied army-leader, queen to whom battle-noises, wars, and fights are a delight" (δεινὴν ἐγρεκύδοιμον ἀγέστρατον ἀτρυτώνην πότνιαν, ᾗ κέλαδοί τε ἅδον πόλεμοί τε μάχαι, Hesiod, *Th.* 925–926). Moreover, this warlike goddess was protectress of the city that was her namesake, an arrangement to which her famous Parthenon bore enduring and elegant witness. She is described with the participial epithet παρούσης (= being by, present [to help]). This verb was descriptive of Athena from early time. As Odysseus was preparing to confront his wife's suitors Athena promised him ἐγώ γε παρέσσομαι (= I will be with you, Homer, *Od.* 13.393). It was characteristic of Athena to stand by her protégés. Indeed, Walter Otto summed up his treatment of her assisting deeds by calling her "die Immernahe" (= the Ever-Near One, cf. *Die Götter Griechenlands*, Bonn: Cohen, 1929, p. 77).

The adjective σύντιμος (= co-worthy) is an ordinary compound (σύν + τίμ[ι]ος) but otherwise unattested (cf. LSJ; *LPGL*). Its meaning comes close to ὁμότιμος (= equally valued) which is documented (cf. LSJ, sub verbum). It may be a coinage from Polemo. The masculine substantive to be mentally supplied with the masculine vocative adjective σύντιμε is unclear. It cannot be the feminine 'hand' (χεῖρ or δεξιά as in A 33, 34, 35, 37). From the immediate context one might consider the substantized τρόφιμε (= foster-child, A 35) or from the wider context πᾶι (= son, A 37, 38, 39). Yet how is a *person* to be thought of as *co-worthy* (σύντιμε) with *struggles* (ἄθλοις)? The syntax of the sentence itself thus seems to require that the vocative ἆθλε (= struggle) be supplied. The noun ἆθλος was the standard term to describe the famous *labors* of Herakles (cf. Apollodorus 2.4.12-2.6.1; Diodorus Siculus 4.11) and the corresponding *ordeals* of Theseus (cf. Diodorus Siculus 4.59; Plutarch, *Thes.* 7.2; 29.3; 30.4). Theseus was the local hero of Athens while Herakles was an apotheosized hero with pan-Hellenic acclaim. Polemo's mention of Athena, Herakles, and Theseus in this context accords with the wall painting of the Marathon battle in the Stoa Poikile which was still visible when Polemo was in Athens (cf. Philostratus, *V. S.* 533, 535) — a mural which no visitor would have neglected to see. In his description of that mural a generation later Pausanias wrote: γεγραμμένος ἐστιν ... καὶ Θησεὺς ἀνιόντι ἐκ γῆς εἰκασμένος Ἀθηνᾶ τε καὶ Ἡρακλῆς (= depicted is ... also Theseus represented as coming up out of the ground, and Athena and Herakles, Pausanias 1.15.3). Further, Plutarch records that the Athenians honored Theseus as a "hero" (ἥρως) because many soldiers at Marathon thought "they saw an apparition of Theseus in arms rushing on in front of them against the barbarians" (φάσμα Θησέως ἐν ὅπλοις καθορᾶν πρὸ αὐτῶν ἐπὶ τοὺς βαρβάρους φερόμενον, Plutarch, *Thes.* 35.5). The belief about Herakles' presence at the battle may have been connected with the recollection that the Greeks had bivouaced by a Herakles shrine at Marathon (Herodotus 6.108, 116).

To view Cynegirus' struggle as co-equal with those of Herakles and Theseus is to attribute to his action mythological status. Because of Theseus' many glorious struggles (ἆθλοι) a popular saying arose about him: Ἄλλος οὗτος Ἡρακλῆς (= He's another Herakles!, Plutarch, *Thes.* 29.3). Now Euphorion is saying the same about Cynegirus! To illustrate his point he offers a concrete comparison: they dragged animals (bulls and lions) = he dragged ships (στόλος). Herakles had brought the Cretan bull to Tiryns (Apollodorus 2.5.7; Diodorus Siculus 4.13.4; Pausanias 1.27.9–10; 5.10.9) while Theseus had driven the Marathonian bull to Athens (Apollodorus, epitome 1.5; Plutarch, *Thes.* 14.1; 25.3; Pausanias 1.27.10) and subdued the Minos-bull (Μινώταυρος) in the labyrinth at Knossos (Plutarch, *Thes.* 15.2; 17.3–4; 19.1). Herakles won renown for killing lions in Cithaeron (Apollodorus 2.4.9–10) and Nemea (Apollodoros 2.5.1; Diodorus Siculus 4.11.3–4). These tales about conquering wild beasts belonged to the standard cycle of hero ἆθλοι (= labors) known across the Greek-speaking world (cf. J. Boardman, et al., "Herakles," *LIMC* V.1.1–71; V.2.6–84). Of equivalent import is Cynegirus' dragging of a *fleet* (στόλος) — in hyperbolic synecdoche one ship has become a whole navy! Earlier it was claimed that Cynegirus had "dashed Asia shattered into the sea" (A 22), now here that he — like Gulliver in Lilliput — "dragged the fleet of Asia".

Such grandiloquence may serve as a case study. It is only a shade less turgid than the notion of 'tying the island of Aegina to Xerxes' ship and dragging it away.' That picture, attributed to Nicetes of Smyrna, the first century teacher of Skopelian, Polemo's teacher, was guffawed at rudely (καταγελάσας πλατύ) by the sober rhetorician Isaeus the Syrian, an older contemporary of Polemo. Isaeus said to an Ionian student admiring this bombast, "Dim-wit! (ἀνόητε), and how will you put to sea?" (Philostratus, *V. S.* 513. The inflated language (μεγαλοφώνως, Philostratus, *loc. cit.*) with which the Smyrnaean sophists liked to speak did not go uncriticized.

36

If the *actions* of Cynegirus are like the *labors of the heroes*, then the *hands* of Cynegirus are like the *instruments of the gods*.

The spear (δόρυ) belonged to the standard identifying accoutrements of Athena as she was depicted in statuary, reliefs, and vase paintings across the Hellenic world (cf. P. Demargne, et al., "Athena," *LIMC*, II.1.955–1050; II.2.706–769). In ancient warfare it was one of the basic weapons of attack.

The word δᾷδες (Attic contraction of δαΐδες [plural of ἡ δαΐς = torch]), which belonged to Homeric vocabulary (*Od.* 1.428, 434; 2.105; 18.310, 354) and still survives in modern Greek as δαδί (√ τὸ δᾳδίον), would have had in Polemo's day a slightly archaic ring to it. An unaffected speaker in Hellenistic time would more naturally have used a word like λαμπάς (= lamp) (cf. LSJ, δαΐς). The δᾷς (δαΐς) was a torch (√ δαίω = kindle, burn) consisting of a number of pine splinters bound together (cf. G. Autenrieth, *A Homeric Dictionary*, Norman: University of Oklahoma Press, 1966, p. 70, δαΐς). The phrase δᾷδες τῶν θεῶν (= torches of the god[desse]s!]) appears to be an allusion to the famous mythical scene of Demeter and Hecate carrying torches (δαΐδας) to light the way of Persephone out of Hades (cf. *H. Hom. 2, Dem.* 48, 61). Because of her role Hecate became known by the epithets δᾳδοφόρος (= torch-bearer, Bacchylides, *frag.* 23.1 [= 40]) and φωσφόρος (= light-bearer, Euripides, *Hel.* 569; Aristophanes, *Th.* 858) and artistic representations customarily showed her holding a pair of torches (cf. L. R. Farnell, *The Cults of the Greek States* [New Rochelle: Caratzas, 1977] 2.549-557). In the Eleusynian Mysteries which reenacted the story of these goddesses facilitating Kore's release from Hades those liturgists who carried the torches were called δᾳδοῦχοι (= torch-holders, cf. LSJ, δᾳδουχέω and δᾳδοῦχος).

Orellius (p. 49) wondered whether Polemo's phrase χεῖρες ἐλευθέριον σέλας φέρουσαι (= hands bearing a freedom flame) could intimate that Cynegirus' one hand held the ship while the other hand held a torch with which he intended to set it ablaze. Such a realistic interpretation is out of place in this context and the rebuttal in B 37 disallows it. The phrase is a reminiscence of the Homeric Hymn's description of Hecate as σέλας ἐν χείρεσιν ἔχουσα (= having in her hands a flame, *H. Hom., 2 Dem.* 52). Finally, though there is no tradition of the Olympian Demeter being a patron in war, of the chthonic Hekate Hesiod (*Th.* 431-33) had said:

> ἠδ' ὁπότ' ἐς πόλεμον φθεισήνορα θωρήσσωνται
> ἀνέρες, ἔνθα θεὰ παραγίγνεται, οἷς κ' ἐθέλῃσι
> νίκην προφρονέως ὀπάσαι καὶ κῦδος ὀρέξαι.

And when men arm themselves for destructive war,
then [the] goddess is present for whom she will
to grant victory willingly and to give glory.

Therefore, to summarize these observations regarding Polemo's torch metaphor, the archaizing allusion-packed language suggests the following: Just as the torches of the goddesses Demeter and Hekate lit the way to liberate Persephone from her entrapment in the dark netherworld of the dead, so Cynegirus' hands blazed the Greeks' way to freedom from the ominous Persian threat.

The artfully constructed tricolon (νῦν πρῶτον 3x) shows pleonastic synonymous parallelism which culminates in a slight formal variation (νῦν ἅμα) with a vivid paradox.

Parallelism:

ναυμαχίαν ἐν γῇ
   ἀνδρὸς μάχην καὶ νεώς
      ἀντίπρωρον δεξιάν

boat fight on land
   fight of man and ship
      right hand pitted against prow

Paradox:

χεῖρα μὲν ἀφιεμένην
ναῦν δὲ κρατουμένην

here a hand loosened
there a ship held firm.

Himerius' description of the same event is probably dependent on Polemo (cf. τῆς μὲν χειρὸς ἀφαιρεθείς, τῆς δὲ τριήρους ἐχόμενος [= separated from his hand, but holding on to a trireme], Himerius, *Or.* 2[6].21 [lines 236-237]).

The doubly alliterative parechesis (ἀπεκόπτετο / ἀπῳκίζετο) cannot be effectively rendered in English (sever off / send off; cut away / send away; cut off / colonize; or similar attempts do not fully succeed). The essential point of the word play lies in the unexpressed, but implied agents of the passive verbs:

οὐ ἀπεκόπτετο

   (the hand was not being cut off [*by someone else against its will*])

ἀπῳκίζετο

   (it was being sent away from home [*by Cynegirus willingly*]).

The image of the hands as ἄποικοι (= emigrants) is a variation of the picture of them as ἀπόστολοι (= envoys, A 23).

The final sentence in A 37 resumes the argument in A 25: The living Cynegirus endured sharp pains, the dead Callimachus felt nothing at all. Stephanus called the formulation a *contemptum dictum*: untouched by pain, Callimachus was lost in reveries of the ἐπιτιμία (= respect, good name) which accrued to him on account of the 'polemarch' title. Orellius (p. 51) rendered the sense with: "Und dürfte wohl Callimachus, er, der gar keine Schmerzen empfand, gross thun mit seiner frühern Polemarchenwürde?" (= And indeed could Callimachus — he, who felt no pains at all — legitimately make himself important with his prior polemarch-status?). In other words, while Cynegirus was performing his heroic deeds, Callimachus was wrapped up in his former importance.

37

The right hand is worth as much as life itself, there is nothing more valuable that one could give.

Following the δεξιά (feminine) the κατέσχε τιμωρήσας (masculine) indicates a change in subject. Hinck's emendation to κατέσχες τιμωρήσασα (feminine) is smoother — the [personified] right hand is then addressed in both clauses — but without any MS support.

By restraining the ship Cynegirus avenged the dead Callimachus. This service of vengeance puts Callimachus in Cynegirus' debt. Since οἰκείῳ and νεκρῷ are both adjectives their combination admits two interpretations depending on which one is substantized: Did Cynegirus avenge a "dead countryman" (οἰκεῖος) or a "kindred corpse" (νεκρός)? Polemo uses οἰκεῖος more often as adjective (4x) than substantive (2x) and νεκρός is more often substantive (30x) than adjective (5x) (cf. Index 8). Further, similar combinations with νεκρός as substantive are common in Polemo (cf. ἀγαθοῦ νεκροῦ [= brave corpse], A 2; φανερῷ νεκρῷ [= conspicuous corpse], A 30; φοβεροῦ νεκροῦ [= fear-inspiring corpse], B 12; τῷ μακροβίῳ νεκρῷ [= the long-lived corpse], B 44; cf. also A 12; B 60). Accordingly οἰκείῳ νεκρῷ is to be construed as "kindred corpse." The nuance of this option is noteworthy — to call Callimachus 'corpse' rather than 'countryman' is more of a demotion for him.

The "new design" (καινὸν and νόημα are both without parallel in Polemo) for the body can hardly refer to the avenging — that was an old human behavior. It is rather the 'inaugural' of a man holding a ship — the theme of A 35-37. This was the 'first-time' event (πρῶτον 3x in A 36; πρῶτος 1x in A 37).

Each father labels his son's deed a μέγα θαῦμα (= great wonder, A 33, 37; and B 48) but Callimachus' father does it more so (cf. θαῦμα without adjective, B 56; μέγιστον θαῦμα [= greatest wonder], B 2, 55).

Euphorion likes nautical comparisons for Cynegirus' hands (cf. ὥσπερ ἀγκυρῶν [= like anchors], A 37; καθάπερ πείσματι [= like a ship's line], A 10; ὥσπερ ἀποστόλους [= like naval expeditions], A 23). Afterwards Callimachus' father contrasts Cynegirus' futile grip with a real anchor (B 45).

38

οἷα in an independent sentence introduces an exclamation of wonder (LSJ, οἷος I.1). Such sentences are commonly associated, as is the case here, with vocatives and interjections (*GG*, 2682; cf. A 41; B 33, 37).

The repetition of the verb ἀπαιτῶ (= I demand back) in the bicolon moves from the specific part (the captured Naxos) to the inclusive whole (the Aegean islands). In the island-hopping advance of the Persian fleet prior to their landing at Marathon, Herodotus reported the invasion route from Ionia to Attica: Samos (6.95), Naxos (6.96), Delos (6.97–98), Carystos and Eretria on Euboea (6.99-102), Marathon (6.102–103). Specifically he described the capture of Naxians (6.96) and Eretrians (6.101).

The demands of this lone foot-soldier are uttered out of all proportion, as though he were a conquering general imposing the terms of surrender upon the vanquished foe.

The form μεῖζω (irregular comparative of μέγας) is an Attic contraction of μείζονα (neuter plural accusative): the 'weak' ν drops out and the vowels ο and α contract in accordance with the rule of progressive assimilation where the ο dominates and lengthens (*GG*, 134, 51.a, 59). Of such comparatives "the shorter forms were more frequent in everyday speech than in literature" (*GG*, 293.d). Though Polemo has other examples of the comparative μείζων (A 16, 29; B 21, 32), the contracted form only appears here (cf. the uncontracted μείζονα in B 32). Anyone wanting to prevail over a ship wishes for "things mightier than nature", i.e., supernatural things.

The perfect tense of βεβουλημένε (= having wished) is a "perfect of dated past action" (*GG*, 1949). The reading βεβουλευμένε (= having deliberated with himself) — found in Stephanus, Possinus, and Orellius — is without any MS support.

A grammatical ambiguity of τοῦ σώματος allows for three possible interpretations:

(a) genitive of possession: through inner resolve he made the limbs *of his own body* bolder;

(b) genitive of possession: through his encouraging example he made the limbs *of the body of each fellow soldier* bolder (cf. A 29, 31);

(c) genitive of comparison: he made his limbs [i.e. hands] bolder *than the [rest of his] body* (cf. A 10, 32, 39).

The hand-emboldenment (c) is strained and the idea of emboldening his fellow soldiers through example (b) does not fit well the immediate context; therefore, the translation opts for the self-emboldenment (a) as more natural.

The phrase διὰ τῶν πεδίων καὶ τῶν ὀρῶν (= through the plains and the mountains) reflects the geography of Attica. The road southeast from Eleusis (the home of Cynegirus) to Athens proper traversed 14 miles of plains and hills. From there the march route to the plain of Marathon, 26 miles northeast of Athens on the opposite side of the Attic peninsula, traversed the Attic plain and the Pentelikon mountain range.

Cynegirus is depicted as contemplating (περινόησας) his bold action ahead of time as he marched through this terrain. His action is thus presented as not impetuous but pre-meditated. This is evidence for the calculation (λογισμός) which Euphorion had earlier asserted is a correlate of ἀρετή and requisite for routing an enemy (A 22).

39

The exclamation ὦ δεινῆς μάχης Παναθήναια μεμιμημένης is difficult (Orellius devoted a full page and a half to it, pp. 52-53). As is often the case in Polemo (cf. Index 3), the vocative which belongs with the particle ὦ is omitted and needs to be supplied from the context. The utterance stands within a long series of such exclamations beginning back in A 33, but those eight in the immediate context (A 37-40) suggest supplying παῖ (= son) or possibly τέκνον (= child). The phrase παῖ / τέκνον δεινῆς μάχης (= son / child *of* [the] fierce fight) would mean something like "child *who carried on* the fierce fight."

The last part of the phrase, Παναθήναια μεμιμημένης (= having imitated [the] Panathenaea), is left unexplained in cryptic brevity. The Παναθήναια [sc. ἱερά] (= All-Athenian [Sacred Rites]), established in sixth century Athens, were celebrated annually (every fourth year with special pomp) from the 21st to the 28th of Hekatombaion, the first month of the Attic calendar (July-August), in commemoration of the traditional birthday of Athena. The week-long festivities included music, dancing, poetry recitation contests, athletic competitions, animal sacrifices and festal meals. The highpoint of the ceremonies comprised a youth-led procession at the center of which was the colorful embroidered robe (πέπλος) for Athena. The robe, woven new for each celebration, was hoisted on the mast of a ship set on wheels and brought to the statue of the goddess (for details cf. H. W. Parke, *Festivals of the Athenians* [Ithaca: Cornell University Press, 1977] pp. 29-50). The assertion that Cynegirus' fight imitated the Panathenaic festival only seems to make any sense if it is meant as a reference to this feature of dragging a ship across land. This ship element — not unlike a float in a modern day parade — was still a known aspect of the Panathenaea in Polemo's day as a variety of references from the Roman period attest. Heliodorus mentions the customary ritual Panathenaic procession "when [the] Athenians escort the ship overland to Athena" (ὅτε τὴν ναῦν Ἀθηναῖοι διὰ γῆς τῇ Ἀθηνᾷ πέμπουσιν, *Eth.* 1.10). The scholiast of Aristophanes says the Great Panathenaea is "when also the ship sails among them on the land" (ὅτε καὶ ἡ ναῦς ἐπὶ γῆς πλέει παρ᾽

αὐτοις, Scholia, *Pax* 417). More details can be found in Philostratus (*V. S.* 550). It would seem that Polemo imagined Cynigrus' dragging of the Phoenician ship toward shore to bear some resemblance to the Athenian youths dragging the Panathenaic ship across land.

The past contrary-to-fact condition appears to be disrupted by a lacuna. Hinck (whom the present edition follows) indicates a void beginning after οὐχ ... no doubt because this negative does not go well with the thought of ὑπεδέξαντο (= they [would have] received) and ἐστεφάνωσαν (= they [would have] crowned). In other words, the second of what seems to have been two parallel negative apodoses (οὐκ ... / οὐχ ...) is missing. Its content would presumably have matched the first ("[the barbarians] would not have escaped from the Aegean / [they?] would not ..."). Possibly the gap stemmed from a *lapsus oculi* of an early scribe, perhaps caused by a *homoioteleuton*. Since the extent of the gap is unknown it is also uncertain whether the two following positive apodoses depended on the initial protasis, or whether they had their own protasis which is now also missing.

The mention of the φίλοι Πλαταιεῖ (= allied Plataeans) alongside the πολῖται (= [Athenian] citizens) corresponds to the battle participants. The Boeotian town of Plataea lay ca. 50 miles to the northeast of Athens on the border between Attica and Boeotia. While the Athenians provided the bulk of the defense force, the Plateans had achieved fame by supplying a contingent of a thousand men (cf. Herodotus 6.108, 111; Pausanias 1.32.3; Plutarch, *Par. Gr. R.* 305b).

The adverb βραδέως (from the adjective βραδύς [= slow]) scarcely refers to a gravity-defying slow speed with which the severed hands fell groundward; rather "*slow* falling" must mean "slow (i.e., *reluctant*) to fall," "falling *late* in the struggle" (cf. LSJ, βραδύς II).

The notion of Cynegirus' rest (λοιπός), i.e., the trunk of his body with the amputated arms gone, as a "[victory] trophy" (τρόπαιον) takes up an idea mentioned earlier (A 10). Putting wreaths on tombs and monuments was a common act of commemoration and respectful acknowledgement among the Greeks (cf. W. Peek, *Griechische Grabgedichte*, Berlin: Akademie Verlag, 1960, ## 22 [p. 56]; 81 [p 76]; 206 [p. 136]; 272 [p. 162]; 284 [p. 168]; 344 [p. 200]; et al.

40

The pejorative κακοδαίμονες (= bad spirited, ill-starred, poor devils) is relatively bland (cf. Aristophanes, *Nu.* 104; *Pl.* 386; Euripides, *Hipp.* 1362). A hard-bitten soldier would have let loose nastier obscenities. Such, however, would not be fitting in the mouth either of the youthful Cynegirus or of the eloquent Polemo.

Cynegirus' words Τί φεύγετε ...; στῆτε καὶ τὰς πόλεις ἀπόδοτε ἃς ἐληίσασθε (= Why are you fleeing? Stay and give back the cities which you plundered) are a re-phrasing of his just quoted demand: Νάξον ἀπαιτῶ τὴν ἡρπασμένην, τὰς ἐν Αἰγαίῳ νήσους ἀπαιτῶ. ἀπόδοτε καὶ μὴ φεύγετε (A 38). It was the mark of a skilled rhetorician to be able to repeat a thought, but reformulated in new words. For example, Philostratus says admiringly of Alexander (the 'Clay-Plato'), "The sentiments that he had so brilliantly expressed before Herodes came he now recast in his presence, but with such different words and different rythms, that those who were hearing them for the second time could not feel that he was repeating himself" (τὰς γὰρ διανοίας τὰς πρὶν ἥκειν τὸν Ἡρώδην λαμπρῶς αὐτῷ εἰρημένας μετεχειρίσατο ἐπιστάντος οὕτω τι ἑτέρᾳ λέξει καὶ ἑτέροις ῥυθμοῖς, ὡς τοῖς δεύτερον ἀκροωμένοις μὴ διλογεῖν δόξαι, *V. S.* 572). Philostratus likewise reports how Hippodromus recast a declamation (*V. S.* 619).

Whereas Cynegirus had *"shouted"* (ἐβόησας [√ βοάω], A 38, 40) at the barbarians — a verb with the tone of a military command (cf. B 23, 40, 61) — they in return "were *screaming*" (ἐκραύγαζον [√ κραυγάζω]) back at him. The variant "were *shrieking*" (ἔκραζον [√ κράζω]) was, despite weak attestation (QR [→ ρ]), printed instead by Stephanus, Possinus, and Orellius. Both verbs, virtual synonyms, can be used of animal or bird croaks (LSJ, *sub verba*). The difference between βοάω and κρ[αυγ]άζω is that between discipline and disarray.

The text provides no guidance as to what vocative to supply with the exclamatory ὦ of the fleeing Persians. In accordance with Polemo's style all three instances should best have the same word (cf. A 38; B 12, 51, 54). Inasmuch as the range of possible choices is broad, the translation simply opts for a colorless "you" (σύ).

The word τολμηρία (= insolence) appears to be undocumented in classical Greek (cf. LSJ); outside this passage it is not attested until Christian literature of the 4th century CE (cf. *LPGL*, τολμηρία). Such a late word is unusual for the Atticizing Polemo who preferred to utilize the vocabulary of the classical age.

Homer frequently used the verb μαίνομαι (= rage, be furious) to describe the rage or frenzy of battle (cf. *Il.* 5.185, 717; 6.101; *Od.* 9.350; 11,537), and specifically he spoke of Patroclus' "hands raging" (cf. οἱ τότε χεῖρες ἄαπτοι μαίνονθ᾽ ὁππότ᾽ ἐγώ περ ἴω μετὰ μῶλον Ἄρης [= his hands then rage invincible when I enter the turmoil of Ares], *Il.* 16.244–245) and of a spear "raging in [the] hands" of other heroes (μαίνεται ἐν παλάμῃσι, *Il.* 8.111; 16.74-75). Further, Herodotus says that at Marathon when the Greeks charged on the run, the Persians imputed "madness" (μανίη) to them (6.112). Polemo's expression μαινομένη δεξιά (= raging right hand) may well have this Homeric and Herodotean language in mind.

λήμματος (= of unjust gain?) is more solidly attested than the homonym λήματος (= of insolence). Yet while the former indisputably stood in the medieval archetype (π), it makes poor sense. In all likelihood, therefore, the original spelling (in Π) had only one μ which in the early transcription process was inadvertently doubled — an easy mistake (indicated in the text by the pointed brackets: {μ}. For λῆμα in the bad sense of *insolence* or *arrogance* cf. LSJ, λῆμα II.2).

The synonymous parallelism of the tricolon (ὦ 3x) shows just enough structural variety so as not to be monotonous.

41

Datis was fleet commander for Darius' expedition against Greece and head of naval operations at Marathon (Herodotus 6.94, 97, 98, 118, 119; 7.74). Polemo introduces him here for the first time; as a known quantity he required no explanation. The second declamation also mentions him several times (B 14, 45, 56, 60).

The adjective τροπαιούχος (√ τρόπαιον + ἔχω = *having* or *gaining trophies*) in this passage is taken by LSJ as referring to Datis, i.e., as part of the genitive absolute Δάτιδος ... τοῦ τροπαιούχου ... ὁρμήσαντος (= when ... the trophy-receiving ... Datis ... urged). This interpretation is presented as parallel to the use of the term τροπαίουχος as an epithet of Roman emperors (cf. OGI 723.2; CIG 3992; 4350; SIG 906b). However, given the argument that heroizes Cynegirus, it is more natural to construe the adjective as substantized and as a possessive genitive, taking the phrase τὴν κεφαλὴν τοῦ τροπαιούχου as a unit: "the head of the trophy getter", i.e. the head of Cynegirus who is obtaining the Phoenician ship as trophy of war, and who himself is presented as a turning point (τρόπαιον) in this battle and in the history of warfare.

The adverb ἄνωθεν could refer to either *time* (= again, anew) or *place* (= from on high, from above). Since Datis and his orders have not been previously mentioned, the spatial sense is more likely here. Datis is pictured on board his ship issuing orders from the upper deck. An apt parallel is the description of Themistocles speaking from the deck of his ship (ἄνωθεν τῆς νεὼς διαλέγεσθαι, Plutarch, *Them.* 12.1) or the military use of ἄνωθεν simply to mean "on deck" (Thucydides 7.63.2). This detail suggests that Cynegirus attacked the flag ship of the Persian fleet, or at least a ship anchored close to it. Such a notion is not necessarily inconsistent with the identification of the ship as Phoenician (A 9, 23, 31) because the Phoenician ships constituted the core of the Persian navy (cf. note to A 9).

The voice of ἐγείρεται is ambiguous — it could be a middle (= rouses himself) or passive (= is roused). In view of prior clause which describes the efforts of the commander as ineffective, the passive (which implies the agency of the commander) seems unlikely; the middle (which suggests the initiative of the sailors) is more probable. Within the otherwise consistent use of past tenses in this passage the present ἐγείρεται may be a *lapsus*. It could, however, be construed as an historical present for the sake of liveliness or vividness (cf. *GG*, 1883).

The neuter plural accusative adjective μυρία serves as an adverb (= intensely, arduously) (cf. LSJ, μυρίος I.4).

Datis' frightened sailors let loose a broad-ranging but carefully structured outburst:

    (a) a question addressed to [Persian?] gods
    (b) a question addressed to Greek soldiers
    (c) a double imperative addressed to themselves
    (d) a prediction about Athenian actions

(a) and (b) form a double interrogative; (c) and (d) an either-or sentence.

Presumably it is to Asian gods that the desperate invaders voice their complaint. They are nowhere named (cf. Index 7) and this is the only passage where θεοί denotes non-Greek deities (cf. A 35, 36; B 10, 52, 62). Not in language, but in sentiment this 'prayer' recalls laments of the waiting relatives of the vanquished Persians as portrayed by Aeschylus:

ὦ δυσπόνητε δαῖμον, ὡς ἄγαν βαρὺς
    ποδοῖν ἐνήλου παντὶ Περσικῷ γένει. (*Pers.* 515–516)
O trouble bringing divinity, that such a crushing weight
    you have thrust upon the whole Persian race.
ἰὼ ἰώ, δαίμονες
    ἔθεθ᾽ ἄελπτον κακὸν
    διαπρέπον, οἷον δέδορκεν Ἄτα. (*Pers.* 1005–1007)
Alas, alas, divinities
    you have brought unexpected evil, conspicuous,
      the sort which [the goddess] Calamity causes with her glance.

χαλκόθυμοι (= brazen-spirited) — virtually equivalent to χαλκεοκάρδιος (= brazen-hearted) — is a post-classical word (cf. LSJ, sub verba). Its occurrence here is one of those few late words inadvertently used by the Atticizing Polemo.

The disjunctive particle paired (ἤ ... ἤ) in the sense of "either ... or" occurs in the declamations in only one other place (ἢ φίλων ἢ πολεμίων = either friends or enemies, A 28). Although the antithetical material of the declamations would readily lend itself to the use of this construction it does not appear to be characteristic of Polemo's style.

The alternatives ἢ θᾶττον ... ἢ ἤδη ... make the parallel adverbs virtually synonymous: quickly / immediately. This use of ἤδη referring to the near future is singular in Polemo; all the other occurrences refer to the past: "already" (A 45, 47; B 26, 27, 31, 61).

The fear of capture by Athenian naval or cavalry forces which is attributed to Datis' crew is a pure creation of Polemo: there is no record of Greek ships or horses participating at the battle of Marathon. There the Greek military consisted entirely of hoplite infantry (cf. Herodotus 6.111–117).

The three sentences in the mouths of the Persians have different addressees: (1) accusatory complaint to the barbarian gods, (2) angry vituperation at the fearless Greeks, and (3) desperate exhortation and prediction to the fellow Persians. Together this concise triple summary effectively evokes the plight of the invaders.

42

The mention of "other arrows" (ἄλλα βέλη) implies that the Persian archers made a futile attempt at stopping Cynegirus. This detail remains undeveloped and stands alone; all other mentions of arrows refer to those directed against Callimachus (A 7, 23, 24, 27, 27, 30, 30, 31, 37, 45, 47; B 10, 10, 12, 39, 51, 56, 57, 57, 59; only the arrows in A 35, whose target is indeterminate, could possibly provide a parallel to A 42).

In the comparison of Cynegirus' hand being cut off *like an oak or pine* (ὥσπερ δρῦν ἢ πεύκην) Orellius (p. 56) sees a modified popular adage: πεύκης τρόπον κόπτειν (= to cut in the manner of the pine), πίτυος δίκην ἐκτρίβειν (= to rub out in the way of the pine), the sense of which he gives as *to completely, utterly extirpate* (cf. Zenobius 5.76; Phalaris, *Ep.* 9.48). Herodotus (6.37) twice repeated the maxim πίτυος τρόπον ἐκτρίψειν (= to rub out after the manner of the pine) before explaining that "the pine alone of all trees, when it is cut off, puts forth no shoot but perishes utterly" (πίτυς μούνη πάντων δενδρέων ἐκκοπεῖσα βλαστὸν οὐδένα μετιεῖ ἀλλὰ πανώλεθρος ἐξαπόλλυται). Theophrastus, who carefully distinguished between the πίτυς and the πεύκη, says this characteristic was attributed to the latter, not the former (πεύκην μὲν γὰρ ἐπικαυθεισῶν τῶν ῥιζῶν οὐκ ἀναβλαστάνειν, τὴν πίτυν δέ φασί τινες ἀναβλαστάνειν [= whereas the 'peuke', when its roots are burnt, does not put forth shoots again, some say the 'pitus' does], H. P. 3.9.5). Against Orellius's interpretation, however, it must be said that such botanical lore does not illumine well the image in Polemo. The point is not that Cynegirus or his hand was utterly destroyed, indeed the whole argument is to the contrary (A 10, 11, 23, 31, 36, 40, 42). Moreover, the proverb which Orellius cites does not account for Polemo's parallel mention of the oak. Hence, another explanation may be more likely. The simile of Cynegirus' hand being cut off *like an oak or pine* (ὥσπερ δρῦν ἢ πεύκην) recalls Homer's comparison of Aias in battle sweeping before him horses and men just as (ὡς) a mountain torrent carries away oaks and pines (*Il.* 11.492–497). If Polemo's comparison derives from Homer, it would imply that the violent amputation was not only like the felling of a majestic tree but an event of epic proportion.

The phrase ταύτης οὐδὲν ἐφρόντισεν (= he took thought in no way of this [hand]) follows a common classical construction: the verb (φροντίζω) takes a genitive object (ταύτης) and the negative is expressed with an accusative of respect (οὐδέν). Parallels are easy to find (cf. Περσέων οὐδὲν φροντίζει [= {the land north of the Caucasus} takes thought in no wise of the Persians], Herodotus 3.97; φροντίζοντας οὐδὲν τῆς πολιορκίης [= being concerned in no way about the siege] Herodotus 3.151; cf. also 4.167, 198; Aristophanes, *Lys.* 915; Plato, *Leg.* 888c).

The clause ὥσπερ ἀλλοτρίαν χεῖρα διδοὺς (= as though giving another's hand) is reminiscent of Thucydides' classic description of the Athenians in war: τοῖς μὲν σώμασιν ἀλλοτριωτάτοις ὑπὲρ τῆς πόλεως χρῶνται (= they use their bodies on behalf of the city as though they were the bodies of others, Thucydides 1.70.6). Isocrates praised the Athenians at Marathon for facing overwhelming odds ὥσπερ ἐν ἀλλοτρίαις ψυχαῖς μέλλοντες κινδυνεύειν (= as if they were about to risk the lives of others, *Pan.* 86). Plutarch, echoed this with τοὺς ἐν Μαραθῶνι προκινδυνεύσαντας ὥσπερ ἀλλοτρίαις ψυχαῖς ... ἐναγωνίσασθαι (= those who braved the dangers at Marathon fought as though risking other people's souls) and he glossed the phrase with τὴν τόλμαν αὐτῶν καὶ τὴν ὑπεροψίαν τοῦ ζῆν (= their daring and disdain of life) (Plutarch, *Glor. Ath.* 350d). Thus Polemo employed a stock oratorical phrase which had become part of the patriotic Greek tradition.

The preposition περί with the accusative could express spatial location: the hand *around* or *near* which the fight was occurring (as in B 13, 39; cf.

LSJ, περί I.1). More in keeping with Polemo's hyperbolic style, however, is the sense that the whole Greek army was fighting *for the sake of* Cynegirus' hand (LSJ, περί I.3; cf δι' ἥν [= on account of which {hand}], A 35).

An assured translation of τὰ τραύματα τοῖς στοιχείοις διένειμεν is impeded by two uncertainties: (1) What is the subject of διένειμεν? Did *he* (= Cynegirus) or *it* (= the whole army) distribute (= 'dish out') the wounds? The proximity of the verb to ὅλον τὸ στρατόπεδον speaks for the latter; but the tense of the verb matches the earlier aorist ἐφρόντισεν (= took thought) — as opposed to the imperfects ἔπιπτεν and ἐμάχετο (= was falling, was fighting) — and could speak for the former. (2) What is the precise sense of τοῖς στοιχείοις? Does the noun denote the *physical elements of land and sea* (cf. A 44, 11) or perhaps connote the *military branches of army and navy* (cf. note at A 11)? Further, what is the sense of the dative (which is typically used to indicate the indirect object of this verb, cf. LSJ, διανέμω)? How does one deliver wounds *to* the physical elements?

The English translation opts for the army as the subject of the verb as being grammatically more natural and consistent with the fact nowhere else do the declamations speak of Cynegirus inflicting wounds on the enemy. The dative is taken as contracted (= to [enemy forces on] land and sea).

43

Briareus (Βριάρεως = strong) was one of the "hundred-handed" giants (ἑκατόγχειρος, Homer, *Il.* 1.402) whom mother Earth bore, together with Gyges and Cottus, as her first children of semi-human form (cf. E. Simon, "Hekatoncheires," *LIMC* IV.1.481-482; R. Graves, *The Greek Myths* [New York: Penguin Books, 1960] 1.31-32). According to ancient myth Briareus and his siblings assisted the Olympians in their cosmic war to subdue the Titans (Hesiod 617-735; Apollodorus 1.2.1). The strength and multiple arms of Briareus played a pivotal role in turning the tide against the Titans (Hesiod, *Th.* 664-686, 713-735). Whereas the mythographers spoke specifically of his having *one hundred* hands (e.g., Hesiod, Theogony 147-154; Apollodorus 1.1.1; Virgil, *Aen.* 10.565-566), Polemo used the less definite πολυχειρία (= *many*-handed-ness), a term which could also describe a host of human hands in a military endeavor (cf. Thucydides 2.77; Xenophon, *Cyr.* 3.3.26; Josephus, *Ap.* 1.240). If like the first generation giants Cynegirus had possessed multiple arms he could have held fast not just one ship but all [the ships of] Asia. As though the previous allusion to the epic Trojan war (A 42) were not enough, the image here recalls the theogonic Titanomachy (cf. Apollodorus 1.6.1-2; Ovid, *Met.* 1.151-162; Claudian, *Gig.*). Such hyperbole exceeds all prior comparisons of Cynegirus with heroes and gods (A 35, 36, 42). Beyond that, however, the πολυχειρία cited by Polemo may also quite possibly contain an allusion to the post-classical notion of a Hydra-like capacity of Briareus' hands to regenerate themselves if cut off (cf. *quae brachia centum, quis Briareus aliis numero crescente lacertis* [= what hundred-handed monster, what Briareus, whose arms grew ever more numerous as they were lopped off], Claudian, *Cons. Stil.* 1.303–304). If that were the case the "many-handedness" would refer not so much to multiple hands at birth, but to the hands' replacement and multiplication when severed. This latter interpretation is in some ways more inviting than the former. It would be strengthened if other evidence for a 'regeneration' ability of Briarean hands could be mustered that had an earlier date than Claudian (ca. 400 CE).

Another striking feature of this passage is the unusual μοι (= *for me*). This dative of interest or advantage (*GG*, 1474; 1481) is not likely a *pars-pro-toto* synecdoche = *for us*; to express that he would have used ἡμῖν (as in A 44 and B40). The singular appears intentional but ambiguous. It could mean (a) that Euphorion identifies with his son and in aristocratic self-importance thinks of himself as participating in the battle vicariously (cf. A 1, 12, 28) or (b) that if Cynegirus had restrained more ships he would have provided his father with an even stronger argument to win his own case before the Athenian jury (cf. A 2–4, 12, 15, 47–49).

After a past indicative (ἦσθα) in the main clause the final conjunction ἵνα with an aorist indicative (ἐκράτησας) expresses a consequence which has not followed or cannot follow (LSJ, ἵνα B.I.3.b). Ordinarily the indicative in the main clause (ἦσθα) would stand with ἄν (Plato, *Men.* 89b; Demosthenes 29.17), but Polemo omits the particle: "you *were* ...," instead of "you *would have been* ..."

Of the seven occurrences of φέρω in Polemo (A 14, 17, 23, 36, 43; B 19, 54) only here (and possibly B 54) does it have the sense of *carry away as booty* (LSJ, φέρω A.VI.2). The imperfect ἔφερεν is translated here as though it were an aorist (ἤνεγκε) because "the imperfect of verbs ... which imply continuous action, is often used where we might expect the aorist of concluded action. ... the action is regarded as unfinished since the goal is not [yet] reached" (*GG*, 1891). Naxos and Eretria are specifically named (also in A 30, 38; B 54, 56, cf. 31) because these are the two places that Herodotus had singled out in his description of Persian captive taking (Herodotus 6.96, 101). Indeed, Herodotus included a report about the resettling of the Eretrian captives at Ardericca in the vicinity of Susa (Herodotus 6.119). Epigrams attributed to Plato say the same (*An. Gr.* 7.256, 259). The tradition of an

Eretrian community in Persia and its origins going back to their capture by Darius lived on beyond the time of Polemo at least into the third century CE (cf. Philostratus, *V. A.* 1.23-24).

The verb ἀπάγω has here the sense of *bring back* (cf. ἀπάγοιεν ὀπίσω, Herodotus 9.117) or *bring home* (cf. ἀπήγαγεν οἴκαδε, Homer, *Od.* 16.370; ἀπάξειν οἴκαδ᾽, Sophocles, *Ph.* 941). The picture of King Darius receiving the battle report (φήμη) back home in Persia is inconsistent with other passages in the declamations which imply his presence on the field of battle (A 29; B 40). This image corresponds rather to the scene in Aeschylus' *Persians* which depicts the reaction of the Persian court when the news arrives in Susa of the disasters at Salamis and Plataea (480/479 BCE). However, there is an important difference. Whereas Aeschylus' Persian survivor who brings the bad news home repeatedly attributes the disaster to ill-willed divinities (δαίμονες) and gods (θεοί), or to an avenging (ἀλάστωρ) and deluding spirit (ἄτη) sent by the gods (cf. Aeschylus, *Pers.* 345-347, 354, 361-362, 373, 454-455, 472, 495, 725, 911, 1005), Polemo's Persian escapees give the credit to Cynegirus and "adamantine" Greeks like him.

ἀδαμάντινος is an alpha-privative (√ ἀ + δαμάω) meaning *un-tamable*, *un-conquerable*, but in common parlance it was used to describe the *hardest* of substances, such as steel or diamond (LSJ, ἀδαμάντινος and ἀδάμας). In the metaphorical use here the root meaning still shimmers through.

This report is οὐκ ἀγεννῆ (= not ignoble). This negation of the alpha-privative with an adherescent οὐ is the first of seven examples of *litotes* having this form (e.g., οὐκ ἄκαιρος = not inopportune, B 29; οὔτε ἀνόητος = not senseless, B 33); these occur mostly in the second declamation (cf. Index 5). The negation of the contrary is a type of understatement which intensifies the affirmation (*GG*, 2694; 2695; 3032): a "not ignoble" report is one that pays the *full* tribute that is due.

44

The Plataeans, being participants at Marathon (cf. note at A 39), could chant their hymns of praise (ᾄδουσι) to Cynegirus as first-hand eye-witnesses; the Lacedaemonians, however, who for their own reasons and despite the Athenians' request declined to participate at Marathon (cf. B 5; A 35; Herodotus 6.106), could only learn about him by second-hand hearsay (πυνθάνονται). Polemo employs the politically official and archaic sounding name *Lacedaemonians* (also in B 5) rather than the term *Spartans* which was just as old but did not have the same official character and which eventually in

Hellenistic times came to be the more widely used name (cf. H. Volkmann, "Sparta," *KP*, 5.292-293).

The Marathon traditions remembered an Athenian at the battle who was permanently blinded by an apparition (φάσμα, Herodotus 6.117; Suidas, Πολύζηλος; or φαντασία; Plutarch, *Par. Gr. R.* 305b–c). In the extant testimonia his name varies between *Polyzelus* (Πολύζηλος [= Much Admired]: Plutarch [who makes him out to be a general], *Par. Gr. R.* 305b-c; Diogenes Laertius 1.56; Suidas, Ἱππίας) and *Epizelus* (Ἐπίζηλος [= Enviable]: Herodotus 6.117; Aelian, *N. A.* 7.38). His blindness was a fixture in the tradition, though the language describing it varied (cf. τῶν ὀμμάτων στερηθῆναι ... ἐόντα τυφλόν [= to be deprived of [his] eyes' sight ... being blind], Herodotus 6.117; τὴν ὅρασιν ἀπέβαλε καὶ τυφλὸς ἐγένετο [= he lost his sight and became blind], Plutarch, *Par. Gr. R.* 305c; πηρώθεις [= incapacitated {in his sight}], Suidas, Πολύζηλος and Ἱππίας). Polemo's μὴ τεθεαμένος (= though not seeing) is yet another variant. The artistic portrayal of the Marathon battle in the famous mural at the Painted Portico (Στοὰ Ποικίλη), which every visitor to the Athenian Agora in the classical and Hellenistic periods would have viewed (cf. Aeschines 3.186; Pliny, *N. H.* 35.57; Pausanias 1.15.3), also included the figure of Epizelus/Polyzelus (Aelian, *N. A.* 7.38). Art historians drawing on comparisons with derivative works have variously suggested that his blinding might have been indicated by showing him either with his arm across his face or with his face averted (cf. E. B. Harrison, "The South Frieze of the Nike Temple and the Marathon Painting in the Painted Stoa," *AJA* 76 [1972], pp. 367-368). Regardless of how it was depicted, Polyzelus' blindness was an essential feature of the Marathon tradition. This tradition claimed that despite his blindness "he fought as though seeing and he distinguished between killing comrades and enemies" (ἐμάχετο ὡς ὁρῶν καὶ διέκρινε τῇ φονῇ τοὺς ἰδίους καὶ τοὺς πολεμίους, Suidas, Ἱππίας). It is in line with such a tradition that Polemo says that Polyzelus, despite not seeing (μὴ τεθεαμένος is concessive), "followed these [deeds of prowess]" (ταύταις [sc. ἀριστείαις] ... ἠκολούθησε). The prowess of Cynegirus was so monumental that it could be discerned even without eyesight.

The sea (τὴν θάλασσαν) is the object of both προκατέλαβες (= you seized in advance) and ἐποίησας (= you made). Not mentioning it until the second clause creates a rhetorical tension of anticipation.

The phrase συνέθου τῷ στοιχείῳ φιλίαν (= you concluded a friendship with the element [i.e. the sea, cf. A 11 and 42]) corresponds with the standard language for military and political treaty arrangements: συντίθεμαι [middle] +

accusative + dative (= to conclude a pact with someone) (LSJ, συντίθημι B.II.1 and 3). This classical expression was used with a variety of accusative objects (cf. ξενία [= friendly relation], Herodotus 1.27; 3.39; 8.120; ὁμαιχμία [= defense league], Herodotus 7.145; 8.140; συμμαχία [= military alliance], Herodotus 5.73). The phrase φιλότητά τε καὶ συμμαχίην συνεθήκατο (= he arranged a friendship and military alliance, Herodotus 2.181) provides a precise exegesis of Polemo's συνέθου ... φιλία. By making the sea a Greek domain unsafe for the Persian navy Cynegirus brought the element into a kind of friendship pact with the Greeks.

In doing this he acted like an ambassador who concludes a treaty ὑπὲρ τῆς πατρίδος (= on behalf of the home country). Both fathers use the preposition ὑπὲρ to argue that their sons acted *on behalf of, in defense of* or *for* their homeland (A 25, 44, 44, 49; B 8, 64).

Linguistically the following sentence (with slightly rearranged word order) presents a nearly perfect parallel:

συνέθου   τῷ στοιχείῳ   φιλίαν   ὑπὲρ τῆς πατρίδος·
ἔδωκας   τῇ θαλάσσῃ   τὴν δεξίαν   ὑπὲρ ἡμῶν.

The second sentence has a double entendre, one side of which nearly matches the first sentence. The literal meaning is, of course, that he surrendered his hand to the sea — when it got chopped off, it fell into the water. Matching the previous sentence, however, is the additional figurative sense which derives from the common idiom διδόναι δεξιάν τινι (= to give [the] right hand to someone [as a sign of friendship and trust]). This 'hand-shake' expression is wide-spread (cf. δεξιὰς δεδομένας μὴ ἀδικήσειν ἀλλήλους [= having given right hands {as pledges} not to harm one another], Xenophon, *An.* 2.5.3); δὸς ἡμῖν δεξιὰς καὶ παυσάσθωσαν οἱ Ιουδαῖοι πολεμοῦντες ἡμᾶς [= give us right hands and let the Jews stop fighting us], 1 Macc 11:50; cf. also Diodorus Siculus 16.43.4; Gal 2:9; Josephus, *A. J.* 18 § 326). From Pergamum comes an inscription with an unusual form of this phrase, namely one which simply has χείρ (= hand) instead of δεξιά (= right hand): δοῦναι τὰς χεῖρας ἡμῖν εἰς σύλλυσιν (= to give the hands to us for agreement, cf. A. Deissmann, *Bible Studies* [Edinburgh: Clark, 1901] 251). In Polemo, therefore, the second sentence in the couplet acts as an epexegetical concretization of the first: Like an official representative on behalf of the Greeks (ὑπὲρ ἡμῶν) Cynegirus 'gave' (ἔδωκας = extended) his right hand to the sea — carrying out the pledge gesture customary in treaty conclusions.

Here the term σχήματα (the plural is infrequent in Polemo, cf. A 26, 28, 44; B 17) comes closer to meaning active *gestures* (cf. B 35, 42; LSJ, σχῆμα

7) rather than passive appearances as is normally the case in Polemo (cf. Index 8).

The expression ἐκ σιδήρου χεῖρες (= hands out of iron) is military terminology for *grappling irons*. Thucydides, for example, speaks of χειρῶν σιδηρῶν ἐπιβολαί (= throwings of iron hands [grappling irons]), to hold fast an enemy ship (Thucydides 7.62.3). Reminiscent of the argument that Cynegirus fought a sea and land battle simultaneously (A 8, 11, 28) is the statement σιδηρᾶς χεῖρας ἐπιβάλλοντες ἠνάγκαζον τοὺς ἀντιταττομένους ἐπὶ τῶν νεῶν πεζομαχεῖν (= throwing iron hands [grappling irons] they compelled the opponents on the ships to fight a foot soldier battle, Diodorus Siculus 13.16.1). Appian has a similar description of a naval battle (*Syr.* 5.105). Like the Greeks, the Romans too called this military device *manus ferreae* (= hand of iron, Frontinus, *Strat.* 2.3.24; Livy 26.39.12) or *ferreae manus harpago* (= grappling hand of iron, Curtius 4.2.12). Livy described these grappling irons (*harpagones*) as *asseres ferreo unco praefixi ...catenas* (= poles with an iron hook affixed [at one end] ... and chains [at the other end]) (Livy 30.10.16) and he recounted their effectiveness in ship warfare (30.10.17–20). Pliny attributed their invention to Pericles (*N. H.* 7.[56].209). At Syracuse Archimedes was famed for having devised a mechanical way to pick up attacking ships with iron claws (χερσὶ σιδηραῖς) on a crane-like structure and to dash them against the rocks (Plutarch, *Marc.* 15.2). Polemo's formulation does not push the traditional invention date any earlier but does make Cynegirus the impetus for the invention.

The grammar of ἐπὶ ναῦς ἐπιβολάς (preposition + two accusatives) is hard. Hence, previous editors have viewed it as a textual corruption and have proposed a variety of 'corrections':

1. ἐπὶ ναυτῶν ἐπιβολάς   (= for assaults of sailors)   [Stephanus]
2. ἐπὶ νεῶν ἐπιβολάς   (= for assaults of ships)   [Stephanus]
3. ἐπὶ ναῶν [νεῶν] ἐμβολάς   (= for forays of ships)   [Jacobs]
4. ἐπὶ ναῦς καὶ ἐμβολάς   (= for ships and forays)   [Jacobs]
5. καὶ ἐπὶ ναῦς ἐπιβολαί   (= and forays against ships)   [Hinck]
6. καὶ ἐπὶ ναῦς ἐμβολαί   (= and assaults against ships)   [Hinck]

Conjectures 1-3 dissolve the double accusative by changing the first accusative to a genitive (subjective [1, 2?, 3?] or objective [2?, 3?]). Conjecture 4 coordinates the two accusatives by inserting the copula καί. Conjectures 5 and 6 dissolve the double accusative by changing the second one to a nominative and inserting the copula καί before the phrase to produce a second subject (forays/assaults) for the verb (γενήσονται) alongside χεῖρες (hands). All these conjectures are smoother than the reading in the text. Any one is plausible, but none has MS attestation. Therefore, the translation retains the difficult reading of the MSS and accounts for the anacoluth by assuming the author's ellipsis [unusual!] or a copyist's omission [haplography] of a second ἐπί with ἐπιβολάς. The [double] preposition is used then in two senses: *for* (purpose) and *against* (hostile opposition) (LSJ, ἐπί C.III.1 and C.I.4).

Agreement in gender, number, and case grammatically links the participle ἔχουσαι (= having) to χεῖρες (= hands). However, unless Polemo actually means that the iron hooks will have embossed on them images or pictures (εἰκόνας) of Cynegirus' fight, which seems unlikely, it is better to construe the participle — contrary to grammar but according to sense — with ἐπιβολάς: naval attacks with grappling hooks will have resemblances (εἰκόνας) to Cynegirus' struggle which prefigured them.

45

Beginning the clause with πολλά and postponing the corresponding noun ἐγκώμια to the end is characteristic of Polemo's style (e.g., πολλὰς ... ναῦς, A 9; πολὺν ... φόνον, B 9; πολλὴ ... σχολή B 13; cf. also A 20, 20; B 10, 46, 47). This rhetorical device has the effect of sharpening the listener's attention: one looks for the resolution: much/many ... what?

Aristotle had distinguished ἐγκώμιον (= commendation) from ἔπαινος (= praise) by saying that the latter dealt with a person's ἀρετή (in the broad sense of 'virtue') while the former set forth a person's ἔργα (= achievements) (*Rh.* 1367b28; *E. N.* 1101b33): "We pronounce an encomium upon those who have achieved [something]" (ἐγκωμιάζομεν πράξαντας, *Rh.* 1367b33). Though the term ἐγκώμια could be used for praises of the living (e.g., Aristophanes, *Nu.* 1205; Theophrastus, *Char.* 3.2), it often referred to *eulogies* of the dead as is the case in Polemo (A 45; B 16; cf. Plato, *Prot.* 326a; T. Job 43).

Depending on the meaning of the verb φυλάττω, the second clause of the sentence may be taken in either of two ways: (1) φυλάττω (= *keep, save,* i.e. until the end): By common custom (κοινῷ νόμῳ) [i.e., in the oratorical tradition] the best (τὰ κάλλιστα) arguments are *kept in store until last.* (2) φυλάττω (= *notice, observe, heed*): ... *not all* encomiums are noted, *just the best* ones. The first interpretation has to do with *sequence,* the second with *selectivity.* For the first sense of φυλάττω it is hard to locate a lexicographical parallel and difficult to pin down precisely what that best encomium is which Euphorion has saved till last. For the second sense of φυλάσσω clear parallels are also not easy to find (LSJ, φυλάσσω B.3 and 5), but "the best encomiums" need not be singled out from the numerous praises in the speech — they comprise all the ones mentioned. The second interpretation, therefore, seems the more likely: Euphorion has not wearied his audience with *all* of the many panegyrics he could have trotted out, but has simply focussed on the *best* ones.

The two questions to the father of Callimachus are in nature rhetorical (negative answers are obviously expected) and in tone sneering.

In the verb μεγαληγορέω the root (-ηγορέω) derives etymologically from ἀγορεύω (= speak in the public assembly [ἀγορά]). The compound follows the pattern of related verbs (cf. ἀλλ-ηγορέω [= speak otherwise, allegorize], κατ-ηγορέω [= speak against, accuse], συν-ηγορέω [= speak for, advocate]). Literally the verb μεγαλ-ηγορέω means *talk big*. Ordinarily it has a negative connotation: *to brag arrogantly or inordinately*. However, occasionally, as here, it means *to boast proudly with legitimation* (cf. Xenophon, *Cyr.* 4.4.2 where the verb is used for soldiers proudly describing their courage in battle, words for which they are commended; Plutarch says there are times when in order to put down the self-willed and audacious person it is "not amiss ... to boast" (οὐ χεῖρον ... μεγαληγορῆσαι, *Inv. Laud.* 544f; cf. 540e). The elliptical accusative interrogative phrase ποίαν τὴν στάσιν (= what sort of stance?) is parallel to τοιοῦτον τινα λόγον (= any such word) in the previous question; to complete the thought the verbs of that sentence (ἔχεις ... μεγαληγορῆσαι) must be mentally supplied.

ἵστημι is one of those rare verbs having both a first (transitive) and a second (intransitive) aorist (*GG*, 361, 554e) and Polemo uses both (first: A 45; B 11, 12, 53; second: A 40; B 8, 39, 47, 55, 58, 62). Here the object of the transitive aorist ἔστησαν (= made to stand) is Greece (τὴν Ἑλλάδα). Both speakers make the same claim about their sons: 'Cynegirus' hands *made Greece to stand* when it was already falling' (A 45); 'Callimachus by himself *made Greece to stand*, not permitting Athens to fall' (B 12).

In sentences with both subject and predicate noun the former is distinguised from the latter by its article (cf. *GG*, 1150). In the μέν clause the anarthrous βέλη βάρβαρα (= barbarian arrows) is thus predicate noun; in the δέ clause the predicate noun, αἱ χεῖρες (= the hands) does, to be sure, have an article but that is because it refers to definite hands previously mentioned (*GG*, 1152). Hence, τὰ σώματα is the subject of both clauses. For rhetorical emphasis it is saved until the very end. This rhetorical subtlety is hard to capture in an uninflected language like English. Because τὰ σώματα (= the bodies) seems difficult, Jacobs conjectured that it was a corruption out of στερεώματα (= solid supports [√ στερ- = stiff, hard, rigid; cf. German *starr* = stiff]). Hinck (p. 16) emended the text accordingly but kept the article τά. This hypothesis is simple and appealing but without any MS support. Hence this edition retains the attested τὰ σώματα but understood in a sense close to στερεώματα, namely as *corporeal substances, solid bodies* (cf. LSJ σῶμα III.1).

A number of sharp contrasts are packed into this short μέν - δέ sentence:
(1) *your* [singular = personal]   vs. *all* [= communal];
(2) [dead] *corpse*   vs. [living] *Greece*;
(3) *barbarian* [= non-Greek]   vs. *our* [plural = family, Greek];
(4) *arrows*   vs. *hands*.

46

The two brusque imperatives (ἄπελθε = get out of the way!, παραχώρησον = make room!) are mitigated by a weak concession: 'Don't worry, I'll also put a plug for your son; after all, he did get to serve as commander over such a magnificent soldier as Cynegirus.' But this is a bogus consolation, damning through faint praise.

The negative μή with the present imperative (ἐπιχείρει) is ambiguous. The present tense may have either (a) iterative or (b) inceptive sense. (a) would mean: "cease working on," "don't continue working on" [a speech you have already started]. (b) would mean: "abstain from working on", "don't begin working on" [a speech you have not yet started]. The iterative sense denoting the interruption of an action already begun would attribute to Callimachus' father more presumptuous confidence in victory than the inceptive sense which urges resistance to an action still lying in the future (cf. *GG*, 1841).

The circumstantial participle ὤν has causal sense.

The μή with ταφῆναι θέλοντος is jarring. Does the corpse not want to be buried because it would lose the acclaim it has in the standing position? Perhaps the verb [ἐ]θέλω does not express volition but used with an inanimate (or here no-longer-animate) body rather expresses futurity, disposition, or what is accustomed: the corpse *is not about to be, is not naturally inclined to be, does not need to be* buried (cf. LSJ, ἐθέλω II.1 and 2) — because it is already entombed in the pile of arrows.

47

For the possessive adjective the first person ἡμετέρων (= our) is the better attested reading and surely stood in the medieval ancestor (π). Yet the second person ὑμετέρων (= your [plural]) fits the argument much better. In the Byzantine period both were pronounced alike (iotacism) so that they were often interchanged. Indeed, confusion between η and υ was "so widespread ...

that the testimony of even the best manuscripts respecting personal pronouns is liable to suspicion, and one's decision between such variant readings must turn upon considerations of fitness in the context." (B. Metzger, *The Text of the New Testament. Its Transmission, Corruption and Restoration*, 2nd ed. [New York: Oxford University Press, 1968], p. 192). Here in Polemo it is highly likely that the original (Π) had the second person ὑμετέρων.

The πάλαι (= long ago) is repeated three times for emphasis (*anaphora* or *epanalepsis*). Since Callimachus has *long since* been buried by arrows, the time for his burial eulogies is *long past*. Any funeral words now from his father come too late to be appropriate.

Euphorion, on the other hand, is more appropriately suited (ἐπιτηδειότερος) for the state funeral speech. His son, after all, was not buried prior to being interred in the official grave for the fallen at Marathon — this argument is not stated, but only implied by way of contrast with the case of Callimachus. The explicit reasons for why Euphorion is the more suited speaker are threefold:

(1) He is father "of him" (αὐτοῦ), i.e. of Cynegirus — who is the only 'war hero' under consideration now that Callimachus has been 'disqualified'. This point of paternity is a return to the beginning argument (0; A 1).

(2) Of all the 'important' people (τῶν μεγάλων) in Athenian society who could be considered as candidates he is the "most notable" (ὀνομαστότατος). The adjective ὀνομαστός (√ ὄνομα) denotes a person of repute (cf. Theognis 23; Herodotus 5.102; 6.114; 7.224); the superlative was reserved for those of special fame (cf. Herodotus 7.98; 9.72). Information about Euphorion's social status is not provided in the declamation; knowledge about his being an aristocratic landowner of a Eupatrid family is simply assumed (cf. note to 0). A significant factor in his claim to fame was also, no doubt, that he had fathered both Cynegirus and Aeschylus.

(3) Euphorion's third argument that he has an able "tongue" (γλῶττα) can be taken in two ways: either (a) he himself has a gifted tongue and is an eloquent speaker, or (b) he has a gifted son, the renowned playwright Aeschylus, who as 'ghost-writer' can compose an eloquent speech for him. The entire declamation Euphorion is delivering would support the former; the request he makes immediately following to Aeschylus (envisioned as part of the audience) to write the speech for him (A 49) supports the latter. Indeed, the phenomenon of speech writers — often hired — was widespread in antiquity.

The attestation for σήματι (= at the grave mound) is evenly balanced with that for σώματι (= at the body), but the former fits the context better. Ever since Homer the term σῆμα (= sign) could, among its many significations, denote the *grave marker* (*Il.* 2.814; 6.419; 7.86, 89; 23.331; *Od.* 1.291). Most of its other varied meanings were gradually displaced by σημεῖον, but σῆμα continued into late antiquity to denote the grave (LSJ, σῆμα 3). Alongside τάφος (= grave) and μνῆμα (= tomb) the term σῆμα had the special sense of the *mound* or *barrow* heaped up over the grave (Plutarch, *Oth.* 18.1).

48

The construction ἐάσατέ με (= permit me) + accusative + infinitive (2x) is standard (LSJ, ἐάω I.a).

The first infinitive τραγῳδῆσαι (= to declaim in tragic style) is coupled with its cognate noun τραγῳδία (= solemn poetry) to give added sonorous weight to the solemnity. Such hymnic commemoration of death is a far cry from the Stoic down-playing of its significance popular in Polemo's day. Epictetus, for example, argued, "Why say 'to die'? Don't make a tragedy of the matter, but talk [about it] as it is" (τί λέγεις ἀποθανεῖν; μὴ τραγῴδει τὸ πρᾶγμα, ἀλλ᾽ εἰπὲ ὡς ἔχει). It is, as he goes on to explain, simply the return of material (ὕλη) to the elements from which it came (Arrian, *Epict. Dis.* 4.7.15).

In the second infinitive παραγαγεῖν (= to lead [forward/past] the precise sense of the παρά prefix may be debated. It could mean that Euphorion wants to lead the triumphal parade *past* or *by* the standing Athenians lined up along the 'parade ground' (cf. Herodotus 4.158; 9.47). Or that he wants to bring the chorus *forward*, i.e., to *present* it or *introduce* it (similar to εἰσάγειν ... τὸν χόρον [= to lead in ... the chorus], Aristophanes, *Ach.* 11; LSJ, παράγω III.1.a.b.c). In view of the co-ordinated reference to poetry recitation [an act] the χορός denotes more likely the *dance* than the *band of dancers* at the public religious ceremony (LSJ, χορός I. and II.). Hearing this noun modified by the adjective ἐπινίκιος (= of/for victory) Polemo's listeners would probably have thought of something like the Latin *triumphus* (→ θρίαμβος) of their day — the triumphal procession of a Roman general after obtaining an important victory. In fact, the act of leading a Roman triumph is expressed precisely by this verb (cf. παρήγαγε ... θρίαμβόν [= he led ... a triumph], Appian, *B. C.* 101; ἕτεροι τῶν θριάμβους παραγόντων [= others of those leading triumphs], Appian, *Mith.* 117). Hence, the prepositional prefix of Polemo's παραγαγεῖν is not to be milked because the compound verb is simply idiomatic for leading a festal procession.

The imperative (ἐάσατε = permit) is followed by a prohibitive subjunctive (μὴ φθονήσητε = do not refuse to grant). "Sometimes ... μή with the aorist subjunctive marks the speaker's interruption, by anticipation, of a mental ... action that is being done by the person he addresses. ... [It] often expresses impatience" (*GG*, 1841.b; 1800.a). The positive and the negative are here then merely alternately formulated requests for the same thing. In other words, the exegesis of the unusual expression "Marathonian drama" is to be found in the previous imperative sentence. This δρᾶμα (= action, [√ δράω = act, do]) consists of reciting solemn funeral poetry extolling the valor displayed at Marathon and performing a dance enacting and celebrating the victory achieved there.

49

   Structurally there is a resemblance to the previous clauses in that a sentence with imperatives (ποίησον [= make] / συγκόσμησον [= confer honor on]) is again followed by a prohibitive subjuntive (μή ... ἀτιμάσητε [= don't dishonor]). Further the λόγον here corresponds to the τραγῳδίαν ἐπιτάφιον there; and the Μαραθωνίῳ there returns as Μαραθῶνος here. But the resemblance ends with this formal similarity. Here the positive and the negative have different addressees: the second person singular imperatives are spoken to Aeschylus; the second person plural prohibitive subjunctive is directed at the jurors (cf. A 47). Moreover, in contrast to the previous pair, the two requests here are not identical: Aeschylus is to prepare the speech; and the jurors should grant Euphorion the privilege to deliver it — to deny him that would be to dishonor him.

   The nominative pronoun σύ [= you] is not needed with the imperatives, it is added for emphasis (indicated in the translation by italics). The celebrated Aeschylus is to do this *for* his father Euphorion (μοι [= *for* me] and τῷ πατρί [= *for* the father] are datives of advantage or interest, cf. *GG*, 1474, 1481), not — interestingly enough — for his fallen brother Cynegirus. This small detail reflects not just the egoism of the aristocrat but also mirrors the general self-importance of rhetoricians in the Second Sophistic. Does the request that Aeschylus "make" (ποίησον) the speech mean that he should (a) *compose* it or (b) both *compose* and *deliver* it? The concluding lines suggest the former. In either case Aeschylus is to become what was called in the late empire an ἐπιτάφιος σοφιστής (= funeral rhetorician, cf. Achilles Tatius 3.25.7).

   Five short, emotion-filled sentences ring down the curtain on Euphorion's performance. Each is signaled by a verb in the first person:

προτείνω (= I stretch out)
ἔχομαι (= I lay claim to)
λαμβάνομαι (= I take hold of)
οὐκ ἀφίσταμαι (= I am not withdrawing from)
ἐπιτίθημι (= I put my hands on).

To stretch out the hands is an act of supplication (cf. προτείνω χεῖρα καὶ προίσσομαι [= I stretch forth my hand and I beg], Archilochus 130; προτείνουσαι τὰς χεῖρας ... ἐποιοῦντο τὴν λιτανείαν [= stretching out their hands ... they made entreaty], 2 Macc 3:20). The father's comparison of his own extended hands as similar (ὅμοιος) to the severed ones of his son is overdrawn.

The verb ἔχομαι (middle) with a genitive object means to cling to or lay hold on in the sense of *lay claim to* (cf. Herodotus 2.27). The λόγος is, of course, the ἐπιτάφιος λόγος (= funeral oration).

The last three sentences are linked as a group through their related objects, each in a different case: του τάφου (= the grave) [genitive]; τὸ πολυάνδριον (= the mass grave) [accusative]; τῷ σώματι (= the body) [dative]. The literal meaning of πολυάνδριον is: [the burial place] of *many men*. The term here is not to be confused with the 'common grave' or burial place for paupers or the dishonored — a denotation which it often had (Aelian, for example, distinguished between the family graves of honor [αἱ πατρῷαι ταφαί or τὰ οἰκεῖα ἠρία] and the πολυάνδριον where cowards in battle were buried, *V. H.* 7.21). In Polemo the term clearly refers to the burial mound on the battlefield where those who died honorably were interred (note the Attic inscription which speaks of commemorative rituals at το [ε]μ Μ[αρ]αθωνι πολυανδρε[ιον] for those who died defending freedom, IG II (2).1006.68; cf. the πολυάνδριον at Thermopylae where the brave Spartans were buried who died defending the pass, Strabo 9.4.16; Pausanias 8.41.1; 9.40.10).

As is typically the case with verbs of touching or taking hold of λαμβάνομαι has a genitive object (*GG*, 1345).

The construction οὐκ ἀφίσταμαι τὸ πολυάνδριον διεξιών is difficult. Because of its prepositional prefix (ἀπό) the verb ἀφίστημι ordinarily takes a genitive object. In rare cases where it does have an accusative object it usually means *avoid, shrink from* (e.g., the sun [τὸν ἥλιον], Xenophon, *Cyn.* 3.3; a fistfight [τὴν πυγμήν], Philostratus, *Gym.* 20; someone [τινάς], Euripides, *frag.* 1006), but this sense does not fit well here with the 'mass grave.' In view of the context the accusative (τὸ πολυάνδριον) probably appears instead of the genitive more for the sake of case variety than grammatical nuance. On that assumption the translation renders the sense of ἀφίσταμαι as though the object were in the genitive: *abandon claim to, withdraw from* (cf. Demosthenes 21.181; 19.147; Thucydides 7.28). The meaning of the circumstantial participle διεξιών (= going out through [√ διέξειμι {-εῖμι}]) is fuzzy. Is it temporal (when I go out through), concessive (although I go ...), or attendant circumstance (in that I go out ...)? In any case it would appear to refer to the act of leaving the assembly once the deliberations are over.

The references to the grave and the body suggest that the location where the jury is gathered and the physical scene of the declamation is to be imagined as the grave site at Marathon, not the ordinary place of assembly in Athens.

The final reminder that Euphorion is father of Cynegirus is a return once again to the legitimating argument of paternity with which the speech began (0; A 1).

Picking up on the comparison of the father's hands with the son's, the declamation concludes with extended pathos: 'Any juror who wishes may cut off *also* Euphorion's extended hands.' The καί of the final clause is not conjunctional (= and), rather it is *adverbial* (= *also, too*) (cf. GG, 2881; LSJ, καί B.2.). The one so disposed may cut off Euphorion's hands *too* (i.e., in addition to the hands of Cynegirus). In other words: Whoever votes to deny Euphorion the privilege of delivering the funeral oration will be acting like the enemy who chopped off Cynegirus' hands. Using a colloquial American idiom one might say that Euphorion's final word to the jury 'lays a guilt-trip' on them. This function of the third person aorist imperative ἀποκοψάτω (= let him cut off) may remind a modern reader of a similar imperative in Jesus' famous dictum: ὁ ἀναμάρτητος ... πρῶτος ... βαλέτω λίθον (= Let the one without sin throw the first stone, John 8:7).

Notes and Commentary on the Second Speech (B)

(The Speaker is the Father of Callimachus)

B.

1

The separation of the noun (νόμον) from its article (τὸν) creates a subtle tension in the sentence. This rhetorical device is a frequent characteristic of Polemo's style in both declamations.

"Adorning the grave" (κοσμοῦντα τὸν ... τάφον) is a common expression (cf. A 12; also τοὺς τάφους ... κοσμῇ, Xenophon, *Mem.* 2.2.13; κοσμεῖτε τὰ μνημεῖα, Matt 23:29) which ordinarily refers to putting some physical ornamentation on it, e.g, a marble stone (cf. 1 Macc 13:27), a stele or inscription (cf. Herodotus 7.228; 4 Macc 17:8), wreaths or flowers (cf. IG II[2] 1006.68). With κοσμέω the means of adornment is customarily expressed by an instrumental dative (cf. A 12; B 12, 56; LSJ, κοσμέω III.1 and 2). Here the adverbial καί (= also) with λόγῳ presupposes the material ornamentation; in addition there is *also* adornment *with a speech* (cf. κοσμεῖ τῷ λόγῳ [= he adorns with the talk], Plato, *La.* 197c; 196b; ἁγίῳ κοσμεῖσθαι λόγῳ [= to be adorned with a holy word], Clemens, *Paed.* 2.12 [p. 228.5; 540c]).

The rationale (cf. γάρ) for praising the Athenian custom of the funeral speech is given in the form of a perfectly balanced aphorism with verbs and adverbs in chiastic order: ἔργων εὖ πραχθέντων / λόγοι ῥηθέντες καλῶς (= deeds well done / words spoken beautifully). The genitive absolute is temporal: Beautifully spoken words (λόγοι) are not hollow when they come *after* deeds (ἔργα) performed well (cf. ὑπ' ἐμοῦ λέγοντος καλῶς τιμηθῆναι τὸν τάφον [= for the grave to be honored by me speaking beautifully], A 12).

The passage ἐμοὶ δὲ αὐτῷ ... δείξω τὸν λόγον poses problems. Possinus and Orellius both struggled with it. The ἐμοί is made emphatic through the addition of αὐτῷ. The attestation for the adverb προσφόρως (→ γ) is balanced with that for the adjective πρόσφορος (→ δ). This edition sides with the γ reading because the point of the argument is not that the valor is fitting (πρόσφορος ... ἀρετή), but that the funeral speech fittingly should belong to Callimachus' father. Thus the beginning and the end of the sentence seem best taken together, framing the sentence like brackets: ἐμοὶ δὲ αὐτῷ μὲν προσφόρως ... δείξω τὸν λόγον [supply a verb like προσήκειν, cf. Orellius p. 68] (= I will show that the speech ... fittingly [belongs] to *me*). These two elements are thus like bookends between which the rest of the sentence stands. Such a sandwich effect is a form of what the rhetoricians called *epanadiplosis* or *inclusio*.

Callimachus' ἀρετή (= valor) outlived his ψυχή (= soul) — that much is clear. But other elements are dark. Wherein does the μέν - δέ contrast consist and how does the dangling prepositional phrase διὰ τὴν ... προτίμησιν (= on account of the ... preferential honor) connect with the rest of the passage? And how does the whole sentence hang together? Possinus's wordy Latin paraphrase (pp. 59–60) provides little help. His verbosity is probably a reflection of his own desperation. It is hard to have confidence in this tangle; the English translation offered here is provisional at best.

The term ἀνδραγαθία (= bravery, manly virtue) — only here in the declamations — serves as an exegetical synonym for the thematic ἀρετή.

2

In classical Greek the verb πρέπω appears mostly in the impersonal 3rd person (LSJ, πρέπω III.4; GG, 1985). It is rare for this verb to have a personal subject as here (LSJ, πρέπω, III.3): *I* am fit. The supplementary infinitive ἑστάναι (= to stand) is a perfect ([literally] = to have stood). Used of the future, the perfect tense may indicate the certainty of the action (GG, 1865.c).

The comparative μᾶλλον (= more) stands with a genitive of comparison παντὸς ἄλλου (= than everyone else) (cf. also B 41, 47).

Regarding the βῆμα (= raised place) at the state funeral for the war dead, Thucydides says that at the proper time near the end of the ceremonies the speaker advanced from the tomb and took his stand "upon a platform which had been built high in order that he might be heard as far as possible in the throng" (ἐπὶ βῆμα ὑψηλὸν πεποιημένον, ὅπως ἀκούοιτο ὡς ἐπὶ πλεῖστον τοῦ ὁμίλου, Thucydides 2.34.8)

The term ἡγεμών (= leader) could designate any *military commander* of higher rank (cf. Herodotus 5.121; 6.43; 7.62; 9.77) or more specifically a στρατηγός (= *general*, cf. Herodotus 7.158).

Since the term πολέμαρχος seems redundant and clumsy Hinck, following Jacobs, bracketed it for deletion. It need not, however, be stricken; it can be taken as an apposition.

In a rare future most vivid condition (cf. Index 2) the unthinkableness of a post-mortem reversal in rank is contemplated. The protasis verb ἡττάομαι (= be less than, inferior to) is a denominative verb formed from ἥττων, the irregular comparative of μικρός (= small) or κακός (= bad). The apodosis verb ὑβρίζω (= to insult, maltreat) is also denominantive (√ ὕβρις = insolence, wanton violence). To make Callimachus *less* than he was is to commit an *outrage* against him. The future middle ὑβριεῖται (instead of the future passive ὑβρισθήσεται) — syntactically parallel to ἡττηθήσεται — must have a passive sense (= he will be insulted, insolently treated). It would appear that Polemo has committed here a *lapsus linguae*.

Given the 'passive' quality of the verb, the accusatives τὴν ἀρχήν and τὴν ἀρετήν cannot be construed as direct objects but must be accusatives of respect: *regarding* office and valor. The subsequent accusative τὴν αἰτίαν (= the cause) is accusative by virtue of apposition. In view of the cumbersome length of the original the English translation divides the sentence and renders τὴν αἰτίαν as though it were a predicate nominative of the second sentence. Grammatically viewed the αἰτία could include both the ἀρχή and ἀρετή. In the μέν clause one might argue that the *office* of Callimachus was the cause of the whole victory because it was his vote (among the divided generals) that brought about the Greek attack (Herodotus 6.109). However, the general tenor of the argument in both μέν and δέ clauses is that it was Callimachus' *valor* that was determinative.

Of all the marvels (θαύματα) at Marathon Callimachus was the greatest (cf. B 55, 56, 48, 64). The wonder is described in two ways: (1) Callimachus fought χωρὶς ψυχῆς (= without a soul), i.e., even after the life had gone out of him. This unusual assertion is expressed with the — for Polemo unusual — improper preposition χωρίς (cf. Index 6). Elsewhere Polemo expresses the same thing with the alpha-privative ἄψυχος (= 'soul-less,' lifeless, B 11; cf. A 25). (2) Callimachus' corpse was θανάτου κρείττονα (= stronger than death), i.e. too strong for death to overpower it right away (*GG*, 1077).

3

The expression κοινωνῆσαι τοῦ τάφου (= to have a share in the grave) is classical (cf. κοινωνεῖν τάφου, Euripides, *Or.* 1055). The parallelism of the infinitives κοινωνῆσαι τοῦ τάφου and πεισεῖν (= to fall) implies that as long as Callimachus was still standing he was not yet effectively dead. From μόγις ἔπεισα (= I scarcely persuaded) one gets the picture of the father on site after the battle talking directly to the upright corpse of his son and entreating it to fall over and accept the fact of death.

The pair of simple infinitives is followed by a pair of compound ones: ἀπ-ελθεῖν (= to go away from) and ὑπο-πεσεῖν (= to fall under), whereby the last infinitive picks up on the first one of the former pair (πεσεῖν / ὑπο-πεσεῖν). Polemo likes to play subtly with words. The sentences are pleonastic. In essence all four infinitives have equivalent meaning: to fall = to have a share in the grave = to depart the standing position = to succumb to the ambitions of others.

The "others" (ἑτέρων) are, as the following clause immediately makes clear, the invaders from Asia. The here unnamed "one [ruling] over all Asia" (τὸν ὑπὲρ τῆς Ἀσίας) is Darius I, Achaemenid king of Persia from 521 to 486 BCE (cf. B 8, 5, 52, 56, 60).

ἀξιόω (= I deem worthy) + accusative (τὸν ... βεβιασμένον) is common (LSJ, ἀξιόω I.2). The participle βεβιασμένον (= [the one] having forced) is a middle with active sense from the deponent βιάζομαι (= act with violence, use force). Its separation from τὸν ὑπὲρ τῆς Ἀσίας to which it belongs and its postponement until the end of the sentence is consonant with Polemo's style, but is stilted here.

The construction of βιάζομαι + infinitive (ὁμολογῆσαι [= to concede]) in the sense of "to force [someone] to do [something]" is common idiom (cf. Xenophon, *An.* 1.3.1; Aristotle, *frag.* 44). The subordinate clause ὅτι τέθνηκεν (= that he has died) is the object of the infinitive ὁμολογῆσαι. Taking into consideration the previous reference to "the ambitions of others" (ταῖς ἑτέρων φιλοτιμίαις), i.e., of Persians, the meaning of the sentence is then as follows: Callimachus did not regard the overly ambitious Persian king Darius, who with so many arrows had forced him (Callimachus) to concede that he had died, as worthy of recognition; hence, he remained standing despite the fact that the Persians had killed him.

4

ἀγαθός has the sense of *brave, valiant* (LSJ, ἀγαθός I.2); κρείττων is its irregular comparative (ibid. III; Index 4). This sentence beginning and ending with ἀγαθός is a clear example of the figure called *epanadiplosis*, the immediate repetition of this adjective in the next clause an example of *anastrophe*. The qualified lauditory remark about Cynegirus on the part of Callimachus' father initially makes him look a little more magnanimous than Euphorion. Subsequent critical comments of his, however, will remove that impression (cf. B 7, 13, 23–24, 26–28, 31–37, 40–49, 63).

The denominative verb ἡττάομαι (√ ἥττων [= less, inferior]) in the sense of *to be less than, inferior to* typically puts its object in the genitive (Καλλιμάχου), a kind of genitive of comparison (LSJ, ἡττάομαι 1; *GG*, 1401–1403).

The paired demonstrative and relative τοσοῦτον ὅσον (cf. also A 2, 23, 23, 43) introduce here two comparisons of degree or proportion (*GG*, 2468–2469) just like Latin *tantus quantus* (= to the degree that ... to the same degree ...): (a) those prone are inferior to those standing; (b) an incomplete corpse is inferior to courage of a brave man. This pair has chiasm of the cases: (a) κείμενοι (nominative) / ἐστηκότων (genitive), (b) θάρσους (genitive) / νεκρός (nominative). The first comparison (a) is of persons, the second (b) of things. The former is natural, the latter strained. For that reason Orellius (p. 70) wondered whether instead of θάρσους ἀγαθοῦ (= courage of a brave [man]) the text ought not to read ἀνδρὸς ἀγαθοῦ (= a brave man), but the MSS provide no support for this.

5

Whether ἅπαν is construed as nominative subject (= everything) or as adverbial accusative (= with respect to everything; always) the sense comes out the same. The phrase ἅπαν τυγχάνει is an idiom in which the verb τυγχάνει comes close to being the same as ἐστί (= it is) (LSJ, τυγχάνω A.II.1 and 2).

The στόλος (√ στέλλω [= furnish, prepare, dispatch]) is a *military expedition* by land or, more frequently, by sea (LSJ, στόλος 1 and 3). Herodotus had used the term to describe Darius' invasion force (6.44) and that of Xerxes too (7.20, 137, 147).

The verb ἀπέβαινε (√ ἀπο-βαίνω) literally means *step off from*, i.e., from the ships (cf. ἀποβᾶσαι ἀπὸ τῶν πλοίων [= stepping off from the boats], Herodotus 4.110; ἐκ τῶν νεῶν ἀποβεβηκότες [= having stepped off from the ships], Xenophon, *Hell.* 5.1.12). Polemo uses the verb absolutely in the sense of *disembark, land* (cf. Herodotus 2.29; Thucydides 1.111). The imperfect may be construed as *continuative* (= was [in the process of] disembarking) or *inceptive* (= was beginning to disembark). In either case the thrust of the tense is that the bridgehead was growing.

The εἰρωνεία (= *dissembling, feigning, pretending*) of the Lacedaemonians is a reference to Herodotus' claim that the Spartans did not immediately come to the aid of Athens when bidden (on the 9th day of their late summer month Carneius), but temporized with the explanation that their law did not permit them to set out on an expedition until the moon was full (i.e., on the 15th day) (Herodotus 6.106, 107, 120). At this juncture in his account Herodotus did not explain the law, but it was connected with the fact that in this month from the 7th to the 15th the Spartans celebrated the Carneia festival in honor of Apollo Carneius and during that week refrained from warfare (cf. Herodotus 7.206; Thucydides 5.54, 75; cf. W. Burkert, *Greek Religion* [Cambridge: Harvard University Press, 1985] 234-236). Later authors mistakenly took this 'full moon' explanation to apply to *every* month of the year (cf. Pausanias 1.28.4; Plutarch, *Herod.* [26] 861e-862c), and, hence, saw it as a bogus claim (Plutarch, ibid.). Not all accounts, however, assert a Spartan delay; Isocrates, for instance, credits them with setting out posthaste with a relief force on the same day that the news of the invasion arrived (*Pan.* 86-87). Polemo was probably aware of this more complimentary tradition — a case can be made for his acquaintance with Isocrates' *Panegyricus* (cf. note at A 42) — yet Polemo sides with the interpretation that attributed a delay to the Spartans for disingenuous reasons. In connection with Polemo's use of εἰρωνεία it is worth noting that Demosthenes, when criticizing the Athenians for delaying to face the threat from Macedon, could speak in one breath of their εἰρωνεία and βραδυτής (= dilitoriness, Demosthenes 4.37). And Theophrastus, in his characterization of εἰρωνεία, observed that the dissembler "enjoins those in haste wishing to make an appeal to go back home" (τοῖς ἐντυγχάνειν κατὰ σπουδὴν βουλομένοις προστάξαι ἐπανελθεῖν, Theophrastus, *Char.* 1 εἰρωνεία).

The dilemma facing the Athenians is posed with a μέν - δέ contrast: the Persian beachhead at Marathon to the northeast, the hesitating Spartans to the southwest. Should Athens confront the growing danger alone or wait for help? Would time work for them or against them?

According to Herodotus the Athenian generals were evenly divided on this issue (Herodotus 6.109). Polemo's unexpanded mention of Miltiades' position assumes knowledge of the Herodotean report: in a private conversation General Miltiades had persuaded the polemarch Callimachus to cast the swing vote against any further delay (Herodotus 6.109). In the first declamation Euphorion's reference to this incident wanted to give the credit for this to Miltiades rather than Callimachus (cf. A 16). That cannot be the intention of Callimachus' father (despite B 20-21). Hence, the καί before τῷ στρατηγῷ Μιλτιάδῃ is better construed as adverb (= also) than as conjunction (= and). The distinction is not unimportant, it implies a subtle suggestion: Miltiades *too* was of the same opinion as Callimachus, namely, to meet the threat head-on, τὴν ταχίστην [sc. ὅδον] (= by the quickest [way], cf. Xenophon, *An.* 1.2.20; Lucian, *Rh. Pr.* 4), i.e. most quickly. This phrase is often used to describe military decisiveness (e.g., Herodotus 3.64; 4.125, 135; Xenophon, *Hel.* 1.6.37; 1.7.2; Polybius 1.33.4; Arrian, *An.* 2.13.6).

6

The adverb of place ἐνταῦθα (= to there, thither) refers of course to Marathon which was just mentioned (B 5).

Callimachus led (ἦγε) the whole Greek army to Marathon for two reasons: (1) the external νόμος (= law) required him as polemarch to do so, and (2) his internal σπουδή (= zeal) drove him to deeds of glory. Historical record established the first point (cf. τοῦ μὲν δεξιοῦ κέρεος ἡγέετο ὁ πολέμαρχος Καλλίμαχος· ὁ γὰρ νόμος τότε εἶχε οὕτω τοῖσι Ἀθηναίοισι, τὸν πολέμαρχον ἔχειν κέρας τὸ δεξιόν [= The polemarch Callimachus was leader of the right wing; for the Athenians had a law at that time that the polemarch should have the right wing], Herodotus 6.111). This first point concedes the argument of Euphorion that Callimachus acted out of duty (cf. A 5, 14, 18, 19). The second point, however, — a Polemonic creation — rejects Euphorion's inference that Callimachus therefore fought only out of obligation, not because of any eager enthusiasm (cf. A 5, 18, 19).

7

The description of Cynegirus as εἷς τις ὢν τῶν πολλῶν (= being one [more] somebody of the many) denies him any special recognition and submerges him in the mass of anonymous soldiers who conducted themselves in a fashion which no one could lable μεμπτός (= blameworthy). Polemo's two limiting expressions demote Cynegirus to the category of the ordinary.

Construed as a middle the verb ἠπείγετο (√ ἐπείγω [= press, urge]) would mean Cynegirus "was pressing [*himself*] forward"; as a passive it would mean he "was being urged forward [*by the commander*]." The middle gives Cynegirus more credit than the passive. While the voice may be intentionally ambiguous, the tenor of the argument makes it more likely that the passive is intended.

The participle συμμίξαντες (√ συμ-μ[ε]ίγνυμι [= to mix together]) has hostile sense: 'mix up with' = meet in close fight, come to blows (LSJ, συμμείγνυμι II.3). Its object (τοῖς βαρβάροις) is in the dative because of the compound verb's prefix σύν. The verb is a graphic term for engaging in hand-to-hand combat (cf. συμμῖξαι ... ἐς χειρῶν τε νόμον ἀπικέσθαι [= to clash together ... and to come to the 'principle' of hands], Herodotus 9.48; εἰς χεῖρας συμμίξοντας τοῖς πολεμίοις [= grappling with the enemy hand-to-hand], Xenophon, *Cyr.* 2.1.11).

In the phrase ἐν δὲ τοῖς ἔργοις the preposition ἐν reinforces the dative of instrument: *by* or *through* his works (LSJ, ἐν A.III.1; *GG*, 1511, 1687.c). Polemo also has other examples of ἐν expressing means or instrument (cf. A 27; B 12, 17, 20, 27).

The ἔργα (= deeds) of Callimachus authenticated him as polemarch. This statement is a response to Euphorion's argument that it is not titles but deeds that count (A 14).

8

Although the weight of the MSS speaks for the personal pronouns αὐτῷ and αὐτόν (smooth breathing) in the medieval ancestor (π), the context makes clear that behind these the original text (Π) must have had the reflexive pronouns αὑτῷ and αὑτόν (rough breathing).

Two circumstantial participles each having temporal sense (παρακελευσάμενος αὑτῷ [= after exhorting himself] and ἀντιτάξας αὑτὸν [= after ranging himself against]) provide the skeleton of the subordinate clauses which begin one of the longest periods in the declamation (all of B 8). With its lack of inflection English will not allow such a cumbersome length. For the sake of readability, therefore, the translation breaks up the period into four separate sentences.

The construction with the first participle — a deponent verb (παρακελευσάμενος [= exhorting]) + dative (αὑτῷ [= himself]) + infinitive (ἀναλῶσαι [= to expend]) — is standard (cf. Plato, *Phd.* 60e; Lysias 28.15; Xenophon, *Hel.* 1.1.24). The κοινὴ ἐλευθερία (= common freedom) for which Callimachus gave his all is the *liberty jointly shared* by all the citizens of Athens (cf. ἡ δὲ πόλις κοινωνία τῶν ἐλευθέρων ἐστίν [= the city-state is a community of the free {citizens}], Aristotle, *Pol.* 1279a21).

The construction with the second participle — verb (ἀντιτάξας [= arraying opposite]) + accusative (αὑτόν [= himself]) + πρός (= against) — is also standard (LSJ, ἀντιτάσσω I). The choice of the active verb (ἀντιτάσσω) instead of the middle (ἀντιτάσσομαι) allows the use of the reflexive pronoun again — parallel to the previous clause — which intensifies the focus on the *individual* Callimachus versus the whole Asian army. The ὡς ἄν with a participle (ὤν) is uncommon (cf. ὡς ἄν + optative, B 14). Typically ὡς alone with a nominative participle indicates the reason or motive for an action (LSJ, ὡς C.III.1). Here the unusual addition of the ἄν qualifies the rationale; that is, it allows an uncertainty about Callimachus being ἀξιόμαχος (= a match for the battle; cf. Herodotus 3.19; 8.63; Thucydides 8.80; Aeneas Tacticus 2.5). But he resolved to act *as if he were able to cope with* the invaders.

The assertion that Callimachus *willingly* (ἑκών) withstood Darius' army is a rejection of Euphorion's claim (A 24) that Callimachus acted *unwillingly* (ἄκων → ἀέκων).

Attestation for the variants προσκαλούμενος (= inviting, summoning) and προκαλούμενος (= calling out to fight, challenging) is evenly balanced (γ vs. δ — hence the bold type in the text), yet because of its military connotations the latter is to be preferred. The middle προ-καλέομαι in the sense of *calling forth [to fight]* is as old as Homer (cf. προκάλεσσαι ... μαχέσασθαι [= {Paris should} challenge {Menelaus} to fight], *Il.* 3.432; also 7.39-40; 13.809; *Od.* 8.142; προκαλέσσατο χάρμη [= {Hector} challenged {Ajax} to battle], *Il.* 7.218). Ever since Homer this verb continued to connote the fight one-on-one (cf. ἐς μονομαχίαν προκαλεῖται [= {Lepreus} challenges {Herakles} to single combat], Aelian, *V.H.* 24.14-15). Hence, Polemo's formulation depicts Callimachus — who in this regard surpasses any ancient hero — challenging the entire Persian army to a μονομαχία (= single combat). With the main verb ἔστη (= he stood) the circumstantial participle προκαλούμενος indicates manner or attendant circumstance (cf. *GG*, 2060, 2062, 2068, 2069).

The verb ἐκχέω (= pour out) is properly used to describe liquids (LSJ, ἐκχέω I.1; II.1), but here the description of all Asia "pouring out" (ἐκχεομένην) of their ships is metaphorical of persons (cf. Μυρμιδόνες ... ἐκ νηῶν ἐχέοντο [= Myrmidons ... poured forth from the ships], Homer, *Il.* 16.266-267; υἷες Ἀχαιῶν ἱππόθεν ἐκχύμενοι [= sons of Achaeans pouring out from the {wooden} horse], Homer, *Od.* 8.514-515). Possibly Polemo had in mind Homer's image of the Trojans, aroused by Patroclus, "pouring forth like wasps" (σφήκεσσιν ἐοικότες ἐξεχέοντο, *Il.* 16.259).

With ἐδέχετο the added emphatic pronoun αὐτός has the sense of *by himself, unaided, alone* (*GG*, 1209.a). This inserted intensive αὐτός is a typical example of the kind of overstatement to which Polemo is given. The verb ἐδέχετο has here the sense of *received as an enemy, awaited the attack of* (LSJ, δέχομαι II.2).

260 *The Severed Hand and the Upright Corpse*

The triad of instrumental datives (ῥώμῃ, τόλμῃ, θυμῷ) covers the totality of Callimachus' military response.

The term ῥώμη denotes *physical strength* (cf. ῥώμη σώματος [= strength of body], Herodotus 1.31; γυίων ῥώμη [= strength of limbs], Aeschylus, *Pers.* 913; ῥώμη τῶν χειρῶν [= by strength of the hands], Antiphon 4.3.3). Callimachus' bodily might was "stronger than [that of] men" (ἀνθρώπων κρείττονι; the genitive of comparison precedes the comparative of κρατύς as in A 34 and B 2).

The term τόλμα, which the speaker uses both positively (= *boldness, courage*, B 8, 40; also A 5, 14, 20, 22, 25) and negatively (= *over-boldness, recklessness*, B 33, 33, 35), is qualified by the compound adjective παράλογος (= beyond reckoning, unexpected, unlooked for). English idiom would speak of 'courage above and beyond the call of duty'.

The term θυμός refers to the *spirit* and *principle of life* or the *seat of the emotions*, much like the Latin *animus* (cf. LSJ, θυμός). English would say 'heart and soul'.

The three terms — reflecting a tri-partite anthropology: body, will [or mind], and emotion [or soul] — express the 'whole-heartedness' with which Callimachus gave himself to the battle. One may compare the famous phrase in Israel's Shema which urges undivided devotion to the Lord with all the heart (לְבָב), soul (נֶפֶשׁ), and strength (מְאֹד) (Deut 6:5; cf. διάνοια/καρδία, ψυχή, δύναμις, LXX Deut 6:5; καρδία, ψυχή, διάνοια, ἰσχύς, Mark 12:30; Matt 22:37; Luke 10:27). The three components named by Polemo in connection with Callimachus (ῥώμη, τόλμα, θυμός) were attributed also to Cynegirus in the first declamation (A 22). This or a similar combination of elements was probably traditional (cf. ῥώμῃ καὶ τόλμῃ, Demosthenes 18.220).

The passive συνεπλάκη (√ συμπλέκω [= intertwine]) is often used of combatants engaged in close fight: one *gets entangled with* one's opponent (LSJ, συμπλέκω II.1).

Two parallel κατά phrases — κατ' αὐτὸ τὸ τοῦ πολέμου στόμα (= over against the very jaws of the war) and κατὰ τὴν ἀκμαιοτάτην τῶν βαρβάρων ἐμβολήν (= over against the fiercest attack of the barbarians) lend color to the passive expression. The first phrase is metaphorical. The personification of war as a monster with a mouth (στόμα) that devours is as old as Homer (cf. πτολέμοιο μέγα στόμα πευκεδανοῖο [= wide mouth of destructive war], *Il.* 10.8; πολέμου στόμα ... αἱματόεντος [= mouth of bloody war], *Il.* 19.313; cf. 20.359). Closely related is the widespread image of the sword with a [devouring] mouth (cf. Asclepiodotus 3.5; Sir 28:18; Luke 21:24). The second, more literal κατά phrase provides an epexegetical clarification of the first: the teeth of the war is where the attack is the fiercest (ἀκμαιοτάτην [√ ἀκμαῖος] = most vigorous, at the height). The two κατά phrases together form a kind of extended *hendiadys*.

The assertion that Callimachus "sufficed for all [the enemies]" (πᾶσιν ἐξήρκεσεν) serves as an *a posteriori* corroboration of his *a priori* resolve to act as though he were ἀξιόμαχος (= a match for the battle).

After the double κατά comes a double οὔτε (= neither ... nor) which provides an opportune juncture for dividing the Greek period and beginning a new sentence in English. This translation solution for the unwieldy Greek requires rendering the participles (ἐκπλαγείς [= being panic stricken] and ἀξιώσας [= deeming]) as finite verbs in English.

The passive of ἐκπλήσσω can sometimes take an accusative object (e.g., Sophocles, *Ph.* 226; *El.* 1045) but because the agent causing the fear is here expressed by the ὑπὸ τοῦ ... πλήθους (= by the ... din) the translation construes the accusative τὴν ὄψιν (= the sight) as adverbial, i.e., as an accusative of respect.

Since the genitive singular of the two-ending adjective συμμιγής, -ές (= mixed up together, commingled) has the same form in all three genders (συμμιγοῦς) it cannot be determined morphologically whether it modifies the feminine τῆς βοῆς (= the shout) or the neuter τοῦ ... πλήθους (= the ... multitude). Both connections yield good sense with little difference in meaning. In view of the word order one might be inclined to connect the adjective with τοῦ ... πλήθους (attributive position between article and noun). The translation, however, links it with βοῆς because classical parallels for that combination can be adduced (cf. συμμιγῆ βοήν [= clamorous cry], Aristophanes, *Av.* 771; βοὰ [συ]μμι[γ]ής [= conglomerate shout], Timotheus, *Pers.* 35 [= frag. 15] — admittedly this could also be restored as [πα]μμι[γ]ής [= all-blended shout]; cf. παμμιγῆ βοὴν [= a cry mixed of all sorts], Lycophron, *Alex.* 5).

The noun ἰταμότης (= effrontery) is formed by the addition of the suffix -της/-τητ to the stem of the adjective ἰταμός (= bold, reckless) to produce a feminine substantive expressing an abstract quality much like the English suffixes -*ness* or -*hood* (*GG*, 840.b.4). This type of vocabulary formation belongs to Polemo's style (cf. θερμότης [= heat] B 24 √ θερμός [= hot]; κακότης [= baseness] B 27 √ κακός [= bad]; νεότης [= youth] A 20 √ νέος [= young]). The meaning of such nouns derives from their adjectival root. The sense of the adjective ἰταμός (= insolent, audacious) is close to ἀναιδής (= shameless) (cf. Menander, *Epit.* 311) and it was listed with τολμηρός (= bold) and πλεονεκτικός (= greedy) among the attributes of πονηρία

(= wickedness) (cf. Demosthenes 25.24). The denominative ἰταμότης was sometimes coupled with θράσος/θάρσος (= insolence, impudence) (cf. Julian, Or. 7.225c; Plutarch, *Quest. Conv.* 715d) and the cognate ἰταμία (= insolence) was used by the Septuagint to render the Hebrew זָדוֹן (= presumptuousness) (cf. Jer 49:16 = 30:10 LXX). Hence, with the term ἰταμότης Polemo points to that wanton quality of the Persian invasion which classical authors circumscribed with the quasi-theological concept of *hybris* (cf. Aeschylus, *Pers.* 808, 821; Herodotus 7.16; Xenophon, *An.* 3.1.21), a term which Polemo did not employ.

The phrase κατ᾽ οὐδέν (literally = in accordance with nothing) is classical (Plato, *Pol.* 302.b.1; *Tim.* 52.e.1; Demosthenes 18.166; 37.24). It is the equivalent of κατ᾽ οὐδένα/μηδένα τρόπον (= in no way, cf. Plato, *Dem.* 383.e.1; 2. Thess 2:3). The negative οὐδέν strengthens the negative οὔτε which it follows (cf. μὴ λειπομένοις κατὰ μηδένα τρόπον [= not remitting in any way], 3 Macc 4:13; μή τις... ἐξαπατήσῃ κατὰ μηδένα τρόπον [= let no one lead astray in any way], 2 Thess 2:3).

The last clause in this lengthy period has the standard construction of indirect discourse: a verb of thinking (ἀξιώσας) + accusative (τὴν ... ἰταμότητα) + infinitive (εἶναι) + predicative adjective (φοβεράν).

Occupying the final position in the sentence and thus bearing all the rhetorical emphasis is the instrumental dative ἀρετῇ: all the heroic achievements described were made possible by Callimachus' *valor*.

9

The circumstantial participle ἐργασάμενος (= working, bringing about) has causal sense.

The εἰς τουτί (→ τοῦτο + deictic suffix -ι for emphasis, *GG*, 333.g) stands with αὐτοὺς ... κατέστησεν (= even to *this* he brought them). The construction καθίστημι + εἰς commonly expresses *bringing* [someone] *into* [dire straights] (cf. ἐς ἀπόνοιαν καταστήσαντας αὐτούς [= bringing them to desperation], Thucydides 1.82.4; ἐς ἀπορίαν καθίστασαν [= they drove {them} to perplexity], 7.75.3; με εἰς τοιαύτην ἀνάγκην κατέστησεν [= he brought me into such a necessity], Lysias 3.3).

The genitives ὀργῆς (= from anger) and ἀνάγκης (= from necessity) are 'ablatival', that is, they indicate the cause or source of the action in the ὥστε clause (*GG*, 1405–1411).

The ὥστε clause is epexegetical: it explains the "this" (τουτί) to which Callimachus brought the enemy. In the ὥστε clause the four varied occurrences of πᾶς (namely: πάντα / πάντες / πάντες / ἅπασι) indicate the massive

Persian effort to deal with Callimachus. Unfortunately in English an uninflected, fourfold "all" would be stylistically languid. The translation tries to get around this somewhat by rendering the plural ἅπασι with a singular "for everyone."

The string of progressive stem verbs (καταλιπόντες [= abandoning], ἐπεχέοντο [= they were streaming], ἐστοχάζοντο [= they were aiming at], ἔφασκον [= they were saying]) lends liveliness and vividness to the description. The present participle of attendant circumstance (καταλιπόντες) and the inceptive imperfect (ἐπεχέοντο) represent one thought unit: *leaving their positions they were streaming* to Callimachus. Whether ἐπεχέοντο is middle or passive the sense remains the same (= stream against, LSJ, ἐπιχέω B.2 and C.2). The metaphorical use of the verb for *soldiers* [rather than liquids] *running* goes back to Homer (*Il.* 15.654; 16.295). It is similar to the metaphorical use of ἐκχέω (= pour out) in B 8.

The following set of verbs poses a second thought unit: they were all *aiming at* (ἐστοχάζοντο) and for all *the goal was to hit* (ἦν σπούδασμα ... τὸ ... βαλεῖν) Callimachus. The articular infinitive is epexegetical — it explains what the σπούδασμα (= earnest endeavor) was: the shooting of Callimachus. A σπούδασμα (verbal abstract from σπουδάζω [= be eager, earnest]) is a *pursuit* or *work done with zeal*. The term could cover a whole range of human endeavors, including military undertakings (cf. Arrian, *An.* 7.7.7).

The γάρ clause offers the reason for the concerted Persian action in the form of indirect discourse: verb of saying (ἔφασκον) + accusative (τὰς 'Αθήνας) + infinitive (εἶναι). ἔφασκον is a durative or iterative imperfect: the repetition of a remarkable utterance is ascribed to the Persians for as long as (temporal genitive absolute) Callimachus (τούτου) was present and helping (παρόντος, cf. LSJ, πάρειμι [-εἰμι] I.1,3.4). Namely, they were saying: "Athens is *in him* (ἐν τούτῳ)." Included in the range of ways that Polemo uses the preposition ἐν (cf. Index 6) is *local*: e.g., barbarians are *in* the land (ἐν τῇ χώρᾳ, B 40); Eretrians are *in* the ships (ἐν ταῖς ναυσιν, B 54); a soul (ψυχή) is *in* the body (ἐν τῷ σώματι, B 11) or *in* the right hand (ἐν τῇ δεξιᾷ, B 43). The use of the preposition in B 9, however, is different from all other local usages in Polemo in that the 'contents' (Athens) is greater than the 'container' (Callimachus). The striking understanding of Callimachus imputed here to the Persians comes close to a conception that Christians would later call ἐνσωμάτωσις (= embodiment) or ἐνσάρκωσις (= incarnation).

10

The adverb of place ἔνθα is used twice for the specific site where Callimachus held his ground (B 10, 59), and twice for the location of Cynegirus' heroic deed (A 8, 11).

Callimachus resolutely endured (LSJ, ὑποδέχομαι II.2) the whole Persian arsenal. Listed are three specific weapons and a miscellaneous catch-all category:

(1) The βέλος by itself can refer to any missile or weapon in general (LSJ, βέλος 1 and 2); in the declamations, however, inasmuch as it is kept in a quiver (φαρέτρα, B 39) it clearly denotes the *arrow*. Of all the various weapons it is the one Polemo names most frequently. With few exceptions the arrows are mentioned in connection with Callimachus' stand (cf. A 7, 23, 24, 27, 27, 30, 30, 37, 45, 47; B 10, 10, 12, 39, 51, 56, 57, 57, 59).

(2) The κοντός is the pike or *javelin* (cf. Lucian, *Tox.* 55).

(3) The ξίφος is a *double-edged sword*, usually kept in a sheath; it was described already by Homer (*Il.* 1.194; 4.530; 21.118).

(4) For the sake of completeness the list is rounded off with "shots of every kind" (παντοδαπῶν βλημάτων).

Four comparisons — each described by a noun with a modifier — underscore how Callimachus withstood the Persian assaults. Calliamchus was like (ὥσπερ) a:

(1) ἐξ ἀδάμαντος ὢν πύργος (= tower made [→ being] from steel). The πύργος, a fortified tower often attached to city walls, was a common defense structure in the ancient Mediterranean world (LSJ, πύργος I.1.a). Undocumented, however, is such a construction out of ἀδάμας (√ ἀ + δαμάω [= not to be tamed]), the hardest known substance, steel or possibly diamond (cf. LSJ, ἀδάμας I.1 and 2), though it is worth noting that Demosthenes is said to have described Athens' defense alliance with Euboea and Thebes metaphorically as ἀδαμάντινα τείχη (= steel walls) (Aeschines 3.84). The Greeks had a long tradition of describing a person of strength metaphorically as a tower. Ajax was termed a "tower" for the Achaeans (Homer, *Od.* 11.556). Oedipus was called a πύργος for the land of Thebes (Sophocles, *O.T.* 1201). Medea longed for a rescuer, a "tower of safety" (Euripides, *Med.* 390). Polemo follows in this tradition.

(2) τεῖχος ἄρρηκτον (= invulnerable wall). A τεῖχος is the defense wall of a city (LSJ, τεῖχος I). Already Homer had coupled this noun with the modifier ἄρρηκτον (alpha-privative from ῥήγνυμι [= to break, burst]) (cf. τεῖχος ... ἄρρηκτος ... εἶλαρ [= wall ... unbreakable ... bulwark], *Il.* 14.56; τεῖχος χάλκεον ἄρρηκτον [= a wall of unbreakable bronze], *Od.* 10.4).

However, in contrast to πύργος, Greek speakers do not seem commonly to have used τεῖχος as a metaphor for persons. To be sure, the Christian seer John described the wall (τεῖχος) of the end-time Jerusalem as having gates and foundations identified with tribes and apostles (Rev. 21:12, 14), and this in an apocalypse which was sent among other places to Smyrna where Polemo later taught (Rev. 1:11; 2:8-11). Yet it would be hard to argue that Polemo was familiar with this image, let alone this document. If not wholly original Polemo's comparison was more likely prompted by something indigenous in the Greek tradition. For example, according to a popular *chreia* "a Laconian, when asked where the walls (τείχη) of Sparta were, extended his spear and said, 'Here'" (cf. R. F. Hock and E. N. O'Neil, *The Chreia in Ancient Rhetoric*, Vol. 1. *The Progymnasmata* [Atlanta: Scholars Press, 1986], pp. 256; 328-329). Such a saying may have provided the seed-bed for Polemo's metaphor.

(3) ἀντίτυπος πέτρα (= rigid rock). The πέτρα is a steep ridge or massive stone (cf. ἠλίβατος πέτρη [= sheer rock], Homer, *Il.* 15.273; *Od.* 10.87-88; Xenophon, *An.* 1.4.4; [= massive boulder], Homer, *Od.* 9.243; Hesiod, *Th.* 786). Ever since archaic times the πέτρα served as symbol of firmness. Homer said that when Odysseus was attacked by Antinous ἐστάθη ἠύτε πέτρη ἔμπεδον (= he stood like a firm rock, *Od.* 17.463). This Homeric simile might well be the origin of Polemo's analogy. The adjective ἀντίτυπος was synonymous with σκληρός (= hard, cf. Plato, *Tim.* 62e; *Tht.* 155e) and στερρός (= solid) (cf. Herodian 6.7.7). However, in view of its etymology (√ ἀντί + τύπτω [= strike against]) Polemo may intend here a more active sense: *repelling* (cf. LSJ, ἀντίτυπος II.1). The Spartan Agesilaus demonstrated his courage and valor by overcoming his enemies μάχῃ ἀντιτύπῳ (= with stubborn fighting, cf. Xenophon, *Ag.* 6.2); in close combat (πρὸς τὴν συστάδην μάχην) the Germans were repellent (ἀντιτυπεῖς) fighters (Herodian 6.7.8).

(4) θεὸς ἀνθρώποις μαχόμενος (= a god fighting with men). With μάχομαι the dative ἀνθρώποις has hostile sense: fighting with, i.e., *against*, men (LSJ, μάχομαι I.1; *GG*, 1523.b). The god is here indeterminate, though elsewhere Callimachus is cast in the image of Ares (B 52).

Clear progression is visible in the four comparisons both with (a) the nouns and (b) the modifiers: (a) *tower* [single construction] / *wall* [extensive construction] / *rock* [much bigger than tower or wall] / *god* [above all man-made or natural fortifications]; (b) *of adamant* [passive] / *unbreachable* [functional] / *repellent* [re-active] / *fighting* [active].

Callimachus continued expending (ἀναλῶσαι) his own body and soul (B 8) until he consumed (ἕως ἀνήλωσε) all their missiles. The assertion that Callimachus caused the Persians to 'run out of ammunition' appears here for the first time; hereafter it is often repeated as one of the linchpins of the whole argument (B 13, 38, 39, 51, 56, 57).

The verb καμεῖν (√ κάμνω) has the basic meaning of *to toil* or *be weary*, but in military contexts it can have the sense of to *be distressed* or even to *meet with disaster* (cf. στρατοῦ καμόντος καὶ κακῶς σποδουμένου [= with the fleet distressed and sorely buffeted], Aeschylus, *Ag.* 670; νεὼς καμούσης ποντίῳ πρὸς κύματι [with a ship distressed in a tossing sea], Aeschylus, *Th.* 210). Pindar's reference to the Medes 'toiling' (κάμον/καμόντων) at Salamis (480 BCE) and by Cithaeron (= Plataea, 479 BCE) means disastrous defeat (*Pyth.* 1.78, 80).

In the expression τὴν πολλὴν δύναμιν the adjective πολύς has the sense of *great, mighty* (LSJ, πολύς I.2.a; cf. τὸν πολὺν Κυναίγειρον [= the mighty Cynegirus], A 32). Here, as also in B 6 and 8, the term δύναμις (= force) is the equivalent of *army* (LSJ, δύναμις I.3). The phrase "mighty army of the king" is a slight variant of "all the army of the king" (B 8).

11

The simplex καρτερέω means to *persevere*; the prefix διά in the compound διακαρτερέω strengthens the sense to *persevere through* (i.e., to the end). Callimachus' soul held out in his body long beyond any normal time. In so doing it was striving against nature (ἐρίζουσα πρὸς τὴν φύσιν). Nature (φύσις) is that universal order of the world (cf. τῷ κοινῷ τῆς φύσεως νόμῳ [= the common law of nature], B 50) which places the limitations of mortality on all human beings (cf. ἡ τῶν ἀνθρώπων φύσις θνητὴ οὖσα [= the nature of human beings is mortal], Aelian, *V. H.* 8.11). Pindar had advised χρὴ δὲ πρὸς θεὸν οὐκ ἐρίζειν [= one must not strive against God], *Pyth.* 2.88), Stoics later urged not to strive against nature. Rather, one should act κατὰ φύσιν (= in accordance with nature, Zeno, *frag.* 183, Antipater, *frag.* 57; Diogenes Babylonius, *frag.* 44) or ἀκολούθως τῇ φύσει (= following nature, Chrysippus, *frag.* 6). Callimachus, who belonged to an earlier era, was, however, not a post-classical Stoic — he heroically resisted the bounds of nature and delayed his soul's departure (cf. B 50, 50, 52).

The imperfect ἐβιάζετο is conative (= he *tried* [unsuccessfully!] to force his way). The construction βιάζομαι + εἰς is classical (cf. βουλόμενοι βιάσασθαι ἐς τὸ ἔξω [= wishing to force their way to the outside],

Thucydides 7.69.4; εἰ βιάσαιντο εἴσω [= if they should force their way inside], Xenophon, *Cyr.* 3.3.69).

The noun formation ἀθανασία (α-privative + θάνατος + -ια suffix of abstract quality [= death-less-ness]) is attested since Isocrates (*Phil.* 33, 134; *Hel.* 61) and Plato (*Pol.* 270a; *Tim.* 90c; *Leg.* 721b-c). According to Greek consensus immortality was enjoyed by the undying (ἀθάνατοι) gods (Isocrates, *Pan.* 260), but whether that was also the case for the human soul stood under debate. Plato was the chief spokesman for the immortality of the soul (cf. *Phdr.* 246a; *Phd.* 95c) while many others rejected the notion. In the Greek world there was great longing for immortality but little belief in it. Polemo in any case says that it is ἀδύνατον ἀνθρώποις (= impossible for humans).

The language in this sentence is curiously reminiscent of two notorious Gospel sayings: πᾶς εἰς αὐτὴν [τὴν βασιλείαν τοῦ θεοῦ] βιάζεται (= everyone forces his way into it [the kingdom of God]), Luke 16:16; and σωθῆναι ... παρὰ ἀνθρώποις ἀδύνατον (= to be saved ... [is] impossible for humans), Mark 10:27.

For all practical purposes the line about 'nature' and 'impossible immortality' serves — not in form, but in substance — as the major premise of a classic syllogism. The following line presents the minor premise and conclusion:

Major premise: All men are mortal.
Minor premise: Callimachus was a man.
Conclusion: Callimachus was mortal.

The term θνητός — from the same root as θνήσκω (= to die) and θάνατος (= death) — means *liable to death*. The multitude of Callimachus' wounds finally made that clear.

In this clause the grammatical subject of ἠναγκάζετο (= was compelled) is Callimachus, but in the context the logical subject is his soul: for a while the soul persisted in the body (ἐν τῷ σώματι διεκαρτέρησεν ἡ ψυχή) but it was finally forced to depart from the body (τοῦ σώματος ἀπελθεῖν ἠναγκάζετο). Callimachus is identified with his soul.

The act of dying (ἀπέθανε) is equated with the soul going out (ἐξιοῦσα ἡ ψυχὴ) of the body. At first the soul had persevered (διεκαρτέρησεν) in the body; when it finally left it urged the body to persist (καρτερεῖν) without it. It is part of Polemo's style to play with the variations between simple and compound verb (cf. e.g., κόπτω / ἀποκόπτω A 10; τάττω / παρατάττω A 18-19; βάλλω / παραβάλλω A 27; μάχομαι / ἀπομάχομαι A 28; πλέω / ἐκπλέω A 45).

The verb ἐνετείλατο (= he enjoined) appears with the standard classical construction: dative [because of the ἐν prefix] (τῷ σώματι) + infinitive (μένειν / καρτερεῖν / μάχεσθαι). Ordinarily this is a *dative of person* (= command *someone* to do ..., cf. LSJ and BAGD, ἐντέλλω; MM, ἐντέλλομαι). Thus what is striking in Polemo is that the *body* is treated as a *person*.

The three infinitives are virtually synonymous: βεβαίως ... μένειν (= to remain steadfast) / καρτερεῖν (= to persist) / μάχεσθαι τὴν ... μάχην (= to fight the fight). Pleonasm is another characteristic feature of Polemo's style. Inhering in the present tense of these infinitives is the mode of *continuance* (*GG*, 1865.a).

The prior assertion that death-less-ness (ἀθανασία) is impossible (ἀδύνατον) for humans underscores the paradox of the notion that for those who are soul-less (τοῖς ἀψύχοις) a fighting is still possible (δυνατήν). The adjective ἄψυχος (= lifeless, inanimate) is often used to describe statues of gods (cf. BAGD, ἄψυχος). The command of Callimachus' soul to his dying body could thus mean that it should remain standing in a fighting position like so many statues of militant Greek deities. Indeed, subsequently Polemo calls Callimachus a "statue (ἄγαλμα) of Ares" (B 52).

The soul's command to the body had been "to remain steadfast" (βεβαίως μένειν). The body (τὸ [sc. σῶμα]) obeyed the command 'to the letter': it "remained steadfast" (βεβαίως ἔμεινεν) as though it had put down roots (ὥσπερ ἐρριζωμένον). Such a metaphorical use of this verb was not uncommon (cf. LSJ, ῥιζόω I).

The circumstantial participle ἐξιοῦσα is concessive (= although [the soul] was going out).

For a long time (πολὺν χρόνον) the soul had persisted in the body; after it departed the 'ruse' of a fighting corpse deceived (ἐξηπάτησεν) the enemy for yet another long time (πολὺν χρόνον). This double "long time" outdoes the single "long time" (πολὺν χρόνον) during which Cynegirus held the Phoenician ship (cf. A 10).

The preposition ἐξ prefixed to the verb ἀπατάω (= deceive) has perfective or intensifying sense: *thoroughly, completely* (*GG*, 1648, 1688.2).

The γάρ clause explains the deception with the standard form of indirect discourse: verb of thinking (ᾤετο) + accusative (τὸν ἑστηκότα) + infinitive (τεθνάναι).

12

A sudden series of eleven exclamations functions more as emotional outburst than logical argument. Each is introduced with an exclamatory ὦ accompanied by an expressed or implied vocative (cf. Index 3). Despite the similarity in form there is artful variety in composition and content. The first nine are nominal, the last two verbal. The second, third, and fourth have comparative adjectives with genitives of comparison. There is *ellipsis* (- / - / - / ἀρετή), *anaphora* (σῶμα / σῶμα; ψυχῆς / ψυχῶν), *anastrophe* (ὀρθόν / ὀρθήν), *chiasmus* (νικηφόρον ὅπλοις / βέλεσι κεκοσμημένον) and *paranomasia* (ψυχῶν / ἔμψυχον). While there appears to be no significance attached the number of exclamations the last two with their longer verbal form represent a clear climax.

(1-4) For the sake of rhetorical emphasis the vocative ἀρετή which belongs with the first four instances of ὦ is postponed until the end of the series. Because of the lack of inflection in English it is not possible to replicate this ellipsis in the translation. Hence, for the sake of clarity the vocative "valor" is supplied in brackets after each exclamation.

(1) Polemo variegates his use of the adjective φοβερός (= causing φόβος [fear]): The Persians' methodical advance across the Aegean inspired fear in the Greeks (cf. B 31), but not in Callimachus (cf. B 8), on the contrary he — or rather his corpse — instilled fear in the invaders (B 12).

(2) The term ἡ εἱμαρμένη (= destiny [a substantized perfect passive participle from μείρομαι = receive one's alloted portion]) was in earlier Greek understood with μοῖρα (= fate), often unexpressed. In the course of time εἱμαρμένη came to stand alone and was frequently personified by itself as Destiny or one of the Fates (Plato, *Gorg.* 512e; *Phd.* 155a; Demosthenes 18.205). The Stoics identified εἱμαρμένη with λόγος (= reason) and πρόνοια (= providence) and Zeus (J. von Arnim, *Stoicorum Veterum Fragmenta* [Leipzig: Teubner, 1903; reprint Dubuque: Brown, 1967], II.913, 937). For the Greeks the moment of death was fated — one could not outlive the alloted span of time (cf. ζῆν μὲν γὰρ καὶ τεθνάναι μεμοίραται ἡμῖν, καὶ οὐκ ἔστι τὸ χρέος φυγεῖν [= to live and to die have been fore-ordained for us, there is no escaping fate], Alciphron 2.4; θανατόν γε μεμορμένον [= fated death], Apollonius Rhodius 3.1130).

Few words in the declamations are as long as the heptasyllabic πολυχρονιωτέρου (comparative from πολυχρόνιος [= long-lived]). Because of its unusual length and its final long open syllable this word may have been deliberately chosen to underscore with its form the notion of longevity. Callimachus wrested from fate *more time* than was originally allotted him.

(3) The comparative adjective μακροτέρα (vocative agreeing with the unspoken ἀρετή) refers here clearly to time as is often the case (LSJ, μακρός II.1): it means *longer(-lasting)*. The valor of Callimachus lasted longer in Hellenic memory than his life did in his body.

(4) The meaning of the fourth exclamation is ambiguous. Is πιστοτέρα (comparative of πιστός) *passive* (= trustworthy, reliable, worthy of credit) or *active* (= faithful, loyal, obedient)? Does πνεῦμα denote *wind* or *breath*? Several interpretations are plausible. The few other occurrences of these words in Polemo offer little guidance. Callimachus is said to be πιστὸς εἰς μαχήν (B 46) — but is that meant passively (= he *could be relied upon* [by his fellow soldiers] in battle) or actively (= he was *faithful* [to his duty] in battle)? The two other instances of πνεῦμα (plurals) denote "winds" (A 35; B 41). The English translation takes its cue from parallels in the previous exclamation (μακροτέρα / πιστοτέρα and ψυχῆς / πνεύματος): "O valor more reliable [passive] than the [human] spirit (or breath)!"

(5) The adjective ἰσόρροπος (ἴσος + ροπή [√ ρέπω = tip the scale] = equally-balanced, well-matched) ordinarily stands with a dative or a preposition to indicate *with* (LSJ, ἰσόρροπος), but there are Classical instances of it linked, as here, with a genitive (e.g., ἰσόρροπος ... ὁ λόγος τῶν ἔργων [= the reputation equally balanced *with* the deeds], Thucydides 2.42.2). The (soul-less) body (of Callimachus) was a match for the many souls (of the Persians).

(6) The derivative noun φρόνημα (= mind, purpose [√ φρονέω = be minded]) was often qualified with limiting epithets (LSJ, φρόνημα I.1). The adjective ὀρθός (= erect, upright) is used here in a metaphorical sense (= right, just, true; cf. LSJ, ὀρθός III.2-4). In a subsequent, much longer series of ὦ exclamations (B 51–56) φρόνημα is the only item to reappear from this first series (cf. B 53). It was Callimachus' *single-minded purpose* to repel the threat to Greek freedom. In the words of Kierkegaard: "Purity of heart is to will one thing."

(7) Callimachus' ἄψυχον σῶμα (= soul-less body, cf. B 11) is here paradoxically said to be ἔμψυχον (= 'in-souled', animate). Cf. πᾶν γὰρ σῶμα, ᾧ μὲν ἔξωθεν τὸ κινεῖσθαι, ἄψυχον, ᾧ δὲ ἔνδοθεν αὐτῷ ἐξ αὐτοῦ, ἔμψυχον (= every body whose motion is from without is soul-less, but that whose [motion] is from within itself has a soul, Plato, *Phdr.* 245e). With ἔμψυχον Polemo means that the body devoid of life behaved as though it still had life.

(8) Hinck changed σῶμα before νικηφόρον to σῆμα, the sign (cf. σημεῖον) by which a grave is known — usually, but not always, a raised mound or cairn (cf. LSJ, σῆμα 3). Hinck's emendation would identify Callimachus' arrow-pierced, erect corpse as the marker of the Marathonian grave for the fallen Greeks — a marker more resembling a στήλη (= upright gravestone) than a σῆμα (= upraised mound). His alteration, however, has no MS support. Polemo speaks of the body (σῶμα).

The epithet νικηφόρος (= victory bringing [√ νίκη + φέρω]) which was often applied to gods and kings could also be used of things and abstractions (LSJ, νικηφόρος II). The σῶμα which it modifies here is on the borderline between person and object — it is an 'animate thing'.

The instrumental dative ὅπλοις (= with weapons) could be construed grammatically with either (a) νικηφόρον or (b) κεκοσμημένον. Each option yields good but different sense:

(a.1) body bringing victory with [well-used Greek] weapons and adorned with [Persian] arrows.

(a.2) body bringing victory with ['captured' Persian] weapons and adorned with [Persian] arrows.

(b) victory-bringing body adorned with [Persian] weapons and arrows.

The first two options (a.1 and a.2) take the modifiers of σῶμα to be a chiasmus in both form and thought: νικηφόρον ὅπλοις / βέλεσι κεκοσμημένον, the two phrases being parallel. The first option seems unlikely because no case is otherwise made for Callimachus' adept use of weapons. The second option is, however, consonant with the frequent argument that Callimachus facilitated the Greek victory by forcing the Persians to use up all their weapons on him (cf. B 13, 38, 39, 51, 56, 57).

Nevertheless, the third option (b) — also consistent with the notion of 'captured' weapons — appears to be more natural because it does not require that 'captured' be supplied and it certainly provides smoother English. Here the mental comma comes not before but after νικηφόρον. This is the understanding represented in the translation.

(9) Polemo portrays Callimachus' body itself, impaled and held erect by so many arrows, as a human τρόπαιον — the first *trophy* erected at Marathon, and during the battle at that. (For the origin and significance of the term τρόπαιον and the Greek practice with war trophies cf. the note at A 10). This view of Callimachus as 'victory monument' (it is reiterated in B 61) counterbalances the same claim that was earlier made about Cynegirus (cf. A 10, 39).

(10-11) The last two exclamations shift from nominal to verbal form. The two vocatives (ὦ τηρήσας ... and ὦ στήσας ...) are clarified by the verb εἴασας (= you permitted) in the concluding clause: in both cases the vocatives must be a second person "you" (= O [you who] preserved ... / O [you who] made to stand ...).

(10) What Callimachus kept *safe* (LSJ, ὀρθός III.1) was ἐλευθερία (= liberty). In the mouth of Callimachus' father this term refers to the αὐτονομία or *independence* of the Athenian state over against subjugation to the Persian empire (Herodotus 7.147; 8.143; 9.41, 98). In the ears of Polemo's audience, however, who six centuries later lived under Roman domination, the term will have had a different ring. Greek listeners in Athens, Smyrna, and other cities in Asia Minor would have thought of the 'freedom' — stability, prosperity, and privileges — accorded to them by the *pax Romana*.

(11) The first aorist στήσας has transitive sense: he *caused* Greece to stand (cf. note on ἵστημι at A 45).

The variants αὐτῷ (→ γ) and ἑαυτῷ (→ δ) are best explained as both deriving from the reflexive pronoun αὐτῷ which will have stood in the medieval progenitor (π). The reflexive pronoun of the third person could sometimes be used for that of the first or second person (*GG*, 1230; LSJ, ἑαυτοῦ, II). Since ἐν αὐτῷ is here followed by a finite verb in the second person (εἴασας) it must be construed as "by *your*self."

(10-11) The varied expression of the last three clauses does not mask the synonymous parallelism:

You kept safe [liberty]   for   Athenians
You made stand   Greece
You did not let fall   Athens.

This tricolon deftly winds up what was becoming an unwieldy miscellaneous list.

13

A long subordinate clause introduced by ἐπειδή is followed by the main clause beginning with πολλὴ μέν. For the sake of readable English the translation divides the Greek period into several independent English sentences.

The temporal conjunction ἐπειδή (= when) belongs with the aorist indicative ἔφυγον (= they fled) and its accompanying participle of attendant circumstance, the second aorist passive τραπέντες, which may be taken either as intransitive (= turning),) or passive (= being turned, i.e., routed) (cf. *GG*, p. 718, τρέφω; LSJ, τρέφω III).

The participles in the parenthetical τὰ μὲν ..., τὰ δὲ ..., τὰ δὲ ... are best understood as indicating cause or possibly attendant circumstance. These τά articles may be taken as accusatives of respect.

The prefix in the compound verb περι-έβλεπον graphically portrays the fleeing soldiers looking *around* (desperately!) in every direction for some possible escape. After the perfects (πεπονηκότες, ἀφωπλισμένοι, πεφοβημένοι) and aorists (τραπέντες ἔφυγον) the imperfect (περιέβλεπον) serves to heighten the vividness of the narrative description (*GG*, 1898–1899).

The genitive absolute (Καλλιμάχου ... πεποιηκότος) is causal.

The phrase πολλὴ μὲν ἦν τοῖς βουλομένοις σχολή has troubled both copyists and editors. Variant readings in the MSS (ἦν / οὖν; σχολή / σπουδή) and conjectured 'corrections' in the editions (φοβουμένοις [Jacobs] or ἡγουμένοις [Hinck] instead of βουλομένοις) clutter the discussion. Such *Verschlimmbesserungen* are unnecessary. Despite the ineptness of the μέν - δέ contrast the simplest understanding is to take the substantized participle τοῖς βουλομένοις (= the [ones] wishing) as eliptical, with something like διώκειν (= to pursue) to be supplied (cf. *tum otium persequendi fuit* [= there was time then for {those} pursuing], Possinus, p.66).

The designation of Cynegirus as "one of those who followed" (εἷς τῶν ἀκολουθησάντων) — it had already appeared proleptically in the first speech (A 13) — not only puts him below the officers but it also denies him the πρόμαχος (= front-fighter) status claimed for him by Euphorion (A 22, 34). Many reached the beach ahead of Cynegirus, he was merely one of those who 'got on the band-wagon' and followed.

The ἀκροστόλιον of a ship is its terminal ornament, a carved figurehead crowning either the stern (Ptolemaeus, *Alm.* 8.1) or more commonly the prow (Callixinus 1; Plutarch, *Dem.* 43). In war it was typically taken as booty (Strabo 3.4.3; Diodorus Siculus 18.75; Plutarch, *Alc.* 32.1; Appian, *Mith.* 25). According to Herodotus (6.114) Cynegirus grabbed an ἄφλαστον (= Latin *aplustre*), the curved stern of a ship with its carved wood ornament. That Cynegirus grabbed hold of this object suggests that he was after a trophy of war. When Callimachus' father describes it as "*some* figurehead," the addition of the indefinite pronoun (τινος) serves to devalue the object. Indeed, Euphorion had not used this term, rather he had spoken of Cynegirus grabbing the τρόπις (= keel) or πρύμνα (= stern or rudder) (A 9, 11).

The construction ἁπτόμενος ἀκροστολίου (= grabbing hold of an ornament) is standard classical: verb of touching + genitive (*GG*, 1345, 1345; LSJ, ἅπτομαι II). However, the construction τὴν χεῖρα ἀπεκόπη

(= {regarding?} the hand he was cut off, i.e., 'he got his hand cut off') is unusual, if not awkward: accusative + passive (*GG*, 1747). It appears to be an idiom which Polemo borrowed from Herodotus (cf. Κυνέγειρος ... τὴν χεῖρα ἀποκοπείς [= Cynegirus ... being cut off {with respect to?} the hand], 6.114; for another example of this idiomatic construction cf. τοὺς θλαδίας καὶ ἀποκεκομμένους τὰ γεννητικά [= the eunuchs and those having been cut away {with respect to?} the genitalia], Philo, *L. A.* 8; *Spec.* 1.325).

The term παιδίον (diminutive of παῖς) denotes a very young child, perhaps up to seven years old (cf. παιδίον ἐστιν ἄχρις ἑπτὰ ἐτέων ὀδόντων ἐκβολῆς [= one is a 'little child' up to seven years, {the time} of shedding of teeth], Hippocrates, *Sept.* 5; Philo, *Op.* 105). The application of this term to Cynegirus in the parenthetical comparison ὥσπερ παιδίον (= like a child) intends to belittle his action even further — idiomatic English might translate, 'Typical of a little kid!'

The μέν - δέ sentence will have been spoken in a tone of scorn: not only did he get his hand lopped off unnecessarily, but the consequence was that he himself also fell next to the wasted hand.

What disclosed (ἐμήνυσε √ μηνύω = make known what was hitherto not evident) the weakness (ἀ-σθένεια = lack of strength [σθένος]) of Cynegirus' constitution was a *single* wound (τραῦμα). Polemo consistently uses the plural τραύματα to describe the many wounds Callimachus received (A 24; B 11, [44], 47), but he reserves the singular τραῦμα for the sole wound that Cynegirus suffered (B 13, 44). Indeed, one of the main points in the argument specifically hinges on this contrast (cf. τραῦμα ἕν vs. μυρία {τραύματα} [= *one* wound vs. *countless* {wounds}], B 44; πληγὴ μία vs. πολλὰ τραύματα [= *one* blow vs. *many* wounds], B 47; also τὸ πλῆθος τῶν τραυμάτων [= the *multitude* of wounds], B 11; πολύτρωτος [= *much* wounded], B 57).

14

The spelling of εἰστήκεις (= you had stood, [2nd pluperfect from ἵστημι]) is anomalous (instead of εἰστήκης). For the most part the father of Callimachus speaks of his son in the third person. Nevertheless, there are passages where he addresses him in the second person as though he were present; this 'enlivening' practice which first appeared at the end of the series of exclamations (B 12) and is resumed here (B 14) does not reappear until the end of the declamation (cf. B 47, 48, 51, 62, 64).

The καί with the genitive absolute narrows its function to *concessive* (καὶ Δάτιδος ἀποπλέοντος = *even though* Datis was sailing away). The compound verb ἐπι-τηρέω (= watch over) in the sense of *supervise* appears to be post-classical (LSJ, ἐπιτηρέω II).

The adverb ἀνδρείως (= in a manly fashion [√ ἀνήρ = man]) occurs only here and outside of ἀνδραγαθία (= manly virtue, B 1) no other cognates (e.g., ἀνδρεῖος [= manly], ἀνδρεία [= manliness], ἀνδρειότης [= manliness],) appear in the declamations. This absence is striking in light of the main theme, ἀρετή (= valor). For whatever reasons Polemo did not find this traditional classical term for courage as useful for explaining valor as other concepts such as ἀγαθός (= brave), ἀδεῶς (= fearless), ἀριστεία (= prowess), θρασύς (= bold), προθυμία (= eagerness), or the many derivations from the stem τολμ- (= daring, cf. τόλμα, τολμάω, τόλμημα, τολμηρία, τολμηρός) (cf. Index 8).

The colorless ταῦτα (= these things) is immediately pigmented by the two chiastically arranged appositional phrases: (1) the barbarians' flight (φυγή) and (2) the purging of the enemies from Marathon (καθαρὸν γενέσθαι τὸν Μαραθῶνα = Marathon becoming clean).

The preposition ἐπί + genitive has here the sense *before, in the presence of* (LSJ, ἐπί A.I.2.e). It is often used this way in the language of lawsuits (cf. BAGD, ἐπί I.1.a.δ) and in that regard can also be coupled, as it is here, with the noun μάρτυς (= [eye- or ear-] witness) (cf. οὐ γὰρ ἐπὶ μαρτύρων ἀλλὰ κρυπτόμενα πράσσεται τὰ τοιαῦτα [= such things are not done in the presence of witnesses but secretly], Antiphon 2.3.8). In legal language ἐπὶ μαρτύρων (= in front of witnesses) is but another variant of phrases like ἐπὶ μάρτυσι (cf. Heb 10:28; Appian, *B. C.* 3.2.14; 3.10.73; ἐνώπιον μαρτύρων (1 Tim 6:12), or ἐναντίον μαρτύρων (Antiphon 1.28; 6.19, 39; Aristophanes, *Ec.* 448).

The term ἀλλότριος (√ ἄλλος [= other]) is meant here as the opposite of οἰκεῖος (= domestic), i.e., in the sense of *foreign* (cf. εἴτε ἀλλότριος εἴτε οἰκεῖος [= whether stranger or kin], Plato, *Euthphr.* 4b). It is virtually the equivalent of the πολέμιοι (= enemies) in the previous clause (LSJ, ἀλλότριος II.1). Callimachus stayed erect so that no barbarian could witness him falling and thus derive encouragement for the battle (cf. B 40) or afterward bring home such a report (cf. A 43, 44; B 60, 61).

The final verb in the sentence has given copyists and editors a headache. The second generation archetypes divided between πεσούσης (→ γ) and πέσῃς (→ δ). J. Casparus proposed πέσειας (1st aorist optative ending on a 2nd aorist stem — a post-classical form; cf. Orellius, p. 80) and Hinck reconstructed πεσοίης (2nd aorist optative ending on a 2nd aorist stem; cf. *GG*, 460). The rule of preferring the *lectio difficilior* (πεσούσης) cannot be made to apply here

— a feminine genitive participle is grammatically untenable. Thus, while an optative would be smoother, this edition accepts the subjunctive πέσῃς (= you would fall) as having stood in the medieval progenitor (π). Whether that reading also stood in the original text (II) is another matter.

15

The enclitic pronouns in the MSS (ταῦτά με ... ταῦτά μοι) Hinck emended to emphatic pronouns by changing the final α in ταῦτα (elision) to an initial ε in the pronouns (ταῦτ᾿ ἐμὲ ... ταῦτ᾿ ἐμοί). The alteration is unnecessary. The forward position of the personal pronouns and possessive adjective in the three successive clauses (με ... μοι ... ἐμόν ...) is sufficient for rhetorical emphasis: It's these things that cause *me* to go up; it's these things that grant to *me* the burial speech; *mine* is the major part of the ceremony.

ἀναβιβάζω is the causal form of ἀναβαίνω (= go up). As is clear from the following clause "cause me to go up" has the sense "give me the right to go up," "legitimate my ascending." παραδίδωσιν + dative has the sense of *grant to* or *bestow upon* (LSJ, παραδίδωμι II).

The first mention of τάφος denotes the *physical tomb* or *grave mound* (as in e.g., Aeschylus, *Pers.* 686; Herodotus 2.136; Thucydides 1.26) whereas the second occurrence refers to the *funeral rites* or *burial ceremonies* (as in e.g., B 16; Homer, *Il.* 23.619; *Od.* 4.547; Sophocles, *Aj.* 1170).

Since the main feature (τὸ κεφάλαιον) of these ceremonies was the funeral oration (τὸν ἐπιτάφιον λόγον), that was the 'prize' for which the two fathers contested.

The μόγις clause reformulates a remark at the opening (πεσεῖν μὲν οὖν αὐτὸν καὶ κοινωνῆσαι τοῦ τάφου μόγις ἔπεισα, B 3) using different words: κεῖσθαι (to lie, B 15) → πεσεῖν / κοινωνῆσαι τοῦ τάφου (to fall / to have a share in the grave, B 3); ἐκίνησα / παρεκάλεσα (I moved / exhorted, B 15) → ἔπεισα (I persuaded, B 3). Though the thought is the same, verbal equivalence between the two sentences appears only in the disclaimer, μόγις (= scarcely, hardly).

The expression εἰσέρχεται εἰς τὸν τάφον (= he goes into the grave) means burial (cf. οὐ μὴ εἰσέλθῃ τὸ σῶμά σου εἰς τὸν τάφον τῶν πατέρων σου [= your body will not go into the grave of your fathers], 3 Kgdms 13:22).

The construction ἄξιος + ὑμῖν (dative of person) + τιμῆς (genitive of thing) is classical (cf. ἡμῖν δ᾿ Ἀχιλλεὺς ἄξιος τιμῆς [= among us Achilles is worthy of honor], Euripides, *Hec.* 309; πολλῶν ἀγαθῶν ἄξιος ὑμῖν [= in your eyes worthy of many goods], Aristophanes, *Ach.* 633; cf. LSJ, ἄξιος II.2.b). The dative of reference (GG, 1496) has the same sense as if it were expressed with the preposition παρά (cf. θείας τινὸς τιμῆς ἄξια παρὰ πάντων ὁπόσοι ἀρετὴν ἐπαίνουσιν [= deserving of some divine honor *from* all who praise valor], Lucian, *Tox.* 3).

The infinitive λέγειν (= to speak) is epexegetical: it is an appositive to ταύτης τῆς τιμῆς (= this honor) which it explains (*GG*, 1987). The subject of the infinitive (τὸν πατέρα τὸν ἐκείνου) is expressed in the accusative (*GG*, 1972). The identification with ἐκείνου rather than αὐτοῦ is emphatic: *his very own* father (*GG*, 1259).

The prefix προ of the verb προκριθέντα yields the sense of *preferred before* [others], *selected ahead of* [others] (LSJ, προκρίνω 1.a). Callimachus' father should be ranked *in front of* Euphorion.

The designation κοινὸν σῆμα (= common grave) is an alternate term for πολυάνδριον (= mass grave, A 49). In classical Athens it was customary to bury those fallen in war in the δημόσιον σῆμα (= People's Grave) in the Outer Cerameicus, a prominent suburb. An exception, however, was made for the fallen at Marathon: because of their pre-eminent valor they were buried on the battlefield where they fell (Thucydides 2.34.5). That special grave mound was still visible in Polemo's day, and after visiting it Pausanias termed it the τάφος Ἀθηναίων (= grave of the Athenians) (Pausanias 1.32.3).

16

The phrases οὗ ζῶντος (= his while living) and τούτου ... τεθνεῶτος (= his ... having died) are not genitive absolutes but attributive participles with possessive genitive pronouns.

Two things are δίκαιον (= meet, right, fitting): (1) that the ἡγεμονία (= leadership) for the war belonged to him while he was still alive [in the past] and (2) that the pre-eminent honors belong to him now that he is dead [in the present]. The former is expressed with a copula (indicative) and nominative subject (ἦν + ἡ ἡγεμονία), the latter with a copula (infinitive) and accusative subject (εἶναι + τὰς πρώτας τιμὰς).

The term ἡγεμονία often refers to the authority of a military officer (cf. Thucydides 4.91; 7.15; Plutarch, *Cam.* 23). Here, as is typical, the qualifier κατὰ τὸν πόλεμον (= for the war) specifically denotes *military command* (cf. βασιλεῖς ... κύριοι δ᾽ ἦσαν τῆς τε κατὰ πόλεμον ἡγεμονίας [= kings ... were supreme authorities of the command in war], Aristotle, *Pol.* 1285b9; τὴν ἡγεμονίην τοῦ πρὸς Δαρεῖον πολέμου [= the leadership of the war against Darius], Herodotus 6.2; ὅσα δεῖ τὸν μέλλοντα στρατηγὸν ἔσεσθαι, τάς τε τάξεις καὶ τὰς ἡγεμονίας τῶν στρατοπεδῶν [= what is needful for him who would be general: the tactics and the leadership of armies], Plato, *Euthd.* 273c).

The term τιμαί frequently designates the *honors* accorded to superiors as reward for their services (LSJ, τιμή I.1; cf. B 1, 17).

The fourfold prefixing of the grammatically unnecessary nominative personal pronoun ἡμεῖς (= we) to the verbs is emphatic (*GG*, 1190). There is an emotional intermixing of father and son in the four actions, a kind of inter-generational identity or familial solidarity whereby the father takes credit for the military actions of the son. Conversely, this "we" also implies that the son will participate in the funeral oration of the father.

The triad of parallels shows more variation in the first member than the second. Whereas the parallels ἐροῦμεν / ἐπαινεσόμεθα / τὰ ἐγκώμια (= we will speak / we will praise / the encomiums) all refer to the same upcoming funeral oration, the parallels ἤγομεν / ὡπλίζομεν / τὰ συνθήματα (= we were leading / we were arming / the battle signals) show differentiation. ἤγομεν (= we were leading [√ ἄγω]) is a verbal recasting of the noun ἡγεμονία (= leadership) — a comprehensive concept. ὡπλίζομεν (= we were arming) connotes action preparatory for war: equipping, arming, training, getting ready (LSJ, ὁπλίζω 3). τὰ συνθήματα refers to specific critical moments on the battlefield.

The συνθήματα are the predetermined *signals for battle* (cf. Polybius 1.27.10; 1.45.5; Plutarch, *Sul.* 28.7). In some situations these were **visible** (cf. οὐκ ... ἐπιθήσεσθαι, οὐδὲ πρότερον ἢ τὸ σύνθημα σφι ἔμελλε φανήσεσθαι [= not to attack before the signal should be seen by them], Herodotus 8.7; τὸ σημεῖόν τε τοῦ πυρός ... ἀνέσχον ... ἰδὼν τὸ ξύνθημα ἔθει δρόμῳ [= they raised the sign of fire ... seeing the signal he set off at a run], Thucydides 4.111–112; σύνθημα δ᾽ ἦν ... ποιεῖσθαι τὴν ἀρχὴν τῆς ... προσβολῆς, ὅταν ἴδωσιν ἀρθεῖσαν ... σινδόνα [= the signal to make the beginning of the assault was when they saw the linen raised], Polybius 2.66.10). On other occasions the σύνθημα was **audible** (cf. διὰ τῶν σαλπιγκτῶν ἀποδοὺς ... τὸ σύνθημα ... τὴν προσβολὴν ἐποιεῖτο [= through the trumpeters he gave the signal ... they made the attack], Polybius 4.71.8; τὸ πρῶτον σύνθημα Λακεδαιμονίοις πρὸς τὴν μάχην ὁ αὐλὸς ἐνδίδωσιν [= the flute gives the first signal for the battle to the Spartans], Lucian, *Salt.* 10 κατεβόων· τοῦτ᾽ ἦν σύνθημα [= they were shouting; this was the signal], Josephus, *B. J.* 2.325–326;).

From the perspective of a military historian or theoretician the pre-determination of the right σύνθημα and its well-timed use belonged to the fundamental elements upon which the success or failure of any military operation depended. Polybius, for example, listed the συνθήματα ὡρισμένα

(= definite signals) among the few essentials that a successful commander must pay attention to or otherwise court disaster (cf. Polybius 9.12.1–9.13.9; 9.17.1–10). In Polemo's declamation there is no hint of what kind of signals Callimachus employed. There is simply the presumption that they were well-planned and aptly utilized. The statement by Callimachus' father that the battle signals came "from us" (παρ' ἡμῶν) does not mean to say that he co-issued the signals on the battlefield, but it could imply that he wants to take credit for participating in the advance decision as to what these signals would be.

17

Four parallel prohibitive subjunctives (μὴ λυπήσητε [don't grieve], μὴ καθέλητε [don't pull down], μὴ ἀποχειροτονήσητε [don't vote against], μὴ ... παρ' ὑμῖν ὀφθῇ [let him not be viewed by you]) want to dissuade the jury from a negative decision.

The verb συνίημι means to *perceive* and *take notice of* (LSJ, συνίημι II; cf. εἰδὼς καὶ συνιείς [= knowing and perceiving], A 25). The assertion here that the dead Callimachus is still aware (συνιέντα) of earthly matters goes against traditional Hellenic belief. Homer's portrayal of the dead as insensate (ἀφραδέες, *Od.* 11.476) dominated in the classical world. The depiction of the seer Teiresias as retaining his mind and faculties (φρένες ἔμπεδοι ... νόον ... πεπνῦσθαι) in Hades was an exception that confirmed the rule (*Od.* 10.493–495). Since Callimachus was cognizant (i.e., of the deliberations in Athens) he could also be "grieved" by an unfavorable decision. This is a reversal; ordinarily it is the survivors, not the deceased, who experience grief (cf. λύπη as a motif in Greek epitaphs, W. Peek, *Griechische Grabgedichte* [Berlin: Akademie-Verlag, 1960] # 67 [p. 72], # 98 [p. 82], # 310 [pp. 180/182], # 416 [p. 236]).

If the Athenian jurists were to "pull down (καθέλητε) the one who stood erect" they would accomplish precisely what the Persians had failed to do (cf. κατελεῖν, B 58).

The verb ἀποχειροτονέω (= stretch out the hand away from [i.e., *vote against*]) is a technical term for *rejection* used in the voting assembly (LSJ, sub verbum II.). It, of course, derives from its counterpart χειροτονέω (= stretch out the hand [i.e., *vote for*]) (LSJ, sub verbum I and II.a). Alongside the practice of voting by a show of hands the Greeks also utilized the voting pebble (ψῆφος), the white representing *for*, the black *against*. According to Athenian custom the stone was used in judicial and legislative questions; in civic matters — as was the case surrounding Cynegirus and Callimachus — the show of hands was more common.

The comparative ἀτιμότερος ([literally] = more dishonored, more unhonored) means simply *less honored*. Already Theognis had complained about the overturning of values: τίς κεν ταῦτ' ἀνέχοιτ' ἐσορῶν, τοὺς ἀγαθοὺς μὲν ἀτιμοτέρους, κακίους δὲ λαχόντας τιμῆς (= who can bear to behold such things — the good being less honored, the bad having obtained honor? Theognis 1110–1111).

The speaker urges that Callimachus not be viewed as deserving less honor than ἑνὸς καὶ δευτέρου τῶν νενικηκότων (= one [who is] even second [best] of the victors). This clumsy phrase appears to be a disparaging reference to Cynegirus. It is possibly a strained allusion to that incident where Achilles admonishes Patroclus not to fight without him (cf. ἀτιμότερον δέ με θήσεις [= you will make me less honored], Homer, *Il.* 16.90).

It is hard to choose between the evenly balanced readings παρ' ὑμῖν (→ γ) and παρ' ἡμῖν (→ δ). With a passive verb (ὀφθῇ [=be seen]) this dative phrase expresses the *sphere of judgment* (GG, 1692.1.b and 2.b; cf. τί ἄπιστον κρίνεται παρ' ὑμῖν; [= why is it judged incredible in your eyes?], Acts 26:8; ὅσος παρ' ὑμῖν ὁ φθόνος φυλάσσεται [= what malice is maintained among you!], Sophocles, *O.T.* 382).

The common phrase οὐ ... μόνον ... ἀλλὰ καί (= not only ... but also) appears just one other time in Polemo (A 30).

The accusatives τὴν πολεμαρχίαν (= the office of general-in-chief) and τὰς ἀρχάς (= the authorities) are the subjects of their respective infinitives ἀγγέλλεσθαι (= to be proclaimed) and ἀξιοῦσθαι (= to be esteemed) (GG, 1972). With these passive infinitives stand instrumental datives. The first three dative nouns describe pre-war *externals*: ὀνόματα, with the specfic sense of *titles* (as in A 13, 14, 18), are distinguished from deeds (cf. ἐξ ἔργων, οὐκ ἐξ ὀνομάτων [= based upon deeds, not titles], A 14). σχήματα which connote *outward appearances* are hollow (cf. σχῆμα κενόν [= empty appearance], A 27; μόνον ἐν τῷ σχήματι [= only in appearance], B 20). The στολή is an *outer garment* in which one is clothed (cf. ἐνδὺς τὴν ... στολήν [= having put on the garment], B 52; cf. στολήν γ' Ἕλληνα ..., τὰ δ' ἔργα βαρβάρου χερός [= Greek garb ..., but deeds of a barbarian hand], Euripides, *Heracl.* 130–131). The fourth noun, τιμαί, denotes *commendation* bestowed by society *after* the war. τῶν ἔργων may be taken as a genitive of source or possession (= honor *arising out of* or *belonging to* the deeds)

18

A crisp imperative exhorts the audience to consider the arguments as presented by the speaker: οὕτως οὖν σκοπεῖτε (= examine, therefore, [the matter] so). Though the verb σκοπέω appears only here in Polemo, variations of this phrase are extremely common in the classical orators. Demosthenes alone has more than four dozen examples (e.g., οὑτωσὶ δὲ σκοπεῖτε 10.37; 25.3; σκοπεῖτε γὰρ οὑτωσί 25.38; cf. also 38.12; 45.11; 9.3; et al.). It belonged to the stock phraseology of an Attic speech (cf. Lysias 19.31, 34; Aeschines 2.69, 160; 3.121; Antiphon, 5.21, 25, 49; Dinarchus, 1.67, 111). With this expression Polemo simply reflects his indebtedness to the Attic tradition.

The adverb οὕτως (= thus) refers to what follows (LSJ, οὕτως I; *GG*, 1248), namely the two conditions. The first condition — εἰ + ἠμφισβήτουν (imperfect indicative) / ἄν + διεκρίθη (aorist indicative) and [ἄν +] ἐπῆνεσε (aorist indicative) — is a mixed contrary to fact condition (present protasis / past apodosis). The second condition — εἰ + παράσχῃ (aorist subjunctive) / ἄν + δῶτε (aor subj) — does not conform to any standard Attic conditional syntax. The particle εἰ with the subjunctive expresses a future condition more distinctly and vividly than εἰ with the optative but less so than εἰ with the indicative (LSJ, εἰ B.II.1). In the apodosis ἄν with the subjunctive — ordinarily confined to epic literature — is virtually equivalent to a future indicative (LSJ, ἄν A.II). Normally Polemo's conditional sentences exhibit all the earmarks of the standard classifications (cf. Index 2); in this instance the anomalies show that he can occasionally take some liberty with the rules.

With περιγενόμενοι (= surviving) the τῆς μάχης (= the battle) is a genitive of the thing escaped *from* (LSJ, περιγίγνομαι II.1). The circumstantial participle περιγενόμενοι is conditional with the same sense as εἰ ... ἠμφισβήτουν: *if* they had survived and *if* they had disputed.

The genitive τῆς παρούσης τάξεως (= the present ranking) indicates the thing *about* which the dispute revolves (LSJ, ἀμφισβητέω I.3).

An ἰδιώτης is a private soldier with no rank as opposed to an officer (LSJ, ἰδιώτης II.1; cf. the contrast with στρατηγός, Xenophon, *An.* 1.3.11).

In common parlance the substantized attributive participle τοὺς πεσόντας (= the fallen) is the usual term for *those fallen in battle* (LSJ, πίπτω B.II.1; cf. A 6).

The three rapid questions introduced by οὐχ expect a positive answer (LSJ, οὐ A.II.12; *GG*, 2651). Elided in all three cases, and to be supplied, is ἄν ἦν (= would be).

The three substantized participles appear to represent concepts regarding preparation for war.

Because of its ambiguity the first term, ὁ πιάσας (= the one pressing, √ πιάζω [= late Attic for πιέζω]) has troubled scribes and editors alike. Yet none of the many variants — κοπιάσας (= toiling) [→ β ι], ρίσας (= ?) [→ M], παρακαλέσας (= summoning) [→ FKG], and ὁπλίσας (= arming) [cf. Hinck, in assimilation to ὡπλίζομεν, B 16] — has sufficient weight to supplant πιάσας (= pressing) [→ α {→ γ → π} ε {→ δ → π}]. This picture of one *pressing* could admit of several understandings. He pressed them:

(a) in rigorous discipline of military training
(b) closer together to form a tight battle line
(c) hard against the enemy

(cf. LSJ, πιέζω I; II.2).

The verb τάσσω means to *draw up in battle order, assign one's battle station* (LSJ, τάσσω I; cf. A 18). Hence, the second designation, ὁ τάξας, describes the role of the tactician and battle commander.

Thirdly, the παρασχών (√ παρέχω = *produce, bring about*; cf. B 2, 6, 28, 29, 61) describes the one who *produced* such [heroic soldiers as the fallen] by his leadership and example.

The object of the three participles is τοὺς πεσόντας (= the fallen) which is comprised in the backward pointing demonstrative pronoun of quality, τοιούτους (= such) (GG, 333e, 1180, 1245).

The speaker answers his own questions with the phrase ἐμοὶ μὲν δοκεῖ (= it seems [so] to me). This common idiom (LSJ, δοκέω II,4) serves as the affirmative response expected by the three οὐχ questions.

In the second condition of this passage the apodosis is framed as another interrogative introduced by οὐκ, that is, expecting an affirmative answer: even if commander and 'grunt' showed equal valor, wouldn't the nod still go to the leadership (ἡγεμονία)?

The word νή, a variant of ναί (= yea, yes), is an Attic particle of asseveration which regularly stands with the accusative of the divinity invoked (accusative Δία from nominative Ζεύς). In this common oath formula all sorts of named or unnamed gods could be cited but Zeus was especially popular (GG, 1596.b; 2923; LSJ, νή I). The phrase νὴ Δία (= by Zeus) often, as here, stands simply as a strong affirmative answer following questions introduced by οὐ (cf. Plato, Phd. 94e; Prot. 312a; Xenophon, Mem. 2.2.13).

19

Arising out of the affirmative "By Zeus ..." (*GG* 2952) the inferential οὐκοῦν (cf. A 13, 14, 18; B 35) has the sense of *surely then* (LSJ, οὐκοῦν II.1).

The separation and sequence of ἥν ... προτίμησιν ... ταύτην (= which [relative pronoun] ... preference [noun] ... that [demonstrative pronoun]) is awkward. The translation reorders the three and puts them together at the front of the sentence. Happily this stilted construction is rare in Polemo's style.

The reading εἴπερ ἦσαν (→ γ I μ) is better attested than εἰ περιῆσαν (→ ε) and surely represents what stood in the medieval progenitor (π). Nonetheless behind the text of π may well have stood a reading resembling that of ε because the verb ἦσαν here has the sense *were* [*alive*] (LSJ εἰμί A.I) and thus is virtually synonymous with περιῆσαν (LSJ περίειμι [-ειμί] III.1; cf A 22; B 19, 19, 22). Elsewhere Polemo uses forms of περιγίγνομαι which likewise means *survive* (LSJ, περιγίγνομαι II.1; cf A 6; B 18). He interchanges them solely for the sake of variety.

The inference signaled by οὐκοῦν is expressed with a past contrary to fact condition (cf. Index 2). The protasis has εἰ with imperfect indicative (ἦσαν), the apodosis has an aorist indicative (ἔσχε) whereby the understood ἄν is omitted and to be supplied from the previous sentence (*GG*, 1767).

The circumstantial participle τεθνεὼς (= having died) may be construed as temporal (= after), attendant circumstance (= now that), or concessive (= even though).

The construction δίκαιος (masculine) φέρεσθαι is personal: *he* is just[ified] to be paid that honor. English typically expresses the same impersonally: *it* is right that he be accorded the honor. The translation opts for an idiomatic rendering.

The preposition ἐκ expresses cause (LSJ, ἐκ III.6; cf A 20, 23, 23, 24, 24; B 24, 28, 31). The phrase ἐκ ... ὧν (= out of which things) is singular in Polemo. The twice repeated ἐξ ὧν in A 23 is not an apt parallel. There, within the sentence, it lacks the transitional function in the argument that it has here, at the beginning of the clause, where it serves almost like an emphatic inferential οὖν: *accordingly, therefore*. In this connection it is worth noting that Polemo rarely uses the post-positive οὖν alone (only A 17; B 18, 20); he much prefers the combination μὲν οὖν followed by a δέ contrast whereby the inferential function of the particle οὖν gets submerged (cf. A 2, 4, 9, 10, 11, 14, 14, 42; B 2, 3, 4, 11, 25, 27, 40, 43).

The type of condition (contrary to fact) is clear not so much from the truncated language as from the context. The conditional participle περιών stands in place of the protasis εἰ περιῆν (= if he had survived); in the apodosis an ἄν again needs to be supplied with the ἦν (= he would be) (*GG* 1767).

The predicate adjective κρείττων (= better) is a comparative (from ἀγαθός) taking a genitive of comparison (Κυναιγείρου) which in turn is modified by a participle (περιόντος) with conditional sense (= better than Cynegirus had he survived).

In the idiomatic phrase ταῦτα καὶ νῦν ἔχει it can be debated whether ταῦτα is a nominative subject (= these things) or an adverbial accusative similar to οὕτως (= thus, so). Despite grammatical ambiguity the sense is clear: *the matter is even now so* (LSJ, οὗτος C. VII.2, 4).

It is characteristic of Polemo's use of the articular infinitive (11x) that he often sandwiches other words or phrases between the article and infinitive (cf. A 15, 22, 25; B 9, 26, 26). Here the perfect infinitive προκεκρίσθαι (= to have been chosen) is inserted into τὸ ... δοκεῖν (= the seeming). The text has no other example of such an articular double infinitive construction. This articular infinitive is the subject of ὑπάρξει which, linked with αὐτῷ (= him), means *will fall to, will belong to* (LSJ, ὑπάρχω B.III.1).

The verb προτιμάω (= honor above [another]; prefer before [another]) is virtually synonymous with the προκρίνω used in the subject's double infinitive. The verb is altered simply to avoid wooden repetition. The participial form (προτιμωμένου) is conditional (cf. Index 2).

Striking here is the *plural* τῶν ἄλλων πατέρων (= the other fathers). Beyond Euphorion and the father of Callimachus the declamations nowhere else indicate that there were additional contenders for the right to deliver the eulogy. Indeed, the form of the traditional pro- and con- *controversiae* genre practically rules this out (cf. the introduction 0). In light of that and the specific statement that the only other legitimate candidate, Miltiades, laid no claim to the speech (A 21), how is this plural (the other fathers) to be understood? Unless one takes it to be a simple *lapsus* two interpretations seem possible: (1) Prior to the present contest between the two fathers there was an earlier 'preliminary round' at which other fathers of fallen heroes also argued their cases (for the purpose of arriving at a short list of two); the plural in B 19 is a veiled reference to that 'semi-final'. (2) The plural simply means that Callimachus' father is not only the best of the two choices at hand but the best of all possible choices. The former interpretation is stretched, the latter is far more natural.

The protasis (εἰ + future indicative [ἔσται]) and apodosis (future indicative [τεύξεται]) yield a future emotional (= future most vivid) condition (cf. Index 2). In such conditions "the protasis commonly suggests something undesired, or feared, ...; the apodosis commonly conveys a threat, a warning, or an earnest appeal to the feelings" (*GG*, 2328).

τὰ τοιαῦτα (= such things) refer back to the "what if" arguments in the hypothetical survival of Cynegirus and Callimachus.

The preposition παρά with the dative (here with τεθνηκότι [= one having died], indicates a kind of possessor relation (*GG* 1692.b). The construction is uncommon (LSJ, παρά B) but not unknown (cf. τὸ μὲν βασιλικὸν χρυσίον παρὰ τούτῳ, οἱ δὲ κίνδυνοι παρ' ὑμῖν [= the royal gold is for him, but the dangers for you], Aeschines 3.240). Hence, the various attempts to 'correct' ἔσται παρὰ τῷ πολέμῳ τεθνηκότι are unnecessary (cf. e.g., ἔσται παρὰ τῷ πολέμῳ τεθνηκότος [= will be now that he has died from the war], QR Stephanus; ἔσται τῷ πολεμάρχῳ τεθνηκότι [= will be for the polemarch who has died], Orellius, pp. 84/86; παρέσται τῷ πολεμάρχῳ τεθνηκότι [= will be possible for the polemarch when he has died], Hinck, p. 22 apparatus).

The interrogative of quality (ποίων) corresponds to the demonstrative of quality (τὰ τοιαῦτα) — ποῖος; / τοιοῦτος = Latin: *qualis? / talis*. With the genitive (ποίων) the verb τεύξεται (future of τυγχάνω) has the sense of *meet with* [*misfortunes*] (cf. τραυμάτων ... τόσων ἐτύγχανεν [= he met with so many wounds], Aeschylus, *Ag.* 866; κακῶν ... τυχεῖν [= to meet with evils], Euripides, *Hec.* 1280). The English would emphasize: what *will* he meet with?

The preponderance of MSS makes clear that an accented interrogative τίς (= what?) stood after προεδρία in the medieval progenitor (π). Despite that reading, an indefinite τις (any) is surely what stood in the original text (Π). There is no instance in the declamations of an interrogative τίς following its noun, it always precedes it (cf. B 36, 36, 46, 56, 56). It is the indefinite which follows its noun (cf. ἀνάγκη τις, A 18; εἷς τις, B 7; τιμή τις, B 20). The term προεδρία denotes a *front seat* in the theater, at public games, and in festal and civic assemblies. Such seats of honor were regularly set aside for victorious generals (cf. Aeschines 2.80; Aristophanes, *Eq.* 573–575; IG, III.248) and certain office holders like priests, archons, ambassadors, judges (LSJ, προεδρία). On occasion, however, they could also be bestowed on an individual as special recognition of some boon or benefit which that person had provided to the *polis*. Indeed, for his services to Smyrna that city granted to Polemo himself and to his descendents the right to sit in front (προκαθῆσθαι) at the Smyrnaen Olympic Games founded by emperor Hadrian (Philostratus, *V. S.* 530; here προκαθῆσθαι may also have the additional specific sense of *to preside over*, cf. LSJ, προκάθημαι II.1). If one could assume that the front-seat privilege which Polemo himself enjoyed prompted the mention of this honor as a parade example then this detail could provide a clue regarding the *terminus a quo* for the composition of the declamation, namely, it would be after Hadrian's institution of the Smyrnaean Games (between 123 and 129 CE).

The front seats themselves (stone or wood) sometimes bore inscriptions indicating for whom the place was reserved (C. Fensterbusch, "Prohedria," *RE* 23.1 [1957] 114–115; M. Maass, *Die Prohedrie des Dionysostheaters in Athen* [Vestigia, Beiträge zur alten Geschichte 15; München: Beck, 1972]). The granting of front seat privileges was of such import that it was effected through the state assembly and proclaimed by an inscription on a *stele* set up in a public place. There are literally hundreds of such inscriptions attesting the award of front seat privileges. According to these inscriptions this honor was also frequently coupled with other forms of recognition, e.g., σίτησις (= free meals at public expense) in the Prytaneum, ἀτέλεια (= exemptions from public burdens), a gold στέφανος (= wreath), a bronze εἴκων (= image), or the like. The reasons for these state awards were often noted, typically with a formulaic ἕνεκα (= on account of) + genitive. Alongside such reasons as εὔνοια (= benevolence), φιλοτιμία (= munificence), εὐταξία (= discipline), ἐπιμέλεια (= diligence), or δικαιοσύνη (= justice) the inscriptions also frequently name ἀρετή, a term which covers a range of merits, including *valor* in war. According to the epigraphical evidence the bestowal of a front seat privilege persisted as one of the most important forms of civic recognition from classical times through the late Roman period. To survey here all the data would exceed the scope of this study; excerpts from three Attic examples can suffice to indicate the flavor of the material:

(1) δοκεῖ τῇ βουλῇ ἐπαίνεσθαι τοὺς ταξιάρχους ... καὶ στεφανῶσαι αὐτοὺς χρυσῷ στεφάνῳ κατὰ τὸν νόμον ἀρετῆς ἕνεκα καὶ ἀνδραγαθίας τῆς εἰς τὸν δῆμον τὸν Ἀθηναίων. εἶναι δ' αὐτοῖς καὶ προεδρίαν ἐν ἅπασιν τοῖς ἀγῶσιν οὕς ἂν ἡ πόλις τιθεῖ. τὸν δὲ ἀρχιτέκτονα κατανέμειν αὐτοῖς τὴν θέαν ἀεὶ οὗ ἂν τοῖς στρατηγοῖς κατανέμηται· ἀναγράψαι δὲ τόδε τὸ ψήφισμα τὸν γραμματέα τὸν κατὰ πρυτανείαν ἐν στήλει λιθίνει ...

(= it seems [right] to the council to praise the commanders and to crown them with a gold wreath in accordance with the law on account of [their] valor and bravery for the people of Athens; and for them to have a front seat at all the games which the city might institute; and for the commissioner always to allot to them the seat whenever he allots it to the generals; and for the secretary of the Prytaneum to write this decree on a stone stele) ... (IG II [2] 500, 23–39).

(2) εἶναι δὲ αὐτῷ καὶ σίτησιν ἐν πρυτανείῳ αὐτῷ καὶ τῶν ἐκγόνων ἀεὶ τῷ πρεσβυτάτῳ, καὶ προεδρίαν ἐν πᾶσι ἀγῶσιν ... ἀναγράψαι δὲ τόδε τὸ ψήφισμα ... ἐν στήλῃ λιθάνει καὶ στῆσαι ἐν ἀκρόπολει ...

(= for there always to be free meals in the Prytaneum for him and for the oldest one of his sons, and a front seat at all the games ... and to write this decree ... on a stone stele and to set it up on the acropolis) (IG, II [2] 510, 1-9.

(3) ὑπάρχειν μὲν Εὐθυδήμῳ ... καὶ τοῖς προγόνοις αὐτοῦ ... προεδρίαν αὐτῷ καὶ ἐγγόνοις ... ἀρετῆς ἕνεκα καὶ εὐνοίας ...

(= to be for Euthydemus ... and for his parents ... a front seat for him and for his children ... on account of valor and benevolence) (IG, II [2], 1194, 10-19).

The προεδρία inscriptions shed light on several points in the Polemo text. First, they show that the front row seat is one of the highest civic honors that could be bestowed by the state. Polemo is not speaking here of something trivial. Second, they clarify the puzzle of how a dead war hero could arrive (ἑπομένῳ) at the theater or assembly looking for a seat. That riddle had led Orellius (pp. 84/86) to label the text corrupt and in need of emendation. However, the προεδρία inscriptions show that this privilege often applied also to the oldest male offspring and occasionally to the parents of the honored. Thus Callimachus' father appears here to be asking whether his being rejected as speaker at the state funeral would also mean that he would be deprived of the 'box seat' which he as father of a posthumously decorated war hero might expect. At issue then on such an understanding would be not only the slight of Callimachus but also the bruised ego of the father. Third, what in the next sentence looks like an oddly abrupt mention of inscribed *steles* makes perfect sense in connection with the front seat privilege award. It was customary to publicize that award with *stele* texts.

The verb προετάττετο (imperfect of customary action = he *used to be* placed in front) is separated from its subject modifying nominative πρῶτος (= first) by the insertion of the genitive absolute τῶν ὀνομάτων τῶν ἐν ταῖς στήλαις γραφομένων (= when the names [i.e.,] those in the *steles* were written). Stylistically this word order achieves two things: It avoids the infelicitous redundancy of a conjoined **πρῶτος** **προετάττετο** and the postponing of the adjective gives it added emphasis.

Problematic is the rationale given for Callimachus' customary first place status: διότι πρεσβύτερος τούτων ἦν ἀπὸ τῆς οἰκείας αὐτοῦ γενέσεως (= since he was older than them because of his family origin). Unclear is whether this amounts to *one* or to *two* reasons. In other words: is the ἀπό clause (1) simply an epexegetical clarification of the διότι clause or (2) another explanation for the front seat status? Both causal indicators represent classical usage (διότι [√ διὰ τοῦτο ὅτι = on account of this that ...]; cf. LSJ, διότι I.1; ἀπό [= in consequence of], LSJ, ἀπό A.III.6). If only a single reason is meant the formulation is a silly tautology: primogeniture because of his family birth (for γένησις in the sense of *birth*, cf. LSJ, sub verbum II). If two reasons are meant the asyndetic juxtaposition is awkward, if not inconsistent: (a) primogeniture, (b) family ties (for γένησις in the sense of *origin*, cf. LSJ, sub verbum I). Hinck's solution was to mark διότι πρεσβύτερος τούτων ἦν for deletion. Though it remains a mystery why such a mindless gloss would find its way into the text the present edition concurs with Hinck that it represents a secondary interpolation and has set it apart with pointed brackets.

The conclusion of the argument in B 19 has a lifeless formulation despite the fact that the grammar is clean and classical: impersonal δεῖ (= it is necessary) + infinitive, ἀκούειν (= to hear) + accusative of thing heard, τὸν ... λόγον (= the word) + genitive of person from whom it is heard, ἡμῶν (= us) + supplementary participle in agreement, λεγόντων (= speaking) (*GG*, 1361). For the plural *us* instead of *me* see the notes to B 16 and 42. The sense is simply: 'Therefore, you have to pick me as speaker of the eulogy' (cf. B 1, 2, 15).

Despite its unusual position vis-à-vis τὸν ... λόγον the adjectival participle εἰωθότα (perfect from ἔθω [= to be accustomed]) must be taken as attributive (*GG*, 1166).

20

Countless inscriptions show that the στέφανος was an honorary *wreath* or *crown*, frequently worked in gold, awarded for service in war or peace. Since such wreaths were frequently dedicated in temples or presented in religious ceremonies (cf. LSJ, στέφανος II.2.b), Polemo characterizes it as *sacred* (θεῖος).

The argument introduced by δικαίως οὖν (= rightly in fact) is based on the logic *a minore ad majus*: The στρατηγός has less stature than the πολέμαρχος — if some honor (τιμή τις) has been conferred on the general, then even more so does the general-in-chief deserve a token of recognition (γέρας). This term can describe the final honors paid to the dead (cf. ταρχύσουσι ... τύμβῳ τε στήλῃ τε· τὸ γὰρ γέρας ἐστὶ θανόντων [= they will solemnly bury ... with mound and marker; for this is the due of the dead], Homer, *Il*. 16.456-457). In Polemo the term γέρας receives its specificity from the entire context and from the following line in particular. Awarding the speakership to Callimachus' father will provide the fitting acknowledgement of Callimachus' valor.

The temporal clause ὅταν ... ἀναβιβάσῃ (= when ... he uplifts) refers to the future and is analogous to the protasis of a future more vivid condition. The principal clause has, instead of a future indicative, an aorist imperative (δότε) which, of course, refers to the future (τότε). The syntax is in accord with classical usage (*GG*, 2401). As it stands, however, the main clause is very difficult. Medieval scribes tried to lessen the difficulties by writing ἐπὶ τούτῳ instead of ἐπὶ τοῦτο. Possinus (p. 120), who described the clause as *perintricata* (= very entangled), suspected a textual corruption but was unwilling to propose an emendation. Jacobs (cf. Hinck, p. 23) suggested changing δότε ἐπὶ τοῦτο to δώσετε, λείπουσαν (= you will give him [his] missing voice). Hinck (p. 23) for his part posited a lacuna after ἐπι which he suggested filling out with something like ἐπι[φέροντες λεῖπον] τοῦτο (= supplying what is missing). The obscurity is compounded by the fact that the last three nouns in the sentence (πίστις, σωτηρία, σχῆμα) are all capable of a range of connotations (cf. LSJ, sub verba). Polemo's vocabulary usage provides no help: πίστις is a *hapax legomenon*; σωτηρία appears in only one other place and there quite possibly with a different meaning (cf. B 27); and σχῆμα can be used in a positive (cf. A 27, 44; B 47, 52, 52, 53, 63), a negative (cf. A 2, 7, 26, 27, 28; B 33, 35, 42) or a neutral (cf. A 7, 27; B 63) sense. Thus what is offered as an English translation of all these ambiguities is no more than an exasperated guess.

21

The argument continues with another past contrary-to-fact condition (cf. Index 2). In the protasis the verb ἠμφισβήτει (√ ἀμφισβητέω = contest, dispute) stands with the genitive (τοῦ λόγου) of thing about which the dispute revolves (LSJ ἀμφισβητέω I.3; cf. A 16; B 18, 39). In the apodosis, from which ἄν is omitted (*GG*, 1767), the verb παρεχώρησα (√ παραχωρέω = yield, concede) stands with the dative of person to whom the concession is made (LSJ, παραχωρέω 1.b; 3; 4) — αὐτῷ (= to him) is understood and then explained by ὡς ἀρχῇ μείζονι (= as to a greater authority).

The point of Callimachus' father mentioning Miltiades yet again is to show that he, the father, is not making an inordinate request. Indeed, he, contrary to Euphorion (cf. B 22), recognizes full well and accepts the prevailing military and societal hierarchy. This point is designed to make him appear more sympathetic to the jury than the immoderate Euphorion.

The use of the attributive participle ἀποιχόμενος meaning *departed* in the sense of *dead and gone* is common (LSJ, ἀποίχομαι 3). Only here in Polemo is Callimachus called ἄρχων. The term cannot be taken in the specific titular sense of *chief magistrate* — in Athens the office of πολέμαρχος was distinuished from that of ἄρχων — but in the general sense of *commander* (LSJ, ἄρχων I).

The long construction within the articular infinitive τὸ ... σχεῖν (= the ... having) is plain enough: τὸν ἀποιχόμενον ἄρχοντα (= the departed commander) is accusative subject of the infinitive, ἔλαττον ἢ πρότερον γέρας (= less recognition than before) is accusative object.

Beyond that the sentence is a nightmare of syntactical ambiguities. Is the articular infinitive (τὸ ... σχεῖν) nominative or accusative? What is designated as εἰκός (= fair, reasonable)? — τὸ σχεῖν (= the having)? τὸ ἐνδεές (= the lack)? or something which has dropped out of the text? The genitive τῆς μοίρας is clearly dependent on τὸ ἐνδεές (LSJ, ἐνδεής; *GG*, 1314, 1396) but the genitival connection of τῆς τιμῆς is less certain. Does it belong with μοῖρα (= the portion of honor) (LSJ, μοῖρα I.2)? Is it to be connected with τῆς τιμῆς παραμυθουμένης as genitive absolute (= since honor consoles)? How is the dative τῷ πλείονι to be understood?

As it stands, the clause following σχεῖν resists a meaningful translation. Orellius (p. 86/88) called the text *mutilis* (= mutilated) and Hinck (p. 23) posited a lacuna after σχεῖν, suggesting that οἰκτ[ε]ίρειν (= to pity, bewail) or something similar has dropped out. Since the text appears to yield no sense without some emendation, this edition follows Hinck's lead and assumes a lacuna after σχεῖν. Nevertheless, what is offered here in English is no more than a tentative attempt at a reasonable solution.

The genitive absolute τούτου ... ἀφεστηκότος probably describes attendant circumstance (= with him having refrained) though it could also be taken as causal or as having conditional sense and serving as protasis for a present simple condition (cf. Index 2). Inasmuch as the πεῖρα (= *attempt*), i.e., to put himself forward as candidate for eulogy speaker, was not undertaken by Miltiades, no other person of rank beside Callimachus reasonably comes under consideration.

22

λύω has here (contrast A 41; B 26) the sense of *undo* or *annul* in the way one would *repeal* a law or *rescind* a vote (LSJ, λύω II.4.b.). The negative prohibition formed by μη with the *present imperative* (λύε) — instead of with the aorist subjunctive — expresses "an order to stop an action already begun": *do not go on annulling, annul no more* (*GG* 1841.a.e; 1840.B). This construction is characteristic of Polemo's style (cf. A 27, 38, 46; B 23, 41, 41, 41, 56, 57, 60).

The term τάξις refers to the military *hierarchy* or *order of rank* that prevailed at Marathon (LSJ, τάξις II.1. and III): Callimachus was an officer, Euphorion only an enlisted man (cf. πολέμαρχος vs. ἰδιώτης B 18).

The sentence beginning μὴ δ᾽ εἰς τὸ πρόσθεν τῷ πολεμάρχῳ δίδωσι poses difficulties. The negative μή (instead of οὐ) with the indicative δίδωσι is problematic (*GG*, 2702), and after πρόσθεν the dative τῷ πολεμάρχῳ (instead of the genitive τοῦ πολεμάρχου) looks anomalous (LSJ, πρόσθεν A). Already Stephanus (cf. Orellius, p. 80) was troubled by the text. He thought the reading could not stand and conjectured as correction μηδενὶ πρόσθεν τοῦ πολεμάρχου (= to no one before the polemarch). But this emendation still does not explain the combination of μή[δενι] and the indicative (δίδωσι). Hinck's solution was to enclose the sentence in quotation marks — apparently understanding it as Euphorion's words being quoted by Callimachus' father: "The custom of public burial does not give the speech to the polemarch in the forefront" (cf. A 15). On such an interpretation the speaker would no doubt have turned his head to the side and uttered the words with a tone of disdain.

None of these alterations satisfactorily resolves all the difficulties. The bothersome μὴ with indicative remains. When πρόσθεν — normally followed by a genitive — seems to be followed by a dative (as here: τῷ πολεμάρχῳ) this dative must be connected with the verb (here δίδωσι) and the πρόσθεν phrase taken adverbially (= the custom of the public burial gives the speech to the polemarch and not to [anyone] ahead of [him]) (LSJ, πρόσθεν A.II). Yet the Greek word order (μὴδ᾽ εἰς τὸ πρόσθεν at the beginning instead of at the end) seems to militate against this rendering. Accordingly, the English translation ventures here a different solution than any hitherto proposed. It assumes (a) an ellipsis after μὴ δ᾽ (sc. λύε τάξιν from the previous clause) and (b) a different punctuation than in the MSS; namely, the sentence is divided in two after the πρόσθεν which is construed more substantivally than adverbially. This resolves the knotty conjunction of μή with an indicative and it requires no more textual surgery than inserting a mark of punctuation between πρόσθεν and τῷ. Readers who remain unsatisfied are invited to propose a better solution.

It is atypical for Polemo to depart from the standard format for conditions (cf. Index 2) but he does so here. The mood of the verb in the protasis is not secure: the optative τύχοι appears to have stood in γ and the subjunctive τύχῃ in δ. The two, because of iotacism, are homonyms. The choice between them has to be based upon internal evidence. Since a simple εἰ (= if) is used with the optative, but not the subjunctive (LSJ, εἰ B.II, III; *GG*, 2282, 2283) the original text (II) will no doubt have had τύχοι. The construction: εἰ with optative τύχοι (= past general protasis) + present indicative ἐστιν (= present general apodosis) produces a *mixed* general condition (cf. Index 2). The construction of τύχοι (aorist) with the supplementary participle περιών (present) is standard for describing a state as continuing (*GG*, 2096.b). The argument builds on the logic of the hypothetical survival of the general-in-chief (cf. B 18-19). In the case of his returning alive from battle he would normally have been the one in charge of the state funeral. In that capacity his responsibilities are circumscribed by three substantized participles and their respective objects. He is the one (ὁ):

(1) τὴν πρόθεσιν αὐτῶν ποιούμενος (= providing for their laying-out)

(2) καλῶν ἐπὶ τὸν λόγον (= summoning to the oration)

(3) παντὸς ἐπιμελόμενος τοῦ τάφου (= taking care of the whole funeral).

(1) The first task is the most unpleasant one: the πρόθεσις (= *laying-out* [i.e., *of the corpses*]). This technical term refers to an essential element at funerals (cf. πρόθεσις τοῦ τετελευτήκοτος [= laying-out of the deceased], Plato, *Leg.* 959e; Demosthenes 43.64; προθέσεις νεκρῶν [= laying-out of the dead], Plutarch, *Cons. Ux.* 612a). Typically a body was laid out no longer than was requisite to show it was not merely in a faint but really dead — ordinarily no more than two days (cf. Plato, *Leg.* 659a). The αὐτῶν (= of them) after πρόθεσιν clearly refers to those fallen in battle; Hinck's deletion of the pronoun is unnecessary.

(2) The second, more agreeable task, *calling to the oration*, will of course not have been carried out by means of individual invitations, but through an official public announcement indicating the occasion, day or date, and time.

(3) The third item does not refer to a specific task but simply indicates a comprehensive responsibility to *take care of all other necessary funeral arrangements* (e.g., officiants, ushers, processions, interments, grave inscriptions, etc.).

The grammatical variety in this triad shows clearly Polemo's careful attention to style; to avoid repetition he has varied even the smallest details: (1) accusative object / participle; (2) participle / prepositional phrase; (3) participle / genitive object.

23

The text appears not to be intact. One waits in vain for a feminine genitive noun to go with the article τῆς. For that reason Hinck (p. 24) indicated a lacuna and suggested that something like κρίσεως (= criterion) has dropped out (cf. A 14). Whereas an omission here seems certain, its extent is not (one word? one line?); the text critic ought not be too sanguine about filling in the gap. The series of apparent lacunae which have been noted in B 20–23 suggests that in an earlier MS behind π, the archetype from which the known MSS derive, the folio containing B 20–23 may have become defective, perhaps incurring a ragged edge or other damage in a few spots. Such a circumstance might account for the textual problems in the existing MSS.

In their entirety the two declamations constitute an extended comparison. This element, however, which the rhetoricians technically called σύγκρισις, Polemo terms here παραβολή. Despite this constituent element, each father faults the other for the particular comparisons he has drawn (cf. A 27; B 44).

In the ὁ μὲν / ὁ δέ contrasts the articles without nouns have demonstrative force (*GG*, 1106–1107). This 'nounless' article construction is characteristic of Polemo's style (cf. A 7–8, 21, 42; B 24, 26, 32, 43, 44, 45). The first ὁ μὲν / ὁ δέ contrast has more color, the second more concision. The two represent exact parallels of thought. The σύνθημα (singular) mentioned here does not seem to have precisely the same connotation as its earlier mention (plural) where it referred to the *pre-arranged signals to begin the battle* given on the field at Marathon (cf. note to B 16). Here rather it seems to mean the *rallying cry to war* given back in Athens and perhaps repeated for encouragement along the march to Marathon. Or possibly σύνθημα refers to a military standard carried at the front of the marching column (LSJ, σύνθημα I.2, 3).

The verb ἐδέχετο has here the uncommon but attested sense of he was *heeding, giving ear to* (LSJ, δέχομαι I.2.c) as its parallel ἐπείθετο (= he was obeying) makes clear.

The two sentences beginning with the relative ὧν have parallel syntax:

ὧν ... ποιοῦσιν, αἴτιοι τούτων ...

 (= cause of the things which they do)

ὧν ... ἐτόλμησε, ... τούτων ... διδάσκαλος

 (= teacher of the things which he dared)

The demonstrative antecedents (τούτων) are omitted before both relatives (ὧν) but are supplied afterwards in the main clauses (*GG*, 2509, 2526); the relatives are in the genitive case rather than the proper accusative (ἅ) because of attraction into the case of their genitive antecedents (*GG*, 2522, 2524, 2531). The English translation makes the grammar smoother by pulling the antecedent clauses αἴτιοι τούτων (= causes of these things) and τούτων διδάσκαλος (= teachers of these things) up to the front of the sentence.

The sequence πειθόμενοι καὶ κελευόμενοι (= obeying and being commanded) is an instance of *hysteron proteron*, i.e., a "reversing [of] the natural order of time in which events occur. It is used when an event, later in time, is regarded as more important than one earlier in time" (*GG*, 3030).

To support the idea of the real "causes" (αἴτιοι) of military actions being "those who persuade and command" (οἱ πείσαντες καὶ κελεύσαντες) Polemo provides a threefold analogy: teachers (διδάσκαλοι), choir-teachers (χοροδιδάσκαλοι), helmsmen (κυβερνῆται) resemble polemarchs and generals (πολέμαρχοι καὶ στρατηγοί), i.e., "those persuading and commanding." Classical precedent for the three analogies is not hard to find (cf. ἄρχων [= στρατηγός] / διδάσκαλος, Xenophon, *Cyr.* 1.6.20; 3.3.53; στρατηγός / χοροδιδάσκαλος, Xenophon, *Mem.* 3.4.4; στρατηγός / κυβερνήτης, Xenophon, *Mem.* 1.7.3; 2.6.38). Here Polemo's pleonastic style of piling up analogies is ponderous.

To call Callimachus διδάσκαλος (= teacher) is equivalent to calling him αἴτιος (= cause) of the daring deeds of Cynegerius. The rationale for this assertion is supplied by the γάρ clause. ἐγκελευόμενος (= urging on) is a circumstantial participle (manner or attendant circumstance, *GG*, 2062, 2068, 2069) whose present tense has the same progressive thrust as the imperfect main verb ἐβόα (= he was shouting).

The negative command which Callimachus shouted contains two subtle ambiguities. (1) The first derives from the combination of μή with the present imperative (φείδεσθε). This construction may refer to either (a) interrupting a current action or (b) resisting a future action (*GG*, 1841.a). In other words, either (a) "Desist from the timerity you are now showing!" or (b) "Don't hold back when you do clash with the enemy!" Given the earlier assertion that no one of the Greeks was blameworthy (cf. B 7) the negative imperative here more likely means the latter. (2) The second ambiguity arises out of the absence of a possessive pronoun with the accusative objects: *whose* limbs and eyes are not to be spared? Does this refer to (a) the bodies of the barbarians or (b) the Greeks own bodies? In the context of warfare the verb may mean either (cf. LSJ, φείδομαι I and II). The verb usage in B 56 and 57 clearly implies the third person. Nonetheless, given the fact that the argument here wants to make Callimachus the real cause for Cynegirus acting aggressively and thereby losing his hand it seems more likely that this admonition means the Greek soldiers should not worry about their own safety. In other words, with "hands, eyes, and bodies" the reader should probably think (b) ὑμῶν (= your) rather than (a) αὐτῶν (= their).

The verb λαμπρύνομαι ([middle] = to distinguish oneself) ordinarily stands with the dative case ([instrumental] = by) (LSJ, λαμπρύνω II). Thus, ὧν (genitive) probably stands for οἷς (dative), the relative pronoun being attracted into the case of its antecedent, the τούτων which follows in the next clause. Attraction of a dative relative pronoun into the genitive is a rarity (*GG*, 2523).

The οὐδέν troubled Stephanus (who emended it to οὐδενός, cf. Possinus, p. 120) and Hinck (who bracketed it for deletion). Greek does not feel the accumulation of negatives as redundant but as having a re-enforcing effect. Alongside the οὔτε ... οὔτε the οὐδέν is an adverbial accusative (= in no respect).

The construction ποιήσασθαι τὴν ἀναφοράν has the unusual sense of *assign to, give credit for* (LSJ, ἀναφορά II.1).

The one having acted (τὸν πεποιηκότα) refers to Callimachus. It is typical of Polemo's style to designate Callimachus with an articular substantized perfect participle (cf. τὸν βεβλημένον [= the one having been struck] A 27; τὸν ἑστῶτα [= the one having stood] A 33; τὸν ἀνεστηκότα [= the one having stood erect] B 17; τὸν νενικηκότα [= the one having conquered] B 17; τῷ τεθνηκότι [= the one having died] B 19; τὸν ἑστηκότα [= the one having stood] B 44; τὸν μεμαχημένον [= the one having fought] B 50). The force of these perfects is completed action with permanent result (*GG*, 1852.b).

24

The double μέν - δέ contrast is an artful balance with chiastic structure:

(1a) Κυναίγειρος μὲν νεώτερος ὢν ταῦτα ηὐθαδιάσατο,

(1b) Καλλίμαχος δὲ πρεσβύτερος,

ὥσθ᾿ (2a) ὁ μὲν ἡλικίας θερμότητι τολμηρός,

(2b) ὁ δὲ ἀνὴρ ἀγαθὸς ὢν ἀρετῆς ἐβεβαίου κρίσιν

Nothing in 1b corresponds to the ταῦτα ηὐθαδιάσατο (= he did these things rashly) of 1a; as main verb in 1b the copula ἦν (= was) must be supplied. This means that, whereas νεώτερος ὢν (= being younger) is a subordinate clause, πρεσβύτερος [ἦν] (= was older) is the main clause. This grammatical imbalance is neutralized by a counter-imbalance in 2a/b: nothing in 2a corresponds to the ἀνὴρ ἀγαθὸς ὤν (= being a brave man) in 2b — νεώτερος ὤν in 1a is the formal counterpart. As main verb in 2a the copula ἦν must again be supplied ([ἦν] τολμηρός = was reckless) to match ἐβεβαίου κρίσιν (= was securing a decision) in 2b. Therefore, viewed as smaller units the contrasts appear poorly matched; viewed as a whole the double composition is carefully crafted so as not to present a wooden construction.

Cynegirus was younger (νεώτερος), i.e., seventeen or eighteen years old (cf. note at A 5); Callimachus was older (πρεσβύτερος), i.e., as polemarch at least middle aged. From this age difference the two fathers draw radically different conclusions (cf. the arguments of Euphorion at A 5, 20).

Because of his youth Cynegirus acted arrogantly (ηὐθαδιάσατο). The verb αὐθαδ[ε]ιάζομαι is a late post-classical form of αὐθαδίζομαι (LSJ, sub verbum), a denominative verb (GG, 866.6) derived from the noun αὐθάδεια (= willfulness, stubbornness). The etymology is instructive: αὐθ' (→ αυτ' → αὐτός [= self]) + ἅδ (cf. ἅδομαι/ἥδομαι or ἀνδάνω [= enjoy, take pleasure]) = *self pleasing*. To the Greek mind the classic example of this trait was seen in Prometheus' *hybris*, his willful assault on the divine order, which brought upon him the punishment of Zeus (cf. Aeschylus, *Pr.* 1012, 1034). Theophrastus included a portrayal of αὐθάδεια in his characterizations of human defects. He illustrated it largely with examples of mundane surliness, but notably in his final example he cited the refusal to pray to the gods (*Char.* 15). Early Christians paired αὐθάδεια with words like θράσος (= arrogance, 1 Clem 30:8), ὑπερήφανος (= haughty, 1 Clem 57:2) and ὑψηλοφροσύνη (= audacity, Hermas, *Sim.* 9.22,2-3). It was easy for them to include this concept in their lists of vices and sins (Did 5:1; Barn 20:1). Thus for Greek ears the terms αὐθαδιάζομαι and αὐθάδεια (cf. B 35) had a particularly pejorative ring. Because of the parallel phrase ἡλικίας θερμότητι τολμηρός (= bold by reason of 'heat' of [his young] age) the English translation of ηὐθαδιάσατο (= did ... rashly) opts more for a stress on recklessness than arrogance.

In this context the term ἡλικία (= age) has the specific sense of *young age* (cf. μὴ πάντα ἡλικίη καὶ θυμῷ ἐπίτραπε [= do not ever indulge youth or passion], Herodotus 3.36; τῇ ἡλικίῃ εἴκειν [= to yield to youth], Herodotus 7.18). Papyri from the Roman period provide countless examples of ἡλικία having the sense of *immature age* (cf. MM, ἡλικία).

The denominative substantive θερμότης (= heat), like the adjective θερμός (= hot) from which it derives, can be used, as here, metaphorically: *hot-headedness, passion* (LSJ, θέρμος II.1; θερμότης II).

While the adjective τολμηρός can connote a positive attribute (cf. e.g., θαυμαστὸς καὶ τολμηρός [= admirable and daring], B 50) the context here indicates a negative connotation (cf. τολμηρὸν ... μάχεσθαι δὲ εὐβούλως οὐκ ἠπίστατο [= reckless ... he did not know how to fight prudently], B 37). In the μέν - δέ contrast τολμηρός is after all not synonymous with but antithetical to ἀγαθός (= brave).

In military descriptions the term κρίσις refers to the *decision* on the battlefield or the *outcome* of the war (cf. τὴν τοῦ πολέμου κρίσιν [= the decision of the war], Arrian, *An.* 1.13.5; 2.16.7; τὸ Μηδικόν ... δυοῖν ναυμαχίαιν καὶ πεζομαχίαιν ταχεῖαν τὴν κρίσιν ἔσχεν [= the Persian {war} had its outcome {determined} quickly in two sea-fights and two land-battles], Thucydides 1.23.1; cf. Polybius 13.3.4; Appian, *B. C.* 2.10.67). The expression βεβαιόω κρίσιν can only mean *secure a* [favorable] *decision, assure a* [positive] *outcome*.

The ἀρετῆς, a genitive of cause (*GG*, 1405, 1409), is parallel to θερμότητι, a dative of cause (*GG*, 1517) — Polemo employs stylistic variety so as to avoid monotony.

The contrast in ages is highlighted by an argument about bodily strength. τὴν ... ῥώμην is an accusative of respect: with respect to physical strength Callimachus was the weaker (ἐλάττων) of the two because of his advanced age (ἡλικία). In contradistinction to the sense of ἡλικία just applied to Cynegirus, here the term clearly means *mature age* or *old age* (cf. προήκων ἐς βαθὺ τῆς ἡλικίας [= having advanced to the depth of {old} age], Aristophanes, *Nu.* 514; κατ' οἰκίαν τὰ πολλὰ διατρίβοντες ὑπὸ τῆς ἡλικίας [= spending the majority of time at home because of {old} age], Plato, *La.* 180d). This argument based on age is thus the exact opposite of what Euphorion had claimed about Callimachus, namely that because he was older he had more strength (ῥώμην πλείονα, A 20).

Not by strength of body but solely by valor of spirit Callimachus was able to *over*power, *sur*pass, or *out*do the enemy, as the compound verb puts it (ὑπερέβαλλε).

25

While the adjective δεινός (= fearful) is common enough in Polemo (A 22, 25, 39, 40; B 52, 56) only here is it substantized as a neuter plural. Yet the expression τὰ δεινά (= the horrors) is found frequently in texts describing war (e.g., Herodotus 7.50, 145; Thucydides 2.87.4; 4.59.2). The horrors of war repel every ordinary person (cf. εἰκὸς ... τὰ ... δεινὰ ... φοβεῖσθαι [= it is natural to fear the horrors], Thucydides 6.91.6). Hence, it was a striking demonstration of courageous resolve for Callimachus to place himself at the focal point of the horrors (ἐν τῇ τῶν δεινῶν ἀκμῇ; cf. ἐν μέσῳ τῷ δεινῷ, A 22).

Without an accusative object the verb παρετάξατο (√ παρατάσσω) is a genuine reflexive middle: *he drew himself up in battle-order*. The indirect object of this verb — here τοῖς βαρβάροις (= against the barbarians) — stands frequently in the dative (cf. παραταξάμενοι τοῖς πολεμίοις [= drawn up for battle *against* the enemies], Isocrates 12.92; παρεταξαντο ἀλλήλοις [= they drew up for battle *against* one another], Xenophon, *Hel.* 4.3.5). What Polemo expresses here with the dative case he does elsewhere with the preposition πρός and the accusative (cf. πρὸς ... τὰ ... ἔθνη παρετάξατο [= against the hordes he arrayed himself], B 32). Variety of expression is one of Polemo's trademarks.

A simile is signaled by the word δίκην (accusative of δίκη [= custom, usage] with adverbial sense) which serves as an improper preposition (*in the way of, after the manner of*) standing with the genitive (LSJ, δίκη I.2; *GG*, 1700) in postpositive position. The verb ἐπιχωριαζούσης (√ ἐπιχωριάζω) seems to be used in a specialized sense, perhaps rooted in its etymology (ἐπί + χώρα + -άζω [= go against land]). The phrase θαλάττης ἐπιχωριαζούσης δίκην means: *like [the] sea making an inroad* (LSJ, ἐπιχωριάζω 4). Orellius (p. 92) rendered the participle ἐπιχωριαζούσης graphically with *aestuans ac in terram sese effundens* (= surging and pouring forth onto the land).

Previous editors have found the prepositional phrase ἐκ τῆς Ἤλιδος difficult. Orellius (p. 92) suspected that it was a corruption out of ἐκ τῆς Μιλήτου (= out of Miletus). Jacobs (cf. Hinck, p. 24) proposed as original ἐκ σύγκλυδος (= out of [what was] washed together). More complicated was Hinck's suggestion (p. 24) that the original reading was συνήλυδα (= assembled) which was first corrupted into σὺν ἤλιδι (= with Elis) and then into ἐκ τῆς ἤλιδος (= out of Elis). Such emendations are, however, unnecessary. The simplest interpretation is to accept the reading and take the ἐκ as a specification of a genitive of origin or belonging (*GG*, 1688.c; 1297-1298): the advancing sea *of* Elis. The ἐκ is added merely to distinguish the genitive dependent on the δίκην (θαλάττης ἐπιχωριαζούσης) from the genitive of location (τῆς Ἤλιδος). This is consistent with Polemo's style (cf. τὰς ἐξ Αἰγαίου τῶν νήσων ἁρπαγάς [= the seizure of the islands *of* the Aegean], B 5; ὁ Πὰν ἐξ Ἀρκαδίας [= Pan *from* Arcadia], A 35). On this understanding the horde of Asians flowing into Attica's plain of Marathon is compared with the Ionian sea which sometimes washed over the flat alluvial plain of Elis on the northwest shore of the Peloponnesus and in so doing carved into it a series of shallow lagoons (cf. E. Meyer, "Elis," *KP* 2.249). This coastal phenomenon would have been familiar to any who had ever visited the games at Olympia.

The verb ἀπεώσατο (√ ἀπωθέω [middle] = he drove back) is reminiscent of Homer (cf. Τρῶας ἀπώσασθαι [= to drive back the Trojans], *Il.* 8.206; νεῖκος ἀπωσαμένους [= driving back the assault], 12.276; ἀπώσασθαι κακά [= to repel the evil], 15.503). Further, the picture of Callimachus *driving back* the flood recalls the portrayal of Achilles fighting the River Scamander — an epic battle which he won only with the help of Poseidon, Athena, and Hephaestus (Homer, *Il.* 21). Throughout the declamations, whether with specific references or with subtle allusions, Polemo knows how to cast his two fallen soldiers in heroic garb and in epic proportions. Callimachus repelled Asia like a figure of Homeric legend.

The comparison of the invaders with a flood of water, be it surging sea or rushing river, — ῥέουσαν (= flowing) befits more the current of a stream than waves of the sea — was an evocative and long-lived analogy. In later time, for example, when barbarians overran the Roman empire Ammianus Marcellinus recalled the Median hordes (*Medicas acies*) which came to Greece and he used the metaphor of a liquid (cf. *innumerae gentium multitudines per provincias circumfusae* [= countless swarms of nations *pouring through* the provinces], 31.4.7–8).

The metaphor and bombast are rounded off with a sentence that sounds very much like a gnomic saying: 'Every danger an opportunity for valor'.

26

The main clause is sundered: the subject, Cynegirus, stands at the very beginning, the object, μιᾶς νεὼς πρύμνης (= one ship's stern), at the very end; the verb is missing. A few late MSS (QR [→ ρ]) supplied ἔσχε (active) and changed the object to an accusative πρύμναν (= he *held* one ship's stern). Following that lead Hinck supplied ἔσχετο (middle) but retained the genitive πρύμνης (= *had hold of* one ship's stern) in accord with earlier parallels (cf. τῆς πρύμνης εἴχετο [= he had hold of the stern], A 11; μιᾶς Φοινίσσης ... εἴχετο [= he had hold of a Phoenician {ship}], A 9). The English translation adopts Hinck's solution.

Between subject and predicate Polemo has sandwiched a long series of seven genitive absolutes. In rhetoric this bracketing technique is known as *inclusio*. It is virtually impossible to retain this grammatical structure in the translation and still have readable English. The translation, therefore, joins subject and predicate at the end of the sentence and then, in order to suggest the sandwich effect, has divided the participle series, grouping the last six together and setting them apart with dashes. Uninflected English sometimes has to resort to expediencies.

The temporal adverb ἤδη (= already) belongs with the whole series of participles, that is, one must think an *already* with each and every one of the verbs. In other words, *prior* to Cynegirus' assault the Persians were already on the run, terrified by Callimachus. This characterization thus takes virtually all the bravery and all the boldness out of Cynegirus' action.

With the exception of συνεληλαμένων (√ συνελαύνω [= drive together]) — a *hapax legomenon* in Polemo — all the participles in the series represent verbs used frequently in the declamations (cf. Index 8). The seven participles are artfully ordered. The first two, *fleeing* (φευγόντων [active]) and *fearing* (πεφοβημένων [middle]), describe the physical and psychological state of the Persians. The next three, *routed*, *pursued*, and *driven* (τετραμμένων, δεδιωγμένων, συνεληλαμένων [all passives]) describe what happened to them because of the agency of Callimachus (ὑπὸ τοῦ Καλλιμάχου [= by Callimachus]). The last two, *being* (ὄντων [active]) in the ships and *loosening* (λυόντων [active]) the lines, describe again the actions of the Persians. The series unfolds with increasing specificity from the abstract to the concrete, culminating in the last detail designed to evoke a scene of shipboard confusion and panic.

The nautical expression τὰ ἀπόγεια is truncated from τὰ ἀπόγεια [σχοινία] (= the [ropes] from land) (LSJ, ἀπόγειος I.2). By itself ἀπόγειον came then to mean *mooring cable* (cf. λύσας τὰ ἀπόγεια τὸν ὠκεανὸν ἔτεμνε [= loosening the shore lines they began to cut through the ocean], Libanius, *Or.* 59.139; φεύγουσαι νῆες ἀνήγοντο σπουδῇ τὰ ἀπόγεια κόπτοντες [= fleeing ships were putting to sea in haste by cutting the shore lines], Libanius, *Or.* 61.21).

The τὸ μέν / τὸ δέ contrast has about it a gnomic ring. It may represent an expanded maxim, perhaps a sentiment like: 'To fight from valor is one thing, to chase a frightened foe another.'

The genitives ἄκρας εὐτυχίας (= [out] of extreme success) and περιττῆς τινος ἀρετῆς (= [out] of some enormous valor) indicate cause (*GG*, 1405).

The phrase τῶν κρατίστων πολέμων αὐτους ὑφίστασθαι is rough and has caused the editors headaches. Orellius (pp. 92/94) wondered whether it ought not read τῷ κρατίστῳ τῶν πολεμίων ὑφίστασθαι — αὐτούς being dropped — the sense of which he gave as "dem Kern des feindlichen Heeres sich entgegenstellen" (= to oppose the core of the enemy army). Hinck (p. 25) adopted a different emendation: he altered αὐτούς to read ἄθλους (= to undertake *struggles* of the fiercest battles) — a not unknown expression (cf.

ὑφιστάμην τὸν ἄθλον [= I withstood the ordeal], Lucian, *Rh.Pr.* 24). The English translation, however, tries to make sense of the passage without any emendation by taking the personal pronoun αὐτούς (= them) in the sense of the demonstrative pronoun τούτους (= those). Though admittedly inelegant the meaning then would be: *to undertake those of the fiercest battles.* This verb is common in war accounts (cf. τοὺς κινδύνους ... ὑφίστασθαι [= to undergo the dangers], Thucydides 4.59.2; ὑποστάντες ... τὸν πόλεμον τοῦτον [= withstanding this battle], Polybius 1.6.7; cf. also Lysias 9.7; Isocrates 3.28; Thucydides 3.57.3).

The temporal adverb ἤδη has a proleptic position in the sentence. Though in advance of them it modifies the substantized participles τὸν φεύγοντα (= the one *already* fleeing) and τοῖς τετραμμένοις (= the ones *already* routed). This simply repeats the thought of the previous sentence (cf. φευγόντων ἤδη ... τετραμμένων).

The subject of an infinitive (here: διώκειν and ἐπεμβαίνειν) is ordinarily expressed in the accusative (*GG*, 1972). In this construction, however, very unusually and perhaps to avoid confusion with the accusative object τὸν φεύγοντα, the subject of the infinitives is expressed as a genitive (of the agent?): παντὸς ... τοῦ τυχόντος (= every chance person). The substantized aorist participle ὁ τυχών has the sense of *any random person* (LSJ, τυγχάνω A.2.b).

The infinitive ἐπεμβαίνειν (= to trample upon) with the dative (τοῖς τετραμμένοις [= the routed]) could be be taken *literally* (cf. ἐχθροῖσιν αὐτοῦ ... ἐπεμβῆναι ποδί [= to trample underfoot his foes], Sophocles, *El.* 456) or *metaphorically* (cf. ταῖσδ᾽ [γυναιξί] ἐπεμβαίνειν ἀεί [= always to trample on the women]). In Polemo the latter sense would mean to *take advantage of* (cf. ἐπεμβαίνων τῷ καιρῷ [= taking advantage of the opportunity], Demosthenes 21.203). Both meanings work well in this context and the choice makes little difference in the overall picture.

27

Rhetoricians of the Second Sophistic, Polemo included, characteristically punctuated their speeches with interspersed *sententiae*. Unusual here, however, indeed without any real parallel in the declamations, is the piling up of successive gnomic sayings to produce a series of three contiguous double maxims.

(1) The declamations are a man's text about men. The first pair of simple *sententiae* contains one of the three rare references in the text to women (γυναῖκες) — two of these assume their weakness and lesser status (cf. B 27,

63) and a third, the mention of the nameless mother (μήτηρ) of Callimachus, is colorless and neutral (cf. B 64). In this first occurrence the parallel γυναῖκες / κύνες (= women / dogs) mirrors a certain disdain for women:

(1a) γυναῖκες ἀνδράσιν ἐπιτίθενται
(= women attack men)
(1b) κύνες κατὰ λεόντων θρασύνονται
(= dogs are over-bold against lions).

The gender of κύνες is indeterminate — it could be masculine or feminine. More often than not hunting hounds are designated with the feminine (LSJ, κύων I). Here that would not only fit better the structural parallel of the two clauses but it would also underscore the negative assessment of women and hence the corresponding jibe against Cynegirus.

In the middle voice the verb ἐπιτίθενται with the dative ([literally] = put themselves upon) means *attack, make an attempt upon* (LSJ, ἐπιτίθημι, B.III.2). The witless audacity of an assault on the part of those who are outclassed is made more pointed by the parallel verb θρασύνονται (= are overly bold [*in malum sensum*], LSJ, θρασύνω II.2).

If not the first example, then certainly the second one has the air of a gnomic saying. In adages dogs appear frequently as examples of what is irksome or despised (LSJ, κύων I; also Prov 26:11, 17; Sir 13:18; Isa 56:11) while lions typically represent power and ferocity (LSJ, λέων; also Plato, *Resp.* 341c; Prov 19:12; 20:2; 28:1). On occasion the two can be juxtaposed in the same aphorism (cf. χορεία κυνός, ὄνομα λέοντος [= circling of a dog, pretence of a lion], Aesop, *Prov.* 175; ὁ κύων ὁ ζῶν, αὐτὸς ἀγαθὸς ὑπὲρ τὸν λέοντα τὸν νεκρόν [= the living dog is better than the dead lion], Qoh 9:4). Polemo's point and the popular lore he assumes are nicely illustrated by Aesop's fable about the dog and the lion (cf. κύων θηρευτικὸς, λέοντα ἰδὼν, τοῦτον ἐδίωκεν· ὡς δὲ ἐπιστραφεὶς ἐβρυχήσατο, φοβηθεὶς εἰς τοὐπίσω ἔφυγεν. ... ὁ λόγος λεχθείη ἂν ἐπ᾽ ἀνδρῶν αὐθαδείᾳ συνόντων, οἳ κατὰ πολὺ δυνατωτέρων συκοφαντεῖν ἐπιχειροῦντες, ὅταν ἐκεῖνοι ἀντιστῶσιν, εὐθέως ἀναχαιτίζονται [= A hunting dog upon seeing a lion chased it; when it, however, turned and roared {the dog} became frightened and fled in retreat. ... This saying may be applied to insolent men who, when they attempt to oppress those much mightier and these resist, are overthrown immediately], cf. H. C. Schnur, *Fabeln der Antike* [Darmstadt: Wissenschaftliche Buchgesellschaft, 1978] 102).

(2) The second pair of *sententiae* is more complex with each half consisting of a double clause:

(2a) ὅταν γὰρ τὸ τῶν πολεμίων φοβερὸν οἴχηται,
τότε παντὶ τολμᾶν πρόχειρον
(= for whenever the dread of the enemy is gone,
then for everyone [it is] easy to be daring)
(2b) τὸ φρόνημα τῶν ἑλόντων γίνεται οὐκ ἐξ οἰκείας ἀρετῆς
ἀλλ᾽ ἐκ τῆς τοῦ πολεμίου κακότητος πεπορισμένον·
(= the high spirit of those winning comes not from personal valor
but [is] provided by the cowardice of the enemy.)

In contrast to the first couplet of sayings this pair is, except for the παντί and πολεμίου (masculines), almost gender neutral. The present tense verb which speaks of fear going away (οἴχηται) usually carries a perfect sense: *has gone, departed*, (LSJ, οἴχομαι I). Once dread has *vanished* it is easy for boldness to fill the void.

The adjective πρόχειρον (= *easy*) — from πρὸ + χείρ (= at hand) — is used in accord with classical idiom: with the dative (παντί [= for everyone]) and infinitive (τολμᾶν [= to be daring]), and with ἐστι to be supplied (LSJ, πρόχειρος I.3).

The concept φρόνημα (a denominative from φρονέω [= to be minded]) is employed here not merely in a neutral sense (= mind, thought) but in a decidedly good sense (= *high*-mindedness) as is often the case in classical authors (LSJ, φρόνημα II.1). This noble quality is attributed once to Cynegirus (A 19) but three times to Callimachus (B 12, 27, 53), as though his father wanted to drown out Euphorion's claim with repetition.

In classical Greek the verb αἱρέω (→ ἑλόντων) when used in the sense of *win, overcome* normally takes an accusative object (LSJ, αἱρέω A.II.1–3). Here, however, it is employed absolutely.

To qualify valor with the adjective οἰκεῖος is to describe it as *homegrown*, as *one's own, personal, private, innate* valor. So used it is virtually the equivalent of ἴδιος (LSJ, οἰκεῖος III.2.a).

The term κακότης (= badness) describes a base or inferior moral quality. A high fighting morale on the part of winners is less impressive measured against cowards than against a stubborn enemy.

The use of the verb πορίζω (= furnish, provide) in the phrase τὸ φρόνημα τῶν ἑλόντων ... πεπορισμένον (= the high spirit of the winners is furnished) is classical (cf. πορίσαι ... νίκην [= to furnish victory], Aristophanes, *Eq.* 593–594).

(3) The third double maxim, a μέν - δέ contrast, has the subject at the very beginning (ἀρετῆς δὲ ἀγὼν) and the verb at the very end (κρίνεται), a

word order of which Polemo is fond (cf. A 22, 26, 32, 40; B 7, 26, 28, 33, 42, 59, 61).

    (3a) ἀρετῆς δὲ ἀγὼν ἐν ἀντιπάλῳ μὲν τῆς δυνάμεως,
      (= and a contest of valor ... {is decided}
      on the one hand by a struggle of power,)
    (3b) ἀσταθμήτῳ δὲ τῷ τῆς τύχης κρίνεται
      (= on the other hand by the uncertainty of chance { }.)

In light of its obviously neuter counterpart, ἀσταθμήτῳ (= uncertainty), it is probably best to construe the ἀντιπάλῳ also as neuter. This adjective (= struggling [√ ἀντί + πάλη [= struggle against]) in the neuter usually describes power that is *nearly balanced* or *almost matched* (LSJ, ἀντίπαλος I.2).

    The phraseology ἀσταθμήτῳ δὲ τῷ τῆς τύχης (= the uncertainty of chance) is conventional (cf. ἀστάθμητον τὸ τῆς ξυμφορᾶς [= the uncertainty of fortune], Thucydides 3.59; τὸ δὲ ἀστάθμητον τοῦ μέλλοντος [= the uncertainty of the future], Thucydides 4.62). The thought is a commonplace (cf. τύχης ἀσταθμητότερον οὐδέν [= nothing is more uncertain than chance], Philo Mechanicus 2.85). With the passive verb κρίνεται (= is decided) the datives ἀντιπάλῳ and ἀσταθμήτῳ express agency (*GG*, 1494) — a kind of dative of instrument (*GG*, 1507, 1512).

    After the three generalizing *sententiae* Polemo returns to the specifics of the argument. The contrast between the two heroes is taken up again with a long μέν - δέ sentence whose second clause is complicated by another μέν - δέ pair of objects. Fortunately, while Polemo is fond of this idiom, he does not overwork it in this fashion anywhere else in the declamations.

    The antecedant of ἅ (accusative) is in both cases an understood ταῦτα (nomininative) serving as subject of the verbs ἐγένετο and ἦν.

    The series of four articular infinitives in quick succession (τοῦ δρᾶν, τοῦ παθεῖν, τοῦ ποιεῖν, τοῦ μὴ παθεῖν has no parallel elsewhere in the declamations although Polemo does otherwise utilize the construction (cf. A 15, 22, 23, 25; B 9, 19, 26). While having the grammatical character of a substantive the articular infinitive focuses on the verbal action: *acting, suffering, doing, not suffering* (*GG*, 2025). All four have adnominal function (*GG*, 2032.b) — they limit and clarify their respective substantives (χαλεπῷ, φοβερῷ, ἐξουσία, ἄδεια [= difficulty, terror, authority, permission]). Thus, whereas in form the sentence utilizes substantized expression, in effect it is verbal dynamism that is highlighted.

Substantized with the article τό the adjective χεῖρον (irregular comparative of κακός [= bad], *GG* 319.2) has the sense of *inferiority* (LSJ, χείρων III.1).

By being placed at the end of the sentence, φυγῇ (= by flight), a dative of means, receives the emphasis. This rhetorical device is characteristic of Polemo (cf. the concluding ἀρετῇ [= by valor], B 8; αὐθαιρέτῳ σπουδῇ [= by independent zeal], B 32; πείσματι [= by a boat-rope], A 10).

28

Notably the μέν - δέ clauses do not present a material contrast but only a formal parallelism in which the pronominal τά is made specific by πεπραγμένα (= the things done):

τὰ (accusative) μὲν Κυναιγείρου Καλλίμαχος παρεσκεύασεν,

τὰ (nominative) δὲ Κυναιγείρου ... Καλλιμάχου ... ἀριστείαν αἰτεῖ.

Callimachus laid the groundwork for the deeds of Cynegirus,

The deeds of Cynegirus presuppose the prowess of Callimachus.

The preposition ἐκ expresses immediate cause or origin (*GG*, 1688.c; LSJ, ἐκ III.6): ἐκ ... τῆς ... μάχης = *in consequence of, because of* the fight.

The two participial expressions καταπλαγέντες and τὰ νῶτα δείξαντες are parallel in thrust but divergent in conception: the former is passive and abstract (= *being stricken with panic*), the latter is active and graphic (= *showing the[ir] backs*). This latter phrase is a common idiomatic expression for undisciplined flight in war (cf. δεῖξαι τὰ νῶτα ... καὶ φυγὴν ἀπροφάσιστον φυγεῖν [= to show the[ir] backs and to flee with an unhesitating flight], Plutarch, *Marc.* 12.3; ὑπὸ πόδα ἀνεχώρει, νῶτα μὴ δεικνύς [= he retreated step by step, not showing his back], Josephus, *B. J.* 4.35; ἔθνος μαχιμώτατον ... προθύμως ἔθνησκον, ... αὐτῶν οὐδείς, οὐδὲ τὰ νῶτα δεικνύς [= a very warlike people, they were dying readily, none of them showing their backs], Appian, *Hisp.* 305.5 [12.72]).

The phrase τῶν ... λαμπρῶν is neuter; after the article and adjective one must mentally supply a substantive like πεπραγμένων (= things done).

Here, as in philosophical logic, the verb αἰτεῖ has the technical sense of *presuppose, assume* (cf. Aristotle, *An. Pr.* 41b9; *Top.* 163a6).

29

The ὥστε clause is fraught with problems. It is clear that ὥστε with infinitive (παρασχεῖν) indicates result (*GG*, 2011; 2250; 2254) but the phrase τὸν τούτου λόγον is difficult. Orellius (p. 96) regarded this reading as unintelligible and Hinck (p. 26) emended it to read τοῦτο τὸν λόγον. The present edition forgoes emendations. The multivalent term λόγος is taken to mean something like *repute* (LSJ, λόγος VI.2.d), a signification which it admittedly has in no other of the two dozen occurrences in the declamations (cf. Index 8).

θατέρῳ is crasis for τῷ ἑτέρῳ [→ ἀτέρῳ] (*GG*, 69; 337), hence τῷ θατέρῳ contains a redundancy (= for *the the* other) — contrast the anarthrous θάτερος in A 4. The gramatically anomalous expression may have been anchored in colloquial speech by Polemo's time. "The other" refers here to Cynegirus.

Callimachus' fight was a work (ἔργον) of internal might (δύναμις), not of external display (ἐπίδειξις). This contrast between δύναμις and ἐπίδειξις corresponds to the distinction between ἔργα (= deeds) and σχῆμα (= appearance) which Polemo had stressed several times earlier (cf. A 26, 27; B 17): ἐπίδειξις is just like σχῆμα, namely without deed (ἀργός, A 26) and empty (κενός, A 27). Thus Polemo can even combine the two in the phrase ἡ ἐπίδειξις τοῦ ἀπόρου σχήματος (= the display of the impracticable appearance, B 33).

The κράτιστον could be construed as a regular superlative (= mightiest) from κρατύς (= mighty) or an irregular superlative (= best) from ἀγαθός (= good) (LSJ, κράτιστος; *GG*, 319.1).

The three nominatives (κράτιστον ἔργον / τὸ πρεσβύτατον / δύναμις) are grammatically clumsy. In a sentence with multiple nominatives the one with the article is ordinarily the subject (*GG*, 1150-1152) — here that would be τὸ πρεσβύτατον [ἔργον], but that does not seem to work well. To unencumber the syntax Orellius (p. xiv) proposed emending the first phrase to κρατίστων δὲ ἔργων [= of the mightiest deeds]). He (p. 96) interpreted the sentence as follows: "In dieser Reihenfolge von Ursachen ist die tapferste That die zuerst geschieht gleichsam die Kraft, die auf alles folgende einwürkt" (= In this sequence of causes the most courageous act which occurs first is at the same time the force which influences everything following). To support this interpretation of δύναμις he cited Manuel Palaeologus: τροπὶς μὲν ἡ δύναμις ναυσί· καὶ θεμέλιος [sc. λίθος] οἴκοις (= a keel is the *strong basis* for ships; and a foundation [stone] [the *strong basis*] for houses). Hinck's solution (p. 26) to the cumbersome nominatives was more invasive: he deleted δύναμις out-and-out. This present edition refrains from emendations and the translation construes the arthrous phrase (τὸ πρεσβύτατον) as predicative (cf. *GG*, 1152) and δύναμις is taken as epexegetical apposition to it.

In the ancestry of the passage δ had an aorist participle (γενομένων) and γ probably (→ β I) a present (γινομένων). Which preserves the medieval progenitor (π) is uncertain (hence the bold type in the text), but in this condition the punctiliar aorist seems more logical than the continuous present. The genitive absolute (ἔργων ... γενομένων) has conditional sense and serves as the equivalent of a protasis consisting of εἰ γένοιτο (optative); this followed by an apodosis having ἄν εἴη (optative) yields a future less vivid condition.

In all previous occurrences the term ἀρχή had connoted *authority/office* (A 5, 13, 16, 16, 18; B 2, 17, 21); here and in the subsequent occurrences it means *beginning* (B 29, 29, 40), as the immediate parallel with αἰτία (= cause) shows. The double meaning of the noun corresponds to the verbs ἄρχω (= rule) and ἄρχομαι (= begin).

The phrase οὐκ ἄκαιρος (= not inopportune) is an example of *litotes*, an affirmation expressed by the negative of the contrary. Polemo uses this rhetorical device frequently and he is particularly fond of formulating it with a negative and an alpha-privative (A 43, 49; B 17, 29, 33, 33 42). This kind of understatement tends to intensify the assertion (*GG*, 3032).

ταῦτα (= these things) has as referent the valiant actions of Callimachus.

Since Callimachus' father is averse to giving Cynegirus credit for anything "the things well executed" (τῶν ... εὖ ... τεχνηθέντων) are to be taken not as a specific reference to the deeds of Cynegirus, but as comprising all the Greeks' deeds of bravery which led to the victory (cf. B 7, 30, 46).

The ὥσπερ introduces a threefold simile. The first two analogies are specific and appear in chiastic word order:

(1) τὰ θεμέλια τῶν οἰκοδομημάτων (= the foundations of buildings)

(2) τῶν νεῶν αἱ τρόπεις   (= of ships the keels)

Just as foundations and keels are indispensible for the construction of buildings and ships, so also Callimachus' fight was the pre-requisite for what Cynegirus did. The third simile is a general summary of the principle in the first two:

(3) πάντα ὅσα πρῶτα (= everything which [comes] first).

All three items require a strong start. The formulation of the third case with predicate and object has the ring of a gnomic saying:

πάντα ὅσα πρῶτα καὶ τὴν ἀρχὴν ἰσχυρὰν ἔχει.

(= all things which [come] first also have a strong beginning). The expression "strong beginning" is found in other axioms too (cf. ἡ τῶν γεννωμένων ῥίζωσις ἰσχυρὰν ἐν ἰσχυροῖς σώμασιν ἀρχὴν λαβοῦσα καλῶς βλαστάνῃ [= the implanted stock of the offspring, by getting a strong start in strong bodies, attains a noble growth], Plutarch, *Apoph. Lac.* 227d). Polemo's point finds succinct expression in the unattributed proverb: ἀρχὴ ἥμισυ πάντων (= [the] beginning [is] half of everything). The principle that the ἀρχή is determinative for what follows was, as Polemo knew, not absolute. Folk wisdom knew to qualify it (cf. τόλμα πρήξιος ἀρχή, τύχη δὲ τέλεος κυρίη [= courage is the beginning of action, but chance decides the outcome], Democritus, *frag.* 269). Hence, Polemo continues the argument with clarifications.

30

ὅπερ (→ ὅ + enclitic particle περ) is singular in Polemo (elsewhere only in the interpolation at A 16) and has little intensive or limiting force (cf. Denniston, *The Greek Particles* [Oxford: Clarendon, 1954] 490). The ὅπερ as well as the following τοῦτο are probably predicate nominatives (with ἦν understood).

No substantial difference is discernible between the adjectives Μαραθωνικός (only here) and Μαραθώνιος which Polemo otherwise prefers (34, 48; B 22, 42, 52, 54, 55). Both suffixes (-ιος and -ικος) signify *belonging to* or *related to* Marathon (*GG*, 858.2, 6)

The future participle γενησομένας (= being about to occur) is a rare verb form in Polemo (elsewhere only ἐροῦντα, A 1, 15 and δυνησόμενος, B 33). It "marks an action as in prospect at the time denoted by the leading verb" (*GG*, 2044). The feminine plural accusative noun belonging with τὰς αὖθις γενησομένας ἁπάσας (= all the [?] which were to occur afterward) is unexpressed — δυνάμεις (= forceful acts)? μάχας (= fights)? νίκας (= victories)? It would be unconvincing to argue that with the future participle Callimachus' father intended to voice a prediction: e.g., the conflicts or victories which *will* take place against the Persians afterward, i.e., subsequent to Marathon (490 BCE) at Salamis (480 BCE) and Plataea and Mycale (479 BCE). That would be a blatant anachronistic *lapsus* on Polemo's part. Hence, the translation takes the phrase as referring to the many unsung individual fights which would still occur at Marathon after Callimachus' heroic death (cf. B 46). Cynegirus' fight is submerged in these countless other struggles and like them is predicated on the prior resolute stance of Callimachus.

The τόλμημα (= daring) which Euphorion had attributed to Cynegirus (A 24) is here out-trumped by the plural τολμήματα (= daring deeds) of Callimachus. When Callimachus' father attributes τόλμημα to Cynegirus, the term has the negative connotation of *recklessness* (cf. B 33, 34, 36).

The demonstrative τοῦτον (= this one, him) refers to Callimachus. "When reference is made to one of two contrasted objects, οὗτος {as distinguished from ἐκεῖνος} refers to the object nearer to the speaker's thought ... or to the object last mentioned" (*GG*, 1261).

The graphic verb ἀναπνεύω (= breathe again) often appears in battle descriptions to indicate a *respite* or *breathing spell* (cf. ἀπόσχωνται πολέμοιο Τρῶες, ἀναπνεύσωσι ... υἷες 'Αχαιῶν [= the Trojans may hold back from war, and the sons of the Achaeans may catch their breath], Homer, *Il.* 11.800; ἀναπνεύσαντας καὶ ἀναπαυσαμένους ... εἰς μάχην ἰέναι [= recovering your breath and resting yourselves ... to go into battle], Xenophon, *Hel.* 6.4.24; τοῦ δέους τῶν ὅπλων ἀναπνεύσαντες [= catching their breath from the terror of arms], Appian, *B. C.* 1.7.{63}).

The nominative ἰδόντες is a circumstantial participle with temporal or causal sense (= *when* or *since* they saw). The accusative φεύγοντας is a supplementary participle with a verb of perception (*GG*, 2110-2111). Each of the juxtaposed participles is separated from its item of reference (φεύγοντας ... τοὺς βαρβάρους [= the barbarians ... fleeing] and ἰδόντες ... ἐθάρρησαν [= when they saw ... they took courage]) — this produces an interlocking word order held together like links in a chain.

The circumstantial participle ὁρῶν has conditional sense and stands as protasis instead of εἰ with imperfect (ὥρα). This followed by the imperfect (ἠμέλει) in the apodosis produces a past general condition (*GG*, 2336, 2297, 2342, 2060, 2067; cf. Index 2). The indefinite τις (= anyone) who is the subject of this condition is any member of the λοιποί (= rest), i.e., the pronoun refers to Greek soldiers, not Persians.

The split prepositional object phrase τοῦτον ... τὸν ... ὑπεριδόντα τοῦ σώματος (= him ... the one ... overlooking his body) which brackets the conditional sentence is a descriptive circumlocution for Callimachus. The verb ὑπεροράω ([literally] = over-look) with the genitive has the strong sense of *disdain* (LSJ, ὑπεροράω II.2.b).

31

Cynegirus' fight from land against a ship which Euphorion had made so much of and depicted as creative boldness (A. 8, 11, 28, 33, 35-38, 44) is here denigrated as an act motivated by caution. The second clause in apposition to the first makes this clear:

ἐκ γῆς / ἐκ τοῦ βεβαίου καὶ πολλοῦ
(= from land / from the secure and open [spot])
πρὸς ναῦν / πρὸς τὸν ἐν τῷ σφαλερῷ καὶ στενῷ
(= against a ship / against the [enemy?] in the perilous and narrow [spot]).

The substantized adjective βέβαιος (= firm, sure), which does not connote merely *terra firma* but *security* (LSJ, βέβαιος I.1 and 3), is contrasted with σφαλερός (= dangerous, vulnerable; √ σφάλλω [= make to fall, overthrow]). Though there is no parallel elsewhere in Polemo for πολύς as it is used here, its sense must be *wide, open* (LSJ, πολύς I.4) as its antonym στενός (= narrow) makes clear. The imperfect ἐμάχετο is best taken as *conative*: Cynegirus *was trying to fight* — and not doing a very good job of it! — from the safety of open space against a ship whose confined anchorage robbed it of maneuverability. The noun with τόν (after πρός) is indeterminate.   Hinck emended it to τήν to match πρὸς ναῦν in the previous clause.

The imperfect ἐμάχετο in the Cynegirus half of the μέν - δε contrast needs to be supplied with the Callimachus half as well — here, however, better with *durative* sense: Callimachus *continued fighting* against the barbarians who were equally matched (ἰσοστασίους) with him. The picture of an 'equal footing' is then rendered into an understatement by the chain of appositions that follows. Callimachus' opponents: (1) were already masters of the land by virtue of their successful bridgehead, (2) were not cowering in their ships — as was the case with Cynegirus' opponents — but had disembarked from their vessels, (3) had made slaves of the island inhabitants of the Aegean sea (sc. πόντον [= sea] or possibly κόλπον [= gulf] with τὸν Αἰγαῖον; the more common neuter πέλαγος [= sea] cannot stand with the masculine τόν; cf. LSJ, Αἰγαῖος), and (4) were bringing abject terror (κατάπληξιν φοβερὰν) by their plunder of Greece (cf. B 5). Callimachus' opponents were, therefore, in actuality on a *more than equal footing* with him. Others might be intimidated but not Callimachus.

32

Devoid of finite verb, the sentence needs the copula ἦν (= was) to be supplied with the passive participle παρωξυμμένος (= spurred on). The verb serves both the μέν and the δέ clause. From its simplex denominative root ὀξύνω (= sharpen [√ ὀξύς = sharp, keen]) the compound verb παροξύνω ([literally] = over-sharpen) gets the sense of *motivate, stimulate, urge on*. The impersonal agents of the passive παρωξυμμένος are expressed with instrumental datives (ζήλῳ [= by jealousy], φιλοτιμίᾳ [= by ambition], αὐθαιρέτῳ σπουδῇ [= by self-chosen zeal]), the personal agent by ὑπό + genitive (ὑπ' ἄλλου [= by another]) (cf. GG, 1755-1757). Ambition is a typical agent with this verb (cf. φιλοτιμίᾳ, ἥπερ μάλιστα παροξύνει πρὸς τὰ καλὰ καὶ ἔντιμα [= by love of honor which especially motivates to deeds of excellence and renown], Xenophon, *Mem.* 3.3.13; cf. 3.5.3).

Both with the noun ζῆλος (= jealousy) and the verb φιλοτιμέομαι (= be ambitious, emulous) the object of emulation is typically indicated with a preposition — here πρός (LSJ, ζῆλος I.2-3; φιλοτιμέομαι I.2).

The argument that Callimachus was not 'other directed' but rather 'inner directed' is meant to counter-act the same assertion made about Cynegirus (cf. A 5, 18, 19). If Cynegirus was motivated "by self-powered valor" (αὐτοκράτορι ἀρετῇ, A 18), then Callimachus was driven "by self-chosen zeal" (αὐθαιρέτῳ σπουδῇ, B 31). Indeed, the two expressions are virtually synonymous.

Regarding valor Callimachus was the paradigm (παράδειγμα), Cynegirus merely a copy (μίμημα). It is quite common, particularly in Platonic thought, to find the terms παράδειγμα and μίμημα linked as a conceptual pair (e.g., μίμημα παραδείγματος [= imitation of a pattern], Plato, *Tim.* 49e1; τὰ γὰρ μιμήματα ... τὰ δὲ παραδείγματα [= the copies ... and the models], Philo, *Som.* 1.206) whereby παράδειγμα is interchangable with ἀρχέτυπον (= archetype) (e.g., Philo, *Her.* 127; *Cong.* 8; *Aet.* 15) and μίμημα synonymous with terms like εἴκων (= likeness), ἄγαλμα (= image), and ἀπεικόνισμα (= representation) (e.g., Plato, *Tim.* 29b4; 37c8; Philo, *Mos.* 2.11, 74). Inherent in this conceptual pair are several aspects which aid Polemo's argument:

(1) the παράδειγμα has *primacy*, the μίμημα only *secondary* character (cf. κατὰ τὰς τοῦ παραδείγματος συμμετρίας ... τὴν τοῦ μιμήματος γένεσιν ἀπεργάζηται [= he produces the imitation according to the proportions of the original model], Plato, *Soph.* 235d-e; μίμημα καλὸν οὐκ ἄν ποτε γένοιτο δίχα καλοῦ παραδείγματος [= a beautiful copy would never be produced apart from a beautiful pattern], Philo, *Op.* 16; cf. 139).

(2) The μίμημα is *inferior* to the παράδειγμα (cf. ἀπολείπεται ... μίμημα ἀρχετύπου παραδείγματος [= the imitation falls short of the archetypal model], Philo, *Post.* 105; ἀποδεῖ γὰρ τὰ μιμήματα τῶν ἀρχετύπων [= the copies are inferior to the archetypes], Philo, *Op.* 141).

(3) The thought pair fits well with the argument just voiced that Cynegirus was driven by *emulousness* (cf. πᾶν δὲ μίμημα ποθεῖ τοῦτο, οὗπέρ ἐστι μίμημα [= every copy longs for that of which it is a copy], Philo, *L. A.* 2.4.5).

The whole point of the model-copy argument is that it would be absurd to pick the imitation over the real thing (cf. ἄτοπον ... μίμημα ἀρχετύπων φέρεσθαι πλέον [= monstrous ... to prefer an imitation over originals], Philo, *Mig.* 12).

The speaker is racing at this point: in the two previous sentences the copula ἦν was omitted, now a transitive verb is missing — something like [ἐπ-]ἔδωκε (= gave [freely]) must be supplied for both the μέν and δέ clauses (cf. τὰς χεῖρας ἐπεδίδου τὰς ἑαυτοῦ μεμαχημένος [= he was giving freely of his very own hands as he fought], A 28).

The assertion that Cynegirus surrendered only the hand (τὴν χεῖρα μόνην) — singular! — contradicts Euphorion's repeated claim that Cynegirus lost both hands — plural! — (A 10, 11, 1, 23, 24, 28, 31, 32, 34, 36, 37, 39, 43, 44, 45, 49). Callimachus' father speaks consistently only of Cynegirus' severed *hand* (B 13, 33, 37, 39, 42, 43, 44, 45, 60, 63). This singular poses an intentional diminishing of Cynegirus' heroism as represented by Euphorion.

The gender of πᾶσι is indeterminate. (a) If masculine, πᾶσι [τοῖς βαρβάροις or πολεμίοις] would be a dative of person with the verb μάχομαι: he fought with (i.e., *against*) all [the barbarians] (cf. ἀνθρώποις μαχόμενος [= fighting against men], B 10; Δαρείῳ καὶ θανάτῳ μεμαχημένε [= having fought against Darius and death], B 52; cf. LSJ, μάχομαι I.1). This would be parallel to and a variant of πρὸς πάνθ᾽ ... ἔθνη (= against all the hordes) in the next sentence. However, this interpretation leaves opaque the connected clause καὶ τοῦ πολέμου πάντα μείζονα. (b) If neuter, πᾶσι [τοῖς μέρεσι] is an instrumental dative: he fought with (i.e., *using*) all his body parts (cf. ὅλῳ τῷ σώματι ... μεμάχηται [= he fought with his whole body], A 32; LSJ, μάχομαι I.1). This is the preferable interpretation for two reasons: (1) It does justice to the γάρ which as a rule picks up on what precedes and (2) it makes sense out of the καὶ τοῦ πολέμου πάντα μείζονα which follows. The πάντα is neuter, plural, nominative (πάντα [τὰ μέρη]) and the comparative μείζονα denotes excess (cf. *GG*, 1082c): all [his body parts] were adequate for, more than enough for the fight (cf. H. G. Liddel and R. Scott, *An Intermediate Greek-English Lexicon* [Oxford: Clarendon, 1964] μέγας, C.1). The point of the argument is to rebut Euphorion's claims that victory resulted from Cynegirus' hands (A 1, 10, 11, 31–32, 34–37, 42–43).

The argument shifts from the soldiers' own bodies to the objects of their endeavors. Whereas Cynegirus attacked *one* ship, and one that was trying to get away at that (μιᾷ τῶν ἀναγομένων ... νηί), Callimachus stood up against *all* the foreigners *at once* (πάνθ᾽ ὁμοῦ τὰ ... ἔθνη), and indeed even as they were attacking. The king (βασιλεύς) is, of course, Darius. παρετάξατο (√ παρατάσσω [reflexive middle] = draw up oneself in battle-order) means *he stood prepared* (LSJ, παρατάσσω I.2). The expression πρὸς πάνθ᾽ ... ἔθνη παρετάξατο is a variation of the earlier τοῖς βαρβάροις παρετάξατο (B 25). Polemo's style always seeks variety of expression.

33

Immediately preceding were four μέν - δέ contrasts (two with names, two with articles). The continuation with another ὁ μέν (referring to Cynegirus) is anomalous because no counter-balancing ὁ δέ follows.

Although usually said of persons, the alpha-privative ἀνόητος (= devoid of νοῦς [sense], unintelligent) is here applied to a thing, namely, Cynegirus' ἐπιβολή (= attack) (cf. ἐπιθυμίας ἀνοήτους [= senseless desires], 1 Tim 6:9). The adjective is in the predicative position (ἀνόητον ... τὴν ἐπιβολὴν) — [literally] "the one made his attack completely senseless" — but it is smoother to render it as an attributive.

To describe Cynegirus' hope (ἐλπίς) as impossible (ἀδύνατος) is to say that he could not have reasonably expected to attain anything with his attack (cf. πρὸς ἀδυνάτους ἤρτηται ... ἔλπις [= hope attached to the impossible], Pseudo-Dionysius Areopagita, *E. H.* 7.3.6). The phenomenon of empty hope (κενὴ ἐλπίς) had long been pondered by the Greek tradition (cf. e.g., Hesiod, *Op.* 498; Sophocles, *Aj.* 477–478; Marcus Aurelius Antonius 14; *An. Gr.* 7.376). The poets particularly observed the folly of pursuing seductive hopes (e.g., φῦλον ἐν ἀνθρώποισι ματαιότατον, ὅστις ... μεταμώνια θηρεύων ἀκράντοις ἐλπίσιν [= a foolish company among men who ... pursue idle dreams in hopes that shall not be fulfilled], Pindar, *Pyth.* 3.21–23; τυφλὰς ἐν αὐτοῖς [θνητοῖς] ἐλπίδας κατῴκισα [= I have made blind hopes to dwell in mortals], Aeschylus, *Pr.* 250; ἐλπὶς οὐδὲν ὠφελεῖ [= hope profits nothing], Sophocles, *frag.* 205). Plato labeled hope εὐπαράγωγος (= easily leading astray) and said that the one full of empty hopes was the fool (τὸν ἀνοηταίνοντα ... ἀνοήτων ... ἐλπίδων μεστόν) (*Tim.* 69d; *Phlb.* 12d; cf. Pindar, *Ol.* 12.5–7; Aeschylus, *Ag.* 505;). The Greeks' sober critique of ἐλπίς forms the backdrop of Polemo's remark about Cynegirus' impossible hope. Polemo's subsequent disparaging remark about "such a swollenness of hope" (τοσούτῳ ὄγκῳ τῆς ἐλπίδος, B 34) is also to be seen in this tradition.

When Euphorion credited Cynegirus with τόλμα it was always in a positive sense (= courage) and often coupled with ἀρετή (= valor) (A 5, 14, 22, 20, 25). When Callimachus' father, however, speaks of Cynegirus' τόλμα it is shaded negatively (= reckless daring) and coupled with pejorative concepts like ἀνόητος (= senseless), ἠλίθιος (= foolish), ἀλαζών (= pretentious), ἄπορος (= impracticable), μάταιος (= futile), μανία (= madness), ἄχρηστος αὐθάδεια (= useless wilfulness) (B 33, 35).

The folly of Cynegirus' attempt is now unrolled in a flurry of rhetorical questions, conditional sentences, gnomic sayings, and brusk judgments (B 33–37).

In the first question ἄν has been omitted; it needs to be supplied with ἐλάβετο in line with the following ἂν ἐγένετο (*GG*, 1767). The question expresses past potential (*GG*, 1784) and is rhetorical: "How (πῶς) would he have captured a ship *with a hand* (χειρὶ is instrumental dative)?" The expected answer is οὔπως (= no way!).

The following rhetorical question is in the form of an apodosis of a contrary-to-fact condition with a double protasis. This second question expands on the first and by making it more specific also makes Cynegirus' assault more absurd. The ship (ναῦς) is now described as trireme (τριήρης), a vessel well over 100 feet long manned by a crew of some 200 (C. G. Starr, "Trireme," *OCD*, 1095). Further, the χειρὶ (= with a hand) has become δακτύλοις (= with fingers). Thus, in the second question the ship has grown, the hand has shrunk, and the whole endeavor looks even more ridiculous. To the rhetorical question, "Who (τίς) could have held a trireme?" the obvious answer is οὔτις (= no one!).

As with τόλμα so with τόλμημα: The τόλμημα of Cynegirus which Euphorion had spoken of positively (= courageous act, A 24) Callimachus' father regards negatively (= reckless act, B 33, 34, 36). It was just plain ἠλίθιον (= foolish), a word which in modern Greek still describes stupidity.

The past contrary-to-fact condition explored the possibility that Cynegirus might have been ignorant of the futility of his action (cf. εἰ μὲν ἠγνόησε [= if he had been ignorant]). Now a past simple condition poses the alternative that he did indeed recognize the futility of what he was doing (cf. εἰ δ᾽ εἶδεν [= if he did see]) but acted nevertheless. If he was cognizant of the impossibilities (ἀμήχανα) then his action was worse than a silly τόλμημα, it was a προσποίησις (= affectation) which is described as ἀλαζών (= pretentious), an adjective which cannot be used of valor (οὔτε ἀλαζὼν ... ἀρετή).

In the series of past tenses the present tense κρατεῖ (= prevails) stands out — almost as if the sentence were a parenthetical aside about the ongoing human condition, the ever recurring flaw of succumbing to folly.

In summary: in either case (whether ignorance or cognizance) Cynegirus' action was but a display of an impracticable gesture (ἐπίδειξις τοῦ ἀπόρου σχήματος) and the thought behind it vain (ματαία ἡ σκέψις).

This whole section denegrating Cynegirus' action is peppered with a series of predicate adjectives preceeding their respective nouns (ἀνόητον ... τὴν ἐπιβολὴν / ἠλίθιον τὸ τόλμημα / ἀλαζὼν ἡ προσποίησις / οὐκ ἀσφαλὴς οὐδὲ ἀναγκαία ἡ ἐπίδειξις / ματαία ἡ σκέψις / οὔτε ἀλαζὼν οὔτε ἀνόητος ἀρετή). The *pre*-position of the adjectives gives them emphasis and the repetition of this construction has the rhetorical effect of adding still more weight to the negative modifiers.

The wording οἷοι δὲ καὶ has troubled previous editors. Because of the δέ, which Orellius (p. 102) took as adversative, he suspected a corruption and wanted to emend the οἷοι to read ἄνοοι (√ ἄνοος / ἄνους): ἄνοοι δὲ καὶ τυφλοὶ (= but senseless and blind). In his edition Hinck (p. 27) emended the δέ to an emphatic δή (= certainly, in fact). This is not an implausible restoration — already D had read it so — it mitigates the problem and fits the exclamation nicely. The text, however, can stand as it is without emendation. There are a number of δὲ καί juxtapositions in the declamations (A 10, 15, 15,31, 47; B 33, 40, 45); in three instances the δέ is not adversative, but copulative (A 10, 15, 47), and that seems to be the case here.

The οἷοι in an independent sentence introduces an exclamation of astonishment (LSJ, οἷος I.1). Such sentences are common for interjections (*GG*, 2682). In contrast, however, to Polemo's other exclamations of this type (A 38, 41; B 37) this sentence has the ring of a gnomic saying. Following common rhetorical practice Polemo often rounds off a thought with such *sententiae*.

The combination τυφλοὶ πόνοι (= blind pains) is striking. It could possibly be a kind of brachylogy whereby two thoughts are condensed into one: e.g., *pains entered into blindly* or *pains caused by blindness*. Polemo, however, exhibits little use of this kind of *praegnans constructio* elsewhere. Hence, it is probably better to take τυφλοὶ as a genuine attributive adjective. Then "blind" would have the sense of *closed off, with no outlet* (cf. τυφλὴ ῥύμη [= blind alley], *P. Oxy.* I, 99.9 or τυφλαὶ ὁδοί [= blind {i.e. dead-end} streets], Aristotle, *H. A.* 533b3), in other words, *inescapable* (LSJ, τυφλός II.2). The notion of impossible desires (ἀδυνάτους ἐπιθυμίας) is a take-off on the earlier mention of Cynegirus' impossible hope (ἀδύνατος ἐλπίς).

34

The precise import of the χρή sentence almost defies exegesis. The use of χρή (= it is necessary) with the infinitive (here ὁρᾶν [= to see]) is standard (*GG*, 1562, 1985.b) and belongs to Polemo's repertoire (A 1, 16; B 17, 62). When the subject of an infinitive — ordinarily expressed with the accusative — is omitted, as here, it needs to be supplied according to sense (*GG*, 1562; 1985b.c). But what is to be supplied? — "It is necessary [for anyone acting like Cynegirus] to see ..."? or "It is necessary [for every observer today] to see ..."?

In light of the apparent contrast with τέλος the πρότερον more likely denotes temporal sequence (= *earlier*, as in A 22; B 21, 28, 29) than rank order (= *superior*, as in A 25; B 18, 21): One ought not to look at something πρότερον (= preceding) as if it were τέλος (= end, cf. A 21, 29).

The combination οὐδέ - οὔτε (= not - nor) is very unusual. Hinck reversed the order trying to achieve smoother Greek (οὔτε - οὐδέ = neither ... and not ...). Moreover, despite grammatical parallelism the sense of the members remains uncertain:

τέχνην ἔργοις ἐπιτιθεμένην   (= skill applied in deeds)

ἀρετὴν λόγοις ἀπειργομένην   (= valor barred by rational faculties)

Whose skill and valor are referred to? That of Cynegirus? of Callimachus? of soldiers in general? of the enemy? Does the second phrase mean to describe a valor on the part of the Persians being prevented by the words of Cynegirus? Or does λόγοις denote something like calculations (LSJ, λόγος I.1)?   To ἀρετὴν λόγοις ἀπειργομένην Orellius (p. 102) says: "*virtutem rationibus i.e. consilio et prudentia ab ἀπείργω*" (= valor deserted by the faculties of reason, i.e., by good sense and prudence).

The copula ἐστί must be supplied with εἰ δυνατὸν ἔτι ... (= if [it is] still possible). The neuter predicate adjectives δυνατόν (= possible) and ληπτόν (= to be apprehended by the senses) show that the subject of ἐστί is neuter or impersonal. Both gender and sense seem to point to the infinitive ὁρᾶν (= seeing): if seeing is indeed possible and understandable for an inanimate nature (φύσει) — seeing, of course, is possible for a man (ἀνδρί) who is able and tries (δυναμένῳ καὶ πειρωμένῳ). Who is this ἀνήρ? Cynegirus? Any man?

The analysis of this sentence leads at best to uncertainty, at worst to exasperation. The English presented here makes no pretense to accuracy.

The twofold interrogative πῶς (= how) is held in abeyance until after the nominative subject of the double question is named: the entire ship (ἡ ναῦς ὅλη) full (μεστή) of crew (πληρώματος) and well-trained oarsmen (εἰρεσίας συγκεκροτημένης). The term πλήρωμα (= that which fills [√ πληρόω = make full]) when used of a single ship refers to the *full complement*, i.e., the *crew* (as in B 36; cf. LSJ, πλήρωμα 3). The abstract noun εἰρεσία (= rowing [√ ἐρέσσω = row]) is used here in the collective sense of *rowers* (as in A 23; LSJ, εἰρεσία II.1). The passive participle of συγκροτέω (= train) is commonly employed in miltary language to describe *disciplined* soldiers (cf. συγκεκροτημένοι τὰ τοῦ πολέμου [= well-trained in matters of war], Demosthenes 2.17; τὰ πλήθη ταῦτα τοῦ στρατοῦ ... ἐς πολεμικὴν ἄσκησιν συγκεκρότητο [= this large body of troops ... had been trained to war fitness], Herodian 7.2.2). In naval terminology in particular it refers to *disciplined* crews (cf. συγκεκροτημένας ναῦς [= well-trained ships], Xenophon, *Hel.* 6.2.12; πληρώματα συγκεκροτημένα [= well-trained crews], Polybius 1.61.3). Hence, all the vocabulary of the extended subject is designed to underscore the gross mis-match between Cynegirus and the ship he attacked.

The questions may be read in either of two ways: (1) πῶς ἦν ... (past factual = how was ... ?) or (2) πῶς ἦν [ἄν] ... (past potential = how would ... have been ...?). The ἄν may be omitted when it can be supplied from the context (*GG*, 1767, 1784). Either reading fits well with the previous sentences (cf. πῶς ... ἐλάβετο; τίς δὲ ἂν ἐγένετο ...; B 33).

The two predicate adjectives ἐπιλήψιμος (= vulnerable to capture [√ ἐπιλαμβάνω = lay hold on]) and ἀγώγιμος (= liable to seizure [√ ἀγωγή = forcible seizure]) are virtually synonymous. Pleonasm is characteristic of Polemo's style.

The pair of adjectives is followed by a pair of noun phrases. Sarcasm drips from the first phrase, τοσούτῳ ὄγκῳ τῆς ἐλπίδος (= by such a swelling of hope). The term ὄγκος (= mass) has a distinctively negative ring. In a literal sense among medical writers it was commonly connected with medical pathologies — cf. *onco*logy — and painful swellings (cf. ὁ παρὰ φύσιν ὄγκος [= the distension contrary to nature], Galen, *Ars Med.* 1.355, 357, 411; similarly Hippocrates, *Epid.* 6.3.18; Diocles Medicus, *frag.* 43). In a figurative sense it could connote self-importance, pretension, or even bombast (LSJ, ὄγκος II.2 and 3). The combination ὄγκος τῆς ἐλπίδος is, however, unusual and does not appear to derive from classical Greek. Possibly it may represent the Hellenization of a popular Latin expression: *spes inflata* (= inflated hope) (cf. *inflasse vana spe* [= to inflate with vain hope], Livy 35.49.4; *mendaciis ... regis spem inflabat* [= with lies he inflated the hope of the king], Livy 35.42.5; *spe falsa ... animos rumor inflasset* [= a rumor inflated your spirits with a false hope], Cicero, *Pis.* 36.89; cf. Cicero, *Mur.* 15.33; Curtius 3.2.10; 5.10.3). In any case, whether it is a Latinism or his own coinage, Polemo's expression denigrates Cynegirus' inflated hope as 'out of sync' with reality.

Scorn and disdain also exude from the second noun phrase, τῇ προσβολῇ τοῦ τολμήματος (= by the assault of recklessness) (cf. note on τόλμημα in B 33).

35

The first sentence in B 35 was aptly characterized by Orellius (p. 104) as a *locus corruptissimus et misere lacerus* (= a thoroughly corrupted and miserably mangled passage). The skeletal structure of the sentence is fixed by ἤ ... ἤ (= either ... or) — a construction used only one other time in the declamations (A 41; cf. A 18). In the first clause something has clearly dropped out after τήν though the length of the omission is unknowable. The negative μή indicates the omission of a mood other than indicative. The article τήν expects a feminine singular accusative noun — προσβολήν (= attack)? ἐλπίδα (= hope)? Any reconstruction reaching beyond these indicators is groundless conjecture (cf. the imaginative attempts of Orellius, pp. 106, xiv). The original text is beyond recovery.

Nevertheless, the sense of the passage is obviously an out-and-out dismissal of Cynegirus' actions as having lacked any prospect for success and as devoid of any military significance. This is made clear by the substantized adjective τὸ μάταιον (= the futility) together with the string of alpha-privatives, ἄπορον (= impracticable), ἄφρον (= senseless), and ἀπέραντος (= unaccomplishable). Conceivably one could take this last adjective in the lexicographically attested sense of *impassible* or *not allowing escape* (cf. LSJ, sub verbum II). Aeschylus had used the word to describe Tartarus beneath Hades from which there is no exit (*Pr.* 153) or to describe a net of calamity (δίκτυον ἄτης) in which one gets entrapped by one's own folly (ἀνοία) (*Pr.* 1078). The sense would then be that Cynegirus undertook an action from which he could not extricate himself. In light of the other terms in the string, however, it seems more likely that Polemo has invested the adjective ἀπέραντος (√ περαίνω = finish, accomplish) with the otherwise undocumented sense of *unfulfillable*.

With the impersonal verbal adjective νοητέον (= one must conceive) the copula ἐστί is omitted as is typical (GG, 944.b). The objects (τὴν ἀνόητον τόλμαν [= the senseless daring] and τὴν ἄχρηστον αὐθάδειαν [= the useless willfulness]) stand in the accusative because that is the case required by νοέω (= consider, deem), the verb from which the verbal adjective derives (GG, 2152). The denigration of Cynegirus' action continues with more alpha-privatives (ἀνόητον [= sense-less] and ἄχρηστον [= use-less]) and derogatory nouns (μανίαν [= madness] and αὐθάδειαν [= willfulness]).

36

The potential optative (εἴποι + ἄν [= might say]) indicates a possible scenario that might arise (GG, 1824). The construction εὖ φρονῶν αὐτῷ (adverb + verb + dative) is the classical way of saying *be well disposed toward* (cf. εὖ φρονῶν ἐμοί [= being well-minded toward me], Aeschylus, *Ag.* 1436; ᾗσι τ᾽ ἐὺ φρονέῃσι [= toward whom she is well-minded], Homer, *Od.* 7.74).

The imaginary sympathizer poses seven questions which display in fact very little sympathy. His words, like those of Job's friends, do more to chide than empathize. There is a twofold *why* ...? (τί ...;), a twofold *what* ...? (τίς ...;), a twofold *can* ...? (δύναται ...;), and a single *will* ...? (περινοστήσεις ...;).

In the first pair of questions the interrogative τί is used in the adverbial sense of *why?* (cf. A 27; B 56; LSJ, τις, τι B.I.8.e), much a like a shortened form of διὰ τί (= on account of what? LSJ, διά, B.III.2). The two questions form a synonymous parallelism, with the second question clarifying the first:

(1) τί ταῦτα μωραίνεις;

    (= why are you being crazy regarding these things?)

(2) τί δ᾽ ἐπιχειρεῖς ναῦν κατασχεῖν ἀνθρωπίνῃ δεξιᾷ;

    (= why are you trying to restrain a ship with a human right hand?)

They are linked by having the same subject, Cynegirus, contained in both verbs (μωραίνεις and ἐπιχειρεῖς [= why are *you* playing the fool? why are *you* attempting?]) and the same object (ταῦτα = ναῦν κατασχεῖν ἀνθρωπίνῃ δεξιᾷ [these things = to restrain a ship with a human right hand]). From a strictly grammatical perspective the active verb μωραίνεις must be construed not as transitive (= make foolish) but as intransitive (= be foolish), and thus the accusative ταῦτα not as direct object of the verb, but as accusative of respect: Why are you playing the fool regarding these things? (cf. οὐδεὶς ... ταῦτα μωραίνει [= no one acts crazy in these matters], Euripides, *frag.* 282.22). The second question exhibits a standard classical construction: ἐπιχειρεῖς (= attempt) + supplementary infinitive (κατασχεῖν [= to restrain]) (LSJ, ἐπιχειρέω I.4) which for its part stands with an instrumental dative (ἀνθρωπίνῃ δεξιᾷ [= with an ordinary right hand]) (LSJ, κατέχω I.b).

The expression φύσιν οὐκ ἔχει (= it does not have nature) is an idiom meaning *it is unnatural, contrary to nature* (cf. Plato, *Resp.* 489b; Demosthenes 2.26; also in positive form, Herodotus 2.45; Plato, *Resp.* 473a). The first two questions together with this idiomatic conclusion emphasize the *illogic* of Cynegirus' actions.

This point is underscored then by a pair of questions in which the interrogative τίς is used adjectively (*GG*, 1262):

(3) τίς τοῦτο Γλαῦκος πόντιος;   (= *what* { } Glaucus of the sea?)

(4) τίς Τρίτων ἐποίησε;   (= *what* Triton did {this}?)

These two questions are linked by having the same verb (ἐποίησε [= did]), the same object (τοῦτο [= this], i.e., restraining a ship with one hand), and similar subjects, Glaucus and Triton, — both sea deities.

The third and fourth questions operate with the kind of rhetorical argument that Aristotle (*Rh.* 1397b4) called τὸ μᾶλλον καὶ ἧττον (= the more and the less). To be more precise, Polemo's argumentation represents a logic of *a majore ad minus* (= from the greater to the lesser) and it stands in direct line with the example offered by Aristotle (ibid.): εἰ μηδ᾽ οἱ θεοὶ πάντα ἴσασι, σχολῇ οἵ γε ἄνθρωποι (= if not even the gods know everything, hardly can men).

The epithet πόντιος (= of the sea), though here attached grammatically only to Glaucus (cf. Athenaeus 7.296b), belonged traditionally also to the other two gods named here, Poseidon (cf. *H. Hom.* 22.3; Sophocles, *O.C.* 1072) and his son Triton "who owns the depth of the sea" (ὅστε θαλάσσης πυθμέν᾽ ἔχων, Hesiod, *Th.* 931-932).

For Glaucus, whose name is etymologically transparent (= gleaming or *blue-green sea*; LSJ, γλαυκός), the Greeks recounted diverse genealogies including one that made him a son of Poseidon and the sea nymph Naïs (Athenaeus 7.296a-c). Appearances and oracles of this fish-form sea daimon (Plato, *Resp.* 10.611d) were thought to bring good or bad luck to sailors (Pausanius 9.22.7). The extensive lore about Glaucus was widely attested in both the Greek and Latin worlds (cf. H. von Geisau, "Glaukos (1)," *KP* 2.810; M. O. Jentel, "Glaukos," *LIMC* IV.1.271-273), yet despite that Polemo knows of no tradition which credits Glaucus with trying to hold back a trireme with his bare hands.

The name of Triton, the sea divinity, goes back to the same pre-Hellenic root as that of his sea-goddess mother, Amphitrite — 'trit' may mean something like 'water.' He was often depicted as merman with lower body in fish form and upper body in human form — a δεινὸς θεός (= fearful god, Hesiod, *Th.* 930-933). Tritons are, along with centaurs, the only composite figures portrayed by high classical art. Surviving reliefs, sculptures and vase paintings show that Triton was often thought of as having apotropaic function (*GGR*, I, 243; H. Herter, "Triton," *KP* 5.967-969). Yet here too, despite the many various Triton myths, Polemo can find none in which this god tried to restrain a ship with his hands.

If sea gods never tried to hold back a ship with bare hands, how then — following the logic of *a majore ad minus* — how then could a mere human like Cynegirus expect to do so?!

The third pair of questions, expressed without any interrogative pronouns, expects a simple *yes* or *no* (*GG*, 2638, 2641). The answer awaited is, of course, obviously *no*.

(5) μόνον δύναται μειράκιον ναῦν ἐπαγαγεῖν;

(= Can a mere lad draw in a ship?)

(6) ἢ Ποσειδῶνος δεξιὰ ἀνέμοις ἁμιλλᾶσθαι;

(= or a right hand compete with Poseidon's winds?)

The two questions are linked by having the same main verb (δύναται [= can]) and parallel supplementary infinitives (ἐπαγαγεῖν / ἁμιλλᾶσθαι [= to bring in / to compete against]).

In the emphatic position stands μόνον (= alone, by himself). The term μειράκιον (= lad [diminutive from μεῖραξ = boy]) sometimes denoted a stage of development between παῖς (= child) and νεανίσκος (= youth) (Arrian, *Epict, Dis.* 3.9.8), and sometimes it was used synonymously with νεανίσκος (Menander, *Georg.* 67-69). Lucian used the term for a twenty year old (*Dial. Mort.: Simylus and Polystratus* 9[19].362). Polemo, for his part, envisions Cynegirus in his late teens (cf. note at A 5).

Previous editors were bothered by Ποσειδῶνος (= of Poseidon). Jacobs proposed emending it to παιδός (= of a boy) and Hinck (p. 28) marked it for deletion altogether. Emendations, however, are unnecessary — Poseidon was traditionally linked with the winds of the sea (cf. Homer, *Od.* 292–296, 304–305, 317, 330-333; Herodotus 7.191–193).

The series of paired questions is rounded off finally with a single query:

(7) περινοστήσεις τοσούτῳ πληρώματι;

(= will you circumvent so great a crew?)

The verb has the metaphorical sense of *circumvent* (LSJ, περινοστέω 1) and the crew (πλήρωμα) are those just named — both the human oarsmen (εἰρεσία, B 34) as well as Poseidon's winds (ἄνεμοι, B 36) which propel the ship.

Just as a summary statement was inserted after the second question, so now a concluding statement wraps up the whole series of questions:

'Your action, Cynegirus, will not have the desired effect: Rather than you holding back the ship, it will instead sail off taking you with it; rather than you capturing it, it will take you prisoner. And not only is your action counter-productive, it also has a comic effect: you will be dangling (ἐξηρτημένος) from the stern, taken captive by a wooden carving (ἀκροστόλιον), and all that unbeknownst to the enemy' (λήσεις [= you will escape notice], LSJ, λανθάνω, A.2.b).

37

The phrase ἐπὶ ναυσὶ μάχαι (= fights against ships) does not here include ordinary naval battles (ship vs. ship at sea), but refers only to land soldiers fighting against ships, as the τοιαύτην (= such [a fight]) makes clear.

322   *The Severed Hand and the Upright Corpse*

The history of post-Marathon warfare does, of course, include records of anti-ship battles from land (e.g., Thucydides 4.14; 7.36-74; Diodorus Siculus 13.9-19; 17.41-46), but from the vantage point of a speaker in 490 BCE it is a vast overstatement to say that *many* (πολλαί) such have occurred. Nevertheless, this πολλαί has found its way into the speech of Callimachus' father because it was a frequent rhetorical convention in Polemo's day (cf. H. J. Cadbury, "Commentary on the Preface of Luke," *The Beginnings of Christianity* [Grand Rapids: Baker, 1979] 2.492-493; J. Bauer, "πολλοί, Luk. 1,1," *NovT* 4 (1960), 263-266). Nonetheless, Polemo's 'mouthpiece' could cite one pre-Marathon example recorded in Homer (it was typical for the name Ὅμηρος to be anarthrous so as to avoid hiatus, cf. J. F. Kindstrand, *Homer in der zweiten Sophistik* [Studia Graeca Upsaliensia 7], Uppsala: KåWe Composer, 1973, pp. 13-14). The *Iliad* (13-16) recounts a long pitched battle in which the Trojans attacked the Greeks and their ships. Polemo could point out that "no one then had tried to *pull* those ships" (conative imperfect: οὐδέ γε εἶλκέ τις ἐκείνας) because Homer had described at length how the Greek ships had already been beached (*Il.* 13.681-682; 14.30-36, 75-79, 99-102; 15.384-389, 435). The Trojan goal was rather to set the Greek ships ablaze. Hector in particular was intent on burning the ships (cf. Ἕκτορα ... νῆας ἐνιπρῆσαι ... ἐμβάλοι αἰθόμενον δαλὸν νήεσσι [= that Hector fire the ships ... should cast a blazing torch upon the ships], 13.319-320; Ἕκτωρ ... ἐνιπρῆσαι πυρὶ νῆα [= that Hector burn the ship with fire], 15.415-417; Ἕκτωρ δὲ πρύμνηθεν ἐπεὶ λάβεν οὐχὶ μεθίει, ἄφλαστον μετὰ χερσὶν ἔχων, Τρωσὶν δὲ κέλευεν· οἴσετε πῦρ [= when Hector grabbed the stern, he did not loose his hold, but kept the ensign in his hands and called to the Trojans, "bring fire"], 15.716-718; cf. also 15.419-421, 701-702, 731; 16.80-81, 122-127, 293). Polemo sums up this entire Trojan endeavor tidily with πῦρ ἐνέβαλε, δᾷδας ἐκόμιζεν (= he was throwing fire, he was bringing torches). The sequence of Polemo's two phrases is a *hysteron proton* — the natural chronological sequence is reversed to put the more important item first (*GG*, 3030). In keeping with the Homeric reference Polemo employs the archaic δᾷδες (plural of δαΐς = fire-brand) instead of the more pedestrian λαμπάδες (plural of λαμπάς = torch) which was current in his own day (cf. A. Oepke, λάμπω ... λαμπάς, *TWNT* 4.17-18).

Rhetoricians of the Second Sophistic were steeped in Homer and often cited him as primary authority to support their point (cf. J. F. Kindstrand, *Homer in der zweiten Sophistik* [Studia Graeca Upsaliensia 7], Uppsala: KåWe Composer, 1973). Homer's description of the Trojan assault on the Greek ships (*Il.* 13-16) was a rich source of material for sophist rhetoric (cf.

Kindstrand, op. cit., pp. 21-22; 51-52; 80-81). To cite but one example, Dio Chrysostom mentions Hector ὅπου γε τὰς ναῦς ἐμπίμπρησιν (= where he was setting fire to the ships, 21.16) or when παρὰ σμικρὸν ἦλθεν ἐμπρῆσαι τὸν ναύσταθμον (= he barely missed burning the beached fleet, 52.10). Thus, Polemo's reference to this 'land battle against ships' borders on the hackneyed.

The point of Polemo's Homeric example is summarized in a succinct sentence which wedges verb and object (κατέχει ναῦν [= restrains a ship]) between the two halves of the sundered subject (αὕτη μόνη / ἡ λαβή [= this alone / the grip]). The striking rhetorical effect produced by this bracketing technique and the emphasis on the noun λαβή by postponing it until the end cannot be reproduced accurately in English. The memorable point is that even the mighty Hector — the one meant by the indefinite τις — would not have tried Cynegirus' scheme, for he too well knew that the only grip (λαβή) which can restrain a ship is that of fire, not of fingers. The comparing or contrasting of historical persons (here Cynegirus) with Homeric figures (in this case, Hector) was common practice in the Second Sophistic (cf. J. F. Kindstrand, op. cit., pp. 34-36; 62-64; 89-90). Polemo stands firmly in this tradition.

Cynegirus is called τολμηρός (= *daring* in the negative sense of *reckless*, cf. B 24, 37, 50) in line with the pejorative comments about his τόλμα and τόλμημα (cf. the note at B 33).

Here κατεφρόνει (+ genitive) appears to be a conative imperfect with desiderative sense (= he *wanted* to disgregard, care nothing for) (cf. BDR, 326; LSJ, καταφρονέω I.1; BAGD, καταφρονέω 2). The ἠπίστατο may be taken (a) as an imperfect of description (*GG*, 1899) offering a reason for the main action (= *throughout* the battle he did not know how to fight wisely) or (b) possibly even as an imperfect of resistance or refusal (*GG*, 1896) hinting at willful stubbornness (= he *would not*, he *refused to* understand how to fight wisely).

The relative pronoun οἵαν (attracted into the gender and case of its following antecedent δεξιάν, *GG*, 2532) introduces an exclamation of astonishment (*GG*, 2682, 2685; LSJ, οἷος I.1). It is characteristic of Polemo's style to punctuate arguments with interjections of this type (cf. A 38, 41; B 33). Literally οἵαν ἀπώλεσεν εἰκῇ δεξιάν says: "What he destroyed in vain — [his] right hand!". The sense in English is: "What a pointless loss of his right hand!"

38

In the phrase διὰ ταῦτα (= on account of these things), which commonly expresses cause or reason (LSJ, διά B.III.2; BAGD, διά B.II.2), the demonstrative pronoun ταῦτα is used loosely. In the only other occurrence of this phrase in Polemo (A 12) the ταῦτα (= these things) refers to the actions of Cynegirus described immediately beforehand (A 8-11). Here in B 38 the ταῦτα refers, of course, to the actions of Callimachus (B 23-32), but between the pronoun and its referent is interposed the long polemic against Cynegirus (B 33-37). This separation makes the διὰ ταῦτα less apt.

Following the critique of Cynegirus (B 33-37) a series of μέν - δέ comparisons of the two heroes unfolds (B 38-40), but these comparisons are syntactically complicated by insertions: In B 38 between the Καλλίμαχος μέν and its counterpart ὁ δὲ σὸς υἱός is interposed a series of three connective δέ's. In B 39 between the Καλλίμαχον μέν and its counterpart Κυναιγείρου δέ is inserted another separate μέν - δέ series (πάντα μέν ..., πάντα δέ ..., πᾶσαι δέ..., ἄπαντα δέ ...). Only in B 40 is the contrast Καλλιμάχου μέν - Κυναίγειρος δέ uncluttered by any similar insertion.

With the genitive (ἁπάντων = everything) ἔτυχεν means *succeeded at, achieved, attained* (LSJ, τυγχάνω B.I and II.2). Instead of an accusative ἅ (= that) as object of the verb ἠθέλησε (= he wished) the genitive ὧν appears because the relative pronoun is attracted into the case of its antecedant, ἁπάντων (*GG*, 2522a, 2524).

The things Callimachus wanted to achieve are itemized as three. The list of aorists is formally marked by a threefold δέ. The items are linked by labial alliteration (π / φ / β) and rounded off with chiasm:

(1) πολλοὺς δὲ ἀφώπλισε   (= he disarmed many),
(2) πάντας δὲ ἐφόβησεν   (= he frightened all),
(3) ἐφύλαξε δὲ τὴν στάσιν   (= he preserved the standing position).

The first and most imaginative item constitutes an irony. Typically the active verb ἀφοπλίζω describes the victor disarming the defeated foe by forcing the hand-over of weapons at the surrender (LSJ, ἀφοπλίζω). Here, however, it connotes Callimachus forcing the Persians to expend all their weapons on him in battle. Through his resolute stand he set himself up as 'target' (σκοπός, B 51) against which the barbarians used up their 'ammunition' (cf. ἀφωπλισμένοι = devoid of weapons, B 13). That his dead corpse 'disarmed' them is a paradox.

The second item, the assertion that Callimachus *terrified all* (cf. B 13, 26), answers Euphorion's sneering question, "What enemies would the one hidden by many arrows have frightened (ἂν ἐφόβησε)?" (A 30) and it counterbalances Euphorion's claims that Cynegirus "terrified many ships" (πολλὰς ... ἐφόβησε ναῦς, A 9) and that the Phoenicians feared (φοβοῦνται) his hand (A 31).

The third item, the upright corpse, is that feature of the Marathonian tradition which in Roman time stood out as especially memorable. This element served as a basic premise for Polemo's declamations (cf. A 7, 2-24, 26-27, 29-31, 45; B 10-12, 14, 38, 43-44, 47-48, 53-56, 58-61).

The demonstrative adverb ὧδε (= in this wise, thus) refers to the three accomplishments of Callimachus just listed.

The labelling of Cynegirus' action as an "afterthought" (ἐπίνοια) is a rebuttal of Euphorion's argument that Cynegirus had conceived his plan of action in advance (περινόησας) while marching across the plains and mountains on his way to Marathon (cf. A 38). The middle ἐκαρπώσατο (√ καρπός = fruit]) has the sense *enjoy the usufruct, reap the fruit* (cf. LSJ, καρπόω, II.2-4)

39

Orellius (p. 108) and Hinck (p. 29) emended οὐδείς (= no-one) into οὐχ εἷς (= not one). This emendation sharpens the point, but it is unncessary. The argument that no-one [singly] killed Callimachus implies and presumes that Cynegirus, by way of contrast, was killed by a single enemy (cf. Κυναιγείρου πεσόντος ὑπὸ πληγῆς μιᾶς [= Cynegirus falling from one blow], B 47) — later mentioned as a lone "someone" (τις, B 63). Euphorion's speech had admitted as much (cf. τις ... ἔκοπτεν [= someone cut off ...], A 42), though the agent of Cynegirus' death is usually hidden behind passive verbs (e.g., ἀποκοπείσης, A 9; κοπείσης, A 10; τεμνομένης, A 25). Conversely, it took a communal effort (κοινὸν ἔργον) of Asia to kill Callimachus (B 39); he was not to be done in by a single blow.

All the spears (δόρατα), javelins (ἀκόντια), arrows (βέλη), and missiles (τοξεύματα) of the enemy were needed to turn Callimachus into a corpse. These weapons are virtually personified and given a hostile intent of their own (cf. φιλοτιμούμενα [= endeavoring]; μαρτυρούμενα [= testifying]; ἀμφισβητοῦντα [= disputing over]).

In the reference to "*this* hand" (τὴν χεῖρα ταύτη) the demonstrative has a disdainful tone of contempt (LSJ, οὗτος, C.3.a; cf. ὁ υἱός σου οὗτος ὁ καταφαγών σου τὸν βίον μετὰ πορνῶν [= *this* son of yours who squandered your property with whores], Luke 15:30; οὐκ εἰμὶ ... ὡς οὗτος ὁ τελώνης [= I am not as *this* tax collector], Luke 18:11).

No subject appears with the verb ἀπέκοψεν (= ? cut off). The scribe of I smoothed the grammar by adding an indefinite τις (= someone) in conformity with other passages (cf. τις ... ἔκοπτεν [= someone cut off], A 42; τις ἀπέκοψε / τις ἔτεμεν [= someone cut off], B 63). The scribe of ρ (→ QR) 'corrected' by changing the verb to ἀπεκοψάν (= they cut off). Whether the subject is missing due to a transmission error or to a lapsus of Polemo himself cannot be said. In any case it is certainly in accord with the sense to supply τις.

The analogy that some enemy cut off Cynegirus' hand *like a piece of wood* (ὥσπερ ξύλον) stands as a conscious demotion of Euphorion's comparison that someone cut it off *like an oak or a pine* (ὥσπερ δρῦν ἢ πεύκην ἔκοπτεν, A 42). His hand resembles more a measly chunk of lifeless wood than the mighty trunk of a majestic tree.

40

The double subject ἡ τόλμα καὶ μάχη has only one article and stands with a singular verb form (ἐβούλετο): the courage and the fight are viewed as a unitary concept in a *hendiadys* (GG, 3025).

τοῦτο ἐβούλετο (= this he wished) is parallel to the earlier ὧν ἠθέλησε (= what he wanted, B 38). The aim in the earlier expression was clarified with a triad of aorist indicatives, here the aim (τοῦτο) is explained with two epexegetical infinitive phrases framed in chiastic word order:

(1) νικῆσαι τὸν βασιλέως στρατὸν　(= to conquer the king's army)

(2) τὴν Ἀττικὴν αὐτοῖς ἄβατον εἶναι (= for Attika to be impassable for them).

The achievement of the first goal, that of winning the victory is claimed by each parent for his son, though Callimachus' father repeats it several times for good measure (A 32; B 17, 40, 60). Polemo uses στρατός and στρατία synonymously (= army, A 8; B 40, 51) as was common (LSJ, sub verba).

The achievement of the second goal, that of making Attica inaccessible (ἄβατον) for the enemy, is claimed only for Callimachus (B 13, 40). The alpha-privative ἄβατος, which often describes mountains that are impassable or rivers that are not fordable (LSJ, ἄβατος 1), suggests that Callimachus blocked the way like a bulwark of nature.

On the other side Cynegirus' actions are circumscribed by three progressives introduced by καὶ ... καὶ ... καὶ (= both ... and ... and):

(1) φεύγοντας ἡμῖν τοὺς βαρβάρους ἀναιρεῖ
want[s] to carry off the barbarians for us as they were fleeing
(2) κατεῖχεν ἐν τῇ χώρᾳ τοὺς πολεμίους
was trying to hold back the enemies in the land
(3) μάχης ἔπραττεν ἀρχὰς δευτέρας
was bringing about the beginnings of a second battle.

The present ἀναιρεῖ looks out of place with all the past tenses in the context. If it is not a medieval transcription error (instead of ἀνῄρει) it may be taken as an historical present for the sake of vividness (*GG*, 1883, 1884). In sense it matches the following imperfects with conative or desiderative sense. In light of the μέν - δέ contrast with ἐβούλετο (= wished) in the previous sentence the desiderative sense (= he *wanted* to ...) may be better. The accompanying ἡμῖν (= for us) is a dative of advantage or disadvantage, depending on whether viewed from the perspective of Cynegirus or from that of Callimachus' father (*GG*, 1481). The present participle φεύγοντας (= fleeing) represents an imperfect ἔφευγον probably with conative sense (= they were *trying* to flee) or possibly with inceptive sense (= they were *beginning* to flee).

Likewise, the imperfect κατεῖχεν also has conative sense (= he *was trying* to hold back). The term χώρα (= land, country; LSJ, χώρα II.1) may be construed in the narrower sense of *Attica* (cf. οὔτε ἱππάσιμη ἡ χώρη ἦν ἡ Ἀττική [= Attica was no country fit for horses], Herodotus 9.13) or in the broader sense of all *Greece* (cf. γᾶς ἀπ' Ἀσίδος ἦλθε ... ἐφ' Ἑλλάδα χώραν [= from the land of Asia he came against the country Greece], Aeschylus, *Pers.* 270-271). Either connotation fits well with Polemo's conceptualization (Attica, B 5, 25, 40, 41, 55, 56; Hellas, B 12, 52; A 34, 45, 45) though in light of the immediate context (B 40, 41) Attica is probably to be preferred.

The third imperfect, ἔπραττεν (= effect, bring about; LSJ, πράττω, III.1), is probably best taken as having inceptive sense (= he was *starting* to bring about, *GG*, 1900). While the inflection of the adjective δευτέρας could be read as an accusative plural belonging with ἀρχάς (= second beginnings) it makes much better sense to take it as genitive singular belonging with μάχης (= of a second battle). This is also consonant with Polemo's frequent habit of separating noun and adjective and inserting other phrases in between.

Implicit in these imperfect tenses is the misguidedness and failure of Cynegirus' actions.

The participle παρών has conditional sense (= protasis: εἰ + παρῆν [imperfect indicative]). This together with the apodosis: ἄν + ἐποίησεν [aorist indicative] produces a past contrary to fact condition (cf. Index 2). Thus Callimachus' father asks a hypothetical question: 'what would have been the

result if Cynegirus, instead of failing, had succeeded?' In the question τί ...
ἄλλο (= what else) the indefinite adverb ποτε has intensive force: what *in the
world* else, what else *possibly*, what *ever* else ...? (LSJ, πότε, III.3 and II.2).
It lends a tone of exasperation to the question born of Cynegirus' misguided
action.

As usual (A 9, 29, 43; B 8, 32, 40, 41, 51, 56, 61) the anarthrous
βασιλεύς refers to Darius I Hystaspes [522–486 BCE] (cf. B 5, 8, 52, 56).

The evidence of the MSS shows that the imperfect ἀνεβόα (= he was
shouting aloud [√ ἀναβοάω]) stood in the text of the medieval archetype (π).
However, Jacobs (cf. Hinck p. 29) may be right to surmise that originally the
ἀν was not prepositional prefix (ἀν- [ἀνά]) but separate particle (ἄν) so that
the reading was ἄν + ἐβόα (= he would have shouted [√ βοάω]) as in FKG.
In the hypothetical case of Cynegirus' success the Persian king would have
shouted to his fleeing army and he would have commanded ([ἄν] ἐκράτει) his
navy ... At this point there is a lacuna, if not in the MS transmission, then
certainly at least a break in the thought. Here one expects a description of what
the Persian commander would yell to his retreating forces. What follows (B
41), however, are the words of Greeks or of the Greek fatherland yelling to
Cynegirus.

41

Whereas the aorist imperative (ἄφες) refers to a simple action, the
present imperative (μὴ λαμβάνου) indicates continuing action (GG, 1864.a.b.):
"let loose [instantly]! don't [continue to] grasp!" The rationale for this urging
is given in the form of a future more vivid condition (cf. Index 2) in which the
protasis (ἄν [= ἐάν] λαμβάνῃς [= if you continue holding on]) is sandwiched
between two apodoses (μενοῦσιν [= they will stay] / εὑρ[ήσ]ουσιν [= they will
find]).

In the first apodosis the medieval archetype (π) read a present tense
(μένουσιν); the original, however, will certainly have had a future (μενοῦσιν).
On this all the editors agree.

Regarding the verb form in the second apodosis it is hard to choose
between the two contending variants εὕρουσιν [a non-existent form] (→ γ) and
εὕρωσιν [aorist subjunctive] (→ δ) — both are grammatically anomalous. One
would expect εὑρήσουσιν [future indicative] which is what all editors would
like to put here. The readings in the MSS arose no doubt through a text
evolution such as the following: At some point in the medieval transmission
process the original εὑρήσουσιν (Π) was inadvertently mis-copied as εὕρουσιν
(π) which was preserved by γ (→ α β). This *lapsus manus* was then 'corrected'

by the scribe of δ ($\rightarrow$ ι μ ε) into the morphologically acceptable but syntactically impossible εὔρωσιν. The text has been restored accordingly — such restorations without MS support are exceedingly rare in this present edition.

The plural ἀποβάσεις (√ ἀποβαίνω = step off) has substantive sense (= landing spots) in contrast to the singular ἀπόβασις in A 5 which had verbal quality (= landing action) (LSJ, ἀπόβασις I.1).

The same constellation of gods (Pan, Athena, Demeter, Kore) and heroes (Theseus, Herakles) which Euphorion had adduced (A 35) is now cited here by the father of Callimachus. The actions attributed to them, however, are different. There Pan ran from Arcadia for the sake of Cynegirus' hand, here he chases away a ship; there Athena stood by, here she lets a trireme go; there Demeter and Kore were present at the battle, here they send forth a ship. There Herakles and Theseus were remembered for their own 'dragging' struggles (which are superceded by Cynegirus' 'dragging' of the ship), here they are said to be standing by. In other words, whereas in the first declamation the 'superhuman' powers were fighting to help Cynegirus achieve his goal, in the second declamation Cynegirus is fighting at cross purposes with them. In the first declamation they want to capture the ship, in the second they want to be rid of it.

The prohibitive present imperatives (μὴ κράτει and μηδ᾿ ἔχου) urge that Cynegirus desist from an action he has been continuing (= don't keep holding on; don't keep clinging) (*GG*, 1864.a).

Pan, regarded as a son of Hermes, was never admitted to the Olympian pantheon as were the other named deities. This anthropo- and therio-morphic god — usually depicted as a humanoid figure with goat's feet, horns, and shaggy hair — was native to Arcadia. His worship in Athens, however, began soon after the battle of Marathon because the Athenians believed he had promised and provided them help against the Persians. Hence, the city adopted his cult and gave him a cave-shrine on the south slope of the acropolis (cf. Herodotus 6.105.2-3; *GGR*, I.235-236; W. Pötscher, "Pan," *KP* 4.444-447; H. J. Rose, "Pan," *OCD*, 773). Ever since then Pan had a firm place in the Marathon traditions. The assertion of Callimachus' father, however, that the ship which Cynegirus had grabbed was being *driven away* (δεδιωγμένην) by Pan, does not stem from the tradition but from the creativeness of Polemo. It appears to be a picturesque way of saying the Persians were running because of *pan*ic fear (cf. B 9, 13, 26, 38).

Athena, daughter of Zeus and a leading Olympian, was the patron deity of Athens, her namesake. Indeed, Homer had called her ἐρυσίπτολις (= city-rescuing, *Il.* 6.305) and in classical tradition she was often designated with the epithets Πολιάς or Πολιοῦχος (= Guardian of the city) (LSJ, sub verba; L. R. Farnell, *The Cults of the Greek States* [New Rochelle: Caratzas, 1977] 1.392–394, note 35).

Because of Athena's agency the trireme which Cynegirus was trying to restrain is described as ἀφεψαλωμένης (→ γ) or ἐφεψαλωμένης (→ δ). This description is problematic. The perfect passive participle appears to come from a denominative (-οω) verb based on the noun φέψαλος/φεψάλυξ (= spark, ember) or possibly the adjective ἀφέψαλος (= without a spark of fire) (cf. LSJ, sub verba). The verb φεψαλόω/φεψαλόομαι (= burn/be burnt to ashes) is rare but documented in classical Greek (cf. ἐφεψαλώθη κἀξεβροντήθη σθένος [= he was burnt to ashes and his strength blasted from him by lightning], Aeschylus, *Pr.* 364). Since, however, Polemo's verb (ἀφεψαλόω or ἀφεψαλόομαι) does not seem to be otherwise attested, it has been debated whether the beginning α is an alpha-privative with negative force (*GG*, 885.1; LSJ, ἀ- as inseparable prefix, I) or a prothetic vowel prefixed before the aspirate consonant φ to facilitate pronunciation (*GG*, 41; LSJ, ἀ- as prothetic vowel; note the variant ἐφεψαλωμένης). This latter case could simply represent an alternate pronunciation and orthography of the attested classical verb. This seems to be the position of Possinus (p. 121) who nevertheless admitted he could not make sense out of τριήρους ... παρ' Ἀθηνᾶς ἀφεψαλωμένης (= a trireme having been set ablaze by Athena). Indeed, the contrast of Cynegirus' grip with the Trojan 'grip' of fire against ships (cf. B 37) would seem here to rule out any form of φεψαλόομαι. Jacobs (cf. Hinck, p. 30) wanted relieve the problem with an emendation: οὐ φεψαλωμένης (= not having been set ablaze). Orellius (pp. 112/114), on the other hand, argued that the beginning α is indeed a genuine alpha-privative (στερητικόν) and that Polemo thus appears to have coined a new verb unknown to classical Greek. Nonetheless, inasmuch as he failed to find any other supporting example, Orellius ended up proposing that the reading was corrupted — a careless conflation of two words (note *homoioarcton*): ἀφεψάλου ἀφιεμένης (= sent away without the spark of a fire). Orellius interpreted the passage as follows: "Although the tutelary gods of Athens were favorably disposed toward the Athenians, they did not want to have the Persian fleet simply massacred, but strove to have them turned in flight: Pan pressed it to flee by inspiring panic terrors, Athena sent it out unharmed by flames, Demeter and Kore permitted it to go away uninjured, and Theseus and Herakles did not want to detain it either." Despite the possibility of some such interpretation, the lexicographical difficulty invites an emendation. Thus Hinck (p. 30) proposed ἀπεψαλμένης

(= plucked off; √ ἀποψάλλω). This restoration which requires only minor changes (change of labials: φ → π; deletion of ω) is attractive. However, the exact image inhering in the expression is hard to determine. It might suggest the picture of *pulling the cord* which *sets off* a trap (cf. Ἐρινύων πικρὰν ἀποψήλασα κηρουλκὸν πάγην [= *springing* the bitter destruction-bringing trap of the Furies], Lycophron, *Alex.* 406–407) or possibly the picture of Athena pulling on the prow while Callimachus is tugging on the stern. Another emendation possibly worth considering is ἀφεψαλισμένης (= having been cut off [with shears]; √ ἀποψαλίζω). It is less invasive (ω → ισ) though admittedly the imagery is not as clear. In any case, the sense of the expression, whatever reading be accepted, is fixed within the bounds of the synonymous parallelism:

ναῦν ὑπὸ Πανὸς δεδιωγμένην   (= a ship driven away by Pan)

τριήρους παρ' Ἀθηνᾶς ἀφεψαλωμένης   (= a trireme [?] by Athena).

To avoid monotony Polemo varies the prepositional phrases with the passives: ὑπὸ Πανὸς (genitive of agent) and παρὰ Ἀθηνᾶς (genitive of author) (*GG*, 1692.1.b).

The argument that Demeter and her daughter Kore — neither famed for martial feats — participated in the battle of Marathon does not seem to be rooted in the Greek tradition. The rationale for Polemo's assertion of their presence may be that the two, as central deities in the Eleusynian Mysteries, were Attic patrons par excellence. Further, the assertion of the presence of Kore (a winter-time resident of the underworld) may recall the memory of the battle occurring in the warm season (cf. notes to A 35 and B 5).

The verb ἀφίησιν which describes the action of these goddesses has here the genuinely active sense *send away, set loose, discharge* (LSJ, ἀφίημι, II; cf. ἕτεροι [ἠφίεσαν] βέλη [= others were discharging arrows], A 31;). It is virtually synonymous with the subsequent ἐκπέμπει (= [they] are ending away). Hence the third person imperative: 'let it escape! (φευγέτω) — don't buck the will of the gods!'

The reference to the heroes Theseus and Herakles standing by (πάρεστι = is present [so as to help], LSJ, πάρειμι [-ειμί], I.4) is anchored in the Marathon tradition (cf. note at A 35). Their presence, however, is qualified with a strong adversative *but* (ἀλλ[ά]): one may not infer from their famed 'dragging' feats (cf. εἷλκον [= they were dragging], A 35) that their purpose at Marathon was to pull the ship onto the beach. The present κατέχουσι has future sense (present of anticipation), indicating what is likely in the immediate future (*GG*, 1879): they are *not going to restrain* the ship. Following a negative clause ὅτι μή means *unless, except, save that*; since this construction does not ordinarily appear with a different verb than in the main clause (LSJ, ὅτι, II.1; *GG*, 2765), the impersonal συμφέρει which follows must be construed as συμφέρει [κατέχειν] (= it is expedient to restrain) cf. LSJ, συμφέρω, A.II.2).

It is not clear who the first person subject is in ἔχω (= *I* have). Orellius (p. 112) proposed that it is the πάτρις (= fatherland) and he suggested that before ἄφες, ἆφες (B 40/41) a line something like τί δ᾽ ἂν εἶπε καὶ ἡ πατρίς; (= what would the fatherland have said?) has dropped out. Jacobs, following a somewhat similar line of reasoning, emended ἔχω καὶ (= I have also) to read ἔχει ἡ γῆ (= the land has) (cf. Hinck, p. 30).

The winds (πνεύματα) mentioned here (cf. A 35) and the winds (ἄνεμοι) of Poseidon named earlier (B 36) are virtually the same (cf. πνεύματα ἀνέμων [= blasts of winds], Aeschylus, *Pr.* 1086, 1047; Herodotus 7.16α) — they want to blow the Persians away. The notion of πνεύματα συγγενῆ (= related winds) is probably connected with the mythological tradition that Boreas, the North Wind, had a marital kinship (κῆδος) with the Athenians: he had an Attic wife, Oreithyia, daughter of King Erechtheus, and was thus regarded by the Athenians as 'son-in-law' (γαμβρός, cf. Herodotus 7.189; Plato, *Phdr.* 229b-c). As such, it was believed, he had brought help to the Athenians already two years before Marathon by destroying Persian ships in storms on the coasts of Athos (Herodotus 6.44) and, a decade later, on the coasts of Artemisium (cf. Herodotus 7.189-192). These 'Athenian' winds could drive Persian ships aground much more effectively than the lone hand of any Athenian teenager (cf. δυνάμενα ... μᾶλλον [comparative from μάλα] σοῦ [genitive of comparison] [= able ... more than you]).

In the τὰ μὲν - σὺ δέ contrast the neuter article τά refers grammatically to the πνεύματα (= winds), but logically it also includes the four named gods and the two heroes. They all in concert expel (ἐκπέμπει) the fight from Attica. The neuter plural τά is regarded as a collective and thus stands with its verb (ἐκπέμπει) in the singular (*GG*, 958).

That trans-human powers provide assistance because of their favorable disposition (εὔνοια) toward Athens was an established classical belief (cf. ἐπὶ πολλῶν ... τὴν παρὰ τῶν θεῶν εὔνοιαν φανερὰν γιγνομένην τῇ πόλει [= the manifest favor on the part of the gods occurring on many occasions toward the city], Demosthenes 2.1). The focused direction of the εὔνοια is expressed with the preposition πρός + accusative (*GG*, 1695.3.c; LSJ, πρός C.I.6.b) — a typical construction with εὔνοια (cf. εὐνοίαν τὴν πρὸς τὴν πόλιν [= favor toward the city], Aristides 13.134.7, 10; 13.155.30; τῆς πρὸς ὑμᾶς εὐνοίας [= favor toward you], Aristides 32.399.25; τῆς πρὸς τοὺς ἄλλους Ἕλληνας εὐνοίας [= the good will toward the other Greeks], Plato, *Resp.* 470a).

In conflict with the divine expulsion of the fleet, Cynegirus was trying to turn Marathon into a Median harbor. Ever since Herodotus the terms Μῆδος and Μηδικός (= Mede, Median) were standard expressions for "Persian" (J. E. Powell, *A Lexicon to Herodotus* [2nd ed.; Hildesheim: Olms, 1977] and LSJ, sub verba). Polemo uses Μῆδοι/Μηδικός and Πέρσαι/Περσικός together in one breath virtually indiscriminately (A 30, 31; B 47, 60). From the anarthrous accusative ναύσταθμον (= ship station) it is impossible to tell whether Polemo employed the old classical neuter noun or the later, more popular masculine ναύσταθμος (cf. LSJ, sub verba).

The μέν - δέ contrast is not entirely symmetrical. While ἐκπέμπει τὸν πόλεμον ἐκ τῆς Ἀττικῆς is balanced by ναύσταθμον Μηδικὸν τὸν Μαραθῶνα ποιεῖς there is no counterpart in the δέ clause for the διὰ τὴν εὔνοιαν τὴν πρὸς ἡμᾶς (= on account of their goodwill toward us) in the μέν clause. The omitted contrast is intentional; the silence implies a subtle insinuation that Cynegirus acted out of κακόνοια (= ill will) toward Athens (for κακόνοια as opposite of εὔνοια cf. LSJ, κακόνοια). Innuendo was one of the tools of the sophists' trade.

The repeated vocative ὦ Κυναίγειρε — now the third time in this passage — has the tone of wearied exasperation because of Cynegirus' misguided undertaking.

Anyone with common sense can see that in Cynegirus' ναυμαχία (= naval battle), which Euphorion had so trumpeted in his argument (A 36, 8, 11, 44), the victory will go to the king (i.e., Darius) who in a synecdoche stands for the entire Persian force. The subject of the verb νικήσει (= will prevail) is saved until the end of the sentence to give it rhetorical emphasis. Personalizing the enemy in the figure of the king heightens the dramatic effect. The battle at Marathon almost becomes a duel between Cynegirus and Darius.

The outrageous projection that the king would feel grateful to Cynegirus alone for providing him the victory in battle is framed in a classical idiom: τῆς μάχης (genitive of reason) μόνῳ Κυναιγείρῳ (dative of indirect object) εἴσεται (√ οἶδα) χάριν (accusative of direct object). This mode of expression (οἶδα χάριν + dat. {+ gen.}) was old and common (cf. οὐδεὶς ... ἐμοὶ τούτων χάριν εἴσεται [= no one will be grateful to me for these things], Xenophon, *Cyr.* 1.6.11; ἑτέροις τῆς σωτηρίας χάριν εἰδέναι [= to acknowledge thanks to others for salvation], Lysias 2.23; cf. also Homer, *Il.* 14.235; Herodotus 3.21; Isocrates 2.175).

The rationale for this projection is framed in a near perfect parallelism: by making his φυγή (= flight) ἄπορος (= blocked) / he was making his νίκη (= victory) ἀναγκαία (= necessary). The circumstantial participle ποιῶν

(= making) more likely expresses means than cause (*GG*, 2063; 2064). Like the active ποιῶν the middle deponent εἰργάζετο has transitive sense (= was making; LSJ, ἐργάζομαι II.1).

Hinck emended εἰργάζετο (= *he* was making) to read εἰργάζου (= *you* were making). His 'correction' would extend the prior quote to include also this sentence among the chiding words of the fatherland (or fellow soldiers?). Such a 'restoration' may be appealing but it is pure conjecture and unnecessary. The third person verb signals that already in this sentence, and not first in the following one, a speaker-shift occurs back to the father of Callimachus.

42

Subtle wordplays with compounds of -νοια (= thought [√ νοέω = think]) are woven into this section of the argument. Cynegirus' undertaking was an ἐπίνοια (= afterthought) which had come to him after seeing Callimachus' heroism (B 38). In contrast to the εὔνοια (= good will) of the gods there was an implicit κακόνοια (= ill will) of Cynegirus (B 41). Finally, now Cynegirus is said to have acted out of a διανοία (= intention) which brought or could have brought the Greeks harm. (Though διάνοια is more common, the paroxytonal διανοία was occasionally used, cf. LSJ, sub verba). Behind διανοία in the medieval progenitor (π) may possibly have stood δι᾽ ἀνοίας (= through lack of thought) in the original (Π) (cf. B FG). The διανοία would correspond with ἑκόντες (= intentionally) of the next sentence, the ἀνοία with ἄκοντες (= unintentionally). Assuming διανοίας is the accepted reading ἔβλαπτε could be an imperfect of continuance or description: he *was harming* (*GG*, 1890; 1898) or a desiderative or conative imperfect: he *wanted to harm*, he *was trying to harm* us (*GG*, 1895). The latter understanding would, of course, be a monstrous claim, but not inconsistant with other outrageous assertions about Cynegirus (e.g., he wanted exemption from suffering, B 27; he was a swaggering show-off, B 33; a madman, B 35, 42; and a deserter, B 44).

τἀληθῆ is crasis for τὰ ἀληθῆ (= the true [things], i.e., the truth). The verb εἰρήσεται (√ εἴρω; *GG*, p. 695) is a future perfect passive (= will have been told) with future passive sense (= will be told). Though archaic, it appears frequently instead of the future passive ῥηθήσεται (= will be told) (LSJ, ἐρῶ; cf. Homer, *Il.* 23.795; Pindar, *Isth.* 6.59; Sophocles, *Ph.* 1276). The interjection τἀληθῆ γὰρ εἰρήσεται (= for the truth will be told) is a rhetorical flourish employed in the Second Sophistic (cf. εἰρήσεται γὰρ τἀληθές, Lucian, *Dial. Mar.* 13.1). It is counter-part to a similar phrase in the first declamation, δεῖ μηδὲν ὀκνήσαντα τἀληθὲς εἰπεῖν (= it is necessary to speak the truth withholding nothing, cf. note at A 26).

The verb ἐμαίνετο (= he was driven mad) picks up on the expression μαινομένη δεξιά (= frenzied hand) in the first declamation (cf. note at A 40) and works with its inherent *double-entendre*: it connotes (a) a fury in fighting and (b) a derangement of the mind.

Ever since Homer the verb described a warrior *raging* in battle (cf. μαίνετο δ᾽ ὡς ὅτ᾽ Ἄρης ἐγχέσπαλος [= {Hector in his attack on Greek ships} was raging like spear-brandishing Ares], Homer, *Il.* 15.605; ὃδὲ λίην μαίνεται οὐδέ τίς οἱ δύναται μένος [= this man {Diomedes} rages exceedingly and no one can match his fury], *Il.* 6.100-101; cf. also 5.185-186; 16.244-245; 21.5; *Od.* 9.350; Sophocles, *Ant.* 135-137). Indeed, the verb μαίνομαι describes the very action of the war god himself, Ares (cf. εἰ οὕτω μαίνεσθαι ἐάσομεν οὖλον Ἄρηα [= if thus we allow destructive Ares to rage], *Il.* 5.717; οἷά τε πολλὰ γίγνεται ἐν πολέμῳ, ἐπιμὶξ δέ τε μαίνεται Ἄρης [= as often occurs in war, for Ares rages confusedly], *Od.* 11.537; cf. Aeschylus, *Th.* 343-344).

On the other side the verb μαίνομαι denotes the pathology of *losing one's mind* (cf. οὔτε μαίνομαι οὔτε ἀπονενόημαι [= neither am I mad nor have I lost my senses], *P. Oxy.* I.33; ἀνόητον αὐτὴν ἡγοῦντο καὶ μαίνεσθαι ἔφασκον [= they considered her senseless and said she was crazy], Dio Chrysostom 12.8; δαιμόνιον ἔχει καὶ μαίνεται [= he has a demon and is gone mad], John 10:20).

Martial and mental aspects are both inherent in Polemo's use of the verb. Since, however, on the martial side, Callimachus' father does not view Cynegirus on a par with a Hector, Diomedes, or Ares, the tone is sarcastic. On the mental side, the emphasis is, of course, negative (cf. notes at B 33 and 35). Callimachus' father regards Cynegirus' headlong rush into a grisly and pointless death in the same way that Antiochus Epiphanes viewed the eagerness of the Jewish priest Eleazar and his sons to endure torture and martyrdom, namely as needless *madness* (cf. συμβουλεύω μὴ μανῆναι τὴν αὐτὴν τῷ προβασανισθέντι γέροντι μανίαν [= I counsel {you} not to be crazy with the same madness as the old man just tortured], 4 Macc 8:5; μὴ μανῇς ... τοῖς ἀδελφοῖς σου τὴν αὐτὴν μανίαν [= do not be crazy with the same madness as your brothers], 4 Macc 10:13).

This passage collapses the time between the battlefield events and their legendary assessment afterwards. The fame which accrued to Callimachus later is retrojected back into the perception of the battle participants (cf. τὸν Καλλιμάχου νεκρὸν ὁρῶν εὐδοκιμοῦντα [= seeing the corpse of Callimachus being esteemed]) and the motivation of Cynegirus during the battle is explained by his anticipating future legends about himself at Marathon (= cf. ἐπεθύμει ... ὅπως ἄν ἐν γένηται τῶν Μαραθωνίων διηγημάτων [= he was desiring that he might become one of the Marathonian tales]).

The intransitive verb εὐδοκιμέω (= be well proven, of good repute, highly esteemed; LSJ, εὐδοκιμέω, I.1) was often used to describe military renown (cf. ἔς τε πολέμους ... εὐδοκιμέειν [= to obtain renown in wars], Herodotus 1.37; εὐδοκιμήσας ἐν τῇ ... στρατηγίῃ [= achieving a reputation in the generalship], Herodotus 1.59; ἐν δὲ τῇ μάχῃ ... ηὐδοκίμησαν [= they distinguished themselves in the battle], Xenophon, *Cyr.* 7.1.46). Unusual in Polemo is that this high repute is attached to a *corpse* (νεκρός)!

In the period of the pre-Socratics, when this speech pretends to have been given, the terms ἐπιθυμέω and ἐπιθυμία (= desire) did not yet have a negative ring but were neutral. With the rise of Stoicism in the third century, however, these concepts began to be ranked with other πάθη (= emotions) which a disciplined man was taught to resist as contrary to his own best interest (cf. F. Büchsel, ἐπιθυμία, ἐπιθυμέω, *TWNT* 3.168-169). This intellectual development is reflected in the negative texture of Polemo's usage (cf. B 33, 35, 42). The imperfect ἐπεθύμει has inceptive sense: he *began to desire* (*GG*, 1900).

The term σχῆμα, by which Polemo usually means appearance as opposed to substance (cf. note at A 2), here seems to have the connotation of *gesture* or *posture* (LSJ, σχῆμα, 7; cf. A 44; B 33, 35). Accordingly, its qualifier ἄλλος has the sense of ἀλλοῖος (= of another sort, different) (LSJ, ἄλλος, III.1).

In Euphorion's presentation the severed right hand (δεξιά) of Cynegirus had a 'life' and prowess all its own (cf. A 3, 11, 23, 31, 32, 35, 36, 37, 40, 41). Callimachus' father, however, does not talk this way. Typically when he mentions that right hand it is either an an instrumental dative in connection with Cynegirus' action (cf. B 33, 36, 42) or as a lifeless object (B 37, 63). Only in this passage (B 42) of his speech does he come close to according independence to the hand. In light of that the modifier applied to the hand, ἀλαζών (= pretentious, cf. B 33, 35), is all the more telling.

The construction ὅπως ἄν + subjunctive (γένηται) — only here in Polemo — signals a final clause denoting purpose (*GG*, 2193; 2201; 2202; LSJ, ὅπως, B.I.1.b). Hence, the claim is that Cynegirus consciously desired to lose (ἀπολέσαι) his boastful hand *in order to* become the subject of a Marathonian legend. This argument, which attributes to him a morbid and self-centered ambition, is designed to undermine Euphorion's argument that Cynegirus acted *on behalf of* (ὑπέρ) Greece (A 25, 44, 44, 49). While the claim strains credulity it is consonant with the sophists' rhetorical practice of denegrating opponents in every way possible.

Derivative nouns with the suffix -μα[τ] express the result of an action (*GG*, 841.2): διήγημα (= narrative) is the consequence of διηγέομαι (= set out in detail, describe). The term has here the quality of *legend* (cf. ἐξ ἱστορίας ἀναιρεθείσης τῆς ἀληθείας τὸ καταλειπόμενον αὐτῆς ἀνωφελὲς γίνεται διήγημα [= if the truth is removed from history what is left of it becomes an idle tale], Polybius 1.14.6; ἐὰν μὴ εἰσακούσῃς τῆς φωνῆς κυρίου ... ἔσῃ ...ἐν ... παραβολῇ καὶ διηγήματι [= if you do not obey the voice of the Lord ... you will become a proverb and a byword {διήγημα → שְׁנִינָה}], Deut 28:15, 37). Thus, the expression ἓν τῶν Μαραθωνίων διηγημάτων (= one of the Marathonian tales) reflects a later era, a time long enough after the battle for a series of legends about it to have become established in the cultural tradition. Herodotus, over a half century after the war, did not yet use the term διήγημα for his narration of the battle; the expression "Marathonian tale" will probably have arisen in Hellenistic time.

The pronoun ἡμεῖς (= we), which is inserted for emphasis (*GG*, 930, 1190, 1191), expresses a solidarity between father and son. This expression of family identity appeared already in B 16 and recurs in B 50 and B 64. It corresponds to a similar mode of expression on the part of Euphorion (A 14, 28). As so often in Polemo's style the subject (ἡμεῖς) at the beginning and predicate (ἐβλάπτομεν [= were harming]) at the end form brackets around the rest of the sentence.

The pairing of ἑκών (= willing) and its opposite, ἄκων [Attic contraction of ἀ-έκων] (= unwilling), is found throughout Greek literature (cf. ἕκοντα μηδ᾽ ἄκοντα ... μεθεῖναι ταῦτα [= neither willingly nor unwillingly to relinquish these things], Sophocles, *Ph.* 771; εἴτε ἑκὼν εἴτε ἀέκων ἁμαρτὼν τοῦ χρησμοῦ [= whether intentionally or unintentionally he missed the meaning of the oracle], Herodotus 4.164). The examples can be easily multiplied (e.g., Homer *Il.* 4.43; 7.197; Sophocles, *Ant.* 276; *O. T.* 1229–1230; Herodotus 4.120; 1 Cor 9:17). This combination, like its Latin counterpart, *nolens volens* (= unwilling, willing), conveys a sense of completeness and absoluteness.

Since the point of the argument is about damage of persons (ἡμᾶς ἔβλαπτε [= he was harming *us*], B 42), not materials, the neuter accusative οὐδέν with ἐβλάπτομεν is to be construed not as direct object (= we were damaging *nothing*) but as adverbial accusative (= we were harming *in no way*) (LSJ, οὐδείς III; *GG*, 1606, 1608, 1609).

Aristotle (*Rh.* 1.10.3) had defined injustice (τὸ ἀδικεῖν) as τὸ βλάπτειν ἑκόντα παρὰ τὸν νόμον (= voluntarily causing injury contrary to the law). To deny having done this belonged to the genre of the *apologia* (cf. πέπεισμαι ἐγὼ ἐκων εἶναι μηδένα ἀδικεῖν [= I am convinced that I have intentionally wronged no one], Plato, *Ap.* 37a). The statement of Callimachus' father is a defense against the very charge he just had raised against Cynegirus (ἡμᾶς ἔβλαπτε [= he was harming us], B 42). The [οὐ] ἐβλάπτομεν can be taken as an imperfect of continuance (= we were not harming), of intention (= we did not wish to harm), or of refusal (= we would not harm) (cf. *GG*, 1890, 1895, 1896).

43

The argument shifts to a pair of past contrary-to-fact conditions (cf. Index 2; *GG*, 2297; 2305; 2309c). The first focuses on the Greeks and Callimachus, the second on the barbarians and Cynegirus.

(1) The first hypothetical situation which imagines πάντες ὅμοιοι Καλλιμάχῳ (= all similar to Callimachus) recalls the notion of Callimachus as imitatable ἀρετῆς παράδειγμα (= model of valor) mentioned earlier (B 32). The preposition κατὰ + accusative (ἐκείνην τὴν ἡμέραν) expresses here a definite indication of time: *during, in the course of, on* (cf. κατὰ ταυτὴν ἡμέραν ἠρίστευσαν Ἀθηναῖοι [= on this day the Athenians excelled], Herodotus 8.17; LSJ, κατά, B.VII; BAGD, κατά II.2.a). With this protasis stands a double apodosis: (a) ἂν ἐλείφθη (= [no-one] would have been left) and (b) ἂν εἵλομεν (= we would have captured).

(a) Here the verb ἐλείφθη (√ λείπω) means *to be left over, remain alive* (cf. πολλοὶ μὲν γὰρ τῶν γε δάμεν, πολλοὶ δὲ λίποντο [= many of them were slain, but many were left {alive}]), Homer, *Od.* 4.495; ἡττηθέντων δὲ αὐτῶν οὐδεὶς ἂν λεφθείη [= if they should be defeated, not one of them would be left {alive}], Xenophon, *An.* 3.1.2). Polemo's notion of *not a single survivor* is, of course, hyperbole. The Persian numbers, not stated by Herodotus and grossly exaggerated by later tradition, will probably not have exceeded two infantry divisions and a small cavalry force — perhaps 20,000 to 30,000 altogether. The number of enemy actually slain in the battle was recorded as 6,400 (Herodotus 6.117) — no doubt an exaggeration, but probably accepted by Polemo's audience. To envision an entire army put to the sword strains the imagination.

(b) The second apodosis, ἂν εἵλομεν (√ αἱρέω [= take]), which imagines the possibility of capturing *all* the Persian ships, stands in stark contrast to the *seven* ships that were in fact seized according to Herodotus who admitted that most of the navy had escaped (Herodotus 6.115). The additional detail that the ships would have been captured empty (κενάς) underscores the notion of no survivors.

(2) The second condition imagines a situation in which the Persians might actually have paid attention to Cynegirus instead of disregarding him as no more than an insignificant irritant (cf. note on πάρεργον, B 49). The term λαβή (= hold, grip, [√ λαμβάνω = take hold of, grasp]) as used here stems from the world of wrestling (cf. ὥσπερ παλαιστής, τὴν αὐτὴν λαβὴν πάρεχε [= like a wrestler, offer the same hold], Plato, *Resp.* 544b; ὥσπερ δεινὸς ἀθλητὴς λαβὴν ζητῶν [= like a skilled athlete seeking a grip], Plutarch, *Fab.* 5). Since Callimachus' father is consistent in only speaking of Cynegirus' right hand (cf. B 32, 33, 36, 37, 39, 42, 43, 44, 45, 63) — in clear contradistinction to Euphorion who argued that Cynegirus lost both hands (A 10, 11, 24, 28, 32, 34, 43, 45, 49) — his reference here to the plural τὰς λαβάς (= the grips) is not an inadvertant *lapsus* but intentional. In other words, rather than referring to alternate grips first of the one hand and then of the other, it must mean *several successive grips of the one right hand*. The plural then subtly suggests a series of ineffectual holds attempted one after the other by an unskilled athlete. This image is designed to counteract Euphorion's picture of a firm and persistent grip (A 10, 11), of a hand showing prowess (A 32) and equal to whole ships (A 43).

In the apodosis the adjective ἄκοντες (= unwilling) does not mean that they would have acted *against* their own will, but rather *instinctively*. The term ἧττα (Attic for ἧσσα [= defeat]), which is etymologically related to the irregular comparative ἥσσων (= inferior, weaker, cf. LSJ, sub verbum), serves in military terminology as the antonym of νίκη (= victory) (cf. εἴτε νίκη εἴτε ἧττα ἢ πολέμου ἢ καὶ ἄλλης τινὸς ἀγωνίας [= whether victory or defeat either in war or in any other contest], Plato, *La.* 196b; νίκας δὲ καὶ ἥττας ἐκτὸς λόγου τὰ νῦν θῶμεν [= let us leave victories and defeats out of the discussion for now], Plato, *Leg.* 638b). The expression τὴν ἧτταν ἀνεμαχέσαντο (= they would have fought back again from the defeat) corresponds to typical military language (cf. μετὰ δὲ τοῦτο τὸ τρῶμα ἀνέλαβον τε καὶ ἀνεμαχέσαντο [= after this disaster they rallied and fought again], Herodotus 5.121; ἄνδρας ἐς ἀναγκαίην ἀπειληθέντας νενικημένους ἀναμαχεσθαί τε κεὶ ἀναλαμβάνειν τὴν προτέρην κακότητα [= defeated men driven into necessity rally and retrieve the former mishap], Herodotus 8.109; τοῖς πολεμίοις παρέσχον ἀναμαχέσασθαι τὸ πταῖσμα [= they gave to the enemies {a chance} to retrieve their defeat], Julian, *Or.* 1.24c).

In this passage the concept θάρρος (Attic for θάρσος) does not describe the internal mental or emotional state of courage, but rather the external *source which gives courage* (cf. ὀλολυγμὸν ... θάρσος φίλοις, λύουσα πολέμιον φόβον [= a triumphal shout ... a source of courage for friends, dissolving the fear of the enemy], Aeschylus, *Th.* 268-270; στρατῷ τε θάρσος τῷδε πυργηρουμένῳ [= a source of courage for the beleaguered army], *Th.* 184). Similarly δέος does not here denote the inner psychic state of fear but the external *reason for fear* (cf. οὔ τοι ἔπι [= ἔπεστι] δέος [= there is not {any} cause of fear for you {= Zeus}], Homer, *Il.* 5.515; δεινότερόν τι τούτου {= θανάτου} δέος [= some terror more dreadful than death], Thucydides 3.45.4).

The statement that Cynegirus was *doing nothing* (δράσας οὐδέν) but getting his hand chopped off is a response to Euphorion's claim (cf. A 23) that Cynegirus had acted (ἔδρασε) while Callimachus had only suffered (ἔπαθε), and that action is more decisive than suffering (τὸ δρᾶν τοῦ πάσχειν κυριώτερόν ἐστι, A 23). The argument of Callimachus' father is an ironic expansion of his earlier charge that what Cynegirus wanted was ἐξουσία μὲν τοῦ ποιεῖν, ἄδεια δὲ τοῦ μὴ παθεῖν (= license to act, but exemption from suffering, A 27). For his part Callimachus had done *both*: he had endured in τῷ χαλεπῷ τοῦ δρᾶν καὶ φοβερῷ τοῦ παθεῖν (= the hardship of action *and* the horror of suffering, A 27).

The active verb ἀποτέμνω (= cut off), which has its direct object in the accusative and its indirect object in the genitive or dative, when converted to the passive retains the accusative of the direct object while the indirect object becomes the nominative subject of the passive (*GG*, 1748.b). Hence, the seemingly jarring construction of passive ἀποτμηθείς with accusative τὴν χεῖρα (= he was cut off {regarding?} the hand) is in fact a very common idiom (cf. ἀποτμηθέντες τὰς κεφαλὰς ἐτελεύτησαν [= they were killed by being beheaded], Xenophon, *An.* 2.6.1; τετελεύτηκε βιαίῳ θανάτῳ ... τὴν γλῶτταν ἀποτμηθείς [= he met his end in a violent death ... having his tongue cut off], Aeschines 1.172; κἂν τὸν τράχηλον ἀπετμήθη [= he would even have had his neck cut off], Arrian, *Epict. Dis.* 1.2.27).

The verb ἔπεσεν (= he fell) is used in the military sense of *he died* (cf. πεσεῖν ... καὶ κοινωνῆσαι τοῦ τάφου [= to fall and to share in the grave], B 3; cf. A 6, 42; B 13, 18, 47, 59).

The claim that Cynegirus fell as soon as he lost his right hand, as though he did not have a second hand, is a direct contradiction of Euphorion's claim that after losing the right hand he continued the struggle using the left hand until he lost that too (A 10). The detail that Cynegirus' death came immediately (εὐθύς) counteracts the claim that Cynegirus fought for a long time (πολὺν χρόνον, A 10), right up to the end of the battle (A 21), and that his hands fell 'slowly' (βραδέως, A 39).

The construction of ὥσπερ + participle (ἔχων ... κειμένης) offers the reason for the immediate death (LSJ, ὡς, I) or a limitation on the assertion (LSJ, ὥσπερ, II). Contrary to convention the posited rationale does not envision the soul as 'housed' in the body, but in the severed and useless hand (cf. B 13) — a striking 'transfer of residence' no doubt prompted by the bold claims of Euphorion (cf. A 11, 23, 37). The picture of the 'soul in the hand' (ἐν τῇ δεξιᾷ τῆς ψυχῆς αὐτῷ κειμένης) may possibly be connected with a Greek idiom. For example, a paramour sneaking in to see a married woman could be described as "always trembling and frightened ... fearful, having the soul in the hand" (ἐν τῇ χειρὶ τὴν ψυχὴν ἔχοντα), Xenarchus, Pentathlum fragment, cited in Athenaeus 13.569c) — an expression much like the English 'taking your life in your hands'. Even more common appears to be the idiom ἐπὶ τοῖς χείλεσι τὴν ψυχὴν ἔχειν (= to have the soul on the lips, cf. Herodas 3.4; Dio Chrysostom 32.50; Aulus Gellius 19.11). To locate the soul not at the core of the body but at its extremities is a way to express its fragility and vulnerability (cf. *senilis anima in primis labiis esset, nec magna vi distraheretur a corpore* [= an old man's soul is on his lips and with not much force it is disengaged from the body], Seneca, *Ep.* 30.14).

The reaction to Callimachus of friends (φίλοι) and barbarians (βάρβαροι) — a variation on friends and foes (φίλοι and πολέμιοι) in the previous sentence — is given as a response to the derisive question of Euphorion: "what enemies would the one hidden by many arrows have frightened or what friends would he have benefited?" (A 30).

Here the term τάξις denotes *battle post* or *battle station* (cf. LSJ, τάξις, I.2 and 5; contrast earlier occurrences in the sense of 'ranking', B 18, 22). In military descriptions the phrase ἐν τῇ τάξει μένοντα (= remaining in the battle post) is a common expression for bravery, resolve, and commitment to duty (cf. οὐκ ἐῶν φεύγειν ... ἐκ μάχης, ἀλλὰ μένοντας ἐν τῇ τάξει ἐπικρατέειν ἢ ἀπόλλυσθαι [= not permitting {them} to flee from battle, but {requiring them} to remain in the battle position and either to prevail or to perish], Herodotus 7.104; οὗτοι μὲν ἔφευγον ... οἳ δε ... ἔμενον ἐν τῇ ἑωυτοῦ τάξι ἕκαστος [= these fled ... but others remained, each in his battle position], Herodotus 3.158).

Whereas Callimachus' determined perseverance elicited from the Greeks awe (ἠδοῦντο → αἰδέομαι [= stand in awe], √ αἰδώς [= awe, respect, reverence]), it produced terror in the Persians. In classical times the participle τρέσας (√ τρέω = flee in terror) had virtually become a substantive and technical term for *runaway*, *coward* (cf. πάντας τοὺς τρέσαντας ἀτίμους εἶναι τοῦ νόμου κελεύοντος [= since the law decrees that all who run away {in battle} shall be deprived of civic rights], Plutarch, *Apoph. Reg.* 191c; τοῖς ἐν τῇ μάχῃ καταδειλιάσασιν, οὓς αὐτοὶ τρέσαντας ὀνομάζουσιν, ὀκνοῦντες τὰς ἐκ τῶν νόμων ἀτιμίας προσάγειν [= upon those who had shown cowardice in the battle, whom they themselves called 'runaways', they hesitated to inflict the dishonors required by the laws], Plutarch, *Ages.* 30.2; ἔπαινοι ... τῶν τεθνηκότων ὑπὲρ τῆς Σπάρτης ... καὶ ψόγοι τῶν τρεσάντων [= praises of those who died for Sparta ... and censure of the cowards], Plutarch, *Lyc.* 31.1). The imperfect ὑπεχώρουν (→ ὑποχωρέω [= give way, withdraw]) may be taken as inceptive or continuative (*GG*, 1900, 1890). By itself the verb could describe *retreat* in battle (cf. Homer, *Il.* 6.107; 22.96; Thucydides 4.43.3) and thus the combination τρέσαντες ὑπεχώρουν is a doubly strong expression of contempt.

The case of τὸ σύμπαν is not certain. It may be taken as either subject nominative (= the *sum* of the *whole* matter [is this]:) or as adverbial accusative (= *on the whole*, *in general*; so A 2; cf. LSJ, σύμπας, II). There is, however, no difference in sense.

Whereas the previous occurrence of ἔπεσεν (= he fell) a few lines earlier had meant he *died*, here it does not have that connotation — both men after all died — but it refers to the body being *physically horizontal* instead of vertical. This is clear from the immediately following contrasts: ὀρθὸν ἢ κείμενον, ἑστηκότα ἢ ἐρριμμένον (= erect or prone, standing or prostrate, B 44). Polemo plays with the polyvalence of the verb πίπτω.

44

The verb ὑπολαμβάνω (= suppose) is often used to indicate an assumption or introduce an hypothesis for the sake of discussion (cf. LSJ, sub verbum III.1; BAGD, sub verbum 4). Here the conditional participle ὑπολαβόντες (= ἐὰν ὑπολάβωμεν [= if we assume]) serves as protasis of a future more vivid condition whose apodosis is a question, πότερον στεφανώσομεν; (= which will we crown?) (cf. Index 2).

Athletic metaphors were frequent among classical authors and comparisons of well-trained athletes with skilled soldiers were commonplace (cf. ὥσπερ δὲ ἀθλητάς τε πολέμου [= like 'athletes' of war], Plato, *Resp.* 543b; ἀθλητὰς ... τῶν {πολεμικῶν} ἔργων [= 'athletes' of {military} operations], Aristotle, *Pol.* 1321a26; ἀθληταὶ τρόπου τοιούτου μάχης [= 'athletes' in this kind of fighting], Josephus, *A. J.* 17.259). Here in Polemo the context makes clear that the term ἀθλητής (√ ἀθλεύω / ἀθλέω [= contend for a prize]) does not just mean 'athlete' in general, but *prize-fighter* in particular, namely a boxer or possibly a pankration-fighter (cf. τέκτον' ἀθληταῖσιν ἔμμεν[αι] ... πυκτᾶν [= to be a master among athletes ... a boxer], Pindar, *Nem.* 5.49, 52; ἀθλητὴς τυπτόμενος [= an athlete under blows], 4 Macc 6:10; μεγάλου ἐστὶν ἀθλητοῦ τὸ δέρεσθαι καὶ νικᾶν [= it is {the mark} of a great athlete to be battered and to win], Ignatius, *Pol.* 3:1).

Organized fist-fighting was at least as old as Homer (cf. *Il.* 23.664-699; *Od.* 18.25-107) and by the 23rd Olympiad (688 BCE) boxing had become part of the regularly scheduled contests (cf. Pausanius 8.10.7, 9; Diogenes Laertius 8.47-48) so that a post-Marathon speaker could already look back on several centuries of prize-fighting. The boxing tradition continued throughout antiquity until the games were abolished by the Christian emperor Theodosius I in 393 CE so that Polemo's audience was also familiar with the sport (cf. Plutarch, *Quest. Conv.* 638b-640a; Philostratus, *Gym.* 9, 58; Lucian, *Smp.* 19).

In classical athletic contests the victors received as prize of honor a στέφανος (= wreath, garland [of interwoven leaves]), ordinarily placed on the head (cf. W. Grundmann, στέφανος, *TWNT* 7.619-620). The denominative verb στεφανόω (= to crown, i.e., bestow the στέφανος) was regularly used to express winning the prize in all types of athletic competitions (cf. Pindar, *Ol.* 7.81; 14.24; *Pyth.* 8.19; *Nem.* 6.19; Herodotus 8.26; Aristotle, *E. N.* 1099a4), including boxing (cf. εὐθυμάχαν ... ἄνδρα ...στεφανωσάμενον αἰνέσω πυγμᾶς ἄποινα [= I will praise the fair-fighting man who was crowned as reward for boxing], Pindar, *Ol.* 7.15-16; πυγμαχίας ἔνεκεν ... στεφάνῳ χρυσέας ἐλαίας [= on account of fist-fighting ... a crown of golden olive], *Ol.* 11.12-13; τίς δὴ ποταίνιον ἔλαχε στέφανον χείρεσσι; ... Δόρυκος δ᾽ ἔφερε πυγμᾶς τέλος [= who won the fresh crown with {his} hands? ... Doryclus won the prize in boxing], *Ol.* 10.60-62, 67).

A classical boxing match had neither rounds nor time limit. The two pugilists simply went at each other unabated until one emerged as victor. The decision was reached basically in one of two ways: one fighter became either (a) unable or (b) unwilling to continue the fight. (a) A boxer could be rendered unable either by knock-out (cf. Homer, *Il.* 23.690-691; *Od.* 18.95; Nonnus, *Dion.* 37.538-539) or worse, by death (cf. Apollonius Rhodius 2.98, Valerius Flaccus 4.310). (b) On the other hand, a boxer could admit defeat by raising his open hand as signal of giving up (cf. Philostratus, *Im.* 2.6 [349]; Theocritus 22.129-131; Plutarch, *Lyc.* 19.4). (For a thorough treatment of boxing in antiquity, cf. J. Jüthner and E. Mehl, "Pygme," *RE*, Suppl. 9.1306-1352). It is the former manner of decision which is envisioned in Polemo's analogy: the victor is the one who remains erect (ὀρθὸν [= upright], ἑστηκότα [=standing]), the defeated is the one on the ground (κείμενον [= lying outstretched], ἐρριμμένον [= prostrate] √ ῥίπτω [= throw down]).

παύσῃ (= you will cease) is a standard contraction of παύσεσαι (future middle indicative 2nd singular): the intervocalic σ of the uncontracted ending drops out and the first of the two vowel sounds (ε / α) dominates and lengthens (*GG*, 48.a; 51.b; 628).

The question οὐ παύσῃ παραβάλλων (= will you stop comparing ...?) is counterpart to the imperative μὴ παράβαλε (= do not compare ...) in the first speech (A 27). However, whereas Cynegirus' father had rebutted three comparisons (corpse / soldier; one struck / one striking; appearance / deed, A 27), Callimachus' father rejects four:

(1) ἀνδρὶ χεῖρα
  (= a hand with a man)
(2) τραῦμα ἒν μυρίοις
  (= one wound with myriads)
(3) τὸν λειποτακτήσαντα τῷ μακροβίῳ νεκρῷ
  (= the deserter with the long-lived corpse)
(4) τὸν ἠκρωτηριασμένον τῷ ... ὁλοκλήρῳ
  (= the mutilated with the intact)

The accusatives describe Cynegirus, the datives Callimachus. This syntax corresponds to its counterpart where Euphorion also spoke of his own son in the dative and the other son in the accusative (cf. A 27). In the first two items the cases appear in chiastic order (dative - accusative / accusative - dative), the order of the third and fourth conform to the second (accusative -dative). That is the reverse of the pattern in A 27 (dative - accusative / accusative - dative / accusative - dative). This refinement is intentional and studied down to the last detail.

In the series of comparisons the images get progressively more graphic:

(1) a *hand* (i.e., a part of a man) compared with a (whole) *man*. The chiastic word order in ἀνδρὶ χεῖρα καὶ τραῦμα ἒν μυρίοις is hard to replicate in an uninflected English; the translation does not reflect the chiasm.

(2) *one wound* compared with *myriads* (of wounds). This picture of a single wound is consonant with the consistent position of Callimachus' father that Cynegirus lost only one hand, not both (cf. note at B 43). In Callimachus' case both fathers mention the arrows (plural!) which had struck him (cf. A 7, 24, 27, 30, 45; B 12, 56, 57, 59, 61). But only Callimachus' father developed the point and spoke of *all sorts* (παντοδαπά) of missiles (B 10), of *many* (πολλά) arrows (B 10, 12), of being *struck many times* (πολλὰ βαλλόμενος,

B 56), indeed, of taking *all* (πάντα) the arrows and weapons (B 39). Hence he could speak of Callimachus being done in by the *multitude of his wounds* (τῷ πλήθει τῶν τραυμάτων, B 11) or by *so many wounds* (πολλὰ τοιαῦτα τραύματα, B 47). All of these details are comprised in the expression *myriads* [of wounds] (μυρίοις [τραύμασι]) which is not so much bombast as it is a conscious outdoing of Euphorion's claim that every crewman had labored *incessantly* (μυρία καμών) against Cynegirus (cf. A 41).

(3) the one abandoning his post compared with the long-lived corpse. The startling contention that Cynegirus was a *deserter who left his post* derives apparently from Euphorion's depiction of Cynegirus getting past the front line (where he had been stationed) and rushing out to the beach (cf. ὑπερβὰς τὴν φάλαγγα ... ἐκδραμὼν πρὸς αὐτὴν ἐπεξῆλθε τὴν ἠόνα, A 8). This characterization of Cynegirus as "one who left his post" (τὸν λειποτακτήσαντα) is intended as a contrast to Callimachus who "remained at his post" (ἐν τῇ τάξει μένοντα, B 43). The term, however, is particularly jarring because in military language the compound verb λ[ε]ιποτακτέω (√ λείπω + τάξις = leave one's post) along with the derivative nouns λιποτάκτης, λιποταξία, and λιποταξίον served as standard technical terminology for *desertion* (cf. LSJ, sub verba) — a punishable act of insubordination. Athenian law prescribed penalties for three military crimes: (1) refusal of service (ἀστρατεία), (2) desertion from the ranks (λιποταξία), and (3) cowardice (δειλία). Punishment involved loss of citizenship rights (ἄτιμος εἶναι) and/or confiscation of property (τὰ χρήματα δημευθῆναι) (cf. Demosthenes, 15.32; Lysias 14.9; Aeschines 3.176) or even death (cf. Lycurgus, *Leoc.* 147-150; for an overview of the legalities, cf. T. Thalheim, Λιποταξίου γραφή, *RE* 13.1.723). The repugnance felt toward λιποταξία was, of course, not limited to Athens. Spartan culture, for example, preferred death to such a disgrace (cf. Λάκαινα τὸν υἱὸν λιποτακτήσαντα ὡς ἀνάξιον τῆς πατρίδος ἀνεῖλον [= a Spartan woman killed her son who had deserted his post on the ground that he was unworthy of his fatherland], Plutarch, *Apoph. Lacaen.* 241a; the famed Spartans who died defending the pass at Thermopylae against the Persians thought it οὐκ ἔχειν εὐπρεπέως ἐκλιπεῖν τὴν τάξιν ἐς τὴν ἦλθον φυλάξοντες ἀρχήν [= not to be seemly to abandon the post which they had first come to defend], Herodotus 7.220; cf. *An. Gr.* 7.431). Later, in the Roman military, desertion was a crime that could be punished, as Polemo's audience well knew, by death (cf. Dionysius Halicarnassus 8.79.2; Josephus, *B.J.* 5.124). At all times abandonment of one's assigned post was an act so grave that prosecution was regarded as unavoidable (cf. προσήκει τῶν λιπόντων τὴν τάξιν κατηγορεῖν [= it is incumbent to bring a charge against

the ones who deserted their post], Lysias 14.21; τὴν ἐκ τῶν νόμων τάξιν λιπών, οὗ δίκην ὀφείλει τῇ πόλει δοῦναι [= he deserted the post {assigned} by the laws, on account of which he is bound to be punished by the state], Demosthenes 21.166). The specific character and profound seriousness of λιποταξία was so deeply ingrained in Greek thought that the terminology has continued uninterrupted in the language right into modern Greek in which λιποτάχτης, λιποταξία, and λιποτακτῶ still describe the soldier who has deserted his post or gone AWOL.

Ordinarily in classical times λιποταξία was conceptually connected with *cowardice* and *retreat away from battle* (cf. τὸν δὲ νόμον κελεύειν, ἐάν τις λίπῃ τὴν τάξιν εἰς τοὐπίσω δειλίας ἕνεκα, μαχομένων τῶν ἄλλων, περὶ τούτου τοὺς στρατιώτας δικάζειν [= the law commands, if anyone leaves his post and retreats to the rear out of cowardice while the others are fighting, that soldiers be prosecuted for this], Lysias 14.5; νόμος ... κεῖται ... ὅσοι ἂν μάχης οὔσης εἰς τοὐπίσω ἀναχωρήσωσι [= the law covers whoever retreats to the rear during the battle], Lysias 14.6; ἐὰν δὲ στρατεύσηται μέν τις, μὴ ἀπαγαγόντων δὲ τῶν ἀρχόντων οἴκαδε προαπέλθῃ τοῦ χρόνου, λειποταξίου τούτων εἶναι γραφάς [= if someone goes on military service, but goes away back home before the {discharge} time without leave from the officers, that soldiers are to be indicted for desertion], Plato, *Leg.* 943d; cf. also Aeschines 1.29).

To accuse Cynegirus, however, of cowardice and running away from battle would be, of course, a grotesque distortion. Not even the denegrations of Callimachus' father were ready to go this far (cf. B 4, 7, 23, 28, 33–35, 50). Hence, the labeling of Cynegirus as λειποτακτήσαντα seems rather to have in mind the same kind of paradoxical situation that Greek historians more than once noted in the Roman military. There was the case, for example, of General Aulus Postumius in the victorious battle against the Aequi (425/424 BCE): "his own son in eagerness leaped forward from the station assigned to him by his father, and his father, preserving the ancient discipline, had his own son executed as one who had left his station" (κατὰ γὰρ τὴν μάχην τὸν υἱὸν διὰ τὴν προθυμίαν προεκπηδῆσαι τῆς ὑπὸ τοῦ πατρὸς δεδομένης τάξεως· τὸν δὲ πατέρα τηροῦντα τὸ πάτριον ἔθος τὸν υἱὸν ὡς λελοιπότα τὴν τάξιν ἀποκτεῖναι, Diodorus Siculus 12.64.3). A parallel situation was recounted about the Roman commander Manlius and his brave but insubordinate son in the Gallic War: "when his son distinguished himself in battle he honored him for his bravery with the crowns awarded for superior valor but then, charging him with disobedience in not staying in the fort in which he was posted but leaving it contrary to the command of the general in order to take part in the struggle, he put him to death as a deserter" (τὸν υἱὸν ἀριστεύοντα κατὰ πόλεμον τῆς μὲν ἀνδρείας ἔκενα τοῖς ἀριστείοις στεφάνοις ἐκόσμησεν, ἀπείθειαν δ᾽ ἐπικαλῶν, ὅτι οὐκ ἐν ᾧ ἐτάχθη φρουρίῳ ἔμεινεν ἀλλὰ παρὰ τὴν ἐπιταγὴν τοῦ ἡγεμόνος ἐξῆλθεν ἀγωνιούμενος, ὡς λιποτάκτην ἀπέκτεινε, Dionysius Halicarnassus, *Ant.* 8.79.2). The matter is similar in Polemo's declamation: the term λειποτακτήσας implies not cowardice but insubordination — a war crime not mitigated by bravery (cf. μηδεμιᾶς συγγνώμης τοὺς ἀκοσμοῦντας ἐν τῷ πολέμῳ τυγχάνοντας [= those who are insubordinate in war obtain no pardon], Lysias 14.13). The charge here of λειποταξία is related to but goes beyond the earlier allegation of αὐθάδεια (= willfulness, B 24, 35). Whereas αὐθάδεια is a moral defect or character flaw, λειποταξία is a culpable act, a crime punishable by law. The deep-rooted pejorative sense of the term λειποτακτήσαντα is meant to derail the impression of selfless valor created by Euphorion.

The compound adjective μακρόβιος (= long-lived) ordinarily describes longevity of the living, i.e., a long span of life *prior to death* (cf. Herodotus 1.23, Hippocrates, *Aër.* 4.29; Aristotle, *Rh.* 1361b33). Hence, to speak of the 'long life' of a dead corpse (νεκρός) is a striking oxymoron. Comparable paradoxes occur also in other phrases of Polemo (cf. ἔμψυχος καὶ τεθνεὼς ὤν [= animate even though being dead], B 55; τῆς εἱμαρμένης πολυχρονιωτέρου [= having more duration than apportioned by destiny], B 12; ἄτρωτε καὶ πολύτρωτε [= unwounded and much wounded], B 51). Contradictory juxtapositions appear characteristic of Polemo's style.

(4) the one mutilated compared with one completely intact. Denominative verbs formed with -αζω denote action (*GG*, 866,6). The verb ἀκρωτηριάζω acquired early the connotation of *cutting off* ἀκρωτήρια (= extremities [of the body], i.e., fingers or hands, toes or feet). Literally the verb means 'to de-extremitize'. Hence, the term could be used in the clinical médical sense of amputating limbs (cf. LSJ, ἀκρωτηριάζω I.3). But in political and military accounts it often has a much more sinister coloring: to viciously *mutilate* or *maim* in acts of vengeance or torture (cf. ἀκρωτηριάζων δὲ καὶ φονεύων καὶ στρεβλῶν πολλοὺς διέφθειρε [= by mutilating, killing, and stretching on the rack he destroyed many], Polybius 5.54.10; τῶν αἰχμαλώτων τὰς χεῖρας ἀπέκοπτον, οὐκ ἀρκούμενοι ταῖς παρὰ τοὺς καρποὺς τομαῖς, ἀλλὰ σὺν αὐτοῖς τοῖς βραχίοσιν ἀκρωτηριάζοντες [= they cut off the hands of the captives, but not being content with the severings at the wrists they lopped off arms and all], Diodorus Siculus 34.8; ἔκθυμος δὲ γενόμενος ... προσέταξεν γλωσσοτομεῖν περισκυθίσαντας ἀκρωτηριάζειν [= falling into a rage he ordered them to cut out the tongue, to scalp him, and to cut off his

extremities], 2 Macc 7:4). Thus the term ἀκρωτηριάζω often describes a brutalization and humiliation of the powerless — and that is certainly what Polemo wants to convey: the mutilated Cynegirus (τὸν ἠκρωτηριασμένον) was a wretched victim to be pitied, not a model soldier to be heroized. This distasteful description of Cynegirus concretizes and shades the earlier, more innocuous one of him as a νεκρὸς οὐχ ὁλόκληρος (= a corpse not complete, B 4), i.e., a dead body without all its parts.

The dismembered corpse presents no real comparison with the one remaining whole up to the present (τῷ μέχρι νῦν ὁλοκλήρῳ). Callimachus, whose body remained intact, did not lose his dignity — he retains it right up to the very present (cf. the temporal μέχρι νῦν in Diodorus Siculus 17.110; Longus 4.16.2; Xenophon Ephesius 1.4.1; Ignatius, *Magn.* 8:1).

In place of the four comparisons allegedly espoused by Euphorion and then rejected by Callimachus' father a more fitting contrast (ὁ μέν / ὁ δέ) is proposed: Cynegirus let go of the ship, Callimachus held on to the shield. These brief clauses show a deft play on words: Euphorion said that Cynegirus had *let go* (ἀφίημι) of his **hands** (A 11, 31, 36) and *held on* (κρατέω / κατέχω) to the **ship** (A 4, 10, 35, 36, 37); Callimachus' father says that Cynegirus *let go* of the **ship** (B 44, cf. 45). If one wants to speak of holding on, it was Callimachus who *held on* (the imperfect ἐκράτει has durative sense), and, namely, to his **shield**. The reference to Callimachus retaining his shield — a detail otherwise unmentioned in the declamations — is a subtle jibe at Euphorion's claim that Cynegirus fought almost γυμνὸς (= naked, A 8), i.e., without shield or armor (cf. γυμνόν, ἄτερ κόρυθος τε καὶ ἀσπίδος [= naked, without helm and shield], Homer, *Il.* 21.50; με γυμνὸν ἐόντα, ... ἐπεί κ' ἀπὸ τεύχεα δύω [= me being naked, when I have put off {my} armor], *Il.* 22.124). To abandon one's shield in battle was ordinarily a sign of flight and cowardice. The unsubstantiated assertion that someone had "thrown away the shield" was regarded by Athenian law as a grievous slander and liable to prosecution (cf. Lysias 10.9). The Spartans likewise saw abandoning one's shield as an act of humiliating cowardice (cf. their saying: τὴν ἀσπίδα ... ἢ τὰν ἢ ἐπὶ τας [= {come home} either {carrying} the shield or {being carried} upon it], Plutarch, *Apoph. Lacaen.* 241f). Cynegirus obviously could not reasonably be accused of cowardice; nevertheless, the argument that Callimachus had held on to his shield was, of course, a reminder that Cynegirus had not done so — an innuendo that would not have gone lost on Polemo's audience.

45

The present tense of the imperatives λέγε and τραγῴδει does not indicate time but continuance of action (*GG*, 1864): *keep talking* and *go on declaiming*.

The λέγε here could possibly have the pejorative sense of 'wagging the tongue', 'blabbering', though that is hard to document. Coupled with τραγῴδει (= tell in tragic style) it more likely means *boast, brag* (cf. λέγων δὲ ἕκαστος ὑμῶν τὴν ἑαυτοῦ ῥώμην [= each of you talking up his own strength], Xenophon, *Cyr.* 1.3.10) or *sing poetically* (cf. θέλω λέγειν Ἀτρείδας [= I wish to tell of Atrides], Anacreontea 23.1).

Similarly the imperative τραγῴδει has the sense of *overstate, dress up in solemn words* (cf, τραγῳδεῖν ... μᾶλλον ἢ ἀληθεύειν [= to exaggerate rather than tell the truth], Galen, *U. P.* 16.4; μὴ τραγῴδει τὸ πρᾶγμα, ἀλλ' εἰπὲ ὡς ἔχει [= make no tragic parade of the matter, but tell it as it is], Arrian, *Epict. Dis.* 4.7.15).

The γάρ offers an explanation for Euphorion's tendency to exaggerate: "like father, like son," or here rather: "like son, like father." Aeschylus was given to poetic exaggeration; this he got, it is implied, from his father.

Possinus (p. 86) latinized the phrase τὴν χεῖρα ὄρος ἐποίεις (= you were making the hand [into] a mountain) with "*montem ex manu facis*" (= you are making a mountain out of a hand), a paraphrase which comes close to the English expression "to make a mountain out of a molehill." In Latin the phrase *montes promittere / polliceri* (= to promise mountains) was an idiomatic expression for 'boasting' or 'making empty promises' (cf. Terence, *Ph.* 68 [1.2.18]; Sallust, *Cat.* 23.3; Persius 3.65). Polemo likely employed here a classical idiom. The widely quoted quip ὤδινεν ὄρος, τὸ δ' ἔτεκε μῦν (= the mountain was in labor, but it brought forth a mouse; cf. Aesop 520 [= Phaedrus 4.24]; Plutarch, *Ages.* 36.5; Athenaeus, 4.616d; Horace, *A.P.* 139) shows that it was proverbial to contrast a mountain with something insignificant. Thus Euphorion's grandiose claims about Cynegirus' hand are as laughably disproportionate as the proverbial mountain in birth pangs for a mouse.

To show the silliness of the exaggeration three hyperbolic assertions from Euphorion are quickly cited and rebutted:

(1) Ἐκ γῆς ἐναυμάχει (= from land he was fighting a naval battle, cf. A 8, 36): If one wants to talk about Cynegirus conducting a sea fight from land, then with equal justification one must speak of Datis carrying on an infantry battle from the sea (Δάτις δ' ἐκ θαλάττης ἐπεζομάχει). This simple *correlation* neutralizes or nullifies Euphorion's first claim.

(2) Κατέσχε τὴν ναῦν (= he restrained a ship, cf. A 10, 35, 37):   If the argument is that Cynegirus held a ship, that is nothing impressive — a thin line does that. A καλῴδιον (diminutive of κάλως = rope) is a slim but sturdy cord. Though strong enough to support the weight of a man (cf. Aristophanes, *Ves.* 379-381; Josephus, *A. J.* 2 § 31; Appian, *B. C.* 1.10.87) a καλῴδιον was light enough to be attached to a spear for use in fishing (cf. Polybius 34.3.5) or for a swimmer to use in water when pulling food sacks behind him (cf. Thucydides 4.26.8). Such lines were used for pulling in ships or holding floating objects (cf. Appian, *B.C.* 5.12.118; 5.12.119; *Pun.* 11.77 [356]; *Hisp.* 15.91 [398]). This mundane likening of Cynegirus' grasp to a light line is belittling enough. The additional remark about an anchor doing a better job is an unnecessary afterthought which limps; it is attached only for the sake of the sarcasm. A simple *comparison* deflates Euphorion's second claim.

(3) Κατέσχε τοὺς πλέοντας (= he restrained those trying to sail, cf. A 9, 11, 23). The present participle represents a conative imperfect: they were *attempting* (unsuccessfully) to sail. If the assertion is that Cynegirus held back those trying to flee, then it is patently untrue, or at best only momentarily valid, because the enemies did in fact make good their getaway (οἱ δὲ καὶ ὅμως ἐξέπλευσαν). This rebuttal by Callimachus' father is an allusion to the well-known Herodotean tradition about the outcome of the shore battle (cf. ἑπτὰ μὲν δὴ τῶν νεῶν ἐπεκράτησαν τρόπῳ τοιῷδε ᾿Αθηναῖοι· τῇσε δὲ λοιπῇσι οἱ βάρβαροι ἐξανακρουσάμενοι [= the Athenians mastered seven of the ships in this manner; with the rest the barbarians pushed off from shore], Herodotus 6.115). The rebuttal by Callimachus' father selectively focused on the bulk of the navy that escaped, ignoring the few ships that were captured. Thus the *historical recollection* of the Persians' flight renders Euphorion's third claim hollow.

Between the second and third 'quotation-rebuttal' another argument is inserted which departs from the pattern: ὁ μὲν ἐλάβετο, ὁ δ' ἀπέκοψε. The phrase ἐλάβετο (= he grabbed on) does not quote any language from Euphorion's speech, rather it repeats an expression in the speech of Callimachus' father (cf. B 33, 41). Thus this μέν - δέ contrast works as an aside. One may imagine Polemo perhaps turning his head here and disdainfully lowering his voice in the delivery. The brief parenthesis deftly disparages Cynegirus in two ways. The action of the first verb (ἐλάβετο [= he grabbed on]) is, of course, shown to be futile by the counter-action of the second verb (= ἀπέκοψε [he chopped off]). More subtle is the deprecating effect of the parallelism of the subjects in the contrast ὁ μέν / ὁ δέ (= the one / the other):

the would-be hero (Cynegirus) is left unnamed and correlated with his anonymous nemesis, the nameless axe-wielding Persian who worked his demise.

46

The double vocative ἄνδρες 'Αθηναῖοι (= gentlemen Athenians) is the counterpart of ὦ ἄνδρες δικασταί (= O gentlemen jurors) in the first declamation (A 47). The two addresses are extremely common and virtually interchangable in Greek oratory. They may be interjected often and anywhere in a single speech. A random speech from Demosthenes is typical: ἄνδρες δικασταί (56.1, 2, 6, 8, 16, 17, 19), ἄνδρες 'Αθηναῖοι (56.5, 14, 24, 33, 40, 44, 48). Indeed, Lucian panned the overuse of these vocatives in the rhetoric of the Second Sophistic as a cover for lack of substance (cf. κἄν ποτε ἀπορήσῃς πράγματος ᾠδικοῦ, τοὺς ἄνδρας τοὺς δικαστὰς ὀνομάσας ἐμμελῶς πεπληρωκέναι οἴου τὴν ἁρμονίαν [= and if ever you are at a loss for matter to intone, say "gentlemen of the jury" elegantly and consider the harmony {of the sentence} complete], *Rh. Pr.* 19). The fact that Polemo has but one lone example in each declamation shows measured restraint in the use of this rhetorical commonplace.

The circumstantial participle περιελθόντες has conditional sense and stands for the protasis: ἐάν with subjunctive περιέλθητε (= if you go around). This together with the future indicative εὑρήσετε (= you will find) in the apodosis yields a future more vivid condition (*GG*, 2297; 2323-2326). The admonition to the audience to walk about in the encampment (στρατόπεδον) and take note of the many mangled Greek bodies presupposes as setting of the declamations the plain of Marathon shortly after the battle. This scene is consistent spatially, but not temporally, with that presupposed in the first declamation which concludes with Euphorion laying his hands dramatically on the grave mound of the *already buried* Greeks (cf. A 49).

The range of Greek casualties is crisply mentioned with a pair of μέν - δέ clauses. The masculine articles τοὺς μὲν ... τοὺς δὲ do not refer to the neuter σωμάτων (= bodies), as do the neuter ἑτέρων μὲν ... ἑτέρων δὲ; rather they must refer to the masculine νεκρούς (= corpses) which are mentioned subsequently.

The improper preposition ἄνευ (= without) — denoting the opposite of σύν (= with, cf. LSJ, ἄνευ, I) — stands here in post-position with the genitive χειρῶν (cf. the pre-position ἄνευ χειρῶν, A 11) and needs to be supplied also with the following ποδῶν: without hands ... [without] feet. In the ancient world to have one's ear hacked off could be a mark of shame and humiliation (cf.

Herodotus 3.118, 154, 157; 9.112; M. Rostovtzeff, "Οὖς δεξιὸν ἀποτέμνειν," *ZNW* 33 [1934] 196-199). In this grisly picture, however, of missing hands, feet, ears, and heads the mutilation seems rather designed to underscore that the fallen defenders bravely gave their all. The range of mutilations shows not only the fury of the battle, but also that there was nothing unique about Cynegirus' injury.

The terms ὅμοιος (= similar) and ἰσοστάσιος (= equivalent) are used here virtually synonymously. It is characteristic of Polemo to strive for variety in vocabularly and nuance in meaning. Though many are *like* the mutilated Cynegirus, no one is *like* the wounded Callimachus. Analogies to the pronc Cynegirus can be found all over the battlefield, nowhere are any to the upright Callimachus to be seen. Two rhetorical questions underscore this point. (1) In the first question the speaker shifts to the second person, addressing his dead son directly: What corpse is *identical* to you? The adjective ἰσοστάσιος (literally = *equal standing*) is deliberately chosen here. (2) In the second question he returns to the third person which had marked the previous train of thought: What soldier was so obedient to his calling? The adjective πιστός was used with a variety of prepositions (e.g., ἐν, περί, ἐπί) but the construction with εἰς rare in classical Greek (cf. LSJ sub πιστός). Here the phrase πιστὸς εἰς μάχην (= ἐν μάχῃ) may well represent a 'correction' in conformity with the idiom of a Byzantine copyist (in the evolution of demotic Greek εἰς has supplanted ἐν).

47

ἐθαύμασα (= I marveled) is a dramatic aorist expressing a present state of mind (*GG*, 1936, 1937). With the comparative μᾶλλον (= more [√ μάλα]) stands the genitive of comparison, Κυναιγείρου: "At you, Callimachus, I marvel *more than at Cynegirus*" (*GG*, 1069, 1431; cf. παντὸς ἄλλου πρέπω μᾶλλον [= I am more suited than anyone else], B 2; μᾶλλόν σου ... δυνάμενα [= more able than you], B 41).

The contrast between the single wound which felled Cynegirus and the multiple wounds that failed to bring down Callimachus is a recurring theme in the argument of Callimachus' father (cf. B 10-13, 32, 39, 46, 51).

The present tense ἄπεισιν (√ ἀπ-εῖμι [= go away]) is for vividness. With a verb of going the participle διελὼν (√ διαιρέω [= cut apart]) specifies the manner of going and contains the main idea (*GG*, 2099). This participle is graphic and the picture grisly (cf. {τὸν παῖδα} κατὰ μελέα διελών [= cutting up {the boy} limb by limb], Herodotus 1.119; τὸν λαγὸν ... διελεῖν [= to cut apart the rabbit], Herodotus 1.123; cf. διαίρεσις [= a cutting apart] as term for mutilating a body in torture and execution, Ignatius, *Rom* 5:3). Thus here διελών refers to the Persian practice of desecrating the bodies of enemies by mutilation (cf. dismemberment of the defeated κατά τινα νόμον Περσῶν [in accordance with a law of the Persians], Plutarch, *Art.* 13.2; cf. also Xenophon, *An.* 1.9.13; Herodotus 3.118; 9.112).

In keeping with his tendency to pleonasm Polemo lists four different assault weapons, each identified by its own national origin (cf. post-positive adjectives with suffixes -ικος and -ιος):

(1) ἀκινάκης Μηδικός   (= Median sword)
(2) κοπὶς Περσική   (= Persian chopper)
(3) αἰχμὴ Βαβυλωνία   (= Babylonian spear)
(4) πέλεκυς Φοινίκιος   (= Phoenician axe)

The gentilic or toponymic attributives are linked with their nouns as much for reasons of assonance as for military tradition: (1) palatals κ κ κ, (2) palatals/labials κ π π κ, (3) labials μ β β, (4) labials/palatals π κ φ κ.

(1) The ἀκινάκης (a Persian word) was, according to Herodotus (7.45), a term for the Περσικὸν ξίφος (= Persian sword) — a short weapon for which the Persians were well known in the Greek (cf. Herodotus 3.118, 128; 9.107; Xenophon, *An.* 1.2.27) as well as the Latin world (cf. *Medus acinaces*, Horace, *Od.* 1.27.5; cf. also Curtius 3.3.4; 4.15.17).

(2) The κοπίς (= cleaver [√ κόπτω = cut]) was a broad curved knife characteristic of Persian military equipment. The term could be used almost interchangably with σάγαρις (= sabre, cf. Xenophon, *An.* 1.2.9; 2.1.9; 4.2.22; 6.2.10).

(3) The αἰχμή (√ ἀκμή ? [= point], cf. Latin *icere* [= strike, stab]) is a generic word for any spear-like weapon. Greek provided a wide range of terms describing pointed shafts, pikes, javelins, and spears and Polemo availed himself of many of them (e.g., δόρυ, A 36, B 39; κοντός, B 10; ἄκων, A 24, B 42, 43; ἀκόντιον, B 39). Here for the sake of variety of expression he chooses αἰχμή.

(4) The πέλεκυς (= battle-axe) is the only term of the four which is mentioned elsewhere in the declamations (cf. A 42; B 63 is probably an interpolation). It was two-edged or double-bladed (cf. πέλεκυν ... ἀμφοτέρωθεν ἀκαχμένον [= an axe sharpened on both sides], Homer, *Od.* 5.234-235; πελέκεως δίστομος γένυς [= double edges of the axe], Euripides, *frag.* 530.5). This final item in the quartet is a dig at Cynegirus — it was a Phoenician axe which cost him his hand and his life (A 9, 23, 31; B 40, 47; and A 42; B 63) but such did not touch Callimachus.

Three exclamations (ὦ ...) give expression to the wonderment which Callimachus' father had spoken of just before his list of weapons (cf. ἐθαύμασα, B 47).

The first ὦ exclamation speaks to Callimachus' upright corpse — a circumstance which his father often referred to (cf. B 3, 11–12, 14, 17, 43–44, 54–56, 60–61) and Euphorion had not contested (A 7, 23, 24, 27, 33, 45). The address μὴ ζηλούμενε (= not being emulated) expresses again the *uniqueness* of Callimachus: "no one is like Callimachus" (B 46). Hinck (p. 32) emended the unanimously attested ζηλούμενε to read ζῆν ἀπιστούμενε (= suspected of being alive). As rationale for his alteration he pointed to quasi-parallels in the declamations (cf. νεκρὸς τὸν θάνατον ἀπιστούμενος [= a corpse being disbelieved regarding death], B 55; οὐδεὶς γὰρ ᾤετο τεθνάναι τὸν ἑστηκότα [= for no one thought the one standing had died], B 11). In Hinck's emendation the μή with the infinitive ζῆν would be 'sympathetic', i.e., confirming the negative idea of the leading verb, ἀπιστέω (*GG*, 2739. 2740). Ingenious as this conjecture may be it is without any MS support. Emendation is unnecessary — the text is unproblematic and may stand as it is.

Just as the horde of Persian missiles around Callimachus "testified" (μαρτυρούμενα) to their massive efforts against him (B 39), so his continued stance "testified" (μαρτυρούμενος) to the Greek victory. His σχῆμα (= appearance) was not empty as Euphorion had claimed (A 2, 7, 26, 27) but emblematic (cf. B 53).

In the genitive absolute τῆς ψυχῆς ἀπελθούσης the participle has concessive sense: "*although* the soul had departed." To speak of 'the soul going away' was a common expression for dying (cf. LSJ, ψυχή, I; BAGD, ψυχή, 1). The literature on Greek conceptions of the soul and death is enormous and cannot be reviewed here (cf. E. Rohde, *Psyche. The Cult of the Souls and Belief in Immortality Among the Greeks* [London: Harcourt, Brace, Routledge & Kegen Paul, 1960]; J. Bremmer, *The Early Greek Concept of the Soul*, Princeton: Princeton University Press, 1983; A. Dihle, ψυχή, *TWNT*, 9.604–614; C. Brown. "Soul," *DNTT*, 3.676–689). Suffice it to note that Polemo uses many variations of the expression (e.g., ἀφῆκε τὴν ψυχήν [= he let go of his soul], A 11; τὴν ψυχὴν ἀναλῶσθαι [= expend the soul], B 8; ἐξιοῦσα ἡ ψυχή [= as the soul went out], B 11; προέσθαι τὴν ψυχήν [= give up the soul], B 64; χωρὶς ψυχῆς [= without a soul], B 2). Despite the departure of his soul (i.e., his life) he was like one still fighting (cf. B 11, 50, 52, 53, 60). At that one must marvel.

48

In the second exclamation the vocative awaited after ὦ is absent as is often the case in Polemo (cf. Index 3). Any number of concepts could be plausibly supplied. The immediate context (cf. τῷ μαχομένῳ) suggests μεμαχημένε (= fighter, cf. ὦ δύο μεγάλας μάχας Δαρείῳ καὶ θανάτῳ μεμαχημένε [= O one having fought two great fights with Darius and death], B 52). Among other possible candidates might be considered ὦ παῖ (= O son, cf. the third exclamation immediately following) or ὦ ἀρετή (= O valor, cf. B 12 and the larger context).

The utterance ὦ τοῦ μεγάλου θαύματος (= O [...] of the great marvel) matches verbatim an exclamation of Euphorion about his son (A 33, cf. also ὦ παῖ, ὦ μέγα θαῦμα [= O son, O great wonder], A 37), but Callimachus' father makes the 'wonder' motif more like a refrain in his speech (cf. τὸ μέγιστον ... τῶν ἐν Μαραθῶνι θαυμάτων [= the greatest of the wonders at Marathon], B 2; ὦ μέγιστον τῶν Μαραθωνίων θαυμάτων [= O greatest of the Marathonian wonders], B 55; ἐκεῖνο τὸ θαῦμα Καλλίμαχος ἦν [= that marvel was Callimachus]; also B 64).

The νῦν πρῶτον (= now for the first time) matches verbally the same phrase thrice repeated in Euphorion's speech (A 36). If Euphorion wanted to claim the fight of his son's severed hands was unprecedented, then Callimachus' father can make the same claim about the fight of his son's 'deathless corpse' (ἀθάνατος νεκρός) — the marvel is expressed with an oxymoron, a figure of which Polemo is fond (cf. τῷ μακροβίῳ νεκρῷ [= the long-lived corpse], B 44; νεκρὸς τὸν θάνατον ἀπιστούμενος [= a corpse belying death], B 55; ἔμψυχος καὶ τεθνεὼς [= animated though dead], B 55).

The passive ὤφθη ([√ ὁράω] = was seen) emerged in Attic Greek with the sense *appear* (LSJ, ὁράω, II.4.b; BAGD, ὁράω, 1.a.δ; cf. ὀφθῇ, B 17).

The noun μάντευμα (√ μαντεύομαι = divine, prophesy) is not used in the technical cultic-mantic sense of 'oracle' or bona fide prediction delivered by a traditional medium such as could be consulted at classical sites like Delphi, Dodona, Didyma, or Claros. Rather it is used in the looser sense of a *presaging* or *foreshadowing* (cf. LSJ, μαντεύομαι, I.2) given wide credence in folk culture. The basic idea here is that inherent in a person's name — τοὔνομα is crasis for τὸ ὄνομα (= the name) — are the essential traits of his character or as the Latin puts it: *nomen est omen* (= a name is a portent). The ancient world is replete with examples of this notion accompanied by folk etymologies of proper names (e.g., Ajax [Pindar, *Isth.* 6,34–54]; Oedipus [Sophocles, *O.T.* 711–725; Abraham [Gen 17:5], Jesus [Matt 1:21]; such examples can be easily multiplied, cf. P. B. R. Forbes "Etymology," *OCD*, 411–412; I. Opelt, "Etymologie," *RAC* 6.797–844).

Aristotle had ranked arguments from etymology among the legitimate devices (ἐνθυμήματα) in persuasive and dissuasive rhetoric (*Rh.* 2.23.29). Thereafter the use of etymologizing became a standard 'topos' in the handbooks on rhetoric (cf. Quintilian 1.6.38-38; 5.10.55; 7.3.25). Thus Polemo's employment here of etymological argument is part of the rhetorician's stock-in-trade. The root elements of Callimachus' name — κάλλι- (= beautiful) and μάχ- (= fight) — portend the superior valor in which his life culminated at Marathon.

The clause ᾧ καὶ τὸ συμβὰν ἄδηλον εἶναι ὄνομα τῷ ἐρευνᾶν βουλομένῳ (= for the one wishing to inquire the outcome [appears] to be unclear) is itself unclear. Medieval scribes struggled to make sense out of it. One attempt was to read ὡς (→ δ) instead of ᾧ (→ γ), i.e., "as/since" instead of "for whom." Another approach (AO → α) was to insert the words ἀνακάλει νῦν πολλὰ τὸν Κυναίγειρον (= go on calling out again and again the [appellation] Cynegirus) before the clause in question. This addition makes explicit what seems to be implicit in the difficult clause following, namely the etymology of the name Κυναίγειρος (√ κυ[ω]ν- [= dog] + ἀγειρ- [= gather] → 'dog-catcher'?, 'hound-herder'?). In contrast to the clear and noble meaning of Callimachus' name, the apparent etymology of Cynegirus' name can only bring a sneer. The interpolation is ingenious but too narrowly attested to be considered authentic. Of the third generation MSS (α β ι μ ε) only α (→ AO) had this reading. It did not appear in the second generation MSS, γ and δ, and consequently was absent in their progenitor π and the underlying original Π. All previous editions of Polemo's declamations printed these words as part of the text; but now, with the reconstruction of the stemma of MSS in this edition, it is no longer possible to accord such weight to A or related witnesses. Despite that this gloss may well capture the sense of the difficult sentence.

The relative ᾧ (= for whom) appears to be proleptic, anticipating the substantized participle τῷ ἐρευνᾶν βουλομένῳ (= for the one wishing to investigate). The verb ἐρευνάω (= search, examine) can connote scientific research or academic inquiry, in particular also philological study (cf. γραμματικὴ μὲν ποιητικὴν ἐρευνῶσα [= grammar doing research into poetry], Philo, *Cher.* 105; ἐρευνᾶτε τὰς γραφάς [= search the scriptures], John 5:39); here with ὄνομα (= name) as object it must refer to etymological analysis. The substantized participle συμβάν has the sense of *result, outcome* (LSJ, συμβαίνω III.3) — namely of the etymological inquiry. Some finite verb (e.g., δοκεῖ [= it seems]) needs to be supplied with the infinitive εἶναι (= to be). What remains less certain is the referent of ὄνομα. While one might construe it as referring to Callimachus or any name in general it seems more likely that the interpolation by α (→ AO) has understood it aright as denoting Cynegirus.

49

The term πάρεργον (√ παρά [= beside] + ἔργον [= work]) is difficult to capture in English with one word. German provides an exact equivalent with *Nebensache* (= side issue). Literally the Greek has the sense of *beside the main subject*, i.e. incidental, insignificant, trifling (LSJ, πάρεργος II). Cynegirus is relegated to an inconsequential side event which barely troubled the barbarians.

In contrast Callimachus was the pivotal figure at Marathon controlling all the events. He had this role because of his περιουσία of valor. This term may be understood quantitatively (= surplus, abundance) or qualitatively (= superiority). Polemo no doubt intends both.

If the phrase τῆς νῦν τελουμένης τιμῆς (= the honor now being performed) were understood in a straight literal sense the honor would have to refer to debate between the two fathers currently taking place before the Athenian assembly. The νῦν (= now), therefore, is better understood as denoting not the present, but rather the immediate future: *presently* (LSJ, νῦν I.3) and the present participle τελουμένης (= being performed) as having future sense (a "present of anticipation," *GG*, 1879), and referring to the state funeral rites which were *going to be performed* shortly. The verb τελέω often serves as technical term for *performing* a variety of religious and state ceremonies, including rites for the dead (cf. περὶ τελευτήσαντας ... τὰ νόμιμα ... ὅσα προσήκει τελεῖσθαι [= regarding the deceased ... the funeral rites which are appropriate to be performed], Plato, *Leg.* 958d; cf. LSJ, τελέω III.3; G. Delling, τελέω, *TWNT*, 8.59). Moreover the term τιμή (= honor) can be used to denote the *final honors* accorded to the dead at funeral ceremonies (cf. ἡ πόλις αὐτοὺς ... ἔθαψε δημοσίᾳ καὶ ἔδωκεν ἔχειν αὐτοῖς ... τὰς αὐτὰς τιμὰς τοῖς ἀστοῖς [= the city gave them a public funeral and granted to them to have the same honors as the citizens], Lysias, *Epit.* 66; θάπτονται δημοσίᾳ ... τοὺς ἐν τῷ πολέμῳ τετελευτηκότας ταῖς αὐταῖς τιμαῖς καὶ τοὺς ἀθανάτους τιμᾶσθαι [= they are given a public funeral ... those having died in war {are worthy} to be honored with the same honors as the immortals], Lysias, *Epit.* 80). Indeed the erection of a gravestone itself could be called a τιμή of the dead person (MM, τιμή 1).

The γάρ sentence gives the rationale for calling Callimachus the αἴτιος (= cause) of everything that happened: When prior to the battle the ten generals — πολέμαρχοι is used here synonymously with στρατηγοί — were deadlocked regarding a tactic of defense versus offense, it was Callimachus' vote that broke the tie in the meeting (συμβολή) and set the battle in motion (cf. Herodotus 6.109–110). Originally the ψῆφος was the white or black pebble used for voting, but it gradually came to denote the vote itself (LSJ, ψῆφος II.5.a, b).

His vote "made that it was necessary to fight it out" (ἐποίησε ... ὅπως δεῖ ἀπομάχεσθαι). The indicative δεῖ (= it is necessary) stands in place of the more usual optative δέοι which one would expect after the secondary tense (ἐποίησε), but the retention of the indicative is not unclassical (*GG*, 2615). What is unclassical, however, is the use of the indicative after ὅπως — the subjunctive or optative being the norm (cf. LSJ, ὅπως, B; *GG*, 2578.d, 2929, 2209-2220, 2228, 2230, 2231). Here in Polemo ὅπως — otherwise only in B 42 — has the sense of ὡς or ὅτι (= that) introducing a dependent statement (cf. Luke 24:20). Polemo employs the optative relatively infrequently (cf. Index 1).

Strictly speaking "the other polemarchs" can only refer to the five who had opted for a defensive strategy. Polemo's imprecise expression, however, would like to suggest that *all* of them were inhibited by timidity (δειλία) in the face of the horde (πλῆθος) of invaders. By Polemo's day it had become legendary that the number in the Persian force was too enormous to be calculated (cf. Xenophon, *An.* 3.2.12; Plutarch, *Herod.* 26-27 [862b-c]; Aelian, *V. H.* 2.25). Polemo's term πλῆθος (= multitude) stands in this tradition. The portrayal of an indecisive general staff is designed to contrast with Callimachus' decisiveness. He was not riled by the numbers (cf. B 8). The argument of Callimachus' father is meant to counter that of Euphorion who had given the credit for this decision to Miltiades for persuading Callimachus to vote for attack (cf. A 16). Thus Callimachus is to be regarded as the reason for the success (κατορθώματος αἴτιος). The term κατόρθωμα (= success, √ κατορθόω [= set upright]) was commonly used to describe a battlefield victory (e.g., Polybius 1.9.12; Diodorus Siculus 13.22.5; Josephus, *B. J.* 1.39, 66; Plutarch, *Mar.* 10.2).

50

The demonstrative τοῦτο (= this) refers to the fact of Callimachus being the αἴτιος (= reason) for the triumph.

In *one* (ἑνὶ) pivotal question (ἐρώτημα [√ ερωτάω = ask]) Euphorion can offer *no refutation* (ἀνανταγωνίστῳ → α + ἀντ{ί} + ἀγων{ιστ-} [= no counter-argument]). That issue is the boundary set by death: Cynegirus' valor ceased at death, Callimachus' valor continued after death.

The argument is presented by citing the position of Euphorion and then showing its limits. Euphorion had claimed that Cynegirus had done amazing things (cf. θαυμαστόν A 11, 26), was most admirable (cf. θαυμασιώτερος A 23), and had shown daring (cf. τόλμα A 5, 14, 22, 25; τόλμημα A 24; τολμηρία A 40; τολμάω A 26). Callimachus' father summarizes that argumentation in one succinct sentence: "Cynegirus was an admirable and daring (θαυμαστὸς καὶ τολμηρὸς) man." But he gives this fair summary only for the purpose of demonstrating its limitations.

The parallel between τοῦ βίου and τῆς ψυχῆς shows that *life* and *soul* are synonymous, just as the parallel between θάνατον and τῷ κοινῷ τῆς φύσεως νομῷ shows that *death* and *the common law of nature* are identical. The parallels, likewise, between the verbs ὡμολόγησε (= he conceded) and ἡττήθη (= he was defeated) are mutually explanatory. ὡμολόγησε has the sense: he *acknowledged* death (LSJ, ὁμολογέω II.2).

The crucial term in the summary of the argument does not enjoy a consensus in the MSS. Already the second generation MSS appear to have been divided: On the one side ἄριστος (= most excellent) appeared in γ; on the other side the reading in δ seems less certain. The reading in the third generation μ is unestablished — its fourth generation descendents are divided (ἄριστος → F / καλλίστη → M). However, μ's sibling, the third generation ε (→ E CN DHP), clearly read ἀόριστος (= bound-less). In the face of the diverging external evidence the internal evidence is determinative. The whole jist of the argument in B 50 is that Callimachus' valor transcended the bounds of nature. Hence ἀόριστος should probably be taken as the original reading (→ ε → δ → π → Π). A subsequent inadvertent alteration to ἄριστος is easily understandable — the two words sound nearly alike and the change represents a common vocable which *prima facie* would seem to fit the general tenor. As in the previous lines, the parallels φύσεως περιττοτέρα (= greater than nature), τὴν ψυχὴν ὑπερβαίνει (= transcends the soul), and τοὺς κοινοὺς τῆς φύσεως ... παρελθόντα ὅρους (= going beyond the common boundaries of nature) all corroborate the reading ἀόριστος (= unbounded [by death]). It is a pivotal point and the phrase φύσεως περιττοτέρα is afterward repeated almost verbatim (cf. τῆς φύσεως περισσότερε, B 52).

The verb form εὕροις (= you would find) is a potential optative (*GG*, 1814; 1821) best understood as the apodosis of a future less vivid condition resumed from or predicated upon the future more vivid condition in B 46 (cf. περιελθόντες το στρατόπεδον ... εύρήσετε [= if you go around the camp ... you will find]).

The Macedonians played no role at the battle of Marathon (490 BCE). Indeed before the rise of Philip II (359–336 BCE) and the battle of Chaeroneia (338 BCE) they were hardly a force to be reckoned with in the Greek world. Their appearance here, therefore, must represent a later interpolation. Why this mindless anachronistic gloss would find its way into the text is unclear. Perhaps in light of the Alexander saga (336–323 BCE) a Byzantine scribe viewed the Macedonians as the quintessential 'Greek' soldiers and so unthinkingly inserted them here as expressive of the epoch-making Greek-barbarian struggle.

The claim that Callimachus alone is ἀνείκαστον (= *incomparable* — literally 'un-depictable' → ἀ + εἰκάζω [√ εἰκώς = like; εἰκών = image]) is, as it were, a response to the earlier rhetorical question: Who is ἰσοστάσιος (= equivalent) to Callimachus? (B 46). It is indicative of the connotations of the word that among the Patristic writers it became a favorite descriptor in connection with Christ (cf. ὁ διάβολος ... ἐκρατήθη ὑπὸ τοῦ ἀνεικάστου ... ἀγκίστρου τῆς θεότητος [= the devil was conquered by the unimaginable hook of divinity], Athanasius, *Quest. Al.* 793.36; ὧ φιλανθρωπία Δεσπότου ἀνείκαστος [= O the Lord's unimaginable love for humanity], John Chrysostom, *Pseud.* 59.566.22; ἀνείκαστος ἡ κατὰ τὸ ἀνθρώπινον τοῦ κυρίου ὑπεροχή [= unimaginable in human terms {is} the superiority of the Lord], Procopius Gazaeus, *Is.* 2:1f {*MPG* 87.1872b}).

With typical pleonasm Callimachus is characterized by a series of four substantized participles in apposition:

(1) τὸν ἐν τῷ βίῳ μόνον μεμαχημένον
   (= the one having fought alone in life)
(2) τόν μὴ δὲ ἐν θανάτῳ καμόντα
   (= the one not tiring in death)
(3) [τὸν] μετὰ βίον ἄνδρα ἀγαθὸν γενόμενον
   (= the one proving to be a brave man after life)
(4) [τὸν] τοὺς κοινοὺς τῆς φύσεως καὶ ἀρετῆς παρελθόντα ὅρους
   (= the one going beyond the common bounds of nature and valor)

Both fathers use the perfect participle μεμαχημένος (= having fought) as a descriptor for their sons (A 1, 28; B 2, 50, 52; cf. A 32; B 32). "The perfect denotes a completed action the effects of which still continue in the present" (*GG*, 1945) — the victory of their struggle endures.

The aorist participle καμόντα (√ κάμνω = *being weary* or *outworn*) was often used of the dead or those meeting with disaster (LSJ, κάμνω II.5). The μή negates the notion that Callimachus was *worsted* by death in combat.

Together with ἄνδρα ἀγαθόν (= a brave man) the aorist participle γενόμενον has the sense of *having proved to be*. This phrase (cf. also A 6) was a frequent expression in Herodotus' account of the Persian war (e.g. 6.14, 15, 114, 117, 137; 7.53, 106, 181, 224, 226) and perhaps Polemo picked it up from him. What is unique here, however, is that this bravery occurred μετὰ τὸν βίον (= after his life [was over])!

The aorist participle παρελθόντα is multivalent. Literally it means *going past* or *beyond*, but it also can have the sense of *outstripping, outwitting* or *eluding* (LSJ, ἔρχομαι II.1 and 2). The limits (ὅρους) of nature and valor to which men are commonly subjected were breached by Callimachus in that he continued the fight even after his death.

51

The peroration begins here with a long series of 28 exclamations introduced by ὦ (B 51-56). Polemo is fond of this exclamatory form — there are over 90 examples of it in the declamations (cf. Index 3). In comparison with its use in other rhetoricians, however, Polemo's list is disproportionately long. This particular section constitutes over 5% of the total text of the declamations, and over 8% of the second declamation. It serves as a counter-weight to a similar series of exclamations in the first declamation (A 33-40), but it is longer — if in nothing else, Callimachus' father will outdo Euphorion in quantity.

(1) The initial exclamation comprises two pairs of vocative adjectives showing paronomasia. Polemo plays with the hero's name by making an adjective out of it and coordinating it with a like sounding attribute: καλλίμαχε καὶ καλλίνικε (= beautiful fighter and beautiful conquerer). Assonance and rhythm are standard tools in the sophist's kit.

In the second pair of alliterative vocatives the variation is in the prefix instead of the suffix, producing a paradox: ἄτρωτε καὶ πολύτρωτε (= not wounded and much wounded). The root concept (√ τρω [→ τιτρώσκω = inflict a wound]) appears elsewhere in the declamations only in the noun τραῦμα (= wound), a concept central to the arguments of both fathers (cf. A 24, 48; B 11, 13, 44, 47). This juxtaposition of contradictory adjectives yields a striking oxymoron, a figure of speech of which Polemo is fond. That Callimachus was "much wounded" was an uncontested 'fact' in both declamations (cf. A 7, 23, 24, 27, 30, 45, 47; B 9-12, 32, 38-39, 44, 47, 51-52, 57-59, 61); that he was "not wounded" was the provocative claim only of Callimachus' father. It is a striking and original reformulation of the argument that wounds and death did not terminate his fight.

After the first exclamation there is an interim comment that prepares the way for the long series of exclamations to come. The form ἐπαινέσειε (√ ἐπαινέω = praise) is more common for the aorist optative than ἐπαίνεσαι (*GG*, 668; 383). With ἄν it is a potential optative referring to future propriety (*GG*, 1824): "How *should* someone *praise* you in accordance with your merit (ἀξία)?"

The second mention of Aeschylus (cf. B 45) along with "such [other second rate] poets and orators" represents another dig at that playwright and, by association, at his father Euphorion and his brother Cynegirus. For the likes of Callimachus more suitable praise would require the voice of a Homer or a comparable epic poet. The term τραγῳδία could be used not only in the narrower sense of the tragedies of the classical playwrights (Aeschylus, Sophocles, Euripides), but also in the wider sense of any serious, majestic, or epic poetry. Hence, Homer could be called a composer of tragedy (cf. Plato, *Tht.* 152e). Throughout the Greek world Homer was recognized as the epic poet *par excellence*. However, that the Smyrnaean sophist Polemo elevates him over the Attic tragedians may also be a subtle reminder of local pride — among the Ionians who laid claim to Homer's place of birth Smyrna was a strong contender (cf. Pindar, *frag.* 279).

Unfortunately, there is no Homer to sing Callimachus' praises. What comes instead is a monody of intemperate length — a torrent of twenty seven more vocative ὦ exclamations in a row is the best Polemo can do (B 51-56).

(2) To call Callimachus the common target (κοινὸς σκοπός) of Asia is to say that all the Persians aimed at him (cf. πάντες ὥστε τοξόται σκοποῦ τοξεύετ᾽ ἀνδρὸς τοῦδε [= you all shoot at this man like archers at a target], Sophocles, *Ant.* 1033-1034; κατέστησέν με ὥσπερ σκοπόν, ἐκύκλωσάν με λόγχαις [= he has set me up as his target, they surround me with spears], Job 16:12-13).

(3) The third vocative exclamation comprises two parallel participial constructions in chiastic order — the first beginning with the participle σκυλεύσας, the second ending with the participle κατασχών.

The verb σκυλεύω normally refers to the despoiling of a slain enemy; that is, it describes *the living stripping the dead* of arms or clothes (cf. σκυλεύσας τοὺς Ἀργείων νεκροὺς καὶ προσφορήσας τὰ ὅπλα πρὸς τὸ ἑωυτοῦ στρατόπεδον [= stripping the Argive dead and carrying the weapons to his own camp], Herodotus 1.82; σκυλεύειν ... τοὺς τελευτήσαντας ... ὅπλων, ἐπειδὰν νικήσωσιν [= to strip the dead of weapons after they have won], Plato, *Resp.* 469c; cf. Herodotus 9.80; Thucydides 4.44, 97; Lysias 12.40; Xenophon, *An.* 6.1.6; *Hel.* 2.4.19). Polemo's use of σκυλεύω, therefore, represents an ironic reversal: *the dead Callimachus stripped the living Persians* of their weapons.

A similar irony appears also in the second clause which says that Callimachus possessed most of the Persian arrows as λάφυρα (= spoils of war). [τὰ] λάφυρα (√ λαβ → λάμβανω [= take]) ordinarily denotes *spoils taken* from those defeated in battle. It is a very common term in accounts of military conquest (e.g., Polybius 2.62.1, 12; 5.16.5; Diodorus Siculus 11.25.1; 11.88.2; 13.51.8; Dionysios Halicarnassus, *Ant.* 1.44.1; 2.34.1; 3.49.3; Josephus, *A. J.* 10.224; *B. J.* 2.279; 7.15, 20) and typically denotes things of value — gold, silver, jewelry, art, etc. Such booty could be distributed to the victorious soldiers as a bonus for their exertions or sent back home as an infusion to the state treasury. Its value was frequently recorded in current monetary units and its sale (λαφυροπωλεῖον) brought economic gain. Indeed, those who bought and sold the loot of war constituted a special profession, the booty dealer (λαφυροπώλης), and it was a lucrative business (cf. LSJ, sub verba). Thus, in light of this language usage, Polemo's labeling of all the arrows in or around Callimachus as λάφυρα represents a drastic departure from the ordinary idiom. The arrows and spent weapons would have little value on the open market nor would they add any revenue to the exchequer. Moreover, it was not a live Callimachus who plundered the 'loot' from the corpses or captives, rather it was a dying and dead Callimachus who collected the 'valuable' missiles in his own body. Polemo's image stands the conventional language on its head in a jarring paradox. It is worth comparing this unusual picture with the Patristic metaphor of Christ's crucifixion as taking λάφυρα from the devil (cf. τὰ λάφυρα κρέμαται ἄνω ... ἐπὶ τοῦ σταυροῦ [= the spoils hang up on the cross], Joannes Chrysostomus, *Coemet.* 3[2.402b]; τὸ τρόπαιον ... τοῦ σταυροῦ ... τὰ λάφυρα τοῦ Χριστοῦ [= the trophy of the cross, the spoils of Christ], Joannes Chrysostomus, *Matt.* 57.24.34-35). Inasmuch as the concept of λάφυρα does not appear in the NT or Apostolic Fathers it would be worth exploring how the Patristic notion of Christ on the cross taking λάφυρα from the devil might be related to Polemo's memorable image of Callimachus as 'despoiler'

(4) An ἀνάθημα (= ἀνάθεμα [√ ἀνατίθημι = set up]) is that which is *set up* or dedicated to a deity such as a statue or votive offering in a temple (cf. Herodotus 1.92, 164, 183; 2.44, 111; 2 Macc 2:13; Jdt 16:19). Sometimes the ἀνάθημα represented a memorial dedication for victory in war (cf. μετὰ τὴν

... νίκην ἀναθήμασί τε κοσμῆσαι τὸ ἱερόν [= after the victory to adorn the temple with votive offerings], Strabo 13.1.26; τῆς ... ἱππομαχίας, ἣν ... ἐνίκησαν ... ἐπεχείρησεν ἀνάθημα ... ποιῆσαι [= because of the cavalry battle which they won he undertook to make a dedication] Plutarch, *Pel.* 25.5). The erect corpse of Callimachus is addressed as such a stately monument of war (σεμνὸν ἀνάθημα πολέμου). The adjective σεμνός (= august, revered) recurs as characteristic of Callimachus (cf. A 26; B 51, 62).

52

(5) The Orellius/Hinck verse division between the fourth and fifth exclamation is infelicitous. The division would be better placed before the fourth because the fifth exclamation stands in synonymous parallelism with the fourth and makes it more concrete. The parallel vocative nouns and genitive qualifiers stand in chiastic order:

σεμνὸν ἀνάθημα πολέμου (= majestic offering of war)

καλὸν Ἄρεος ἄγαλμα   (= fine Ares' image)

The expression Ἄρεως ἄγαλμα is polysemous. On the one hand, as close parallel to the preceding ἀνάθημα πολέμου, it connotes a *votive offering dedicated to Ares*, the god of war. The term ἄγαλμα (√ ἀγάλλω = glorify, exalt) often has the sense of votive offering (cf. ἄγαλμα θεῶν θελκτήριον [= offering pleasing to the gods], Homer, *Od.* 8.509; τρίπους ... Ἀπόλλωνι ... ἄγαλμα [= a tripod as thank offering to Apollo], Herodotus 5.60, 61). Thus ἄγαλμα and ἀνάθημα can be nearly equivalents (cf. ἄγαλμα δέ ἐστι ... τὸ ... ἀνάθημα [= the dedication is an image], Pausanias 2.31.6; 13.6.2; τοῦ ... ἀναθήματος ἄλλο ἐστὶν ἄγαλμα [= from the dedicatory offering another is an image], Pausanias 5.27.8).

On the other hand ἄγαλμα, as parallel to εἴδωλον (= image) in the following clause, connotes a statue or likeness. In that sense Ἄρεος ἄγαλμα denotes an *image of the war god Ares*. This genitive construction for identifying statues is common (e.g., τοῦ Ἄρεος τὸ ἄγαλμα [= the image of Ares], Herodotus 4.62; τὸ ἄγαλμα τοῦ Ἡρακλέους [= the image of Herakles], Pausanias 13.6.2; cf. also Herodotus 2.42; 4.81; IG, XI.2144b5; ID 617.1). That ἄγαλμα and εἴδωλον are virtually synonyms is evidenced by the fact that the LXX used both terms to translate the Hebrew פֶּסֶל (= image, likeness) (cf. Isa 21:9; Exod 20:4; Deut 5:8; Hos 4:17; 8:4; 13:2). In epigraphy καλὸν ἄγαλμα (= fine statue) was a standard expression for describing a high quality work of art (cf. IG I (2), 522.1; 810.1; IG II (2) 4828.2; DAA 4.1; 181.1; 244.1; SEG 13.26.1; AM 67.59.99.2). Images of gods were made from a range of hard materials — typically from metals, stone, marble, or wood (cf. Pausanias 8.37.12; 9.17.3; 10.8.7; IG II (2) 1076.fr.a–h27; IG II (2) 1390.2; 1410.7; SEG 33.140.5). It is unusual, therefore, when Polemo speaks of an image of Ares presented by the *fleshly corpse* of Callimachus.

Though the war god Ares — mentioned only here in Polemo — was reckoned among the Olympians, he was the least significant in the pantheon (cf. προσέφη ... Ζεύς· ἔχθιστος δέ μοί ἐσσι θεῶν οἳ Ὄλυμπον ἔχουσιν [= Zeus said to {Ares}: you are the most hateful to me of the gods who hold Olympus], Homer, *Il* 5.888–890; τὸν ἀπότιμον ἐν θεοῖς θεόν [= the god least honored among gods], Sophocles, *O. T.* 215). Today the paucity of Ares artifacts — very few inscriptions, coins, dedications, or statuary survive — reflects the limited extent of his cult in antiquity (cf. P. Bruneau and C. Augé, "Ares," *LIMC* II.1.479–498; II.2.358–374). The mythology about him was meager because Ares was more a personification of war than a real personality. The graphic arts usually depicted him in group reliefs, individual images were rare. Nonetheless, ἀγάλματα of Ares are occasionally mentioned in written records (cf. Herodotus 4.62; Pausanias 2.25.1; 2.35.9; 7.21.10; 8.48.4), even one by the famous sculptor Alcamenes (Pausanias 1.8.4), but no description of the appearance of any of them survives. Polemo's exclamation, therefore, about Callimachus being a noble image of Ares is due more to his own idealization of the tenacious warrior than to any identifiable cult statuary or any recognizable cultural or religious traditions. (For Ares in myth and cult cf. L. R. Farnell, *The Cults of the Greek States* [New Rochelle: Caratzas, 1977] 5.396-414; *GGR*, 1.517–519; R. Graves, *The Greek Myths* [New York: Penguin, 1980] 1.73–74; W. Burkert, *Greek Religion* [Cambridge: Harvard University Press, 1985] 169–170.)

(6) The term πολέμαρχος (= war leader) does not appear in archaic Greek, but first emerges in the classical era as a military or political office (cf. note at A 5). It was not, therefore, an archaic epithet of Ares. Moreover it does not seem to be attested as a title for the god in the classical or hellenistic periods either. No doubt it was the analogy that Polemo drew between Callimachus (the polemarch) and Ares which prompted the unique lable "polemarch god."

Callimachus was a δεινὸν εἴδωλον (= fearful replica) of that god. The term εἴδωλον (√ ειδ- [= see] → εἶδος [= form]) — among Greeks never a designation for cult images — has here the sense of *reflection, replica* (cf. λέγω δὲ τὰς ὁμοιότητας, ὅτι παραπλήσια συμβαίνει τὰ φαντάσματα τοῖς ἐν τοῖς ὕδασιν εἰδώλοις [= Regarding likenesses I say that the mental pictures are like the reflections in water], Aristotle, *Div. Somn.* 464b9; cf. Plato, *Soph.* 266b).

So far the sixth exclamation exhibits near synonymous parallelism with the fifth and fourth exclamations (σεμνὸν ἀνάθημα πολέμου / καλὸν Ἄρεος ἄγαλμα / πολεμάρχου θεοῦ δεινὸν εἴδωλον). But, like climatic parallelism in the Bible, the final phrase brings an additional feature into the picture: *surrounded by the missiles of Asia.* To be sure, this detail reiterates a recurring motif in the declamations (cf. A 7, 23, 24, 27, 30, 45, 47; B 9–12, 32, 38–39, 44, 47, 51–52, 57–59, 61). But in light of the religious undertones of the terminology (cf. ἀνάθημα, ἄγαλμα, εἴδωλον) this picture of an enclosure fence of countless Asian arrows stuck close together in the ground surrounding Callimachus (τὰ τοξεύματα περιβεβλημένον) becomes an allusion to the wall which typically surrounded the sacred precinct (τέμενος) of any sanctuary. Such a wall, usually of stone and about the height of a man (cf. W. Burkert, *Greek Religion* [Cambridge: Harvard University Press, 1985] 86), marked the boundary of the shrine and the area which was off-limits (ἄβατον, ἄδυτον) for the profane. This enclosed area was called the περιβόλιον or περίβολος (cf. LSJ, sub verba). The sacrosanct images of the honored gods were housed within the enclosure marked by this wall. Thus Callimachus, like a Greek god, was set apart from the ordinary world.

(7) The seventh exclamation recasts the metaphor of the sixth: from sanctuary fence (περίβολος) to military uniform (στολή). The arrows are now not a demarcation wall thrown up around him by Persians (περιβεβλημένον is passive), but rather a garment which Callimachus himself put on (ἐνδύς is active). The picture of Callimachus putting on the hostile arrows like a robe is original, the language (ἐνδὺς τὴν τοῦ πολέμου στολήν), however, is conventional (cf. ἔνδυσαι τὴν στολὴν τῆς ἱερατείας [= put on the robe of the priesthood], T.Levi 8:2; στολὴν δόξης ἐνδύσῃ αὐτήν {i.e., σοφίαν} [= you will put on wisdom as a robe of glory], Sir 6:31). This phraseology with military metaphors also lent itself to moralizing and mysticism (cf. ἐνδυσώμεθα τὰ ὅπλα τοῦ φωτός [= let us put on the armor of light], Rom 13:12; ἐνδύσασθε τὴν πανοπλίαν τοῦ θεοῦ [= put on the whole armor of God], Eph 6:11; cf. also 1 Thess 5:11; Eph 6:14; Isa 59:17–18; Sap 5:18). Not only does Polemo's particular metaphor appear to be original but it applies solely (μόνος) to Callimachus.

(8) and (9) The eighth and ninth exclamations form a pair both in sound and in sense. The vocative noun is the same in both (σχῆμα) and the suffix of the pentasyllabic adjectives (ἐλευθέριον / Μαραθώνιον) is likewise the same (-ιον). The result is identical rhythm in the two. Cadences like these will have

enhanced the sing-song style of delivery which characterized 'Asianist' rhetoric and which fell under the critique of the Atticists (cf. Dio Chrysostom 32.68; Philostratus, *V. S.* 491; 513; 589; 620; Lucian, *Dem.* 12; *Rh. Pr.* 19). The term σχῆμα (= figure) is devoid of any of the negative connotations which otherwise often mark it in the declamations (cf. A 2, 7, 26, 27; B 33, 35, 42). Here it means *exemplary form*, almost like παράδειγμα (= model, B 32). Picking up on an earlier note the qualifier ἐλευθέριον means *freedom preserving* (B 8, 12) and thus *freedom symbolizing*. The parallel adjective Μαραθώνιον takes on then similar meaning. The battle at Marathon had become emblematic of the Greek struggle for liberty.

(10) The tenth exclamation is a graphic exegesis of the previous two 'abstract' vocatives, and thus forms a triad with them. Callimachus was the freedom-bringing figure at Marathon because he did not allow Greece to become supine or prostrate (μὴ κλίνας [cf. in*cline*, de*cline*, re*cline*).

The next half dozen exclamations form a group of two triads with the one group bracketing the other. The 'frame' (short nominal phrases) is marked by those with the comparative forms and their accompanying genitives of comparison: (11) τῆς φύσεως περισσότερε [= greater than nature], (15) πλέον τοῦ βίου [= more than life], (16) ζώντων μαχιμώτερε [= more warlike than the living]. Inserted between (11) and (15/16) is the other triad (longer phrases) which with its own formation produces yet another *inclusio*: the verbal phrases (12) ὦ ... μεμαχημένε [= O {you} who have fought] and (14) ὦ μὴ ... ἀφείς [= O {you} who did not leave] bracket the remaining nominal exclamation (13) ὦ κοινὸν ... κατόρθωμα [= O joint success]. The series is bound together by conscious alliteration: (11) φύσεως περισσότερε (labials: φ / π); (12) δύο μεγάλας μάχας Δαρείῳ ... μεμαχημένε [δ / μ]; (13) κοινὸν ... κατόρθωμα [κ / κ]; (14) μὴ μετὰ ... ἀρετὴν ἀφείς [μ / α]; (15) φρόνημα πλέον ... βίου [labials: φ / π / β]. Polemo is conscious and careful of his craft.

(11) The expression "greater than nature" is repeated from a previous line where it refers to Callimachus 'living on' after death (cf. B 50).

(12) The two great battles were fought on different levels or in different realms. The fight with Darius — metonymy for the Persian army — took place on a human level. Callimachus and Cynegirus both struggled on this plain (though the latter on a much smaller scale). On the other hand the fight with death — almost personified — occurred on a 'higher' level. In general Polemo treats death as a natural phenomenon (cf. A 25; B 50, 51, 53. 55), but here (and possibly in B 2) θάνατος comes close to the personification Death. The Greek notion of Death as person, though undeveloped, goes back to archaic times (cf. Homer, *Il.* 16.671-683; 14.231; Hesiod, *Th.* 211-212; 756-766;

Euripides, *Alc.* passim) and this mythologoumenon survived into Polemo's world (cf. Rev 6:8; 20:14). Like a Herakles Callimachus pitted himself against the ἄνθρωπος Darius and against the δαίμων Death.

(13) As often in Polemo attribute (κοινόν [= common]) and noun (κατόρθωμα [= success]) are separated so as to form brackets for the rest of the clause. κατόρθωμα connotes the battlefield success in the double struggle against Darius and Death (cf. note at B 49). The genitives (ζώντων / νεκρῶν = [the] living / dead) are not dependent on the noun, but on the adjective (cf. κοινὸν τοῦ τὲ ἄρρενος καὶ θήλεος [= shared by male and female], Plato, *Smp.* 189e; τὸ ἐν Πλαταιαῖς ἔργον ... κοινὸν ... Λαδεδαιμονίων τε καὶ Ἀθηναίων [= the exploit at Plataea shared by both Lacedaemonians and Athenians], Plato, *Mx.* 241c; ὁ ὅρος ὁ κοινὸς τοῦ φωτὸς καὶ τῆς σκίας [= the boundary shared by light and shadow], Aristotle, *Pr.* 913a12). The concept κοινόν (= shared) offers a balance to the notion μόνος (= alone) in exclamation 7: The fruits of the military success achieved *alone* through Callimachus are *shared jointly* by both those who survived and those who fell.

(14) It seems awkward at best to describe Callimachus as not letting go or giving up valor μετὰ ζώντων (= with [the] living). Hinck, therefore, emended the phrase to read μετὰ ζωῆς (= with life): 'Callimachus did not surrender valor with [the surrender of his] life.' One might imagine the emergence of such a faulty reading through a *lapsus oculi* (cf. the *homoioarcton* ζώντων in the lines directly before and after) but it is methodologically more sound to make do with the attested text. Hence Possinus probably did better when he retained the text and rendered: "*Tu, tu virtutem, quae sola esse spirantium putabatur, etiam mortuis vindicasti*" [= you, you have laid claim to {?} valor, which was thought to be {a matter} of the living, even among the dead], Possinus, p. 91; Orellius, p. 131). In other words, the sense of μετὰ ζώντων is probably: 'Callimachus did not leave valor to be exhibited *just among the living* but he continued showing valor even after he had died.'

53

(15) The φρόνημα (= high aspiration) which Euphorion had attributed to his son Cynegirus as an innate quality (A 19) the father of Callimachus had insinuated to be a result of the enemy's cowardice (B 27). And the φρόνημα which Callimachus' father had claimed earlier for his own son as authentic (ὀρθόν) (B 12) he now boosts to the level of πλέον τοῦ βίου (= greater than life). The expansion is probably to be taken temporally: it lasted *longer than the* [earthly] *life* of Callimachus (cf. LSJ, πλείων I.1).

(16) Euphorion had spoken of his [living] son Cynegirus being more warlike (μαχιμώτερος) than a whole Persian ship (A 31). Using the same term of his own son Callimachus' father advances the notion: his [dead] son Callimachus was more warlike (μαχιμώτερος) [than the living barbarians? Greeks?]. Indeed, he puts the same notion on the lips of the barbarian reporters (cf. B 60). Polemo's technique is repeatedly that of subtle 'one-up-man-ship'.

Between the 16th and 17th vocative exclamation comes an interlude, a parenthetical statement in the third person with polysyndeton. Comparable breaks in the indicative are also inserted after the 1st, 18th, 23rd, 26th, and 27th exclamations. Clearly Polemo made an attempt to mitigate the monotony of this unduly long series.

With the anarthrous ψυχήν the attributive adjective ἀρίστην may be taken as *relative* superlative (expressing the highest degree of quality): *a most noble soul*. As quasi-predicative adjective in apposition μεγίστην is better construed as *absolute* superlative (expressing a very high degree of a quality: *a very great* [soul] (*GG*, 1085).

The concept of a "second" (δευτέραν) soul is without analogy. The notion that a person could have 'another' soul in reserve which could 'replace' the 'first' soul after it gets 'used up' runs counter to all traditional Greek conceptualization. The universally known myth of Admetus and Alcestis is emblematic of the idea that a person is limited to only one soul. Admetus can only escape looming death by offering the substitute life of another instead, and Alcestis volunteers to die in his place (cf. Ἄδμητον ἤδην τὸν παραυτίκ᾽ ἐκφυγεῖν, ἄλλον διαλλάξαντα τοῖς κάτω νεκρόν [= Admetus shall escape the imminent [trip to] Hades if he gives another corpse as ransom to those below], Euripides, *Alc.* 13–14), but it is a 'solution' which does not work (cf. "Alcestis," *OCD*, 36; R. Graves, *The Greek Myths* [New York: Penguin, 1980] 1.223-225). The answer to Jesus' rhetorical question, "what could a man give as exchange (ἀντάλλαγμα) for his soul?" (Mark 8:37) was plain to the whole Hellenistic world. Polemo's unique conception of a 'deutero-psyche' or 'back-up' soul that goes on warring and fighting — πολεμοῦσαν and ἀγωνιζομένην are pure pleonasm — under its own power (διὰ τῆς ἰδίας δυνάμεως) constitutes creative hyperbole on a bold new level.

(17) The 17th exclamation picks up on the 'first time' motif. Euphorion had claimed that Cynegirus was the *first* (πρῶτος) to fight a sea-battle from land (A 8, 36) and the *first* (πρῶτος) to show a hand's prowess (A 32, 37). That novelty, however, is out-trumped by Callimachus' own unprecedented act. Callimachus' father had countered that in his son for the first time

(πρῶτον) an undying corpse (ἀθάνατος νεκρός) was seen (B 48). That alpha-privative abstraction is 'animated' in this exclamation with the more graphic picture of the first human being exhibiting the fight of a corpse (πρῶτος ... ἀνθρώπων νεκροῦ μάχην). It is characteristic of Polemo in the second speech not only to counter-balance the arguments in the first speech, but to out-do them.

(18) The 18th exclamation introduces a new metaphor into the declamations, namely a *juridical* analogy. διαδικασία is technical terminology for a *law suit* (cf. LSJ, sub verbum) to be decided before a court (δικαστήριον). It denotes a legal proceeding to which one may be officially *summoned* — a less onerous term than *dragged* (often with force) — by the authorities (cf. προσεκαλέσαντο τὴν γυναῖκα ... εἰς διαδικασίαν [= they summoned the woman to trial], Demosthenes 43.7.5; cf. also 43.15.3; Εὐπόλεμον προσεκαλέσατο εἰς διαδικασίαν [= he summoned Eupolemos to court], Libanius, *Arg. Dem.* 56.3.3). In B 8 the γ variant Καλλίμαχος ... τὴν Ασίαν **προσκαλούμενος** (= Callimachus *summoning* Asia), instead of the δ reading **προκαλουμενος** (= *challenging*), may have in view the διαδικασία imagery in B 53.

"Those who were running for [dear] life" (τοὺς πρὸς βίον τρέχοντας), i.e., to save their necks, Callimachus was *dragging to a judicial settlement* (ἕλκων ἐπὶ διαδικασίαν). This 'dragging' idiom was common though the expression varied widely (cf. ἑλκόμενος περὶ πραγματίου [= being dragged {into court} concerning a law suit], Aristophanes, *Nu.* 1004; cf. 1217; ἕλκουσιν ὑμᾶς εἰς κριτήρια [= they drag you into courts], Jas 2:6; εἵλκυσαν εἰς τὴν ἀγορὰν ἐπὶ τοὺς ἄρχοντας [= they dragged {them} into the forum before the authorities], Acts 16:19). Moreover, it appears also in connection with verdicts of guilt (cf. εἷλκον με εἰς τὸ δεσμωτήριον [= they were dragging me to the prison], Achilles Tatius 7.15.4; τοῦτον ἐκ βίης ἕλκεις ἐς τὰς ἀνάγκας [= him you drag forcibly to punishment], Herodas 5.58–59; Θηραμένην ... εἵλκυσαν ἐπὶ τὸν θάνατον [= they dragged Theramenes to his execution], Diodorus Siculus 14.5.3). In his declamations, therefore, Polemo plays with this concept of "dragging." Euphorion had claimed that Cynegirus had dragged a ship, and he likened this to Herakles and Theseus dragging mythological beasts (A 35). Callimachus' father, however, had rejected Cynegirus' ship-dragging as ineffectual (B 37). His own son, by way of contrast, 'dragged' the fleeing Persian army 'to account before his tribunal' for their war crimes of invasion and devastation. The 'juridical' dragging of Callimachus supercedes the 'mythological' dragging of Cynegirus.

Between the 18th and 19th exclamation a short set of explanatory statements provides another break in the long ὦ series. Both the μέν - δέ and the ὡς sentences have a postpositive γάρ signalling a reason for the preceding and following clauses (*GG*, 2803, 2810-2811). The μέν clause refers to Callimachus' *ante mortem* actions, the δέ clause to his *post mortem* stance.

Euphorion had called his son a "soldier" (στρατιώτης) in the sense of 'a man's man', but without any real qualifiers — simply "such" (τοιοῦτος) a soldier (A 46) and contrasted with a corpse (A 2, 27). Callimachus' father too lays claim to the honorific "soldier" for his son, but he adds attributes: a soldier "more long-lived than fated" (B 12), "faithful in battle" (B 46), and now in this ὦ exclamation "fighting for the fatherland" (B 53). Once again Callimachus' father does not just match Euphorion, he outdoes him.

The explanation that Callimachus remained standing because "he agreed with his soul" refers to his *ante mortem* soul, not his 'second' soul. It is a reformulation of the earlier presentation that Callimachus' departing soul had enjoined his body to remain standing and to continue to fight (B 11). The statement that "he obeyed and remained steadfast" (ἐπείσθη καὶ βεβαίως ἔμενεν, B 11) is recast here as "he agreed with his soul" (ὡμολόγησε τῇ ψυχῇ).

54

(19) In the long series of exclamations the 19th (μεγάλη στάσις [= great stance]) is unrivaled in brevity (5 syllables in 2 words). It acts like a punctuation mark in the list separating the foregoing from the following. στάσις (= standing posture) is the term used in both speeches to denote the upright corpse of Callimachus — described negatively in the first speech (A 7, 22, 24, 26, 27), positively in the second (B 3, 38, 54).

(20) (21) (22) (23) The next four exclamations form a conceptual unit whose common theme is summarized in the adjectives of the interlude sentence which follows them: ἀκίνητος, στασιμώτερος, βεβαιότερος [= unmoved, stationary, steadfast]. Callimachus was bonded with the land.

(20) Callimachus was 'co-souled' (σύμψυχος) with the earth. The term σύμψυχος (= united in soul) does not seem to be documented prior to the NT (cf. τὸ αὐτὸ φρονῆτε ... σύμψυχοι, τὸ ἕν φρονοῦντες [= think the same thing ... in mutual accord, being of one mind], Phil 2:2), but it does appear often later in patristic literature (e.g., *Const. Ap.* 2.47.2; Eusebius Caesariensis, *H. E.* 7.21.3; Eusebius Nicomediensis, *Lib. Poen.* 65.14 [variant for συμψήφους [M 67.113a]; Joannes Chrysostomus. *hom.in Phil.* [5.1] 62.213.6; 62.214.1, 13,16; Basilius, *Ep.* 204.7.12; *Asc. Mag.* 31.1005.35; 1184.15;

1204.50; *Reg. Mor.* 31.796.4; 816.6; Amphilochius, *Ep. Syn.* 76). The patristic passages — virtually all dependent on Phil 2:2 — refer to unison among Christians. Polemo is distinctive in that he uses the term to describe a harmony between Callimachus and the earth (γῆ); it is thus, as it were, a trans-human concept. Ordinarily Polemo's vocabulary is in conscious conformity with Classical Attic usage. The compound σύμψυχος, however, appears to be one of those rare linguistic anachronisms in Polemo where a Hellenistic coinage is projected back into the Classical period.

(21) (22) The unity between the man and the earth which was hailed in the 20th exclamation is portrayed in the next two exclamations with the botanical imagery of root and plant.

(21) Being the *lectio difficilior* the nominative βαλλόμενος (→ γ) is to be preferred over the vocative βαλλόμενε (→ δ). Amidst the series of vocatives the nominative is conspicuous, but "the nominative may be used in exclamations as a predicate with the subject unexpressed" (*GG*, 1288). Attestation for the expression ρίζας ... βαλλόμενος (= putting down roots) is scant but it appears to have been a relatively common idiom. In Job 5:3, for instance, the LXX translated the Hiphil participle מַשְׁרִישׁ (√ שׁרשׁ [= taking root]) with ρίζαν βάλλοντας (= throwing down root), a phrase which 1 Clement (39:8) had no trouble repeating (cf. also ρίζαν δ' οὐκ ἀπὸ γῆς μητρὸς βάλεν, ἀλλ' ἀπὸ πέτρης [= she struck root not from mother Earth, but from a rock], *An.Gr.* 9.307.5). Thus βάλλω ρίζας (= put down roots) is a periphrastic version of ριζοβολέω (= strike root, cf. LSJ, sub verbum) and an alternate way of saying ριζόω (= become rooted). The 21st exclamation, in fact, recasts an earlier image with precisely that verb (cf. βεβαίως ἔμενεν ὥσπερ ἐρριζωμένον [= he remained firm as though rooted], B 11). Despite the ferocity of the battle Callimachus was able to fasten roots, that is, remain firm, because of his valor (ἐξ ἀρετῆς). Conceptually this image is similar to the allegorical interpretation of the seed on rocky ground in Jesus' parable of the sower (cf. οὐκ ἔχουσιν ρίζαν ... ἀλλὰ πρόσκαιροί εἰσιν, εἶτα γενομένης θλίψεως ἢ διωγμοῦ ... εὐθὺς σκανδαλίζονται [= they do not have root but are ephemeral, when trouble or persecution occurs they are immediately caused to fall], Mark 4:17). In Polemo's metaphor it is, of course, not Christian faith (πίστις) but Greek valor (ἀρετή) which enables the firm rootedness.

(22) The 22nd exclamation expands the preceding metaphor — Callimachus with *roots* becomes himself a *plant*. Before Polemo φυτόν had already been used metaphorically of human beings in both the Greek and Jewish worlds (cf. ἡμᾶς ... ὄντας φυτὸν οὐκ ἔγγειον ἀλλ' οὐράνιον [= us ... being not an earthly but a heavenly plant], Plato, *Tim.* 90a; ὁ Πλάτων ...

ἀθάνατόν σε λέγων καὶ φυτὸν οὐράνιον [= Plato ... calling you immortal and a heavenly plant], *An. Gr.* 10.45; ὡς γὰρ φυτὸν ἧς εὐώδους μήλου συνανθῶν [= you were blossoming as a plant of fragrant fruit], *T. Job* 32:6). The Hebrew tradition had long used the plant metaphor (cf. a Torah observer "like a tree planted by streams of water" (כְּעֵץ שָׁתוּל עַל־פַּלְגֵי מָיִם [→ ὡς τὸ ξύλον τὸ πεφυτευμένον παρὰ τὰς διεξόδους τῶν ὑδάτων], Ps 2:3; Israel as "shoot planted by the Lord" (נֵצֶר מַטָּע יהוה [→ φύτευμα], Isa 60:21); the Qumran community as "eternal planting" [מַטַּעַת עוֹלָם 1QS 8:5; 11:8; CD1:7; 1QH 6:15; 7:19; 86-10]). What is unique to Polemo, therefore, is the specific *Marathonian location* of the plant. The image of Callimachus as lone sturdy plant — surely he means a tree (cf. LSJ, φυτόν I.1) — on the plain of Marathon counters the picture of Cynegirus as oak or pine (cf. A 42), a simile which Callimachus' father had already debased to a piece of wood (cf. B 39).

(23) The metaphor shifts from botany to topology. Parallel to νήσων (= islands), δήμων must here mean *lands* (LSJ, δῆμος I). Coming on the heels of the plant metaphor the adjective βεβαιότερε (= more solid) may have in mind the *roots* and the λαμπρότερε (= more brilliant) the *foliage*.

Between the 23rd and 24th exclamation another break is inserted to alleviate the underlying monotony of the unwieldy ὦ series. The interruption has the form of a double μέν - δέ contrast: (a) Eretrians and Naxians removed versus Callimachus unmoved; (b) mainland and islands quaking versus corpse unshaken.

(a) Naxos and Eretria suffered the brunt of the Persian naval invasion before the landing at Marathon (cf. the notes at A 38, 43). The fate of the two is described in synonymous parallelism: ἡρπασμένη (= seized) / αὔτανδρος (= men and all). The compound adjective αὔτανδρος (→ αὐτός + ἀνήρ) expresses *entirety* (cf. ναῦν αὔτανδρον [the ship and its entire crew], Polybius 1.25.3; 128.14; τὰς οἰκίας αὐτάνδρους [= the houses and everyone in them], Josephus, *B. J.* 6.404; τὸν δῆμον αὔτανδρον [= the people to the last man], Josephus, *B. J.* 2.492; 4.302). Thus Νάξος αὔτανδρος (= Naxos and its entire [male?] population) represents a gross exaggeration on Polemo's part. In actuality the Naxians had fled to the mountains prior to the Persians' arrival so that the invaders only caught the stragglers (cf. Herodotus 6.31). Here Polemo has probably extrapolated from the general Persian policy of putting out the 'dragnet' over an entire island when it was captured (cf. Herodotus 6.31). For the fate of the Eretrians see the note at A 43.

The parallel verbs πλεῖ (= sets sail) / ἐν ταῖς ναυσὶν ἐτέθη (= was put in the ships) present a *hysteron proteron* — a reversal of the natural order in time in order to put the stress on the later event as more important (*GG*, 3030). It corresponds with the inverted chronology of Naxos and Eretria.

In contrast to this mass movement of captives Callimachus remained ἀκίνητος, a description which connotes both *unmoved* (cf. ὦ ... μὴ κεκινημένε [= O {you who} have not moved], B 47) as well as *unmovable* (cf. κινῆσαι δὲ οὐδεὶς ἠδύνατο [= no one was able to move], B 58). The term ἀκίνητος refers primarily to *physical* motionlessness (cf. also B 58). But simultaneously it also connotes figuratively steadfastness of *character* (cf. LSJ, ἀκίνητος II.3; BAGD, ἀκίνητος 2). This description *via negativa* is 'fleshed out' positively with a pair of comparisons in apposition — "more stationary than the mountains and more steadfast than the peaks." Such pleonastic synonymous parallelism has the function, as in the Psalter, of investing the words with more weight.

(b) The second μέν - δέ contrast shifts from the human to the geological realm. Polemo cites two examples of seismic phenomena: earthquakes on the mainland (γῆ ἐσείσθη) and disappearances of whole islands (νήσους ὅλας ... φερομένας) — the former more frequent (πολλάκις [= many times], the latter more drastic (εἶδον ἄνθρωποι [= men take note]). The chosen terminology is conventional for seismic disasters (cf. LSJ, σείω I.2 [earthquakes]; φέρω B.I.1 [being swept away involuntarily]). The inexorable tectonic movement beneath the Aegean world left a deep impression on the Greek psyche (cf. only the popular etymology of Ποσειδῶν as earth**shaker**: ἀπὸ τοῦ σείειν ὁ σείων ὠνόμασται· πρόσκειται δὲ τὸ πῖ καὶ τὸ δέλτα [= from his shaking he has been called the Shaker, the pi and delta are added], Plato, *Crat.* 403a; cf. Herodotus 7.129). Countless quakes were recorded in Greece proper as well as Ionia (Polemo's own Smyrna was devastated by a severe earthquake in 178 CE). And reduced or submerged islands were part of Greek lore (cf. Thera and Atlantis). For the cultural significance of earthquakes in the classical world cf. A. Hermann, "Erdbeben," *RAC*, 5.1070–1113.

Having named the literal natural phenomena Polemo shifts to a figurative mode of speech — earthquake becomes a metaphor for war, a not uncommon occurrence in the classical world (cf. *dissensio civilis quasi permixtio terrae* [= civil dissension like an upheaval of the earth], Sallust, *Jug.* 41.10; *sumite nunc gentes accensis mentibus arma, ... ipsa tremat tellus* [= take up arms now, you peoples, while your spirit is hot ... let the earth herself quake], Petronius 124, 283 and 287; ἀνετράπετ᾽ ἠΰτε πύργος ... κραδαινομένης βαθὺ γαίης [= {Achilles} fell like a tower when the earth is deeply shaken], Quintus Smyrnaeus 3.63, 65). So gravely was the Greek world shaken by the Persian invasion that the war could be measured on the Richter scale. But this upheaval did not rattle (οὐ διέσεισε) Callimachus. The compound verb διασείω means *confound, throw into confusion* (cf. ἦν μέν νῦν μὴ συμβάλωμεν, ἔλπομαι τινὰ στάσιν μεγάλην διασείσειν ἐμπεσοῦσαν τὰ 'Αθηναίων φρονήματα ὥστε μηδίσαι [= if we do not now give battle I suppose some great upheaval bursting in will shake the minds of the Athenians so that they side with the Medes.], Herodotus 6.109). Here Polemo plays with the simple and compound verb: σείω and διασείω. Such punning is characteristic of Polemo's style (e.g., ἔχω / κατέχω A 9–10; B 36, 41; τάσσω / παρατάσσω A 18–19; μάχομαι / ἀπομάχομαι A 28; πίπτω / ὑποπίπτω B 3; κελεύω / ἐγκελεύω B 23; πλέω / ἐκπλέω B 45). Even the corpse of Callimachus was not disturbed.

55

(24) The τεῖχος (= city-wall) — distinguished from τοῖχος (= house-wall) — was a defense fortification known from gray antiquity (cf. Homer, *Il.* 21.295, 446; *Od.* 6.9; Herodotus 1.26, 80, 141, 150, 163). In the LXX τεῖχος is the standard translation of חוֹמָה (= city defense wall). Polemo's image thus excedes the conventional concept for he does not speak of the wall of Athens (city) but of Attica (district), a triangular territory of some 1000 square miles (cf. the τεῖχος of the gargantuan endtime Jerusalem, Rev. 21:12–18). Aristotle had discussed the advantages and disadvantages of city walls (*Pol.* 1330b33–1331a24) and, recognizing that "the superior numbers of attackers may be too much for the human valor among those [who are] few" (ἐνδέχεται πλείω τὴν ὑπεροχὴν γίγνεσθαι τῶν ἐπιόντων τῆς ἀνθρωπίνης τῆς ἐν τοῖς ὀλίγοις ἀρετῆς), he argued that fortified walls represent the securest and most warlike strategy (*Pol.* 1330b38–40).

Occasionally τεῖχος could be used figuratively to describe strong-willed people (cf. Jer 1:18; 15:20; Cant 8:9-10) or formidable soldiers (cf. 1 Sam 25:16 and note at B 10), but this was not common in the Greek tradition. Nevertheless, Polemo likes the metaphor and uses it three times of Callimachus (B 10, 55, 59; cf. note at B 10). Within the secure Roman empire of Polemo's day the fortification wall will not have carried the same significance as in ancient Greece. Yet the nostalgia of the Attic revival felt the wall to be a powerful metaphor. What would have been the outcome without the wall of valor presented by the resolute Callimachus? (cf. ὥσπερ πόλις τὰ τείχη καταβεβλημένη καὶ ἀτείχιστος, οὕτως ἀνὴρ ὃς οὐ μετὰ βουλῆς τι πράσσει [= just like a city {whose} walls are breached and {which is} unwalled, so is a man who does not do anything with determination], Prov 25:28).

(25) The 25th exclamation takes up the recurring θαῦμα (= marvel) motif. Both fathers view their sons as an object of wonder (Cynegirus: A 25, 33, 37; Callimachus: B 2, 48, 55, 56, 64). On this score, however, each father deals with the claim of the other differently. Euphorion deflates the marvel of Callimachus by pointing out that the amazing thing (τὸ θαυμαστόν) occurred after he could no longer be aware of it — and there is no valor without a perceiving soul (A 25). For his part, Callimachus' father simply ignores the θαῦμα claim for Cynegirus. His strategy is instead to outdo Euphorion quantitatively and qualitatively. He reiterates the term for Callimachus more often (B 2, 48, 55, 56, [64]) and he attaches here superlatives to the term: the great (μέγα) wonder of Cynegirus (A 33, 37) is out-trumped by the greatest (μέγιστον) and the most divine (θειότατον) of the Marathonian wonders — Callimachus.

(26) On the surface the 26th exclamation appears to restate the 25th using different words in synonymous parallelism, but it actually goes slightly beyond it:

25th	26th
Μαραθωνίων (= Marathonian)	→ ἐκεῖ (= there)
θαυμάτων (= marvels)	→ φασμάτων (= portents)
μέγιστον, θειότατον (= greatest, most divine)	→ ἐξαίρετον (= exceptional)

The advance occurs in the term φάσμα (√ φαίνω [= appear]) which connotes a *supernatural appearance* or phenomenon (LSJ, sub verbum). Herodotus' account of the battle of Marathon provided the precedent for equating the terms θαῦμα and φάσμα. There θῶμα/φάσμα referred to an unidentified *apparition* that appeared to Epizelus, blinding him and killing a comrade (Herodotus 6.117), an incident that was retold many times in the Greek tradition (cf. A 44; Plutarch, *Athen.* 347d; *Par. Gr. R.*305b-c; Aelian, *N. A.* 7.38; Diogenes Laertius 1.56; Suidas, Πολύζηλος; Ἱππίας). Plutarch represents a version of this tradition when he records that "of those fighting at Marathon against the Medes not a few thought they saw an apparation (φάσμα) of Theseus in arms rushing on in front of them against the barbarians" (Plutarch, *Thes.* 35.5). In this 26th exclamation Polemo, in his own version, does something otherwise undocumented in the φάσμα legend, namely, he identifies the φάσμα with Callimachus. This is repeated more explicitly in the 28th and final exclamation (B 56). This unique identification not only elevates Callimachus to a trans-human level on a par with the demi-god Theseus, but it also has the corollary function of relegating to a lower level the prowess of Cynegirus. (Recall Euphorion had claimed that Polyzelus, despite being blinded by the φάσμα, could still see the prowess of Cynegirus, A 44).

Between the 26th and 27th exclamation Polemo inserts yet another prose interlude. The increasing frequency of such 'breaks' in this ὦ series betrays Polemo's awareness that the spontaneity of the outbursts has been dissipated and that the series cannot be naturally sustained.

In Polemo's day the adjective εὐσχήμων was popularly used to describe the socially prominent or decorous (cf. LSJ, BAGD, and MM, sub verbum; H. Greeven, εὐσχήμων, *TWNT* 2.768-770). The second century Atticist Phrynichus, however, rejected that connotation of externals and, as purist, argued for a signification of inward ethical-aesthetic values (cf. εὐσχήμων· τοῦτο μὲν οἱ ἀμαθεῖς ἐπὶ τοῦ πλουσίου καὶ ἐν ἀξιώματι ὄντος τάττουσιν· οἱ δ' ἀρχαῖοι ἐπὶ τοῦ καλοῦ καὶ συμμέτρου [= εὐσχήμων: the unlearned utilize this word for the one who is rich and in a position of rank, but the ancients {utilized it} for the one who is noble and {does things} in due proportion], *Ecl.* 309). It is that older sense, close to the classical understanding of ἀρετή (= virtue, excellence, nobility, valor), that Polemo means here. The etymological components of εὐ-σχήμων are still felt by Polemo: Callimachus' corpse was elegant in figure, winsome in mien.

In saying that the corpse stood *in the foremost position* (ἐν τῇ πρώτῃ στάσει) Polemo uses the term στάσις differently than elsewhere in the declamations. Otherwise it connotes Callimachus' *upright posture* (cf. A 7, 22, 24, 26, 27, 45; B 3, 38, 54). Here, however, it designates his *location* or *position* in the front line (cf. LSJ, στάσις, B.I.2). This description of his battle station — a variation of his being in the 'teeth' (στόμα) of the battle where the assault was 'fiercest' (ἀκμαιοτάτην) (B 8) — is formulated to counter Euphorion's argument that Cynegirus 'got past the front line of battle' (ὑπερβὰς τὴν φάλαγγα) and fought on the beach against the 'toughest' (μαχιμώτατον) enemy (A 8). Callimachus' father had already delegitimized that action of Cynegirus by labeling it an 'abandoning of his assigned post' (λειποτακτήσαντα, cf. note at B 44). That negation is now outstripped by the positive picture of Callimachus' adherence to his front line position.

The phrase τὸν θάνατον ἀπιστούμενος is ambiguous. The participle could be construed as a middle with active sense and having an accusative direct object: Callimachus' 'corpse disbelieved the death' that came over it and so continued as though it were not true (cf. ἐν σελήνῃ ... τὴν δὲ γνῶσιν τοῦ οἰκείου ἀπιστεῖσθαι [= in moonlight to distrust the recognition of their own friends], Thucydides 7.44.2). On the other hand the participle could be taken as a passive standing with an accusative of respect: the 'corpse was disbelieved {by the Persians} regarding its death' (cf. ἄνθρωποι ... ἐπειδὰν γνῶσιν ἀπιστούμενοι, οὐ φιλοῦσι τοὺς ἀπιστοῦντας [= men when they are mistrusted regarding their knowledge do not love those mistrusting {them}], Xenophon, *Cyr.* 7.2.17). In light of the active ἔστη preceding and the middle αἰσχυνόμενος following, the middle interpretation of ἀπιστούμενος seems more likely.

The construction αἰσχυνόμενος πεσεῖν (the verb αἰσχύνομαι + infinitive) is classical: *being ashamed to fall* essentially means 'he would be ashamed if he did fall' (*GG*, 2126; LSJ, αἰσχύνω B.II.2.c). The later expansion of the phrase to μετὰ τοσούτων αἰσχύνῃ πεσεῖν; (= with so many [looking on] are you ashamed to fall?, B 60), shows that this shame has more to do with losing face outwardly than feeling guilt inwardly. The language reflects a 'shame culture' rather than a 'guilt culture' (cf. E. R. Dodds, *The Greeks and the Irrational* [Berkeley: University of California Press, 1971] 28-63). In other words, the concern is not for moral virtue but for 'what will people say?'.

The phrase νεκρός ... γέγονεν ἔμψυχος (= [the] corpse became 'insouled') reformulates the earlier exclamation ὦ σῶμα ἔμψυχον (= O 'animated' body, B 12). This restatement does not diminish the paradox; it underscores it by adding the concessive participial phrase καὶ τεθνεὼς ὤν (= even though he had died). It is instructive to compare Polemo's νεκρὸς ... γέγονεν ἔμψυχος with a similar phrase in Sophocles: ἔμψυχον ἡγοῦμαι νεκρόν (= I consider [Creon] a living corpse, *Ant.* 1167). The predecessor, though linguistically identical, has the opposite sense of Polemo: Creon — having in *hybris* caused the suicides of Antigone, Haemon, and Eurydice, and brought down on himself the curse of the gods — is, though still alive, an ἔμψυχον νεκρόν (= breathing corpse) doomed to a miserable existence and a worse death. In contrast Callimachus is a νεκρὸς ἔμψυχος (= corpse instilled with a soul) which despite death continued the courageous struggle displayed while still alive. Sophocles' phrase describes a tragic wretch, Polemo's a noble hero.

(27) The determinative concept in the penultimate exclamation, namely τῆς ψυχῆς τὴν ὁδόν (= the way of the soul), is singular in Polemo. Indeed, it is hard to find an equivalent expression anywhere in Greek literature. In philosophy, religion, and the vernacular the term ὁδός was a versatile concept (cf. W. Michaelis, ὁδός, *TWNT* 5.42-101). When used figuratively its multivalence was usually narrowed with qualifiers, e.g., a *preposition* (cf. ὁδὸν εἰς εὐδοξίαν [= way to glory], Heraclitus, *frag.* 135; τὴν ὁδὸν ... ἐπὶ τὸν βίον [= the path for life], Xenophon, *Mem.* 2.1.21), an *adjective* (cf. ἄδικον ὁδόν [= unjust path], Thucydides 3.64.4; χαλεπὴν καὶ μακρὰν ὁδόν [= difficult and long way], Xenophon, *Mem.* 2.1.29), or a *genitive* (cf. πολλαὶ δ' ὁδοὶ ... εὐπραγίας [= many paths of prosperity], Pindar, *Ol.* 8.13-14; τοῦ βίου ταύτην τὴν ὁδόν [= this path of life], Isocrates 1.5). In such constructions the

qualifier is essential for the specific understanding of ὁδός. Despite the genitive, however, in Polemo's phrase, the precise meaning of τῆς ψυχῆς τὴν ὁδόν is elusive.

The semantic content of ψυχή varies in the declamations. Sometimes it connotes the *impersonal basis of life* or *life itself* (cf. μέχρι τοῦ βίου / μέχρι τῆς ψυχῆς [= as long as life/soul {lasted}], B 50; also A 11, 37; B 1, 12, 47, 60) and sometimes *personal conscious individuality* (cf. ἡ ψυχὴ ... τῷ σώματι ... ἐνετείλατο ... μάχεσθαι [= the soul enjoined the body to fight], B 11; also B 2, 8, 12, 13, 43, 53, 56). That τῆς ψυχῆς is an objective genitive is unlikely, for it is hard to imagine how the corpse of Callimachus could go the way that leads to life or to the soul (cf. ἡ ὁδὸς τῆς ζωῆς [= the way of life], Did 1:2 = ἡ ὁδὸς ἡ ἀπάγουσα εἰς τὴν ζωήν [= the way leading to life], Matt 7:14). It is, therefore, best taken as a subjective genitive: the ψυχή is not the destination to which the path leads but rather the entity which follows the path and 'makes its way'. Mentions of the ψυχή immediately before and after refer clearly to Callimachus' own personal soul (cf. B 53, 55) and that seems to fit best here too. Nonetheless, the omission of the vocative after ὦ, though a common stylistic feature in Polemo (cf. Index 3), leaves a certain vagueness. *What* (or *who*) does the seeing or imitating? The preceding context suggests that νεκρέ (= corpse) be supplied, though one might perhaps argue for Καλλίμαχε (= Callimachus), ψυχή (= [departed] soul). The vocative makes some difference in the conceptualization.

More well-known ὁδός metaphors do not satisfactorily illumine Polemo's "way of the soul." The tradition, for example, that the departed soul upon arrival in the underworld is directed to one of two "ways" (ὁδοί) — Elysium or Tartarus (cf. Plato, *Gorg.* 524a; *Resp.* 10.614b-e; Virgil, *Aen.* 6.540-543) — sheds as little light on Polemo as Prodicus' fable of Herakles at the crossroad having to chose between the two "ways" (ὁδοί) of virtue (ἀρετή) or of vice (κακία) (cf. Xenophon, *Mem.* 2.1.21-34). Nevertheless, Orellius' interpretation (p. 132) of Polemo's expression seems to be guided by some such mythological or moral conception (cf. μιμούμενος τῆς ψυχῆς τὴν ὁδόν, *quae scil. e corpore excedens sursum tendit ad loca coelestia* [= imitating the way of the soul which, it is evident, as it was going out of the body tended upwards to the heavenly realm]). In other words, the dead Callimachus conformed to the 'upward path of the [departing] soul'! The picture, however, of a soul striving toward heaven is not only without analogy in Polemo but it also is at direct odds with the sentence immediately following.

For the meaning of Polemo's distinctive phrase, therefore, the context has to be determinative. Accordingly, the implied vocative subject of the verbs *seeing* (βλέπων) and *imitating* (μιμούμενος) is the 'de-souled' corpse of Callimachus. The disjunctive ἤ (= or) between the participles seems rough. The scribe of ρ (followed by QR, Stephanus, Possinus, and Orellius) altered it to an asyndetic ὤ, thereby putting the participles in apposition. Hinck (p. 35), for his part, emended it to a conjunctive καί (= and). Such changes, however, are unnecessary. The "or" may stand with the sense: "seeing *or* [*rather, to say it better,*] imitating." The sense of the whole striking exclamation is then quite simple: the lifeless corpse of Callimachus saw (i.e., remembered) and copied the conduct of Callimachus' fighting body while it was still being animated by the soul before its departure.

56

Between the final two exclamations Polemo inserts one last prose interlude which helps clarify the exclamations bracketing it. Only here does Callimachus' father refer to himself with the emphatic pronoun *I* (ἐγώ), the less measured Euphorion had done that four times (A 2, 15, 32, 33). The verb of thinking (οἶμαι) + accusative (τὴν ψυχήν) + infinitive (συμμάχεσθαι / ἐγγυᾶσθαι) represents the classical construction for indirect discourse (*GG*, 2016, 2018, 2022).

Key to understanding the picture is the noun to be supplied with the prepositional phrase ἐκ τ᾿ ἀφανοῦς [elision for τοῦ ἀφανοῦς] = from the unseen ...). From the unseen *what*? The alpha-privative adjective ἀφανής (= un-seen [√ φαίνομαι = appear]) belonged to the vocabulary of poets and playwrights who ventured to speak of Hades and the underworld (cf. **Ταρτάρου** πυθμὴν πιέζει σ᾿ **ἀφανοῦς** σφυρηλάτοις ἀνάγκαις [= the depth of **unseen Tartarus** oppresses you with hard-forged necessities], Pindar, *frag.* 207, quoted by Plutarch, *Cons. Ap.* 104a; ἐρέσσετ᾿ ... δι᾿ ᾿Αχέροντ᾿ ... τὰν ἄστολον μελάγκροκον ναύστολον θεωρίδα, τὰν ἀστιβῆ ᾿πόλλωνι, τὰν ἀνάλιον πάνδοκον εἰς **ἀφανῆ** τε **χέρσον** [= row over Acheron the ungirded, dark, dispatched ferryboat {of Charon} to the {land} untrodden by Apollo, to the sunless, all-receiving {land}, to the **unseen land**], Aeschylus, *Th.* 855–860; κατθάνοισα δὲ κείσῃ ... **ἀφάνης** κἀν ᾿Αίδα δόμῳ [= but when you die **you will lie** there ... **unseen** even in the house of Hades], Sappho 55 {→ Plutarch, *Conj. Pr.* 146a; Stobaeus 3.4.12}; cf. also Sophocles, *O. C.* 1551–1552, 1557–1560). Thus, Polemo's phrase ἐκ τ᾿ ἀφανοῦς (= from the unseen [----]) comes out of poetic tradition; the omission of a substantive (e.g., Hades, Tartarus, Erebos, or the like) may reflect a kind of folk piety or superstition — one does not name things that should not be conjured up (cf. 'Speak of the devil and he appears'). For those steeped in the Greek tradition the meaning of the truncated phrase will have been clear.

It remains unclear how Polemo imagined the soul of Callimachus participating in the battle from the nether realm of Hades. Did he stay below and fight at a distance with, as it were, 'long arms'? Or did he take a 'leave of absence' and temporarily remain at Marathon until the victory was achieved? The description of the soul as παροῦσαν (= standing by) suggests the latter.

As a rule in classical Greek verbs of promise, like ἐγγυᾶσθαι (= pledge oneself), are followed by a future infinitive (LSJ, ἐγγυάω II.2), particularly in indirect discourse (*GG*, 1865d, 1866c, 1867c 1868, 1999, 2024). That the infinitive following should be a present as here (ἀνέχειν [= to hold up]) is rare, but not unknown (*GG*, 1868).

(28) The final exclamation in the ὦ series does contain a vocative, the participle κεκοσμημένε (= adorned, honored), but as with the participles in the previous exclamation (βλέπων / μιμούμενος) a masculine substantive still needs to be supplied mentally. It would be most natural, though not necessary, to think the same noun as before (corpse? fighter?).

This last exclamation rephrases the φάσμα motif of the 26th exclamation (cf. note at B 55): the corpse was adorned with a "great apparition" (μεγάλῳ φάσματι). The perfect participle (κεκοσμημένε = has been clothed) "denotes a completed action the effects of which still continue in the present" (*GG*, 1945, cf. 1872d, 2043). In other words, the 'epiphanic' quality of Callimachus' corpse endures.

This φάσμα (= supernatural appearance) motif constitutes the culmination of the entire series of exclamations. Polemo expands and makes explicit what was implied in the 26th exclamation. The φάσμα which had become an established feature in the Marathon tradition is here explicitly and uniquely identified with Callimachus himself! On this point Polemo stands alone in the record.

The reading τουτὶ δὲ Πολύζηλος (= and this very [φάσμα] Polyzelos), which according to the evidence of the MSS stood in the medieval progenitor π, represents an incomplete sentence — a verb of seeing needs to be supplied. Hence, the variant of the μ group of MSS, namely τουτ᾽ εἶδε Πολύζηλος (= this [φάσμα] Polyzelus saw), may well reconstruct the earlier reading of Π which stood behind π. For the equation φάσμα = θαῦμα, cf. the note at B 55.

While Polemo did attribute to Callimachus' corpse the act of standing and the act of fighting, he could not bring himself to attribute to it the act of talking — that would have been too much apparently even for the bombast of Polemo. So in a sort of 'mini-flashback' he places the utterance to follow on the lips of

Callimachus *while he was still alive* (ζῶν ἔτι ... ἔστηκε βοῶν [= while he still living he stood shouting]). Euphorion had cited two brief shouts of Cynegirus at the enemy (A 38, 40). Now Callimachus' father, who had earlier cited one short command of his son to the troops (B 23), outdoes all these staccato quotes with a much longer 'challenge speech' of Callimachus to the enemy. At a length of 89 words it is the longest quoted 'speech' within the declamations.

Two adjectival phrases describe the speaker Callimachus: δεινὸς πολεμίοις (= fearful to enemies) and ἀκόρεστος μάχης (= insatiate in battle). The first is uncommon though it or something like it is attested (cf. τοῖς μὲν πολεμίοις δεινὸς ἦν [= he was fearful to the enemies], Xenophon, *Ag.* 6.8.2; δεινότατος ... τοῖς ἐναντίοις [= most fearful to the opponents], Thucydides 7.42.3). The second phrase copies formulaic epic language describing heroes and gods — ἀκόρεστος is a late form of ἀκόρητος (√ κορέννυμι [= satisfy, satiate]) — (cf. Achilles μάχης ἀκόρητον [= insatiate in battle], Homer, *Il.* 20.2; Ajax μόθου ἀκόρητος [= insatiate in fight], *Il.* 7.117; Ares ἀκόρητος αὐτῆς [= unsated in {battle}], Hesiod, *Sc.* 346; cf. also Homer, *Il.* 12.335; 13.621, 639; Aeschylus, *Pers.* 998). The epic ring of the expression was familiar to anyone raised on Homer.

In classical literature the insertion of speeches into narrative or argument had many notable precedents in epic (cf. Homer, Virgil), historiography (cf. Herodotus, Thucydides), and philosophy (cf. Plato, Xenophon). Callimachus' lengthy speech which throws down the gauntlet to the Persians stands in this literary tradition.

The opening address, "O barbarian slaves (δοῦλοι βάρβαροι) of Darius!," is rude — no *captatio benevolentiae* is needed in a taunt speech. The term βάρβαροι is the standard designator for the Persians in Polemo's declamations (32x; cf. Index 8), but only here is it used in the vocative. Precedent for this nomenclature for the invaders was provided by Aeschylus (cf. *Pers.* 255, 377, 391, 423, 434, 475, 798) and Herodotus (cf. 6–9, passim). Inasmuch as βάρβαροι at its root denotes *non-Greek speakers* (cf. J. Jüthner, "Barbar," *RAC*, 1.1173-1176; H. Windisch, βάρβαρος, *TWNT* 1.544-547) there is a certain irony in Callimachus addressing them in Greek. Polemo, however, will not have reflected on the illogic of this situation. For him the term was suitable because of its tone of disdain.

The companion term δοῦλοι (= slaves) is singular in Polemo. For a sense of the invaders as slaves one need only recall the classic image of the Persian commanders urging their men forward under the lash (Herodotus 7.223, 56, 22, 103). The distinction between the barbarians as slaves and the Greeks as free is alluded to in Polemo but never really developed (cf. A 36; B 8, 12, 31).

(1) The first point in the speech lies in the contrast between Scythia and Attica regarding the way each dealt with the Persian invaders.

The Scythians, an Indo-European nomadic people, had their home on the north coast of the Black Sea. From the Greek perspective they were, among the barbarian peoples, the wildest and most savage (cf. Herodotus 4; 2 Macc 4:47; 3 Macc 7:5; 4 Macc 10:7; Pliny, *N. H.* 7.2.9–10) or, as J. A. Bengel put it, *barbaris barbariores* (= more barbarian than the barbarians) (*Gnomon Novi Testamenti* [Stuttgart: Steinkopf, 1915] at Col 3:11, p. 806). In 513 BCE Darius had invaded Scythian territory, crossing both the Bosphorus and the Danube by means of boat-bridges, and attempted to conquer the Scythians. Rather than face the Persians in direct combat the Scythians opted for a calculated retreat with a dual tactic. On the one hand they scorched the earth behind them as they retired, on the other hand their mounted archers harassed the Persians as was opportune until they were finally compelled to retreat back across the Bosphorus (cf. Herodotus 4.83–143). It is that campaign 23 years earlier which Callimachus contrasts with the battle at Marathon.

Four negatives (οὐ + οὐδέ 3x) signal the obstacles which the Persians faced in their Scythian campaign. These are arranged in pairs: Σκύθαι and ποταμός (nouns alone) followed by πλάνης ὅμιλος and ἅμαξαι ζηλούμεναι (nouns with adjectives).

The first pair is comprised of an ethnic designation, the *Scythians* themselves, and a geographical one, the ποταμός (= river), presumably the Danube, or as the Greeks called it, the *Ister* (Ἴστρος). This river, which posed a kind of boundary between the nomadic tribes to the north and the urban peoples to the south, was regarded as the largest river of Europe (cf. Herodotus 4.48, 53; Hesiod, *Th.* 339) and marking the border of Scythia (Herodotus 4.49, 99).

The second pair refers to peculiar cultural traits of the Scythians. As a *wandering throng* (πλάνης ὅμιλος) they were able to pick up easily and go. Their *wagons* (ἅμαξαι) represented a kind of 'mobile home' — both dwelling place and means of family transport (cf. Herodotus 4.28, 114, 121). Thus Herodotus described the Scythians as *house-bearers* (φερέοικοι) who carried their dwellings on carts drawn by yoked animals (οἰκήματα ... ἐπὶ ζευγέων) in which the women and children stayed (Herodotus 4.46, 121).

What Polemo means by calling these wagons ζηλούμεναι (= *envied*) is obscure. Possibly he imagines the pursuing Persians as wishing that they too possessed such vehicles, or at least wishing the Scythians did not. Or perhaps it is an allusion to the attitude of the Amazon women (riders and hunters) being unwilling to share their lot with the Scythian women (domestics living and working in these wagons) though this was not really from envy or jealousy (cf. Herodotus 4.114). Instead of ζηλούμεναι the scribe of ε (→ E CN DHP) wrote ζητούμεναι (= sought for), apparently understanding that the wagons were sought after by the Persians (cf. Herodotus 4.121). This is an appealing interpretation but not supported by the evidence of the MSS.

These four items of the Scythian world are set in contrast with two Greek elements.

The first name (nominative singular Ἀττική) is clear: *Attica* comprises the easternmost promontory of central Greece, the large territory of which Athens was the political and cultural center (cf. B 5, 25, 40, 41, 55).

The second name (genitive plural Πελοπιδῶν) is problematic: The genitive Πελοπιδῶν (→ γ → π) is more difficult than the nominative Πελοπίδαι (→ δ) which smoothens the text by making a clean parallel with the nominative Ἀττική. The *lectio difficilior* has the clear priority, but what does it derive from? If it were from the adjective Πελοπηΐς, -ΐδος (the feminine form of the adjective Πελόπιος/Πελοπήϊος [√ noun Πέλοψ = Pelops, the mythological eponymous ancestor of the Peloponnesus]), one would expect it to be accented Πελοπίδων (cf. LSJ, sub verba). It is unclear, however, who would be meant by the feminine plural genitive adjective 'of the Pelopian [-----s]' or what nominative noun (parallel with Attica) should be supplied here with the genitive (of possession?). Because of these difficulties Possinus (p. 123) suggested emending Πελοπιδῶν to Πέλοπος χθών (= Pelops' land) so as to produce a better parallel with Attica. In Possinus's notes the last syllable of Πέλοπος (genitive of masculine noun Πέλοψ) is poorly printed — consequently Orellius (p. 134) read it as Πέλοπις (nominative of feminine adjective Πελοπηΐς) and corrected the accent to Πελοπὶς χθών (= Pelopian land). In either case Possinus and Orellius wondered how Attica could be called *Pelopis terra* (= Pelops' ground). Peloponnesians did not after all, as Polemo pointed out (B 5), participate in the battle at Marathon. In light of these problems, therefore, it is probably better to construe Πελοπιδῶν as deriving rather from Πελοπίδας (= Pelopidas, the famous Theban leader [ca. 410-364 BCE], contemporary with Epaminondas and captain of the Sacred Band, cf. Plutarch, *Pel.* passim). That seems in any case to have been the understanding of the δ MSS. Πελοπίδαι would apparently then refer to descendants or followers of Pelopidas — in other words, to Thebans or Boeotians. If so, the designation would seem to have in mind the (Boeotian) Plataeans, the only allies of Athens to participate in the battle at Marathon (cf. οἱ φίλοι Πλαταιεῖς [= the allied Plataeans], A 39, 44; Herodotus 6.108, 111, 113; Pausanias 1.15.3; 1.32.3). Plataea was a border town between Boeotia and Attica, long under dispute between the two. After the fourth century its brave inhabitants might conceivably have been referred to poetically as 'Pelopidas-ites' though there seems to be no recorded evidence for this. This interpretation of the passage presumes an omission of some nominative noun — parallel to Attica — before Πελοπιδῶν (e.g., χώρα [= land], Πλάταια [= Plataea], or the like). Admittedly, such an understanding has its own difficulties, foremost of which is that it involves an anachronism — Polemo would be putting a late classical designation on the lips of an early classical speaker. Possibly this anachronism is a gloss inserted by the same slow-witted scribe who interpolated the anachronistic Μακεδόνας in B 50. In any case the word upon which the genitive Πελοπιδῶν depends is missing.

No verb appears in the sentence. It is less likely that Polemo left it out in the rush of delivery than that it dropped out in the transmission process. The accusative object ταῦτα (= these things) indicates that a transitive verb needs to be supplied — perhaps something like *achieve* or *accomplish* (ἐποίησαν ? εἰργάσαντο ?). The whole point of the argument is that even the formidable Scythians did not succeed in destroying the Persian invaders, only the disciplined Greeks under Callimachus were able to do this.

(2) The second point of the taunt-speech shifts the focus of attention to Callimachus himself — he speaks in the first person: I stand (ἕστηκα), I await (περιμένω), [I am] being hit (βαλλόμενος), [I am] being shot (τοξευόμενος), [I am] being crowned (στεφανούμενος), I say (λέγω).

The variants ἐν ταύτῃ (= in this [Attic land]) and ἐνταῦθα (= here) have equally strong attestation (γ versus δ) but it is easier to imagine the latter arising out of the former than vice-versa. The present ἀπόλλυται is used instead of the future to convey what is immediate, certain, and threatening (*GG*, 1879: a "present of anticipation"). The participles βαλλόμενος and τοξευόμενος are concessive. The simile ὡς τισιν ἄνθεσι στεφανούμενος (= as if being wreathed with some flowers) belittles the efforts of the Persian bowmen. Their many arrows are to him like a victor's crown (cf. ἄνθεσι Διαγόρας ἐστεφανώσατο δίς [= Diagoras {boxing champion} has twice crowned himself with flowers], Pindar, *Ol.* 7.80–81; παγκρατίῳ ... νικῶντ᾽ ... ἄνθεων ... στεφανώματα [= in the pancratium winning ... crowns of flowers], Pindar, *Nem.* 5.54; also Philostratus, *Her.* 720.8 [12a.2]; *Ep.* 1.4.4).

(3) The third point of the taunt shifts attention to the enemy archers — the verbs are second person plural. The *present* imperatives denote *continuance* (*GG*, 1864a): βάλλετε (= *keep on* shooting) and μὴ φείδεσθε (= *don't go on* holding back). The present indicative βάλλετε is also iterative (*GG*, 1852):

"Why don't you *continue* shooting?" i.e., 'why are you letting up?' The tone is contemptuous: 'You aren't doing enough, try harder!'

(4-5) The remaining 'stanzas' of the taunt vascillate rapidly between the first and second person (a few third person verbs represent merely stylistic variations of direct second person address).

(4) With a genitive object (βελῶν [= arrows]) the deponent δέομαι means to *be in need of* (LSJ, δέω B.II.1.b). In the fourth 'stanza' this striking notion of 'needing' arrows is explained with a double rationale:

(a) ἐπεὶ χωρεῖ τὸ σῶμα (= since the body has room [for them]). With the verb χωρεῖ (= have room) the same object needs to be supplied mentally as with δέομαι, but in the accusative (βέλη or the pronoun αὐτά). The verb pictures the body 'three-dimensionally' as a *container* which is not yet filled to capacity (LSJ, χωρέω III).

(b) τόπον ὑγιῆ ἔχον (= since it [the body] [still] has a healthy spot). The 'two-dimensional' expression τόπον ὑγιῆ refers to body *surface* which is as yet unscathed. The phrase appears comparable to one in Galen who distinguished the skin area inflamed by a poisonous bite from τὸν ὑγιῆ τόπον (= the healthy spot), i.e., from that skin area not afflicted by the venom (Galen, *Ther.* 14.227.5, 10). Skin surface remains on Callimachus that has not yet been punctured; there is still room on the target for more arrows.

(5) The fifth 'stanza' contrasts the captured islanders (Naxians, Eretrians) and the challenging mainlander (Callimachus). The adjectives ἄθλιος (= miserable [√ ἄθλος = ordeal]) and ταλαίπωρος (= distressed [√ τάλας = suffering + πωρός = miserable]) both connote — as they still do in modern Greek — the *endurance of hardship*. They are virtual synonyms and were used in combination also by other orators (cf. Demosthenes 21.104; Aristides 56.1.4.1). For the fate of Naxos and Eretria see notes at A 38, 43; B 54.

Though solidly attested, the dative ἐμοί before περίστητε (= you surrounded) is difficult because the verb regularly takes an accusative object (LSJ, περιίστημι A.I.1; B.I.2.). Several attempts to 'fix' the grammar have been tried: the scribe of B changed it to an accusative (ἐμὲ) and Hinck (p. 35) transposed it after the verb so as to take it — now an emphatic double ἐμοὶ — with the following verb περιτείνατε (= stretch around) which does stand with the dative. These unsupported emendations only serve to highlight the difficulty of the text. If the ἐμοί (dative of advantage? of relation?) is accepted it would seem to have the sense of *instead of me*, though admittedly an analogous construction is not to be found. If the wording is corrupted, the original is not recoverable.

δίκτυον — a *net* for snaring fish or game (LSJ, sub verbum 1 and 2) — is used here metaphorically: *the net of war* (cf. δίκτυον ἄτης [= net of calamity], Aeschylus, *Pr.* 1078; δίκτυόν τι Ἅιδου [= a net of Hades], Aeschylus, *Ag.* 1115). In the declamations the image has a double reference. On the one hand it alludes to the general Persian military practice of taking captives by 'sweeping with the dragnet' (cf. the following σαγηνευσάτω in B 56 and the note at A 30). On the other hand it refers specifically to the picture of the tight mesh of arrows enclosing Callimachus (cf. τοῖς βέλεσιν ἐσαγηνεύσαμεν [= we have netted {him} with our arrows], A 30).

(6) The sixth point of the argument shifts from specific victims to specific villains. With proper names the interrogative τίς is used adjectively: *What Datis, what Tissaphernes?* (LSJ, τίς B.I.3; *GG*, 1262). The verb must be supplied from the previous sentence (either περιστήσει [= will surround] or περιτενεῖ [= will stretch out]) or from the general sense (e.g., πειράσεται [= will try], cf. B 34, 58 or ἐπιχειρήσει [= will try], cf. B 36).

Datis was the commander of the Persian fleet at Marathon (cf. note at A 41) and he figures several times in Polemo's portrayal of the battle (cf. A 41; B 14, 45, 60). The name Tissaphernes, though anchored in the MSS, is an historical error on Polemo's part. Tissaphernes, son of Hydarnes, was the satrap in Anatolia who intervened in the Peloponnesian War against Athens during the years 412–395 BCE (cf. H. Volkmann, "Tissaphernes," *KP*, 5.867). His name is confused here with that of Artaphernes, son of Artaphernes and nephew of Darius, the co-commander (with Datis) of the Persian expedition at Marathon in 490 BCE (cf. Herodotus 6.94, 119; 7.74). Confusion of the two names, which arose no doubt out of *homoioteleuton* (-αφέρνης) and their shared anti-Athenian policy, is found also in other writers (e.g., Pompeius Trogus). Editorial emendation to Intaphernes (α followed by AO, Stephanus and Possinus) or Artaphernes (Orellius and Hinck) is unwarranted. Polemo's *lapsus* remains.

With ὦ πάντες (= O all [of you]) Callimachus challenges commanders and subordinates alike. His declaration that he stands *ready* (ἕτοιμος) is carefully indeterminate. Ready for what? — the explanatory infinitive or prepositional phrase common with ἕτοιμος in military parlance is left out (cf. ἕτοιμα ... διαμάχεσθαι [= ready to fight hard], Plato, *Smp.* 207b; ἕτοιμοι εἰς πόλεμον [= ready for battle], 1 Macc 3:44; 5:39; 12:50; ἕτοιμος τελευτᾶν [= ready to die], Diodorus Siculus 13.98.1; cf. 2 Macc 7:2; 8:21; 4 Macc 9:1). Callimachus is prepared for whatever may come.

(7) The final element of the taunt is formulated as a parallelism. Third person imperatives (θυέτω [= let {someone} slay]; σαγηνευσάτω [= let {the

king} catch in the dragnet]) are relatively rare in Polemo (only 8x); they occur particularly in the fabricated quotes placed on the lips of the dramatized characters (cf. ἀποτεμνέτω, λυσάτω A 41; φευγέτω B 41). This mood adds a direct liveliness to the quoted sayings. The verb θύω (= slay) is here devoid of any of the cultic-sacrificial connotations originally and commonly associated with it — in Polemo it simply means *kill* (like Euripides, *Iph. T.* 621; Sir 34:20; 1 Macc 7:19; John 10:10). For the parallel verb σαγηνευσάτω see the note at A 30).

In the final pair of challenges the former is directed to anyone (τις), the latter, upping the ante, is addressed to the king himself (βασιλεύς). The parallels εἰ δύναται (= if he can) and εἰ ἔξεστιν (= if it is possible) are designed to needle the enemy right up to the last word.

57

The verb ἔπηξεν appears to be a rare 1st aorist from ἐπάγω (= direct against) (far more common is the 2nd aorist, cf. ἐπαγαγεῖν, B 36). That it could be an aorist from ἐπαίσσω (= rush upon, assault) seems to be ruled out by the syntax (accusative ὅλα τὰ βέλη + prepositional phrase ἐπ᾽ αὐτῷ) (cf. LSJ, ἐπαΐσσω).

In view of the audible quotations immediately preceding and following, the phrase λέγων πρὸς ἑαυτόν (= saying to himself) might seem to mean that Callimachus actually spoke out loud to himself. However, the subsequent formulation τοιοῦτον εἶπε τὸν λόγον πρὸς ἑαυτόν (= he said some such word word to himself, B 58) suggests rather that Callimachus' father is reconstructing the inner thoughts of his dying son.

The plural verb (ἀπεδύσαμεν) which Callimachus uses for himself is more a plural of majesty than modesty (*GG*, 1006; 1008); with the accusative object of person (τὴν ᾽Ασίαν) one must supply the accusative object of thing from the context (ὅλα τὰ βέλη): "we have stripped Asia [of all its arrows]" (cf. the double accusative: τὴν δὲ ἐσθῆτα ... ἀπέδυσαν αὐτόν [= they stripped him of his clothing], Lucian, *Nigr.* 13).

After his taunt-speech to the Persians and his 'self-congratulatory' word comes Callimachus' three point command to his soldiers: 'smite, cut down, don't hold back.' With the present imperative παίετε (= continue smiting) the present participle κατακεντοῦντες (= cutting down) expresses manner (*GG*, 2062). The prohibition, μὴ φείδεσθε (= don't hold back, cf. also B 23), is a commonplace in military commands (cf. παραγγείλας κτείνειν τὸν παρατύχοντα καὶ μηδενὸς φείδεσθαι [= commanding to kill every person encountered and to spare no one], Polybius 10.15.4; δόγμα θέμενοι μηδενὸς φείδεσθαι [= issuing a decree to spare no one], Plutarch, *Mul. Virt.* 244b; μὴ φείδεσθε ... καὶ μὴ ἐλεήσητε [= don't hold back and don't show mercy], Eus. *Sermo* 5; also Polybius 11.18.1; Diodorus Siculus 12.62.2; Plutarch, *Pel.* 9.5; *Dio.* 47.3; *Brut.* 5.1). The Greeks can now fight with abandon because the enemy is 'out of ammunition' (οὐκέτι γὰρ ἔχουσι βέλη [= for no longer do they have arrows]). This is accounted for in a reformulation of the previous quote:

γυμνοὺς ὑμῖν αὐτοὺς ἐποίησα   (→ τὴν Ἀσίαν ἀπεδύσαμεν)
I made them 'naked' for you   (→ we have stripped Asia).
Here γυμνός means *unarmed* (cf. LSJ, sub verbum 2).

58

ἐπειρῶντο is an imperfect of continuance or repeated action (*GG*, 1890): they *kept on* trying. Typically this verb takes an infinitive which may sometimes be understood (*GG*, 1992a; LSJ, πειράω B.I). Here the infinitives (κινῆσαι [to move] and καθελεῖν [to destroy]) are separated from the verb by the epexegetical aside καὶ πᾶς ἔβαλλε (= and everyone was shooting). In other words, the infinitives belong to both of the μέν - δέ clauses: all were trying and none was succeeding (πάντες ἐπειρῶντο ... οὐδεὶς ἠδύνατο). The object of their efforts was the man 'affixed stiff to the earth' (πεπηγότα [√ πήγνυμι = stick fast, fix in]). The elusively active (rather than passive) participle — having fixed [himself?] — suggests that he remained upright more by virtue of his own resolve than by the impalement of the enemy's arrows.

The substantized participles οἱ καθελόντες (= the ones destroying) and οἱ βιασάμενοι (= the ones using force) follow in apposition to the subject οἱ βάρβαροι (= the barbarians). The objects in these participial phrases stand in stark contrast to the transfixed Callimachus. The Persians succeeded at pulling down Babylon's massive dykes and defense embankments (cf. Herodotus 1.184-192; also note on χώματα, A 30), but they failed to pull down Callimachus. They employed too much (ἄγαν) force on the Bosporus (cf. the Persian boat-bridge spanning the formidable straights for the invasion of Scythia, Herodotus 4.83-89), but they did not have enough force to overcome Callimachus. The description of the Bosporus as having a strong current (ῥοώδης) corresponds with empirical observation (cf. Aristotle, *Mete.* 366a25; Strabo 1.3.11-12) — in the narrowest spot it reaches a speed of over five miles per hour. Its characterization as a "Scythian sea" is loose at best. These Thracian narrows (17 miles long, 3300 to 600 yards wide) connecting the Pontus with the Propontis hardly fit the picture of a θάλασσα (= sea). The straights are "Scythian" insofar as they demarcate the southernmost natural boundary of the territory of the Scythians. For his terminology Polemo need not have been dependent on ancient descriptions of this waterway (cf. Herodotus 4.83-87; Polybius 4.38-44; Strabo 7.6.1-2; Dionysius Byzantius, *Bosp.*) — in his travels he may well have seen it himself.

The πᾶς μὲν ἔβαλλε (= everyone was shooting) resumes the καὶ πᾶς ἔβαλλε of the previous sentence. A new element appears, however, with πᾶς ἐφονεύετο καὶ τῷ Καλλιμάχῳ προσέπιπτεν (= everyone was being slain and was falling before Callimachus). The implied agent of the passive ἐφονεύετο is, of course, Callimachus, but the restraint in the expression is noticeable. The declamation makes many assertions about Callimachus — that he instigated the battle, fought tenaciously, inspired terror, routed many, suffered countless wounds, and the like — but the claim that he *killed* many Persians is first introduced in this passage (B 58-59). Indeed, the core of the argument is more about what Callimachus endured than what he inflicted. The reference to his direct victims remains quite undeveloped.

The verb προσπίπτω (= fall at someone's feet or knees) is often used to express supplication (cf. LSJ, sub verbum III; BAGD, sub verbum 1) and here a connotation of Callimachus' victims begging for mercy may actually shimmer in the background.

καθάπερ (√ καθ᾽ [→ κατ᾽ → κατὰ] + ἄ + περ = according as, just as) introduces the simile of the rock (λίθος) jutting into the sea (cf. A 10, 30). This is a variation on the earlier comparison of Callimachus with a resistant rock (cf. ὥσπερ ... ἀντίτυπος πέτρα, B 10). The perfect participle which describes the rock *leaning forward* (προνενευκότι) reflects a customary expression for promontories (cf. LSJ, προνεύω).

The active participle ἐρείσας (√ ἐρείδω = prop up) with accusative object ἑαυτοῦ τὸ σῶμα (= propping up his own body) is the equivalent of the reflexive middle ἐρεισάμενος (= planting himself) common since Homer (cf. στῆ ... ἐρεισάμενος [= he stood planting himself], *Il.* 12.457; τὸν {πέτρον} ἧκε δ᾽ ἐρεισάμενος [= and planting himself he hurled the stone], *Il.* 16.736). But with this verb Homer often named the means of support, e.g., spear, scepter, hand, etc. (cf. *Il.* 2.109; 5.309; 14.38; 22.225; 23.735) which Polemo does not do. It is surely deliberate that the supporting props are not specifically identified, for this would be a tacit acknowledgement of Euphorion's recurring argument that the one praising Callimachus is actually praising the enemy arrows that held him up (cf. A 27, 7, 23, 24, 45).

The text critical choice between the adjective τελευταῖον [→ γ] (= last [word]) and the participle τελευτῶν [→ δ] (= as he was dying) is a hard call (hence the bold font in the Greek). The two words are nearly homonyms, they have equally balanced MS support (γ versus δ), and in the context both work equally well. This edition opts for the adjective because (a) it is attested in Polemo's vocabulary (cf. B 28) while the verb τελευτάω is not, and (b) when all other things are equal the nod goes to γ as the better MS (cf. Appendix 2).

The final word from Callimachus' lips is a self-exhortation: "Stand unmoved!" This ἀκίνητος is a fitting conclusion to his conscious action — it sums up a central theme in the father's argument (cf. Καλλίμαχος δὲ ἀκίνητός ἐστι [= Callimachus is immovable], B 54; τὸν μὲν δὴ μόγις ἐκίνησα [= I barely moved him], B 15; ὦ ... μὴ κεκινημένε [= O you who have not been moved], B 47; κινῆσαι δὲ οὐδεὶς ἠδύνατο [= no one was able to move {him}], B 58). In function one might compare the σήμερον (= today) in Jesus' word from the cross in Luke (23:43) which sums up a 'present eschatological' outlook in Luke's gospel (cf. Luke 2:11; 4:21; 5:26; 13:32, 33; 19:5, 9).

59

The comparison of Callimachus with a strong wall (ὥσπερ τείχει ... καρτερῷ) is variation of the earlier simile 'like an unbreachable wall' (ὥσπερ ... τεῖχος ἄρρηκτον, B 10).

προσβάλλω with the dative has the sense of *strike against, make an assault upon* (LSJ, sub verbum III.1). The expression δράω (= do, accomplish) + πλέον οὐδέν (= nothing more) is a widespread idiom meaning *avail nothing at all* (cf. Euripides, *Hipp.* 284; *Iph.A.* 1373; Andocides, *Myst.* 149; *Alc.* 20; Plato, *Phd.* 115c; Athenaeus 8.344b).

Euphorion had described Callimachus as "the one hidden by the many arrows" (ὁ κρυπτόμενος ὑπὸ τῶν πολλῶν βελῶν) and hence of no consequence for friend or foe (A 30). Using similar language Callimachus' father now puts a different slant on the 'concealment'. Callimachus was hidden (ἐκρύπτετο) by the *enclosure* (περιβολή) of arrows. This picture of the περιβολή invests the previous image of the τεῖχος (= wall) with new meaning — ἡ περιβολή (like ὁ περίβολος and τὸ περιβόλιον) can describe the demarcation wall enclosing a sacred temple precinct (cf. LSJ, sub verba; and the note on τὰ τοξεύματα περιβεβλημένον, B 52). Thus the earlier sacral imagery (Callimachus as ἀνάθημα, ἄγαλμα, and εἴδωλον surrounded by the 'temenos' fence of arrows, B 52) is resumed here with alternate language. This shrine precinct term brings with it the implication that those assaulting him are guilty of a kind of ἱεροσυλία (= sacrilege). Their deaths *there* (ἔνθα = in specific close proximity, cf. A 8, 11; B 10) may be understood as the due punishment for their 'temple desecration'.

The characterization of the Persians as 'toiling' or 'exhausting themselves' (κάμνοντες) appears in both fathers (cf. πᾶς ἀνὴρ πρὸς χεῖρα μυρία καμών [= every man laboring mightily against the hand {of Cynegeirus}], A 41; καμεῖν ἐποίησε τὴν πολλὴν δύναμιν τοῦ βασιλέως [= {Callimachus} made the great army of the king to be exhausted], B 10). Only Callimachus' father, however, brought this concept into contrast with his son, the one *not growing weary* in death (cf. τὸν μὴ δέ ἐν θανάτῳ καμόντα, B 50).

The statement πολλοὶ ... ὑπὸ τῶν Καλλιμάχου βλημάτων ἀπώλοντο (= many perished from the wounds [inflicted] / missiles [cast] {?} by Callimachus) is difficult. Are the βλήματα to be understood as *projectiles* hurled by Callimachus or as *wounds* caused by him? (cf. LSJ, βλῆμα 1 and 2). In the former case how would Callimachus have had at his disposal numerous spears or javelins? Further, were the enemy deaths produced by the still *living* Callimachus or by his standing and fighting *dead* corpse? The context would seem to suggest the latter, yet in the view of Possinus that would be "an absurd and immoderate hyperbole". Hence, he proposed taking βλήματα Καλλιμάχου in a passive sense: when *the missiles hurled against Callimachus* went astray from their target they wounded and felled many other Medes! (cf. Possinus, p. 123). Such an interpretation, however, strains the Greek. It must be acknowledged that Polemo's formulation leaves unexplained the source of Callimachus' 'ammunition' and that it leaves vague whether the agent of the deaths was *ante-* or *post-mortem*. Furthermore, overdrawn bombast does not seem elsewhere to have given Polemo any embarassment, so there is little reason to assume that it would do so here.

60

In contrast to the many who were *laboring* stands Datis who was *watching* (πολλοὶ μὲν κάμνοντες ... Δάτις δὲ ὁρῶν): while the Persian soldiers were dying (ἀπώλοντο) their commander was merely becoming infuriated (ὠργίζετο). The picture of Datis as frustrated observer stands in stark relief to the image of Callimachus as engaged combatant.

Datis' ineffectual command (ἐνεκελεύετο) to his troops turns into a desperate lament over the superiority of the Greeks. His lengthy complaint stands in antithesis to the long taunt of Callimachus (B 56).

(1) The first element in the quote is a plea to the Persian troops in the form of a double question: "Won't you knock over and won't you remove the bothersome corpse?" οὐ κλινεῖτε and οὐκ ἀναιρήσετε are jussive futures; coupled with the interrogative οὐ they express an imperative sense of urgency (*GG*, 1917; 1918). The adjective φιλόν[ε]ικος ([literally] = fond of victory) is,

of course, used here in a bad sense: *quarrelsome, disputatious, contentious* (LSJ, sub verbum 1; BAGD, sub verbum 1). This qualifier seems to focus particularly on the taunt-speech which Callimachus had just delivered (B 56).

(2) The second element is a scolding of Callimachus in the form of four short questions. He is addressed directly with a brusk vocative: ἄνθρωπε δαιμόνιε (= marvelous fellow, honorable sir [with an ironic tone]), a classical address which traditionally introduced words of indignation or reproach (cf. δαιμόνι᾿, Homer, *Il.* 2.200; 3.399; 4.31; *Od.* 18.15; δαιμόνιε ἀνδρῶν, Herodotus 4.126; 7.48; δαιμόνι᾿ ἀνθρώπων, Aristophanes, *Av.* 1638).

(a) The question, "Are you ashamed to fall?" (αἰσχύνῃ πεσεῖν; cf. αἰσχυνόμενος πεσεῖν [= being ashamed to fall], B 55) is qualified by the phrase "amidst so many" (μετὰ τοσούτων). This 'arena', however, is indeterminate: amidst so many [Persians]? so many [Greeks]? so many [dead]? Each possibility lends a slightly different color to the question.

(b) The second question is truncated, but easily filled out: "Do you still remain (μένεις) [standing]?" (cf. ἔμενεν ἐν τῷ τῆς στάσεως σχήματι [= he remained in the standing posture], A 7; βεβαίως ἔμενεν [= he remained firm], B 11; τὸν ... ἐν τῇ τάξει μένοντα [= the one remaining at his post], B 43).

(c) The third question, too, is shortened: "Are you [though dead] still fighting?

(d) In the fourth question, "How many *souls* (= lives) do you still have?" the plural ψυχάς is unusual, but the earlier mention of a "second soul" (B 53) has prepared the way for the notion of multiple souls.

The questions to Callimachus do not expect answers — dead men don't talk. They are not designed for responses but rather to express Datis' exasperation.

(3) The third 'stanza' is introduced by οἴμοι (properly οἴ μοι = ah me, woe to me), an onomatopoetic exclamation of fright, pain, grief, or self-pity widely used by the tragedians, but documented as early as Theognis (LSJ, οἴ and οἴμοι; cf. the similar Hebrew אוֹי or הוֹי which could be translated by οἴ[μ]μοι [Jer 4:31; 15:10; 22:18; 51:3] or the Latin oi / oiei).

The reason for the *alas* follows immediately: victory over the Persians is being won by an Athenian corpse! The word order of the lament diverges in the γ and δ MSS (νικᾷ stands at the beginning in γ, at the end in δ) and it is hard to decide between them. At issue is the rhetorical emphasis which falls on the last word. Given the Ἀθηναῖοι two lines later, it seems more likely that the complaint ended with Ἀθηναῖος.

Datis' command to stop shooting (μηκέτι βάλλετε) counters specifically Callimachus' taunt requesting more arrows (βάλλετε καὶ μὴ φείδεσθε. τί δ᾽

οὐ βάλλετε; [= Keep shooting and don't let up. Why aren't you shooting?], B 56).

The participle ἀποθνῄσκοντες (= dying) has temporal or conditional sense: *when* or *if* they die, the Athenians become more warlike (μαχιμώτεροι). In so saying, Datis chimes in with the view of Callimachus' father (cf. ὦ νεκρὲ ζώντων μαχιμώτερε [= O corpse more warlike than the living], B 53; cf. Euphorion's claim that Ἀθηναίων ἕκαστος ὅλης νεὼς βαρβάρου μαχιμώτερος [= each of the Athenians is more warlike than a whole barbarian ship], A 31). In other words, 'stop shooting, because when you kill Athenians you make matters worse, not better' — their dead soldiers are better fighters still.

(4) Since classical times the term δεσπότης (= overlord, master) was used for the Persian emperor to indicate his absolute authority (Plato [*Leg.* 859a] equates δεσπότης with τύραννος [= tyrant], and Herodotus [3.89] describes a δεσπότης as χαλεπός ... καὶ ὠλίγωρος [= harsh and contemptuous]). In Polemo's sources the vocative δέσποτα was a standard mode of address to the Persian king (cf. Aeschylus, *Pers.* 666; 1049; Herodotus 1.90; 3.34, 35, 62, 85; 5.105; 7.5, 9, 38, 147; 8.88, 100, 102, 118; 9.111, 116) and Polemo follows this convention.

Datis' exasperation is visible in his question to Darius: "Who deluded (ἐξηπάτησεν) you?" One may chide inferiors or peers this way, but not a monarch. It is unwise, if not dangerous, to accuse a despot of being misled or deceived. The king's misguidedness, however, is evidenced in his orders to attack a superior foe.

In the phrase ἐπ᾽ ἀθανάτους ἀνθρώπους ἡμᾶς ἔπεμψας the ἀνθρώπους is grammatically ambiguous. It may be taken syntactically either with the preceding ἐπ᾽ ἀθανάτους (= you sent us against deathless men) or with the following ἡμᾶς (= you sent us humans against immortals). The scribe of α (→ AO) transposed the word order of ἀνθρώπους ἡμᾶς to make clear the latter understanding. The difference is slight, but noteworthy. In the former case ἄνθρωποι denotes the Greeks, in the latter case the Persians. More importantly, in the latter case the ἄνθρωποι (humans) stand in contrast to the substantized ἀθάνατοι (= immortals), a designation for the *gods* (cf. Homer, *Il.* 1.503, 520, 525; 2.14, 31, 49, 68, 306, 814; etc.; Pindar, *Pae.* 6.50; Herodotus 7.140, 148). This latter sense fits the previous allusions to 'divinization' of Callimachus (cf. B 56, 59). Immortals, by definition, do not fall.

(5) The 'arts' (τέχναι) of the '*Magi*' (Μάγοι) which were ineffective (ἀπρακτοῦσιν) against Callimachus are understood by Orellius (p. 140) as the witchcraft of oriental sorcerers employed in war to disable the enemy. In

support of this he cited a passage from Arnobius to the effect that Easterners used magicians and Chaldeans in warfare to work ill-will by means of occult practices (cf. adv. Gentes 1.5). That interpretation, however, is dubious. In Polemo the τέχναι which availed nothing against Callimachus are not specifically identified — they can only be inferred from those practicing them and from the situation to which they are applied. They are held in repute (δοκούμεναι, cf. LSJ, δοκέω II.5; BAGD, δοκέω 2.b) by Πέρσαι, Μῆδοι, and Μάγοι. Strictly speaking the Persians and the Medes were two distinct, though closely related, Indo-European peoples who occupied the Iranian plateau — the Persians in the south with the capital cities of Susa and Persepolis, the Medes in the north with the chief cities of Ecbatana and Rages. Each territory constituted separate satrapies in the empire. Yet for all practical purposes from the Greek perspective the two were not really distinguished. Herodotus, for example, often uses the two names interchangably. Polemo likewise names Persians and Medes side by side without apparent differentiation (cf. A 30, 31; B 60). In question here then is whether the Magians (Μάγοι) are of the same order. Throughout Greek records at least four different senses attach to this name: (a) members of the Persian priestly caste, (b) possessors and practitioners of supernatural knowledge and ability, (c) magicians and sorcerers, (d) swindlers and deceivers (cf. G. Delling, μάγος, *TWNT* 4.360–361). It seems unlikely, however, that Polemo had in mind any of these meanings. On the one hand, a 'professional' category fits poorly with the first two 'ethnic' groups in the triad; and on the other hand, what business would priests, dream interpreters, magic workers, or charlatans have in the pitched battle at Marathon? More likely is that Polemo's Μάγοι constitute another 'national' group alongside the Persians and Medes. Herodotus (1.101) had named the Μάγοι as one of the six constituent tribes of the Medes, and Polemo is probably thinking imprecisely in this vein so that his triad of 'Persians, Medes, and Magians' represents the entire composite of 'ethnic' groups at the heart of the Persian empire (cf. "Medes and Persians and Phoenicians," A 31). Thus — contrary to Orellius — the τέχναι are not arts of sorcerers or devices of spell-casters for which Persia was well-known, not artifices of malevolent magic (e.g., curse uttering, bone pointing, jar breaking, or the like) directed against Callimachus on the battle field, but rather simply the '*arts of war*' (cf. αἱ πολεμικαὶ τέχναι [= the arts pertaining to war], Xenophon, *Cyr.* 1.6.26; 1.6.41; 8.1.37; ἡ πολεμικὴ τέχνη [= the art of war], Plato, *Resp.* 522c; Xenophon, *Oec.* 4.4; ηὑρημένας εἰς πόλεμον τέχνας [= arts invented for war], Xenophon, *Cyr.* 1.16.14). Such *military* τέχναι covered the whole gamut of battle skills from strategems for attack (cf. Thucydides 5.8.2) to use of weapons (cf. Xenophon, *Hel.* 3.3.7; *Cyr.* 1.6.13) to manoeuvering ships at sea (cf. Thucydides 7.36.4; Xenophon, *Hel.* 7.1.4). Given the situation with Callimachus, Polemo's mention of τέχναι will have had in mind foremost the legendary *archery skills* of the Persian bowmen — their shooting abilities had little effect on Callimachus. Polemo's formulation is possibly related to a soldiers' maxim (cf. φόβος γὰρ μνήμην ἐκπλήσσει, τέχνη δὲ ἄνευ ἀλκῆς οὐδὲν ὠφελεῖ [= Fear drives away presence of mind, and skill without courage is of no use], Thucydides 2.87.4).

(6) The climactic parallelism of Datis' final stanza restates the main argument of Callimachus' father: death was not a real barrier for Callimachus — his valorous fight continued on after his death. Callimachus' father had argued that his son's case was *sui generis* (cf. B 46). Datis, however, pluralizes the corpse of Callimachus to "the corpses of the Athenians" — from the Persian perspective Callimachus' post-mortem fight epitomizes the indefatigability of all the Athenians. Killing them achieves nothing because the number of fighters is not thereby diminished — the dead continue fighting alongside the living.

In view of the facts that (a) the final line of Datis' speech stands in parallelism with the previous line about Callimachus, and (b) this line is placed on Datis' lips by the father of Callimachus, the δεξιὰ νεκροῦ πολεμοῦσα (= the corpse's fighting right hand) must refer to the right hand of *Callimachus*, not of Cynegirus. That makes this passage singular in the declamations, for all the other occurrences of δεξιά refer to the right hand of Cynegirus (cf. A 3, 10, 11, 11, 23, 31, 32, 35, 35, 36, 37, 40, 40, 41, 43, 44, 47; B 33, 36, 37, 42, 43, 63). This unique detail is a clever calculation on Polemo's part. It means that from the Persian perspective the right hand of Callimachus made more of an impact than the right hand of Cynegirus. This final point of Datis' speech delivers the *coup de grâce* to Euphorion's whole case.

61

Since the anarthrous βασιλεύς (= king) refers to Darius himself (cf note .at A 9), its construction with ἰδών ... ἐβόα (= seeing ... he began shouting) presupposes his actual physical presence at the battlefield. On this point the declamations are inconsistent — in some passages he is thought of as present at Marathon (A 30; B 40, 41, 60, 61), in another he is imagined to be home in Persia (A 43). Possinus (p. 125), who would like to evade the implication of this passage that Darius was present at Marathon, suggests that βασιλεύς (= king) has the sense here of στρατηγός (= general), a *regius miles* (= 'royal soldier'), and is thus a reference to Datis. That connotation of βασιλεύς, however, finds no corroboration in Polemo.

In the picture of the upright (ὀρθόν, cf. B 44) corpse surrounded (περιβεβλημένον, cf. B 52, 59) by countless weapons the lines are fuzzy. The weapons may be envisioned as either *in* him or *around* him, i.e., as either having found their target or having missed their mark. The two conceptions are not mutually exclusive and they can blur together.

Subjunctives are relatively infrequent in Polemo (17x, cf. Appendix 1) and outside of this φεύγωμεν, πλέωμεν (= let us flee, let us sail) there is in the declamations only one other example of a hortatory subjunctive (κρινώμεθα [= let us judge], A 17). The cohortatives form a lively expression of defeat on the lips of Darius himself.

Earlier in the declamation the father of Callimachus had interpreted his son's necro-stance as the equivalent of a battlefield τρόπαιον (B 12). Now he depicts the Persian monarch as voicing the same opinion (δόγμα). The term δόγματα is used in its primal sense of *things that seem* to be (√ δοκέω [= seem]), i.e., *opinions*, *beliefs* (cf. LSJ, δόγμα 1).

This portrayal of the Persians as recognizing and understanding the Greek custom of victory monuments (cf. note on τρόπαιον at A 10) is not peculiar to Polemo. Pausanias, a younger contemporary, does the same and goes a step further. He attributes to the Persians the same practice. Pausanias says that the Persians were so confident of their upcoming victory that they had brought with them to Marathon a piece of Parian marble out of which they intended to make their own τρόπαιον. With fitting irony Pausanias concludes this tale by noting that after the battle the Greeks came into possession of this stone and fashioned from it a statue to the goddess Nemesis which they set up at Rhamnous on the coast about eleven miles north of Marathon (Pausanias 1.33.2).

62

The final ὦ exclamations appear as a pair (the three ὦ's that follow merely introduce simple vocatives of address, cf. B 62, 64, 65):

ὦ σεμνὸν πολέμου τέρας·

(= O revered portent of war)

ὦ τῶν συμμάχων θεῶν ἄξιον θέαμα.

(= O sight worthy of the co-fighting gods)

Both exclamations rework earlier formulations. The former reframes ὦ σέμνον ἀνάθημα πολέμου (= O revered votive offering of war [said of Callimachus], B 52), and the latter expands ὦ θέαμα τῶν θεῶν ἄξιον (= O sight worthy of the gods [said of Cynegirus], A 35). The first counters Euphorion's statement that "the revered thing of Callimachus was merely an idle appearance" (τὸ μὲν Καλλιμάχου σέμνον σχῆμα μόνον ἀργὸν ἦν, A 26). The second, — applied now to Callimachus, not Cynegirus — by adding the attribute συμμάχων to the gods, recalls that the divine fought on the side of Callimachus, and not against him as was said to be the case with Cynegirus (cf. B 41, 36).

From after the two ὦ exclamations (B 62b) up to the end of the declamations proper (B 64a), i.e., until the juncture where the secondary Ending (B 64b-65) is attached, the wording of the text has suffered considerably at the hands of the scribes. The scribal alterations occurred in two phases:

(1) In the earlier phase prior to the medieval progenitor MS π (11th century?) a number of interpolations appear to have been secondarily added to the text:

(a) τῷ πελέκει τις ἀπέκοψε τὴν Κυναιγείρου δεξιάν
    (= someone cut off the right hand of Cynegirus with an axe)

(b) οὐκ αὐτοῦ μέν ὑπάρχουσαν, ἐκείνου δέ
    (= not being his, but that one's)

(c) αἱ μὲν γὰρ ἄλλαι δεξιαὶ τῶν στρατιωτῶν πρὸ τῶν ἱερῶν θυρῶν
    ἔμειναν ὑπὸ σπάρτων ἐχόμεναι ἐν τῷ τῆς λαβῆς σχήματι
    (= for the other right hands of the soldiers remained before
    the sacred doors being held by ropes in the form of a grip)

(d) τρεῖς παῖδες παλαιοί
    (= three aged sons)

and possibly also

(e) αὐτόχθονες μέν ἐσμεν ὡς αληθῶς
    (= we are truly sprung from the land)

Originally these all appear to have been glosses (in the margin?) which subsequently found their way into the text itself. Whether they all stem from the same scribe or a succession of copyists cannot be determined. In any case these interpolations stood in π, the common progenitor of all our MSS, and they were duly copied by both γ and δ.

(2) In the later phase (12th-15th century) the copyists of γ and δ and their successors made a more than average number of changes in the received text.

The critical apparatus shows the wide range of variants, some inadvertent, some deliberate.

Despite the many variants of the later phase, however, their type and distribution allow the reconstruction of γ and δ with near certainty and the recovery of π with some confidence. Regarding the interpolations of the first phase and the reconstruction of the pre–π wording (→ Π ?) there may legitimately be some debate.

The sorry state of the last lines of the text may perhaps be accounted for by an evolutionary development such as described in the following hypothesis:

(α) First Stage: in a medieval ancestor text behind π the final folio of the declamations got separated and lost. The last words at the bottom of the last surviving *verso* page were ἡ μήτηρ καὶ τὸν μέν Ἡρακλέος (B 64a).

(β) Second Stage: this defective MS was then copied so that the final lines up to and including these words (B 62 [?] - B 64a) ended up covering only the top part of the final page of the new MS — leaving the bottom of that last page partially blank.

(γ) Third Stage: subsequent scholiasts or glossators added a variety of comments or study notes in the empty space at the bottom of that last page.

(δ) Fourth Stage: later a copyist of this 'glossated' MS incorporated the notes into the newly copied text itself thus producing an 'expanded' version of the 'truncated' text (the form represented by π in the 11th century).

(ε) Fifth Stage: In the 14th century there emerged an ending to the declamations (B 64b–65) which was attached secondarily to some, but not all, of the existing Polemo MSS deriving from π (it was added namely to: A, B, ρ, μ, E, and ν; but not added to: O, M, and η).

(ζ) Sixth Stage: In the 15th century a number of MSS with the secondarily added ending were copied so that the ending appears in them in the first hand as part of the text (namely, in: Q R (→ ρ), F (→ μ), K G (→ F), C N (→ ν). Alongside these MSS with integrated endings other 15th century 'ending-less' MSS existed which were copied from *Vorlagen* without the ending (namely: D and H [+ P] (→ η).

Euphorion had claimed that both gods and heroes — specifically Pan, Demeter, Kore, Athena, Herakles, and Theseus — had fought on Cynegirus' behalf (cf. A 35). That claim was refuted by Callimachus' father with the counter-argument that these same divine figures had actually worked against Cynegirus (cf. B 41). Now Callimachus' father makes the claim that the deities and heroes were really the allies of Callimachus. The allied gods (σύμμαχοι θεοί) are named in a list that varies slightly from the two earlier catalogues. The gods are addressed in the second person in a kind of mini-hymn of praise:

(a) "You Pan aided (ἐβοήθησας) [sc. Callimachus]." The verb recalls the tradition that Pan assisted Athens at the battle of Marathon (cf. Herodotus 6.105-106; Pausanias 1.28.4; cf. note at A 35).

(b) "You Hera applauded (συνεκρότησας) [sc. Callimachus]." The verb suggests not so much active intervention as observer approval (cf. LSJ, συγκροτέω I.2). Hera replaces Demeter (her sister) and Kore (Demeter's daughter) who were named in the earlier lists. As the sister–wife of Zeus, Hera enjoyed a pre-eminent position among the Olympians. Her patronage thus (rather than that of Demeter + Kore) represents a 'step up' for Callimachus.

(c) The third-named god is Pallas [Athena]. This name is, to be sure, text-critically insecure — δ had read πολλῶν and γ had πολλάς. Neither makes much sense and the scribe of B was surely correct in emending the πολλάς of his *Vorlage* (β [→ γ → π ?]) to read Παλλάς, the spelling that in all likelihood had stood in Polemo's original (Π). Παλλάς was an old epithet of Athena (cf. Παλλὰς 'Αθήνη, Homer, *Il.* 1.400; 4.78, 541; 5.1, 61, 121; Hesiod, *Th.* 577; *Op.* 76) but was later used alone as equivalent of Athena (cf. Bacchylides, *Ep.* 5.92; *Dith.* 15.3; Aeschylus, *Eum.* 21, 224, 629; *Th.* 130; Herodotus 5.77). The etymology of Παλλάς remains obscure; it was sometimes interpreted as *maiden* (√ παλλάς / πάλλαξ = youth), sometimes as *brandisher* [of the spear] (√ πάλλω = brandish), but the word may well have a pre-Hellenic origin (cf. W. Fauth, "Athena," *KP*, 1.681-686). Polemo will have chosen it instead of Athena for the sake of variety of language and an archaic ring. Literary texts and plastic arts often depicted Athena equipped with spear, sword, and shield — hence the attribute ὡπλισμένη (= armed). This perfect participle (→ ὁπλίζω = arm [√ ὅπλα = weapons]) can be construed as either middle or passive; both yield good sense. However, it is more likely that Athena was thought of as having armed herself (middle) than that she was armed (passive) by another (e.g., by Hephaistos). As armed goddess she was envisioned as Protectress of the City Athens and so titled (cf. Παλλὰς Πολιοῦχος [= Pallas, Guardian of the City], Pindar, *Ol.* 5.10; Aristophanes, *Eq.* 581; 'Αθήνα Πολιοῦχος [= Athena, Guardian of the City], Aristophanes, *Nu.* 601; 'Αθάνα Πολιάς [= Athena, Protectress of the City], Sophocles, *Ph.* 134; Herodotus 5.82). Of Athena's arms it is her shield (ἀσπίς) that is highlighted in the verb ὑπερήσπισας ([√ ὑπέρ + ἀσπίζω] = you held the shield over [him]).

(d) (e) With Herakles and Theseus the verbs shift from the second to the third person. In contrast to the direct acknowledging address to the gods, the heroes are not spoken *to*, but *about*. Their active presence is described for the listeners (cf. notes on Heracles and Theseus at A 35; B 41). The expression περὶ σὲ ἔστη (= he stood close by you) is a personalizing reformulation of the earlier πάρεστι Θησεύς, πάρεστιν Ἡρακλῆς (= Theseus stood by, Herakles stood by, B 41). The περὶ σέ with the Herakles verb is to be supplied also with the Theseus verb. The text-critical choice between the singular σεμνυνόμενος (→ δ) and the plural σεμνυνόμενοι (→ γ) is uncertain. Does the qualifying adjective *revered* belong to Theseus alone, or to both heroes? It seems more likely that a scribe would have changed a singular into a plural in order to have the adjective apply to both than that a plural would have been changed to a more limiting singular, but this is may be debated. The denominative verb σεμνύνω (√ σεμνός = august) means to *accord dignity, solemnity, or majesty* to someone.

The paired clauses χρὴ ... προτιμᾶσθαι (= it is necessary to be preferred) and ἀγορεύειν ... ἁρμόττει (= to speak is fitting) have chiastic construction. The 'modal' verbs χρή and ἁρμόττει are parallel. The accusative subject of προτιμᾶσθαι is σέ (= you [Callimachus]) while the accusative subject of ἀγορεύειν is τὸν πατέρα τὸν σόν (= your [Callimachus'] father). This parallel syntax shows that the honor of Callimachus and the dignity of his father are intertwined — recognition of the one means the same for the other.

The verb προτιμᾶσθαι (√ προ + τιμάω) connotes *honoring* one *before* another, *preferring* one *above* another. The 'lesser' party is expressed in the genitive (τῶν ... κειμένων [= those lying {at Marathon}]), the case being dependent on the prepositional prefix πρό (cf. LSJ, sub verbum I.1; *GG*, 1694). The point here is an extension of the earlier argument that the one standing erect deserves the honor over the one lying prostrate (cf. B 44).

The impersonal ἁρμόττει (= it is fitting) is the Attic form of ἁρμόζει (√ ἁρμός / ἁρμή = a joint, junction, fitting). The construction with accusative (τὸν πατέρα τὸν σόν [= your father]) and infinitive (ἀγορεύειν [= to speak]) conforms to standard classical idiom (cf. LSJ, ἁρμόζω II.3). ἀγορεύω means to *speak publicly* (√ ἀγορά [= Assembly]); λόγον is short for ἐπιτάφιον λόγον, the state funeral oration.

63

Linked with the imperative θάπτε (= bury!), the participle ἀπελθών (= going away) takes on imperative sense: *go off!* (cf. παίετε κατακεντοῦντες [= smite, cut down!], B 57). The imperatives dismiss Euphorion bruskly. The double θάπτε has a double set of objects: (1) Bury Cynegirus' corpse, and (2) bury his severed hand.

(1) Each phrase in the series of asyndetic appositions expresses increasing denegration: (a) τὸν σεαυτοῦ νεκρόν (= your *own* corpse) — it represents your private misery, not public pride; (b) τὸν χαμαί (= the [one] on the ground) — in contrast to the resolutely upright body of Callimachus; (c) τὸν ἐν ὄχλῳ νεκρῶν καὶ πεπατημένον (= the [one] in the mass of corpses and trampled underfoot) — Cynegirus' corpse is in no way distinctive compared with the rest of the dead, indeed, worse, it has been desecrated by being trodden on. In this third phrase νεκρῶν has weak attestation. It was missing in δ and what γ had is uncertain: α (→ AO) had νεκρῶν, but what β had is unclear (B copied νεκρόν and ρ [→ QR] omitted the word); the similarity of AO and B suggests that a form of νεκρ-ν stood in γ — probably the plural νεκρῶν because the singular would be redundant from the first phrase. The editors have given the nod to γ over δ (cf. Appendix 2).

(2) Bury the hand too. The wording of the object clause after θάπτε τὴν χεῖρα has been corrupted with interpolations. The words τῷ πελέκει τις ἀπέκοψε τὴν Κυναιγείρου δεξιάν (= someone cut off the right hand of Cynegirus with an axe) clearly represent a useless scribal gloss secondarily incorporated into the text.   The rather awkward words οὐκ αὐτοῦ μὲν ὑπάρχουσαν, ἐκείνου δέ (= not belonging to him, but to that one) may be the phrase that prompted that gloss.   Whether these latter words *in toto* or in part were original to the text or themselves also an (earlier?) interpolation is harder to answer.   If original, the wording is probably truncated or garbled. The likely interpolations are noted in the text with pointed brackets { }. Setting these aside, the object of the second θάπτε is τὴν χεῖρα (= the hand) followed by a simple relative clause ἣν ὅπλῳ γυναικῶν τις ἔτεμεν (= which someone lopped off with a women's weapon). This relative clause with its misogynist tone disparages the hand with as much force the previous phrases did the body.

As it stands the syntax of the clause beginning with ἀκροστόλιον (whether nominative or accusative) is opaque. The translation assumes that the case of ἀκροστόλιον (= ship's ornament, cf. notes at B 13, 36) is accusative and that perhaps — despite the postpositive γάρ — before it originally stood some preposition (ἐπί, πρός, παρά, or εἰς). The assumption here of textual corruption is not without warrant given the demonstrably poor state of the text in this passage.

The subject of ἀπέκοψεν (= cut off) is the same as that of the previous ἔτεμεν (= hacked off), namely the anonymous τις (= someone). The same τις is also subject of the following verb ἐπέσχε (= kept in check). The

construction of ἐπέχω (= hinder) + accusative (γλῶσσαν [= tongue])
+ genitive (τῶν ἀπειλητικῶν λήρων [= from the threatening trumperies])
corresponds to standard idiom (cf. ὧν ἐπισχήσω σ᾽ ἐγώ [= from which I will
stay you], Euripides, *Andr.* 160; τῆς ὁρμῆς ἐπέσχον τοὺς στρατιώτας [they
kept the soldiers from their ardor], Diodorus Siculus 13.87.3). The severing of
Cynegirus' hand proved to be a mortal blow that prevented him from
continuing the sort of blustering words that Euphorion had attributed to him
(cf. A 38, 40). The noun λῆρος (= nonsense, humbug) in Polemo's phrase
ἀπειλητικῶν λήρων (= threatening trumperies) constitutes a deliberate 'put
down' of Cynegirus' shouts in that it alludes to but simultaneously distorts a
common expression with more substance (cf. ἀπειλητηρίους λόγους
[= threatening words], Herodotus 8.112; ῥήσεις ἀπεικλητικάς [= threatening
speeches], Plato, *Phdr.* 268c; cf. also *Leg.* 823c;).

With the participle οὖσαν the ὡς sets forth the ground or belief on which
the agent acts. It may be rendered *in the opinion that, on the ground that* (*GG*,
2086). The notion that the tongue is more *intemperate* (ἀκρατεστέραν,
comparative of ἀκρατής [= immoderate, incontinent]) than other parts of the
body was a commonplace (cf. οὐκ ἔστι γλώσσης ῥεούσης ἐπισχέσις [= there
is no checking a loose tongue], Plutarch, *Gar.* 509d; γλῶσσα θνατοῖσιν δολία
νόσος, ἃς ἀχάλινος ἀφροσύνα τίκτει πολλάκι δυστυχίαν [= a guileful
plague to mortals is the tongue, whose unbridled madness gives birth often to
calamity], *An. Gr.* 16.132; ἡ γλῶσσα μικρὸν μέλος ἐστὶν καὶ μεγάλα αὐχεῖ
[= the tongue is a small member and boasts great things], Jas 3:5; cf.
Plutarch, *Gar.* 506c; *An.Gr.* 16.131; 11.321; Ps 11:4; Prov 10:31; 17:20;
21:23; Jas 3:8).

It is hard to regard as original the sentence about "the other right hands":
αἱ μὲν γὰρ ἄλλαι δεξιαὶ τῶν στρατιωτῶν πρὸ τῶν ἱερῶν θυρῶν ἔμειναν ὑπὸ
σπάρτων ἐχόμεναι ἐν τῷ τῆς λαβῆς σχήματι (= For the other right hands of
the soldiers remained before the sacred doors being held by ropes in the form
of the grip). These words make no sense in Polemo and are best construed as a
secondary interpolation. The δεξιαί (= right hands) and ἱερῶν θυρῶν
(= sacred doors, doors of temples) may somehow vaguely have in mind a
passage in Herodotus (6.91):

"The rich men of Aegina gained the mastery over the commoners
who had risen against them ... and having made them captive led them
out to be slain. ... and as they led these out for slaughter one of them
escaped from his bonds and fled to the temple gate (πρόθυρα) of Demeter
the Lawgiver where he laid hold of the door-handles and clung to them
(ἐπιλαμβανόμενος δὲ τῶν ἐπισπαστήρων εἴχετο). When his enemies

could not drag him away despite their efforts they cut off his hands (ἀποκόψαντες αὐτοῦ τὰς χεῖρας) and so brought him away; and those hands were left clinging fast to the door-handles (αἱ χεῖρες δὲ ἐκεῖναι ἐμπεφυκυῖαι ἦσαν τοῖσι ἐπισπάστροισι)" (Herodotus 6.91). Orellius (p. 146) thinks that Polemo has built on this Herodotean passage and fashioned the brutality and impiety of the Persians in accordance with it. That view is unconvincing because it does not account for the ropes (σπάρτα) and because the whole sentence makes more the impression of being a foreign body than a part of the text. Jacobs is surely closer to the mark with his suspicion that the sentence is a scholiast's addition, perhaps based on a (garbled?) recollection of Herodotus (cf. Hinck, p. 38). The sentence probably appeared as an obscure marginal note in an early medieval MS which a later scribe unwisely incorporated into the text. Every attempt to integrate the words into the declamations or squeeze sense out of them remains unsatisfying.

The assertion that Cynegirus' hand was beaten off (ἀπεκρούσθη) from the stern without gaining possession (μήτε ... κατασχοῦσα) of it is a final rejection of Euphorion's portrayal of the hands continuing to hold on even after they were severed (cf. A 11, 23, 36, 37). Earlier Callimachus' father had portrayed Cynegirus' hand as letting go as soon as it was severed (B 13, 43, 44). Here that point is underscored with a verb often used to describe the beating off of an attack (cf. LSJ, ἀποκρούω).

The expression ξύλου ... Σιδονίων (= wood of Sidonians) is a double *synecdoche*: the wood stands *pars pro toto* for the entire ship and the city of Sidon stands for the whole country of Phoenicia. This is a subtle turn because otherwise Polemo had only spoken of the Phoenician ship (cf. A 9, 23, 31; B 40). π appears to have read ξύλ without the inflected ending being written. In medieval MSS 'shorthand' was a not uncommon phenomenon in cases where clarity would be presumed. Unfortunately in this instance there is ambiguity with the result that the copyists produced a range of endings (-ου, -ον, -α, -ων). The verb κατέχω may stand either with the accusative (= restrain) or genitive (= gain possession of), the standard case with verbs of 'taking hold of' (*GG*, 1345; LSJ, κατέχω I.2). In all other occurrences of κατέχω Polemo regularly construes it with the accusative (A 29, 35, 37; B 33, 36, 37, 40, 41, 45, 51). While that could work also here, the genitive seems to fit better with the trope and context. Hence the editors have followed the scribe of α (→ AO). But the bold print (**ξύλου**) in the text indicates the uncertainty.

64

The high expectation (cf. LSJ, δόξα I) for Callimachus was old or long-standing (cf. LSJ, παλαιός II.2) b) in the sense that it was there since his childhood — the phrase τοῦ ... πρώτου γένους means *the first stage of life* (cf. γένος ... καθ᾽ ἡλικίαν, οἷον παῖς ἢ ἀνὴρ ἢ γέρων [= 'genus' according to age — child or man or old man], Aristotle, *Rh.* 1408a27; γένει ὕστερος ἦεν [= in stage of life he was the younger], Homer, *Il.* 3.215). The expectation to which Polemo refers is probably that inherent in the name given to him at birth: Callimachus (Καλλί-μαχος) = Noble Fighter (cf. B 48).

ἐπιστώσω (= you confirmed [√ πιστόω]) is a standard contracted form of the middle aorist indicative second singular ἐπιστώσασο — the intervocalic σ of the ending (-ασο) drops out, then α and ο contract to ω with regressive assimilation because an *o* sound always prevails over an *a* sound (*GG*, 120; 51.a; 59). Callimachus 'confirmed' in the sense that he '*lived up to*' the expectations placed on a good fighter.

Hinck (p. 38) was surely right to regard τρεῖς παῖδες παλαιοί (= three aged sons) as an interpolation. The words are completely unrelated to the context and make no sense in the declamations. Possibly they became attached because of the catch-word παλαιάν in the previous line, but that is only a guess.

One might legitimately ask if the first part of the sentence, αὐτόχθονες μέν ἐσμεν ὡς ἀληθῶς (= we are in truth sprung from the land), should not also be regarded as part of the interpolation. From a methodological standpoint one should, of course, be cautious about identifying glosses, but in this case the following sentence, οὕτως ἀνέσχε Καλλίμαχον ἡ μήτηρ ... (= thus the mother held up Callimachus ...) seems to follow upon τὴν παλαιὰν δόξαν τοῦ σοῦ πρώτου γένους ἐπιστώσω (= you confirmed the old expectation from your first time of life) more smoothly than upon αὐτόχθονες μέν ἐσμεν ὡς ἀληθῶς (= we are native to the land in the true sense).

If this last clause does belong to the original text then the ἐσμεν (= *we are*) includes both Callimachus and his father. αὐτόχθονες (= sprung from the land itself, native born, not settlers) is the antonym of ἐπήλυδες (= immigrants, foreigners, cf. Herodotus 1.78; 4.197; 8.73; Lysias 2.43) and προσήλυτοι (= sojourners, outsiders, cf. Lev 16:29; 17:15; 24:16; Num 9:14; 15:30). The term αὐτόχθονες had become a common shibboleth in Greek patriotism (cf. Demosthenes 19.261; 59.74; 60.4; Isocrates 4.24, 63; 8.49; 12.124; Lycurgus, *Leoc.* 41, 100; Lysias 2.17, 43; Xenophon, *Hel.* 7.1.23; Euripides, *Ion* 29, 589). Here, however, it is more than a mandatory patriotic slogan; it serves to counter-balance Euphorion's argument that "the earth had brought forth [Cynegirus'] right hand for the Greeks" (cf. δεξιὰ ἦν ἀνέτειλε τοῖς Ἕλλησιν ἡ γῆ, A 35). The counter-claim of Callimachus' father is both more concise and more comprehensive.

The formulation ἀνέσχε Καλλίμαχον ἡ μήτηρ can only mean: the mother lifted up the *infant* Callimachus — possibly in a presentation act before the family or in a cultic act of dedication.

The final words of the 'second generation' MSS γ and δ were καὶ τὸν μὲν Ἡρακλέος (= and on the one hand the [.....] of Herakles). This termination point is unequivocally clear from the existing MSS (cf. the critical apparatus for B 64b–65 and chapter 2 "The Ending of the Manuscripts," pp. 67–71). These words, therefore, represent the breaking-off point for the medieval progenitor π, the ancestor of all the existing MSS. The syntactical relationship of these words to the preceding ἀνέσχε clause remains unclear. It is possible that the τόν is an object (parallel with Καλλίμαχον) of that verb, but this is by no means necessary.

About the missing text which was broken off only two things can be said with any confidence: (1) the article τόν expects a masculine noun in the accusative, and (2) the μέν anticipates a correlate δέ. To be sure, there are a few scattered examples of a lone μέν in Polemo (B 3, 23, 56, 63, 64) but with one exception (B 56) these stem from ellipsis (B 23), interpolations (B 63, 64?), or a combination with οὖν (B 3). In the overwhelming majority of cases (102x) μέν is always paired with δέ — this is an earmark of Polemo's style. It may, therefore, reasonably be assumed that the broken-off text continued with an accusative noun and a δέ clause. Beyond that nothing can be said with certainty. The length and content of the missing text are simply not knowable without additional MS evidence independent of π.

The Ending (= Z)

For a discussion of the nature, history, and origins of the Ending the reader is referred above to the chapter 2, "The Ending of the Manuscripts," pp. 67–71 and Appendix 3. Apart from a few inconsequential variants the text of the ending is homogenous in all the MSS. The homogeneity is a result of its not being copied as part of the scribal transmission process which produced the various MSS. Rather it appeared first in the 14th century and was secondarily appended in a short span of time to a half dozen different Italian MSS (A B ρ μ E ν). From these then it was copied as integral to the next generation of MSS (QR [→ ρ + Z] F [→ μ + Z] KG [→ F] CN [→ ν + Z]).

64b

The Doric word γεννάδας connotes *nobility* and *magnanimity* (cf. διαλάμπει τὸ καλόν, ἐπειδὰν φέρῃ τις εὐκόλως πολλὰς καὶ μεγάλας ἀτυχίας, μὴ δι' ἀναλγησίαν, ἀλλὰ γεννάδας ὢν καὶ μεγαλόψυχος [= the nobility shines through when someone bears many and great misfortunes calmly, not owing to insensibility, but from generosity and greatness of soul], Aristotle, *E.N.* 1100b32; γεννάδας τὴν ψυχὴν καὶ μεγαλόψυχος [= generous with respect to the soul and having a big heart], Diogenes Laertius 3.89; χρηστὸς ... καὶ γεννάδας [= valiant and noble], Aristophanes, *Ra.* 179). It is very hard to make the text critical choice between the accusative γεννάδαν (QR [→ ρ+Z] FKG [→ μ+Z]) and the dative γεννάδα [= γεννάδᾳ] (A B E CN [→ ν]). As accusative it is apparently to be construed with the previous article: τὸν μὲν Ἡρακλέος γεννάδαν (= the high-born of Herakles); as dative (of standard of judgment? of respect?, *GG*, 1512, 1516) it would be part of a longer phrase: τὸν μὲν Ἡρακλέος γεννάδᾳ οὕτω λαμπρόν (= the one so illustrious when measured on the nobility of Herakles {?}). In his edition Hinck emended γεννάδα[ν] to read γένηημα (= child). However, if the 19th century's willingness to reconstruct old readings by emendation may be called cavalier, then that procedure is certainly unwarranted in the case of this Ending with its demonstrably short transmission history.

The parallel phrases οὕτω λαμπρὸν (= so brilliant) and τόσον ... σπουδαῖον (= so significant) are nearly synonymous. The former has more of a visible, the latter more of a moral quality. The οὕτω / τόσον are followed by ὡς + infinitive (προέσθαι [√ προίημι = give up, let go, cf. LSJ, sub verbum A.I]): *so much ... so as to give up* (cf. LSJ, οὕτω[ς] III; τόσος I.1 and II.1).

The claim that Callimachus surrendered his soul *on behalf of the fatherland* (ὑπὲρ πατρίς) is reminiscent of the earlier statement that he died fighting for the fatherland (θνήσκων ... πατρίδος ὑπερμαχῶν, B 53), It serves as a counter-weight to Euphorion's claim that Cynegirus made a friendship pact with the sea "on behalf of the fatherland" (ὑπὲρ τῆς πατρίδος, A 44). Indeed, Polemo often uses the preposition ὑπέρ to express the selfless action of his heroes *for* the common weal (cf. ὑπὲρ τοῦ παντὸς στρατοπέδου [= for the whole army], A 25; ὑπὲρ ἡμῶν [= for us], A 44; ταῖς [χείραις] ὑπὲρ ὑμῶν κειμέναις [= the hands lying outstretched for us], A 49; ὑπὲρ τῆς κοινῆς ἐλευθερίας [= for the common freedom], B 8).

Despite the problematic character of the untranslatable dangling article οἱ (= the [plural]), the scribes all retained it. Subsequent editors, however, have sought to eliminate the problem by emendation: Jacobs altered it to δή

(= certainly, manifestly) and Hinck to τοι (= mark you, surely) — ingenious solutions, but pure conjecture.

The preposition ἐπί + dative (θαύματι) appears to connote here *end* or *purpose* (cf. LSJ, ἐπί B.III.2). Yet while Polemo frequently has ἐπί with the dative (cf. A 1, 3, 3, 3, 17, 27, 28, 47; B 15, 16, 19, 29, 37, 57, 62) nowhere else does it have this sense. Nonetheless, the term θαῦμα (= wonder, marvel) is part of Polemo's vocabulary (cf. A 25, 33, 37; B 2, 48, 55, 56). The specific *marvel* to which this refers is, of course, the dead corpse standing and fighting (cf. B 2, 48, 55, 56).

65

The compound particle τοιγαροῦν (τοι + γάρ + οὖν) functions as an emphatic inferential conjunction: *therefore, accordingly*. In classical Greek it regularly stood, as an expression of its strength, first in the sentence (*prepositive*), and that practice lasted into the first century CE (cf. 1 Thess 4:8; Heb 12:1; 1 Clem 57:4, 6; Josephus, *B. J.* 4.168; *Ap.* 2.178); in late imperial Greek, however, it could be postponed to the second position (*postpositive*) — as here and in B 20 (cf. LSJ, τοιγάρ II.1; *GG*, 2987; J. D. Denniston, *The Greek Particles* [2nd ed.; Oxford: Clarendon, 1954] 566–567). It is a fitting connective for the conclusion.

In this conclusion, however, the rhetorical emphasis lies on the very first word, the possessive adjective ἐμόν (= *my*) which, though separated from it, goes with τὸν παῖδα (= the son). This ἐμὸν ... τὸν παῖδα (= *my* son) stands in contrast with τὸν σὸν [παῖδα] (= *your* son) in the final sentence. Thus, the polarity which is constitutive for whole text of Polemo's declamations poses the structural basis for the final sentences.

In an independent sentence without ἄν the optative εἴη (√ εἰμί) expresses a wish referring to the future: *may* [it] *be* (*GG*, 1814). The optative is very rare in Polemo's declamations (only 6x: τύχοι, B 22; εἴη, B 29; εἴποι, B 36; νομίζοιτο, B 49; εὕροις, B 50; ἐπαινέσειε, B 51) and none of these occurrences represents an optative of wish. This rarity does not rule out the possibility of Polemonic authorship of the Ending, but it does feed suspicion about authenticity.

The first thing (τὸ ... πρῶτον) at the funeral ceremonies (τοῖς ἐπιταφίοις) refers more to rank order than chronological order: *the main thing, the most important thing* (cf. LSJ, πρότερος B.I.4. and 5).

The two infinitives κοσμεῖν (= to honor) and τραγῳδεῖν (= to recite) are predicate nominatives explaining τὸ πρῶτον: the main obligation is actually twofold: (1) to honor the son (τὸν παῖδα κοσμεῖν) means to allow Callimachus' father to deliver the ἐπιτάφιον λόγον (= funeral oration) (cf. 0; A 1-3; B 1) in which no doubt Callimachus' valor would be celebrated. (2) to recite the victory hymn (τὸν ἐπινίκιον τραγῳδεῖν) which would presumably include stanzas dedicated to Callimachus' exploits.

With the phrase τὸν ἐπινίκιον one must mentally supply a noun, most likely ὕμνον or παιᾶνα: *the victory hymn* or *paean* (cf. ᾄδοντες ὕμνον ἐπινίκιον [= singing the victory hymn], Diodorus Siculus 5.29; ἐπινικίους ὕμνους ᾖδον [= they were singing victory hymns], Plutarch, *Sert.* 22.2; ᾄδων ... παιᾶνας ἐπινικίους [= singing victory paeans], Plutarch, *Marc.* 8.2). Of course, the adjective ἐπινίκιος could be substantized and stand alone (cf. τὸν ἐπινίκιον ᾄδοντες [= singing the victory song], Aristides 49.379; ποίους ἐπινικίους ... ᾀσόμεθα [= which victory songs will we sing?], Aristides 29.374). Such victory hymns were composed for the occasion by recognized poets, e.g., Pindar (cf. Nem. 4.78-92), Euripides, Leophron, Callimachus (cf. Athenaeus 1.5; 4.25) or by the Muses themselves (cf. Dio Chrysostom 2.58). The hymns could be sung or solemnly recited which is what the verb τραγῳδεῖν (= declaim in tragic style) has in mind (cf. LSJ, τραγῳδέω II).

The Ending closes with a brusk imperative addressed to Euphorion: σὺ δὲ τὸν σὸν ... θρήνει ([contraction of θρήνε-ε] = but you sing a dirge [θρῆνος] for your son). This clever conclusion gets one final dig in at Euphorion because the θρῆνος (= lament, sad strain) is the exact opposite of the victory paean (cf. ἀντὶ δὲ θρήνων ἐπιτυμβιδίων παιὰν μελάθροις ἐν βασιλείοις [= in place of dirges over a tomb, a paean in royal halls], Aeschylus, *Ch.* 342-343). When the main attraction is finished, Euphorion can sound his sad lament for his uselessly mutilated son as a kind of pitiful afterthought (μεθύστερον) — that is, assuming that the jurymen give their permission (συγχωρούντων τῶν δικαστῶν). This concluding genitive absolute phrase has conditional sense with a twofold function: (1) On the one hand it gives public recognition to the authority and discernment of the δικασταί who are judging the debate — a subtle note designed to keep their favor in their subsequent deliberations and vote. In that regard it is more politic than the conclusion of the first declamation which weighs in on the emotions of the jury (cf. A 49). (2) On the other hand, though, it insinuates that Euphorion's words — a predicted mournful lamentation — would be a minor blemish on the state funeral and it is left to the descretion of the jury whether that consolation to Euphorion should be granted at the expense of the solemn dignity that the Athenians have a right to expect from the ceremony.

Appendix 1: Description of the Manuscripts

None of the actual MSS were examined on site. The descriptions which follow are based upon a study of microfilm or photographic copies. On this basis it was not possible to make determinations about (a) the writing materials, (b) the bindings or contents of the codices, or (c) the dimensions of the individual MSS. Hence information about these matters is necessarily absent from the following overviews. In these descriptions the term "ending" denotes the last 43 words in the declamations (i.e., from γεννάδαν οὕτω to τῶν δικαστῶν [B 64b-65]).

A   Florence: Biblioteca Medicea Laurentiana, gr. 56, 1
13/14th century
folios 43r–51v (= 0/A1–B65)

The text of the declamations covers less than 17 full pages having uniformly 34 lines per page with an average of 54 ± 3 letters per line. The lines and narrow margins are clean and straight. The small angular, precise, vertical script was produced by a steady, skilled hand. The smooth breathing marks are ordinarily round while the rough breathing marks vary between round and square. Abbreviations for the inflected endings appear in the standard superposition while the occasional contractions of *nomina sacra* (e.g. ἄνθρωπος, πατήρ) appear on the line. Punctuation consists primarily in the raised dot; commas occur much less often. The final movable ν is employed frequently, even when a consonant follows. When noted (seldom), the mute *iota* is adscript. Proper nouns are usually marked with a short horizontal line drawn over the name.

The last page (51v) — containing the ending — is written in a second hand whose script is similar but not identical. The ending stems from the very same hand that also added the ending to B. Beginning on the second last page (51r) corrections are indicated by underlining the word or letters in question and then writing the correction above the word (B 63, 64) or in the adjacent margin (B 63, 64). These corrections are from a different hand than the one which completed the final page (51v).

The MS has unfortunately suffered from what appears to be water damage and has a large stain across the top and outside corner. The first two lines are entirely, the next fourteen partially affected. Particularly along the edge of the stain the text is difficult to read; on the whole, however, the MS is still quite legible.

B Florence: Biblioteca Medicea Laurentiana, gr. 87, 14
13th century
folios 134r–143v (= 0/A1–B65)

The text of the declamations extends over 20 pages which have uniformly 29 lines per page with an average of 48 ± 3 letters per line. The inner margins are narrower than the outer ones. The letters of the somewhat round script lean forward slightly and vary in size so that they do not mechanically hug the line. The spaces between words is barely more than that between letters. Breathing marks are round. The vowels *iota* and *upsilon* are often, but not always, written with double dots over them. Punctuation consists predominately in the raised dot, but also in occasional commas. The standard modes of short-hand — superposition, combination, and suspension of letters — are found on every page, though on the whole they are used with restraint. Several abbreviations are regularly employed (e.g., for ἄνθρωπος, μήτηρ, πατήρ). The text is devoid of linear or interlinear overwrites — the hand was steady. While the script itself exhibits a certain latitude in letter formation, the scribe appears to have taken great care in copying.

Beginning on the fourth line of the last page (143v) the ending of the text is written clearly in a second hand whose smaller script makes no attempt to replicate the first hand. This ending is from the very same hand that added it also to A.

C Florence: Biblioteca Medicea Laurentiana, gr. 59, 37

15th century

folios 55r–68r (= 0/A1–B65)

The text of the declamations extends over 27 pages, each page having uniformly 26 lines with an average of 45 ± 2 letters per line. The beginning of the first declamation is marked by an elaborate winding vine-like design at the top of the page occupying 3 lines of space.

The first declamation concludes on line 25 of folio 59v. The 26th and final line has the subscription ὁ Κυναίγειρος πατήρ. Above the beginning of the second declamation stands the superscription ἐκ τοῦ ἐναντίου ὁ Καλλιμάχου πατήρ. The fact that this superscription appears above the standard 26 lines and that both it and the immediately preceding subscription are written with a lighter, thinner point suggests that both sub- and superscription may have been secondarily added.

The script is vertical and despite letter extensions above and below the line the general impression is a script of uniform size, i.e., 'bilinear' (fitting between the two guide-lines). The use of ligatures and connected letters is common. The breathing marks are round and the circumflex is often connected to its vowel. Punctuation varies between upraised dots and commas. Notably words divided between two lines are often hyphenated. A grave accent frequently appears on the enclitic τις. The *iotas* and *upsilons* have above them sometimes a single dot and sometimes double dots. Occasionally where corrections have been inserted an upward pointing arrow beneath the line marks the place of correction (cf. e.g., B 19, 20). Along with the full range of standard abbreviations for inflected endings the copyist also employed the καί-compendium and the contraction for ἄνθρωπος. The text is the product of an experienced scribe with a steady, skilled hand.

D Florence: Biblioteca Medicea Laurentiana, gr. 70, 28
15th century
folios 235r–254v (= 0/A1–B64)

The Polemo text extends over 40 pages with very uneven format and unusually irregular script. Prior to writing no guidelines were marked out on the pages; the result is that the lines of text are neither straight, parallel, equidistant, nor uniform in number. On the earlier folios 235r–248r the number of lines per page varies between 20 and 27 (243v with 31 lines is an exception) with the number of letters per line ranging between 20 and 30. In the later folios 248v–254v more text is squeezed onto each page. On these later folios the number of lines per page ranges between 25 and 34 with the number of letters per line increased to between 25 and 35. The text is without the ending; it stops at the word Ἡρακλέος in B 64 — at the bottom of the page but in the middle of the line. Moreover, an upraised punctuation dot marks this as conclusion. This format shows that the termination is not accidental. The scribe was obviously copying from a MS which ended at this point.

Letters that extend above or below the line provide opportunities for great swirling flourishes. Breathing marks are round and the (often erratic) accents are on occasion connected to the letters beneath. When written, the mute *iota* is usually adscript. Proper nouns are typically marked by a short horizontal line over them.

The entire MS is characterized by innumerable careless mistakes: misspellings; inadvertent omissions of words, phrases, or whole lines; haplographies; dittographies; and transpositions. The whole text was shoddily copied by an incompetent scribe (or possibly several?) with an unsteady hand and no experience or natural talent. The irritated reader is minded to attribute the wretched quality to either disinterest or dyslexia. But it may perhaps merely represent an initial practice exercise of an unenthused novice. If so, however, after seeing the results of the probe the teacher or abbot will in all likelihood have advised the unpromising pupil to pursue other endeavors in life.

Whatever its origin, this MS will certainly not have served as basis for any subsequent copies. And it has little direct value for reconstructing the text of the declamations. Its main usefulness today lies in the evidence it provides about its parent text (η) — the same *Vorlage* that H used. In view of its inferior quality it is no great misfortune that this MS, like that other Florentine MS B, has suffered water damage which has left the top four or five lines badly stained and difficult to read.

E Rome: Biblioteca Apostolica Vaticana, gr. 96 (103)
14th century
folios 11r–18v (= 0/A1–B65)

The declamations cover 16 pages. The number of lines per page varies between 32 and 34 with an average of 50 ± 3 letters per line. Large margins frame the text. Simple wavy designs occupying one line mark the beginnings of both declamations. In addition, side rubrics are noted in the margins at the beginning of each speech: ὁ Κυναιγείρου πατήρ (right margin) and ὁ Καλλιμάχου πατήρ (left margin).

The script is vertical, angular, and compact. It is relatively consistent but lacks elegance. Breathing marks are round; grave and acute accents are clearly distinguished by their 45 ° and 135 ° slants. The *diaeresis* appears frequently but only over the *iota*, not over the *upsilon*. Punctuation is limited to the upraised dot and the comma. Abbreviations of inflected endings are standard: common are superposition, suspension, ligatures, and the καί-compendium.

The ending (the last five lines of the text) comes from a second hand whose script closely resembles that of the first hand, but some of whose letter formations (e.g., δ, θ, ρ, φ, ω) are nevertheless characteristically different from those in the first hand.

In the entire text only one marginal note appears (by A12/13): ἀντίθεσις / λύσις which seems to mark the transition from the topic of Cynegirus to that of Callimachus. It is apparently a rhetorical observation on the part of the copyist (it seems to be in the same hand). Except for occasional smudges or partially faded lines the text is generally quite legible.

F Rome: Biblioteca Apostolica Vaticana, gr. 1297 (Orsini 9)
14/15th century
folios 408v–413r (= 0/A1–B65)

The entire text of the declamations is squeezed onto 9½ pages which uniformly have 37 lines per page, except for the last page which only has 19 lines of text leaving blank the bottom half of the partially cut off page. The very compact script (73 ± 2 letters per line) is written with a fine point as though the cardinal scribal virtue were economy of space. No other MS compresses the Polemo text onto so little surface. The scribe employed the standard ligatures and abbreviated inflexions along with a few idiosyncratic abbreviations of his own, to which the reader quickly becomes accustomed. Tiny script, superposition of endings, suspension of letters, contractions of *nomina sacra* (e.g., ἄνθρωπος, πατήρ), and the καί-compendium all contribute to the visible compression. Double dots typically appear over both the *iota* and the *upsilon*; on occasion the dots are written so close together that the ink merges giving the appearance of a single dot. Breathing marks are round and accents distinct. Interlinear dots are used to signal the existence of alternate readings (cf. e.g., B 40, 41). Punctuation consists in the upraised period and, less often, the comma.

The superscription of the first speech (ὁ Κυναιγείρου πατήρ) is written in the left margin next to the opening line; the superscription of the second speech (εἰς τὸ ἐναντίον. Καλλιμάχου πατήρ) is linear. The initial calligraphic *epsilon* in the opening word (ἐπειδή) of the first speech is written enlarged (3 lines high) in the left margin. The corresponding letter *tau* in the opening word (τὸν) of the second speech has inadvertently been left out. The scribe began the second speech by writing ὸν on the line and then completed the sentence without remembering to return afterward to write the enlarged letter *tau* in the margin — a *lapsus* due to simple inattention on the part of the scribe or the calligrapher.

The inner margins are narrow (width of 4-5 letters) while the outer margins are over twice as wide. It is hard to determine with certainty whether the few glosses and variant readings (A 7, 12, 13; B 8) in the outer margins stem from the first or second hand. The marginal notes at A 12/13 (ἀντίθεσις / λύσις) — also in the margins of E and L at the same passage — seem to be observations on the rhetorical transition.

Hinck (p. 38) judged the ending (the last four lines) to have been written by a second hand. That is an assessment with which it is hard to concur. A careful analysis of the handwriting does not lend support to it. For every character and combination of characters in the ending exact matches can be found in the text. If it is from another hand the second scribe was remarkably successful in replicating the original script. There is no discontinuity in the ink or size and shape of the script. Any minor differences thought to be perceived in the last lines may be attributed to the scribe's relief at approaching the end.

The MS is the work of an accomplished scribe with a confident hand. It is devoid of erasures or overwrites. It makes a businesslike impression, almost pedantic, yet with just enough flair to avoid monotony. The whole carefully copied text is in good condition (no stains, tears, blotchs, or fading) and virtually every letter, despite Lilliputian dimensions, is clearly legible.

G Rome: Bibliotheca Apostolica Vaticana, gr. 1415

15th century

folios 23v–52r (= 0/A1–B65)

The MS spreads out the text of the declamations over 55 pages (more pages than any other Polemo MS). Each page has an identical format: 17 lines per page with 30 ± 1 letters per line, and very large margins so that the text itself barely occupies half the width of the page. With a relatively wide point the scribe produced thick-lined letters with such abundant ink that the writing sometimes bled through to the opposite side of the page making the letters on both sides difficult to read. With its uneconomic use of writing surface and its thick script this MS is visually the polar opposite of F.

Despite his prodigal non-use of available writing surface the scribe still employed the standard abbreviations, ligatures, and contractions. Since this was obviously not with a view to saving space it must have been to save time. This interpretation is corroborated by the highly developed, forward leaning cursive handwriting which the scribe used. He liked to connect letters; two or three connected letters are normal, as many as five linked letters are not uncommon. Other clues that he wrote quickly are his fondness for elisions which have no parallels in the other MSS (e.g., ποτ᾽ ἂν B 40; δ᾽ ὦ B 41; δ᾽ οὔ B 43; δ᾽ ἕνα B 54; σ᾽ ἐξηπάτησε B 60) and his careless omissions of articles (e.g., A 17; B 26) or whole lines (e.g., A 27). Omissions are occasionally corrected utilizing an insertion sign in the text (an upright pointing arrow under the line) where the correction is to be added (e.g., A 27; B 26, 31). Alternate readings or corrections are occasionally noted in the side margin (cf. A 23, 49; B 8, 51). Breathing marks and letters are rounded. His style has a number of notable characteristics: *iota* subscripts are indicated with a dot under the letter; the enclitic τις is often written with a grave accent instead of placing an acute on the last syllable of the previous word; misplaced accents are subsequently corrected; hyphens show the division of words at the end of a line. Unique to this Polemo MS is the scribe's practice of repeating below the last (17th) line of every *verso* page the same word or phrase which begins the top of the next (*recto*) page. This sort of duplication appears only once at the bottom of a *recto* page (41r bottom / 41v top) — a *lapsus* due no doubt to simple inattention.

Despite the inevitable mistakes that come with speed writing and the smudging that comes from excessive ink, one will have to credit the scribe with skill and care. He seems to have counted time as important and prized speed as the mark of an accomplished professional. In this regard he probably pushed himself to the limit. Consequently on rare occasions he exceeded his limits and unwittingly forfeited accuracy for the sake of efficiency. Nevertheless, visually his product is a handsome MS of which he may rightfully have been proud.

H   Paris: Bibliotheque Nationale, gr. 3017
14/15th century
folios 114r–122r (= 0/A1–B64)

The text of the declamations, which does not contain the ending, occupies 17 pages of the codex; the number of lines per page vascillates between 34 and 35 (folio 120v with 33 lines is an exception) with an average of 50 ± 4 letters per line. The tiny inconsistency in the number of lines and the very slight deviations of the individual lines from the straight are barely noticable, but they indicate that the scribe was skilled and confident enough to proceed without first marking out guidelines on the page. Despite that every page presents a remarkably uniform format. The narrow inside margins vary somewhat in width (ca. 3-6 letters); in general the outside margins are about twice as wide as the inside ones. The margins are clean; only one marginal note appears in the entire text (the variant reading λοιποί at B 30).

The script is angular and nearly vertical. The breathing marks while technically round make the impression of a right angle shape. The transition from the older period of square breathing marks is probably not far removed. The scribe utilized the full range of conventional abbreviations. Apart from double character ligatures the letters are rarely connected. The text is largely a 'printed' product of the sort pre-dating the development of continuous cursive script like that found, for instance, in G. In general the script is lower case with a number of letters (e.g., α, π, and σ) occurring in several different minuscule forms. Some letters, however, appear regularly in upper case form (e.g., H) while others appear in both upper and lower case (e.g., Γ/γ, Δ/δ). The text is clear and legible throughout.

I Paris: Bibliotheque Nationale, Ancien gr. 1733

15th century
folios 245r–253v (= 0/A1–B64)

This Polemo text, which is without the ending, is the joint work of at least three hands:

(1) 245r-249r   (= 0/A1-B13), 31-34 lines per page with 50 ± 3 letters per line
(2) 249v   (= B13-B19), 31 lines on the page with 44 ± 3 letters per line
(1?) 249v-251v (= B19-B42), 31-32 lines per page with 49 ± 2 letters per line
(3) 252r-253v (= B42-B64), 35-37 lines per page with 41 ± 3 letters per line

Thus altogether the text extends over 18 pages. The script of the first hand is vertical and angular. Some letters extend far above and below the line (e.g., β, γ, κ, τ, χ). Initial and final letters are sometimes in superposition. The script of the second hand is very similar but a bit darker, heavier, and slightly rounded. The third hand produced a much more rounded script which leans forward and tends toward connecting the letters in cursive fashion. In all three hands the breathing marks are round. The diaeresis with *iota* and *upsilon* is present in all three hands, but noticably darker in the second hand. In the third hand it is not uncommon for the dots to be set inside a wide mouthed *upsilon*.

The inner margins are extremely narrow (2-3 letters wide), the outer margins are larger (7-8 letters wide). The MS is in poor condition. Repair tape has been applied to frayed outer edges at a number of places. The last three folios (251r-253v) are noticably and unevenly discolored on the inner portion of the pages. The entire MS is so badly rubbed that in many places the text is a struggle to read. In nine passages the outer margins contain smudged or faded notes that unfortunately are nearly impossible to decipher (cf. A 1, 3, 14, 25, 31, 37, 43; B 3).

The MS is a maverick in that it derives from a 'composite' *Vorlage*. That is, its variant readings sometimes side with the γ group (AO BQR) and sometimes with the δ group (MFKG J EL CN HPD). Therefore, I — or more likely its parent ι (cf. Chapter 2, "The Hybrid Manuscripts," pp. 61–63) — utilized two *Vorlagen* (one from each side of the stemma: γ and δ) and proceeded in eclectic fashion, choosing here from γ, there from δ. As *mixtum compositum* I (or more likely its parent ι) arose after the second generation split into two families. It is, therefore, a fourth generation MS, or, much less likely, a third generation MS.

J Rome: Biblioteca Apostolica Vaticana, Palatinate gr. 93
13th century
folio 10r (= 0/A1–A13)

This witness consists of a single page with 35 lines of Polemo text averaging 73±2 letters per line. Early on in the first declamation the text breaks off mid-sentence at A 13 after the words τῆς ἀρχῆς ἔχει without any punctuation marks. At this point the scribe was in the middle of his line and he left the remainder blank. There are no apparent reasons or clues as to why the scribe interrupted his copying here without completing even one full page. Beneath, filling up the rest of the page, there are seven more lines of completely unrelated notes in two other hands.

The script in the Polemo text is very small and leans slightly forward. The breathing marks are round. On this single page the entire gamut of conventional abbreviations for inflected endings is displayed. Despite the tiny script, the text, what little there is of it, is fully legible. The initial *epsilon* of the opening ἐπειδή is not — in contrast to all the other MSS (except D) — written with calligraphic enlargment. Further, it is also visually distinguished from all other Polemo MSS in that the text of the preludium (0) is underlined.

It could be that from the outset this page was only intended to be a practice exercise or trial run. If so, in that respect it might be analogous to D. Yet in spite of its brevity, the existence of J is of great importance, for it is one of the oldest existing witnesses to Polemo's declamations. While it is unfortunate that J is so brief, it is nevertheless valuable because it contains enough material to establish that J belongs to the ε family of MSS (J EL CN DHP). J demonstrates, therefore, that the ε archetype was even older (12th century?). It thus makes an important contribution to the reconstruction of the stemma of the δ family of MSS (MFKG J EL CN DHP).

K Rome: Biblioteca Apostolica Vaticana, gr. 928
15th century
folios 196v–202v (=0/A1–B65)

The declamations cover almost 13 pages of this MS. The number of lines per page ranges between 32 and 36 with an average of 70±7 letters per line. The inner margins are very narrow (3-4 letters across), the outer margins are disproportionately wide (over one third the width of the text) and devoid of any notes or glosses.

The script is small and efficient, but without grace. Breathing marks are round, but in a shape reminiscent of their square ancestry. The *diaeresis* appears over *iotas* and *upsilons*, but not regularly. A wide range of abbreviations is employed: superposition, ligatures, καί-compendia, and inflection shorthand. Punctuation consists in period and comma. Between sentences the scribe often leaves a tiny but discernable space (1-2 letters wide). The entire text is clear and legible. The MS presents nothing particularly noteworthy or problematic.

L   Rome: Biblioteca Apostolica Vaticana, gr. 1898
15/16th century
folios 220r–223v (= A1–49)

This MS covering 8 pages is unique in that it contains only the first of the two declamations (A1-49). The introduction which explains the contest between the two fathers (0) — found in all the other MSS — has been omitted and replaced by the otherwise unattested phrase ἐπιτάφιος εἰς Κυναίγειρον ἀπὸ τοῦ πατρός (= funeral speech for Cynegirus by his father). This remark (which is inaccurate) shows that it was the scribe's intention from the outset to produce a copy only of the first speech. No other MSS offer any parallel to this phenomenon. Thus it seems fair to assume that the truncation derives from this scribe and not from any *Vorlage* of his.

All the pages have uniformly 30 lines. On the first page (220r), after the title line, the second and third lines are left blank and the text begins on the fourth line. On the last page (223v) near the end of the 30th line, after the words ὑπὸ τῶν βελῶν in A 47, the few remaining sentences of the first declamation (A 47-49 from εἰμὶ δέ, ὦ ἄνδρες ... to ὁ θέλων ἀποκοψάτω) are squeezed into the lower margin in five lines of microscopic script. This writing is barely legible and it is impossible to determine with certainty whether it stems from the same or a different scribe. It seems likely, however, that the original scribe, not wanting to start a new folio for the few remaining sentences, simply compressed the final words into the available space at the bottom of the page — an economic procedure disregarding any aesthetic sensitivity or myopia of the reader.

In the MS the script sits largely on the line. Letters and abbreviations in superposition are employed but with great restraint. Two or three letters are often connected, the linking of four (or more) letters is extremely rare. Breathing marks are round. In form the *diaeresis* appears both as two dots and as a small stroke resembling a circumflex. The use of the *diaeresis* over *iota* and *upsilon* is irregular. The ink is inconsistent — it is darker in some places, lighter in others.

Except for the marginal comment at A 12/13 (ἀντίθεσις / λύσις) — similar to E and F — the margins are clear of glosses. A large dark stain appears in the outer upper margin (9 lines high) on pages 220r-222v, but fortunately it does not affect the text itself.

M   Naples: Biblioteca Nazionale, gr. III, 16 (338)
14th century
folios 43v–48v (= 0/A1–B64)

The text, which does not have the ending, is squeezed onto a little over ten pages of the codex. The script is small and the lines narrow. The number of lines per page varies between 38 and 44 with an average of 74 ± 4 letters per line. In spite of the small script the margins are generous — each margin (inner and outer) has a width of about 15-20% that of the written text. In the left margin of the first declamation this MS has the most elaborate calligraphic initial *epsilon* (17 lines high) of all the extant MSS. The initial *tau* in the margin at the start of the second declamation is small and plain by comparison (2 lines high). Beyond that the margins are free of glosses.

The MS is somewhat frayed on the edges. Because of folio damage, five to ten letters on some of the top ten lines in the inner margin are missing. The bottom line on some pages is also partly missing. Repair tape on the inner margin occasionally obscures a few letters. In many places the script is so rubbed or faded that some letters or words are uncertain. Yet in spite of these physical defects the skill and ability of the scribe is clear.

The characters are uniform, leaning slightly forward, and connected two or three at a time. Letters and endings in superposition are relatively rare. Breathing marks are small and usually round, though some have almost right angles. The script is business-like and not given to unnecessary flourishes. Normally the *diaeresis* over the *iota* and the *upsilon* consists in two dots, though a short horizontal stroke can also do the job. The mute *iota* can appear as adscript or subscript, or more often not at all. Abbreviations of the usual 'nomina sacra' (e.g., ἄνθρωπος, πατήρ) are employed. Although a few idiosyncratic ligatures take some getting used to, the script as a whole is easy to read.

The last page of the declamation only has four lines on it with the rest of the page left blank. This page is in poor condition and repair tape on the inner margin covers over about 18-20 letters. Nevertheless, it appears that the text terminated in B 64a with the phrase τὸν μὲν Ἡρακλέους. Inasmuch as there was plenty of room to continue, it may be reasonably concluded that the scribe's *Vorlage* also stopped at that point.

N   Naples: Biblioteca Nazionale, gr. II, E, 21 (16)
15th century
folios 1r–22r (= 0/A1–B65)

The declamations cover 43 pages of the codex. Prior to writing the scribe appears to have marked out on each page all the margins (top, bottom, left, right) forming a rectangular area for writing. Within this space he then wrote the text without pre-marked horizontal lines for the text. With the help of the margin lines he appears simply to have 'eyeballed' the text lines as he wrote. The resulting lines of text are remarkably straight, but not uniform. The number of lines per page varies between 20 and 23 with an average of 35±4 characters per line. The script beginning on the lines at the left delineates an absolutely straight left margin. The right margin guideline, however, served more as a 'target'. Sometimes he undershot it, sometimes he overshot it. The result is only an approximately straight right margin. Horizontal strokes in the last letter of the line often trail off into the margin to a distance equal to 8 or 10 letters.

The nearly vertical and somewhat rounded script is large and flowing. Even the 'straight' strokes have a slight curve or wave in them. No distinction is made between medial and final *sigmas*. When the *sigma* is C-shaped it often embraces the next letter; likewise his *omicron* sometimes surrounds the following *sigma*. Some letters appear in both upper and lower case forms (e.g. γ / Γ). The scribe employed the full range of superposition shorthand endings. Abbreviations of *nomina sacra* are irregular: ἄνθρωπος and πατήρ are sometimes abbreviated, sometimes not; πνεῦμα and σωτήρ are never abbreviated. The scribe wrote the *iota* subscript often, but not always. The *diaeresis* appears only rarely, and then just with the *iota*, not the *upsilon*. Proper names are marked with a short horizontal stroke over them. His use of accents and apostrophes is sometimes anomalous: there are missing accents and extra unnecessary apostrophes. Breathing marks and accents often are placed over the first rather than the second vowel of a diphthong. From start to finish the script is uniform (large, dark, clear) and has grace. Of all the existing Polemo MSS this one is a ranking contender for first place in ease of reading.

O   Milan: Biblioteca Ambrosiana, gr. D. 42 sup.
14th century
folios 90r–101v (= 0/A1–B64)

The Polemo text occupies 24 pages of the codex. The text is without the ending; it breaks off in B 64 after the word Ἡρακλέους. The concluding punctuation mark of the period and the half empty page at the end make clear that the truncation was not due to a transmission accident. The ending obviously must have been absent from the parent text also. The ink employed by the scribe was a tad too thin with the result that the letters do not exhibit a uniform darkness, occasionally they have run together, and in some instances they have faded or smeared.

The number of lines per page varies from 26 to 30 with the last page having only 12 lines and the remainder left blank. Although the scribe wrote without pre-marked guidelines, the resulting text still has acceptably straight lines. In the margins the 'left justification' turned out better than the 'right justification'. The outer margins are about twice the width of the inner ones which are ca. 3-7 letters wide. With the exception of the marginal note at A 20 (ἐνέλαβε) the margins are completely devoid of any glosses.

Whereas the script as a whole makes the visual impression of being relatively consistent, the size of individual letters varies so that the number of characters per line ranges from about 37 to 55, the average being 43 ± 3. The scribe wrote largely on the line and placed letters in superposition relatively infrequently, noticably more often at the end of lines in the interest of 'right justification.' Abbreviations are used sparingly and standard ligatures occur alongside the same individual letters written *plenum*. The *diaeresis* is used regularly with the *iota* and *upsilon*. Breathing marks are ordinarily round, though square ones appear intermittantly. Large C-shaped sigmas often encircle the subsequent vowel letter. Overwrites are rare (cf. A 16, B 1, 9, 32); despite the unevenness of the script size the copyist wrote with a steady regularity.

P   Milan: Biblioteca Ambrosiana, gr. I, 49 sup.
  15th century
  folios 99r–110v (= 0/A1–B64)

The text, which does not contain the ending, covers 24 pages of the codex. Each page has uniformly 28 lines with an average of 47 ± 3 characters per line. The remarkably consistent script leans slightly forward, is rounded, and represents a stage in the evolution of handwriting on its way to becoming fully cursive. The script literally flows — five to eight sequentially connected letters are common. The script throughout is 'bilinear' — the tops and bottoms of the letters follow rigorously straight and parallel lines. The scribe employs many standard shorthand symbols but only rarely does he write letters or abbreviations for inflected endings in superposition, and then most often at the end of a line in order to achieve a very straight margin. Breathing marks are round; accents are ordinarily written separately from their vowels though on occasion they may be a continuation of the final stroke of the letter. When the *diaeresis* is used (irregularly) it is more with the *upsilon* than the *iota*. The script shows a playful artistry. Letters, for instance, which should immediately follow an *omicron* are sometimes written inside it, and letters which by nature extend above or below the line (e.g., γ, δ, ξ, ρ, ϕ) provide occasions for an intermittant artistic flourish. The MS is the work of a master scribe who wrote with a sure hand. The result is of unusual visual quality and virtually free of correcting overwrites (the few interlinear letters in A 26 are a lone exception).

The margins are clean and the entire MS is in excellent condition. The only blemish is a small dark blotch on lines 10 and 11 by the inner margin — perhaps caused by an ink spill on 107v where it is the worst. The fluid, however, has bled through the adjacent pages in both directions so that the discoloration is visible at the same spot on pages 101r though 110v. Consequently a few letters on pages 104r-109v are not legible. But in the face of the elegance of the whole this flaw is negligible.

Q   Vienna: Nationalbibliothek, Suppl. gr. 135
  15th century
  folios 1r–9v (= 0/A1–B65)

The declamations fill 18 pages that have uniformly 30 lines apiece, except for the last page (9v) which only uses the first 16 lines, leaving the bottom half of the page empty. The number of characters per line varies from 51 to 64, with the average being 56±3. The margins are generous: the inner margins are 20% the width of the text, the outer ones often 25%. One distinguishing feature of this MS is the high number of corrections or alternate readings from a second hand noted both between the lines (some 104 altogether) and in the margins (97 in all). Another distinctive feature of the MS is the appearance at the bottom of the *verso* pages (below the end of the 30th line) of the first two or three letters of the word which begins the next *recto* page. Of the other Polemo MSS only G shares an analogous phenomenon.

The scribe has an even and polished script. For inflected endings he employs a limited number of shorthand signs in superposition. Word divisions at the end of a line are usually indicated with a hyphen. With *iota* and *upsilon* the *diaeresis* appears, but irregularly. The standard *nomina sacra* and their cognates are written with abbreviations (e.g. ἄνθρωπος, ἀνθρώπινος, πατήρ, πατρίς, σωτήρ, σωτηρία). Such features suggest scribal skill and experience.

Yet a number of other elements reflect the copyist's carelessness and indicate that his knowledge of Greek was extremely limited. Apart from the fact that the scribe of Q dutifully copied his *Vorlage* with all its mistakes, even when they represented gibberish (cf. description of ρ below), he also produced a host of his own peculiar variants. A broad selection of these is worth noting so as to demonstrate his own limited abilities. Odd iotacisms are noticable (e.g., κρήττω [for κρείττω] A 4; τετραμμένης [for τετραμμένοις] B 26; ἀκινάκι [for ἀκινάκη] B 47). Confusion of the vowels o and ω is common (e.g., λαχόν A 14; νεκρῶν A 27; ζόντων B 52). Other letters, too, are mixed up (e.g., βοβερῷ [for φοβερῷ] B 27; κούς [for τούς] B 40). Often dropped are single letters (e.g., Κα[λ]λίμαχος A 21; περι[ν]όησας A 38; ν[α]ῦν B 31; ἐρρι[μ]μένου B 44) or multiple letters (e.g., ἐπέ[δι]δου A 28; [στοι]χείοις] A 42; [βοη]θεῖν B 5; [κα]μεῖν B 10; πορι[ζο]μένων] B 27). One can understand the dittographies (e.g., νῶνῶτα B 28; νενεκρός B 50), but it is harder to account for other extra letters which are nonsensical (e.g., πολειμάρχους A 17; συνιθέντα B 17; πόντινος B 36; γάρετῆς B 50). Morphological anomalies also mar the text (e.g., πυνθάνοντες; ἡττηθήσθσαι B 2). Typical are careless omissions both of single words (cf. A 26, 27; B 26, 29, 41, 54) and of multiple words (e.g., 4 words in B 9; 14 words in B 11; 18 words in B 63). Many of these readings suggest that the scribe either had poor vision or was perhaps dyslexic or both. Often, however, variants cannot be plausibly explained. The one may make sense best as *lapsus oculi*, another as *lapsus auris*, and yet another as *lapsus manus*. Moreover, if one were to hypothesize that the text was produced by dictation, it is would be hard to say whether a given variant stemmed from a mistake in the hearing of the scribe or from an erroneous pronunciation of the one dictating. At any rate the scribe of this MS displays a peculiar mix of abilities — adept in his script but unskilled in the Greek language.

One important value of the MS lies in its unique 'composite' testimony to both major text traditions. The Q text itself was copied from a *Vorlage* belonging to the γ family (its parent text was a MS closely resembling B, here designated ρ). On the other hand, the interlinear and marginal corrections in Q^2 stem from a MS in the η sub-group (HPD), a MS which by a process of elimination can be identified as H (cf. Chapter 2, "The Hybrid Manuscripts," pp. 64–66). Thus, the MS Q/Q² stands as tangible evidence for the phenomenon of the cross-fertilization of MSS and provides an example of the stage of development that may precede the production of a 'mixed' text which exhibits few telltale glosses (such as the hybrids I and M).

R   Munich: Bayerische Staatsbibliothek, gr. 99
   15/16th century
   folios 187r–197r (= 0/A1–B65)

The declamations extend over 21 pages with uniformly 30 lines apiece having an average of 52 ± 2 characters per line. On the first page, between the calligraphic design which occupies the first line and the introduction starting on the third line, the second line is blank. On the last page the final thirteen lines of text gradually narrow down to a single word in the center. The last six lines of the page are left unutilized.

The script is remarkably uniform throughout. It leans forward and frequently employs double letter ligatures. The scribe tended toward an economy of strokes, often connecting three or four letters and sometimes as many as six or seven together. Despite the cursive character of the script it still makes an angular appearance. The C-shaped *sigma* sometimes surrounds the following letter. *Iota* subscript and *diaeresis* are used, but not consistently. '*Nomina sacra*' (e.g., ἄνθρωπος, σωτηρία, πνεῦμα, πατήρ) are written in standard abbreviated form with a horizontal stroke over them. In general the scribe's practice is to write all words *plenum* with all the letters on the line. Inflected endings abbreviated in superposition are quite rare, though they sometimes are found at the end of a line in the interest of a straight margin.

Visually and superficially this MS gives the impression of scribal competence, but a closer reading discloses many serious shortcomings. Odd iotacisms reveal a poor knowledge of orthography and grammar (e.g., πίσματι [for πείσματι] A 10; δίκτιον [for δίκτυον] B 56; ἡ [for οἱ] B 58). The letters ο and ω are very often confused (e.g., στρατιοτῶν A 6; ὥστις A 15; ἔχον A 45; ἐκαρπόσατο B 39; μακρωβίῳ B 44; καλοδίου B 45; ἐπείροντο B 58). Other vowels too are frequently mixed up (e.g., ταθνεώς [for τεθνεως] B2; ἀξιοῦσα [for ἐξιοῦσα] B 4; νηῶν [for νεῶν] B 29; ἀπ᾽ [for ὑπ᾽] B 32; ἀνίητον [for ἀνόητον] B 33; ἡπίστετο [for ἡπίστατο] B 37; οὐ [for οἱ] B 45; ἔψασθαι [for ὄψεσθε] B 46). Consonants likewise are often confused (e.g., ψευγετε [for φεύγετε] A 40; σίπτουσαν [for πίπτουσαν] A 45; ἀργηδόνος [for ἀλγηδόνος] B 36; ἀπήγατον [for ἀπήγαγον] B 43; ὦρ᾽ [for ὡς] B 63; ἐπὶ ταρίοις [for ἐπιταφίοις] B 65). Moreover, vowels can even be confused with consonants (e.g., εἰούς [for τούς] B 40; εἰδύς [for ἐνδύς] B 52; ἀκοπέλων [for σκοπέλων] B 54; ἄντανδρος [for αὔτανδρος] B 54). Whereas the confusion between ο and ω might be construed as a *lapsus auris*, the other letter confusions make much more sense as *lapsus oculi*. Such mistakes did not always yield orthographic nonsense. It is easy, for example, to see how the scribe could read πράγματα for τραύματα, A 42 or πόταμον for πόλεμον, B 41. Many dropped letters may be due as much to bad vision as to haste or carelessness (e.g., ἀμελέσε[ι]ν A 20; Ἀθηναίο[ι]ς A 31; μένει[ν] B 47; Μα[ρα]θώνιον B 54; [σ]τῆθι B 59; ὑπάρ[χ]ουσαν B 63). Added letters sometimes yield forms that are morphologically if not syntactically possible (e.g., θαλάσσης A 11; μέχρις A 21; βεβληκέναι A 25; βασιλεῦς A 43). Sometimes the result of additional letters is just plain nonsense (e.g., Κυναιγείρων B 46; ἧσθαι B 47). From all of these bizarre readings it can be seen that the scribe's knowledge of Greek morphology and grammar did not go much beyond that of a mediocre student in Greek 102. Moreover, one will have to infer that he had little understanding of what he was copying.

Nevertheless, despite its manifold flaws, R is still important for two reasons: (1) together with Q it bears witness to their common parent (ρ) — a MS closely related to B. The confirmed existence of ρ and then the assumption of its use also by M satisfactorily explains the presence of all the γ readings in that δ MS. R thus makes a significant contribution to the reconstruction of the stemma of the MSS. (2) The collations show that R was the "other" MS used by Stephanus in his *editio princeps* of the declamations. Many idiosyncratic readings of this MS, to which Stephanus gave credance, were thus unfortunately perpetuated into the era of the printed editions. The study of R and the recognition of its inferior quality now provide the objective basis for dismissing the odd readings presented in Stephanus's edition.

The no longer extant, but partially reconstructable ancestor MSS behind the eighteen extant MSS

α ('parent' of A and O; 'child' of γ) not extant
Italy; 12/13th century.
(contents: 0/A1–B64a)

It is from their common *Vorlage* α that the 59 variants peculiar to A and O have derived. These reveal several characteristic features of α. That MS contained many inconsequential orthographic variants (e.g. movable ν [ἐτόλμησεν, A20; παρήγγελλεν, B 57]; vowel instead of apostrophe elision [δὲ, A 46; κατὰ, B 8; ξύλου, B 63]). With some minor orthographic variants the change was probably inadvertent (e.g., breathing mark [εἱμαρμένης for εἰμαρμένης, B 12; ἀμιλλᾶσθαι for ἀμιλλᾶσθαι, B 36], confusion of letters [αὐτὸ for αὐτῷ, A 30; Ἐνέτρια for Ἐρέτρια, B34; ἀνάθεμα for ἀνάθημα, B 51], omission of letter (βεβαίου for ἐβεβαίου, B 24) . Other small variants appear to be deliberate (e.g., addition of καί [A 20; B 21, 37, 51] or τε [B 29]; addition of a single letter [χαλκέοθυμοι for χαλκόθυμοι, A 41; τοῦτον for τὸ τὸν, B 21], omission of a monosyllable [e.g., καί, A ll; γάρ, B 21; ἤ, B 35; μέν, B 64]).

In a number of instances while the variants do make a difference in the sense, it is not possible to know if they were intentional or accidental (e.g., λήματος for λήμματος, A 40; ἀκοντῶν for κόντων, B 10; ἄπορον for ἄπειρον, B 35; ἀρετήν for ἀρίστην, B 53). Any number of variants may go back to a lapse of the eye or ear (e.g. ἐπιδραμοῦσαι for ἐπιδραμοῦσα, A 41; ἀναλῶσαι for ἀναλῶσθαι, B 8; παρασχῶν for παρασχεῖν, B 29; προελθόντα for παρελθόντα, B 50).

It is, however, worth noting that in a number of cases the scribe of α untertook deliberate alterations of the text in the interest of clarification or interpretation. Particularly striking are his addition of the words ἀνακάλει νῦν πολλὰ τὸν Κυναίγειρον, B 48 (which expand the etymological argument); his change of the name Τισσαφέρνης to Ἰνταφέρνης, B 56 (which unsuccessfully tries to make an historical correction); his transposition of the words ἀνθρώπους ἡμᾶς to ἡμᾶς ἀνθρώπους, B 60 (which identifies the Persians not the Greeks as "human"); and the alteration of Μαραθωνικὴ δύναμις to Μαραθῶνι νίκη ἐδυνάμωσε, B 30 (which seeks to smooth a difficulty). Lesser changes too appear to represent deliberate stylistic 'improvements' (e.g. ἔτυχεν for ἐτύγχανεν, B 38; κατασχεῖν for κατέχειν, B 30; ἀγάλλεσθαι for ἀγγέλλεσθαι, B 17; αὔξεσθαι for ἀξιοῦσθαι, B 17; παρά for περί, B 13). Despite the fact that the scribe of α was a relatively careful copyist he did not escape the errors endemic to his trade. Ironically his biggest flaw was his acumen. He sought not only to 'improve' the text here and there by slight alterations, but he also occasionally introduced into the text deliberate interpretive changes. These were taken over by the next generation of MSS (→ A O) from which they then unfortunately found their way into the printed editions of the modern era.

β 'Parent' of B and ρ; 'Child' of γ
    Italy: 12/13th century (not extant)
    Contents: 0/A1–B64a

The divergent readings shared by the MS group BQR and found either nowhere else or in unrelated δ MSS reflect the wording in β. It is striking that there are only a handful of such readings peculiar to β. Of these a few are inconsequential orthographic variants (Πολύξυλος for Πολύζηλος, A 44; θάλατταν, not θάλασσαν, B 26; δὲ for δ', B 44; Ἐρέτρια for Ἐρετρία, B 54; προσβαλλόντες for προσβαλόντες B 59). There are also a few omissions (τόν, 0; καί [after ἀφανῶς], A 19; σοῦ, B 48). Finally, several minor substitutions fill out the list (μόλις for μόγις, B 3; αὐτό for αὐτός, B 8; ἀνηλῶσθαι for ἀναλῶσθαι, B 8; κοπίασας for πίασας, B 18; τέχνης for τύχης, B 27; γινωμένων for γενωμένων, B 29; φύσει for φύσεως, B 50; στρατιώταις for συστρατιώταις, B 57). Altogether such unique variants number only seventeen. Therefore, of all the reconstructable third generation MSS (α β ι μ ε) β is far and away the one with the fewest divergent readings. In other words, of all the MSS of its generation β did the best job of carefully preserving the wording of its *Vorlage* (in this case, γ) and it may thus be safely regarded as the most reliable witness of its age.

γ 'Parent' of α and β; 'Child' of π
    Italy: 11/12th century (not extant)
    Contents: 0/A1–B64a

For the characteristic and salient features of this 'second generation' MS see Appendix 2: γ versus δ.

δ 'Parent' of μ and ε; 'Child' of π
Italy: 11/12th century   (not extant)
Contents: 0/A1-B64a

For the characteristic and salient features of this 'second generation' MS see Appendix 2: γ versus δ.

ε 'Parent' of J, E, ν, and η; 'Child' of δ
Italy: 12/13th century   (not extant)
Contents: 0/A1-B64a

At least four MSS (E J ν η) were copied from the *Vorlage* termed here ε, a MS in the δ family. (The wording of ν can be recovered from the agreements in its 'children' C and N; likewise the readings of η can be recovered from the common readings in its 'offspring' D and H.) In A 1-13 (which is the extent of J) where at least three of the four derivative MSS agree, the wording of ε may be regarded as recovered. In A 13 – B 64 where at least two of the three witnesses agree, ε may be regarded as recovered. By this procedure ca. 30 divergent readings peculiar to ε may be reconstructed. These are of various sorts. Omissions (ἦν, A 19) and iotacisms (ὑμῶν for ἡμῶν, A 41) are rare. Transpositions are more frequent (ἅπασαν δύναμιν for δύναμιν ἅπασαν, B 6; τολμᾶν παντί for παντὶ τολμᾶν, B 27; δὲ μὴ for μὴ δὲ, B 50). ε appears to have truncated some case endings (τοῦτ for τούτοις, A 17; ἀκροστόλ for ἀκροστόλιον, B 63) and changed others (θατέρα for θάτερος, A 4; παραμύθιον for παραμυθία, A 13; ζῶντος for ζῶντι, A 26; θερμότατα for θερμοτάτην, B 6; ἀκμαιότατα for ἀκμαιοτάτην, B 8 τούτῳ for τοῦτο, B 20; βασίλεια for βασιλέως, B 32; πρῶτον for πρῶτος, B 56). Only rarely is there an actual word substitution (φιλίαις for φιλοτιμίαις, A 3; παραγενόμενοι for περιγενόμενοι, B 18; εἰ περιῆσαν for εἴπερ ἦσαν, B 19). In verbs both endings and tenses could be changed (τραγωδεῖν for τραγωδῆσαι, A 48; παράγειν for παραγαγεῖν, B 48; ἀνηλῶσθαι for ἀναλῶσθαι, B 8; ἁρμόττον for ἁρμόττει, B 62) as well as the stems (ἐπέβαινε for ἀπέβαινε, B 5; ζητούμεναι for ζηλούμεναι, B 56). Most of these changes are quite minor and many are understandable. Hence, one may conclude that in general the scribe of ε was a careful copyist who seldom deliberately introduced his own 'improvements' into the text. The fact that it was later copied at least four times suggests that the MS probably had a neat appearance and engendered confidence in its reliability.

η 'Parent' of D and H; 'Child' of ε
Italy [France?]: 14/15th century (not extant)
Contents: 0/A1–B64a

The unique readings common only to D and H [+ PQ²] are derived from their common *Vorlage*, here called η. At least 34 such peculiar variants can be tabulated, enough to reflect the character of η. This MS in the δ family was marred by many omissions — both single word omissions (καί [before ταύτης], A 10; κοινοῦ, B 2; ἐκ, B 8; καί [after ξιφῶν], B 10; ταῖς, B 29; νηί, B 32; πολλοῖς, B 61) and multiple word omissions (ἐμοὶ δὲ ὀφείλεται τιμῆς παραμυθία, A 13; νῦν πρῶτον ἀνδρὸς μαχὴν καὶ νεώς, A 36; τὰ δὲ πεφοβημένοι, B 13). The misspellings are of less significance (οὑμος for οὐμος, A 6; κατακενοῦντες for κατακεντοῦντες, B 57; ἐδύνατο for ἠδύνατο, B 58; ἔβαλε for ἔβαλλε, B 58; ἀκροστόλ[ου?] for ἀκροστόλιον, B 63). Of more significance are the many substitutions. Some of these are striking (δυνάμεις for δεξιάς, A 31; Ἀθηναίους for Ἀθήνας, A 41; καί τοι for ὅτι, B 6 αὐτόν for τὸν τάφον, B 15; πολλοί for λοιποί, B 30; βάλλειν for βασιλεύς, B 56) while others simply represent a change of gender, number, or case (Μιλτιάδῃ for Μιλτιάδην, A 16; ὅλος for ὅλης, A 31; πρῶτος for πρῶτον, A 36; ἀσάλευτα for ἀσάλευτον, A 37; ταύτην for ταύτας, A 49; τοῦ κοινοῦ σήματος for τῷ κοινῷ σήματι, B 15; ταῖς στολαῖς for τῇ στολῇ, B 17; ναῦς for ναῦν, B 37; φοινικῷ for φοινικίῳ, B 47; ρίζα for ρίζας, B 54; τοιοῦτος for τοσοῦτος, B 54). Only one variant in the lot involves a verb (πεποίηκας for ἐποίησας, A 44). Few of these omissions or substitutions appear to be intentional, most seem to have resulted rather from inattention. Thus the MS was produced by a relatively competent but somewhat careless scribe. Visually it will probably have given a positive impression and appeared to be a trustworthy exemplar — after all, it served at least twice as model for later copyists.

ι 'Parent' of I; 'Child' of both δ and γ together
Italy: 12/13th century (not extant)
Contents: 0/A1–B64a

For the characteristic and salient features of this mixed '3rd generation' MS see Chapter 2: "The Hybrid Manuscripts," pp. 62–63.

μ 'Parent' of M and F; 'Child' of δ
Italy: 12/13th century   (not extant)
Contents: 0/A1–B64a (→ M); later + B64b–65 (→ F)

The dozen and a half variants found only in M and F (+ KG) and nowhere else are evidence of their common parent text, here called μ. An overview of those peculiar variants shows that in comparison with its *Vorlage* (δ) this MS had only one single omission (δή, B 27). That remarkable completeness suggests a certain mechanical care on the part of the scribe of μ. On the other hand, the scribe was prone to small transpositions (πρόσφορος μέν instead of μέν πρόσφορος, B 1; τοῦ σου instead of σου τοῦ, B 48; κατὰ τὴν ἀξίαν ἐπαινέσειε instead of ἐπαινέσειε κατὰ τὴν ἀξίαν, B 51) and tiny additions (τοῦτο + νῦν, B 5; μὲν + τῷ, B 27; τὸν + μέν, B 51; δὲ before μὴ δὲ, B 50). Changes in inflected endings sometimes occurred in accord with the scribe's *Sprachgefühl* (τῇ θαλάσσῃ becomes τῆς θαλάσσης, A 8; βαρβάρου becomes βαρβάρων, A 31; μέρη is changed to μέρος, A 32; μόνον to μόνην, B 18; τῶν βαρβάρων to τοῦ βαρβάρου, B 51). Some changes are probably due more to confusion of sound than intent to alter the language (ὑβριεῖτε instead of ὑβριεῖται, B 2; οἰητέον in place of νοητέον, B 35). Other variants, however, appear to be deliberate (συμπλοκήν in place of ἐμβολήν, B 8; συμπερινοστήσεις for περινοστήσεις, B 36; ἐπεθύμησε replaces ἐπεθύμει, B 42). Thus, in general the scribe of μ was faithful to his *Vorlage*, yet he could on occasion make conscious 'improvements' — the sign of one well schooled in Greek.

In both M and F the script is very small and pedantic; and in both cases the declamations occupy less than ten pages — these two MSS are far and away the most compact of all the existing MSS. It is, therefore, not unreasonable to assume that their common *Vorlage* μ probably exhibited the same compactness: the declamations in μ were very likely in tiny script squeezed onto relatively few folios. At the time when μ was copied by M, μ had no ending (the text broke off at τὸν μὲν Ἡρακλέος in B 64). By the time that μ was copied by F, however, the Ending (B 64b–65) had been appended to μ so that it appeared integrated in F. Hence, near the end of its career (in the 14th century) μ belonged to those MSS which were 'updated' with the Ending. That ending will have been appended in continuing lines (as in F) and not in diminishing lines tapering down to a point (as in A B Q R).

ν 'Parent' of C and N; 'Child' of ε

Italy: 14th century (not extant)

Contents: 0/A1–B64a; later + B64b–65

The variants appearing in C and N but not in other MSS will have derived from their common *Vorlage*, here called *ν*. There are some 44 such peculiar variants stemming from *ν*. Over half (23 instances) of these are a matter simply of a confusion, metathesis, addition or omission of one letter, or occasionally two: **confusion** (περιέναι for παριέναι, A 16; προτιμώτερος for προτιμότερος, A 23; ὄρθου for ὥρθου, A 27; κρεῖτον for κρείττων, A 35; ὡρμήσαντος for ὁρμήσαντος, A 41; μέλη for βέλη, A 42; ἡμῖν for ὑμῖν, B 2; βαλομένοις for βουλομένοις, B 13; ἡμφισβήτη for ἡμφισβήτει, B 21; δεξιᾷ for δεξιά, B 36; Θυσεύς for Θησεύς, B 41), **metathesis** (ἐθράσυνας for ἐθάρσυνας, A 31), **addition** (ἐπέρριψεν for ἐπέρριψε, A 10; παρέττατεν for παρέταττε, A 19), **substitution** (βάσεως for βασιλέως, A 9; μέλετε for μέλλετε, A 41; ἀρετή for ἀρετῆς, B 24; ἁμιλᾶται for ἁμιλλᾶσθαι, B 36; ἐρριμένον for ἐρριμμένον, B 44; παρήγγελε for παρήγγελλε, B 56; προβαλόντες for προσβαλόντες, B 59; γλῶσαν for γλῶσσαν, B 63). Another half dozen variants are comprised by single and multiple word **omissions** (τὸν τάφον ὅν ἐκόσμησα, A 12; καὶ (before περιὼν), A 22; τὰς ἑαυτοῦ, A 28; τῶν, B 1; ἐπεὶ δ᾽ [for ἐπειδὴ δὲ], B 13; εὐ, B 29) and a **transposition** (τοῖς βαρβάροις παρέσχες for παρέσχες τοῖς βαρβάροις, B 61). Together these sorts of variants constitute over two thirds of the divergent readings. Virtually all of these are inadvertent and of no consequence, but they do show repeated 'peccadillos' by the scribe of *ν* which may possibly have been due to poor eyesight.

While some of the remaining variants are minor substitutions (τἀληθῆ for ταληθές, A 26; ἐκ τοῦ ἐναντίου for εἰς τὸ ἐναντίον, B 1; τοῦ for τήν, B 1; πρῶτον for πρῶτα, B 29; βασιλεία for βασελέως, B 30; βασιλεῖ for βασελεύς, B 56), others are more significant (πτερομάτων for πνευμάτων, A 35; σῶμα for σέλας, A 36; ἐπιτιμήσεως for ἐπιτιμίας, A 36; σπουδή for σχολή, B 13; βοηθῶν for βοῶν, B 56). These, coupled with a few additions (end of first declamation + ὁ Κυναιγείρου πατήρ, A 49; ὧν (φτερ ὠσθ᾽) + ὁ, B 23; ἐβεβαίου + τὴν, B 24), may in fact be deliberate alterations of the text. Even so, they are noticably few.

From another aspect one may assume that *ν* was a MS in which the initial letters of both declamations (namely ε [ἐπειδή] and τ [τόν]) probably stood enlarged in the left margin with calligraphic embellishments. This deduction stems from looking at the appearance of the 'offspring' of *ν*, namely at C and

N. Among all the MSS C displays some of the most elaborate calligraphic letters (here it takes second place only to M Q R). In N it is clear from the truncated forms πειδὴ (instead of ἐπειδὴ) in A 1 and ὸν (instead of τὸν) in B 1 that the scribe had intended decorative letters to be inserted in the left margin. Unfortunately that task was left undone so that a comparison between the calligraphy of C and N can not be made. Nevertheless, the fact that the decorative letters were not drawn at the outset is an indication that they were to be more elaborate than just enlarged letters. The calligraphic letters of C and the planned calligraphy of N point no doubt to a *Vorlage* which itself exhibited especially decorative letters.

In summary one can say that ν was a MS copied with considerable care, but nonetheless because of a deficiency of the scribe — perhaps he was an old man — it was marred by many tiny flaws. Fortunately, most of these did not alter the text in any substantial way. The script and the calligraphy of ν will have been aesthetically pleasing — both C and N sought to match that impression — and inspired the confidence of those who later copied it.

ρ 'Parent' of Q, R, and M; 'Child' of β

Italy: 13/14th century   (not extant)

Contents: 0/A1–B64a (→ M); later + B64b–65 (→ Q R)

The nearly 300 variants common to Q and R but to no other MSS prove that the two are related. Further, the scores of variant readings unique to each MS alone but not found in the other show that neither MS can be understood as dependent upon the other. The only cogent explanation is that Q and R have a common parent (ρ — so designated because of its parentage to R). Here the demonstrated limitations of the scribes of both Q and R can be made to yield a positive result. The two scribes were such novices in Greek that they could do little more than woodenly, indeed one might say slavishly, copy their *Vorlage*, even when it presented bad Greek or patent gibberish. Their language ability was too minimal to undertake any independent 'corrections' or 'improvements' of their *Vorlage*. Thus, wherever Q and R agree, a hypothetical reconstruction of the *Vorlage* (ρ) may be undertaken with some certainty.

Though of inferior quality, ρ will no doubt visually or superficially have inspired a sense of confidence — in that respect similar to Q and R. After all, a scribe does not knowingly copy what is manifestly flawed. The initial letters (ε and τ) of the two declamations will have been written in the left margin, enlarged, and in strikingly elaborate calligraphy. This may be inferred from the unusual and similar calligraphic letters in its three offspring Q, R, and M.

Further, in the 14th century, between the time when ρ was consulted by M and the time when it was copied by Q and R the ending (B 64b-65) was secondarily added. As in the last 4 lines of Q and the last 13 lines of R, the ending in ρ will no doubt have progressively narrowed down to a single word. The same format is also found in the last 3 lines of A and the last 4 lines of B. This phenomenon stands in contrast to the δ MSS containing the ending (FKG E CN) which simply continue writing on the line right up to the last word, finishing without any artistic flourish.

A reconstruction of ρ from the agreements in Q and R shows that the text of ρ is closely akin to AO and B. Where the readings of these MSS diverge, ρ occasionally agrees with A or O, but most often with B. The *circa* 300 variant readings common to Q and R, however, distinguish ρ from the other MSS in the group. Among the distinctive features of ρ is the tendency to change superlatives to comparatives (e.g., θαυμαστότεροι [for θαυμαστότατοι] A 6; θειότερον [for θειότατον] B 55; cf. also ἀθλήτερον [for ἀθλητάς]! B 44) or vice versa (e.g., μάλιστα [for μᾶλλον] A 12). The scribe of ρ preferred perfects (or forms with κ) over aorists (e.g., ἔδωκαν [for ἔδοσαν] A 29; ἀποκέκοπτο [for ἀπεκόπτετο] A 36; ἠμεληκότα [for ὑπεριδόντα] A 30) and in general showed a tendency to change the tenses of verbs (e.g., ἔχομεν [for εἴχομεν] A 29; ἐμνημόνευσεν [for ἐμνημόνευεν] A 36; μεμάχητο [for μεμάχηται] B 32; ἐπεχείρει [for ἐπεχείρησε] B 32). The scribe's proclivity to alter word order is also striking (cf. A 2, 3, 10, 22, 25, 34, 46; B 15, 19, 23, 28, 30, 35, 41, 46, 47, 54, 58, 60).

Alongside such characteristic features in ρ what stands out particularly is the host of orthographic oddities. Confusion of ο and ω is common (e.g. βουλωμένῳ A 30; ἰσώρροπον B 12; πρωτιμουμένῳ B 19; πειρομένῳ B 34; γενώμενον B 50; νεκρόν B 52; μαχιμότερε B 53) but ioticisms are rarer (e.g., μίζονας [for μείζονας] A 29; νενήκημεν [for νενίκημεν] A 32; οἶδεν [for εἶδεν] B 33). Many anomalous forms are simply careless misspellings due to dropped letters (e.g., βασίος [for βασιλέως] A 29; γέμων [for ἡγέμων] B 2; ἐπέσθη [for ἐπείσθη] B 11; ἀνέπευσαν [for ἀνεπνευσαν] B 30; δύμις [for δύναμις] B 31), added letters (e.g., πευσεῖν [for πεσεῖν] A 7; ἤρκεσει [for ἤρκεσε] A 21; λυσάστω [for λυσάτω] A 41; ἀκόντινα [for ἀκόντια] B 39), metathesized letters (e.g., ὄκνῳ [for ὄγκῳ] B 34; κύσθαι [for σκύθαι] B 56), wrong letters (τᾶττον [for θᾶττον] A 11; μενπτός [for μεμπτός] B 7; παντᾰδαπῶν [for παντοδαπῶν] B 10; ῥύμην [for ῥώμην] B 24; παρατάξετο [for παρατάξατο] B 32), or faulty word separation (e.g., εἶχε τό [for εἴχετο]

A 9; ὑπεδέξα τό [for ὑπεδέξατο] B 10; ἤδη μήτηρ [for ἡ Δημήτηρ] B 41). Forms that are theoretically possible but non-existent also appear (e.g., ἀδύναται A 26; Γλαύκων B 36). Besides all this there also stood uncorrected gobbledegook (e.g., ὥσπερ ὑπερ ὑπʼ A 37; οὐκ ἀλάττων [for ἐλάττων] B 24).

In view of all of his obvious limitations it is, therefore, all the more striking that the scribe of ρ occasionally undertook to 'improve' the choice of words in his text (cf. e.g., ἄτερος [for θάτερος] A 4; ὕστερος [for δεύτερος] A 22; γένη [for βέλη] A 27; ἑτέρας [for ἄλλας] B 41; οἰκείας [for ἰδίας] B 53; νήσεις [for νήσους] B 54).

This text of ρ, with all its varied mistakes and idiosyncratic readings, the scribes of Q and R dutifully and uncritically copied. For the modern critic, however, their slavish ignorance turns out to be a boon — it is what allows the reconstruction of their *Vorlage*. That reconstructed text, ρ, despite all its flaws, is valuable because it supplies an additional contemporary witness alongside and related to AO and B. This on the one hand enables the reconstruction of the γ family and on the other hand it provides some balance to the δ family of witnesses which is much larger.

π 'Parent' of γ and δ; 'Child' of unknown ancestry
  Italy: 11th[?] century (not extant)
  Contents: 0/A1–B64a

All the extant Polemo MSS go back to this single medieval MS. Either this MS or its *Vorlage* was in all probability brought to Italy from the Byzantine world. The Greek text presented in Chapter 3 is a reconstruction of the entire text of π as best as it can be recovered on the basis of the extant MSS. In several dozen passages there may be legitimate debate about the wording. These are all cases where the reconstructed readings of γ and δ diverge and yet appear equally plausible (see Appendix 2: γ versus δ) — these cases are indicated in the text by bold font.

Nothing can be said about the actual MS itself. The number of folios or their dimensions, the nature of the script or the visual image of the page, the condition or physical defects of the MS at the time it was copied by γ and δ — all of that eludes our knowledge. However, two things about the MS may be said with certainty: (1) The MS did not contain the ending (B 64b–65). And (2) the scribe of π appears occasionally to have truncated inflected endings in such a way that it was not always clear to subsequent copyists what the abbreviation stood for (e.g., cf. the critical apparatus in the following cases:

βασιλ´ [= βασιλεύς ? βασιλεῖ ?], B 56; πολλ [= πολλάς ? πολλῶν ?], B 62; ἀκροστόλ [= ἀκροστόλιον ? ἀκροστόλου ? ἀκροστόλον ?], B 63; ξύλ [= ξύλον ? ξύλου ? ξύλα ? ξύλων ?], B 63). This abbreviation practice accounts for at least some of the divergencies between the first copies (γ and δ) made of π.

The ancestral lineage behind the medieval π — be that of its immediate *Vorlage* or the original second century Π itself — cannot be addressed without additional and older MS evidence. This edition, therefore, contents itself with the reconstruction and interpretation of π. Other than the identification of a half dozen glosses in π, further conjectural reconstructions are studiously avoided.

Π Original text of Polemo's declamations

Asia Minor: 2nd century   (not extant)
Contents: 0/A1–B64a + a now lost ending

This MS may well have been produced in Smyrna though that is not demonstrable. Whether Polemo himself, an amanuensis, or possibly a devoted student, first wrote it down remains beyond our ken. In light of the abrupt break at B 64a in the medieval MSS, it may be taken as certain that the original Π included an ending extending beyond B 64a, but which has since gotten lost. The extent of that missing ending, however, is unknown. Yet given the considerable length of the extant peroration (B 51–64a), it seems unlikely that very much has disappeared. The degree to which Π is mirrored in π, its 11th century descendent, can be a matter of debate. The editorial judgments in this matter (recorded in the critical apparatus beneath the English translation in Chapter 3) are, all things considered, relatively conservative. It will probably be safe to say that what survives represents a close approximation of the original.

Appendix 2: γ versus δ

In this appendix the designators γ and δ do not have the same connotation as in the critical apparatus (where they indicate a unanimous consensus of all the extant MSS dependent on γ and δ respectively). Rather in this appendix *γ and δ refer to the no longer extant second generation* (12th century?) *MSS themselves* and their respective reconstructed wordings (which were not always reproduced by all the descendants).

The structure of the stemma and the breadth of the data are such that in most cases they permit the reconstruction of the wording of both γ and δ with high probability, if not certainty. Where α and β agree, the wording of γ may be regarded as recovered. Likewise, where μ and ε agree, the agreement may be viewed as representing the wording of δ. Where a pair of siblings disagrees, the reading in ι may occasionally help to resolve the case. Where γ and δ agree, the wording of their common *Vorlage*, the (11th century?) medieval progenitor π, may be regarded as recovered. It is where γ and δ diverge that the reading of π may be in dispute.

As it turns out there are about 170 instances where γ and δ are not in agreement. Fortunately, the vast majority of these divergencies are of relatively little significance. The transpositions of word order are for the most part without any change in meaning (17x). The orthographic variants (legitimate 22x; illegitimate 7x; ambiguous 6x) rarely affect the sense. The omissions are in general quite minor (single words 24x; multiple words 4x). Most substitutions too are of small consequence: changes in gender (6x), number (9x), case (18x), tense (10x), mood (5x), and person (1x). There

439

remain only about 30 substitutions of any substance at all: verbal variations (roots,[1] prepositional prefixes,[2] endings[3]) and nominal variations (nouns / pronouns,[4] adjectives / adverbs[5]). Taken as a whole, therefore, the text tradition may be regarded as sound and stable.

In each of these 170 cases where γ and δ do diverge — be the variants 'minor' or 'major' — a choice between the two options must be made which cannot rely solely or even primarily on the external witness of the MSS. The decision ordinarily hinges on a weighing of the internal evidence. In general that reading is to be preferred which best explains the rise of the other. Certain established text critical 'rules of thumb', when applied judiciously, are helpful. Often the more difficult reading (*lectio difficilior*) is to be preferred because a scribe is more likely to smooth over a difficulty than introduce one. The old rule of preferring the shorter reading (*lectio brevior*) — because copyists tend more to expand than contract a text — is less applicable because in most of the relevant cases it is a matter of inadvertent omissions on the part of δ due to inattention. When other things are equal that reading may be preferred which appears more consistent with the vocabulary, syntax, or style of the established passages — this might be termed the *principle of coherence* or *consistency*.

Utilizing such criteria an arguably clear choice between γ and δ presents itself in about 144 of the 170 cases of divergency. In connection with these cases the important point to be stressed is the *ratio* of the choices: *In 114 instances γ seems preferable* to the present editors, *in only 30 cases δ*; in the remaining 25 cases it appears to be an even choice. In other words, in the 144 'clearer' cases the readings of γ were chosen over those of δ in a ratio of about 4 to 1. This leads to the conclusion that γ *is a more reliable witness than δ* in the reconstruction of their common medieval *Vorlage*, π. Compared with the γ form of the text, the δ form is characterized by more omissions, transpositions,

---

[1] Cf. μάχεσθαι / δέχεσθαι (A 19); συγκόσμησον / συγκόμισον (A 49); εὕρομεν / ἐροῦμεν (B 16); ἐπικαλούμενος / ἐπιμελούμενος (B 22).

[2] Cf. ἐπεξῆλθε / ἐπῆλθε (A 8); βεβηκέναι / συμβεβηκέναι (A 25); ἔκοπτεν / ἐξέκοπτεν (A 42); προσκαλούμενος / προκαλούμενος (B 8); κατέστησεν / παρέστησεν (B 9); ἐστοχάζοντο / κατεστοχάζοντο (B 9); ἀποβάντες / ἐπιβάντες (B 31); ἐπαγαγεῖν / ἀπαγαγεῖν (B 36); ἀφεψαλωμένης / ἐφεψαλωμένης (B 41).

[3] Cf. λέγεις / λέγειν (A 28); ἤπτοντο / ἤπτετο (A 42); ἀμιλλᾶσθαι / ἀμιλλᾶται (B 36); εὕρουσιν / εὕρωσιν (B 41); τραγῳδεῖ / τραγῳδίαν (B 45); τελευταῖον / τελευτῶν (B 58).

[4] Cf. πλήρης / τρόπαιον (A 32); οἵαν / ἥν (A 45); παιδεύσεως / κελεύσεως (B 23); πολεμίου / πολέμου (B 27); τέχνης / τύχης (B 27); σκέψις / σκῆψις (B 33).

[5] Cf. γενναιότερον / κυριώτερον (A 23); προσφόρως / πρόσφορος (B 1); ἄριστος / ἀόριστος (B 50); ἐν ταύτῃ / ἐνταῦθα (B 56).

substitutions, and misspellings. Hence, in the several dozen cases of γ - δ divergency, where the internal evidence provides no clear guidance and where in the end the choice seems to come down to a 'coin-toss', the editors were in general inclined to give the nod to the reading in γ.

Documentation for the all these observations regarding γ - δ divergencies is presented in the following comprehensive chart which shows: (1) the location of the passage by verse number; (2) the divergent readings in γ and in δ, with the preferred reading in bold print; (3) the type of variant, indicated with the signs used in the critical apparatus (uncertainty about addition or omission is indicated by the inclusion of both signs: + ○); (4) the preferred MS noted in separate columns with the signs γ or δ, or with ? in the case of uncertainty.

#	Reading in γ	Reading in δ	Type of Variant	Preferred Reading	
0	Καλλίμαχον καὶ **Κυναίγειρον**	Κυναίγειρον καὶ Καλλίμαχον	∩	γ	
A					
1	-- **Μαραθῶνι**	ἐν Μαραθῶνι	+	γ	
1	συμβαλλόμενος	**συμβαλόμενος**	⫢		δ
2	**Καλλιμάχου**	Καλλίμαχον	>	γ	
3	**λέγῃ** [?]	λέγοι [?]	> +		?
3	**οὕτως**	οὕτω	⊥	γ	
3	**ὁμότιμοι πάντων αἱ χεῖρες**	πάντων αἱ χεῖρες ὁμότιμοι	∩	γ	
4	**θάτερος**	θατέρα	>	γ	
7	**τε**	--	○	γ	
8	**ἐπεξῆλθε**	ἐπῆλθε	>	γ	
10	**ἐρηρεισμένη**	ἠρεισμένη	⫢	γ	
12	**μᾶλλον δίκαιον**	δίκαιον μᾶλλον	∩		?
14	**τῆς πολεμαρχίας**	τοῦ πολεμάρχου	>	γ	
14	**ἐπολεμάρχησε**	ἐπολεμάρχει	>	γ	
15	----	**φημι**	○		δ
16	**ἐστιν**	ἐστί	⊥		δ
17	**τούτοις**	τούτ	+		?
19	**καὶ ... μάχεσθαι**	--- ... δέχεσθαι	>		?
22	πρότερος [?]	**πρότερον**	>		δ
23	**καὶ** (before Καλλίμαχος)	---	○	γ	
23	γενναιότερον	**κυριώτερον**	>		δ
23	**Κυναίγειρος θαυμασιώτερος**	θαυμασιώτερος ὁ Κυναίγειρος	∩ +	γ	

#	Reading in γ	Reading in δ	Type of Variant	Preferred Reading	
25	βεβηκέναι	συμβεβηκέναι	>		?
25	συνιεὶς	ξυνιεὶς	±		?
27	τί	ἔτι	>		?
28	λέγεις	λέγειν	>	γ	
28	μόνῃ	μόνον	>		?
29	τοῖς βαρβάροις	**τοὺς βαρβάρους**	>		δ
30	τοι τούτῳ τῷ Καλλιμάχου	τούτῳ τῷ Καλλιμάχῳ	○ >	γ	
30	εἰς	ἐς	±		δ
31	σεαυτοῦ	ἑαυτοῦ	>	γ	?
32	πλήρης	τρόπαιον	>	γ	
33	μικρὸν	μικρὰ	>		?
34	Μαραθώνιαι	Μαραθώνιοι	>	γ	
34	σωτῆρες	σώτειραι	>	γ	
35	μακροτέρας	μακροτέρων	>	γ	
37	ψυχῆς ἰδίας	ἰδίας ψυχῆς	∩	γ	
39	σου	---	+○		δ
41	ἐβόησεν	ἐβόησαν	>	γ	
41	ἀποτεμνέτω	ἀποτεμέτω	∓	γ	
42	ἥπτοντο	**ἥπτετο**	>		δ
42	ἔκοπτεν	ἐξέκοπτεν	>	γ	
43	Ἐρέτριαν	Ἐρετρίαν	∓	γ	
44	ταύταις	**ταύτῃ**	>		δ
44	μὴ	--	○	γ	
44	Ἀθηναίοις	Ἀθηναίους	>	γ	
45	οἵαν	ἦν	>	γ	
47	σώματι	**σήματι**	>		δ
47	γλῶτταν	γλῶσσαν	±	γ	
48	με	--	○	γ	
48	παραγαγεῖν	παράγειν	>	γ	
49	συγκόσμησον	συγκόμισον	>	γ	
B					
1	**ῥηθέντες καλῶς**	καλῶς ῥηθέντες	∩	γ	
1	**προσφόρως**	πρόσφορος	>	γ	?
2	καὶ (before τεθνεὼς)	---	○	γ	
3	οὐδὲ	οὐδ᾽	±	γ	
5	ἐξ Ἀιγαίου	ἐν Ἀιγαίῳ	>	γ	?
5	Λακεδαιμονίων	Λακεδαιμονίαν	>		?
8	προσκαλούμενος	**προκαλούμενος**	>		δ
8	ἐκ τῶν νεῶν ἐκχεομένην	ἐκχεομένην ἐκ τῶν νεῶν	∩	γ	
9	--	τε	○		δ
9	κατέστησεν	παρέστησεν	>	γ	
9	ἐστοχάζοντο	κατεστοχάζοντο	>	γ	

#	Reading in γ	Reading in δ	Type of Variant	Preferred Reading
10	βλημάτων	βλήματα	>	γ
11	ἐν τῷ σώματι διεκαρτέρησεν ἡ ψυχὴ	ἡ ψυχὴ διεκαρτέρησεν ἐν τῷ σώματι	∩	γ
11	ἔμεινεν	ἔμενεν	>	δ
11	τοιοῦτο	τοιοῦτον	>	?
13	ἐπειδὴ δὲ	ἐπείδ'	>	γ
13	ἐπὶ τὸν αἰγιαλὸν	--- --- --------	○ +	γ
13	ἀκροστολίου	ἀκροστόλου	⊤	γ
14	ταῦτα	ταύτην	>	γ
14	ἐπιτηρῶν τῶν βαρβάρων	τῶν βαρβάρων ἐπιτηρῶν	∩	γ
14	πεσούσης	πέσῃς	⊤	δ
16	τῷ τάφῳ	τὸν τάφον	>	γ
16	εὕρομεν	ἐροῦμεν	>	δ
17	δὲ (before καθέλητε)	--	○	γ
17	ὑμῖν	ἡμῖν	>	γ
18	πρότερος	πρῶτος	>	?
18	ἴσην τὴν ἀρετὴν	τὴν ἀρετὴν ἴσην	∩	?
19	αὐτῷ	αὐτοῦ	>	γ
19	δὲ	δ'	≐	γ
19	τῶν ὀνομάτων	--- --------	○	γ
20	δὲ	--	○	γ
22	τὸν λόγον ὁ νόμος	ὁ νόμος τὸν λόγον	∩	γ ?
22	τύχοι	τύχῃ	>	?
22	ἐπικαλούμενος	ἐπιμελούμενος	>	δ
22	τοῦ	---	○	γ
23	παιδεύσεως	κελεύσεως	>	γ
23	μήτε χειρῶν μήτε ὀφθαλμῶν	μήτε ὀφθαλμῶν μήτε χειρῶν	∩	γ
24	ηὐθαδιάσατο	ηὐθαδειάσατο	≐	γ
24	δὲ	δ'	≐	γ
24	ὑπερέβαλλε	ὑπερέβαλε	±	?
25	θαλάττης	θαλάσσης	≐	γ
26	θάλατταν	θάλασσαν	≐	γ
27	ἀλλ'	ἀλλὰ	≐	γ
27	ἐκ	--	○	γ
27	πολεμίου	πολέμου	>	γ
27	τέχνης [?]	τύχης	>	δ
28	προτέρας	πρότερον	>	δ ?
28	ῥᾳδίως	ῥᾳδίαν	>	δ
28	Κυναιγείρου	Κυναιγείρῳ	>	γ
29	τῷ	--	○	γ
29	γινομένων	γενομένων	>	δ ?

#	Reading in γ	Reading in δ	Type of Variant	Preferred Reading	
29	[εὖ] τε [?]	[εὖ] --	+	δ	
30	καὶ (Κυναιγείρῳ)	--- (Κυναιγείρῳ)	O	γ	
30	ὁρῶντες	ὡρῶν τις	>	δ	
31	τῷ (σφαλερῷ)	-- (σφαλερῷ)	O +	γ	?
31	κυρίους, τοὺς	-------, ----	O	γ	
31	ἀποβάντες	ἐπιβάντες	>	γ	
32	δὲ (after Καλλίμαχος)	δ'	⫤	γ	
32	παρωξυμμένος	παροξυνόμενος	>	γ	?
32	γὰρ	---	O	γ	
33	δὲ	δ'	⫤	γ	
33	δακτύλοις	δακτύλῳ	>	γ	
33	ἄλλως	ἀλλ' ὡς	> ⫤	δ	
33	σκέψις	σκῆψις	>	γ	
33	- (ἀρετή)	ἡ (ἀρετή)	O	δ	
33	πόνοι πάντες	πάντες πόνοι	∩	γ	
35	ἀπολύσαι	ἀπολῦσαι	⊤	δ	
36	δὲ	δ'	⫤	γ	
36	δ'	δὲ	⫤	γ	
36	ἐπαγαγεῖν	ἀπαγαγεῖν	>	γ	
36	ἀμιλλᾶσθαι	ἀμιλλᾶται	>	γ	
36	ακροστολίου	ἀκροστόλου	⊤	γ	
37	τοιαύτην	τοιαύτας	>	γ	?
37	μειράκιον τολμηρὸν	τολμηρὸν μειράκιον	∩	γ	
37	δὲ	δ'	⫤	γ	
38	ἀπάντων	-------	O	γ	?
39	καὶ (after ψαῦσαι)	---	O	γ	
39	Κυναιγείρου	Κυναίγειρος	>	γ	
40	ἀρχὰς	ἀρχὴν	>	γ	
41	λαμβάνῃς	λάβῃς	>	γ	
41	εὕρουσιν	εὕρωσιν	>		?
41	ἀφεψαλωμένης	ἐφεψαλωμένης	>	γ	
41	νικήσει	νικήσας	>	γ	
42	οὔτε	οὔτ'	⫤	γ	
43	ἂν (after ναῦς)	--	O	γ	
43	δὲ	δ'	⫤	γ	
44	δὲ	δ'	⫤	γ	
45	τραγῴδει	τραγῳδίαν	>	γ	
45	εἰ	--	O	γ	
45	θαλάττης	θαλάσσης	⫤	γ	
47	κεκινημένε	κεκινημένος	>	γ	
47	μὴ (before ζηλούμεναι)	--	O	γ	
48	πρῶτον	πρῶτος	>	γ	

#	Reading in γ	Reading in δ	Type of Variant	Preferred Reading
48	ᾧ	ὡς	>	γ
49	ὅς	ὁ σὸς	>[+]	δ
49	δὲ	δ'	⩲	γ
50	ἄριστος	ἀόριστος	>	δ
50	φύσει	φύσεως	>	δ
50	μὴ δὲ	δὲ μὴ	∩	γ
51	τοιούτων ποιητῶν καὶ ῥητόρων	τοιούτου ποιητοῦ καὶ ῥήτορος	>	γ
53	ἡμῖν δείξας ἀνθρώπων	ἀνθρώπων δείξας ἡμῖν	∩	γ
54	βαλλόμενος	βαλλόμενε	>	γ
54	Ἐρέτρια	Ἐρετρία	⧺	γ
56	Πελοπιδῶν	Πελοπίδαι	>	γ
56	ἐν ταύτῃ	ἐνταῦθα	>	γ
56	ὑγιὲς	ὑγιῆ	>	δ
58	τελευταῖον	τελευτῶν	>	γ
60	νικᾷ νεκρὸς ἡμᾶς Ἀθηναῖος	νεκρὸς ἡμᾶς Ἀθηναῖος νικᾷ	∩	γ
61	αὐτὸν ὀρθὸν	ὀρθὸν αὐτὸν	∩	γ
62	Πολλὰς	πολλῶν	>	γ
62	ὑπερήσπισεν	ὑπερήσπισας	>	δ
62	σεμνυνόμενοι	σεμνυνόμενος	>	δ
62	-- (before Μαραθῶνι)	ἐν (before Μαραθῶνι)	+	γ
63	νεκρῶν	------	○	γ
63	ἐκείνου δὲ	------- --	○	γ
63	ἀκροστόλιον	ἀκροστόλ	⧺	γ
63	γὰρ (after ἀκροστόλιον)	δὲ (after ἀκροστόλιον)	>	γ
64	πρώτου	-----	○	γ

Appendix 3: The Ending in the Manuscripts (B 64b–65)

The term "ending" denotes the last 43 words of the declamations:

64b ἐγεννάδαν οὕτω λαμπρὸν καὶ τόσον ὑπὲρ τῆς πατρίδος σπουδαῖον ὡς ὑπὲρ αὐτῆς προέσθαι οἱ ἐπὶ θαύματι τὴν ψυχήν.   **65** ἐμὸν τοιγαροῦν, ὦ Εὐφορίων, εἴη τὸ τοῖς ἐπιταφίοις πρῶτον τὸν παῖδα κοσμεῖν καὶ τὸν ἐπινίκιον τραγῳδεῖν. σὺ δὲ τὸν σὸν μεθύστερον θρήνει συγχωρούντων τῶν δικαστῶν.

Of the vocabulary in this ending 7 words occur only here in the declamations while the other 36 words are found one or more times elsewhere in the text.

The *hapax legomena* are (in alphabetical order):

γεννάδας	B 64
θρηνέω	B 65
μεθύστερον	B 65
προίημι	B 64
σπουδαῖος	B 64
συγχωρέω	B 65
τόσος	B 64

447

The words attested elsewhere in the declamations are (in alphabetical order):

αὐτός	B 64	*passim*	
δέ	B 65	*passim*	
δικαστής	B 65	1x	A 47
εἰμί	B 65	*passim*	
ἐμός	B 65	8x	A 8, 12, 18, 32; B 6, 15, 43, 49
ἐπί	B 64	33x	cf. Index 6
ἐπινίκιος	B 65	1x	A 48
ἐπιτάφιος	B 65	6x	0, A 15, 46, 47, 48; B 15
Εὐφορίων	B 65	3x	B 22, 37, 63
θαῦμα	B 64	7x	A 25, 33, 37; B 2, 48, 55, 56
καί	B 64, 65	*passim*	
κοσμέω	B 65	4x	A 12; B 1, 12, 56
λαμπρός	B 64	3x	A 7; B 28, 54
ὁ, ἡ, τό	B 64, 65, 65, 65	*passim*	
οὕτω(ς)	B 64	7x	A 3, 31, 37; B 18, 27, 46, 64
παῖς	B 65	21x	cf. Index 8
πατρίς	B 64	2x	A 44; B 53
πρῶτος	B 65	17x	cf. Index 8
σός	B 65	7x	A 32, 46; B 37, 38, 49, 62, 62
σύ	B 65	8x	A 31, 35, 35, 40, 45; B 14, 41, 64
τοιγαροῦν	B 65	1x	B 20
τραγῳδέω	B 65	2x	A 48; B 45
ὑπέρ	B 64, 64	6x	A 5, 44, 44, 49; B 3, 8
ψυχή	B 64	19x	cf. Index 8
ὦ	B 65	82x	cf. Index 3
ὡς	B 64	18x	A 5, 11, 16, 31, 31, 37, 40; B 8, 21, 33, 33, 34, 42, 47, 53, 56, 63, 64

Out of the 43 words in the ending 36 (= 84%) are thus demonstrably 'Polemonic,' whereas 7 (= 16%) are otherwise unattested in the declamations. In comparison with the full text of the declamations this ratio between words of singular occurrence and of multiple occurrence is somewhat different. The full text of the declamations (not including the ending) contains 6000 words; of these about 570 (= 9.5%) are *hapax legomena* (cf. Index 8). Thus the two ratios (ca. 1:10 [declamations] and 1:5 [ending]) are not the same; but given the brevity of the ending the difference is probably not significant. From the statistical standpoint of word usage, therefore, the vocabulary of the ending does not necessarily militate against authenticity. Nevertheless, these numbers also do not prove the genuineness of the ending. There is nothing particularly unusual about any of this vocabulary. It would not be hard for a careful reader of the declamations to imitate Polemo's word usage for the few lines in this short ending. At any rate, in all fairness it must be conceded that statistics and observations about style based upon such meager material cannot be conclusive either way.

Chronology is more telling. There is no MS evidence that the 43 word ending existed or was copied prior to the 14th century. If it is authentic then its ancestry must be traced to a MS not connected with the stemma to which the 18 extant MSS belong because neither of the 2nd generation MSS (γ and δ) from which all the others derive contained the ending. The supposition of a Polemo MS not derivative from π and yet whose existence and text is only attested by the ending "preserved" from it is unconvincing. Rather than argue that the ending goes back through a different (otherwise unpreserved) line to the 2nd century II, it seems far more plausible that the 43 word ending first emerged in the 14th century as the creation of an Italian (or immigrant Greek) scribe unsatisfied with the abrupt termination of the declamations at καὶ τὸν μὲν Ἡρακλέος (B 64). The long history of the transmission of texts is rife with such scribal fabrications and secondary interpolations. To posit a secondarily fabricated ending for Polemo's declamations is not particularly unusual and strains credulity less than the hypothesis of an entire or even fragmentary Polemo MS independent of the existing evidence, a text, moreover, which has now gone completely lost apart from its ending.

This present edition thus assumes as more likely that the ending does not preserve an ancient tradition, but instead that it is the product of a creative medieval scholar. Identifying the actual source of the words (be it scribal school or geographical location) can only be a subject for speculation.

Appendix 4: A Messenian Contest About Valor

To provide some comparative literary background for Polemo's declamations Stephanus included in his *editio princeps* (1567) an appendix with a *circa* 750 word Greek text having the title Περὶ δύο ἀνδρῶν ἀριστευσάντων ἐν πολέμῳ καὶ ἀγωνιζομένων περὶ πρωτείων (= Concerning two men who showed valor in battle and who contested for first place). This instructive text he simply identified as coming from "someone anonymous" (ἀνωνύμου τινος). Orellius in his edition of the declamations (1819) reprinted this text in full (cf. pp. 150–154), but now fortunately identifying the author as Diodorus Siculus. The credit for ferreting out this attribution he gave to Isaac Vossius (cf. Orellius, p. xv).

Because this Diodorus text provides such valuable background material for Polemo's declamations, this current appendix, following the precedent set by Stephanus and Orellius, also supplies the complete passage (Diodorus Siculus 8.12.1–16) but supplements it now with a corresponding English translation.

Background for the story is the long intra-Peloponnesian conflict between Messenia and Sparta. Whether the Diodorus narrative is based upon events in the Second War (ca. 650 BCE) or the Third War (ca. 490 BCE) is in dispute. It is worth noting, however, that Plato gave the latter as the reason for the Spartans arriving one day too late to help at the battle of Marathon (*Leg.* 698d–e; cf. Polemo, B 5). The specific battle to which the Diodorus text refers is known as the "Battle of the Great Ditch" (cf. Pausanias 4.7–10). The unnamed king in the text who convened the 'trial about valor' (8.12.1, 2, 3, 5), is the Messenian ruler Euphaes. The two contestants, Cleonnis and

451

Aristomenes, — the quasi-counterparts to Polemo's Cynegirus and Callimachus — are legendary heroes of Messenian resistance to Sparta.

The Diodorus text pre-dates Polemo's declamations by at least 150 years. While it cannot be demonstrated that Polemo was familiar with this Diodorus text, it is not implausible. At any rate, among Greeks there was general historical knowledge about the long-standing Messenian-Spartan conflict and about the rivalries between leading Messenians, including Cleonnis, Aristomenes, and others (cf. Pausanias 4.10.5-7). Such knowledge may be reasonably be presumed also on the part of a sophist like Polemo.

To be sure, Polemo's declamations and Diodorus' text share much characteristic terminology, but more important is their parallel conceptualization: After the battle and in accordance with the νόμος an official public dispute or competition (κρίσις, Diodorus 8.12.1, 2, 5, 10; ἅμιλλα, Polemo A 14) was held to determine which soldier had fought most bravely and to whom the honor of first place (πρωτεία, Diodorus 0, 6; αἱ πρῶται τιμαί, Polemo B 16) in valor (ἀρετή, Diodorus 2, 3, 10, 13, 14; Polemo, *passim*, 35x) belonged. In both texts two competitors come forward. In the Diodorus text the contestants are surviving war heroes who each present their own cases whereby the arguments of the second speaker (Aristomenes) are more extensive that those of the the first (Cleonnis). In the Polemo text the actual contenders (Cynegirus and Callimachus) are dead — they had fallen in battle — so their respective fathers argue their cases for them. Here, too, the second speech is longer than the first. Whereas in his conclusion Diodorus says that the judges unanimously voted for the second speaker, Aristomenes, in the surviving Polemo text the judges' decision is not recounted. From the length and tenor of the second speech, however, Callimachus presumably won the decision. At stake in the Polemo contest was the right to deliver the eulogy at the state funeral (cf. 0). The prize in the Diodorus trial, however, is not specified. Inasmuch as the Messenian king, Euphaes, was childless the prize may have had to do with the throne succession (cf. Pausanias 4.10.5). In any case, despite the comparative brevity of the Diodorus text, the parallels with Polemo's declamations are patent.

Diodorus Siculus 8.12.1–16

The Greek Text
(on the left)

The English Translation
(on the right)

περὶ δύο ἀνδρῶν ἀριστευσάντων ἐν πολέμῳ

καὶ ἀγωνιζομένων περὶ πρωτείων.

(Diodorus Siculus 8.12.1-16)

1 ὁ μὲν βασιλεὺς ἀναλαβὼν ἑαυτὸν ἐκ τῶν τραυμάτων προέθηκε κρίσιν ἀριστείου. κατέβησαν μὲν οὖν ἐπὶ τὸν ἀγῶνα δύο, Κλεοννίς τε καὶ Ἀριστομένης, ὧν ἑκάτερος εἶχεν ἴδιόν τι πρὸς δόξαν. **2** ὁ γὰρ Κλεοννις ὑπερασπίσας τὸν βασιλέα πεπτωκότα τῶν ἐπιφερομένων Σπαρτιατῶν ὀκτὼ νεκροὺς ἐπεποιήκει· καὶ τούτων ἦσαν δύο ἡγεμόνες ἐπιφανεῖς· πάντων δὲ τῶν ἀναιρεθέντων ὑπ' αὐτοῦ τὰς πανοπλίας ἐσκυλευκὼς ἐδεδώκει τοῖς ὑπασπισταῖς, ἵνα ἔχῃ σημεῖα τῆς ἰδίας ἀρετῆς πρὸς τὴν κρίσιν. πολλοῖς δὲ περιπεσὼν τραύμασιν ἅπαντ' ἔσχεν ἐναντία, μέγιστον παρεχόμενος τεκμήριον τοῦ μηδενὶ τῶν πολεμίων εἶξαι. **3** ὁ δ' Ἀριστομένης ἐν τῷ περὶ τοῦ βασιλέως ἀγῶνι πέντε μὲν ἀνῃρήκει τῶν Λακεδαιμονίων, καὶ τὰς πανοπλίας ἐσκυλεύκει τῶν πολεμίων ἐπικειμένων. καὶ τὸ μὲν ἑαυτοῦ σῶμα διεφύλαξεν ἄτρωτον, ἐκ δὲ τῆς μάχης ἀπερχόμενος εἰς τὴν πόλιν ἔργον ἐπαινούμενον ἔπραξεν. **4** ὁ μὲν γὰρ Κλεοννις ἀσθενῶς ἐκ τῶν τραυμάτων διακείμενος οὔτε βαδίζειν καθ' αὑτὸν οὔτε χειραγωγεῖσθαι δυνατὸς ἦν· ὁ δ' Ἀριστομένης ἀράμενος αὐτὸν ἐπὶ τοὺς ὤμους ἀπήνεγκεν εἰς τὴν πόλιν, οὐδὲν δὲ ἧττον κομίζων τὴν ἰδίαν πανοπλίαν, καὶ ταῦτα τοῦ Κλεόννιδος προέχοντος τῶν ἄλλων μεγέθει τε καὶ ῥώμῃ σώματος. **5** τοιαύτας δ' ἐχόντων ἀφορμὰς εἰς τὴν ὑπὲρ τῶν ἀριστείων κρίσιν, ὁ βασιλεὺς ἐκάθισε μετὰ τῶν ταξιάρχων κατὰ τὸν νόμον. προλαβὼν οὖν τὸν λόγον ὁ Κλεοννις τοιούτοις ἐχρήσατο λόγοις.

6 Βραχὺς μέν ἐστιν ὁ περὶ τῶν ἀριστείων λόγος· κριταὶ γάρ εἰσιν οἱ τεθεαμένοι τὰς ἑκάστων ἀρετάς· ὑπομνῆσαι δὲ δεῖ με, διότι πρὸς τοὺς

Concerning two men who showed valor in battle
and who contested for first place.
(Diodorus Siculus 8.12.1-16)

1 After the king had recovered from his wounds, he proposed [that they hold] a trial for the prize of valor. Two, therefore, entered the contest, Cleonnis and Aristomenes, each of whom had his own particular claim to fame. **2** For Cleonnis had protected the king with his shield when he had fallen and had brought about the death of eight onrushing Spartans — and of these two were distinguished commanders. From all those killed by him he had stripped the complete armor and had given it to his shield-bearers, in order that he might have tokens of his own personal valor for the trial. And though he had received many wounds, he got them all in front, providing [the] greatest proof that he had given way to no one of the enemy. **3** And Aristomenes in the struggle over the king had killed five attacking Lacedaemonians and had stripped the complete armor from the[se] enemies. He kept his own body free of wounds, and on his way back to the city from the battle he performed a deed to be praised. **4** For Cleonnis lay so weakened by his wounds that he was not able to walk by himself nor to be led by the hand. Aristomenes, lifting him on his shoulders, brought him back to the city, notwithstanding that he was [also] carrying his own full armor and that Cleonnis surpassed the others in size and strength of body. **5** Inasmuch as they had such arguments [to bring] to the trial for the prize of valor, the king took his seat with the commanding officers in accordance with the law. Delivering his speech first Cleonnis argued his case with the following words:

6 The speech for the prize of valor is [going to be] brief because the judges are those who [themselves] have witnessed the brave deeds of each [of us]. But, since we both fought against the same men at one [and the same]

αὐτοὺς ἄνδρας ἐκατέρων διαγωνισαμένων ὑφ᾽ ἕνα καιρὸν καὶ τόπον ἐγὼ πλείους ἀπέκτεινα. δῆλον οὖν ὡς κατὰ τὴν αὐτὴν περίστασιν ὁ πρότερος ἐν ἀριθμῷ τῶν ἀναιρεθέντων προτερεῖ καὶ τοῖς εἰς τὸ πρωτεῖον δικαίοις.   7 ἀλλὰ μὴν καὶ τὰ σώματα ἐκατέρων ἐμφανεστάτας ἀποδείξεις ἔχει τῆς ὑπεροχῆς· ὁ μὲν γὰρ πλήρης ὢν τραυμάτων ἐναντίων ἀπελύετο τῆς μάχης, ὁ δ᾽ ὥσπερ ἐκ πανηγύρεως, ἀλλ᾽ οὐ τηλικαύτης παρατάξεως ἐξιὼν οὐκ ἐπειράθη, τί δύναται πολεμίων σίδηρος.   8 εὐτυχέστερος μὲν οὖν ἴσως Ἀριστομένης, ἀγαθώτερος δ᾽ ἡμῶν οὐκ ἂν δικαίως κριθείη. πρόδηλος γὰρ ὁ ὑπομείνας τοσαύτας διαιρέσεις τοῦ σώματος ὡς ἀφειδῶς ἑαυτὸν ἐπέδωκεν ὑπὲρ τῆς πατρίδος· ὁ δ᾽ ἐν πολεμίων συμπλοκῇ καὶ τοιούτων κινδύνων τηρήσας ἑαυτὸν ἄτρωτον εὐλαβείᾳ τοῦ παθεῖν τι τοῦτ᾽ ἐνήργησεν.   9 ἄτοπον οὖν εἰ παρὰ τοῖς ἑωρακόσι τὴν μάχην ὁ τῶν πολεμίων μὲν ἐλάττους ἀνελών, τῷ δ᾽ ἰδίῳ σώματι κινδυνεύσας ἧττον, προκριθήσεται τοῦ πρωτεύοντος ἐν ἀμφοτέροις. ἀλλὰ μὴν καὶ τὸ μηδενὸς ἔτι κινδύνου ὑπάρχοντος βαστάσαι τὸ σῶμα καταπεπονημένον ὑπὸ τῶν τραυμάτων ἀνδρείαν μὲν οὐδεμίαν ἔχει, σώματος δ᾽ ἴσως ἰσχὺν ἐπιδείκνυται. ἱκανά μοι ταῦτα εἴρηται πρὸς ὑμᾶς· πρόκειται γὰρ ἀγὼν οὐ λόγων, ἀλλ᾽ ἔργων.

10 Παραλαβὼν δ᾽ ἐν μέρει τὸν λόγον Ἀριστομένης, Θαυμάζω, φησίν, εἰ μέλλει περὶ ἀριστείων ἀμφισβητεῖν ὁ σωθεὶς τῷ σώσαντι· ἀναγκαῖον γὰρ ἢ τῶν δικαζόντων αὐτὸν ἄνοιαν καταγινώσκειν ἢ τὴν κρίσιν δοκεῖν ἐκ τῶν νῦν λεγομένων, ἀλλ᾽ οὐκ ἐκ τῶν τότε πεπραγμένων ἔσεσθαι. οὐ μόνον δὲ Κλέοννις δειχθήσεται κατ᾽ ἀρετὴν λειπόμενος, ἀλλὰ καὶ τελέως ἀχάριστος. 11 ἀφεὶς γὰρ τὸ τὰ συντελεσθέντα ὑπ᾽ αὐτοῦ καλῶς διαπορεύεσθαι, διέσυρε τὰς ἐμὰς πράξεις, φιλοτιμότερος ὢν ἢ δίκαιον· ᾧ γὰρ καὶ ἰδίας σωτηρίας τὰς μεγίστας ὀφείλει χάριτας, τούτου τὸν ἐπὶ τοῖς καλῶς πραχθεῖσιν ἔπαινον διὰ φθόνον ἀφῄρηται. ἐγὼ δὲ ὁμολογῶ μὲν ἐν τοῖς τότε

time and place, I must remind you that I killed more [men]. It is obvious, then, that in the same circumstance the one first in the number of slain is first also in the just [claims] on the prize of valor.   **7** Furthermore, the bodies of both of us provide the most visible proofs of the superiority: for the one being full of wounds in the front [clearly] came away from a battle, while the other, going out as if from a festal assembly and not from such a pitched fight, did not experience how powerful the enemy's iron [arms] were.   **8** Perhaps Aristomenes [may be judged to be] luckier, but he may not justly be judged [to be] the braver of us [two]. For it is absolutely clear that the one who endured such lacerations of the body gave of himself unflinchingly for the fatherland; whereas the other, in [his] encounter with the enemy and such perils, kept himself unwounded [and] did that through caution about suffering anything.   **9** [It would be] absurd then if, before those who [themselves] saw the battle, the one who killed fewer enemies and ran less risk to his own body shall be ranked ahead of the one who holds first place on both these counts. Moreover, his carrying a body completely exhausted by its wounds, especially when there was no longer any danger, is no [indication of] bravery, though it does perhaps show strength of body. What has been said to you is enough for me; for the contest is a matter not of words but of deeds.

10 Then Aristomenes in turn taking up the speech said: I am astonished that the one who was rescued intends to wrangle with his rescuer for the prize of valor. For [it would be] necessary for him either to regard the judges [as having] no sense, or to think that the decision will be [arrived at] from the words now spoken, not from the deeds done then. But not only will Cleonnis be shown [to be] wanting in valor, but completely ungrateful as well.   **11** For, omitting to enumerate the things well accomplished by him, he tried to disparage my deeds, since he is more ambitious than just. Indeed, from the one to whom he owes the greatest gratitude for his own rescue he, on account of envy, has taken away the praise [based] upon the things done well.

γεγενημένοις κινδύνοις εὐτυχὴς ὑπάρξαι, φημὶ δὲ πρότερον ἀγαθὸς γενέσθαι. **12** εἰ μὲν γὰρ ἐκκλίνας τὴν τῶν πολεμίων ἐπιφορὰν ἄτρωτος ἐγενόμην, οὐκ εὐτυχῆ με προσῆκεν ὀνομάζειν, ἀλλὰ δειλόν, οὐδ᾿ ὑπὲρ ἀριστείων λέγειν κρίσιν, ἀλλὰ ταῖς ἐκ τῶν νόμων τιμωρίαις περιπεπτωκέναι· ἐπεὶ δ᾿ ἐν πρώτοις μαχόμενος καὶ τοὺς ὑφισταμένους ἀναιρῶν οὐκ ἔπαθον ἅπερ ἔπραξα, ῥητέον οὐκ εὐτυχῆ με μόνον, ἀλλὰ καὶ ἀγαθόν. **13** εἴτε γὰρ οἱ πολέμιοι καταπλαγέντες τὴν ἀρετὴν οὐκ ἐτόλμησαν ἀμύνασθαι, μεγάλων ἐπαίνων ἄξιος ὃν ἐφοβήθησαν, εἴτ᾿ ἐκείνων ἀγωνιζομένων εὐθύμως ἐγὼ φονεύων τοὺς ἀνθεστηκότας καὶ τοῦ σώματος ἐποιούμην πρόνοιαν, ἀνδρεῖος ἅμα καὶ συνετός. **14** ὁ γὰρ ἐν αὐτῷ τῷ θυμομαχεῖν ἐμφρόνως ὑπομένων τὸ δεινὸν ἑκατέρας ἔχει τὰς ἀρετάς, σώματός τε καὶ ψυχῆς. καίτοι γε ταῦτα τὰ δίκαια πρὸς ἑτέρους ἦν μοι ῥητέον ἀμείνους τούτου. ὅτε γὰρ Κλέοννιν παραλελυμένον ἐκ τῆς μάχης εἰς τὴν πόλιν ἀπήνεγκα τἀμαυτοῦ σώζων ὅπλα, καὶ ὑπ᾿ αὐτοῦ κεκρίσθαι νομίζω τὸ δίκαιον. **15** καίτοι γε παρορaθεὶς τόθ᾿ ὑφ᾿ ἡμῶν ἴσως οὐκ ἂν ἤριζε νῦν ὑπὲρ ἀριστείων, οὐδὲ διασύρων τηλικοῦτον μέγεθος εὐεργεσίας ἔλεγε μηθὲν εἶναι μέγα τὸ πραχθὲν διὰ τὸ κατ᾿ ἐκεῖνον τὸν καιρὸν ἀποχωρεῖν ἐκ τῆς μάχης τοὺς πολεμίους. τίς γὰρ οὐκ οἶδεν, ὅτι πολλάκις οἱ διαλυθέντες ἐκ τῆς μάχης ἐξ ὑποστροφῆς εἰώθασιν ἐπιτίθεσθαι καὶ στρατηγίᾳ ταύτῃ χρησάμενοι τυγχάνειν τῆς νίκης; ἱκανά μοι τὰ ῥηθέντα· λόγων γὰρ πλειόνων οὐκ οἶμαι ὑμᾶς προσδεῖσθαι.

16 Τούτων ῥηθέντων οἱ δικάζοντες ὁμογνώμονες γενόμενοι προέκριναν τὸν Ἀριστομένην.

I concede that in the dangers occurring then I was lucky, but I maintain that I was pre-eminently brave. **12** If I had come off unwounded by avoiding the enemy onslaught, it would have been fitting for me to call myself not lucky, but cowardly, and not to lay claim on the prize of valor, but to have been subjected to the punishments [prescribed] by the law. Since, however, I was fighting in the front lines and killing those who opposed me [and yet] I did not suffer what I inflicted [on others], it must be said not only that I was lucky but also brave. **13** For either [it is the case that] the enemy did not dare to face my valor because they were terrified [and I] whom they feared [am] deserving of great praise; or [it is the case that] though they fought with zeal I slaughtered them as they resisted **and** took thought for my body since I was at the same time courageous **and** cunning. **14** For the one who, in the very pitched fighting endures the terror, keeping his wits about him, has double valor, both of body and of soul. And yet these just [claims] ought to be spoken against other men better than this one. For when I carried Cleonnis disabled away from the battle to the city, preserving my own weapons too, I think that the justice [of my claim] was acknowledged by him. **15** And yet, if he had been neglected by us at that time, he would perhaps not now be contending for the prize of valor, nor would he, disparaging such a great benefaction, by saying that the great deed performed [by me] was nothing, because by that time the enemy had withdrawn from the battle. Who, indeed, does not know that many times those who have retired from the battle-field have been accustomed by wheeling about to renew the attack, and with this strategy to win the victory? The things said suffice for me, for I do not think you have need of further words.

16 When these things were said the judges unanimously voted for Aristomenes.

Index 1: Analysis of the Verb Forms

The following comprehensive table of all the verbs appearing in Polemo's declamations is provided to serve three purposes:

(1) For the beginner in Greek who has not yet mastered the inflection of the verb and who may be struggling with this or that passage, this list with its analytical parsing of all the verb forms in their order of occurrence should help clarify difficult grammar.

(2) For those more advanced in Greek who want to examine Polemo's syntax and usages of specific aspects of the verb, this list can quickly provide all the occurrences of any selected aspect of the verb. By consulting the appropriate column for tense or mood, for example, one can readily find every example of the imperfect, optative, or participle.

(3) Finally, presenting the verb analyses in this separate list makes it possible to pass over a discussion of the verbs in the commentary. Reducing some of the 'morphology' clutter in an already very 'busy' commentary will hopefully make it a bit easier to read.

461

#	text form	lexicon form	tense	voice	mood	person gender	number	case
A	ὄντος	εἰμί	pres	act	part	masc	sing	gen
	ἀποθανόντος	ἀποθνήσκω	aor	act	part	masc	sing	gen
	λέγειν	λέγω	pres	act	inf			
	δικάζονται	δικάζω	pres	mid	ind	3rd	plur	
1	χρή	χρή	pres	act	ind	3rd	sing	
	εἶναι	εἰμί	pres	act	inf			
	κειμένοις	κεῖμαι	pres	mid	part	masc	plur	dat
	ἐροῦντα	λέγω	fut	act	part	masc	sing	acc
	φημὶ	φημί	pres	act	ind	1st	sing	
	προσήκειν	προσήκω	pres	act	inf			
	ὤν	εἰμί	pres	act	part	masc	sing	nom
	τετολμημένων	τολμάω	perf	pass	part	neut	plur	gen
	συμβαλόμενος	συμβάλλω	aor	mid	part	masc	sing	nom
	μεμαχημένον	μάχομαι	perf	mid	part	masc	sing	acc
2	ἐπειπεῖν	ἐπιλέγω	aor	act	inf			
3	ποιοῦμαι	ποιέω	pres	mid	ind	1st	sing	
	διαθήσεται	διατίθημι	fut	mid	ind	3rd	sing	
	κειμένων	κεῖμαι	pres	mid	part	masc	plur	gen
	ἐστιν	εἰμί	pres	act	ind	3rd	sing	
	εἴπῃ	λέγω	aor	act	subj	3rd	sing	
	ἔσονται	εἰμι	fut	mid	ind	3rd	plur	
	συγκινδυνεύουσιν	συγκινδυνεύω	pres	act	ind	3rd	plur	
4	ὁρᾶτε	ὁράω	pres	act	impv	2nd	plur	
	κρατεῖν	κρατέω	pres	act	inf			
	κρατῶν	κρατέω	pres	act	part	masc	sing	nom
	ἀπέθανεν	ἀποθνήσκω	aor	act	ind	3rd	sing	
	εἰδόσι	οἶδα	perf	act	part	masc	plur	dat
	πεπραγμένα	πράσσω	perf	pass	part	neut	plur	acc
	συν-	συν-						
	-αγωνίζεται	-αγωνίζομαι	pres	mid	ind	3rd	sing	
	λεγόμενα	λέγω	pres	pass	part	neut	plur	nom
	ἔσται	εἰμί	fut	mid	ind	3rd	sing	
5	ἦγεν	ἄγω	impf	act	ind	3rd	sing	
	βουλόμενον	βούλομαι	pres	mid	part	masc	sing	acc
	ἀμύνασθαι	ἀμύνω	aor	mid	inf			
	ὤν	εἰμι	pres	act	part	masc	sing	nom
	μετέσχε	μετέχω	aor	act	ind	3rd	sing	
	ὀρεγόμενος	ὀρέγω	pres	mid	part	masc	sing	nom
6	ἐγένετο	γί[γ]νομαι	aor	mid	ind	3rd	sing	
	πέσοντες	πίπτω	aor	act	part	masc	plur	nom
	περι-	περι-						
	-γενόμενοι	-γι[γ]νομαι	aor	mid	part	masc	plur	nom
	ἐφάνησαν	φαίνω	aor	pass	ind	3rd	plur	
7	ἐκθεὶς	ἐκτίθημι	aor	act	part	masc	sing	nom
	περιχυθέντων	περιχέω	aor	pass	part	neut	plur	gen
	κατεσχέθη	κατέχω	aor	pass	ind	3rd	sing	

#	text form	lexicon form	tense	voice	mood	person gender	number	case
	ἔμενεν	μένω	impf	act	ind	3rd	sing	
	ἐδόκει	δοκέω	impf	act	ind	3rd	sing	
	ἑστάναι	ἵστημι	perf	act	inf			
	ἐδόκει	δοκέω	impf	act	ind	3rd	sing	
	ἑστάναι	ἵστημι	perf	act	inf			
	πεσεῖν	πίπτω	aor	act	inf			
	δυνάμενος	δύναμαι	pres	mid	part	masc	sing	nom
	ἐστι	εἰμί	pres	act	ind	3rd	sing	
	ζῶντος	ζάω	pres	act	part	masc	sing	gen
8	ὑπερβὰς	ὑπερβαίνω	aor	act	part	masc	sing	nom
	ἐκδραμών	ἐκτρέχω	aor	act	part	masc	sing	nom
	ἐπεξῆλθε	ἐπεξέρχομαι	aor	act	ind	3rd	sing	
	ἦν	εἰμί	impf	act	ind	3rd	sing	
	μαχόμενος	μάχομαι	pres	mid	part	masc	sing	nom
	ἐπέβη	ἐπιβαίνω	aor	act	ind	3rd	sing	
	ἐναυμάχησεν	ναυμαχεώ	aor	act	ind	3rd	sing	
9	ἐφόβησε	φοβέω	aor	act	ind	3rd	sing	
	ἐπιβαλὼν	ἐπιβάλλω	aor	act	part	masc	sing	nom
	εἴχετο	ἔχω	impf	mid	ind	3rd	sing	
	φεύγειν	φεύγω	pres	act	inf			
	ἐπιτρέπων	ἐπιτρέπω	pres	act	part	masc	sing	nom
10	κατείχετο	κατέχω	impf	pass	ind	3rd	sing	
	ἐρηρεισμένη	ἐρείδω	perf	pass	part	fem	sing	nom
	ἀποκοπείσης	ἀποκόπτω	aor	pass	part	fem	sing	gen
	ἐπέρριψε	ἐπιρρίπτω	aor	act	ind	3rd	sing	
	ἐγίνετο	γί[γ]νομαι	impf	mid	ind	3rd	sing	
	κοπείσης	κόπτω	aor	pass	part	fem	sing	gen
	ἦν	εἰμί	impf	act	ind	3rd	sing	
11	κατ-	κατα						
	-εμέμφετο	-μέμφομαι	impf	mid	ind	3rd	sing	
	ἀπῆτει	ἀπαιτέω	impf	act	ind	3rd	sing	
	εἴχετο	ἔχω	impf	mid	ind	3rd	sing	
	φεύγουσιν	φεύγω	pres	act	part	masc	plur	dat
	ἀφῆκε	ἀφίημι	aor	act	ind	3rd	sing	
	ἐγένετο	γί[γ]νομαι	aor	mid	ind	3rd	sing	
	ναυμαχῶν	ναυμαχέω	pres	act	part	masc	sing	nom
	διώκουσα	διώκω	pres	act	part	fem	sing	nom
	πληρώσας	πληρόω	aor	act	part	masc	sing	nom
	ἔκειτο	κεῖμαι	impf	mid	ind	3rd	sing	
	μεμερισμένος	μερίζω	perf	mid	part	masc	sing	nom
12	ποιεῖ	ποιέω	pres	act	ind	3rd	sing	
	προσήκειν	προσήκω	pres	act	inf			
	δεῖ	δεῖ	pres	act	ind	3rd	sing	
	λέγοντος	λέγω	pres	act	part	masc	sing	gen
	τιμηθῆναι	τιμάω	aor	pass	inf			
	ἐκόσμησα	κοσμέω	aor	act	ind	1st	sing	

#	text form	lexicon form	tense	voice	mood	person gender	number	case
13	φησιν	φημί	pres	act	ind	3rd	sing	
	εἶναι	εἰμί	pres	act	inf			
	ἀκολουθησάντων	ἀκολουθέω	aor	act	part	masc	plur	gen
	τετίμηται	τιμάω	perf	pass	ind	3rd	sing	
	ἔχει	ἔχω	pres	act	ind	3rd	sing	
	ὀφείλεται	ὀφείλω	pres	pass	ind	3rd	sing	
14	γίνεται	γί[γ]νομαι	pres	mid	ind	3rd	sing	
	ἐστι	εἰμι	pres	act	ind	3rd	sing	
	φιλοτιμούμεθα	φιλοτιμέομαι	pres	mid	ind	1st	plur	
	κοινωνεῖ	κοινωνέω	pres	act	ind	3rd	sing	
	παρούσης	πάρειμι	pres	act	part	fem	sing	gen
	ἐπολεμάρχησε	πολεμαρχέω	aor	act	ind	3rd	sing	
	λαχών	λαγχάνω	aor	act	part	masc	sing	nom
	φέρει	φέρω	pres	act	ind	3rd	sing	
15	δεδήλωται	δηλόω	perf	pass	ind	3rd	sing	
	ἀνακεῖσθαι	ἀνακεῖμαι	pres	mid	inf			
	ἦν	εἰμί	impf	act	ind	3rd	sing	
	ἐδέδοκτο	δοκέω	plperf	pass	ind	3rd	sing	
	εἶναί	εἰμί	pres	act	inf			
	φημι	φημί	pres	act	ind	1st	sing	
	ἐροῦντα	λέγω	fut	act	part	masc	sing	acc
	ᾖ	εἰμί	pres	act	subj	3rd	sing	
	εἰπεῖν	λέγω	aor	act	inf			
	χρῆναι	χρή	pres	act	inf			
	λέγειν	λέγω	pres	act	inf			
	ἔχει	ἔχω	pres	act	ind	3rd	sing	
16	διοριζομένῳ	διορίζω	pres	mid	part	masc	sing	dat
	ἀμφισβητεῖν	ἀμφισβητέω	pres	act	inf			
	ἔδει	δεῖ	impf	act	ind	3rd	sing	
	ἐστι	εἰμί	pres	act	ind	3rd	sing	
	μετα-	μετα-						
	-κεχειρισμενος	-χειρίζω	perf	mid	part	masc	sing	nom
	ἐστὶν	εἰμί	pres	act	ind	3rd	sing	
	ἐφεὶς	ἐφίημι	aor	act	part	masc	sing	nom
	δεδήλωκεν	δηλόω	perf	act	ind	3rd	sing	
	χρὴ	χρή	pres	act	ind	3rd	sing	
	παριέναι	πάρειμι (εἶμι)	pres	act	inf			
17	φέρε	φέρω	pres	act	impv	2nd	sing	
	κρινώμεθα	κρίνω	pres	mid	subj	1st	plur	
	ὁρᾷς	ὁράω	pres	act	ind	2nd	sing	
	ἄγοντας	ἄγω	pres	act	part	masc	plur	acc
18	ἦγεν	ἄγω	impf	act	ind	3rd	sing	
	ἐξῆρχε	ἐξάρχω	impf	act	ind	3rd	sing	
	ἔταττεν	τάσσω	impf	act	ind	3rd	sing	
	αἰδούμενος	αἰδέομαι	pres	mid	part	masc	sing	nom
	δυσωπούμενος	δυσωπέω	pres	pass	part	masc	sing	nom

#	text form	lexicon form	tense	voice	mood	person gender	number	case
	ἀκολουθῶν	ἀκολουθέω	pres	act	part	masc	sing	nom
	χρώμενος	χράω	pres	mid	part	masc	sing	nom
	ἐφάνη	φαίνω	aor	pass	ind	3rd	sing	
19	παρέταττε	παρατάσσω	impf	act	ind	3rd	sing	
	ἦν	εἰμί	impf	act	ind	3rd	sing	
	λαθεῖν	λανθάνω	aor	act	inf			
	γενομένῳ	γί[γ]νομαι	aor	mid	part	masc	sing	dat
	ζῆν	ζάω	pres	act	inf			
	μάχεσθαι	μάχομαι	pres	mid	inf			
20	ὤν	εἰμί	pres	act	part	masc	sing	nom
	ἔχων	ἔχω	pres	act	part	masc	sing	nom
	μέλλων	μέλλω	pres	act	part	masc	sing	nom
	ἀμελήσειν	ἀμελέω	fut	act	inf			
	εἶχε	ἔχω	impf	act	ind	3rd	sing	
	κινδυνεύειν	κινδυνεύω	pres	act	inf			
	ἐτόλμησε	τολμάω	aor	act	ind	3rd	sing	
	ἐξιών	ἔξειμι (εἶμι)	pres	act	part	masc	sing	nom
	περιεῖδε	περιοράω	aor	act	ind	3rd	sing	
	ἐνέβαλε	ἐμβάλλω	aor	act	ind	3rd	sing	
21	ἀπέθανεν	ἀποθνήσκω	aor	act	ind	3rd	ind	
	ἀντισχών	ἀντέχω	aor	act	part	masc	sing	nom
	ἤρκεσε	ἀρκέω	aor	act	ind	3rd	sing	
	ἐξητάσθη	ἐξετάζω	aor	pass	ind	3rd	sing	
	ἐπολέμησεν	πολεμέω	aor	act	ind	3rd	sing	
22	εἱστήκει	ἵστημι	plperf	act	ind	3rd	sing	
	περιών	περίειμι	pres	act	part	masc	sing	nom
	κατήρραξεν	καταράσσω	aor	act	ind	3rd	sing	
	ἐδεῖτο	δέω	impf	mid	ind	3rd	sing	
	διωκόντων	διώκω	pres	act	part	masc	plur	gen
	ἑστηκότων	ἵστημι	perf	act	part	masc	plur	gen
	διώκειν	διώκω	pres	act	inf			
	τρέπεσθαι	τρέπω	pres	pass	inf			
	γίνεται	γί[γ]νομαι	pres	mid	ind	3rd	sing	
	ἀπέθανε	ἀποθνήσκω	aor	act	ind	3rd	sing	
	προὐμάχει	προμαχέω	impf	act	ind	3rd	sing	
23	ἔπαθε	πάσχω	aor	act	ind	3rd	sing	
	ἦν	εἰμί	impf	act	ind	3rd	sing	
	ἐνεχθέντων	φέρω	aor	pass	part	neut	plur	gen
	ἀνέστησεν	ἀνίστημι	aor	act	ind	3rd	sing	
	ἔδρασε	δράω	aor	act	ind	3rd	sing	
	θαυμάζεται	θαυμάζω	pres	pass	ind	3rd	sing	
	πέμπων	πέμπω	pres	act	part	masc	sing	nom
	ἀμυνόμενος	ἀμύνω	pres	mid	part	masc	sing	nom
	δρᾶν	δράω	pres	act	inf			
	πάσχειν	πάσχω	pres	act	inf			
	ἐστι	εἰμί	pres	act	ind	3rd	sing	

#	text form	lexicon form	tense	voice	mood	person gender	number	case
24	βουλόμενος	βούλομαι	pres	mid	part	masc	sing	nom
	ἐχρήσατο	χράω	aor	mid	ind	3rd	sing	
	συνέπεσεν	συμπίπτω	aor	act	ind	3rd	sing	
	ἐφῆκε	ἐφίημι	aor	act	ind	3rd	sing	
	συνεκάλεσε	συγκαλέω	aor	act	ind	3rd	sing	
	ἐπανέτεινε	ἐπανατείνω	aor	act	ind	3rd	sing	
25	ἐστιν	εἰμί	pres	act	ind	3rd	sing	
	βεβηκέναι	βαίνω	perf	act	inf			
	ἔχει	ἔχω	pres	act	ind	3rd	sing	
	ἔστιν	εἰμί	pres	act	ind	3rd	sing	
	εἰδὼς	οἶδα	perf	act	part	masc	sing	nom
	συνιεὶς	συνίημι	pres	act	part	masc	sing	nom
	τεμνομένης	τέμνω	pres	pass	part	fem	sing	gen
	καρτερῶν	καρτερέω	pres	act	part	masc	sing	nom
	ποιούμενος	ποιέω	pres	mid	part	masc	sing	nom
	ὀφείλεται	ὀφείλω	pres	pass	ind	3rd	sing	
	πέπονθεν	πάσχω	perf	act	ind	3rd	sing	
	πεποίηκεν	ποιέω	perf	act	ind	3rd	sing	
26	δεῖ	δεῖ	pres	act	ind	3rd	sing	
	ὀκνήσαντα	ὀκνέω	aor	act	part	masc	sing	acc
	εἰπεῖν	λέγω	aor	act	inf			
	δοκοῦσα	δοκέω	pres	act	part	fem	sing	nom
	ἐστι	εἰμί	pres	act	ind	3rd	sing	
	πράττειν	πράσσω	pres	act	inf			
	ζῶντι	ζάω	pres	act	part	masc	sing	dat
	τετολμημένη	τολμάω	perf	pass	part	fem	sing	nom
	ἦν	εἰμί	impf	act	ind	3rd	sing	
27	παράβαλλε	παραβάλλω	pres	act	impv	2nd	sing	
	βάλλοντι	βάλλω	pres	act	part	masc	sing	dat
	βεβλημένον	βάλλω	perf	pass	part	masc	sing	acc
	ἐπαινῶν	ἐπαινέω	pres	act	part	masc	sing	nom
	ἐπαινεῖ	ἐπαινέω	pres	act	ind	3rd	sing	
	ἐμπαγέντα	ἐμπήγνυμι	aor	pass	part	neut	plur	nom
	περιπεσόντα	περιπίπτω	aor	act	part	neut	plur	nom
	βουλόμενον	βούλομαι	pres	mid	part	neut	sing	nom
	ἀνεῖχε	ἀνέχω	impf	act	ind	3rd	sing	
	ὤρθου	ὀρθόω	impf	act	ind	3rd	sing	
	δεδεμένον	δέω	perf	pass	part	masc	sing	acc
	συνεχομένων	συνέχω	pres	pass	part	neut	plur	gen
28	ἐπεδίδου	ἐπιδίδωμι	impf	act	ind	3rd	sing	
	μεμαχημένος	μάχομαι	perf	mid	part	masc	sing	nom
	λέγεις	λέγω	pres	act	ind	2nd	sing	
	ἐπεδείξατο	ἐπιδείκνυμι	aor	mid	ind	3rd	sing	
	μεμαχήμεθα	μάχομαι	perf	mid	ind	1st	plur	
	ἀπεμάχεσθε	ἀπομάχομαι	impf	mid	ind	2nd	plur	
	φυγεῖν	φεύγω	aor	act	inf			

#	text form	lexicon form	tense	voice	mood	person gender	number	case
	ποιοῦντες	ποιέω	pres	act	part	masc	plur	nom
	ἀφιστάμεθα	ἀφίστημι	pres	mid	ind	1st	plur	
29	ἐγένοντο	γί[γ]νομαι	aor	mid	ind	3rd	plur	
	κατέχωσαν	κατέχω	aor	act	ind	3rd	plur	
	ἀναδραμόντες	ἀνατρέχω	aor	act	part	masc	plur	nom
	εἶχον	ἔχω	impf	act	ind	3rd	plur	
	ἐμιμήσατο	μιμέομαι	aor	mid	ind	3rd	sing	
	ἔδοσαν	δίδωμι	aor	act	ind	3rd	plur	
	κατακοπέντες	κατακόπτω	aor	pass	part	masc	plur	nom
	ἔσχε	ἔχω	aor	act	ind	3rd	sing	
	ἀναδησάμενοι	ἀναδέω	aor	mid	part	masc	plur	nom
	εἴχομεν	ἔχω	impf	act	ind	1st	plur	
30	ἐφόβησε	φοβέω	aor	act	ind	3rd	sing	
	κρυπτόμενος	κρύπτω	pres	act	part	masc	sing	nom
	ὤνησε	ὀνίνημι	aor	act	ind	3rd	sing	
	φρονοῦντες	φρονέω	pres	act	part	masc	plur	nom
	ἔλεγον	λέγω	impf	act	ind	3rd	plur	
	ἐσαγηνεύσαμεν	σαγηνεύω	aor	act	ind	1st	plur	
	ἦν	εἰμί	impf	act	ind	3rd	sing	
	περιπίπτων	περιπίπτω	pres	act	part	masc	sing	nom
	βουλομένῳ	βούλομαι	pres	mid	part	masc	sing	dat
	λαθεῖν	λανθάνω	aor	act	inf			
	ἀνεστηκότι	ἀνίστημι	perf	act	part	masc	sing	dat
31	ἐθάρσυνας	θαρσύνω	aor	act	ind	2nd	sing	
	δεικνὺς	δείκνυμι	pres	act	part	masc	sing	nom
	ἠφίεις	ἀφίημι	impf	act	ind	2nd	sing	
	κατέπληττες	καταπλήσσω	impf	act	ind	2nd	sing	
	δεικνὺς	δείκνυμι	pres	act	part	masc	sing	nom
	δηλῶν	δηλόω	pres	act	part	masc	sing	nom
	εἰσιν	εἰμί	pres	act	ind	3rd	plur	
	ἐκάλυψαν	καλύπτω	aor	act	ind	3rd	plur	
	φοβοῦνται	φοβέω	pres	mid	ind	3rd	plur	
	κειμένην	κεῖμαι	pres	mid	part	fem	sing	acc
32	ἦν	εἰμί	impf	act	ind	3rd	sing	
	μεμάχηται	μάχομαι	perf	mid	ind	3rd	sing	
	νενίκηκεν	νικέω	perf	act	ind	3rd	sing	
	ἔδειξεν	δείκνυμι	aor	act	ind	3rd	sing	
	εἶ	εἰμί	pres	act	ind	2nd	sing	
	ἐδεξάμην	δέχομαι	aor	mid	ind	1st	sing	
	ἦν	εἰμί	impf	act	ind	3rd	sing	
33	ἐπαινεῖς	ἐπαινέω	pres	act	ind	2nd	sing	
	ἑστῶτα	ἵστημι	perf	act	part	masc	sing	acc
	διαφέροντα	διαφέρω	pres	act	part	masc	sing	acc
34	τεθραμμέναι	τρέφω	perf	pass	part	fem	plur	voc
35	ἀνέτειλε	ανατέλλω	aor	act	ind	3rd	sing	
	κατέσχες	κατέχω	aor	act	ind	2nd	sing	

#	text form	lexicon form	tense	voice	mood	person gender	number	case
	ἀναγομένην	ἀνάγω	pres	mid	part	fem	sing	acc
	ἐρεττομένην	ἐρέσσω -ττ-	pres	pass	part	fem	sing	acc
	ὥρμισας	ὁρμίζω	aor	act	ind	2nd	sing	
	ἔδραμεν	τρέχω	aor	act	ind	3rd	sing	
	παρ- -εγένοντο	παρα- -γί[γ]νομαι	aor	mid	ind	3rd	plur	
	παρούσης	πάρειμι	pres	act	part	fem	sing	gen
	εἷλκον	ἕλκω	impf	act	ind	3rd	plur	
	εἷλκες	ἕλκω	impf	act	ind	2nd	sing	
36	ἦν	εἰμί	impf	act	ind	3rd	sing	
	φέρουσαι	φέρω	pres	act	part	fem	plur	nom
	εἶδον	ὁράω	aor	act	ind	masc	plur	
	ἀφιεμένην	ἀφίημι	pres	pass	part	fem	sing	acc
	κρατουμένην	κρατέω	pres	pass	part	fem	sing	acc
	ἀπεκόπτετο	ἀποκόπτω	impf	pass	ind	3rd	sing	
	ἀπῳκίζετο	ἀποικίζω	impf	pass	ind	3rd	sing	
	ἐμνημόνευεν	μνημονεύω	impf	act	ind	3rd	sing	
	αἰσθανόμενος	αἰσθάνομαι	pres	mid	part	masc	sing	nom
37	κατέσχε	κατέχω	aor	act	ind	3rd	sing	
	τιμωρήσας	τιμωρέω	aor	act	part	masc	sing	nom
	ἔδειξας	δείκνυμι	aor	act	ind	2nd	sing	
	μένουσαν	μένω	pres	act	part	fem	sing	acc
38	φασι	φημί	pres	act	ind	3rd	plur	
	βοᾶν	βοάω	pres	act	inf			
	ἐχόμενον	ἔχω	pres	mid	part	masc	sing	acc
	ἀπαιτῶ	ἀπαιτέω	pres	act	ind	1st	sing	
	ἡρπασμένην	ἁρπάζω	perf	pass	part	fem	sing	acc
	ἀπαιτῶ	ἀπαιτέω	pres	act	ind	1st	sing	
	ἀπόδοτε	ἀποδίδωμι	aor	act	impv	2nd	plur	
	φεύγετε	φεύγω	pres	act	impv	2nd	plur	
	βεβουλημένε	βούλομαι	perf	mid	part	masc	sing	voc
	ποιήσας	ποιέω	aor	act	part	masc	sing	voc
	περινοήσας	περινοέω	aor	act	part	masc	sing	voc
	ἄγειν	ἄγω	pres	act	inf			
39	μεμιμημένης	μιμέομαι	perf	mid	part	fem	sing	gen
	εἴχομεν	ἔχω	impf	act	ind	1st	plur	
	ἐξῆλθον	ἐξέρχομαι	aor	act	ind	3rd	plur	
	ὑπεδέξαντο	ὑποδέχομαι	aor	mid	ind	3rd	plur	
	πεσούσας	πίπτω	aor	act	part	fem	plur	acc
	ἐστεφάνωσαν	στεφανόω	aor	act	ind	3rd	plur	
40	ὑποστὰς	ὑφίστημι	aor	act	part	masc	sing	nom
	ἐβόησας	βοάω	aor	act	ind	2nd	sing	
	φεύγετε	φεύγω	pres	act	ind	2nd	plur	
	στῆτε	ἵστημι	aor	act	impv	2nd	plur	
	ἀπόδοτε	ἀποδίδωμι	aor	act	impv	2nd	plur	
	ἐληίσασθε	ληίζομαι	aor	mid	ind	2nd	plur	

#	text form	lexicon form	tense	voice	mood	person gender	number	case
	ἐκραύγαζον	κραυγάζω	impf	act	ind	3rd	plur	
	φεύγοντες	φεύγω	pres	act	part	masc	plur	nom
	μαινομένης	μαίνομαι	pres	mid	part	fem	sing	gen
	ἐπιστρέψει	ἐπιστρέφω	fut	act	ind	3rd	sing	
41	κόπτειν	κόπτω	pres	act	inf			
	ὁρμήσαντος	ὁρμάω	aor	act	part	masc	sing	gen
	μείναντος	μένω	aor	act	part	masc	sing	gen
	ἐγείρεται	ἐγείρω	pres	mid?	ind	3rd	sing	
	καμών	κάμνω	aor	act	part	masc	sing	nom
	ἰσχύσας	ἰσχύω	aor	act	part	masc	sing	nom
	ἐβόησεν	βοάω	aor	act	ind	3rd	sing	
	ἠγάγετε	ἄγω	aor	act	ind	2nd	plur	
	μέλλετε	μέλλω	pres	act	ind	2nd	plur	
	ἀποτεμνέτω	ἀποτέμνω	pres	act	impv	3rd	sing	
	λυσάτω	λύω	aor	act	impv	3rd	sing	
	ἐπιδραμοῦσα	ἐπιτρέχω	aor	act	part	fem	sing	nom
	κομιοῦσι	κομίζω	fut	act	ind	3rd	plur	
42	ἥπτετο	ἅπτω	impf	mid	ind	3rd	sing	
	ἔκοπτεν	κόπτω	impf	act	ind	3rd	sing	
	ἐφρόντισεν	φροντίζω	aor	act	ind	3rd	sing	
	ἀφαιρουμένης	ἀφαιρέω	pres	pass	part	fem	sing	gen
	διδοὺς	δίδωμι	pres	act	part	masc	sing	nom
	ἔπιπτεν	πίπτω	impf	act	ind	3rd	sing	
	ἐμάχετο	μάχομαι	impf	mid	ind	3rd	sing	
	διένειμεν	διανέμω	aor	act	ind	3rd	sing	
43	ἦσθα	εἰμί	impf	act	ind	2nd	sing	
	ἐκράτησας	κρατέω	aor	act	ind	2nd	sing	
	ἀντήρκεσας	ἀνταρκέω	aor	act	ind	2nd	sing	
	ἔφερεν	φέρω	impf	act	ind	3rd	sing	
	ἀπήγαγον	ἀπάγω	aor	act	ind	3rd	plur	
	λέγοντες	λέγω	pres	act	part	masc	plur	nom
	ἐπλεύσαμεν	πλέω	aor	act	ind	1st	plur	
	κοπτομένων	κόπτω	pres	pass	part	fem	plur	gen
	μέλει	μέλω	pres	act	ind	3rd	sing	
	παρισουμένας	παρισόομαι	pres	mid	part	fem	plur	acc
	ἀνήχθημεν	ἀνάγω	aor	pass	ind	1st	plur	
44	ᾄδουσι	ᾄδω / ἀείδω	pres	act	ind	3rd	plur	
	πυνθάνονται	πυνθάνομαι	pres	mid	ind	3rd	plur	
	ἠκολούθησε	ἀκολουθέω	aor	act	ind	3rd	sing	
	τεθεαμένος	θεάομαι	perf	mid	part	masc	sing	nom
	προκατ- -έλαβες	προκατα- -λαμβάνω	aor	act	ind	2nd	sing	
	ἐποίησας	ποιέω	aor	act	ind	2nd	sing	
	συνέθου	συντίθημι	aor	mid	ind	2nd	sing	
	ἔδωκας	δίδωμι	aor	act	ind	2nd	sing	
	μιμήσονται	μιμέομαι	fut	mid	ind	3rd	plur	

#	text form	lexicon form	tense	voice	mood	person gender	number	case
	ναυμαχοῦντες	ναυμαχέω	pres	act	part	masc	plur	nom
	γενήσονται	γί[γ]νομαι	fut	mid	ind	3rd	plur	
	ἔχουσαι	ἔχω	pres	act	part	fem	plur	nom
45	λέγειν	λέγω	pres	act	inf			
	ἔχων	ἔχω	pres	act	part	masc	sing	nom
	φυλάττω	φυλάσσω	pres	act	ind	1st	sing	
	ἔχεις	ἔχω	pres	act	ind	2nd	sing	
	μεγαληγορῆσαι	μεγαληγορέω	aor	act	inf			
	ἔστησαν	ἵστημι	aor	act	ind	3rd	plur	
	πίπτουσαν	πίπτω	pres	act	part	fem	sing	acc
46	ἄπελθε	ἀπέρχομαι	aor	act	impv	2nd	sing	
	παραχώρησον	παραχωρέω	aor	act	impv	2nd	sing	
	ἐρῶ	λέγω	fut	act	ind	1st	sing	
	ἦν	εἰμί	impf	act	ind	3rd	sing	
	ἐπιχείρει	ἐπιχειρέω	pres	act	impv	2nd	sing	
	ὤν	εἰμί	pres	act	part	masc	sing	nom
	ταφῆναι	θάπτω	aor	pass	inf			
	θέλοντος	[ἐ]θελω	pres	act	part	masc	sing	gen
47	παρελήλυθεν	παρέρχομαι	perf	act	ind	3rd	sing	
	τέθαπται	θάπτω	perf	pass	ind	3rd	sing	
	εἰμὶ	εἰμί	pres	act	ind	1st	sing	
	ἔχω	ἔχω	pres	act	ind	1st	sing	
48	ἐάσατε	ἐάω	aor	act	impv	2nd	plur	
	τραγῳδῆσαι	τραγῳδέω	aor	act	inf			
	παραγαγεῖν	παράγω	aor	act	inf			
	φθονήσητε	φθονέω	aor	act	subj	2nd	plur	
49	ποίησον	ποιέω	apr	act	impv	2nd	sing	
	συγκόσμησον	συγκοσμέω	aor	act	impv	2nd	sing	
	ἀτιμάσητε	ἀτιμάω	aor	act	subj	2nd	plur	
	προτείνω	προτείνω	pres	act	ind	1st	sing	
	κειμέναις	κεῖμαι	pres	mid	part	fem	plur	dat
	ἔχομαι	ἔχω	pres	mid	ind	1st	sing	
	λαμβάνομαι	λαμβάνομαι	pres	mid	ind	1st	sing	
	ἀφίσταμαι	ἀφίστημι	pres	mid	ind	1st	sing	
	διεξιών	διέξειμι (εἶμι)	pres	act	part	masc	sing	nom
	ὤν	εἰμί	pres	act	part	masc	sing	nom
	ἐπιτίθημι	ἐπιτίθημι	pres	act	ind	1st	sing	
	θέλων	[ἐ]θελω	pres	act	part	masc	sing	nom
	ἀποκοψάτω	ἀποκόπτω	aor	act	impv	3rd	sing	

#	text form	lexicon form	tense	voice	mood	person gender	number	case
B								
1	ἐπαινῶ	ἐπαινέω	pres	act	ind	1st	sing	
	κοσμοῦντα	κοσμέω	pres	act	part	masc	sing	acc
	πραχθέντων	πράσσω	aor	pass	part	neut	plur	gen
	ῥηθέντες	λέγω	aor	pass	part	masc	plur	nom
	εἰσι	εἰμί	pres	act	ind	3rd	plur	
	γενομένη	γί[γ]νομαι	aor	mid	part	fem	sing	nom
	κρίνεται	κρίνω	pres	pass	ind	3rd	sing	
	δείξω	δείκνυμι	fut	act	ind	1st	sing	
2	ὤν	εἰμί	pres	act	part	masc	sing	nom
	πρέπω	πρέπω	pres	act	ind	1st	sing	
	ἑστάναι	ἵστημι	perf	act	inf			
	ζῶν	ζάω	pres	act	part	masc	sing	nom
	ζῶντος	ζάω	pres	act	part	masc	sing	gen
	ἦν	εἰμί	impf	act	ind	3rd	sing	
	τεθνεὼς	[ἀπο]θνήσκω	perf	act	part	masc	sing	nom
	ἡττηθήσεται	ἡσσάομαι	fut	pass	ind	3rd	sing	
	ὑβριεῖται	ὑβρίζω	fut	mid	ind	3rd	sing	
	γενομένην	γί[γ]νομαι	aor	mid	part	fem	sing	acc
	παρασχοῦσαν	παρέχω	aor	act	part	fem	sing	acc
	μεμαχημένον	μάχομαι	perf	mid	part	masc	sing	acc
3	πεσεῖν	πίπτω	aor	act	inf			
	κοινωνῆσαι	κοινωνέω	aor	act	inf			
	ἔπεισα	πείθω	aor	act	ind	1st	sing	
	ἤθελεν	[ἐ]θέλω	impf	act	ind	3rd	sing	
	ἀπελθεῖν	ἀπέρχομαι	aor	act	inf			
	ὑποπεσεῖν	ὑποπίπτω	aor	act	inf			
	ἀξιῶν	ἀξιόω	pres	act	part	masc	sing	nom
	τέθνηκεν	[ἀπο]θνήσκω	perf	act	ind	3rd	sing	
	ὁμολογῆσαι	ὁμολογέω	aor	act	inf			
	βεβιασμένον	βιάζω	perf	mid	part	masc	sing	acc
4	ἦν	εἰμί	impf	act	ind	3rd	sing	
	ἥττηται	ἡσσάομαι	perf	mid	ind	3rd	sing	
	κείμενοι	κεῖμαι	pres	mid	part	masc	plur	nom
	ἑστηκότων	ἵστημι	perf	act	part	masc	plur	gen
5	τυγχάνει	τυγχάνω	pres	act	ind	3rd	sing	
	ἐξετάσατε	ἐξετάζω	aor	act	impv	2nd	plur	
	ἀπέβαινε	ἀποβαίνω	impf	act	ind	3rd	sing	
	βοηθεῖν	βοηθέω	pres	act	inf			
	ἔδει	δεῖ	impf	act	ind	3rd	sing	
	περιμένοντας	περιμένω	pres	act	part	masc	plur	acc
	ἦν	εἰμί	impf	act	ind	3rd	sing	
	ἐδόκει	δοκέω	impf	act	ind	3rd	sing	
	τρέχειν	τρέχω	pres	act	inf			
6	ἦγε	ἄγω	impf	act	ind	3rd	sing	
	ὤν	εἰμί	pres	act	part	masc	sing	nom

#	text form	lexicon form	tense	voice	mood	person gender	number	case
	ἔχων	ἔχω	pres	act	part	masc	somg	nom
	παρασχέσθαι	παρέχω	aor	mid	inf			
7	ὤν	εἰμί	pres	act	part	masc	sing	nom
	ἠπείγετο	ἐπείγω	impf	pass	ind	3rd	sing	
	συμμίξαντες	συμμ[ε]ίγνυμι	aor	act	part	masc	plur	nom
	ἦν	εἰμί	impf	act	ind	3rd	sing	
	ἔδειξεν	δείκνυμι	aor	act	ind	3rd	sing	
	ἦν	εἰμί	impf	act	ind	3rd	sing	
8	παρα-	παρα-						
	-κελευσάμενος	-κελεύομαι	aor	mid	part	masc	sing	nom
	ἀναλῶσθαι	ἀναλίσκω	aor	mid	inf			
	ἀντιτάξας	ἀντιτάσσω	aor	act	part	masc	sing	nom
	ὤν	εἰμί	pres	act	part	masc	sing	nom
	ἔστη	ἵστημι	aor	act	ind	3rd	sing	
	προκαλούμενος	προκαλέω	pres	mid	part	masc	sing	nom
	ἐκχεομένην	ἐκχέω	pres	mid	part	fem	sing	acc
	ἐδέχετο	δέχομαι	impf	mid	ind	3rd	sing	
	συνεπλάκη	συμπλέκω	aor	pass	ind	3rd	sing	
	ἐξήρκεσεν	ἐξαρκέω	aor	act	ind	3rd	sing	
	ἐκπλαγεὶς	ἐκπλήσσω	aor	pass	part	masc	sing	nom
	ἀξιώσας	ἀξιόω	aor	act	part	masc	sing	nom
	εἶναι	εἰμί	pres	act	inf			
9	ἐργασάμενος	ἐργάζομαι	aor	mid	part	masc	sing	nom
	κατέστησεν	καθίστημι	aor	act	ind	3rd	sing	
	καταλιπόντες	καταλείπω	aor	act	part	masc	plur	nom
	ἐπεχέοντο	ἐπιχέω	impf	mid	ind	3rd	plur	
	ἐστοχάζοντο	στοχάζομαι	impf	mid	ind	3rd	plur	
	ἦν	εἰμί	impf	act	ind	3rd	sing	
	βαλεῖν	βάλλω	aor	act	inf			
	παρόντος	πάρειμι	pres	act	part			
	εἶναι	εἰμί	pres	act	inf			
	ἔφασκον	φάσκω	impf	act	ind	3rd	plur	
10	ὑπεδέξατο	ὑποδέχομαι	aor	mid	ind	3rd	sing	
	ὑπέμεινε	ὑπομένω	aor	act	ind	3rd	sing	
	ὤν	εἰμί	pres	act	part	masc	sing	nom
	μαχόμενος	μάχομαι	pres	mid	part	masc	sing	nom
	ἀνήλωσε	ἀναλίσκω	aor	act	ind	3rd	sing	
	καμεῖν	κάμνω	aor	act	inf			
	ἐποίησε	ποιέω	aor	act	ind	3rd	sing	
11	διεκαρτέρησεν	διακαρτερέω	aor	act	ind	3rd	sing	
	ἐρίζουσα	ἐρίζω	pres	act	part	fem	sing	nom
	ἐβιάζετο	βιάζω	impf	mid	ind	3rd	sing	
	ἦν	εἰμί	impf	act	ind	3rd	sing	
	ἀπελθεῖν	ἀπέρχομαι	aor	act	inf			
	ἠναγκάζετο	ἀναγκάζω	impf	pass	ind	3rd	sing	
	ἀπέθανε	ἀποθνήσκω	aor	act	ind	3rd	sing	

#	text form	lexicon form	tense	voice	mood	person gender	number	case
	ἔπεσε	πίπτω	aor	act	ind	3rd	sing	
	ἐξιοῦσα	ἔξειμι (εἶμι)	pres	act	part	fem	sing	nom
	μένειν	μένω	pres	act	inf			
	καρτερεῖν	καρτερέω	pres	act	inf			
	ἐνετείλατο	ἐντέλλω	aor	mid	ind	3rd	sing	
	μάχεσθαι	μάχομαι	pres	mid	inf			
	ἐπείσθη	πείθω	aor	pass	ind	3rd	sing	
	ἔμενεν	μένω	impf	act	ind	3rd	sing	
	ἐρριζωμένον	ῥιζόω	perf	pass	part	neut	sing	nom
	ἐξιοῦσα	ἔξειμι (εἶμι)	pres	act	part	fem	sing	nom
	ἔστησεν	ἵστημι	aor	act	ind	3rd	sing	
	ἐξηπάτησεν	ἐξαπατάω	aor	act	ind	3rd	sing	
	ᾤετο	οἴομαι	impf	mid	ind	3rd	sing	
	τεθνάναι	[ἀπο]θνῄσκω	perf	act	inf			
	ἑστηκότα	ἵστημι	perf	act	part	masc	sing	acc
12	εἱμαρμένης	μείρομαι	perf	pass	part	fem	sing	gen
	κεκοσμημένον	κοσμέω	perf	pass	part	neut	sing	voc
	τηρήσας	τηρέω	aor	act	part	masc	sing	voc
	στήσας	ἵστημι	aor	act	part	masc	sing	voc
	εἴασας	ἐάω	aor	act	ind	2nd	sing	
	πεσεῖν	πίπτω	aor	act	inf			
13	πεπονηκότες	πονέω	perf	act	part	masc	plur	nom
	ἀφωπλισμένοι	ἀφοπλίζω	perf	pass	part	masc	plur	nom
	πεφοβημένοι	φοβέω	perf	pass	part	masc	plur	nom
	τραπέντες	τρέπω	aor	pass	part	masc	plur	nom
	ἔφυγον	φεύγω	aor	act	ind	3rd	plur	
	περιέβλεπον	περιβλέπω	impf	act	ind	3rd	plur	
	πεποιηκότος	ποιέω	perf	act	part	masc	sing	gen
	ἦν	εἰμί	impf	act	ind	3rd	sing	
	βουλομένοις	βουλόμαι	pres	mid	part	masc	plur	dat
	ἀκολουθησάντων	ἀκολουθέω	aor	act	part	masc	plur	gen
	ἐγένετο	γί[γ]νομαι	aor	mid	ind	3rd	sing	
	ἁπτόμενος	ἅπτω	pres	mid	part	masc	sing	nom
	ἀπεκόπη	ἀποκόπτω	aor	pass	ind	3rd	sing	
	ἔπεσεν	πίπτω	aor	act	ind	3rd	sing	
	ἐμήνυσε	μηνύω	aor	act	ind	3rd	sing	
14	εἱστήκεις	ἵστημι	plperf	act	ind	2nd	sing	
	ἀποπλέοντος	ἀποπλέω	pres	act	part	masc	sing	gen
	ἐπιτηρῶν	ἐπιτηρέω	pres	act	part	masc	sing	nom
	γενέσθαι	γί[γ]νομαι	aor	mid	inf			
	πέσῃς	πίπτω	aor	act	subj	2nd	sing	
15	ἀναβιβάζει	ἀναβιβάζω	pres	act	ind	3rd	sing	
	παραδίδωσιν	παραδίδωμι	pres	act	ind	3rd	sing	
	ἐκίνησα	κινέω	aor	act	ind	1st	sing	
	κεῖσθαι	κεῖμαι	pres	mid	inf			
	παρεκάλεσα	παρακαλέω	aor	act	ind	1st	sing	

#	text form	lexicon form	tense	voice	mood	person gender	number	case
	εἰσέρχεται	εἰσέρχομαι	pres	mid	ind	3rd	sing	
	προκριθέντα	προκρίνω	aor	pass	part	masc	sing	acc
	λέγειν	λέγω	pres	act	inf			
16	ζῶντος	ζάω	pres	act	part	masc	sing	gen
	ἦν	εἰμί	impf	act	ind	3rd	sing	
	τεθνεῶτος	[ἀπο]θνῄσκω	perf	act	part	masc	sing	gen
	εἶναι	εἰμί	pres	act	inf			
	ἤγομεν	ἄγω	impf	act	ind	1st	plur	
	ἐροῦμεν	λέγω	fut	act	ind	1st	plur	
	ὡπλίζομεν	ὁπλίζω	impf	act	ind	1st	plur	
	ἐπαινεσόμεθα	ἐπαινέω	fut	mid	ind	1st	plur	
	ἦν	εἰμί	impf	act	ind	3rd	sing	
	ἔστω	εἰμί	pres	act	impv	3rd	sing	
17	λυπήσητε	λυπέω	aor	act	subj	2nd	plur	
	συνιέντα	συνίημι	pres	act	part	masc	sing	acc
	καθέλητε	καθαιρέω	aor	act	subj	2nd	plur	
	ἀνεστηκότα	ἀνίστημι	perf	act	part	masc	sing	acc
	ἀπο- -χειροτονήσητε	ἀπο- -χειροτονέω	aor	act	subj	2nd	plur	
	νενικηκότα	νικάω	perf	act	part	masc	sing	acc
	νενικηκότων	νικάω	perf	act	part	masc	plur	gen
	ὀφθῇ	ὁράω	aor	pass	subj	3rd	sing	
	ἀγγέλλεσθαι	ἀγγέλλω	pres	pass	inf			
	χρὴ	χρή	pres	act	ind	3rd	sing	
	ἀξιοῦσθαι	ἀξιόω	pres	pass	inf			
18	σκοπεῖτε	σκοπέω	pres	act	impv	2nd	plur	
	περι- -γενόμενοι	περι- -γί[γ]νομαι	aor	mid	part	masc	plur	nom
	παρούσης	πάρειμι	pres	act	part	fem	sing	gen
	ἠμφισβήτουν	ἀμφισβητέω	impf	act	ind	3rd	plur	
	διεκρίθη	διακρίνω	aor	pass	ind	3rd	sing	
	ἐπῄνεσε	ἐπαινέω	aor	act	ind	3rd	sing	
	πεσόντας	πίπτω	aor	act	part	masc	plur	acc
	πιάσας	πιέζω/πιάζω	aor	act	part	masc	sing	nom
	τάξας	τάσσω	aor	act	part	masc	sing	nom
	παρασχών	παρέχω	aor	act	part	masc	sing	nom
	δοκεῖ	δοκέω	pres	act	ind	3rd	sing	
	παράσχῃ	παρέχω	aor	act	subj	3rd	sing	
	δῶτε	δίδωμι	aor	act	subj	2nd	plur	
19	ἦσαν	εἰμί	impf	act	ind	3rd	plur	
	ἔσχε	ἔχω	aor	act	ind	3rd	sing	
	τεθνεὼς	[ἀπο]θνῄσκω	perf	act	part	masc	sing	nom
	φέρεσθαι	φέρω	pres	mid	inf			
	ἦν	εἰμί	impf	act	ind	3rd	sing	
	περιὼν	περίειμι	pres	act	part	masc	sing	nom
	περιόντος	περίειμι	pres	act	part	masc	sing	gen

#	text form	lexicon form	tense	voice	mood	person gender	number	case
	ἔχει	ἔχω	pres	act	ind	3rd	sing	
	προκεκρίσθαι	προκρίνω	perf	pass	inf			
	δοκεῖν	δοκέω	pres	act	inf			
	προτιμωμένου	προτιμάω	pres	pass	part	masc	sing	gen
	ὑπάρξει	ὑπάρχω	fut	act	ind	3rd	sing	
	ἔσται	εἰμί	fut	mid	ind	3rd	sing	
	τεθνηκότι	[ἀπο]θνῄσκω	perf	act	part	masc	sing	dat
	τεύξεται	τυγχάνω	fut	mid	ind	3rd	sing	
	ἔσται	εἰμί	fut	mid	ind	3rd	sing	
	ἑπομένῳ	ἕπω	pres	mid	part	masc	sing	dat
	προετάττετο	προτάσσω	impf	pass	ind	3rd	sing	
	γραφομένων	γράφω	pres	pass	part	neut	plur	gen
	ἦν	εἰμί	impf	act	ind	3rd	sing	
	δεῖ	δεῖ	pres	act	ind	3rd	sing	
	θαπτομένοις	θάπτω	pres	pass	part	masc	plur	dat
	εἰωθότα	ἔθω	perf	act	part	masc	sing	acc
	ἀκούειν	ἀκούω	pres	act	inf			
	λεγόντων	λέγω	pres	act	part	masc	plur	gen
20	ἐτιμήσατε	τιμάω	aor	act	ind	2nd	plur	
	ἐδόθη	δίδωμι	aor	pass	ind	3rd	sing	
	γενέσθω	γί[γ]νομαι	aor	mid	impv	3rd	sing	
	λέγων	λέγω	pres	act	part	masc	sing	nom
	ἀναβιβάσῃ	ἀναβιβάζω	aor	act	subj	3rd	sing	
	δότε	δίδωμι	aor	act	impv	2nd	plur	
21	ἠμφισβήτει	ἀμφισβητέω	impf	act	ind	3rd	sing	
	παρεχώρησα	παραχωρέω	aor	act	ind	1st	sing	
	ἀποιχόμενον	ἀποίχομαι	pres	mid	part	masc	sing	acc
	ἄρχοντα	ἄρχω	pres	act	part	masc	sing	acc
	σχεῖν	ἔχω	aor	act	inf			
	ἐστι	εἰμί	pres	act	ind	3rd	sing	
	παρα- -μυθουμένης	παρα- -μυθέομαι	pres	mid	part	fem	sing	gen
	ἀφεστηκότος	ἀφίστημι	perf	act	part	masc	sing	gen
	ἐστιν	εἰμί	pres	act	ind	3rd	sing	
22	λύε	λύω	pres	act	impv	2nd	sing	
	δίδωσι	δίδωμι	pres	act	ind	3rd	sing	
	περιὼν	περίειμι	pres	act	part	masc	sing	nom
	τύχοι	τυγχάνω	aor	act	opt	3rd	sing	
	ἐστιν	εἰμί	pres	act	ind	3rd	sing	
	ποιούμενος	ποιέω	pres	mid	part	masc	sing	nom
	καλῶν	καλέω	pres	act	part	masc	sing	nom
	ἐπιμελούμενος	ἐπιμελέομαι / ἐπιμέλομαι	pres	mid	part	masc	sing	nom
23	δεῖ	δεῖ	pres	act	ind	3rd	sing	
	εἶναι	εἰμί	pres	act	inf			
	ἦγε	ἄγω	impf	act	ind	3rd	sing	

#	text form	lexicon form	tense	voice	mood	person gender	number	case
	ἐδέχετο	δέχομαι	impf	mid	ind	3rd	sing	
	ἐκέλευεν	κελεύω	impf	act	ind	3rd	sing	
	ἐπείθετο	πείθω	impf	mid	ind	3rd	sing	
	πειθόμενοι	πείθω	pres	pass	part	masc	plur	nom
	κελευόμενοι	κελεύω	pres	pass	part	masc	plur	nom
	ποιοῦσιν	ποιέω	pres	act	ind	3rd	plur	
	πείσαντες	πείθω	aor	act	part	masc	plur	nom
	κελεύσαντες	κελεύω	aor	act	part	masc	plur	nom
	εἰσιν	εἰμί	pres	act	ind	3rd	plur	
	ἐτόλμησε	τολμάω	aor	act	ind	3rd	sing	
	ἐβόα	βοάω	impf	act	ind	3rd	sing	
	ἐγκελευόμενος	ἐγκελεύω	pres	mid	part	masc	sing	nom
	φείδεσθε	φείδομαι	pres	mid	impv	2nd	plur	
	ἐλαμπρύνετο	λαμπρύνω	impf	mid	ind	3rd	sing	
	ἔστι	εἰμί	pres	act	ind	3rd	sing	
	ποιήσασθαι	ποιέω	aor	mid	inf			
	πεποιηκότα	ποιέω	perf	act	part	masc	sing	acc
24	ὤν	εἰμί	pres	act	part	masc	sing	nom
	ηὐθαδιάσατο	αὐθαδιάζομαι	aor	mid	ind	3rd	sing	
	ὤν	εἰμί	pres	act	part	masc	sing	nom
	ἐβεβαίου	βεβαιόω	impf	act	ind	3rd	sing	
	ὑπάρχων	ὑπάρχω	pres	act	part	masc	sing	nom
	ὑπερέβαλε	ὑπερβάλλω	aor	act	ind	3rd	sing	
25	παρετάξατο	παρατάσσω	aor	mid	ind	3rd	sing	
	ἐπιχωριαζούσης	ἐπιχωριάζω	pres	act	part	fem	sing	gen
	ῥέουσαν	ῥέω	pres	act	part	fem	sing	acc
	ἀπεώσατο	ἀπωθέω	aor	mid	ind	3rd	sing	
	ἦν	εἰμί	impf	act	ind	3rd	sing	
26	φευγόντων	φεύγω	pres	act	part	masc	plur	gen
	πεφοβημένων	φοβέω	perf	pass	part	masc	plur	gen
	τετραμμένων	τρέπω	perf	pass	part	masc	plur	gen
	δεδιωγμένων	διώκω	perf	pass	part	masc	plur	gen
	συνεληλαμένων	συνελαύνω	perf	pass	part	masc	plur	gen
	ὄντων	εἰμί	pres	act	part	masc	plur	gen
	λυόντων	λύω	pres	act	part	masc	plur	gen
	ἔστι	εἰμί	pres	act	ind	3rd	sing	
	ὑφίστασθαι	ὑφίστημι	pres	pass	inf			
	τυχόντος	τυγχάνω	aor	act	part	masc	sing	gen
	διώκειν	διώκω	pres	act	inf			
	φεύγοντα	φεύγω	pres	act	part	masc	sing	acc
	τετραμμένοις	τρέπω	perf	pass	part	masc	plur	dat
	ἐπεμβαίνειν	ἐπεμβαίνω	pres	act	inf			
27	ἐπιτίθενται	ἐπιτίθημι	pres	mid	ind	3rd	plur	
	θρασύνονται	θρασύνω	pres	mid	ind	3rd	plur	
	οἴχηται	οἴχομαι	pres	mid	subj	3rd	sing	
	τολμᾶν	τολμάω	pres	act	inf			

#	text form	lexicon form	tense	voice	mood	person gender	number	case
	ἐλόντων	αἱρέω	aor	act	part	masc	plur	gen
	γίνεται	γί[γ]νομαι	pres	mid	ind	3rd	sing	
	πεπορισμένον	πορίζω	perf	pass	part	neut	sing	nom
	κρίνεται	κρίνω	pres	pass	ind	3rd	sing	
	ἠρίστευσεν	ἀριστεύω	aor	act	ind	3rd	sing	
	δρᾶν	δράω	pres	act	inf			
	παθεῖν	πάσχω	aor	act	inf			
	ἐγένετο	γί[γ]νομαι	aor	mid	ind	3rd	sing	
	ἠθέλησε	[ἐ]θέλω	aor	act	ind	3rd	sing	
	ποιεῖν	ποιέω	pres	act	inf			
	ἦν	εἰμί	impf	act	ind	3rd	sing	
	παθεῖν	πάσχω	aor	act	inf			
	ὡμολογηκότων	ὁμολογέω	perf	act	part	masc	plur	gen
	ποριζομένων	πορίζω	pres	mid	part	masc	plur	gen
28	παρεσκεύασεν	παρασκευάζω	aor	act	ind	3rd	sing	
	γενομένης	γί[γ]νομαι	aor	mid	part	fem	sing	gen
	καταπλαγέντες	καταπλήσσω	aor	pass	part	masc	plur	nom
	δείξαντες	δείκνυμι	aor	act	part	masc	plur	nom
	παρεῖχον	παρέχω	impf	act	ind	3rd	plur	
	ἐπιφερομένοις	ἐπιφέρω	pres	pass	part	masc	plur	dat
	πεπραγμένα	πράσσω	perf	pass	part	neut	plur	nom
	αἰτεῖ	αἰτέω	pres	act	ind	3rd	sing	
29	παρασχεῖν	παρέχω	aor	act	inf			
	ἐστιν	εἰμί	pres	act	ind	3rd	sing	
	γενομένων	γί[γ]νομαι	aor	mid	part	neut	plur	gen
	εἴη	εἰμί	pres	act	opt	3rd	sing	
	ἦν	εἰμί	impf	act	ind	3rd	sing	
	τεχνηθέντων	τεχνάομαι	aor	pass	part	neut	plur	gen
	ἔχει	ἔχω	pres	act	ind	3rd	sing	
30	γενησομένας	γί[γ]νομαι	fut	mid	part	fem	plur	acc
	ἀνέπνευσαν	ἀναπνεύω	aor	act	ind	3rd	plur	
	φεύγοντας	φεύγω	pres	act	part	masc	plur	acc
	ἰδόντες	ὁράω	aor	act	part	masc	plur	nom
	ἐθάρρησαν	θαρσέω	aor	act	ind	3rd	plur	
	ὁρῶν	ὁράω	pres	act	part	masc	sing	nom
	ἠμελει	ἀμελέω	impf	act	ind	3rd	sing	
	ὑπεριδόντα	ὑπεροράω	aor	act	part	masc	sing	acc
31	ἐμάχετο	μάχομαι	impf	mid	ind	3rd	sing	
	ἀποβάντας	ἀποβαίνω	aor	act	part	masc	plur	acc
	δεδουλωμένους	δουλόω	perf	pass	part	masc	plur	acc
	ἐπιφέροντας	ἐπιφέρω	pres	act	part	masc	plur	acc
	συνειλημμένων	συλλαμβάνω	perf	pass	part	masc	plur	gen
32	παρωξυμμένος	παροξύνω	perf	pass	part	masc	sing	nom
	φιλοτιμούμενος	φιλοτιμέομαι	pres	mid	part	masc	sing	nom
	μεμάχηται	μάχομαι	perf	mid	ind	3rd	sing	
	ἀναγομένων	ἀνάγω	pres	mid	part	fem	plur	gen

#	text form	lexicon form	tense	voice	mood	person gender	number	case
	ἐπεχείρησε	ἐπιχειρέω	aor	act	ind	3rd	sing	
	παρετάξατο	παρατάσσω	aor	mid	ind	3rd	sing	
33	ἐποιήσατο	ποιέω	aor	mid	ind	3rd	sing	
	ἦν	εἰμί	impf	act	ind	3rd	sing	
	ἐλάβετο	λαμβάνω	aor	mid	ind	3rd	sing	
	ἐγένετο	γ[ί]γνομαι	aor	mid	ind	3rd	sing	
	ἠγνόησε	ἀγνοέω	aor	act	ind	3rd	sing	
	κατασχεῖν	κατέχω	aor	act	inf			
	δυνησόμενος	δύναμαι	fut	mid	part	masc	sing	nom
	προσεδόκησε	προσδοκέω	aor	act	ind	3rd	sing	
	βιάσασθαι	βιάζω	aor	mid	inf			
	εἶδεν	ὁράω	aor	act	ind	3rd	sing	
	κρατεῖ	κρατέω	pres	act	ind	3rd	sing	
	ἦν	εἰμί	impf	act	ind	3rd	sing	
34	χρὴ	χρή	pres	act	ind	3rd	sing	
	ὁρᾶν	ὁράω	pres	act	inf			
	ἐπιτιθεμένην	ἐπιτίθημι	pres	pass	part	fem	sing	acc
	ἀπειργομένην	ἀπείργω	perf	pass	part	fem	sing	acc
	δυναμένῳ	δύναμαι	pres	mid	part	masc	sing	dat
	πειρωμένῳ	πειράω	pres	mid	part	masc	sing	dat
	συγκεκροτημένης	συγκροτέω	perf	pass	part	fem	sing	gen
	ἦν	εἰμί	impf	act	ind	3rd	sing	
35	βουλομένου	βούλομαι	pres	mid	part	masc	sing	gen
	λαβεῖν	λαμβάνω	aor	act	inf			
	ἀπολῦσαι	ἀπολύω	aor	act	inf			
36	εἴποι	λέγω	aor	act	opt	3rd	sing	
	φρονῶν	φρονέω	pres	act	part	masc	sing	nom
	μωραίνεις	μωραίνω	pres	act	ind	2nd	sing	
	ἐπιχειρεῖς	ἐπιχειρέω	pres	act	ind	2nd	sing	
	κατέχειν	κατέχω	pres	act	inf			
	ἔχει	ἔχω	pres	act	ind	3rd	sing	
	ἐποίησε	ποιέω	aor	act	ind	3rd	sing	
	δύναται	δύναμαι	pres	mid	ind	3rd	sing	
	ἐπαγαγεῖν	ἐπάγω	aor	act	inf			
	ἀμιλλᾶσθαι	ἀμιλλάομαι	pres	mid	inf			
	περινοστήσεις	περινοστέω	fut	act	ind	2nd	sing	
	συναπάξει	συναπάγω	fut	act	ind	3rd	sing	
	πλέουσα	πλέω	pres	act	part	fem	sing	nom
	λήσεις	λανθάνω	fut	act	ind	2md	sing	
	ἐξηρτημένος	ἐξαρτάω	perf	mid	part	masc	sing	nom
	γενόμενος	γί[γ]νομαι	aor	mid	part	masc	sing	nom
37	γεγόνασιν	γί[γ]νομαι	perf	act	ind	3rd	plur	
	διηγήσατο	διηγέομαι	aor	mid	ind	3rd	sing	
	εἷλκέ	ἕλκω	impf	act	ind	3rd	sing	
	ἐνέβαλλε	ἐμβάλλω	impf	act	ind	3rd	sing	
	ἐκόμιζεν	κομίζω	impf	act	ind	3rd	sing	

#	text form	lexicon form	tense	voice	mood	person gender	number	case
	κατέχει	κατέχω	pres	act	ind	3rd	sing	
	ἦν	εἰμί	impf	act	ind	3rd	sing	
	κατεφρόνει	καταφρονέω	impf	act	ind	3rd	sing	
	μάχεσθαι	μάχομαι	pres	mid	inf			
	ἠπίστατο	ἐπίσταμαι	impf	mid	ind	3rd	sing	
	ἀπώλεσεν	ἀπόλλυμι	aor	act	ind	3rd	sing	
38	ἐτύγχανεν	τυγχάνω	impf	act	ind	3rd	sing	
	ἠθέλησε	[ἐ]θέλω	aor	act	ind	3rd	sing	
	ἀφώπλισε	ἀφοπλίζω	aor	act	ind	3rd	sing	
	ἐφόβησεν	φοβέω	aor	act	ind	3rd	sing	
	ἐφύλαξε	φυλάσσω	aor	act	ind	3rd	sing	
	τεθνεώς	[ἀπο]θνήσκω	perf	act	part	masc	sing	nom
	ἐκαρπώσατο	καρπόω	aor	mid	ind	3rd	sing	
39	ἀπέκτεινεν	ἀποκτείνω	aor	act	ind	3rd	sing	
	ἐγένετο	γί[γ]νομαι	aor	mid	ind	3rd	sing	
	ἦλθε	ἔρχομαι	aor	act	ind	3rd	sing	
	ψαῦσαι	ψαύω	aor	act	inf			
	φιλοτιμούμενα	φιλοτιμέομαι	pres	mid	part	neut	plur	nom
	ἐκενώθησαν	κενόω	aor	pass	ind	3rd	plur	
	ἔστη	ἵστημι	aor	act	ind	3rd	sing	
	μαρτυρούμενα	μαρτυρέω	pres	pass	part	neut	plur	nom
	ἀμφισβητοῦντα	αφισβητέω	pres	act	part	neut	plur	nom
	ἀπέκοψεν	ἀποκόπτω	aor	act	ind	3rd	sing	
40	ἐβούλετο	βούλομαι	impf	mid	ind	3rd	sing	
	νικῆσαι	νικάω	aor	act	inf			
	εἶναι	εἰμί	pres	act	inf			
	φεύγοντας	φεύγω	pres	act	part	masc	plur	acc
	ἀναιρεῖ	αναιρέω	pres	act	ind	3rd	sing	
	κατεῖχεν	κατέχω	impf	act	ind	3rd	sing	
	ἔπραττεν	πράσσω	impf	act	ind	3rd	sing	
	ἐποίησεν	ποιέω	aor	act	ind	3rd	sing	
	παρών	πάρειμι	pres	act	part	masc	sing	nom
	φεύγουσιν	φεύγω	pres	act	part	masc	plur	dat
	ἀνεβόα	ἀναβοάω	impf	act	ind	3rd	sing	
	ἐκράτει	κρατέω	impf	act	ind	3rd	sing	
41	ἄφες	ἀφίημι	aor	act	impv	2nd	sing	
	λαμβάνου	λαμβάνω	pres	mid	impv	2nd	sing	
	μένουσιν	μένω	pres	act	ind	3rd	plur	
	λαμβάνῃς	λαμβάνω	pres	act	subj	2nd	sing	
	εὑρ[ήσ]ουσιν	εὑρίσκω	fut	act	ind	3rd	plur	
	κράτει	κρατέω	pres	act	impv	2nd	sing	
	δεδιωγμένην	διώκω	perf	pass	part	fem	sing	acc
	ἔχου	ἔχω	pres	mid	impv	2nd	sing	
	ἀφεψαλωμένης	ἀποψάλλω	perf	pass	part	fem	sing	gen
	ἀφίησιν	ἀφίημι	pres	act	ind	3rd	sing	
	φευγέτω	φεύγω	pres	act	impv	3rd	sing	

#	text form	lexicon form	tense	voice	mood	person gender	number	case
	πάρεστι	πάρειμι	pres	act	ind	3rd	sing	
	κατέχουσι	κατέχω	pres	act	ind	3rd	plur	
	συμφέρει	συμφέρω	pres	act	ind	3rd	sing	
	ἔχω	ἔχω	pres	act	ind	1st	sing	
	κατασχεῖν	κατέχω	aor	act	inf			
	δυνάμενα	δύναμαι	pres	mid	part	neut	plur	
	ἐκπέμπει	ἐκπέμπω	pres	act	ind	3rd	sing	
	ποιεῖς	ποιέω	pres	act	ind	2nd	sing	
	νικήσει	νικάω	fut	act	ind	3rd	sing	
	εἴσεται	οἶδα	fut	mid	ind	3rd	sing	
	ποιῶν	ποιέω	pres	act	part	masc	sing	nom
	εἰργάζετο	ἐργάζομαι	impf	mid	ind	3rd	sing	
42	ἔβλαπτε	βλάπτω	impf	act	ind	3rd	sing	
	εἰρήσεται	εἴρω	fut.per	pass	ind	3rd	sing	
	ἐμαίνετο	μαίνομαι	impf	mid	ind	3rd	sing	
	ὁρῶν	ὁράω	pres	act	part	masc	sing	nom
	εὐδοκιμοῦντα	εὐδοκιμέω	pres	act	part	masc	sing	acc
	ἐπεθύμει	ἐπιθυμέω	impf	act	ind	3rd	sing	
	ἀπολέσαι	ἀπόλλυμι	aor	act	inf			
	γένηται	γί[γ]νομαι	aor	mid	subj	3rd	sing	
	ἐβλάπτομεν	βλάπτω	impf	act	ind	3rd	plur	
43	ἐγένοντο	γί[γ]νομαι	aor	mid	ind	3rd	plur	
	ἐλείφθη	λείπω	aor	pass	ind	3rd	sing	
	εἵλομεν	αἱρέω	aor	act	ind	1st	plur	
	εἶδον	ὁράω	aor	act	ind	3rd	plur	
	ἀνεμαχέσαντο	ἀναμάχομαι	aor	mid	ind	3rd	plur	
	ἐγένετο	γί[γ]νομαι	aor	mid	ind	3rd	sing	
	δράσας	δράω	aor	act	part	masc	sing	nom
	ἀποτμηθεὶς	ἀποτέμνω	aor	pass	part	masc	sing	nom
	ἔπεσεν	πίπτω	aor	act	ind	3rd	sing	
	ἔχων	ἔχω	pres	act	part	masc	sing	nom
	κειμένης	κεῖμαι	pres	mid	part	fem	sing	gen
	ὁρῶντες	ὁράω	pres	act	part	masc	plur	nom
	μένοντα	μένω	pres	act	part	masc	sing	acc
	ᾐδοῦντο	αἰδέομαι	impf	mid	ind	3rd	plur	
	τρέσαντες	τρέω	aor	act	part	masc	plur	nom
	ὑπεχώρουν	ὑποχωρέω	impf	act	ind	3rd	plur	
	ἔπεσεν	πίπτω	aor	act	ind	3rd	sing	
44	εἶναι	εἰμί	pres	act	inf			
	ὑπολαβόντες	ὑπολαμβάνω	aor	act	part	masc	plur	nom
	στεφανώσομεν	στεφανόω	fut	act	ind	1st	plur	
	κείμενον	κεῖμαι	pres	mid	part	masc	sing	acc
	ἐστηκότα	ἵστημι	perf	act	part	masc	sing	acc
	ἐρριμμένον	ῥίπτω	perf	pass	part	masc	sing	acc
	παύσῃ	παύω	fut	mid	ind	2nd	sing	
	παραβάλλων	παραβάλλω	pres	act	part	masc	sing	nom

#	text form	lexicon form	tense	voice	mood	person gender	number	case
	λ[ε]ιπο-τακτήσαντα	λ[ε]ιπο-τακτέω	aor	act	part	masc	sing	acc
	ἠκρωτηριασμένον	ἀκρωτηριάζω	perf	pass	part	masc	sing	acc
	ἀφῆκε	ἀφίημι	aor	act	ind	3rd	sing	
	ἐκράτει	κρατέω	impf	act	ind	3rd	sing	
45	λέγε	λέγω	pres	act	impv	2nd	sing	
	τραγῴδει	τραγῳδέω	pres	act	impv	2nd	sing	
	εἶ	εἰμί	pres	act	ind	2nd	sing	
	ἐποίεις	ποιέω	impf	act	ind	2nd	sing	
	ἐναυμάχεις	ναυμαχέω	impf	act	ind	2nd	sing	
	ἐπεζομάχει	πεζομαχέω	impf	act	ind	3rd	sing	
	κατέσχε	κατέχω	aor	act	ind	3rd	sing	
	ποιεῖ	ποιέω	pres	act	ind	3rd	sing	
	ἐλάβετο	λαμβάνω	aor	mid	ind	3rd	sing	
	ἀπέκοψε	ἀποκόπτω	aor	act	ind	3rd	sing	
	κατέσχε	κατέχω	aor	act	ind	3rd	sing	
	πλέοντας	πλέω	pres	act	part	masc	plur	acc
	ἐξέπλευσαν	ἐκπλέω	aor	act	ind	3rd	plur	
46	περιελθόντες	περιέρχομαι	aor	act	part	masc	plur	nom
	εὑρήσετε	εὑρίσκω	fut	act	ind	2nd	plur	
	ἀποτετμημένας	ἀποτέμνω	perf	pass	part	fem	plur	acc
	ὄψεσθε	ὁράω	fut	mid	ind	2nd	plur	
47	ἐθαύμασα	θαυμάζω	aor	act	ind	1st	sing	
	πεσόντος	πίπτω	aor	act	part	masc	sing	gen
	λαβὼν	λαμβάνω	aor	act	part	masc	sing	voc
	κεκινημένε	κινέω	perf	pass	part	masc	sing	voc
	διελὼν	διαιρέω	aor	act	part	masc	sing	nom
	ἄπεισιν	ἄπειμι (-εἶμι)	pres	act	ind	3rd	sing	
	ἀποθανόντων	ἀποθνήσκω	aor	act	part	masc	plur	gen
	πεσὼν	πίπτω	aor	act	part	masc	sing	voc
	ζηλούμενε	ζηλόω	pres	pass	part	masc	sing	voc
	ἔστης	ἵστημι	aor	act	ind	2nd	sing	
	μαρτυρούμενος	μαρτυρέω	pres	mid	part	masc	sing	nom
	ἀπελθούσης	ἀπέρχομαι	aor	act	part	fem	sing	gen
	ἦσθα	εἰμί	impf	act	ind	2nd	sing	
	μαχομένῳ	μάχομαι	pres	mid	part	masc	sing	dat
48	ὤφθη	ὁράω	aor	pass	ind	3rd	sing	
	ἦν	εἰμί	impf	act	ind	3rd	sing	
	συμβὰν	συμβαίνω	aor	act	part	neut	sing	nom
	εἶναι	εἰμί	pres	act	inf			
	ἐρευνᾶν	ἐρευνάω	pres	act	inf			
	βουλομένῳ	βούλομαι	pres	mid	part	masc	sing	dat
49	ἐγένετο	γί[γ]ομαι	aor	mid	ind	3rd	sing	
	ἐκράτησε	κρατέω	aor	act	ind	3rd	sing	
	τελουμένης	τελέω	pres	pass	part	fem	sing	gen
	γέγονεν	γί[γ]ομαι	perf	act	ind	3rd	sing	

#	text form	lexicon form	tense	voice	mood	person gender	number	case
	ἐντιθεμένων	ἐντίθημι	pres	pass	part	masc	plur	gen
	προσγενομένη	προσγίγνομαι	aor	mid	part	fem	sing	nom
	ἐποίησε	ποιέω	aor	act	ind	3rd	sing	
	δεῖ	δεῖ	pres	act	ind	3rd	sing	
	ἀπομάχεσθαι	ἀπομάχομαι	pres	mid	inf			
	τολμᾶν	τολμάω	pres	act	inf			
	ἐκύρωσεν	κυρόω	aor	act	ind	3rd	sing	
	νομίζοιτο	νομίζω	pres	pass	opt	3rd	sing	
50	ἐστί	εἰμί	pres	act	ind	3rd	sing	
	νικήσομεν	νικάω	fut	act	ind	1st	plur	
	ἦν	εἰμί	impf	act	ind	3rd	sing	
	ὡμολόγησε	ὁμολογέω	aor	act	ind	3rd	sing	
	ἡττήθη	ἡττάομαι	aor	pass	ind	3rd	sing	
	ἐστι	εἰμί	pres	act	ind	3rd	sing	
	ὑπερβαίνει	ὑπερβαίνω	pres	act	ind	3rd	sing	
	εὕροις	εὑρίσκω	aor	act	opt	2nd	sing	
	μεμαχημένον	μάχομαι	perf	mid	part	masc	sing	acc
	καμόντα	κάμνω	aor	act	part	masc	sing	acc
	γενόμενον	γί[γ]νομαι	aor	mid	part	masc	sing	acc
	παρελθόντα	παρέρχομαι	aor	act	part	masc	sing	acc
51	ἐπαινέσειε	ἐπαινέω	aor	act	opt	3rd	sing	
	σκυλεύσας	σκυλεύω	aor	act	part	masc	sing	voc
	κατασχών	κατέχω	aor	act	part	masc	sing	voc
52	περιβεβλημένον	περιβάλλω	perf	pass	part	neut	sing	voc
	ἐνδὺς	ἐνδύω	pres	act	part	masc	sing	voc
	κλίνας	κλίνω	aor	act	part	masc	sing	voc
	μεμαχημένε	μάχομαι	perf	mid	part	masc	sing	voc
	ζώντων	ζάω	pres	act	part	masc	plur	gen
	ἀφείς	ἀφίημι	aor	act	part	masc	sing	voc
53	ζώντων	ζάω	pres	act	part	masc	plur	gen
	εἶχεν	ἔχω	impf	act	ind	3rd	sing	
	πολεμοῦσαν	πολεμέω	pres	act	part	fem	sing	acc
	ἀγωνιζομένην	ἀγωνίζομαι	pres	mid	part	fem	sing	acc
	δείξας	δείκνυμι	aor	act	part	masc	sing	voc
	τρέχοντας	τρέχω	pres	act	part	masc	plur	acc
	ἕλκων	ἕλκω	pres	act	part	masc	sing	voc
	ἔπραξεν	πράσσω	aor	act	ind	3rd	sing	
	θνήσκων	[ἀπο]θνήσκω	pres	act	part	masc	sing	nom
	ὑπερμαχῶν	ὑπερμαχέω	pres	act	part	masc	sing	nom
	ἔστησεν	ἵστημι	aor	act	ind	3rd	sing	
	ἔμεινε	μένω	aor	act	ind	3rd	sing	
	ὡμολόγησε	ὁμολογέω	aor	act	ind	3rd	sing	
54	βαλλόμενος	βάλλω	pres	mid	part	masc	sing	nom
	ἡρπασμένη	ἁρπάζω	perf	pass	part	fem	sing	nom
	πλεῖ	πλέω	pres	act	ind	3rd	sing	
	ἐτέθη	τίθημι	aor	pass	ind	3rd	sing	

#	text form	lexicon form	tense	voice	mood	person gender	number	case
	ἐστι	εἰμί	pres	act	ind	3rd	sing	
	ἐσείσθη	σείω	aor	pass	ind	3rd	sing	
	εἶδον	ὁράω	aor	act	ind	3rd	plur	
	φερομένας	φέρω	pres	pass	part	fem	plur	acc
	διέσεισε	διασείω	aor	act	ind	3rd	sing	
55	ἔστη	ἵστημι	aor	act	ind	3rd	sing	
	ἀπιστούμενος	ἀπιστέω	pres	mid	part	masc	sing	nom
	αἰσχυνόμενος	αἰσχύνομαι	pres	mid	part	masc	sing	nom
	πεσεῖν	πίπτω	aor	act	inf			
	γέγονεν	γί[γ]νομαι	perf	act	ind	3rd	sing	
	τεθνεὼς	[ἀπο]θνῃσκω	perf	act	part	masc	sing	nom
	ὤν	εἰμί	pres	act	part	masc	sing	nom
	βλέπων	βλέπω	pres	act	part	masc	sing	voc
	μιμούμενος	μιμέομαι	pres	mid	part	masc	sing	nom
56	οἶμαι	οἴομαι	pres	mid	ind	1st	sing	
	συμμάχεσθαι	συμμάχομαι	pres	mid	inf			
	παροῦσαν	πάρειμι	pres	act	part	fem	sing	acc
	ἐγγυᾶσθαι	ἐγγυάω	pres	mid	inf			
	ἀνέχειν	ἀνέχω	pres	act	inf			
	κεκοσμημένε	κοσμέω	perf	pass	part	masc	sing	voc
	ἦν	εἰμί	impf	act	ind	3rd	sing	
	ζῶν	ζάω	pres	act	part	masc	sing	nom
	ἔστηκε	ἵστημι	perf	act	ind	3rd	sing	
	βοῶν	βοάω	pres	act	part	masc	sing	nom
	ζηλούμεναι	ζηλόω	pres	pass	part	fem	plur	nom
	ἔστηκα	ἵστημι	perf	act	ind	1st	sing	
	περιμένω	περιμένω	pres	act	ind	1st	sing	
	ἀπόλλυται	ἀπόλλυμι	pres	mid	ind	3rd	sing	
	βαλλόμενος	βάλλω	pres	pass	part	masc	sing	nom
	τοξευόμενος	τοξεύω	pres	pass	part	masc	sing	nom
	στεφανούμενος	στεφανόω	pres	pass	part	masc	sing	nom
	λέγω	λέγω	pres	act	ind	1st	sing	
	βάλλετε	βάλλω	pres	act	ind	2nd	plur	
	φείδεσθε	φείδομαι	pres	mid	impv	2nd	plur	
	βάλλετε	βάλλω	pres	act	ind	2nd	plur	
	δέομαι	δέω	pres	mid	ind	1st	sing	
	χωρεῖ	χωρέω	pres	act	ind	3rd	sing	
	ἔχον	ἔχω	pres	act	part	neut	sing	nom
	περιέστητε	περιίστημι	aor	act	ind	2nd	plur	
	περιτείνατε	περιτείνω	aor	act	impv	2nd	plur	
	θυέτω	θύω	pres	act	impv	3rd	sing	
	δύναται	δύναμαι	pres	mid	ind	3rd	sing	
	σαγηνευσάτω	σαγηνεύω	aor	act	impv	3rd	sing	
	ἔξεστιν	ἔξεστι	pres	act	ind	3rd	sing	
57	ἔπηξεν	ἐπάγω	aor	act	ind	3rd	sing	
	ἔχαιρε	χαίρω	impf	act	ind	3rd	sing	

#	text form	lexicon form	tense	voice	mood	person gender	number	case
	λέγων	λέγω	pres	act	part	masc	sing	nom
	ἀπεδύσαμεν	ἀποδύω	aor	act	ind	1st	plur	
	παρήγγελλε	παραγγέλλω	impf	act	ind	3rd	sing	
	παίετε	παίω	pres	act	impv	2nd	plur	
	κατακεντοῦντες	κατακεντέω	pres	act	part	masc	plur	nom
	φείδεσθε	φείδομαι	pres	mid	impv	2nd	plur	
	ἔχουσι	ἔχω	pres	act	ind	3rd	sing	
	ἐποίησα	ποιέω	aor	act	ind	1st	sing	
58	ἐπειρῶντο	πειράω	impf	mid	ind	3rd	plur	
	ἔβαλλε	βάλλω	impf	act	ind	3rd	sing	
	κινῆσαι	κινέω	aor	act	inf			
	ἠδύνατο	δύναμαι	impf	mid	ind	3rd	sing	
	καθελεῖν	καθαιρέω	aor	act	inf			
	πεπηγότα	πήγνυμι	perf	act	part	masc	sing	acc
	καθελόντες	καθαιρέω	aor	act	part	masc	plur	nom
	βιασάμενοι	βιάζω	aor	mid	part	masc	plur	nom
	ὄντα	εἰμί	pres	act	part	masc	sing	acc
	ἔβαλλε	βάλλω	impf	act	ind	3rd	sing	
	ἐφονεύετο	φονεύω	impf	pass	ind	3rd	sing	
	προσέπιπτεν	προσπίπτω	impf	act	ind	3rd	sing	
	προνενευκότι	προνεύω	perf	act	part	masc	sing	dat
	ἐρείσας	ἐρείδω	aor	act	part	masc	sing	nom
	εἶπε	λέγω	aor	act	impv	2nd	sing	
	στῆθι	ἵστημι	aor	act	impv	2nd	sing	
59	προσβαλόντες	προσβάλλω	aor	act	part	masc	plur	nom
	ἔδρων	δράω	impf	act	ind	3rd	plur	
	ἐκρύπτετο	κρύπτω	impf	pass	ind	3rd	sing	
	κάμνοντες	κάμνω	pres	act	part	masc	plur	nom
	ἀπώλοντο	ἀπόλλυμι	aor	mid	ind	3rd	plur	
	ἔπιπτον	πίπτω	impf	act	ind	3rd	plur	
	ἑστηκότα	ἵστημι	perf	act	part	masc	sing	acc
60	ὁρῶν	ὁράω	pres	act	part	masc	sing	nom
	ὠργίζετο	ὀργίζω	impf	pass	ind	3rd	sing	
	ἐνεκελεύετο	ἐγκελεύω	impf	mid	ind	3rd	sing	
	κλινεῖτε	κλίνω	fut	act	ind	2nd	plur	
	ἀναιρήσετε	ἀναιρέω	fut	act	ind	2nd	plur	
	αἰσχύνῃ	αἰσχύνω	pres	mid	ind	2nd	sing	
	πεσεῖν	πίπτω	aor	act	inf			
	μένεις	μένω	pres	act	ind	2nd	sing	
	μάχῃ	μάχομαι	pres	mid	ind	2nd	sing	
	ἔχεις	ἔχω	pres	act	ind	2nd	sing	
	νικᾷ	νικάω	pres	act	ind	3rd	sing	
	βάλλετε	βάλλω	pres	act	impv	2nd	sing	
	ἀποθνήσκοντες	ἀποθνήσκω	pres	act	part	masc	plur	nom
	γίνονται	γί[γ]νομαι	pres	mid	ind	3rd	plur	
	ἐξηπάτησεν	ἐξαπατάω	aor	act	ind	3rd	sing	

#	text form	lexicon form	tense	voice	mood	person gender	number	case
	ἔπεμψας	πέμπω	aor	act	ind	2nd	sing	
	πεσεῖν	πίπτω	aor	act	inf			
	εἰδότας	οἶδα	perf	act	part	masc	plur	acc
	δοκούμεναι	δοκέω	pres	pass	part	fem	plur	nom
	ἀπρακτοῦσιν	ἀπρακτέω	pres	act	ind	3rd	plur	
	μάχονται	μάχομαι	pres	mid	ind	3rd	plur	
	πολεμοῦσα	πολεμέω	pres	act	part	fem	sing	nom
	ἐγένετο	γί[γ]νομαι	aor	mid	ind	3rd	sing	
61	ἰδὼν	ὁράω	aor	act	part	masc	sing	nom
	περιβεβλημένον	περιβάλλω	perf	pass	part	masc	sing	acc
	ἐβόα	βοάω	impf	act	ind	3rd	sing	
	φεύγωμεν	φεύγω	pres	act	subj	1st	plur	
	πλέωμεν	πλέω	pres	act	subj	1st	plur	
	ἤγειραν	ἐγείρω	aor	act	ind	3rd	plur	
	παρέσχες	παρέχω	aor	act	ind	2nd	sing	
62	ἐβοήθησας	βοηθέω	aor	act	ind	2nd	sing	
	συνεκρότησας	συγκροτέω	aor	act	ind	2nd	sing	
	ὑπερήσπισας	ὑπερασπίζω	aor	act	ind	2nd	sing	
	ὡπλισμένη	ὁπλίζω	perf	pass	part	fem	sing	nom
	ἔστη	ἵστημι	aor	act	ind	3rd	sing	
	σεμνυνόμενος	σεμνύνω	pres	pass	part	masc	sing	nom
	χρὴ	χρή	pres	act	ind	3rd	sing	
	προτιμᾶσθαι	προτιμάω	aor	mid	inf			
	κειμένων	κεῖμαι	pres	mid	part	masc	plur	gen
	ἀγορεύειν	ἀγορεύω	pres	act	inf			
	ἁρμόττει	ἁρμόζω	pres	act	ind	3rd	sing	
63	ἀπελθὼν	ἀπέρχομαι	aor	act	part	masc	sing	nom
	πεπατημένον	πατέω	perf	pass	part	masc	sing	acc
	θάπτε	θάπτω	pres	act	impv	2nd	sing	
	ἀπέκοψε	ἀποκόπτω	aor	act	ind	3rd	sing	
	ἔτεμεν	τέμνω	aor	act	ind	3rd	sing	
	ὑπάρχουσαν	ὑπάρχω	pres	act	part	fem	sing	acc
	οὖσαν	εἰμί	pres	act	part	fem	sing	acc
	ἀπέκοψεν	ἀποκόπτω	aor	act	ind	3rd	sing	
	ἐπέσχε	ἐπέχω	aor	act	ind	3rd	sing	
	οὖσαν	εἰμί	pres	act	part	fem	sing	acc
	ἔμειναν	μένω	aor	act	ind	3rd	plur	
	ἐχόμεναι	ἔχω	pres	pass	part	fem	plur	nom
	ἀπεκρούσθη	ἀποκρούω	aor	pass	ind	3rd	sing	
	κατασχοῦσα	κατέχω	aor	act	part	fem	sing	nom
64	ἐπιστώσω	πιστόω	aor	mid	ind	2nd	sing	
	ἐσμεν	εἰμί	pres	act	ind	1st	plur	
	ἀνέσχε	ἀνέχω	aor	act	ind	3rd	sing	
	προέσθαι	προίημι	aor	mid	inf			
65	εἴη	εἰμί	pres	act	opt	3rd	sing	
	κοσμεῖν	κοσμέω	pres	act	inf			

#	text form	lexicon form	tense	voice	mood	person gender	number	case
65	τραγῳδεῖν	τραγῳδέω	pres	act	inf			
	θρήνει	θρηνέω	pres	act	impv	2nd	sing	
	συγχωρούντων	συγχωρέω	pres	act	part	masc	plur	gen

Appendix 2: Analysis of the Conditions

No hypotactic clause in Greek is more important than the conditional sentence. While the recognition of the conditions and their nuances is a *sine qua non* for understanding any Greek text, such sentences are in many cases often not immediately clear. Hence, all the conditional sentences found in the declamations are registered in the following list. The conditions – cited in the order of their appearance — are noted according to their basic component elements: protasis (conjunction [εἰ / ἐάν] + verb) and apodosis (particle [ἄν] + verb). Each condition is classified in terms of time and type.

This schematic analysis of the conditions is intended to provide on the one hand an elucidation of the syntax of individual sentences and on the other hand to give an overview of the full grammatical repertoire which Polemo utilizes.

487

#	Protasis	Apodosis	Time	Type
A				
3	ὅστις ἄν [ ] (subj?) *in place of* [ἐάν τις]	διαθήσεται (fut ind)	future	more vivid
3	ἂν εἴπῃ (subj)	ἐστίν (pres ind)	present	general
3	εἰ μή [ ] (ind?)	συγκινδυνεύουσιν (pres ind)	present	simple
4	λεγόμενα (pres part) *in place of* [ἐὰν λέγῃ] (subj)	ἔσται (fut ind)	future	more vivid
14	λαχών (aor part) *in place of* [εἰ ἔλαχε] (aor ind)	ἂν ἐπολεμάρχησε (aor ind)	past	unreal
15	εἰ ἦν (impf ind)	ἂν ἐδέδοκτο (pluperf ind)	past	unreal
15	ἂν ᾖ (subj)	εἶναι (pres inf) *in place of* [ἐστί] (pres ind)	present	general
15	ὅστις ἔχει (pres ind) *in place of* [εἴ τις ἔχει] (pres ind)	[ ] (pres ind?)	present	simple
19	γενομένῳ (aor part) *in place of* [εἰ ἐγένετο] (aor ind) *or* [εἰ γένοιτο] (opt)	ἦν	past *or* past	simple *or* general
20	εἰ ἐτόλμησεν (aor ind)	[ἦν ?] (impf ind)	past	simple
26	εἰ δεῖ (pres ind)	ἐστί (pres ind)	present	simple
27	ὁ ἐπαινῶν (pres part) *in place of* [εἰ τις ἐπαινεῖ] (pres ind) *or* [ἐάν τις ἐπαινῇ] (subj)	ἐπαινεῖ (pres ind)	present *or* present	simple *or* general

#	Protasis	Apodosis	Time	Type
29	εἰ ἐγένοντο (aor ind)	ἂν κατέχωσαν (aor ind)	past	unreal
		ἂν εἶχον (impf ind)	past	unreal
29	εἰ ἐμιμήσατο (aor ind)	ἂν ἔδοσαν (aor ind)	past	unreal
		ἂν ἔσχε (aor ind)	past	unreal
		ἂν εἴχομεν (impf ind)	past	unreal
31	εἰ [ἐκάλυψαν] (aor ind)	ἐκάλυψαν (aor ind)	past	simple
39	εἰ εἴχομεν (impf ind)	ἂν ἐξῆλθον (aor ind)	past	unreal
		ὑπεδέξαντο (aor ind)	past	unreal
		ἐστεφάνωσαν (aor ind)	past	unreal
43	κοπτομένων (pres part)	μέλει (pres ind)		
	in place of			
	[εἰ κόπτονται] (pres ind)		present	simple
	or		*or*	
	[ἐὰν κόπτωνται] (subj)		present	general

#	Protasis	Apodosis	Time	Type
B				
1	εἰ κρίνεται (pres ind)	δείξω (fut ind)	future	most vivid?
2	εἰ ἡττηθήσεται (fut ind)	ὑβριεῖται (fut ind)	future	most vivid
18	εἰ ἠμφισβήτουν (impf ind)	ἂν διεκρίθη (aor ind)	past	unreal
18		[ἂν] ἐπήνεσε (aor ind)	past	unreal
18	εἰ παράσχῃ (aor subj)	ἂν δῶτε (aor subj)	future?	?
19	εἴπερ ἦσαν (impf ind)	[ἂν] ἔσχε (aor ind)	past	unreal
19	περιών (pres part) *in place of* [εἰ περιῆν] (impf ind)	[ἂν] ἦν (impf ind)	present	unreal
19	προτιμωμένου (pres part) *in place of* [ἐὰν προτίμωμαι] (subj)	ὑπάρξει (fut ind)	future	more vivid
19	εἰ ἔσται (fut ind)	τεύξεται (fut ind)	future	most vivid
19	ἐπομένῳ (pres part) *in place of* [ἐὰν ἔπηται] (subj)	ἔσται (fut ind)	future	more vivid
21	εἰ ἠμφισβήτει (impf ind)	[ἂν] παρεχώρησα (aor ind)	past	unreal
21	ἀφεστηκότος (perf part) *in place of* [εἰ ἔστηκε] (perf ind)	ἐστιν (pres ind)	present	simple
22	εἰ τύχοι (opt) [τύχῃ ?] (subj)	ἐστιν (pres ind)	present	general?
29	γενομένων (aor part) *in place of* [εἰ γένοιτο] (opt)	ἂν εἴη (opt)	future	less vivid
30	ὁρῶν (pres part) *in place of* εἰ ὁρῴη or ὁρῷ (opt) *or possibly* εἰ ὥρα (impf ind)	ἠμέλει (impf ind)	past *or* past	general *or* simple

#	Protasis	Apodosis	Time	Type
33	εἰ ἠγνόησε (aor ind) προσεδόκησε (aor ind)	ἂν ἐγένετο (aor ind)	past	unreal
33	εἰ εἶδεν (aor ind)	ἦν (impf ind)	past	simple
34	εἰ [ἐστί] (pres ind)	χρή (pres ind)	present	simple
40	παρών (pres part) *in place of* [εἰ παρῆν] (impf ind)	ἂν ἐποίησεν (aor ind)	past	unreal
41	ἂν λαμβάνῃς (subj)	μένουσιν (pres ind) (= fut ind ?) εὑρήσουσιν (fut ind)	present future future	general more vivid more vivid
43	εἰ ἐγένοντο (aor ind)	ἂν ἐλείφθη (aor ind) ἂν εἵλομεν (aor ind)	past past	unreal unreal
43	εἰ εἶδον (aor ind)	ἂν ἀνεμαχέσαντο (aor ind)	past	unreal
44	ὑπολαβόντες (aor part) *in place of* [ἐὰν ὑπολάβωμεν] (subj)	στεφαμώσομεν (fut ind)	future	more vivid
46	περιελθόντες (aor part) *in place of* [ἐὰν περιέλθητε] (subj)	εὑρήσετε (fut ind)	future	more vivid
56	εἰ δύναται (pres ind)	θυέτω (pres impv)	present	simple
56	εἰ ἔξεστιν (pres ind)	σαγηνευσάτω (aor impv)	present	simple
60	ἀποθνήσκοντες (pres part) *in place of* [ἐάν/ὅταν ἀποθνήσκωσιν] (subj) *or* [εἴ/ὅτε ἀποθνήσκουσιν] (ind)	γίνονται (pres ind) *or*	present *or* present	general simple
65	συγχωρούντων (pres part) *in place of* [εἰ συγχωροῦσιν] (pres ind)	θρήνει (pres impv)	present	simple

Appendix 3: Analysis of the ὦ Exclamations

Exclamations introduced by the interjection ὦ are unusually frequent in Polemo's declamations (over 90 occurrences). It will be fair to say that they are a distinguishing feature of his style. Notably, in a third of the cases the vocative, that ordinarily would be expected to follow the ὦ, is missing. Its absence sometimes impedes the initial understanding and obstructs a precise translation.

The following comprehensive list of all the exclamations is presented to show Polemo's range of syntactical constructions and thus, by means of the analogies, to suggest possibilities for understanding the elipses.

493

##	ὦ	Vocative	Qualifiers
		Proper Name	
A 43	ὦ	Κυναίγειρε	
B 37	ὦ	Εὐφορίων	
B 41	ὦ	Κυναίγειρε	
B 41	ὦ	Κυναίγειρε	
B 62	ὦ	Πάν	
B 65	ὦ	Εὐφορίων	
		Noun	
A 31	ὦ	τέκνον	
A 37	ὦ	παῖ	
A 38	ὦ	παῖ	
A 39	ὦ	παῖ	
A 40	ὦ	τέκνον	
A 41	ὦ	θεοί	
A 44	ὦ	παῖ	
A 44	ὦ	παῖ	
A 44	ὦ	παῖ	
B 14	ὦ	τέκνον	
B 48	ὦ	παῖ	
B 62	ὦ	τέκνον	
		Names/Nouns in Apposition	
A 47	ὦ	ἄνδρες δικασταί	
A 49	ὦ	Αἴσχυλε παῖ	
B 47	ὦ	Καλλίμαχε τέκνον	
B 60	ὦ	δέσποτα Δαρεῖε	
		Noun	**+ Adjective (in pre-position)**
A 35	ὦ	δεξιά	ἡδεῖα
A 37	ὦ	θαῦμα	μέγα
B 54	ὦ	στάσις	μεγάλη
		Noun	**+ Adjective (in post-position)**
A 34	ὦ	χεῖρες	Μαραθώνιαι
B 12	ὦ	φρόνημα	ὀρθόν
B 12	ὦ	σῶμα	ἔμψυχον
B 52	ὦ	σχῆμα	ἐλευθέριον
B 52	ὦ	σχῆμα	Μαραθώνιον
B 54	ὦ	φυτὸν	Μαραθώνιον

##	ὦ	Vocative	Qualifiers
		Noun	**+ Adjectival Phrase**
A 34	-	χεῖρες	φίλταται κἂν ταῖσδε ταῖς ἐμαῖς χερσὶ τεθραμμέναι
A 35	ὦ	δεξιὰ	βιαιοτέρα πνευμάτων
A 35	ὦ	χεῖρ	κρείττων ῥοθίου βαρβαρικοῦ
A 35	ὦ	θέαμα	τῶν θεῶν ἄξιον
A 37	ὦ	δεξιὰ	ψυχῆς ἰδίας ἀξία
B 12	ὦ	ἀρετὴ	πιστότερα τοῦ πνεύματος
B 12	ὦ	σῶμα	πολλῶν ψυχῶν ἰσόρροπον
B 52	ὦ	κατόρθωμα	κοινὸν καὶ ζώντων καὶ νεκρῶν
B 53	ὦ	φρόνημα	πλεὸν τοῦ βίου
B 53	ὦ	[νεκρὲ]	ζώντων μαχιμώτερε
B 62	ὦ	θέαμα	τῶν συμμάχων θεῶν ἄξιον

		Noun	**+ Attributive Participial Phrase**
A 38	ὦ	παῖ	μείζω τῆς φύσεως βεβουλημένε
B 12	ὦ	σῶμα	νικηφόρον ὅπλοις καὶ βέλεσι κεκοσμημένον
B 52	-	δεινὸν εἴδωλον	τῆς Ἀσιας τὰ τοξεύματα περιβεβλημένον

		Noun	**+ Adjective + Genitive**
A 37	ὦ	νόημα	καινὸν	σώματος
B 12	ὦ	τρόπαιον	πρῶτον	Μαραθῶνος
B 51	ὦ	σκοπὲ	κοινὲ	τῆς Ἀσίας
B 51	ὦ	ἀνάθημα	σεμνὸν	πολέμου
B 52	ὦ	ἄγαλμα	καλὸν	Ἄρεως
B 56	ὦ	δοῦλοι	βάρβαροι	Δαρείου
B 62	ὦ	τέρας	σεμνὸν	πολέμου

		Noun	**+ Genitive**
A 32	ὦ	πάτερ	Καλλιμάχου
A 34	ὦ	σωτῆρες	τῆς πάσης Ἑλλάδος
A 34	ὦ	πρόμαχοι	τῶν Ἀθηναίων
A 34	ὦ	δόξα	Μαραθῶνος
A 35	ὦ	[τρόφιμε]	τῆς παρούσης Ἀθηνᾶς
A 45	ὦ	πάτερ	Καλλιμάχου
B 52	ὦ	πολέμαρχε	πολεμάρχου θεοῦ
B 55	ὦ	τεῖχος	Ἀττικῆς ἀρετῆς

##	ὦ	Vocative	Qualifiers
		Noun omitted, to be supplied from context	+ Adjective or + Adjectival Phrase
A 34	ὦ	[χεῖρες]	κρείττονες τῶν στρατιωτῶν ὅλων
A 35	ὦ	[ἆθλε]	σύντιμε τοῖς Ἡρακλέους ἄθλοις καὶ Θησέως
A 40	ὦ	[?]	κακοδαίμονες (virtually substantized)
B 12	ὦ	[ἀρετή]	μακροτέρα τῆς ψυχῆς
B 35	ὦ	[χεῖρ]	[κρείττων] στολαγωγοῦ καὶ μακροτέρας βελῶν δεξιᾶς
B 51	ὦ	[?]	καλλίμαχε καὶ καλλίνικε
B 51	-	[?]	ἄτρωτε καὶ πολύτρωτε
B 52	ὦ	[?]	περισσότερε τῆς φύσεως
B 54	ὦ	[?]	τῇ γῇ σύμψυχε
B 54	ὦ	[?]	δήμων βεβαιότερε καὶ νήσων πρότερε
B 55	ὦ	[θαῦμα]	μέγιστον τῶν Μαραθωνίων θαυμάτων καὶ θειότατον
B 55	ὦ	[φάσμα]	τῶν ἐκεῖ φασμάτων ἐξαίρετον
B 56	ὦ	[?]	πάντες

		Noun omitted, instead: Substantized(?) Active or Middle Participle	+ Accusative Object Phrase
A 38	ὦ	[παῖ ?] ποιήσας	θρασύτερα τὰ μέλη τοῦ σώματος
A 38	ὦ	[παῖ ?] ὁ περινοήσας	ἄγειν ναῦν Ἀθηναίοις αἰμάλωτον
B 12	ὦ	[σὺ ?] τηρήσας	ὀρθὴν τὴν ἐλευθερίαν Ἀθηναίοις
B 12	ὦ	[σὺ ?] στήσας	ἐν αὐτῷ τὴν Ἑλλάδα
B 47	ὦ	[?] λαβών	πολλὰ τοιαῦτα τραύματα
B 47	ὦ	μόνε [?] τῶν ἀποθανόντων οὐ πεσών	
B 51	ὦ	[?] σκυλεύσας	τῷ θανάτῳ τὴν στρατιὰν βασιλέως
B 51	-	[?] κατασχών	πλεῖστα λάφυρα τῶν βαρβάρων τὰ βέλη
B 52	ὦ	[?] μὴ κλίνας	τὴν Ἑλλάδα
B 54	ὦ	[?] μεμαχημένε	δύο μεγάλας μάχας Δαρείῳ καὶ θανάτῳ
B 52	ὦ	[?] μὴ ἀφεὶς	μετὰ ζωῆς τὴν ἀρετὴν
B 53	ὦ	πρῶτος [ ] ἀνθρώπων δείξας	νεκροῦ μάχην
B 53	ὦ	[?] ἕλκων	θανάτῳ τοὺς πρὸς βίον τρέχοντας ἐπὶ διαδικασίαν
B 54	ὦ	[?] βαλλόμενος	ρίζας ἐξ ἀρετῆς
B 55	ὦ	[?] βλέπων ἢ μιμούμενος	τῆς ψυχῆς τὴν ὁδόν

##	ὦ	Vocative	Qualifiers
		Noun omitted, to be supplied from context	**+ Passive Participial Phrase**
B 47	-	[λαβὼν ?]	μὴ κεκινημένε
B 47	ὦ	μόνε [ ] τῶν ἀποθανόντων	μόνε μὴ ζηλούμενε
B 56	ὦ	[?]	μεγάλῳ φάσματι κεκοσμημένε
		Noun omitted, to be supplied from context	**+ Genitive**
A 33	ὦ	[?]	τοῦ μεγάλου θαύματος
A 39	ὦ	[παῖ ?]	δεινῆς μάχης Παναθήναια μεμιμημένης
A 40	ὦ	[?]	τῆς τολμηρίας
A 40	ὦ	[?]	μαινομένης δεξιᾶς
A 40	ὦ	[?]	τοῦ μεγάλου λήματος
B 12	ὦ	[ἀρετή]	Καλλιμάχου καὶ φοβεροῦ νεκροῦ
B 12	ὦ	[ἀρετή]	στρατιώτου τῆς εἱμαρμένης πολυχρονιωτέρου
B 48	ὦ	[?]	τοῦ μεγάλου θαύματος

Index 4: Comparatives and Superlatives

Synkrisis is an essential element in Polemo's rhetoric. Comparatives and superlatives are found in his declamations in the full range of irregular (-[ι]ων / -ιστος) and regular (-τερος / -τατος) forms. These adjectives also appear in a wide spectrum of syntactical connections. The following comprehensive list, categorized by endings and arranged alphabetically, is presented both to help clarify individual passages and to provide an overview of this facet of Polemo's argumentation technique.

Positive	Comparative	##	Superlative	##
ἀγαθός			ἄριστος	0; B 53
ἀγαθός	βελτίων	A 15		
ἀγαθός	κρείσσων/-ττ-	A 2, 4, 35; B 4, 19, 45	κράτιστος	[B 29?]
κρατύς	κρείσσων/-ττ-	A 34, 35; B 2, 8	κράτιστος	B 26, [29?]
καλός			κάλλιστος	A 26, 45
μάλα	μᾶλλον	A 12; B 2, 41, 47	μάλιστα	A 1; B 49, 50
μέγας	μείζων	A 16, 29, 38; B 21, 32	μέγιστος	A 14, 16; B 2, 53, 55
ὀλίγος	ἐλάσσων/-ττ-	A 20; B 21, 24		
πολύς	πλείων	A 2, 20, 20, 20, 21; B 18, 21, 53, 59	πλεῖστος	A 3, 8, 11, 51
ταχύς	θάσσων/-ττ-	A 11, 41	τάχιστος	B 5

Positive	Comparative	##	Superlative	##
ἀκμαῖος			ἀκμαιότατος	B 8
ἀκρατής	ἀκρατέστερος	B 63		
ἀξιόλογος			ἀξιολογώτατος	A 1
ἄπωθεν	ἀπώτερω	A 16		
ἄτιμος	ἀτιμότερος	B 17		
βέβαιος	βεβαιότερος	B 54, 54		
βίαιος	βιαιότερος	A 35		
[γενναῖος]	[γενναιότερος]	[A 23]		
δίκαιος	δικαιότερος	A 2, 4, 15		
[δύο ?]	δεύτερος	A 2, 22; B 17, 28, 40, 53		
ἔνδικος	ἐνδικώτερος	A 24		
ἐπιτήδειος	ἐπιτηδειότερος	A 47		
θαυμάσιος	θαυμασιώτερος	A 23		
θαυμαστός			θαυμαστότατος	A 6
θεῖος			θειότατος	B 55
θερμός			θερμότατος	B 6
θρασύς	θρασύτερος	A 38		
ἴδιος	ἰδιώτερος	A 24		
κύριος	κυριώτερος	A 23		
λαμπρός	λαμπρότερος	B 54		
μακρός	μακρότερος	A 35; B 1, 12		
μάχιμος	μαχιμώτερος	A 31; B 53, 60	μαχιμώτατος	A 8
νέος	νεώτερος	B 24		
ὀκνηρός	ὀκνηρότερος	A 30		
ὀνομαστός			ὀνομαστότατος	A 47
περισσός/-ττ-	περισσότερος/-ττ	B 50, 52		
πιστός	πιστότερος	B 12		
πολυχρόνιος	πολυχρονιώτερος	B 12		
πρέσβυς	πρεσβύτερος	A 20; B 19, 24	πρεσβύτατος	B 29
πρό	πρότερος	A 22, 25; B 18, 21, 21, 28, 29, 34	πρῶτος	A 8,18,21,32, 36,36,36,36, 37; B 12,16, 19,29,48,53, 55,56,64,65
πρότιμος	προτιμότερος	A 23		
στάσιμος	στασιμώτερος	B 54		
φανερός	φανερώτερος	A 4		
φίλος			φίλτατος	A 34
ὠφέλιμος	ὠφελιμότερος	A 23		

Index 5: Alpha-Privatives

The use of the alpha-privative, particularly in *litotes* (through the negation of the alpha-privative) and in pleonastic expressions, is characteristic of Polemo's rhetorical style. The following list is presented to provide an overview of this Polemonic feature and to facilitate comparisons with other authors regarding this phenomenon.

α-Privative	Root	Affirmed	Negated (+ *οὐ* / *μή*)
ἄβατος	βα	B 13, 40	
ἀγεννής	γεν		A 43
ἀγνοέω	γνο/γνω	B 33	
ἀδάμας	δαμ	B 10	
ἀδεῶς	δϝι	A 8	
ἄδηλος	δηλ	B 48	
ἀδύνατος	δυν	A 26; B 11, 33, 33, 33	
ἀθανασία	θαν	B 11	
ἀθάνατος	θαν	A 31; B 48, 53, 60	
ἄκαιρος	καιρ		B 29
ἀκίνητος	κιν	B 54, 58	
ἀκλινής	κλι[ν]	A 33	
ἀκόρεστος	κορ	B 56	
ἀκρατής	κρα[τ]	B 63	
ἄκων	ἐκ	A 24; B 43	B 42
ἀμελέω	μελ	A 20; B 30	
ἀμήχανος	μηχαν	B 33	
ἀναίσθητος	αἰσθ	A 25	
ἀνανταγώνιστος	αντ-αγων	B 50	
ἀνείκαστος	εἰκ	B 50	
ἀνόητος	νο	B 33, 35	B 33
ἀνοία	νο	B 42	
ἀόριστος	ὁρ	B 50	
ἄπειρος	πειρ	A 20	
ἀπέραντος	περ	B 35	
ἀπιστέω	πιθ	B 55	
ἄπορος	πορ	B 33, 35, 41	
ἀπρακτέω	πραγ	B 60	
ἄπρακτος	πραγ	A 41	
ἀργός	ϝεργ	A 26	
ἄρρηκτος	ρηγ	B 10	
ἀσάλευτος	σαλ	A 37	
ἀσθένεια	σθεν	B 13	
ἀστάθμητος	στα	B 27	
ἀτιμάω	τι[μ]		A 49
ἄτιμος	τι[μ]		B 17
ἄτρωτος	τρω	B 51	
ἀφανής	φα[ν]	B 56	
ἀφανῶς	φα[ν]	A 19	
ἄφρων	φρεν	B 35	
ἄχρηστος	χρα	B 35	
ἄψυχος	ψυχ	B 11	

α-Privatives possibly no longer felt as such by Polemo

ἀδαμάντινος	δαμ	A 43	
ἄδεια	δϝι	B 27	
ἀληθής	λαθ	A 26; B 42	
ἀληθῶς	λαθ	B 64	
ἀσφαλής	σφαλ		B 33

Index 6: Analysis of the Prepositions

In Greek the prepositions constitute the central means for expressing substantival relationships. In Polemo's declamations the entire range of proper prepositions is represented, though not every available case construction is utilized. The use of improper prepositions, however, is quite sparse. Other than that Polemo's use of prepositions, both with cases and in compounds, exhibits nothing unusual. His practice corresponds to the standard Attic idiom.

From the following comprehensive list of preposition occurrences in the declamations one may control the English translation and the interpretation by making quick comparisons with analogous constructions. The overview may also facilitate comparisons of Polemo's language and idiom with that of other authors.

prepo- sition	+ case or as prefix	##
ἀμφί	+ verb	A 16; B 18, 21, 39
	+ adj	A 25; B 19
ἀνά	+ verb	A 15, 23, 24, 27, 29, 29, 30, 35, 35, 43 B 8, 15, 17, 20, 30, 32, 40, 43, 48, 56, 60, 64
	+ noun	B 23, 51
	+ adv	A 41
ἀντί	+ gen	A 33
	+ verb	A 21, 43; B 8
	+ adj	A 31, 36; B 10, 27, 50
ἀπό	+ gen	A 16, 16; B 19
	+ verb	A 4, 10, 11, 11, 21, 22, 28, 28, 31, 36, 36, 36, 38, 38, 38, 40, 41, 42, 43, 46, 49, 49 B 3, 5, 11, 11, 13, 13, 14, 17, 21, 25, 34, 35, 36, 37, 38, 39, 39, 41, 41, 41, 41, 41, 42, 43, 44, 45, 46, 47, 47, 47, 49, 52, 56, 57, 59, 60, 63, 63, 63, 63
	+ noun	A 5, 23
	+ adj	A 16, 20; B 26
διά	+ gen	A 21, 38, 41, 41; B 11, 19, 23, 42, 49, 53
	+ acc	A 7, 12, 35; B 1, 19, 30, 38, 41
	+ verb	A 3, 16, 33, 42, 49; B 11, 18, 37, 47, 54
	+ noun	B 42
ἐς εἰς	+ acc + acc	A 30 0; A 5, 22, 24, 29, 41 B 5, 9, 11, 13, 15, 22, 23, 23, 23, 25, 26, 43, 46
	+ verb	A 15
ἐν	+ dat	A 0, 6, 7, 7, 21, 22, 25, 27, 27, 28, 28, 36, 38, 42 B 6, 7, 9, 11, 12, 17, 19, 20, 25, 25, 26, 27, 27, 31, 33, 40, 43, 50, 50, 54, 55, 56, 63
	+ verb	A 20, 23, 27; B 11, 23, 26, 37, 49, 52, 56, 60
	+ noun	A 45; B 8, 16
	+ adj	A 24; B 21, 55
ἐκ, ἐξ	+ gen	A 1, 8, 14, 14, 20, 23, 23, 24, 24, 35, 43, 44 B 5, 10, 23, 24, 25, 27, 27, 28, 31, 31, 31, 31, 41, 45, 45, 54, 56,
	+ verb	A 7, 8, 18, 19, 20, 21, 39 B 5, 8, 8, 8, 11, 11, 11, 27, 36, 41, 45, 56, 60
	+ noun	A 22, 30
	+ adj	B 55
	+ adv	A 30

prepo-sition	+ case or as prefix	##
ἐπί	+ gen	A 29; B 2, 14
	+ dat	A 1, 3, 3, 3, 17, 27, 28, 47;
		B 15, 16, 19, 29, 37, 57, 62, 64
	+ acc	A 11, 16, 23, 23, 41, 43, 43, 44
		B 13, 15, 20?, 22, 39, 53, 60
	+ verb	A 2,8, 8, 9, 9, 10, 16, 24, 24, 27, 27, 28, 28, 33,
		40, 41, 46, 49; B 1, 7, 9, 14, 16, 18, 22, 25,
		26, 27, 28, 31, 32, 34, 36, 36, 42, 51, 57, 63
	+ noun	A 3, 25, 36, 44; B 29, 29, 33, 33, 33, 34, 35, 38
	+ adj	A 0, 15, 46, 47, 47, 48, 48; B 15, 34, 65, 65
κατά	+ gen	A 9; B 38
	+ acc	A 1, 10, 32, 33; B 6, 8, 8, 8, 16, 24, 43, 51,
	+ verb	A 7, 10, 11, 22, 29, 31, 35, 37; B 9, 17, 28, 33
		36, 37, 40, 41, 41, 44, 45, 45, 51, 57, 58, 58, 63
	+ noun	B 31, 49, 52
	+ adv	A 10, 30, 58
μετά	+ gen	A 26, 29; B 42, 42, 52, 53, 60
	+ acc	A 25; B 5, 50
	+ verb	A 5, 16
	+ adj	B 65
παρά	+ gen	A 11, 25; B 16, 16, 41
	+ dat	B 17, 19, 60
	+ verb	A 13, 13, 14, 16, 19, 27, 35, 35, 43, 46, 47, 48
		B 2, 6, 8, 15, 15, 18, 18, 18, 21, 21, 25, 28, 28,
		29, 32, 32, 40, 41, 41, 44, 50, 56, 57, 61
	+ noun	B 23, 32
	+ adj	A 23, 26, 29; B 36, 49
περί	+ gen	A 46; B 39
	+ acc	A 24, 42; B 13, 13, 33, 39, 62
	+ verb	A 6, 7, 20, 22, 30, 38; B 5, 13, 18, 19, 19, 19,
		22, 46, 52, 56, 56, 56, 61
	+ noun	A 20; B 49, 59
	+ adj	B 26, 50, 52
πρό	+ gen	A 5
	+ verb	A 22, 44, 49; B 8, 15, 19, 19, 19, 58, 62, 64
	+ noun	A 18, 24, 24, 30, 34; B 1, 19, 22
	+ adj	A 23, 25; B 18, 21, 21, 27, 28, 29, 34, 53, 54, 56, 65

prepo- sition	+ case or as prefix	##
πρός	+ dat	A 30
	+ acc	A 8, 23, 40, 40, 41, 47; B 8, 8, 11, 20, 23, 30, 30, 31, 31, 31, 32, 32, 41, 50, 50, 53, 57, 58, 58
	+ verb	A 1, 12; B 33, 49, 58, 59
	+ noun	B 10; B 33, 35
	+ adj	B 1
σύν	+ dat	B 15
	+ verb	A 1, 3, 4, 24, 24, 25, 27, 44, 49 B 7, 8, 17, 26, 31, 34, 36, 41, 48, 56, 62, 65
	+ noun	A 24; B 23, 49, 57
	+ adj	A 2, 20, 35; B 41, 43, 54, 62
ὑπέρ	+ gen	A 25, 44, 44, 49; B 3, 8, 64, 64
	+ verb	A 8; B 24, 30, 50, 53, 62
ὑπό	+ gen	A 5, 7, 12, 18, 30, 30, 37, 41, 47 B 8, 26, 32, 47, 59, 59, 63
	+ verb	A 39, 40; B 3, 10, 10, 19, 26, 43, 44, 63

im- proper prepo- sition		
ἀνεύ	+ gen	A 11, 11; B 46
μέχρι	+ gen	A 21; B 44?, 50, 50
χάριν	+ gen	A 3
χωρίς	+ gen	B 2

Index 7: The Proper Names

The following comprehensive list of proper names (nouns and adverbs) — divided by categories and arranged alphabetically — provides a ready overview of the historical and mythological references in the declamations. It gives a sense of the relative importance of each name in the speeches and it can be useful for relating the declamations to other treatments of the Marathon traditions.

Deities	##
Ἄρης	B 52
Ἀθηνᾶ	A 35, 36; B 41
Βριάρεως	A 43
Γλαῦκος	B 36
Δημήτηρ	A 35; B 41
Ζεύς	B 18
Ἥρα	B 62
Κόρη	A 35; B 41
Παλλάς	B 62
Πάν	A 35; B 41, 62
Ποσειδῶν	B 36
Τρίτων	B 36

Heroes

Ἡρακλῆς	A 35; B 41, 62, 64
Θησεύς	A 35; B 41, 62

Men

Αἰσχύλος	A 49; B 45, 51
Δάρειος	B 5, 8, 52, 56, 60
Δᾶτις	A 41; B 14, 45, 56, 60
Εὐφορίων	B 22, 37, 63, 65
Καλλίμαχος	0, 0; A 2, 2, 5, 7, 19, 20, 21, 22, 22, 23, 23, 24, 26, 26, 27, 28, 29, 30, 30, 31, 32, 37, 45, 47 B 1, 1, 2, 2, 4, 7, 9, 9, 9, 11, 12, 17, 19, 20, 21, 23, 23, 23, 24, 25, 26, 27, 28, 28, 28, 30, 31, 32, 32, 32, 32, 38, 39, 39, 40, 42, 43, 46, 47, 50, 50, 53, 54, 56, 58, 58, 59, 64
Κυναίγειρος	0, 0; A 1, 1, 2, 3, 3, 3, 4, 5, 8, 10, 10, 10, 11, 11, 11, 19, 20, 21, 22, 22, 23, 23, 24, 24, 25, 26, 26, 28, 29, 32, 32, 36, 43, 43, 45, 46, 49 B 2, 4, 7, 13, 19, 23, 23, 24, 26, 27, 28, 28, 30, 31, 32, 32, 36, 39, 40, 41, 41, 41, 41, 43, 43, 46, 47, 50, 50, 63
Μιλτιάδης	A 16; B 5, 20, 21
Ὅμηρος	B 37, 51
Πολύζηλος	A 44; B 56
Τισσαφέρνης	B 56

Peoples

	##
Ἀθηναῖοι	A 31, 31, 34, 38, 44; B 12, 46, 60, 60, 60, 61
Ἀσσύριοι	A 30
Ἕλληνες	A 35; B 31
Ἐρετριεῖς	A 30; B 56
Λακεδαιμόνιοι	A 44; B 5
Μάγοι	B 60
{Μακεδόνες}	B 50
Μῆδοι	A 30, 31; B 60
Νάξιοι	A 30; B 56
Πελοπίδαι	B 56
Πέρσαι	A 31; B 47, 60
Πλαταιεῖς	A 39, 44
Σιδόνιοι	B 63
Σκύθαι	B 56
Φοινῖκες	A 23, 31, 31

Places

Ἀθῆναι	A 29, 41; B 9, 12
Ἀθήνησι	0
Αἰγαῖος	A 38, 39; B 5, 31
Ἀρκαδια	A 35
Ἀσία	A 22, 35, 43; B 3, 8, 10, 25, 39, 51, 52, 57
Ἀττική	B 5, 25, 40, 41, 55, 56
Ἀττικός	A 31
Βαβυλωνία	B 47
Βόσπορος	B 58
Ἑλλάς	A 34, 45, 45; B 12, 52
Ἐρετρία	A 43; B 54
Ἧλις	B 25
Μαραθών	A 1, 5, 32, 34, 49; B 2, 5, 12, 14, 23, 30, 41, 62
Μαραθωνικός	B 30
Μαραθώνιος	A 34, 48; B 22, 42, 52, 54, 55
Μηδικός	B 41, 47
Νάξος	A 38, 43; B 54
Περσικός	B 47
Σκυθικός	B 58
Φοινίκιος	B 47
Φοινίσσα	A 9; B 40

Festivals

Παναθήναια	A 35

Index 8: The Vocabulary

The following list represents a concordance of all the basic vocabulary (verbs, adverbs, nouns, adjectives) appearing in Polemo's declamations. It may be supplemented with the list of prepositions in Index 6 and proper names in Index 7. The vocabulary lists are designed to facilitate exegetical study within the declamations as well as to enable comparisons of Polemo with other authors.

511

Word (Lexicon Form)	Occurrences (##)
ἄβατος	B 13, 40
ἀγαθός	A 2, 6, 24; B 1, 4, 4, 4, 4, 24, 50, 50
ἄγαλμα	B 52
ἄγαν	B 58
ἀγγέλλω	B 17
ἀγεννής	A 43
ἄγκυρα	A 37; B45
ἀγνοέω	B 33
ἀγορεύω	B 62
ἄγω	A 5, 17, 18, 38, 41; B 6, 16, 23
ἀγώγιμος	B 34
ἀγών	B 27
ἀγωνίζομαι	B 53
ἀδαμάντινος	A 43
ἀδάμας	B 10
ἄδεια	B 27
ἀδεῶς	A 8
ἄδηλος	B 48
ἀδύνατος	A 26; B 11, 33, 33, 33
ἄδω	A 44
ἀεί	A 30
ἀθανασία	B 11
ἀθάνατος	A 31; B 48, 53, 60
ἀθλητής	B 44
ἄθλιος	B 56
ἄθλος	A 35
αἰγιαλός	B 13
αἰδέομαι	A 18; B 43
αἱρετός	A 15
αἱρέω	B 27, 43
αἰσθάνομαι	A 36
αἰσχύνω	B 55, 60
αἰτέω	B 28
αἰτία	B 2, 29, 29
αἴτιος	B 23, 49, 49
αἰχμάλωτος	A 29, 38, 41; B 36
αἰχμή	B 47
ἄκαιρος	B 29
ἀκινάκης	B 47
ἀκίνητος	B 54, 58
ἀκλινής	A 33
ἀκμαῖος	B 8
ἀκμή	B 25
ἀκολουθέω	A 13, 18, 44; B 13
ἀκόντιον	B 39
ἀκόρεστος	B 56

Word (Lexicon Form)	Occurrences (##)
ἀκούω	B 19
ἀκρατής	B 63
ἀκρόπολις	A 29
ἄκρος	B 26
ἀκροστόλιον	B 13, 36, 63
ἀκρωτηριάζω	B 44
ἄκων	A 24; B 42, 43
ἀλαζών	B 33, 33, 42
ἀλγηδών	A 25, 36
ἀληθής	A 26; B 42
ἀληθῶς	B 64
ἄλλος	A 1, 17, 29, 42; B 2, 9, 19, 23, 32, 40, 41, 42, 46, 49, 53, 63, 63
ἀλλότριος	A 42; B 14
ἄλλως	B 42
ἅμα	A 36; B 9
ἅμαξα	B 56
ἀμελέω	A 20; B 30
ἀμήχανος	B 33
ἅμιλλα	A 14
ἁμιλλάομαι	B 36
ἀμύνω	A 5, 23
ἀμφισβητέω	A 16; B 18, 21, 39
ἀμφότερος	A 25; B 19
ἄμφω	A 11
ἀναβιβάζω	B 15, 20
ἀναβοάω	B 40
ἀναγκάζω	B 11
ἀναγκαῖος	B 27, 33, 41
ἀνάγκη	A 5, 18; B 9
ἀνάγω	A 35, 43; B 32
ἀναδέω	A 29
ἀνάθημα	B 51
ἀναιρέω	B 40, 60
ἀναίσθητος	A 25
ἀνακεῖμαι	A 15
ἀναλίσκω	B 8, 10
ἀναμάχομαι	B 43
ἀνανταγώνιστος	B 50
ἀναπνεύω	B 30
ἀνατέλλω	A 35
ἀνατρέχω	A 29
ἀναφορά	B 23
ἀνδραγαθία	B 1
ἀνδρείως	B 14
ἀνείκαστος	B 50

Word (Lexicon Form)	Occurrences (##)
ἄνεμος	B 36
ἀνέχω	A 27; B 56, 64
ἀνήρ	A 1, 6, 36, 41, 41, 43, 47; B 1, 2, 24, 27, 34, 35, 44, 46, 50, 50, 57, 58, 60
ἄνθος	B 56
ἄνθρωπος	A 8, 31, 36; B 8, 10, 11, 11, 47, 53, 54, 60, 60
ἀνθρώπινος	B 36
ἀνίστημι	A 23, 30; B 17
ἄνοια	B 42
ἀνόητος	B 33, 33, 35
ἀνταρκέω	A 43
ἀντέχω	A 21
ἀντίπαλος	B 27
ἀντίπρῳρος	A 36
ἀντίρροπος	A 31
ἀντιτάσσω / -ττ-	B 8
αντίτυπος	B 10
ἄνωθεν	A 41
ἀξία	B 51
ἀξιόλογος	A 1
ἀξιόμαχος	B 8
ἄξιος	A 2, 35, 37, 43; B 15, 51, 62
ἀξιόω	B 3, 8, 17
ἀξίωμα	A 14
ἀξίωσις	A 14
ἀόριστος	B 50
ἀπάγω	A 43
ἀπαιτέω	A 11, 38, 38
ἄπας	B 5, 6, 9, 23, 30, 38, 39
ἀπειλητικός	B 63
ἄπειμι (-εἶμι)	B 47
ἀπείργω	B 34
ἄπειρος	A 20; B 35
ἀπέραντος	B 35
ἀπέρχομαι	A 46; B 3, 11, 47, 63
ἀπιστέω	B 55
ἀποβαίνω	B 5, 31
ἀπόβασις	A 5; B 41
ἀπόγειος	B 26
ἀποδίδωμι	A 38, 40
ἀποδύω	B 57
[ἀπο]θνῄσκω	0; A 4, 21, 22; B 2, 3, 11, 11, 16, 19, 19, 38, 47, 53, 55, 60
ἀποικίζω	A 36
ἀποίχομαι	B 21
ἀποκόπτω	A 10, 36, 49; B 13, 39, 45, 63, 63

Word (Lexicon Form)	Occurrences (##)
ἀποκρούω	B 63
ἀποκτείνω	B 39
ἀπόλλυμι	B 37, 42, 56, 59
ἀπολύω	B 35
ἀπομάχομαι	A 28; B 49
ἀπόμαχος	A 20
ἀποπλέω	B 14
ἄπορος	B 33, 41
ἀπόστολος	A 23
ἀποτέμνω	A 41; B 43, 46
ἀποχειροτονέω	B 17
ἀποψάλλω	B 41
ἀπρακτέω	B 60
ἄπρακτος	A 41
ἅπτω	A 42; B 13
ἄπωθεν	A 16
ἀπωθέω	B 25
ἀργός	A 26
ἀρετή	A 2, 2, 4, 5, 14, 14, 16, 18, 18, 22, 25, 26, 28, 45; B 1, 2, 8, 12, 18, 23, 24, 24, 25, 26, 27, 27, 32, 33, 34, 35, 49, 50, 50, 52, 55
ἀριστεία	A 32, 44; B 28
ἀριστεῖος ? [ἀριστέα]	A 15
ἀριστεύω	B 27
ἄριστος (ἀγαθός)	0; B 53
ἀρκέω	A 21
ἁρμόζω	B 62
ἁρπαγή	B 5, 31
ἁρπάζω	A 38; B 54
ἄρρηκτος	B 10
ἀρχή	A 5, 13, 16, 16, 18; B 2, 17, 21, 29, 29, 40
ἄρχω	B 21
ἀσάλευτος	A 37
ἀσθένεια	B 13
ἀσπίς	B 44
ἀστάθμητος	B 27
ἀσφαλής	B 33
ἀτιμάω	A 49
ἄτιμος	B 17
ἄτρωτος	B 51
αὐθάδεια	B 35
αὐθαδιάζομαι	B 24
αὐθαίρετος	B 32
αὖθις	B 28, 30
αὔξω/αὐξάνω	B 17
αὔτανδρος	B 54

Word (Lexicon Form)	Occurrences (##)
αὐτοκράτωρ	A 18
αὐτόχθων	B 64
ἀφαιρέω	A 42
ἀφανής	B 56
ἀφανῶς	A 19
ἀφίημι	A 11, 31, 36; B 41, 41, 41, 44, 52
ἀφίστημι	A 28, 49; B 21
ἀφοπλίζω	B 13, 38
ἄφρων	B 35
ἄχρηστος	B 35
ἄψυχος	A 25; B 11
βαίνω	A 25
βάλλω	A 27, 27; B 9 54, 56, 56, 56, 58, 58, 60
βαρβαρικός	A 35; B 8
βάρβαρος	A 1, 5, 11, 23, 27, 28, 29, 29, 31, 31, 45; B 7, 8, 11, 13, 14, 25, 28, 30, 30, 31, 40, 43, 43, 43, 49, 51, 54, 56, 58, 60, 61
βασιλεύς	A 9, 29, 43, 43; B 8, 10, 32, 40, 40, 41, 51, 56, 61
βέβαιος	B 31, 54, 54
βεβαιόω	B 24
βεβαίως	B 11, 11
βέλος	A 7, 23, 24, 27, 27, 30, 30, 31, 35, 37, 42, 45, 47; B 10, 10, 12, 39, 51, 56, 57, 57, 59
βελτίων (ἀγαθός)	A 15
βῆμα	B 2
βιάζω	B 3, 11, 33, 58
βίαιος	A 35
βίος	A 20, 20; B 50, 50, 50, 53, 53
βλάπτω	B 42, 42
βλέπω	B 55
βλῆμα	A 7; B 10, 59
βοάω	A 38, 40, 41; B 23, 56, 61
βοή	B 8
βοηθέω	B 5, 62
βούλομαι	A 5, 24, 27, 30, 38; B 13, 35, 40, 48
βραδέως	A 39
γένεσις	B 19
γεννάδα	B 64
γένος	B 64
γέρας	B 20, 21
γῆ	A 8, 11, 27, 28, 28, 35, 36; B 13, 31, 31, 45, 54, 54
γί[γ]νομαι	A 6, 10, 11, 14, 19, 22, 29, 44; B 1, 2, 13, 14, 20, 27, 27, 28, 29, 30, 33, 36, 37, 39, 42, 43, 43, 49, 49, 50, 55, 60, 60
γλῶσσα / -ττ-	A 47; B 63
γράφω	B 19

Word (Lexicon Form)	Occurrences (##)
γυμνός	A 8; B 57
γυνή	B 27, 63
δαιμόνιον	B 60
δαίς	A 36; B 37
δάκτυλος	B 33
δεῖ	A 12, 16, 26; B 5, 19, 23, 49
δείκνυμι	A 31, 31, 32, 37; B 1, 7, 28, 53
δειλία	B 49
δεινός	A 22, 25, 39, 40; B 25, 52, 56
δεξιός	A 3, 10, 11, 11, 23, 31, 32, 35, 35, 35, 36, 37, 40, 40, 41, 43, 44, 47; B 33, 36, 37, 42, 43, 60, 63, 63
δεσπότης	B 60
δεύτερος	A 2, 22; B 17, 28, 40, 53
δέος	A 41; B 43
δέχομαι	A 32; B 8, 23
δέω	A 22, 27; B 56
δηλόω	A 15, 16, 31
δῆμος	B 54
δημόσιος	B 22
διαδικασία	B 53
διαιρέω	B 47
διακαρτερέω	B 11
διακρίνω	B 18
διανέμω	A 42
διάνοια	B 42
διασείω	B 54
διατίθημι	A 3
διαφέρω	A 33
διδάσκαλος	B 23, 23
δίδωμι	A 29, 42, 44; B 18, 20, 20, 22
διέξειμι (-εἶμι)	A 49
διηγέομαι	B 37
διήγημα	B 42
δικάζω	0
δίκαιος	A 2, 4, 12, 14, 15; B 16, 19
δικαίως	A 25; B 20
δικαστής	A 47; B 65
δίκη	A 29
δίκην	B 25
δίκτκυον	B 56
διορίζω	A 16
διώκω	A 11, 22, 22; B 26, 26, 41
δίωξις	B 28
δόγμα	B 61
δοκέω	A 7, 15, 26; B 5, 18, 19, 60
δόξα	A 3, 5, 25, 34; B 64

Word (Lexicon Form)	Occurrences (##)
δόρυ	A 36; B 39
δοῦλος	B 56
δουλόω	B 31
δρᾶμα	A 48
δράω	A 23, 23; B 27, 43, 59
δριμύς	A 25
δρῦς	A 42
δύναμαι	A 7; B 33, 34, 36, 41, 56, 58
δύναμις	B 6, 8, 10, 27, 29, 29, 30, 53
δυνατός	B 11, 34
δύο	B 52
δυσωπέω	A 18
ἐάω	A 48; B 12
ἐγγυάω	B 56
ἐγείρω	A 41; B 61
ἐγκελεύω	B 23, 60
ἐγκώμιον	A 45; B 16
ἐθελούσιος	A 5
[ἐ]θέλω	A 46, 49; B 3, 27, 38
ἔθνος	B 32
ἔθω	B 19
εἴδωλον	B 52
εἰκῆ / εἰκῇ	A 35; B 37
εἰκός	A 2, 15; B 21
εἰκών	A 44
εἰρεσία	A 23; B 34
εἰρωνεία	B 5
εἰς	A 9, 11, 13, 32, 32, 33; B 7, 13, 17, 26, 32, 39, 42, 44, 47, 50, 54
εἰσέρχομαι	B 15
εἶτα	A 8
ἕκαστος	A 10, 30, 31, 41
ἐκεῖ	B 55
ἐκπέμπω	B 41
ἐκπλέω	B 45
ἔκπληξις	A 22, 30
ἐκπλήσσω/-ττ-	B 8
ἐκτίθημι	A 7
ἐκτρέχω	A 8
ἐκχέω	B 8
ἑκών	B 8, 42
ἐλάσσων/-ττ- (ὀλίγος)	A 20; B 21, 24
ἐλευθερία	B 8, 12
ἐλευθέριος	A 36; B 52
ἕλκω	A 35, 35; B 37, 53
ἐλπίς	B 33, 34

Word (Lexicon Form)	Occurrences (##)
ἐμβάλλω	A 20; B 37
ἐμβολή	B 8
ἐμπήγνυμι	A 27
ἔμψυχος	B 12, 55
ἐναντίος	A 7; B superscription
ἐνδεής	B 21
ἔνδικος	A 24
ἐνδύω	B 52
ἔνθα	A 8, 11; B 10, 59
ἐνταῦθα	B 6
ἐντέλλω	B 11
ἐντίθημι	B 49
ἐξαίρετος	B 55
ἐξαπατάω	B 11, 60
ἐξαρκέω	B 8
ἐξαρτάω	B 36
ἐξάρχω	A 18
ἔξειμι (-εῖμι)	A 20; B11, 11
ἐξεπίτηδες	A 30
ἐξέρχομαι	A 39
ἔξεστι	B 56
ἐξετάζω	A 21; B 5
ἔξοδος	A 5
ἐξουσία	B 27
ἔπαινος	A 3, 25
ἐπάγω	B 36, 57
ἐπαινέω	A 27, 27, 33; B 1, 16, 18, 51
ἐπανατείνω	A 24
ἐπείγω	B 7
ἐπεμβαίνω	B 26
ἐπεξέρχομαι	A 8
ἐπέχω	B 63
ἐπιβαίνω	A 8
ἐπιβάλλω	A 9
ἐπιβολή	A 44; B 33
ἐπιδείκνυμι	A 28
ἐπίδειξις	B 29, 29, 33
ἐπιδίδωμι	A 28
ἐπιθυμέω	B 42
ἐπιθυμία	B 33, 35
ἐπιλέγω	A 2
ἐπιλήψιμος	B 34
ἐπιμελέομαι / -μελομαι	B 22
ἐπινίκιος	A 48; B 65
ἐπίνοια	B 38

Word (Lexicon Form)	Occurrences (##)
ἐπιρρίπτω	A 10
ἐπίσταμαι	B 37
ἐπιστρέφω	A 40
ἐπιτάφιος	0; A 15, 46, 47, 48; B 15, 65
ἐπιτήδειος	A 47
ἐπιτηρέω	B 14
ἐπιτίθημι	A 49; B 27, 34
ἐπιτιμία	A 36
ἐπιτρέπω	A 9
ἐπιτρέχω	A 41
ἐπιφέρω	B 28, 31
ἐπιχειρέω	A 46; B 32, 36
ἐπιχείρησις	B 34
ἐπιχέω	B 9
ἐπιχωριάζω	B 25
ἔπω	B 19
ἐργάζομαι	B 9, 41
ἔργον	A 5, 14, 14, 21, 26, 27; B 1, 6, 7, 17, 23, 29, 29, 29, 34, 39, 45
ἐρείδω	A 10; B 58
ἐρέσσω	A 35
ἐρευνάω	B 48
ἐρίζω	B 11
ἔρεισμα	A 27
ἔρχομαι	B 39
ἔρως	A 5
ἐρώτημα	B 50
ἕτερος	A 4, 10, 14, 31, 31, 32; B 3, 29, 32, 43, 46, 46
ἐτέρωθι	A 32, 32
ἔτι	A 21, 22, 25, 29; B 14, 31, 34, 35, 56, 60, 60, 60
ἕτοιμος	B 56
εὖ	B 1, 29, 36
εὐβούλως	B 37
εὐδοκιμέω	B 42
εὐθύς	B 43
εὐκόλως	A 31
εὔνοια	B 41
εὐπλοία	B 23
εὑρίσκω	B 41, 46, 50
εὐσχήμων	B 55
εὐτυχία	B 26
ἐφίημι	A 16, 24
ἔχω	A 9, 11, 13, 15, 20, 20, 25, 29, 29, 29, 38, 39, 44, 45, 47, 49; B 6, 19, 19, 21, 29, 41, 41, 43, 53, 56, 57, 60, 63
ζάω	A 7, 19, 26; B 2, 2, 16, 52, 52, 53, 56

Word (Lexicon Form)	Occurrences (##)
ζῆλος	B 32
ζηλόω	B 47, 56
ἡγεμονία	A 18; B 16, 18
ἡγεμών	B 2
ἤδη	A 41, 45, 47; B 26, 26, 27, 31, 61
ἡδύς	A 35
ἠιών	A 8, 29
ἠλίθιος	B 33
ἡλικία	A 5; B 24, 24
ἡμέρα	B 43
ἥμισυς	A 32
ἤπειρος	A 40
ἧσσα / -ττ-	B 43
ἡσσάομαι / -ττ-	B 2, 4, 50
ἡσυχία	A 17
θάλασσα / -ττ-	A 8, 11, 22, 28, 41, 44, 44; B 13, 25, 26, 45, 58, 58
θάνατος	A 25; B 2. 50, 50, 51, 52, 53, 55
θάπτω	A 46, 47; B 19, 63, 63
θαρσέω	B 30
θάρσος / θάρρος	B 4, 43
θαρσύνω	A 31
θάσσων / -ττ- (ταχύς)	A 11, 41
θαῦμα	A 25, 33, 37; B 2, 48, 55, 56, 64
θαυμάζω	A 23; B 47
θαυμάσιος	A 23
θαυμαστός	A 6, 11, 20, 25, 26, 27, 28; B 6, 50
θέαμα	A 35; B 62
θεάομαι	A 44
θεῖος	B 20, 55
θεμέλιον	B 29
θεός	A 35, 36, 41; B 10, 52, 62
θερμός	B 6
θερμότης	B 24
θνητός	B 11
θρασύνω	B 27
θρασύς	A 27, 38
θρηνέω	B 65
θυμός	A 22; B8
θύρα	B 63
θύω	B 56
ἴδιος	A 3, 24, 37; B 6, 53
ἰδιώτης	B 18, 18
ἰδού	B 56
ἱερός	B 63
ἱκανῶς	A 13, 16
ἱππικός	A 41

Word (Lexicon Form)	Occurrences (##)
ἰσόρροπος	B 12
ἴσος	B 18
ἰσοστάσιος	B 31, 46
ἵστημι	A 7, 22, 22, 33, 40, 45; B 2, 4, 8, 11, 11, 12, 14, 39, 44, 47, 53, 55, 56, 56, 58, 59, 62
ἰσχυρός	B 29
ἰσχύω	A 41
ἴσως	B 32
ἰταμότης	B 8
καθαιρέω	B 17, 58, 58
καθάπερ	A 10, 30; B 58
καθαρός	A 18; B 14
καθίστημι	B 9
καινός	A 37
καιρός	A 47; B 25
κακοδαίμων	A 40
κακός	A 19
κακότης	B 27
καλέω	B 22
καλλίμαχος	B 51
καλλίνικος	B 51
κάλλος	B 48
καλός	A 24, 25, 26, 45, 46; B 52
καλύπτω	A 31
καλώδιον	B 45
καλῶς	A 12; B 1
κάμνω	A 41; B 10, 50, 59
καρπόω	B 38
καρτερέω	A 25; B 11
καρτερός	A 10; B 59
κατακεντέω	B 57
κατακόπτω	A 29
καταλείπω	B 9
καταμέμφομαι	A 11
κατάπληξις	B 31
καταπλήσσω	A 31; B 28
καταράσσω / -ττ-	A 22
καταφρονέω	B 37
κατέχω	A 7, 10, 29, 35, 37; B 33, 36, 37, 40, 41, 41, 45, 45, 51, 63
κατόρθωμα	B 49, 52
κεῖμαι	A 1, 3, 11, 31, 49; B 4, 15, 43, 44, 62
κελεύω	B 23, 23, 23
κενός	A 27; B 43
κενόω	B 39
κεφάλαιος	B 15

Word (Lexicon Form)	Occurrences (##)
κεφαλή	A 29, 41; B 46
κινδυνεύω	A 20
κίνδυνος	B 5, 25
κινέω	B 15, 47, 58
κλῆρος	A 14
κλίνω	B 52, 60
κοινός	A 3, 45; B 2, 8, 15, 39, 50, 50, 51, 52
κοινωνέω	A 14; B 3
κοινωνία	B 39
κομιδῆ	A 5
κομίζω	A 41; B 37
κοντός	B 10
κοπίς	B 47
κόπτω	A 10, 41, 42, 43
κοσμέω	A 12; B1, 12, 56, 65
κρατέω	A 4, 4, 36, 43; B 40, 41, 44, 49
κράτιστος (ἀγαθός)	A 26
κράτιστος (κρατύς)	B 26; B 29[?]
κραυγάζω	A 40
κρείττων / -ττ- (ἀγαθός)	A 2, 4; B 4, 19, 45
κρείττων / -ττ- (κρατύς)	A 34, 35; B 2, 8
κρίνω	A 17; B1, 27
κρίσις	B 24
κρύπτω	A 30; B 59
κυβερνήτης	B 23
κύριος	A 23; B 31
κυρόω	B 49
κύων	B 27
λαβή	B 37, 43, 63
λαγχάνω	A 14
λαμβάνω	A 49; B 33, 35, 41, 41, 45, 47
λαμπρός	A 7; B 28, 54, 64
λαμπρύνω	B 23
λανθάνω	A 19, 30; B 36
λάφυρα	B 51
λέγω	0; A 1, 3, 4, 12, 15, 15, 15, 26, 28, 30, 43, 46, 46; B 1, 15, 16, 19, 20, 36, 42, 45, 56, 57, 58
λείπω	B 43
λειποτακτέω	B 44
λέων	A 35; B 27
ληίζομαι	A 40
λῆμ{μ}α	A 40
ληπτός	B 34
λῆρος	B 63
λίθος	B 58
λογισμός	A 22

Word (Lexicon Form)	Occurrences (##)
λόγος	A 1, 3, 3, 12, 16, 16, 45, 46, 47, 49, 49; B 1, 1, 1, 15, 19, 20, 21, 22, 22, 29, 34, 58, 62
λοιπός	A 10, 32, 39; B 30, 47
λυπέω	B 17
λύω	A 41; B 22, 26
μαθητής	B 23
μαίνομαι	A 40; B 42
μακρόβιος	B 44
μακρός	A 35; B 1, 12
μάλιστα (μάλα)	A 1; B 49, 50
μᾶλλον (μάλα)	A 12; B 2, 41, 47
μανία	B 35
μανικός	B 35
μάντευμα	B 48
μαρτυρέω	B 39, 47
μάρτυς	B 14
μάταιος	B 33, 35
μάτην	A 35
μάχη	A 6, 10, 21, 22, 32, 35, 36, 39, 44, 49; B 6, 11, 18, 28, 37, 40, 40, 41, 46, 49, 52, 53, 56, 60, 60
μαχιμός	A 8, 31; B 53, 60
μάχομαι	A 1, 8, 19, 28, 28, 32, 42; B 2, 10, 11, 31, 32, 37, 47, 50, 52, 60
μεγαληγορέω	A 45
μεγαλοψυχία	A 20
μέγας	A 5, 9, 33, 33, 37, 40, 42, 47; B 6, 48, 52, 54, 56, 58
μέγιστος (μέγας)	A 14, 16; B 2, 53, 55
μεθύστερον	B 65
μείζων (μέγας)	A 16, 29, 38; B 21, 32
μειράκιον	A 20; B 36, 37
μείρομαι	B 12
μέλλω	A 20, 41
μέλος	A 10, 11, 38
μέλω	A 43
μεμπτός	B 7
μένω	A 7, 37, 41; B 11, 11, 41, 43, 53, 60, 63
μερίζω	A 11
μέρος	A 1, 21, 32, 42, 43; B 32, 60, 63
μέσος	A 21, 22
μεστός	B 34
μεταχειρίζω	A 16
μετέχω	A 5
μέτριος	A 19
μηδείς	B 14
μηκέτι	B 60
μηνύω	B 13

Word (Lexicon Form)	Occurrences (##)
μήτηρ	B 64
μικρός	A 33
μιμέομαι	A 29, 39, 44; B 55
μίμημα	B 32
μνημονεύω	A 36
μόγις / μόλις	A 43; B 3, 15
μοίρα	B 21
μόνος	A 7, 14, 21, 22, 26, 28, 28, 30, 30, 31, 32; B 17, 18, 20, 23, 24, 32, 36, 37, 41, 47, 47, 49, 50, 50, 50, 52
μυρίος	A 41; B 44
μωραίνω	B 36
ναυάγια	A 29
ναυμαχέω	A 8, 11, 44; B 45
ναυμαχία	A 36; B 41
ναυμάχος	A 33
ναυτής	B 23
ναυτικός	A 9
ναῦς	A 9, 10, 11, 24, 29, 31, 31, 35, 36, 36, 37, 37, 38, 38, 40, 41, 43, 44; B 8, 13, 26, 26, 29, 31, 31, 32, 33, 34, 35, 36, 36, 37, 37, 40, 41, 41, 43, 44, 45, 54, 63
ναύσταθμον /-μος	B 41
νεκρός	A 2, 7, 11, 12, 22, 26, 27, 27, 28, 30, 33, 37, 45, 46; B 2, 4, 12, 39, 42, 44, 46, 48, 52, 53, 53, 53, 54, 55, 55, 60, 60, 60, 60, 63, 63
νέος	A 5; B 24
νεότης	A 20
νῆσος	A 38; B 5, 54, 54
νικάω	A 32; B 17, 17, 40, 41, 50, 60
νίκη	B 2, 41, 47
νικηφόρος	B 12
νῖκος	A 12
νόημα	A 37
νοητέον	B 35
νομίζω	B 49
νόμος	0; A 15, 19, 45; B 1, 6, 22, 50
νῶτον	B 28
ξίφος	B 10
ξύλον	B 39, 63
ὄγκος	B 34
ὁδός	B 55
οἶδα	A 4, 25; B 41, 60
οἰκεῖος	A 1, 15, 23, 37, 44; B 19, 27
οἰκοδόμημα	B 29
οἴμοι	B 60

Word (Lexicon Form)	Occurrences (##)
οἴομαι	B 11, 56
οἴχομαι	B 27
ὀκνέω	A 26
ὀκνηρός	A 30
ὀλίγος	A 11
ὁλόκληρος	B 4, 44
ὅλος	A 31, 32, 34, 42, 43; B 3, 23, 30, 32, 34, 49, 49, 54, 57
ὅλως	A 26; B 28, 33
ὅμιλος	B 56
ὅμοιος	A 49; B 43, 46, 47
ὁμολογέω	B 3, 27, 50, 53
ὁμότιμος	A 3
ὁμοῦ	B 32
ὅμως	B 45
ὀνίνημι	A 30
ὄνομα	A 13, 14, 18; B 17, 19, 48, 48
ὀνομαστός	A 47
ὀξύς	B 5
ὁπλίζω	B 16, 62
ὅπλον	B 12, 61, 63
ὁράω	A 4, 17, 36; B 17, 30, 30, 33, 34, 42, 43, 43, 46, 48, 54, 60, 61
ὀργή	B 9
ὀργίζω	B 60
ὀρέγω	A 5
ὀρθός	B 12, 12, 44, 61
ὀρθόω	A 27
ὁρμάω	A 41
ὁρμίζω	A 35
ὄρος, εος, τό	A 38; B 45, 54
ὅρος, ου, ὁ	B 50
οὐδείς	A 26; B 7, 11, 39, 43, 46, 47, 58, 59
οὐκέτι	B 57
οὖς	B 46
ὀφείλω	A 13, 25
ὀφθαλμός	B 23
ὄχλος	B 63
ὄψις	B 8
παίδευσις	B 23
παιδίον	B 13
παῖς	A 3, 3, 4, 4, 6, 18, 37, 38, 38, 39, 44, 44, 44, 46, 49; B 1, 1, 4, 18, 43, 48, 64, 65
παίω	B 57
πάλαι	A 15, 47, 47, 47
παλαιός	B 64, 64

Word (Lexicon Form)	Occurrences (##)
πάλιν	B 41
πανταχοῦ	A 33
παντοδαπός	B 10
πάντως	A 22
παραβάλλω	A 27; B 44
παραβολή	B 23
παραγγέλλω	B 57
παραγί[γ]νομαι	A 35
παράγω	A 48
παράδειγμα	B 32
παραδίδωμι	B 15
παράδοξος	A 26
παρακαλέω	B 15
παρακελεύομαι	B 8
παράλογος	B 8
παραμυθέομαι	B 21
παραμυθία	A 13
παραμύθιον	A 13
παραπλήσιος	A 29
παράσημος	A 23
παρασκευάζω	B 28
παρατάσσω	A 19; B 25, 32
παραχωρέω	A 46; B 21
πάρειμι (-εἰμί)	A 14, 35; B 9, 18, 40, 41, 41, 56
πάρειμι (-εἶμι)	A 16
πάρεργον	B 49
παρέρχομαι	A 47; B 50
παρέχω	B 2, 6, 18, 18, 28, 29, 61
παρισόομαι	A 43
παροξύνω	B 32
πᾶς	A 1, 3, 6, 6, 15, 21, 22, 25, 27, 29, 29, 29, 34, 39, 41, 43, 45; B 2, 2, 8, 8, 8, 8, 8, 9, 9, 9, 10, 10, 22, 25, 26, 27, 29, 30, 32, 32, 32, 33, 38, 39, 39, 39, 39, 43, 43, 43, 43, 49, 50, 53, 56, 57, 58, 58, 58, 58
πάσχω	A 23, 23, 25; B 27, 27, 63
πατήρ	0, 0, 0; A 1, 3, 13, 16, 17, 32, 32, 45, 46, 47, 49, 49; B 0, 1, 2, 4, 15, 19, 19, 20, 45, 62
πατρίς	A 44; B 53, 64
παύω	B 44
πεδίον	A 38
πεζομαχέω	B 45
πεζομάχος	A 33
πείθω	B 3, 11, 23, 23
πεῖρα	A 20; B 21, 33
πειράω	B 34, 58

Word (Lexicon Form)	Occurrences (##)
πεῖσμα	A 10
πέλεκυς	A 42; B 47, 63
πέμπω	A 23; B 60
περιβάλλω	B 52, 61
περιβλέπω	B 13
περιβολή	B 59
περιγί[γ]νομαι	A 6; B 18
περίειμι (-εἰμί)	A 22; B 19, 19, 22
περιέρχομαι	B 46
περιίστημι	B 56
περιμένω	B 5, 56
περινοέω	A 38
περινοστέω	B 36
περιοράω	A 20
περιουσία	A 20; B 49
περιπίπτω	A 27, 30
περισσός / -ττ-	B 26, 50, 52
περιτείνω	B 56
περιχέω	A 7
πέτρα	B 10
πεύκη	A 42
πήγνυμι	B 58
πιέζω / πιάζω	B 18
πίπτω	A 6, 7, 39, 42, 45; B 3, 11, 12, 13, 14, 18, 43, 43, 47, 47, 55, 59, 60, 60
πίστις	B 20
πιστός	B 12, 46
πιστόω	B 64
πλάνης	B 56
πλεῖστος (πολύς)	A 3, 8, 11; B 51
πλείων (πολύς)	A 2, 20, 20, 20, 21; B 18, 21, 53, 59
πλέω	A 43; B 36, 45, 54, 61
πληγή	B 47
πλῆθος	A 23; B 8, 11, 49
πλήρης	A 32
πληρόω	A 11
πλήρωμα	B 34, 36
πνεῦμα	A 35; B 12, 41
ποιέω	A 3, 12, 25, 25, 28, 38, 44, 49; B 10, 13, 19, 22, 23, 23, 23, 27, 33, 36, 40, 41, 41, 45, 45, 49, 57
ποιητής	B 51
πολεμαρχέω	A 14
πολεμαρχία	A 14, 18; B 17
πολέμαρχος	A 5, 13, 14, 15, 15, 15, 16, 17, 36, 46; B 2, 6, 7, 17, 18, 18, 20, 22, 23, 49, 52, 52
πολεμέω	A 21; B 53, 60

Word (Lexicon Form)	Occurrences (##)
πολέμιος	A 21, 22, 28, 30, 40; B 9, 14, 27, 27, 27, 40, 43, 56
πόλεμος	0; A 16, 21; B 8, 11, 16, 19, 26, 32, 41, 52, 53, 54, 56, 62
πόλις	A 1, 40; B 1
πολίτης	A 39
πολλάκις	A 22; B 45, 54
πολυάνδριον	A 49
πολύς	A 9, 10, 12, 20, 20, 30, 32, 33, 45; B 7, 9, 10, 10, 11, 11, 12, 13, 23, 31, 37, 38, 46, 47, 50, 56, 59, 59, 61
πολύτρωτος	B 51
πολυχειρία	A 43
πολυχρόνιος	B 12
πονέω	B 13
πόνος	A 21; B 33
πόντιος	B 36
πορίζω	B 27, 27
ποταμός	B 56
πότερος	B 44
πούς	B 30, 46
πράσσω / -ττ-	A 26; B 1, 28, 40, 53
πρέπω	B 2
πρέσβυς	A 20; B 19, 24, 29
προαίρεσις	A 24
πρόβολος	A 30
προεδρία	B 19
πρόθεσις	B 22
προθυμία	A 18, 24
προίημι	B 64
προκαλέω	B 8
προκαταλαμβάνω	A 44
προκρίνω	B 15, 19
προμαχέω	A 22
πρόμαχος	A 34
προνεύω	B 58
προσβάλλω	B 59
προσβολή	B 10, 34, 35
προσγί[γ]νομαι	B 49
προσδοκέω	B 33
προσήκω	A 1, 12
πρόσθεν	B 22
προσπίπτω	B 58
προσποίησις	B 33
προσφόρως	B 1
προτάσσω / -ττ-	B 19
προτείνω	A 49
πρότερος (πρό)	A 22, 25; B 18, 21, 21, 28, 29, 34
προτιμάω	B 19, 62

Word (Lexicon Form)	Occurrences (##)
προτίμησις	B 1, 19
πρότιμος	A 23
πρόχειρος	B 27
πρύμνα	A 11; B 13, 26, 36, 63
πρῶτος (πρό)	A 8, 18, 21, 32, 36, 36, 36, 36, 37;
	B 12, 16, 19, 29, 48, 53, 55, 56, 64, 65
πυνθάνομαι	A 44
πῦρ	B 37
πύργος	B 10
ῥᾴδιος	B 28
ῥᾳδίως	B 13
ῥέω	B 25
ῥήτωρ	B 51
ῥίζα	B 54
ῥιζόω	B 11
ῥίπτω	B 44
ῥόθιος	A 35
ῥοώδης	B 58
ῥώμη	A 20, 22; B 8, 24
σαγηνεύω	A 30; B 56
σείω	B 54
σεμνός	A 3, 26; B 51, 62
σεμνύνω	B 62
σέλας	A 36
σῆμα	A 47; B 15
σίδηρος	A 44
σκέψις	B 33
σκόπελος	B 54
σκοπέω	B 18
σκοπός	B 51
σκυλεύω	B 51
σπάρτον	B 63
σπουδαῖος	B 64
σπούδασμα	B 9
σπουδή	A 3; B 6, 32
στάσιμος	B 54
στάσις	A 7, 22, 24, 26, 27, 45; B 3, 38, 54, 55
στενός	B 31
στέφανος	B 20
στεφανόω	A 39; B 44, 56
στήλη	A 33; B 19
στοιχεῖον	A 11, 42, 44
στολαγωγός	A 35
στολή	B 17, 52
στόλος	A 35; B 5, 8
στόμα	B 8

Word (Lexicon Form)	Occurrences (##)
στοχάζομαι	B 9
στρατηγός	A 16, 16; B 5, 20, 20, 21, 23
στρατιά	A 8; B 51
στρατιώτης	A 2, 6, 27, 28, 30, 31, 32, 34, 46; B 12, 15, 23, 44, 46, 50, 53, 62, 63
στρατόπεδον	A 25, 29, 42; B 46
στρατός	B 40
συγγενής	B 41
συγκαλέω	A 24
συγκινδυνεύω	A 3
συγκοσμέω	A 49
συγκροτέω	B 34, 62
συγχωρέω	B 65
συλλαμβάνω	B 31
συμβαίνω	B 48
συμβάλλω	A 1
σύμπαν	A 2; B 43
συμβολή	B 49
συμμάχομαι	B 56
σύμμαχος	A 20; B 62
συμμ[ε]ίγνυμι	B 7
συμμιγής	B 8
συμπίπτω	A 24
συμπλέκω	B 8
συμφέρω	B 41
συμφορά	A 24
σύμψυχος	B 54
συναγωνίζομαι	A 4
συναπάγω	B 36
συνελαύνω	B 26
συνέχω	A 27
συνίημι	A 25; B 17
σύνθημα	B 16, 23
συντίθημι	A 44
σύντιμος	A 35
συστρατιώτης	B 57
σφαλερός	B 31
σχεδόν	A 5, 8
σχῆμα	A 2, 7, 7, 26, 26, 27, 27, 27, 28, 44; B 17, 20, 33, 35, 42, 47, 52, 52, 53, 63
σχολή	B 13
σῶμα	A 7, 32, 36, 37, 38, 39, 45, 49; B 8, 11, 11, 11, 12, 12, 12, 13, 23, 24, 30, 32, 37, 46, 47, 53, 56, 56, 58
σωτήρ	A 34
σωτηρία	B 20, 27
ταλαίπωρος	B 56

Word (Lexicon Form)	Occurrences (##)
τάξις	B 18, 22, 43
τάσσω / -ττ-	A 18; B 18
ταῦρος	A 35
ταφή	B 22
τάφος	A 2, 3, 12, 49; B 1, 3, 15, 15, 15, 16, 22
τάχα	A 40
τάχιστος (ταχύς)	B 5
τεῖχος	B 10, 55, 59
τεκμήριον	A 14
τέκνον	A 31, 40; B 14, 47, 61, 64
τελευταῖος	B 28, 58
τελέω	B 49
τέλος	A 21, 29; B 34
τέμνω	A 25; B 63
τέρας	B 62
τεχνάομαι	B 29
τέχνη	B 34, 60
τηρέω	B 12
τίθημι	B 54
τιμάω	A 12, 13; B 20
τιμή	A 2, 13; B 1, 1, 15, 16, 17, 18, 20, 21, 49
τίμιος	A 28
τιμωρέω	A 37
τόλμα	A 5, 14, 20, 22, 25; B 8, 33, 33, 35, 40
τολμάω	A 1, 20, 26; B 23, 27, 49
τόλμημα	A 24; B 30, 33, 34, 36
τολμηρία	A 40
τολμηρός	B 24, 37, 50
τόξευμα	A 7, 27; B 39, 52
τοξεύω	B 56
τόπος	B 56
τότε	B 27, 56
τραγικός	B 51
τραγῳδέω	A 48; B 45, 65
τραγῳδία	A 48; B 51
τραῦμα	A 24, 42; B 11, 13, 44, 47
τρεῖς	B 64
τρέπω	A 22; B 13, 26, 26
τρέφω	A 34
τρέχω	A 35; B 5, 53
τρέω	B 43
τριήρης	B 33, 41
τρόπαιον	A 10, 39; B 12, 61
τροπαίουχος	A 41
τρόπις	A 9; B 29
τρόφιμος	A 35

Word (Lexicon Form)	Occurrences (##)
τυγχάνω	B 5, 19, 22, 26, 38
τυφλός	B 33
τύχη	A 14; B 27
ὑβρίζω	B 2
ὑγιής	B 56
υἱός	A 15, 18, 32; B 6, 37, 38, 49
ὑπάρχω	B 19, 24, 63
ὑπερασπίζω	B 62
ὑπερβαίνω	A 8; B 50
ὑπερβάλλω	B 24
ὑπερμαχέω	B 53
ὑπεροράω	B 30
ὑποδέχομαι	A 39; B 10
ὑπολαμβάνω	B 44
ὑπομένω	B 10
ὑποπίπτω	B 3
ὑποχωρέω	B 43
ὑφίστημι	A 40; B 26
φαίνω	A 6, 18
φάλαγξ	A 8, 41
φανερός	A 4, 30
φαρέτρα	B 39
φάσκω	B 9
φάσμα	B 55, 56
φείδομαι	B 23, 56, 57
φεύγω	A 9, 11, 28, 38, 40, 40; B 13, 26, 26, 30, 40, 40, 41, 61
φέρω	A 14, 17, 23, 36, 43; B 19, 54
φήμη	A 43
φημί	A 1, 13, 15, 38
φθονέω	A 48
φιλία	A 44
φιλόνεικος	B 60
φίλος	A 28, 30, 34, 39; B 43, 43
φιλοτιμέομαι	A 14; B 32, 39
φιλοτιμία	A 3; B 3, 32
φοβερός	B 8, 12, 27, 27, 31
φοβέω	A 9, 30, 31; B 13, 26, 38
φόβος	A 22; B 9
φονεύω	B 58
φόνος	B 9
φρονέω	A 30; B 36
φρόνημα	A 19; B 12, 27, 53
φροντίζω	A 42
φυγή	A 21; B 14, 27, 41
φυλάσσω / -ττ-	A 45; B 38

Word (Lexicon Form)	Occurrences (##)
φύσις	A 1, 11, 38; B 11, 34, 36, 50, 50, 50, 52
φυτόν	B 54
φωνή	B 20, 51
χαίρω	B 57
χαλεπός	B 27
χαλκόθυμος	A 41
χαμαί	B 63
χάρις	A 25; B 41
χείρ	A 3, 9, 11, 11, 11, 23, 24, 24, 25, 28, 31, 31, 31, 32, 32, 34, 34, 34, 35, 36, 36, 36, 37, 39, 39, 41, 41, 42, 43, 44, 44, 45, 45, 49, 49; B 13, 13, 13, 13, 23, 27, 30, 32, 33, 39, 42, 43, 44, 45, 46, 63
χερσαῖος	A 29
χοροδιδάσκαλος	B 23
χορός	A 48; B 23
χράω	A 18, 24
χρή	A 1, 16; B 17, 34, 62
χρόνος	A 10, 44; B 11, 11
χρῶμα	A 19
χῶμα	A 30; B 58
χώρα	B 40
χωρέω	B 56
χωρίον	B 9
ψαύω	B 39
ψῆφος	B 49
ψυχή	A 11, 37; B 1, 2, 8, 11, 11, 11, 12, 12, 13, 43, 47, 50, 50, 53, 53, 55, 56, 60, 64
ᾠδή	B 23
ὠφέλιμος	A 23

Select Bibliography

Editions of Polemo's Declamations
(in chronological order)

Stephanus, Henricus, *Polemonis, Himerii et aliorum quorundam declamationes nunc primum editae*. Geneva: H. Fugerus, 1567.

Prevosteau, Stephanus, Πολέμωνος σοφίστου ἐπιτάφιοι λόγοι εἰς Κυναίγειρον καὶ Καλλίμαχον. Paris: S. Prevosteau, 1586.

Possinus, Petrus, *Polemonis Sophistae Orationes quotquot extant, duae*. Toulouse: A. Colerium, 1637.

Orellius, Joannes C., *Polemonis Laodicensis Sophistae Laudationes II Funebres*. Leipzig: C. Henricus, 1819.

Hinck, Hugo, *Polemonis Declamationes quae exstant duae*. Leipzig: B. G. Teubner, 1873

Polemo's Life and Work

Bowersock, G. W., *Greek Sophists in the Roman Empire*. Oxford: University Press, 1969.

Cadoux, C. J., *Ancient Smyrna*, Oxford: Blackwell, 1938.

Chowen, R. H., "Traveling Companions of Hadrian," *CJ* 50 (1954) 122–124.

Gleason, M. W., "Eye to Eye. The Physiognomonic *aristeae* of Polemo," American Philological Association Abstracts. Ithaca: Scholars Press, 1987

Gleason, M. W., *Embodying the Rheteoric of Manhood: Self-Presentation in the Second Sophistic*, Berkeley: University of California dissertation, 1990 [now published as: *Making Men. Sophists and Self-Presentation in Ancient Rome*. Princeton: Princeton University Press, 1995.

Förster, R. (ed), *Scriptores Physiognomonici Graeci et Latini*, Vol. 1. Leipzig: Teubner, 1893.

Jüttner, H., *De Polemonis rhetoris vita operibus arte*, *BPhA* 8,1 (1898) [reprint: Hildesheim: Olms, 1968].

Mesk, J., "Die Beispiele in Polemons Physiognomik," *WS* 50 (1932), 51-67.

Stegemann, W., *Antonius Polemon, der Hauptvertreter der zweiten Sophistik*, Stuttgart, 1942.

Stegemann, W., "Polemon (10)," *RE* 21 (1952), 1320-1357.

Declamations, Rhetoric, and Education

Avontins, I., "The Holders of the Chairs of Rhetoric at Athens," *HSCP* 79 (1975) 313-24.

Baumhauer, O. A., *Die sophistische Rhetorik. Eine Theorie sprachlicher Kommunikation*, Stuttgart: Metzler, 1986.

Bevan, E., "Rhetoric in the Ancient World," *Essays in Honor of Gilbert Murray*, ed. H. A. L. Fisher, S. A. de Madariage, and C. Archer. London: Allen and Unwin, 1936, pp. 189-213.

Boissier, G., "The Schools of Declamation at Rome," *Tacitus and Other Roman Studies*. New York: Putnam, 1906, pp. 163-194.

Bonner, S. F., *Roman Declamation in the Late Republic and Early Empire*. Berkeley: University of California Press, 1949.

-----, *Education in Ancient Rome: from the Elder Cato to the Younger Pliny*, Berkeley: University of California Press, 1977.

Bryant, D. C. (ed), *Ancient Greek and Roman Rhetoricians: A Biographical Dictionary*, Columbia, MO: Artcraft, 1968.

Burgess, T. C., "Epideictic Literature," *University of Chicago Studies in Classical Philology* 3 (1902) 89-261.

Caplan, H., "The Decay of Eloquence at Rome in the First Century," *Of Eloquence: Studies in Ancient and Medieval Rhetoric*, ed. A. King and H. North. Ithaca: Cornell University Press, 1970. pp. 160-195.

Chase, J. R., "The Classical Conception of Epideictic," *Quarterly Journal of Speech* 47 (1961) 293–300.

Cizek, A., "Zur Bedeutung der 'topoi Enkomiastikoi' in der antiken Rhetorik," *Topik. Beiträge zur interdisziplinaren Diskussion. Kritische Informationen*, München: Finck, 1981. pp. 33–41.

Clark, D. L., *Rhetoric in Greco-Roman Education.* New York: Columbia University Press, 1957

Clarke, M. L., *Rhetoric at Rome. A Historical Survey.* 2nd ed., London: Cohen and West, 1966.

Cleland, M. R. M., *Sophistic Epideictic Rhetoric: A Classical Theory and a Contemporary Interpretation*, DeKalb: Northern Illinois University dissertation, 1989.

Gwynn, A. O., *Roman Education from Cicero to Quintilian.* Oxford: Oxford University Press, 1926 [reprint 1964].

Hock, R. and E. O'Neil, *The Chreia in Ancient Rhetoric, 1: The Progymnasmata.* Decatur, GA: Scholars Press, 1986.

Hofrichter, W., *Studien zur Entwicklungsgeschichte der Deklamation von der griechischen Sophistik bis zur römischer Kaiserzeit*, Breslau: dissertation, 1935

Johannsen, R. L., "The Greek Rhetoricians on Deistic Reference," *Central States Speech Journal* 12 (1962) 100–05.

Kennedy, G. A., *The Art of Persuasion in Greece*, Princeton: Princeton University Press, 1963.

-----, *The Art of Rhetoric in the Roman World: 300 B.C. – A.D. 300.* Princeton: Princeton University Press, 1972.

-----, "Later Greek Philosophy and Rhetoric," *Ph&Rh* 13 (1980) 181–97.

King, D. B., "The Appeal To Religion in Greek Rhetoric," *CJ* 50 (1955) 363–371, 376.

Kohl, R., *De scholasticarum declamationum argumentis ex historia petitis*, *RhSt* 4. Paderborn: Schöningh, 1915.

Kroll, W., "Rhetorik," *RE* Suppl.VII. (1940) 1039-1138.

Lausberg, H., *Elemente der Literarischen Rhetorik*, 3rd ed., München: Heubner, 1967.

-----, *Handbuch der Literarischen Rhetorik: Eine Grundlegung der Literaturwissenschaft*, 3rd ed. Stuttgart: Steiner, 1990.

Marrou, H. I., *A History of Education in Antiquity*. New York: Sheed and Ward, 1956.

McCall, M. H., *Ancient Rhetorical Theories of Simile and Comparison*, Cambridge: Harvard University Press, 1969.

Parks, E. P., *The Roman Rhetorical Schools as a Preparation for the Courts Under the Early Empire*. Johns Hopkins University Studies in Historical and Political Science 63,2. Baltimore: Johns Hopkins University Press, 1945.

Poulakos, J., "Interpreting the Sophistical Rhetoric: A Response to Schiappa," *Ph&Rh* 23 (1990) 218-28.

Price, B. J., *Paradeigma and Exemplum in Ancient Rhetorical Theory*, Berkeley: University of California dissertation, 1975.

Rinker, C. W., *The Art of Censure. Classical 'Psogos' Rhetoric*. Norman: University of Oklahoma dissertation, 1979.

Rohde, E., "Die asianische Rhetorik und die zweite Sophistik," *RhM* 41 (1886) 170-190.

Russel, D. A., *Greek Declamation*. Cambridge: Cambridge University Press, 1983.

Schamberger, M., *De declamationum Romanorum argumentiis observationes selectae*. Halle: Wischau & Burkhardt, 1917.

Solmsen, F., "The Aristotelian Tradition in Ancient Rhetoric," *AJP* 62 (1941) 35-50, 169-90.

Summers, W. C., "Declamations under the Empire," *Proceedings of the Classical Association* 10 (1913) 87–102.

Vickers, B. (ed), *Schoolroom and Courtroom. Rhetoric Revalued.* Papers from the International Society for the History of Rhetoric. Medieval and Renaissance Texts and Studies 19. Binghamton: SUNY, 1982.

Wehrli, F., "Der erhabene und der schlichte Stil in der poetisch-rhetorischen Theorie der Antike," *Phyllobolia. Für Peter von der Mühll.* Basel: Schwabe, 1946. pp. 9–34.

Wilcox, S., "The Scope of Early Rhetorical Instruction," *HSCP* 53 (1942) 121–155.

The Second Sophistic

Anderson, G., *Philostratus, Biography, and Belles Lettres in the Third Century A.D.* London / Dover, NH: Croom Helm, 1986.

-----, *The Second Sophistic: A Cultural Phenomenon in the Roman Empire.* New York: Routledge, 1993.

Avotins, I., "Prosopographical and Chronological Notes on Some Greek Sophists of the Empire," *California Studies in Classical Philology* 4 (1971) 67–80.

Bowersock, G. W., *Greek Sophists in the Roman Empire.* Oxford: Clarendon, 1969.

-----, *Hellenism in Late Antiquity.* Ann Arbor: University of Michigan Press, 1990.

Bowersock, G. W. (ed), *Approaches to the Second Sophistic.* Papers Presented at the 105th Annual Meeting of the American Philological Association. University Park: The American Philological Association, 1974.

Bowie, E. L., "The Greeks and Their Past in the Second Sophistic," *Studies in Ancient Society* (ed. M. Finley). London / Boston: Routledge & K. Paul, 1974. pp. 166–209.

-----, "The Importance of Sophists," *YCS* 27 (1982) 29–50.

Brunt, P. A., "The Bubble of the Second Sophistic," *BICS* 41 (1994) 25–52.

Campbell, J. M., *The Influence of the Second Sophistic on the Style of the Sermons of St. Basil the Great*. Patristic Studies. Washington: Catholic University of America dissertation, 1922.

Cameron, A. and S. Walker (eds), *The Greek Renaissance in the Roman Empire*. London: University of London, Institute of Classical Studies, 1989.

Fuchs, H., *Der geistige Widerstand gegen Rom in der Antiken Welt*. Berlin: de Gruyter, 1938.

Gerth, K., "Zweite Sophistik," *RE* Suppl. VIII (1956) 719–782.

Jones, C. P., "Prosopographical Notes on the Second Sophistic," *GRBS* 21 (1981) 374–377.

Keil, J., "Vertreter der zweiten Sophistik in Ephesos," *JÖAI* 40 (1953) 5–26.

Reardon, B. P., "The Second Sophistic," *Renaissances Before the Renaissance: Cultural Revivals of Late Antiquity and the Middle Ages*. (ed. W. Treadgold). Stanford: Standford University Press, 1984. pp. 23–41.

Richtsteig, E., "Bericht über die Literatur zur sogenannten Zweiten Sophistik aus den Jahren 1915-1925," *Jahresbericht Über die Fortschritte der Klassischen Altertumswissenschaft* 211 (1927) 1–109; 216 (1928) 1–64.

Stanton, G. R., "Sophists and Philosophers: Problems of Classification," *AJP* 94 (1973) 350–364.

Steinmetz, P., *Untersuchungen zur römischen Literatur des zweiten Jahrhunderts nach Christi Geburt*. Wiesbaden: Steiner, 1982.

Swain, S., "The Reliability of Philostratus' Lives of the Sophists," *CA* 10 (1991) 148–163.

Van Groningen, B. A., "General Literary Tendencies in the Second Century A.D.," *Mnemosyne* 18 (1965) 41–56.